GO!
with Microsoft® Office

Access 2003
Comprehensive

**Linda Foster-Turpen
and Jeffrey M. Howard**

Shelley Gaskin, Series Editor

Upper Saddle River, New Jersey

Library of Congress Cataloging-in-Publication Data

The Library of Congress has catalogued Volume 1 as follows:

Foster-Turpen, Linda.
  GO! with Microsoft Office Access 2003 : volume 1 / Linda Foster-Turpen.
    p. cm.— (Go! with Microsoft Office 2003)
Includes index.
  ISBN 0-13-143427-6 (spiral ed.)—ISBN 0-13-145101-4 (perfect bound ed.)
  1. Database management. 2. Microsoft Access. I. Title. II. Series.
QA76.9.D3F665 2004
005.75'65—dc22

    2003026108

ISBN 0-13-143426-8 (Comprehensive)

Vice President and Publisher: Natalie E. Anderson
Executive Acquisitions Editor: Jodi McPherson
Senior Marketing Manager: Emily Williams Knight
Marketing Assistant: Nicole Beaudry
Senior Project Manager, Editorial: Mike Ruel
Senior Media Project Manager: Cathi Profitko
Editorial Assistant: Alana Meyers
Senior Project Manager, Production: Tim Tate
Manufacturing Buyer: Tim Tate
Design Manager: Maria Lange
Art Director: Pat Smythe
Cover Designer: Brian Salisbury
Cover Photo: Steve Bloom/Getty Images, Inc.
Interior Designer: Quorum Creative Services
Full Service Composition: Black Dot Group
Printer/Binder: Von Hoffmann Corporation
Cover Printer: Phoenix Color Corporation

Credits and acknowledgments borrowed from other sources and reproduced, with permission, in this textbook are as follows or on the appropriate page within the text.

Microsoft, Windows, PowerPoint, Outlook, FrontPage, Visual Basic, MSN, The Microsoft Network, and/or other Microsoft products referenced herein are either trademarks or registered trademarks of Microsoft Corporation in the U.S.A. and other countries. Screen shots and icons reprinted with permission from the Microsoft Corporation. This book is not sponsored or endorsed by or affiliated with Microsoft Corporation.

Microsoft and the Microsoft Office Specialist logo are trademarks or registered trademarks of Microsoft Corporation in the United States and/or other countries. Pearson Education is independent from Microsoft Corporation and not affiliated with Microsoft in any manner. This text may be used in assisting students to prepare for a Microsoft Office Specialist Exam. Neither Microsoft, its designated review company, nor Pearson Education warrants that use of this text will ensure passing the relevant exam.

Copyright © 2004 by Pearson Education, Inc., Upper Saddle River, New Jersey, 07458. All rights reserved. Printed in the United States of America. This publication is protected by Copyright and permission should be obtained from the publisher prior to any prohibited reproduction, storage in a retrieval system, or transmission in any form or by any means, electronic, mechanical, photocopying, recording, or likewise. For information regarding permission(s), write to the Rights and Permissions Department.

10 9 8 7 6 5 4 3 2 1
ISBN 0-13-143426-8

What does this logo mean?

It means this courseware has been approved by the Microsoft® Office Specialist Program to be among the finest available for learning **Microsoft® Office Word 2003, Microsoft® Office Excel 2003, Microsoft® Office PowerPoint® 2003,** and **Microsoft® Office Access 2003.** It also means that upon completion of this courseware, you may be prepared to take an exam for Microsoft Office Specialist qualification.

What is a Microsoft Office Specialist?

A Microsoft Office Specialist is an individual who has passed exams for certifying his or her skills in one or more of the Microsoft Office desktop applications such as Microsoft Word, Microsoft Excel, Microsoft PowerPoint, Microsoft Outlook, Microsoft Access, or Microsoft Project. The Microsoft Office Specialist Program typically offers certification exams at the "Specialist" and "Expert" skill levels.* The Microsoft Office Specialist Program is the only program approved by Microsoft for testing proficiency in Microsoft Office desktop applications and Microsoft Project. This testing program can be a valuable asset in any job search or career advancement.

More Information:

To learn more about becoming a Microsoft Office Specialist, visit
www.microsoft.com/officespecialist

To learn about other Microsoft Office Specialist approved courseware from Pearson Education, visit **www.prenhall.com/phit**

*The availability of Microsoft Office Specialist certification exams varies by application, application version, and language. Visit www.microsoft.com/officespecialist for exam availability.

Microsoft, the Microsoft Office Logo, PowerPoint, and Outlook are trademarks or registered trademarks of Microsoft Corporation in the United States and/or other countries, and the Microsoft Office Specialist Logo is used under license from owner.

GO!
Series for Microsoft® Office System 2003

Series Editor: Shelley Gaskin

Office
Getting Started
Brief
Intermediate
Advanced

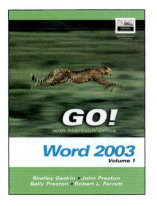

Word
Brief
Volume 1
Volume 2
Comprehensive

Excel
Brief
Volume 1
Volume 2
Comprehensive

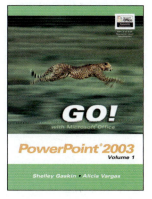

PowerPoint
Brief
Volume 1
Volume 2
Comprehensive

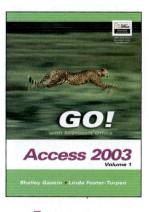

Access
Brief
Volume 1
Volume 2
Comprehensive

GO! Series Reviewers

We would like to thank the following "Super Reviewers" for both their subject matter expertise and attention to detail from the instructors' perspective. Your time, effort, hard work, and diligence has helped us create the best books in the world. Prentice Hall and your author partners thank you:

Rocky Belcher	Sinclair CC
Judy Cameron	Spokane CC
Gail Cope	Sinclair CC
Larry Farrer	Guilford Tech CC
Janet Enck	Columbus State CC
Susan Fry	Boise State
Lewis Hall	Riverside CC
Jeff Howard	Finger Lakes CC
Jason Hu	Pasadena City College
Michele Hulett	Southwest Missouri State U.
Donna Madsen	Kirkwood CC
Cheryl Reindl-Johnson	Sinclair CC
Jan Spaar	Spokane CC
Mary Ann Zlotow	College of DuPage

We would also like to thank our valuable student reviewers who bring us vital input from those who will someday study from our books:

Nicholas J. Bene	Southwest Missouri State U.
Anup Jonathan	Southwest Missouri State U.
Kimber Miller	Pasadena City College
Kelly Moline	Southwest Missouri State U.
Adam Morris	Southwest Missouri State U.
Robert Murphy	Southwest Missouri State U.
Drucilla Owenby	Southwest Missouri State U.
Vince Withee	Southwest Missouri State U.

Finally, we have been lucky to have so many of you respond to review our chapter manuscripts. You have given us tremendous feedback and helped make a fantastic series. We could not have done it without you.

Abraham, Reni	Houston CC	Challa, Chandrashekar		Virginia State University
Agatston, Ann	Agatston Consulting	Chamlou, Afsaneh		NOVA Alexandria
Alejandro, Manuel	Southwest Texas Junior College	Chapman, Pam		Wabaunsee CC
Ali, Farha	Lander University	Christensen, Dan		Iowa Western CC
Anik, Mazhar	Tiffin University	Conroy-Link, Janet		Holy Family College
Armstrong, Gary	Shippensburg University	Cosgrove, Janet		Northwestern CT Community Technical College
Bagui, Sikha	Univ. West Florida			
Belton, Linda	Springfield Tech. Com College	Cox, Rollie		Madison Area Technical College
Bennett, Judith	Sam Houston State University	Crawford, Hiram		Olive Harvey College
Bishop, Frances	DeVry Institute- Alpharetta (ATL)	Danno, John		DeVry University/ Keller Graduate School
Branigan, Dave	DeVry University			
Bray, Patricia	Allegany College of Maryland	Davis, Phillip Md.		Del Mar College
Buehler, Lesley	Ohlone College	Doroshow, Mike		Eastfield College
Buell, C	Central Oregon CC	Douglas, Gretchen		SUNY Cortland
Byars, Pat	Brookhaven College	Driskel, Loretta		Niagara CC
Cacace, Rich	Pensacola Jr. College	Duckwiler, Carol		Wabaunsee CC
Cadenhead, Charles	Brookhaven College	Duncan, Mimi		University of Missouri-St. Louis
Calhoun, Ric	Gordon College	Duvall, Annette		Albuquerque Technical Vocational Institute
Carriker, Sandra	North Shore CC			

Reviewers continues

Reviewers continued

Ecklund, Paula	Duke University
Edmondson, Jeremy	Mount Pisgah School
Erickson, John	University of South Dakota
Falkenstein, Todd	Indiana University East
Fite, Beverly	Amarillo College
Foltz, Brian	East Carolina University
Friedrichsen, Lisa	Johnson County CC
Fustos, Janos	Metro State
Gallup, Jeanette	Blinn College
Gentry, Barb	Parkland College
Gerace, Karin	St. Angela Merici School
Gerace, Tom	Tulane University
Ghajar, Homa	Oklahoma State University
Gifford, Steve	Northwest Iowa CC
Gregoryk, Kerry	Virginia Commonwealth State University
Griggs, Debra	Bellevue CC
Grimm, Carol	Palm Beach CC
Helms, Liz	Columbus State CC
Hernandez, Leticia	TCI College of Technology
Hogan, Pat	Cape Fear CC
Horvath, Carrie	Albertus Magnus College
Howard, Chris	DeVry University
Huckabay, Jamie	Austin CC
Hunt, Laura	Tulsa CC
Jacob, Sherry	Jefferson CC
Jacobs, Duane	Salt Lake CC
Johnson, Kathy	Wright College
Jones, Stacey	Benedict College
Kasai, Susumu	Salt Lake CC
Keen, Debby	Univ. of Kentucky
Kirk, Colleen	Mercy College
Kliston, Linda	Broward CC
Kramer, Ed	Northern Virginia CC
Laird, Jeff	Northeast State CC
Lange, David	Grand Valley State
LaPointe, Deb	Albuquerque TVI
Lenhart, Sheryl	Terra CC
Letavec, Chris	University of Cincinnati
Lightner, Renee	Broward CC
Lindberg, Martha	Minnesota State University
Linge, Richard	Arizona Western College
Loizeaux, Barbara	Westchester CC
Lopez, Don	Clovis- State Center CC District
Low, Willy Hui	Joliet Junior College
Lowe, Rita	Harold Washington College
Lucas, Vickie	Broward CC
Lynam, Linda	Central Missouri State University
Machuca, Wayne	College of the Sequoias
Madison, Dana	Clarion University
Maguire, Trish	Eastern New Mexico University
Malkan, Rajiv	Montgomery College
Manning, David	Northern Kentucky University
Marghitu, Daniela	Auburn University
Marks, Suzanne	Bellevue CC
Marquez, Juanita	El Centro College
Marucco, Toni	Lincoln Land CC
Mason, Lynn	Lubbock Christian University
Matutis, Audrone	Houston CC
McCannon, Melinda (Mindy)	Gordon College
McClure, Darlean	College of Sequoias
McCue, Stacy	Harrisburg Area CC
McEntire-Orbach, Teresa	Middlesex County College
McManus, Illyana	Grossmont College
Menking, Rick	Hardin-Simmons University
Meredith, Mary	U. of Louisiana at Lafayette
Mermelstein, Lisa	Baruch College
Metos, Linda	Salt Lake CC
Meurer, Daniel	University of Cincinnati
Monk, Ellen	University of Delaware
Morris, Nancy	Hudson Valley CC
Nadas, Erika	Wright College
Nadelman, Cindi	New England College
Ncube, Cathy	University of West Florida
Nicholls, Doreen	Mohawk Valley CC
Orr, Claudia	New Mexico State University
Otieno, Derek	DeVry University
Otton, Diana Hill	Chesapeake College
Oxendale, Lucia	West Virginia Institute of Technology
Paiano, Frank	Southwestern College
Proietti, Kathleen	Northern Essex CC
Pusins, Delores	HCCC
Reeves, Karen	High Point University
Rhue, Shelly	DeVry University
Richards, Karen	Maplewoods CC
Ross, Dianne	Univ. of Louisiana in Lafayette
Rousseau, Mary	Broward CC
Sams, Todd	University of Cincinnati
Sandoval, Everett	Reedley College
Sardone, Nancy	Seton Hall University
Scafide, Jean	Mississippi Gulf Coast CC
Scheeren, Judy	Westmoreland County CC
Schneider, Sol	Sam Houston State University
Scroggins, Michael	Southwest Missouri State University
Sever, Suzanne	Northwest Arkansas CC
Sheridan, Rick	California State University-Chico
Sinha, Atin	Albany State University
Smith, T. Michael	Austin CC
Smith, Tammy	Tompkins Cortland CC
Stefanelli, Greg	Carroll CC
Steiner, Ester	New Mexico State University
Sterling, Janet	Houston CC
Stroup, Tracey	Pasadena City College
Sullivan, Angela	Joliet Junior College
Szurek, Joseph	University of Pittsburgh at Greensburg
Taylor, Michael	Seattle Central CC
Thangiah, Sam	Slippery Rock University
Thompson-Sellers, Ingrid	Georgia Perimeter College
Tomasi, Erik	Baruch College
Toreson, Karen	Shoreline CC
Turgeon, Cheryl	Asnuntuck CC
Turpen, Linda	Albuquerque TVI
Upshaw, Susan	Del Mar College
Vargas, Tony	El Paso CC
Vicars, Mitzi	Hampton University
Vitrano, Mary Ellen	Palm Beach CC
Wahila, Lori	Tompkins Cortland CC
Wavle, Sharon	Tompkins Cortland CC
White, Bruce	Quinnipiac University
Willer, Ann	Solano CC
Williams, Mark	Lane CC
Wimberly, Leanne	International Academy of Design and Technology
Worthington, Paula	NOVA Woodbridge
Yauney, Annette	Herkimer CCC
Zavala, Ben	Webster Tech

Dedications

I would like to dedicate this book to my awesome family. I want to thank my husband, Dave Alumbaugh, who always lets me be exactly who I am; my kids, Michael, Jordan, and Ceara, who give me hope and my drive for everything that I do; my mom, who never gives up; and my dad, who has been my light, my rock, and one of my best friends every day that I can remember. I love you all and . . . thanks for putting up with me.

—Linda Foster-Turpen

I would like to dedicate this book to my beautiful wife, Dawn, and to my 5 children, Jacquelynn, Allie, Savannah, Jeffrey, and Jaysen.

—Jeffrey M. Howard

This book is dedicated to my students, who inspire me every day, and to my husband, Fred Gaskin.

—Shelley Gaskin

About the Authors/Acknowledgments

About Linda Foster-Turpen

Linda Foster-Turpen is an instructor in Computer Information Systems at Albuquerque TVI in Albuquerque, New Mexico, where she teaches and has developed computer applications courses. Linda received her B.B.A. in Accounting as well as her M.B.A. in MIS and M.B.A. in Accounting from the University of New Mexico. She has developed new courses for her college including courses in Intranets/Extranets, Management Information Systems, and Distance Learning courses in introductory computer applications and Microsoft Access.

In addition to teaching and authoring, Linda likes to hike and backpack with her family. She lives in Corrales, New Mexico, with her husband Dave, her three children, Michael, Jordan, and Ceara, and their animals.

Acknowledgments from Linda Foster-Turpen

I would like to thank everyone at Prentice Hall (and beyond) who was involved with the production of this book. To my reviewers, your input and feedback were appreciated more than you could know. I would not want to write a book without you! To my technical editors, Jan Snyder and Mary Pascarella, thank you for your attention to detail and for your comments and suggestions during the writing of this book. A big thank you to Emily Knight in Marketing, Gail Steier de Acevedo and Tim Tate in Production, and Pat Smythe and Maria Lange in Design for your contributions. To the series editor, Shelley Gaskin, thank you for your wonderful vision for this book and the entire *GO! Series*. Your ideas and inspiration were the basis for this whole project from its inception. To the Editorial Project Manager, Mike Ruel, thanks for making sure all of my ducks were always in a row, and to the Executive Editor, Jodi McPherson, thank you for your faith and confidence in me from the beginning. A huge thanks to my students, you are the reason these books are written! I would also like to thank my colleagues at TVI for giving me a sounding board from which I could bounce ideas or just vent my frustrations. Any book takes a team of people, and I was most fortunate to have all of you on mine. I also want to thank God for . . . everything.

About Jeffrey M. Howard

Jeffrey M. Howard is a Computer Science instructor at Finger Lakes Community College, State University of New York, Canandiagua, N.Y. campus. He has been teaching for the last 15 years. He currently teaches Microsoft Applications (Word, Excel, PowerPoint, and Access), C++, Java, Assembly, and Engineering. Jeff also teaches Office and Concepts classes online through the SUNY Learning Network. He graduated from the University at Buffalo with a BA and MA in Mathematics.

When not working, Jeff tries to spend as much time as possible with his "beautiful and patient" wife, Dawn, and their children, Jacquelynn, Allie, Savannah, Jeffrey, and Jaysen.

Acknowledgments from Jeffrey M. Howard

I would like to thank my Executive Acquisitions Editor, Jodi McPherson, and Senior Project Manager, Mike Ruel, both at Prentice Hall. My special thanks also goes to Tim Tate, Senior Project Manager in Production.

I would also like to thank the Series Editor, Shelley Gaskin, who was a big help to me.

About Shelley Gaskin

Shelley Gaskin, Series Editor, is a professor of business and computer technology at Pasadena City College in Pasadena, California. She holds a master's degree in business education from Northern Illinois University and a doctorate in adult and community education from Ball State University. Dr. Gaskin has 15 years of experience in the computer industry with several Fortune 500 companies and has developed and written training materials for custom systems applications in both the public and private sector. She is also the author of books on Microsoft Outlook and word processing.

Acknowledgments from Shelley Gaskin

Many talented individuals worked to produce this book, and I thank them for their continuous support. My Executive Acquisitions Editor, Jodi McPherson, gave me much latitude to experiment with new things. Editorial Project Manager Mike Ruel worked with me through each stage of writing and production. Emily Knight and the Prentice Hall Marketing team worked with me throughout this process to make sure both instructors and students are informed about the benefits of using this series. Also, very big thanks and appreciation goes to Prentice Halls' top-notch Production and Design team: Associate Director Product Development Melonie Salvati, Manager of Production Gail Steier de Acevedo, Senior Production Project Manager and Manufacturing Buyer Tim Tate, Design Manager Maria Lange, Art Director Pat Smythe, Interior Designer Quorum Creative Services, and Cover Designer Brian Salisbury.

Thanks to all!
Shelley Gaskin, Series Editor

Why I Wrote This Series

Dear Professor,

If you are like me, you are frantically busy trying to implement new course delivery methods (e.g., online) while also maintaining your regular campus schedule of classes and academic responsibilities. I developed this series for colleagues like you, who are long on commitment and expertise but short on time and assistance.

The primary goal of the **GO! Series**, aside from the obvious one of teaching **Microsoft® Office 2003** concepts and skills, is ease of implementation using any delivery method—traditional, self-paced, or online.

There are no lengthy passages of text; instead, bits of expository text are woven into the steps at the teachable moment. This is the point at which the student has a context within which he or she can understand the concept. A scenario-like approach is used in a manner that makes sense, but it does not attempt to have the student "pretend" to be someone else.

A key feature of this series is the use of Microsoft procedural syntax. That is, steps begin with where the action is to take place, followed by the action itself. This prevents the student from doing the right thing in the wrong place!

The *GO! Series* is written with all of your everyday classroom realities in mind. For example, in each project, the student is instructed to insert his or her name in a footer and to save the document with his or her name. Thus, unidentified printouts do not show up at the printer nor do unidentified documents get stored on the hard drives.

Finally, an overriding consideration is that the student is not always working in a classroom with a teacher. Students frequently work at home or in a lab staffed only with instructional aides. Thus, the instruction must be error-free, clearly written, and logically arranged.

My students enjoy learning the Microsoft Office software. The goal of the instruction in the *GO! Series* is to provide students with the skills to solve business problems using the computer as a tool, for both themselves and the organizations for which they might be employed.

Thank you for using the **GO! Series for Microsoft® Office System 2003** for your students.

Regards,

Shelley Gaskin

Shelley Gaskin, Series Editor

Preface

Philosophy

Our overall philosophy is ease of implementation for the instructor, whether instruction is via lecture, lab, online, or partially self-paced. Right from the start, the *GO! Series* was created with constant input from professors just like you. You've told us what works, how you teach, and what we can do to make your classroom time problem free, creative, and smooth running—to allow you to concentrate on not what you are teaching from but who you are teaching to—your students. We feel that we have succeeded with the *GO! Series*. Our aim is to make this instruction high quality in both content and presentation, and the classroom management aids complete—an instructor could begin teaching the course with only 15 minutes advance notice. An instructor could leave the classroom or computer lab; students would know exactly how to proceed in the text, know exactly what to produce to demonstrate mastery of the objectives, and feel that they had achieved success in their learning. Indeed, this philosophy is essential for real-world use in today's diverse educational environment.

How did we do it?

- All steps utilize **Microsoft Procedural Syntax**. The *GO! Series* puts students where they need to be, before instructing them what to do. For example, instead of instructing students to "Save the file," we go a few steps further and phrase the instruction as "On the **Menu** bar, click **File**, and then select **Save As**."

- A unique teaching system (packaged together in one easy to use **Instructor's Edition** binder set) that enables you to teach anywhere you have to—online, lab, lecture, self-paced, and so forth. The supplements are designed to save you time:

    - ***Expert Demonstration Document***—A new project that mirrors the learning objectives of the in-chapter project, with a full demonstration script for you to give a lecture overview quickly and clearly.

    - ***Chapter Assignment Sheets***—A sheet listing all the assignments for the chapter. An instructor can quickly insert his or her name, course information, due dates, and points.

    - ***Custom Assignment Tags***—These cutout tags include a brief list of common errors that students could make on each project, with check boxes so instructors don't have to keep writing the same error description over and over! These tags serve a dual purpose: The student can do a final check to make sure all the listed items are correct, and the instructor can check off the items that need to be corrected.

- ***Highlighted Overlays***—These are printed and transparent overlays that the instructor lays over the student's assignment paper to see at a glance if the student changed what he or she needed to. Coupled with the Custom Assignment Tags, this creates a "grading and scoring system" that is easy for the instructor to implement.
- ***Point Counted Chapter Production Test***—Working hand-in-hand with the Expert Demonstration Document, this is a final test for the student to demonstrate mastery of the objectives.

Goals of the GO! Series

The goals of the *GO! Series* are as follows:

- Make it *easy for the instructor to implement* in any instructional setting through high-quality content and instructional aids and provide the student with a valuable, interesting, important, satisfying, and clearly defined learning experience.
- Enable true diverse delivery for today's diverse audience. The *GO! Series* employs various instructional techniques that address the needs of all types of students in all types of delivery modes.
- Provide *turn-key implementation* in the following instructional settings:
    - Traditional computer classroom—Students experience a mix of lecture and lab.
    - Online instruction—Students complete instruction at a remote location and submit assignments to the instructor electronically—questions answered by instructor through electronic queries.
    - Partially self-paced, individualized instruction—Students meet with an instructor for part of the class, and complete part of the class in a lab setting.
    - Completely self-paced, individualized instruction—Students complete all instruction in an instructor-staffed lab setting.
    - Independent self-paced, individualized instruction—Students complete all instruction in a campus lab staffed with instructional aides.
- Teach—*to maximize the moment*. The *GO! Series* is based on the Teachable Moment Theory. There are no long passages of text; instead, concepts are woven into the steps at the teachable moment. Students always know what they need to do and where to do it.

Pedagogical Approach

The *GO! Series* uses an instructional system approach that incorporates three elements:

- *Steps are written in* **Microsoft Procedural Syntax**, which prevents the student from doing the right thing but in the wrong place. This makes it easy for the instructor to teach instead of untangle. It tells the student where to go first, then what to do. For example—"On the File Menu, click Properties."

- *Instructional strategies* including five new, unique ancillary pieces to support the instructor experience. The foundation of the instructional strategies is performance based instruction that is constructed in a manner that makes it *easy for the instructor* to demonstrate the content with the GO Series Expert Demonstration Document, guide the practice by using our many end-of-chapter projects with varying guidance levels, and assess the level of mastery with tools such as our Point Counted Production Test and Custom Assignment Tags.

- *A physical design* that makes it *easy for the instructor* to answer the question, "What do they have to do?" and makes it easy for the student to answer the question, "What do I have to do?" Most importantly, you told us what was needed in the design. We held several focus groups throughout the country where we showed **you** our design drafts and let you tell us what you thought of them. We revised our design based on your input to be functional and support the classroom experience. For example, you told us that a common problem is students not realizing where a project ends. So, we added an "END. You have completed the Project" at the close of every project.

Microsoft Procedural Syntax

Do you ever do something right but in the wrong place?

That's why we've written the *GO! Series* step text using Microsoft procedural syntax. That is, the student is informed where the action should take place before describing the action to take. For example, "On the menu bar, click File," versus "Click File on the menu bar." This prevents the student from doing the right thing in the wrong place. This means that step text usually begins with a preposition—a locator—rather than a verb. Other texts often misunderstand the theory of performance-based instruction and frequently attempt to begin steps with a verb. In fact, the objectives should begin with a verb, not the steps.

The use of Microsoft procedural syntax is one of the key reasons that the *GO! Series* eases the burden for the instructor. The instructor spends less time untangling students' unnecessary actions and more time assisting students with real questions. No longer will students become frustrated and say "But I did what it said!" only to discover that, indeed, they *did* do "what it said" but in the wrong place!

Chapter Organization—Color-Coded Projects

All of the chapters in every *GO! Series* book are organized around interesting projects. Within each chapter, all of the instructional activities will cluster around these projects without any long passages of text for the student to read. Thus, every instructional activity contributes to the completion of the project to which it is associated. Students learn skills to solve real business problems; they don't waste time learning every feature the software has. The end-of-chapter material consists of additional projects with varying levels of difficulty.

The chapters are based on the following basic hierarchy:

Project Name
    Objective Name (begins with a verb)
        Activity Name (begins with a gerund)
            Numbered Steps (begins with a preposition or a verb using Microsoft Procedural Syntax.)

Project Name → **Project 1A Exploring Outlook 2003**

Objective Name → **Objective 1**
Start Outlook and Identify Outlook Window Elements

Activity Name → **Activity 1.1 Starting Outlook**

Numbered Steps → **1** On the Windows taskbar, click the Start button, determine from your instructor or lab coordinator where the Microsoft Office Outlook 2003 program is located on your system, and then click Microsoft Office Outlook 2003.

A project will have a number of objectives associated with it, and the objectives, in turn, will have one or more activities associated with them. Each activity will have a series of numbered steps. To further enhance understanding, each project, and its objectives and numbered steps, is color coded for fast, easy recognition.

In-Chapter Boxes and Elements

Within every chapter there are helpful boxes and in-line notes that aid the students in their mastery of the performance objectives. Plus, each box has a specific title—"Does Your Notes Button Look Different?" or "To Open the New Appointment Window." Our GO! Series Focus Groups told us to add box titles that indicate the information being covered in the box, and we listened!

Alert!

> **Does Your Notes Button Look Different?**
>
> The size of the monitor and screen resolution set on your computer controls the number of larger module buttons that appear at the bottom of the Navigation pane.

Alert! boxes do just that—they alert students to a common pitfall or spot where trouble may be encountered.

Another Way

> **To Open the New Appointment Window**
>
> You can create a new appointment window using one of the following techniques:
>
> - On the menu bar, click File, point to New, and click Appointment.
> - On the Calendar Standard toolbar, click the New Appointment button.

Another Way boxes explain simply "another way" of going about a task or shortcuts for saving time.

> **Note** — Server Connection Dialog Box
>
> If a message displays indicating that a connection to the server could not be established, click OK. Even without a mail server connection, you can still use the personal information management features of Outlook.

Notes highlight additional information pertaining to a task.

> **More Knowledge** — Creating New Folders
>
> A module does not have to be active in order to create new folders within it. From the Create New Folder text box, you can change the type of items that the new folder will contain and then select any location in which to place the new folder. Additionally, it is easy to move a folder created in one location to a different location.

More Knowledge is a more detailed look at a topic or task.

Organization of the GO! Series

The *GO! Series for Microsoft® Office System 2003* includes several different combinations of texts to best suit your needs.

- **Word, Excel, Access, and PowerPoint 2003** are available in the following editions:
  - **Brief:** Chapters 1–3 (1–4 for Word 2003)
  - **Volume 1:** Chapters 1–6
    ~ Microsoft Office Specialist Certification
  - **Volume 2:** Chapters 7–12 (7–8 for PowerPoint 2003)
  - **Comprehensive:** Chapters 1–12 (1–8 for PowerPoint 2003)
    ~ Microsoft Office Expert Certification for Word and Excel 2003.

- Additionally, the *GO! Series* is available in four combined **Office 2003** texts:
  - **Microsoft® Office 2003 Getting Started** contains the Windows XP Introduction and first chapter from each application (Word, Excel, Access, and PowerPoint).
  - **Microsoft® Office 2003 Brief** contains Chapters 1–3 of Excel, Access, and PowerPoint, and Chapters 1–4 of Word. Four additional supplementary "Getting Started" books are included (Internet Explorer, Computer Concepts, Windows XP, and Outlook 2003).
  - **Microsoft® Office 2003 Intermediate** contains Chapters 4–8 of Excel, Access, and PowerPoint, and Chapters 5–8 of Word.
  - **Microsoft® Office 2003 Advanced** version picks up where the Intermediate leaves off, covering advanced topics for the individual applications. This version contains Chapters 9–12 of Word, Excel, and Access.

Microsoft Office Specialist Certification

The *GO! Series* has been approved by Microsoft for use in preparing for the Microsoft Office Specialist exams. The Microsoft Office Specialist program is globally recognized as the standard for demonstrating desktop skills with the Microsoft Office System of business productivity applications (Microsoft Word, Microsoft Excel, Microsoft Access, Microsoft PowerPoint, and Microsoft Outlook). With Microsoft Office Specialist certification, thousands of people have demonstrated increased productivity and have proved their ability to utilize the advanced functionality of these Microsoft applications.

Instructor and Student Resources

Instructor's Resource Center and Instructor's Edition

The *GO! Series* was designed for you—instructors who are long on commitment and short on time. *We asked you how you use our books and supplements and how we can make it easier for you and save you valuable time.* We listened to what you told us and created this Instructor's Resource Center for you—different from anything you have ever had access to from other texts and publishers.

What is the Instructor's Edition?

1) Instructor's Edition

New from Prentice Hall, exclusively for the *GO! Series*, the Instructor's Edition contains the entire book, wrapped with vital margin notes—things like objectives, a list of the files needed for the chapter, teaching tips, Microsoft Office Specialist objectives covered, and MORE! Below is a sample of the many helpful elements in the Instructor's Edition.

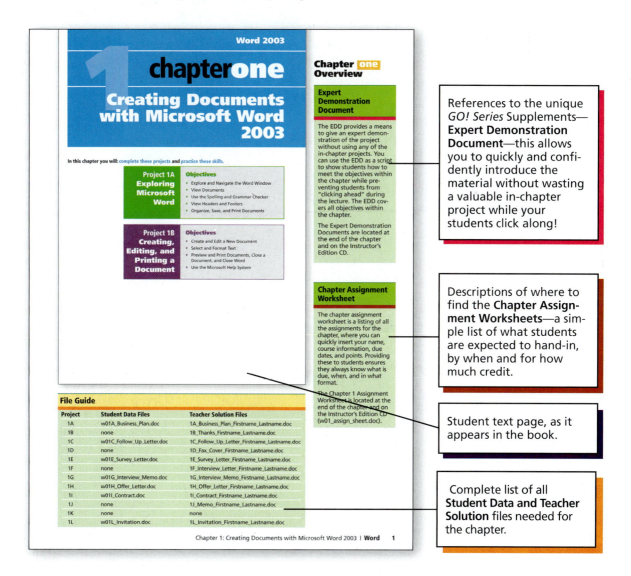

Reference to Prentice Hall's Companion Website for the *GO! Series*: www.prenhall.com/go

The Companion Website is an online training tool that includes personalization features for registered instructors. Data files are available here for download as well as access to additional quizzing exercises.

Each chapter also tells you where to find another unique *GO! Series* Supplement—the **Custom Assignment Tags**—use these in combination with the highlighted overlays to save you time! Simply check off what the students missed or if they completed all the tasks correctly.

Custom Assignment Tags

Custom Assignment Tags, which are meant to be cut out and attached to assignments, serve a dual purpose: the student can do a final check to make sure all the listed items are correct, and the instructor can quickly check off the items that need to be corrected and simply return the assignment.

The Chapter 1 Custom Assignment Tags are located at the end of the chapter and on the Instructor's Edition CD (w01_assign_tags.doc).

The Perfect Party

The Perfect Party store, owned by two partners, provides a wide variety of party accessories including invitations, favors, banners and flags, balloons, piñatas, etc. Party-planning services include both custom parties with pre-filled custom "goodie bags" and "parties in a box" that include everything needed to throw a theme party. Big sellers in this category are the Football and Luau themes. The owners are planning to open a second store and expand their party-planning services to include catering.

© Getty Images, Inc.

Getting Started with Microsoft Office Word 2003

Word processing is the most common program found on personal computers and one that almost everyone has a reason to use. When you learn word processing you are also learning skills and techniques that you need to work efficiently on a personal computer. Use Microsoft Word to do basic word processing tasks such as writing a memo, a report, or a letter. You can also use Word to do complex word processing tasks, including sophisticated tables, embedded graphics, and links to other documents and the Internet. Word is a program that you can learn gradually, adding more advanced skills one at a time.

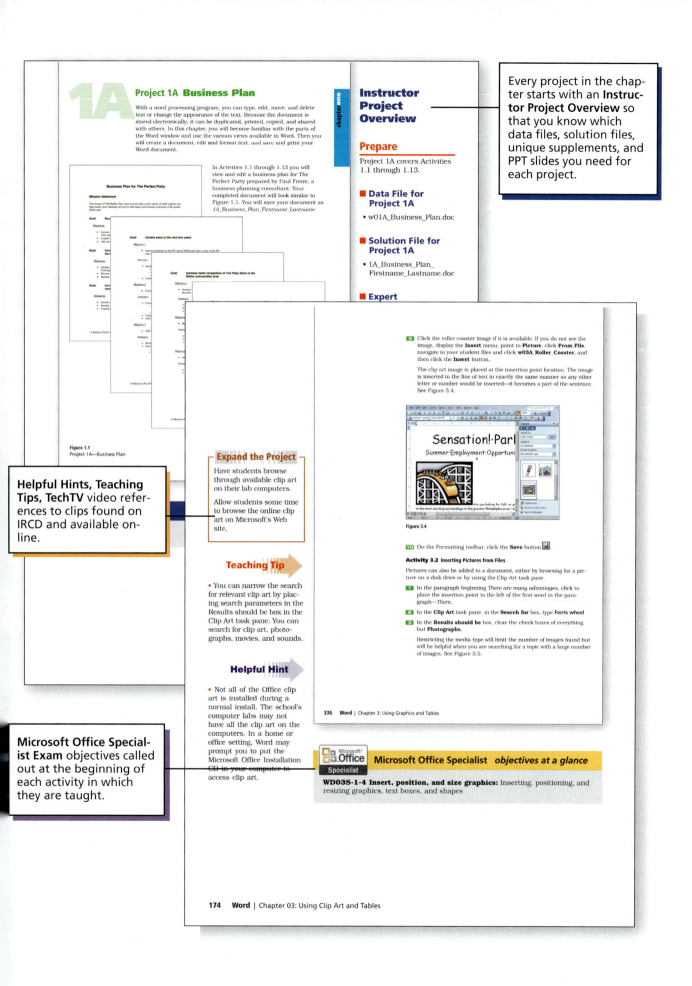

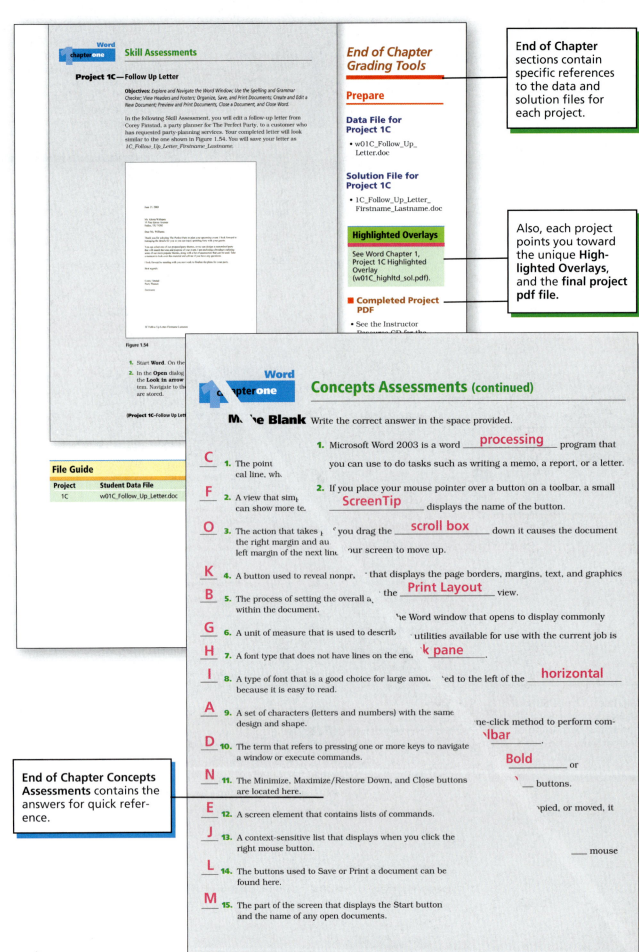

Chapter summary pages contain links to Glossary and Key Terms, as well as information about Online Courses and Prentice Hall's Train and Assess Generation IT—online training and assessment.

Another supplement exclusive to the *GO! Series* is the **Point Counted Production Test.** Reminders are put on each chapter summary page, the printed documents are provided in the back of each chapter, and we also provide electronic versions in Word format on the IE CD-ROM for easy customization.

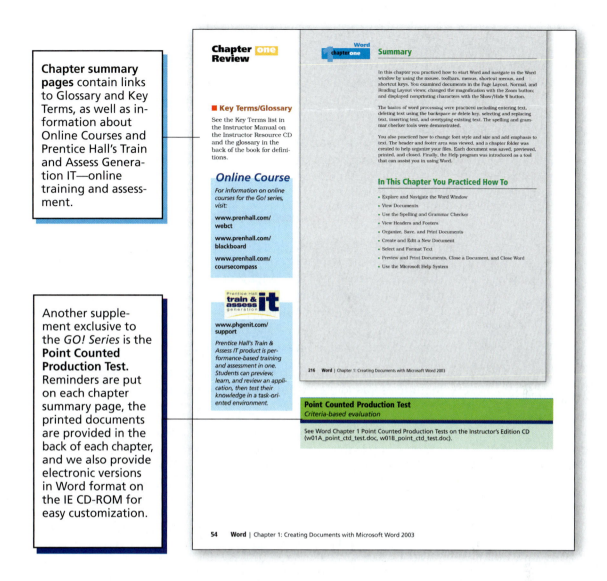

The Instructor's Edition also contains printed copies of these supplement materials *unique* to the *GO! Series*:

- ***Expert Demonstration Document (EDD)***—A mirror image of each in-chapter project, accompanied by a brief script. The instructor can use it to give an expert demonstration of each objective that will be covered in the chapter, without having to use one of the chapter's projects. This EDD also prevents students from "working ahead during the presentation," as they do not have access to this document/project.

- ***Chapter Assignment Sheets***—With a sheet listing all the assignments for the chapter, the instructor can quickly insert his or her name, course information, due dates, and points.

- ***Custom Assignment Tags***—These cutout tags include a brief list of common errors that students could make on each project, with check boxes so instructors don't have to keep writing the same error description over and over! These tags serve a dual purpose: The student can do a final check to make sure all the listed items are correct, and the instructor can check off the items that need to be corrected.

- ***Highlighted Overlays***—These are printed and transparent overlays that the instructor lays over the student's assignment paper to see at a glance if the student changed what he or she needed to. Coupled with the Custom Assignment Tags, this creates a "grading and scoring system" that is easy for the instructor to implement.

- ***Point Counted Chapter Production Test***—Working hand-in-hand with the EDD, this is a final test for the student to demonstrate mastery of the objectives.

2) Enhanced Instructor's Resource CD-ROM

The Instructor's Resource CD-ROM is an interactive library of assets and links. The Instructor's Resource CD-ROM writes custom "index" pages that can be used as the foundation of a class presentation or online lecture. By navigating through the CD-ROM, you can collect the materials that are most relevant to your interests, edit them to create powerful class lectures, copy them to your own computer's hard drive, and/or upload them to an online course management system.

The new and improved Prentice Hall Instructor's Resource CD-ROM includes tools you expect from a Prentice Hall text:

- The Instructor's Manual in Word and PDF formats—includes solutions to all questions and exercises from the book and Companion Website

- Multiple, customizable PowerPoint slide presentations for each chapter

- Data and Solution Files

- Complete Test Bank

- Image library of all figures from the text

- TestGen Software with QuizMaster

  - TestGen is a test generator that lets you view and easily edit test bank questions, transfer them to tests, and print in a variety of formats suitable to your teaching situation. The program also offers many options for organizing and displaying test banks and tests. A built-in random number and text generator makes it ideal for creating multiple versions of tests that involve calculations and provides more possible test items than test bank questions. Powerful search and sort functions let you easily locate questions and arrange them in the order you prefer.

  - QuizMaster allows students to take tests created with TestGen on a local area network. The QuizMaster utility built into TestGen lets instructors view student records and print a variety of reports. Building tests is easy with TestGen, and exams can be easily uploaded into WebCT, Blackboard, and CourseCompass.

3) Instructor's Edition CD-ROM

The Instructor's Edition CD-ROM contains PDF versions of the Instructor's Edition as well as Word versions of the *GO! Series* unique supplements for easy instructor customization.

Training and Assessment— www2.phgenit.com/support

Prentice Hall offers performance-based training and assessment in one product—Train&Assess IT. The training component offers computer-based training that a student can use to preview, learn, and review Microsoft Office application skills. Web or CD-ROM delivered, Train IT offers interactive, multimedia, computer-based training to augment classroom learning. Built-in prescriptive testing suggests a study path based not only on student test results but also on the specific textbook chosen for the course.

The assessment component offers computer-based testing that shares the same user interface as Train IT and is used to evaluate a student's knowledge about specific topics in Word, Excel, Access, PowerPoint, Outlook, the Internet, and Computing Concepts. It does this in a task-oriented environment to demonstrate proficiency as well as comprehension of the topics by the students. More extensive than the testing in Train IT, Assess IT offers more administrative features for the instructor and additional questions for the student.

Assess IT also allows professors to test students out of a course, place students in appropriate courses, and evaluate skill sets.

OneKey—www.prenhall.com/onekey

OneKey lets you in to the best teaching and learning resources all in one place. OneKey for the *GO! Series* is all your students need for anywhere-anytime access to your course materials conveniently organized by textbook chapter to reinforce and apply what they've learned in class. OneKey is all you need to plan and administer your course. All your instructor resources are in one place to maximize your effectiveness and minimize your time and effort. OneKey for convenience, simplicity, and success… for you and your students.

Companion Website @ www.prenhall.com/go

This text is accompanied by a Companion Website at www.prenhall.com/go. Features of this new site include an interactive study guide, downloadable supplements, online end-of-chapter materials, additional practice projects, Web resource links, and technology updates and bonus chapters on the latest trends and hottest topics in information technology. All links to Web exercises will be constantly updated to ensure accuracy for students.

CourseCompass—www.coursecompass.com

 CourseCompass is a dynamic, interactive online course-management tool powered exclusively for Pearson Education by Blackboard. This exciting product allows you to teach market-leading Pearson Education content in an easy-to-use, customizable format.

Blackboard—www.prenhall.com/blackboard

 Prentice Hall's abundant online content, combined with Blackboard's popular tools and interface, result in robust Web-based courses that are easy to implement, manage, and use—taking your courses to new heights in student interaction and learning.

WebCT—www.prenhall.com/webct

Course-management tools within WebCT include page tracking, progress tracking, class and student management, gradebook, communication, calendar, reporting tools, and more. Gold Level Customer Support, available exclusively to adopters of Prentice Hall courses, is provided free-of-charge on adoption and provides you with priority assistance, training discounts, and dedicated technical support.

TechTV—www.techtv.com

 TechTV is the San Francisco-based cable network that showcases the smart, edgy, and unexpected side of technology. By telling stories through the prism of technology, TechTV provides programming that celebrates its viewers' passion, creativity, and lifestyle.

TechTV's programming falls into three categories:

1. **Help and Information**, with shows like *The Screen Savers*, TechTV's daily live variety show featuring everything from guest interviews and celebrities to product advice and demos; *Tech Live*, featuring the latest news on the industry's most important people, companies, products, and issues; and *Call for Help*, a live help and how-to show providing computing tips and live viewer questions.

2. **Cool Docs**, with shows like *The Tech Of...*, a series that goes behind the scenes of modern life and shows you the technology that makes things tick; *Performance*, an investigation into how technology and science are molding the perfect athlete; and *Future Fighting Machines*, a fascinating look at the technology and tactics of warfare.

3. **Outrageous Fun**, with shows like *X-Play*, exploring the latest and greatest in videogaming; and *Unscrewed* with Martin Sargent, a new late-night series showcasing the darker, funnier world of technology.

For more information, log onto www.techtv.com or contact your local cable or satellite provider to get TechTV in your area.

Visual Walk-Through

Project-based Instruction
Students do not practice features of the application; they create real projects that they will need in the real world. Projects are color coded for easy reference.

Projects are named to reflect skills the student will be practicing, not vague project names.

Word 2003

chapter one
Creating Documents with Microsoft Word 2003

In this chapter you will: complete these projects and practice these skills.

Project 1A Exploring Microsoft Word
Objectives
- Explore and Navigate the Word Window
- View Documents
- Use the Spelling and Grammar Checker
- View Headers and Footers
- Organize, Save, and Print Documents

Project 1B Creating, Editing, and Printing a Document
Objectives
- Create and Edit a New Document
- Select and Format Text
- Preview and Print Documents, Close a Document, and Close Word
- Use the Microsoft Help System

Learning Objectives
Objectives are clustered around projects. They help students to learn how to solve problems, not just learn software features.

Each chapter opens with a story that sets the stage for the projects the student will create, not force them to pretend to be someone or make up a scenario themselves.

The Greater Atlanta Job Fair

The Greater Atlanta Job Fair is a nonprofit organization that holds targeted job fairs in and around the greater Atlanta area several times each year. The fairs are widely marketed to companies nationwide and locally. The organization also presents an annual Atlanta Job Fair that draws over 2,000 employers in more than 70 industries and generally registers more than 5,000 candidates.

©Getty Images, Inc.

Getting Started with Outlook 2003

Do you sometimes find it a challenge to manage and complete all the tasks related to your job, family, and class work? Microsoft Office Outlook 2003 can help. Outlook 2003 is a personal information management program (also known as a PIM) that does two things: (1) it helps you get organized, and (2) it helps you communicate with others efficiently. Successful people know that good organizational and communication skills are important. Outlook 2003 electronically stores and organizes appointments and due dates; names, addresses, and phone numbers; to do lists; and notes. Another major use of Outlook 2003 is its e-mail and fax capabilities, along with features with which you can manage group work such as the tasks assigned to a group of coworkers. In this introduction to Microsoft Office Outlook 2003, you will explore the modules available in Outlook and enter data into each module.

Each chapter has an introductory paragraph that briefs students on what is important.

Visual Summary
Shows students up front what their projects will look like when they are done.

Project Summary
Stated clearly and quickly in one paragraph with the Visual Summary formatted as a caption so your students won't skip it.

Objective
The skills they will learn are clearly stated at the beginning of each project and color coded to match projects listed on the chapter opener page.

Teachable Moment
Expository text is woven into the steps—at the moment students need to know it—not chunked together in a block of text that will go unread.

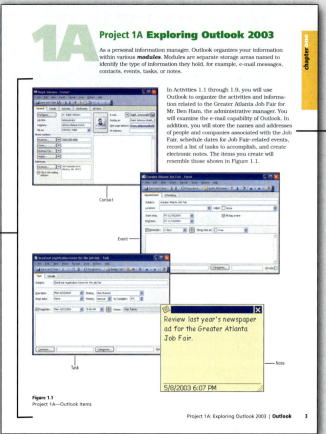

xxviii   Visual Walk-Through

Steps
Color coded to the current project, easy to read, and not too many to confuse the student or too few to be meaningless.

Microsoft Procedural Syntax
All steps are written in Microsoft Procedural Syntax in order to put the student in the right place at the right time.

Sequential Page Numbering
No more confusing letters and abbreviations.

End of Project Icon
All projects in the *GO! Series* have clearly identifiable end points, useful in self-paced or on-line environments.

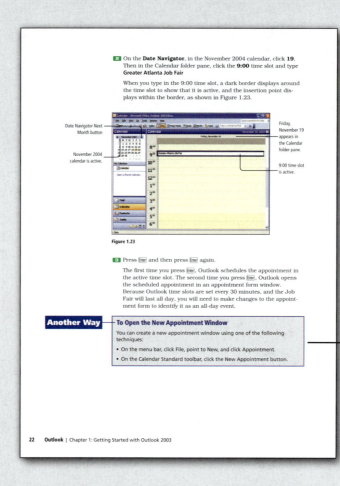

Alert box
Draws students' attention to make sure they aren't getting too far off course.

Another Way box
Shows students other ways of doing tasks.

More Knowledge box
Expands on a topic by going deeper into the material.

Note box
Points out important items to remember.

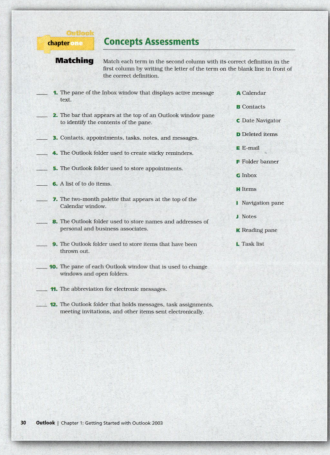

End-of-Chapter Material
Take your pick… Skills Assessment, Performance Assessment, or Mastery Assessment. Real-world projects with high, medium, or low guidance levels.

xxx Visual Walk-Through

Objectives List

Each project in the GO! Series end-of-chapter section starts with a list of the objectives covered, in order to easily find the exercises you need to hone your skills.

Performance Assessments

Project 1D — Creating Folders for College Fairs

Objectives: *Start Outlook and Create Outlook Folders.*

The fairs for Mercer College and Georgia Tech have been set for April 2005. As a result, you need to create folders to hold vendor information for the fairs. When you have created the contact folders for these two fairs, your Contacts list will appear as in Figure 1.35.

Figure 1.35

1. Start Outlook, open the **Contacts** module, open the main **Contacts** folder, and on the menu bar, click **File**, point to **Folder**, and click **New Folder** to open the **Create New Folder** dialog box.
2. In the **Name** text box, type **Mercer College Fair 2005** ensure that **Contact Items** appears in the **Folder contains** text box, and click **OK**.
3. Repeat the procedures in Steps 1 and 2 to create another contacts folder named **Georgia Tech Fair 2005**

End You have completed Project 1D

End of Each Project Clearly Marked

Groups of steps that the student performs; the guided practice in order to master the learning objective.

On the Internet

In this section, students are directed to go out to the Internet for independent study.

On the Internet

Locating Friends on the Web

The World Wide Web not only stores information about companies, Web sites for bidding on items, and so forth, but it also contains telephone book information as well as e-mail addresses for many people—especially those who are students at universities! Search the Web for the colleges that three of your friends attend. After you locate the sites, search each university's e-mail directory for one of your friends. Then record these friends and their university e-mail addresses in your contacts list. Print a copy of each contact form as you create it.

GO! with Help

Training on Outlook

Microsoft Online has set up a series of training lessons at its online Web site. You can access Microsoft.com and review these training sessions directly from the Help menu in Outlook. In this project, you will work your way through the links on the Microsoft Web site to see what training topics they currently offer for Outlook. Log onto the required networks, connect to the Internet, and then follow these steps to complete the exercise.

1. If necessary, start Outlook. On the menu bar, click **Help** and then click **Office on Microsoft.com**.
   The Microsoft Office Online Web page opens in the default browser window.
2. On the left side of the Microsoft Office Online Web page, click the **Training** link.
   The Training Home Web page opens.
3. On the Training Home page, under Browse Training Courses, click **Outlook**.
   The Outlook Courses Web page opens.
4. On the Outlook Courses Web page list, click **Address your e-mail: Get it on the To line fast**.
   The Overview Web page displays information about the training session, identifies the goals of the session, and displays links for continuing the session. Navigation buttons appear in a grey bar toward the top of the Overview page for playing, pausing, and stopping the session. Yellow arrows appear above the navigation bar to advance to the next session page.
5. In the upper right side of the Overview page, on the gray navigation bar, click **Play**.

GO! with Help

A special section where students practice using the HELP feature of the Office application.

Visual Walk-Through xxxi

Contents in Brief

Preface xiii

brief

Chapter 1 **Getting Started with Access Databases and Tables** 1

Chapter 2 **Forms and Reports** 81

Chapter 3 **Queries** 153

volume 1
Chapters 1 through 6

Chapter 4 **Customizing Tables, Data Access Pages, and Converting a Database** 225

Chapter 5 **Building and Maintaining a Relational Database** 291

Chapter 6 **Advanced Forms and Subforms** ... 351

volume 2
Chapters 7 through 12

Chapter 7 **Advanced Reports and Queries** 417

Chapter 8 **Integrating Access with Other Office Applications** 481

Chapter 9 **Macros and Switchboards** 545

Chapter 10 **Access Tools** 609

Chapter 11 **Visual Basic for Applications** 659

comprehensive
Chapters 1 through 12

Chapter 12 **Exporting and Advanced Integration** 707

Task Guide 769

Glossary 799

Index 805

Table of Contents

Preface .... **xiii**

Chapter 1   **Getting Started with Access Databases and Tables** **1**

Objective 1	**Rename a Database**	**4**
Activity 1.1	Renaming a Database	4
Objective 2	**Start Access, Open an Existing Database, and View Database Objects**	**6**
Activity 1.2	Starting Access and Opening an Existing Database	6
Activity 1.3	Viewing the Database Window	12
Activity 1.4	Opening a Table	14
Activity 1.5	Viewing a Table	18
Activity 1.6	Viewing a Query	20
Activity 1.7	Viewing a Form	21
Activity 1.8	Viewing and Printing a Report	23
Objective 3	**Create a New Database**	**28**
Activity 1.9	Creating a New Database	28
Objective 4	**Create a New Table**	**29**
Activity 1.10	Adding Fields to a Table	29
Activity 1.11	Switching Between Views	33
Objective 5	**Create a Primary Key and Add Records to a Table**	**34**
Activity 1.12	Creating a Primary Key in a Table	34
Activity 1.13	Adding Records to a Table	36
Objective 6	**Close and Save a Table**	**37**
Activity 1.14	Closing and Saving a Table	37
Objective 7	**Open a Table**	**38**
Activity 1.15	Opening a Table	38
Objective 8	**Modify the Table Design**	**39**
Activity 1.16	Deleting Fields	39
Activity 1.17	Adding Fields	41
Objective 9	**Print a Table**	**42**
Activity 1.18	Printing a Table	42
Objective 10	**Edit Records in a Table**	**44**
Activity 1.19	Editing a Record	44
Activity 1.20	Deleting a Record	45
Activity 1.21	Resizing Columns and Rows	46
Activity 1.22	Hiding Columns	49
Objective 11	**Sort Records**	**51**
Activity 1.23	Sorting Records in a Table	51
Objective 12	**Navigate to Records in a Table**	**52**
Activity 1.24	Navigating Among Records Using the Navigation Area	52
Activity 1.25	Navigating Among Records Using the Keyboard	53
Objective 13	**Close and Save a Database**	**54**
Activity 1.26	Closing and Saving a Database	54
Objective 14	**Use the Access Help System**	**55**
Activity 1.27	Using the Access Help System	55

Summary	58
In This Chapter You Practiced How To	58
Concepts Assessment	59
Skill Assessments	61
Performance Assessments	69
Mastery Assessments	75
Problem Solving Assessments	79
On the Internet	80
Go! with Access Help	80

Chapter 2   **Forms and Reports** **81**

Objective 1	**View and Navigate to Records with a Form**	**84**
Activity 2.1	Viewing and Navigating to Records Using a Form	84
Objective 2	**Create an AutoForm**	**87**
Activity 2.2	Creating an AutoForm	87
Objective 3	**Save and Close an AutoForm**	**89**
Activity 2.3	Saving and Closing an AutoForm	89
Objective 4	**Use a Form to Add Records to and Delete Records from a Table**	**90**
Activity 2.4	Adding Records to a Table Using a Form	90
Activity 2.5	Deleting Records from a Table Using a Form	91
Objective 5	**Create a From with the Form Wizard**	**95**
Activity 2.6	Creating a Form Using the Form Wizard	95
Objective 6	**Modify a Form**	**98**
Activity 2.7	Switching Between Views in a Form and Adding a Form Header	98
Activity 2.8	Moving and Resizing Fields in a Form	103
Activity 2.9	Adding a Page Footer to a Form	110
Objective 7	**Create a Report with the Report Wizard**	**112**
Activity 2.10	Creating a Report Using the Report Wizard	112
Objective 8	**Save a Report**	**115**
Activity 2.11	Saving a Report	115
Objective 9	**Modify the Design of a Report**	**115**
Activity 2.12	Switching Between Report View and Design View	115
Activity 2.13	Moving and Resizing Fields in a Report	117
Activity 2.14	Adding a Page Footer and a Report Footer to a Report	124
Objective 10	**Print a Report**	**126**
Activity 2.15	Printing a Report	126

Summary	127
In This Chapter You Practiced How To	127
Concepts Assessments	128
Skill Assessments	130

xxxv

Performance Assessments	140
Mastery Assessments	146
Problem Solving Assessments	150
On the Internet	151
GO! with Help	152

Chapter 3 Queries 153

Objective 1 Create a New Select Query — 156
- Activity 3.1 Creating a New Query, Using the Select Query Window, and Adding Fields to the Design Grid — 156

Objective 2 Run, Save, and Close a Query — 161
- Activity 3.2 Running, Saving, and Closing a Query — 161

Objective 3 Open and Edit an Existing Query — 162
- Activity 3.3 Opening an Existing Query and Switching Between Views — 162
- Activity 3.4 Editing a Query — 163

Objective 4 Specify Text Criteria in a Query — 166
- Activity 3.5 Specifying Text Criteria in a Query — 166
- Activity 3.6 Printing a Query — 172

Objective 5 Use Wildcards in a Query — 174
- Activity 3.7 Using the * Wildcard in a Query — 174
- Activity 3.8 Using the ? Wildcard in a Query — 178
- Activity 3.9 Specifying Criteria Using a Field Not Displayed in the Query Result — 180

Objective 6 Specify Numeric Criteria in a Query — 183
- Activity 3.10 Specifying Numeric Criteria in a Query — 183
- Activity 3.11 Using Comparison Operators — 184

Objective 7 Use Compound Criteria — 187
- Activity 3.12 Using AND in a Query — 187
- Activity 3.13 Using OR in a Query — 188

Objective 8 Sort Data in a Query — 189
- Activity 3.14 Sorting Data in a Query — 189
- Activity 3.15 Modifying the Query Design and Sorting Data Using Multiple Fields in a Query — 190

Objective 9 Use Calculated Fields in a Query — 196
- Activity 3.16 Using Calculated Fields in a Query — 196

Objective 10 Group Data and Calculate Statistics in a Query — 201
- Activity 3.17 Grouping Data in a Query — 201
- Activity 3.18 Using the AVG, SUM, MAX, and MIN Function in a Query — 203

Summary	206
In This Chapter You Practiced How To	206
Concepts Assessment	207
Skill Assessments	209
Performance Assessments	216
Mastery Assessments	220
Problem Solving Assessments	223
On the Internet	224
GO! with Help	224

Chapter 4 Customizing Tables, Data Access Pages, and Converting a Database 225

Objective 1 Customize a Field — 228
- Activity 4.1 Changing a Data Type — 228
- Activity 4.2 Changing a Field Size — 232
- Activity 4.3 Entering a Default Value — 234

Objective 2 Specify a Field Format — 235
- Activity 4.4 Specifying a Field Format — 235

Objective 3 Create Input Masks Using the Input Mask Wizard — 237
- Activity 4.5 Creating Input Masks Using the Input Mask Wizard — 237

Objective 4 Create Input Masks Using the Input Mask Properties Box — 240
- Activity 4.6 Specifying Uppercase and Lowercase Text — 240
- Activity 4.7 Specifying Numeric Input Masks — 242

Objective 5 Specify a Required Field — 244
- Activity 4.8 Specifying a Required Field — 244

Objective 6 Validate Data Entry — 246
- Activity 4.9 Using the Expression Builder to Create Validation Rules — 246
- Activity 4.10 Creating Validation Text — 248

Objective 7 Create a Lookup Wizard Field — 250
- Activity 4.11 Creating a Lookup Wizard Field — 250

Objective 8 Find a Record — 252
- Activity 4.12 Finding a Record by Searching a Single Field — 252
- Activity 4.13 Finding a Record by Searching the Table — 254

Objective 9 Display Specific Records — 255
- Activity 4.14 Displaying Specific Records Using Filter By Selection — 255
- Activity 4.15 Displaying Specific Records Using Filter By Form — 257

Objective 10 Create and Use a Data Access Page — 260
- Activity 4.16 Creating a Data Access Page — 260
- Activity 4.17 Viewing the Data Access Page with a Browser — 263
- Activity 4.18 Using a Data Access Page — 265

Objective 11 Convert a Database from a Previous Version of Access — 267
- Activity 4.19 Converting a Database from a Previous Version of Access — 267

Summary	269
In This Chapter You Practiced How To	269
Concepts Assessments	270
Skill Assessments	272
Performance Assessments	280
Mastery Assessments	286
Problem Solving	289
On the Internet	290
GO! with Help	290

Chapter 5 Building and Maintaining a Relational Database 291

Objective 1 Index Fields in a Table — 294
- Activity 5.1 Indexing Fields Without Duplicates — 294
- Activity 5.2 Indexing Fields with Duplicates — 295

Objective 2 View Relationships in a Database — 296
- Activity 5.3 Viewing Relationships in a Database — 296

Objective 3 Establish Relationships Between Tables — 301
- Activity 5.4 Establishing a One-to-Many Relationship and Enforcing Referential Integrity — 301
- Activity 5.5 Printing the Relationships Window — 304
- Activity 5.6 Establishing a One-to-One Relationship — 304
- Activity 5.7 Establishing a Many-to-Many Relationship — 307

Objective 4 Create a Query from Joined Tables — 310
- Activity 5.8 Creating a Query from Joined Tables — 310

Objective 5 Identify and Correct Design Errors in Tables — 313
- Activity 5.9 Finding Duplicate Records — 313
- Activity 5.10 Finding Unmatched Records — 315
- Activity 5.11 Examining Tables to Check for Design Errors — 317
- Activity 5.12 Testing the Design of a Database — 320

Objective 6 Protect and Maintain a Database — 322
- Activity 5.13 Protecting a Database with a Password — 322
- Activity 5.14 Encoding and Decoding a Database — 324
- Activity 5.15 Compacting and Repairing Database Files — 326
- Activity 5.16 Making Backup Copies of a Database and Replicating a Database — 327

Summary — 331
In This Chapter You Practiced How To — 331
Concepts Assessments — 332
Skill Assessments — 334
Performance Assessments — 340
Mastery Assessments — 346
Problem Solving — 349
On the Internet — 351
GO! with Help — 351

Chapter 6 Advanced Forms and Subforms 353

Objective 1 Add Fields to a Form — 356
- Activity 6.1 Adding Fields to a Form — 356

Objective 2 Use Toolbar Buttons to Enhance a Form — 359
- Activity 6.2 Modifying Font Color — 359
- Activity 6.3 Adding a Background Color to a Form — 361
- Activity 6.4 Applying a Border to a Control in a Form — 363

Objective 3 Use Form Control Properties — 366
- Activity 6.5 Changing Text Properties on a Form Using the Property Sheet — 366
- Activity 6.6 Refining Additional Properties on a Form Using the Properties Box — 369

Objective 4 Make a Form User-Friendly — 371
- Activity 6.7 Adding Instructions to the Status Bar of a Form — 371
- Activity 6.8 Creating Custom ControlTips — 373
- Activity 6.9 Adding a Combo Box to a Form — 374
- Activity 6.10 Changing the Tab Order on a Form — 379

Objective 5 Create a Form in Design View — 382
- Activity 6.11 Creating a Form in Design View — 382
- Activity 6.12 Specifying a Picture Background — 385
- Activity 6.13 Adding a Title to the Form — 386

Objective 6 Create a Subform — 388
- Activity 6.14 Creating a Subform — 388
- Activity 6.15 Adding Records Using the Subform — 390

Summary — 393
In This Chapter You Practiced How to — 393
Concepts Assessments — 394
Skill Assessments — 396
Performance Assessments — 406
Mastery Assessments — 411
Problem Solving — 415
On the Internet — 416
GO! with Help — 417

Chapter 7 Advanced Reports and Queries 417

Objective 1 Create a Subreport — 420
- Activity 7.1 Embedding a Subreport in a Report — 420

Objective 2 Group Data in a Report — 427
- Activity 7.2 Grouping Data in a Report — 427

Objective 3 Create Calculated Fields in a Report — 429
- Activity 7.3 Creating a Calculated Field for a Group — 429
- Activity 7.4 Creating a Calculated Field for a Report — 434

Objective 4 Set Report and Report Section Properties — 435
- Activity 7.5 Setting Report and Report Section Properties — 435

Objective 5 Create a Crosstab Report — 437
- Activity 7.6 Creating a Report from a Crosstab Query — 437

Objective 6 Create an Update Query — 440
- Activity 7.7 Creating an Update Query — 440

Objective 7 Create a Delete Query — 444
- Activity 7.8 Creating and Running a Delete Query — 444

Objective 8 Create Special Purpose Queries — 447
- Activity 7.9 Creating a Crosstab Query — 447
- Activity 7.10 Adding Conditions to a Crosstab Query — 450
- Activity 7.11 Creating a Parameter Query — 452

Objective 9 Create Action Queries — 454
- Activity 7.12 Creating a Make-Table Query — 454
- Activity 7.13 Creating an Append Query — 456

Objective 10 View Queries in SQL — 458
- Activity 7.14 Viewing Queries in SQL — 458

Summary	460
In This Chapter You Practiced How To	460
Concepts Assessments	461
Skill Assessments	463
Performance Assessments	470
Mastery Assessments	475
Problem Solving	479
On the Internet	480
GO! with Help	480

Chapter 8 Integrating Access with Other Office Applications 481

Objective 1	**Import Data from a Word Table**	**484**
Activity 8.1	Importing Data from a Word Table	484
Objective 2	**Use Mail Merge to Integrate Access and Word**	**491**
Activity 8.2	Merging an Access Table with a Word Document	491
Objective 3	**Import from Excel**	**496**
Activity 8.3	Importing from Excel	496
Objective 4	**Add Hyperlinks to Word and Excel Files**	**497**
Activity 8.4	Adding Hyperlinks from a Form to a Word Document	497
Activity 8.5	Adding Hyperlinks from a Form to an Excel Worksheet	500
Objective 5	**Link Database Objects to Office Files**	**505**
Activity 8.6	Linking a Form and an Excel Worksheet	505
Activity 8.7	Linking Databases	510
Objective 6	**Add a Chart to a Form**	**514**
Activity 8.8	Adding a Chart to a Form	514
Objective 7	**Add a Chart to a Report**	**519**
Activity 8.9	Linking a Chart in a Report	519

Summary	522
In This Chapter You Practiced How To	522
Concepts Assessments	523
Skill Assessments	525
Performance Assessments	533
Mastery Assessments	539
Problem Solving	543
On the Internet	544
GO! with Help	544

Chapter 9 Macros and Switchboards 545

Objective 1	**View the Macro Window**	**548**
Activity 9.1	Viewing the Macro Window	548
Objective 2	**Create a New Macro**	**551**
Activity 9.2	Creating a New Macro	551
Activity 9.3	Adding Actions to a Macro	553
Activity 9.4	Attaching a Macro to a Command Button	556
Objective 3	**Run a Macro in Response to an Event**	**559**
Activity 9.5	Running a Macro in Response to an Event	559
Activity 9.6	Using Condition Expressions in Macros	564
Objective 4	**Create a Macro Group**	**567**
Activity 9.7	Creating a Macro Group	567
Objective 5	**Create a Switchboard Page**	**571**
Activity 9.8	Creating a Switchboard Page	571
Activity 9.9	Enhancing the Switchboard	574
Activity 9.10	Adding a Second Page to the Switchboard	577
Activity 9.11	Changing Switchboard Properties	579

Summary	583
In This Chapter You Practiced How To	583
Concepts Assessments	584
Skill Assessments	586
Performance Assessments	593
Mastery Assessments	600
Problem Solving	605
On the Internet	607
GO! with Help	607

Chapter 10 Access Tools 609

Objective 1	**Use the Database Wizard**	**612**
Activity 10.1	Using the Database Wizard	612
Objective 2	**Analyze Data with the Table Analyzer**	**617**
Activity 10.2	Using the Table Analyzer	617
Objective 3	**Use the Performance Analyzer**	**621**
Activity 10.3	Using the Performance Analyzer	621
Objective 4	**Manage and Secure a Database**	**623**
Activity 10.4	Setting a Database Password	623
Activity 10.5	Establishing User-Level Security	625
Objective 5	**Create a Replica of a Database**	**632**
Activity 10.6	Creating a Replica of a Database	632
Activity 10.7	Encrypting a Database	635

Summary	637
In This Chapter You Practiced How To	637
Concepts Assessments	638
Skill Assessments	640
Performance Assessments	646
Mastery Assessments	652
Problem Solving	656
On the Internet	658
GO! with Help	658

Chapter 11 Visual Basic for Applications 659

Objective 1	**Convert a Macro to VBA Code**	**662**
Activity 11.1	Converting a Macro to VBA Code	662
Objective 2	**Modify an Existing Procedure**	**667**
Activity 11.2	Modifying an Existing Procedure	667
Objective 3	**Use Immediate Window to Test Statements**	**671**
Activity 11.3	Using Immediate Window to Test Statements	671
Objective 4	**Write a Procedure**	**673**
Activity 11.4	Writing a Procedure	673
Activity 11.5	Writing a Second Procedure	676
Objective 5	**Define Variables in a Procedure**	**679**
Activity 11.6	Defining a String Variable in a Procedure	679
Activity 11.7	Defining a Numeric Variable in a Procedure	681
Objective 6	**Use the Selection Structure**	**684**
Activity 11.8	Using the Selection Structure	684
Objective 7	**Use the Select Case Structure**	**686**
Activity 11.9	Using the Select Case Structure	686
Summary		689
In This Chapter You Practiced How To		689
Concepts Assessments		690
Skill Assessments		692
Performance Assessments		697
Mastery Assessments		702
Problem Solving		705
On the Internet		706
GO! with Help		706

Chapter 12 Exporting and Advanced Integration 707

Objective 1	**Export an Access Table to Excel**	**710**
Activity 12.1	Exporting Data to Excel	710
Activity 12.2	Creating a Chart to Analyze Data in Excel	712
Objective 2	**Export an Access Table to Word**	**715**
Activity 12.3	Exporting an Access Table to Word	715
Objective 3	**Create a Report Snapshot**	**718**
Activity 12.4	Using the Export Command to Create a Snapshot	718
Objective 4	**Create a Custom Data Access Page**	**721**
Activity 12.5	Creating a Custom Data Access Page	721
Activity 12.6	Modifying a Data Access Page	723
Objective 5	**Place a PivotTable in a Data Access Page**	**726**
Activity 12.7	Placing a PivotTable in a Data Access Page	726
Objective 6	**Export Access Data as an XML Document**	**732**
Activity 12.8	Exporting Access Data as an XML Document	732
Activity 12.9	Exporting Forms	735
Objective 7	**Import an XML Document into Access**	**736**
Activity 12.10	Importing an XML Document into Access	736
Summary		738
In This Chapter You Practiced How To		738
Concepts Assessments		739
Skill Assessments		741
Performance Assessments		751
Mastery Assessments		761
Problem Solving		765
On the Internet		767
GO! with Help		767

Task Guide 769

Glossary 799

Index 805

Access 2003

chapter one

Getting Started with Access Databases and Tables

In this chapter, you will: complete these projects and practice these skills.

Project 1A
Opening and Viewing a Database

Objectives
- Rename a Database
- Start Access, Open an Existing Database, and View Database Objects

Project 1B
Creating a Database

Objectives
- Create a New Database
- Create a New Table
- Create a Primary Key and Add Records to a Table
- Close and Save a Table
- Open a Table
- Modify the Table Design
- Print a Table
- Edit Records in a Table
- Sort Records
- Navigate to Records in a Table
- Close and Save a Database
- Use the Access Help System

Lake Michigan City College

Lake Michigan City College is located along the lakefront of Chicago—one of the nation's most exciting cities. The college serves its large and diverse student body and makes positive contributions to the community through relevant curricula, partnerships with businesses and nonprofit organizations, and learning experiences that allow students to be full participants in the global community. The college offers three associate degrees in 20 academic areas, adult education programs, and continuing education offerings on campus, at satellite locations, and online.

© Getty Images, Inc.

Getting Started with Access Databases and Tables

Do you have a collection of things that you like, such as a coin collection, stamp collection, recipe collection, or collection of your favorite music CDs? Do you have an address book with the names, addresses, and phone numbers of your friends, business associates, and family members? If you collect something, chances are you have made an attempt to keep track of and organize the items in your collection. If you have an address book, you have probably wished it were better organized. A computer program like Microsoft Access can help you organize and keep track of information.

For example, assume you have a large collection of music CDs. You could organize your CDs into a database because your CDs are a collection of related items. By organizing your CDs in a database, you would be able to find the CDs by various categories that you define. If the information in your address book were placed in a database, you could produce a list of all your friends and family members who have birthdays in the month of April. In this chapter, you will see how useful a database program like Access can be.

Project 1A Computer Club

Data refers to facts about people, events, things, or ideas. A **database** is a collection of data related to a particular topic or purpose. Data that has been organized in a useful manner is referred to as **information**. Examples of data that could be in a database include the titles and artists of all the CDs in a collection or the names and addresses of all the students in an organization. Microsoft Office Access 2003 is a database program that you can use to create and work with information in databases. Databases, like the ones you will work with in Access, include not only the data, but also tools for organizing the data in a way that is useful to you.

In Activities 1.1 through 1.8, you will create a new folder where you will store your projects. Then you will copy a database to your folder and rename the database so you can use it to complete the steps in this project. In this project, you will open a database and view information about the Club Events sponsored by the Computer Club at Lake Michigan City College. See Figure 1.1. In addition to the Event Name and the date of the event, the information includes the name of the Event Coordinator and the type of event.

Club Events

Event#	Event Name	Date	Event Type	Coordinator
01	New Member Social	08/15	Social	Jordan Williams
02	Bi-Monthly Meeting	08/15	Meeting	Annette Jacobson
03	Bi-Monthly Meeting	09/1	Meeting	Annette Jacobson
04	Making Access work for	09/10	Training	Mike Franklin
05	Introduction to Outlook	09/16	Training	Mike Franklin
06	Bi-Monthly Meeting	09/15	Meeting	Annette Jacobson
07	Bi-Monthly Meeting	10/1	Meeting	Annette Jacobson
08	Bi-Monthly Meeting	10/15	Meeting	Annette Jacobson
09	Bi-Monthly Meeting	11/1	Meeting	Annette Jacobson
10	Bi-Monthly Meeting	11/15	Meeting	Annette Jacobson
11	Bi-Monthly Meeting	12/1	Meeting	Annette Jacobson
12	Annual Party	12/10	Social	Linda Turpen
13	Project 1A	11/18	Training	Firstname Lastname

Thursday, October 16, 2003   Page 1 of 1

Figure 1.1
Project 1A—Computer Club

Objective 1
Rename a Database

To complete the projects in the chapters, you will locate the student files that accompany this textbook and copy them to the drive and folder where you are storing your projects. Databases that you copy to your storage location must be renamed so you can differentiate them from the data files that accompany this book. In this activity, you will learn how to do this.

Activity 1.1 Renaming a Database

1. Using the **My Computer** feature of your Windows operating system, navigate to the drive where you will be storing your projects for this book, for example, Removable Disk (D:) drive.

2. On the menu bar, click **File**, point to **New**, and then click **Folder**.

   A new folder is created, the words *New Folder* display highlighted in the folder's name box, and the insertion point is blinking. Recall that within Windows, highlighted text will be replaced by your typing.

3. Type **Chapter 1** and then press [Enter].

4. Navigate to the location where the student files that accompany this textbook are located, and then click once to select the file **a01A_ComputerClub**.

> **Note** — Using File Extensions
>
> *Access databases use a .mdb extension.*
>
> The computer that you are using may be set such that file extensions display. If so, this file name will display as a01A_ComputerClub.mdb. The .mdb extension indicates that this file is a Microsoft database file.

5. Move the mouse pointer over the selected file name and then right-click to display a shortcut menu. On the displayed shortcut menu, click **Copy**.

6. Navigate to and open the **Chapter 1** folder you created in Step 3. Right-click to display a shortcut menu and then click **Paste**.

   The database file is copied to your folder and is selected.

7 Move your mouse pointer over the selected file name, right-click to display the shortcut menu, and then on the shortcut menu, click **Rename**. As shown in Figure 1.2, and using your own first and last name, type **1A_ComputerClub_Firstname_Lastname**

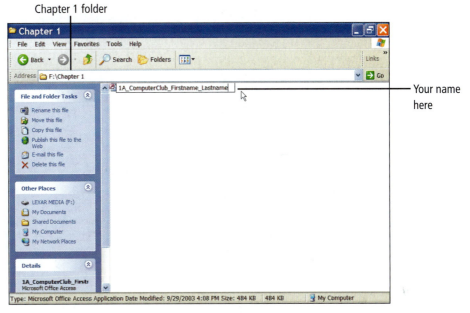

Figure 1.2

8 Press Enter to save the new file name. If the *Confirm File Rename* message displays, click **Yes**. Be sure that the file name is still selected (highlighted), pause your mouse pointer over the selected name, and then right-click to display the shortcut menu.

Note — Naming Files

Use underscores instead of spaces.

The Microsoft Windows operating system recognizes file names with spaces. However, some Internet file transfer programs do not. To facilitate sending your files over the Internet using a course management system, in this textbook you will be instructed to save files using an underscore rather than a space. On your keyboard, the underscore key is the shift of the hyphen key, to the right of the zero key.

9 On the displayed shortcut menu, click **Properties**.

The Properties dialog box with the database name in the title bar displays. The databases provided with this book have a Read-only attribute that protects them from being altered. To use a database, you must first save the database to the location where you are storing your files, rename the database, and then remove the Read-only attribute so you can make changes to the database.

10 At the bottom of the dialog box, click to clear the check mark next to **Read-only**. See Figure 1.3.

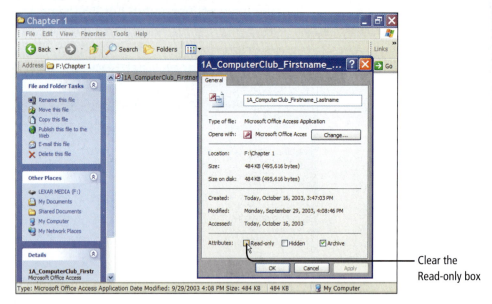

Clear the Read-only box

Figure 1.3

11 Click **OK** to close the dialog box.

12 **Close** the **My Computer** window.

You may want to mark or otherwise make a note of this section for future reference when you need to retrieve, copy, and rename additional databases for use in this textbook.

Objective 2
Start Access, Open an Existing Database, and View Database Objects

Activity 1.2 Starting Access and Opening an Existing Database

Data that is organized in a format of horizontal rows and vertical columns is called a *table*. A table is the foundation on which an Access database is built. In the following activity, you will view a table within a database.

1 On the left side of the Windows taskbar, click the **Start** button .

The Start menu displays.

2 On the computer you are using, determine where the Access program is located and point to **Microsoft Office Access 2003**.

Organizations and individuals store computer programs in a variety of ways. The Access program might be located under All Programs or Microsoft Office or some other arrangement. See Figure 1.4 for an example.

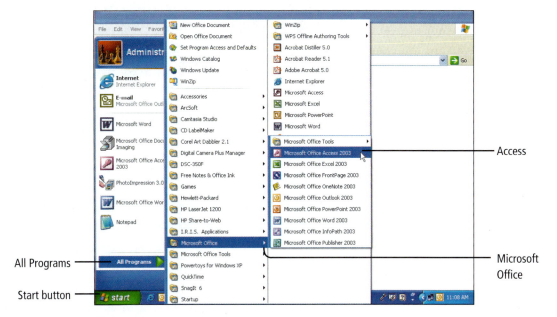

Figure 1.4

3. Click once to open the **Access** program.

The Access program opens. Across the upper portion of the Access window is the title bar, a menu bar, and the Database toolbar. The main window is divided into two sections—the ***task pane*** on the right and a blank gray area on the left. The task pane is a window within a Microsoft Office application that provides commonly used commands. Its location and small size allow you to use these commands while working in your database. A database, when opened, will display in the gray area. See Figure 1.5.

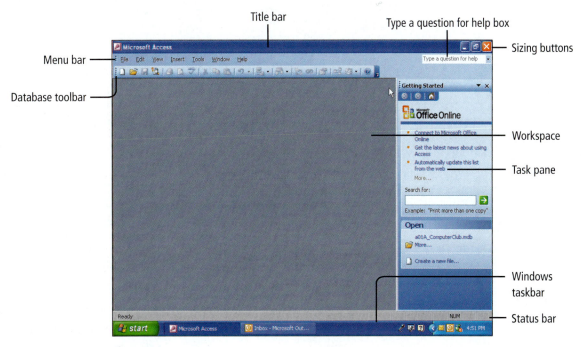

Figure 1.5

Project 1A: Computer Club | **Access** 7

> **Note — Comparing Programs**
>
> *Access opens the program only.*
>
> You may have used Microsoft Word, which opens and displays a blank document, or Microsoft Excel, which opens and displays a blank workbook. Access, however, does not open a blank database—it opens the program only.

4 Take a moment to study the elements of the Access window as shown in Figure 1.5 and as described in the table in Figure 1.6.

Elements of the Access Window

Element	Description
Title bar	Displays the name of the program.
Sizing buttons	Enable you to minimize, maximize, restore, and close the Access window.
Type a question for help box	Allows you to access the Microsoft Access Help feature by typing a question.
Menu bar	Contains the menus of Access commands. Display a menu by clicking on its name in the menu bar.
Database toolbar	Contains a row of buttons that provide a one-click method to perform the most common commands in Access.
Task pane	Displays commonly used commands.
Status bar	Displays information about the task you are working on.
Windows taskbar	Displays the Start button and buttons indicating active windows.
Workspace	Gray area where an open database displays.

Figure 1.6

5 On the Database toolbar, pause your mouse pointer over the **Open** button .

When you position the mouse pointer over a button, Access displays the button's name in a box called a **ScreenTip**. You should see the ScreenTip *Open*.

6 On the menu bar, click **File**.

The File menu displays. When you display a menu in Access, either the short menu, shown in Figure 1.7, or the full menu, shown in Figure 1.8, displays.

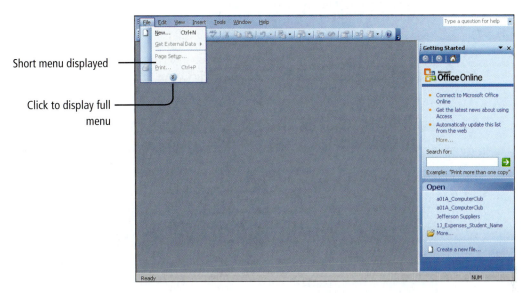

Short menu displayed

Click to display full menu

Figure 1.7

The short menu will display fully after a few seconds. Alternatively, you can click the small double arrow at the bottom of the short menu to display the full menu.

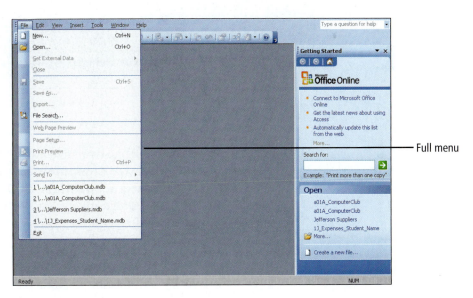

Full menu

Figure 1.8

Project 1A: Computer Club | **Access**

More Knowledge — Displaying the Full Menu

Select the Always show full menus *option.*

If you do not see the short version of the File menu as shown in Figure 1.7, your system has been set so that full menus always display. Many individuals prefer the full menu display. To set a system to always display the full menu, display the Tools menu, click Customize, and then click the Options tab. Select (place a check mark in) the Always show full menus check box. Click Close.

7 On the displayed **File** menu, click **Open**.

The Open dialog box displays.

8 Click the **Look in arrow** shown in Figure 1.9 and then navigate to the location where you are storing your projects for this chapter.

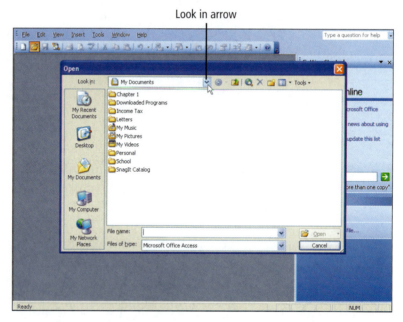

Figure 1.9

9 Locate the database file that you saved and renamed with your name in Activity 1.1. Click the **1A_ComputerClub_Firstname_Lastname** database file once to select it, and then, in the lower right corner, click the **Open** button. Alternatively, you can double-click the name of the database.

10 If the message in Figure 1.10, or similar message, displays on your screen, click **Yes**.

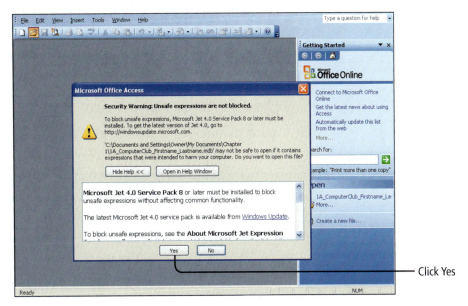

Figure 1.10

11 If another Security Warning message displays, click **Open**.

The ComputerClub Database window opens, as shown in Figure 1.11.

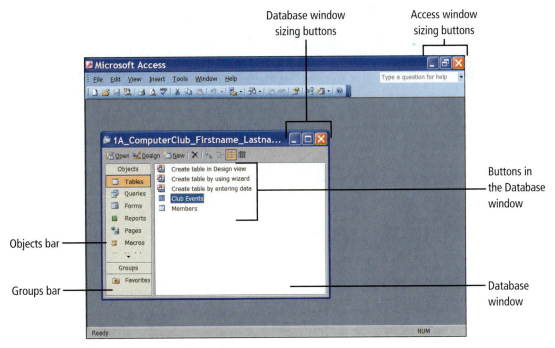

Figure 1.11

Activity 1.3 Viewing the Database Window

The ***Database window*** displays when a database is open. The ***Objects bar*** on the left side of the Database window has buttons—called ***objects***—that you can work with in Access. Objects are the primary components of an Access database.

Just one object—***Tables***—actually *stores* your data; the other objects are used to organize, manage, and manipulate the data. Recall that a table is a collection of data organized in a format of columns and rows. One or more tables can be used to store data in a database.

1 Take a moment to study the elements of the Database window shown in Figure 1.11 and described in the table in Figure 1.12.

Elements of the Database Window

Element	Description
Database window	Displays when a database is open and allows you to access all the database objects.
Objects bar	Contains buttons that activate the objects (tools) of a database.
Groups bar	Contains shortcuts to different types of database objects.
Database window sizing buttons	Enables you to minimize, maximize, and close the Database window.
Buttons in the Database window	Activate commands related to the selected database object.

Figure 1.12

2 In the extreme upper right corner of your screen, locate the **Type a question for help** box. Just above that box, click the Access window's **Minimize** button . See Figure 1.11.

The Access window is minimized and displays as a button on the Windows taskbar at the lower edge of your screen. See Figure 1.13.

Figure 1.13

3️⃣ On the Windows taskbar, click **Microsoft Access**.

The Access window and Database window are restored. Minimizing windows in this manner enables you to view your Desktop.

4️⃣ Look at the Database window (the smaller window) and notice that it also has a set of sizing buttons at the right edge of its title bar. Click its **Maximize** button 🔲.

The Database window fills the entire gray workspace within the Access window. The Database window's title bar no longer displays—the name of the database displays instead on the main title bar enclosed in square brackets. See Figure 1.14.

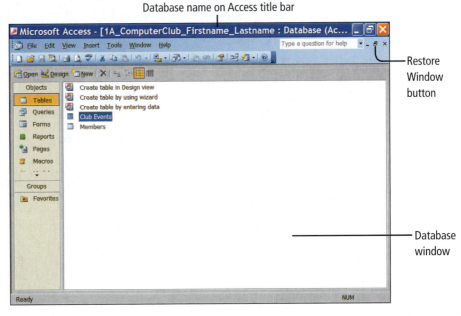

Figure 1.14

Project 1A: Computer Club | **Access** 13

5 To the right of the **Type a question for help** box, click the small **Restore Window** button . See Figure 1.14.

The Database window is restored to its original size and position, as shown in Figure 1.11. You can see that the Database window is a separate window that can be manipulated like other windows.

> **Note** — Sizing the Database Window
>
> *Maximize to fill the gray area.*
>
> You have seen that the Database window can be maximized to fill the gray area, or left in its original size, which is smaller and contained within the gray area. Many Access users prefer keeping the Database window smaller than the gray area of the Access window. This visually separates the Objects bar and the other parts of the Database window from features that are part of the larger Access window.

6 On the Objects bar, notice that *Tables* is selected. With the Tables object selected, point to, but do not click, each of the remaining objects one by one.

The Computer Club Database window displays seven objects: Tables, Queries, Forms, Reports, Pages, Macros, and Modules. Each of these objects is used by Access to manage the information stored in the Computer Club database. As you progress in your study of Access, you will learn more about each of these objects.

Activity 1.4 Opening a Table

Recall that tables are the foundation of your Access database because that is where the data is stored. Each table in an Access database stores data about only one subject. For example, in the Computer Club database, the Club Events table stores data about individual club events and the Members table stores data about the Club's members.

1 On the Objects bar, if necessary, click **Tables** to select it.

Notice that to the right of the Objects bar, three command icons display followed by the names of two tables. The command icons provide three different methods for creating a new table. Following the command icons, the names of the tables that have been created and saved as part of the Computer Club database display. There are two tables in this database, the *Club Events* table and the *Members* table.

2 Click the **Club Events** table once to select it if necessary, and then, just above the Objects bar, click the **Open** button . Alternatively, you can double-click the table name to open it.

The table opens, as shown in Figure 1.15. Here you can see the data organized in a format of columns and rows.

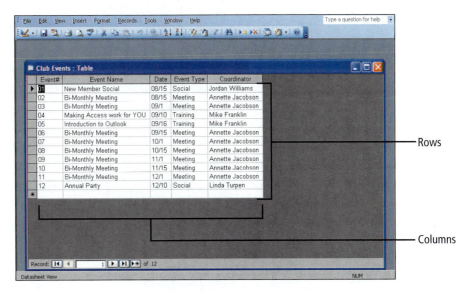

Figure 1.15

3 Along the left side of the open table, move your mouse pointer until it displays as a right-pointing arrow, as shown in Figure 1.16.

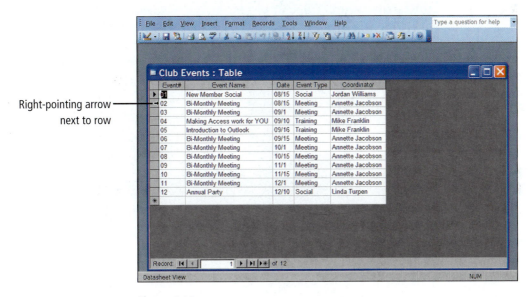

Figure 1.16

Project 1A: Computer Club | **Access**

4 Pause the arrow pointer at the row containing the event *Annual Party* and click once.

The row containing the information for the Annual Party is highlighted in black. Each horizontal row of a table stores all of the information about one database item. You can see that, in the Club Events table, each event has a separate row in the database table. The information in a row is referred to as a **record**.

5 Use the technique you just used in Step 4 to find and select the record for the training event **Introduction to Outlook**.

6 Across the top of the table, move your mouse pointer over the words *Event Type* until it becomes a down arrow, and then click once to select the column. See Figure 1.17.

Each record contains information located in vertical columns, called **fields**, which describe the record. For example, in the Club Events table, each event (record) has the following fields: Event#, Event Name, Date, Event Type, and Coordinator.

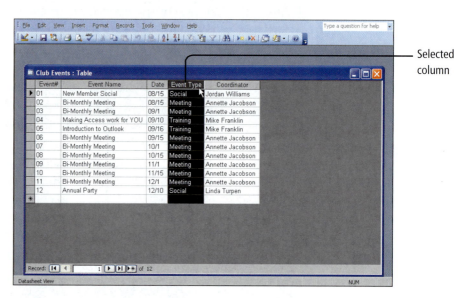

Selected column

Figure 1.17

7 Use your mouse pointer to select the column representing the **Coordinator** field. Take a moment to look at the other column names in the table to familiarize yourself with these *fields*.

16 **Access** | Chapter 1: Getting Started with Access Databases and Tables

8 In the last row of the table, click once in the **Event#** field under the last record in the table. See Figure 1.18.

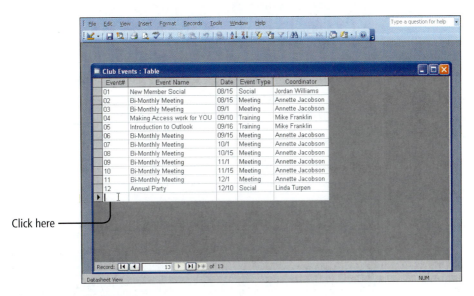

Click here

Figure 1.18

9 In the **Event#** field type **13**

10 Notice the pencil image in the gray box to the left. See Figure 1.19.

In the *row selector*—the small gray box at the left end of a row—a small pencil image displays in the row in which a new record is being entered. The pencil image in the row selector indicates that the information in this record is in the process of being entered and has not yet been saved.

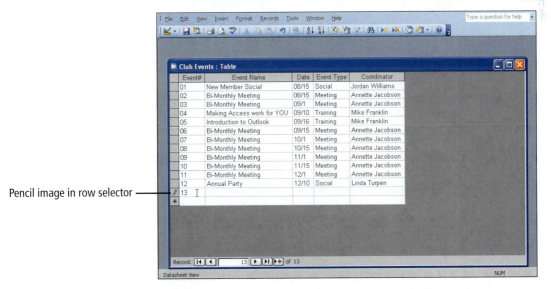

Pencil image in row selector

Figure 1.19

11 Press Tab once.

The insertion point is blinking in the next field to the right, which is the *Event Name* field.

12 In the **Event Name** field, type **Project 1A** and then press Tab.

13 In the **Date** field, type **11/18** and then press Tab.

14 In the **Event Type** field, type **Training** and then press Tab to move to the **Coordinator** field. Using your own first and last name, in the **Coordinator** field, type **Firstname Lastname**

15 Press either Enter or Tab on your keyboard to save the record.

The pencil image no longer displays, indicating that the record is saved. Compare your screen to Figure 1.20.

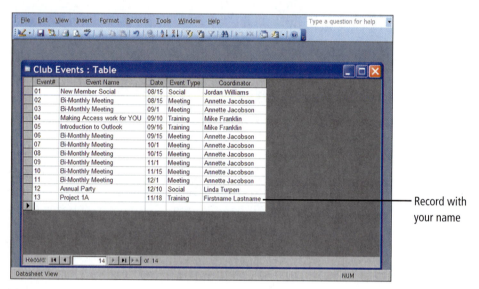

Figure 1.20

Activity 1.5 Viewing a Table

The Tables database object has four ***views***. A view is a way of looking at something such as a table or form. As you work with tables of data, there are two ways to look at tables that are particularly useful—the Datasheet view, which is currently displayed on your screen, and the Design view.

In the previous activity, you opened the Club Events table in the Datasheet view. The Datasheet view displays all the records in a table in a format of columns (fields) and rows (records).

1 On the Table Datasheet toolbar, locate the **View** button, as shown in Figure 1.21.

Its picture, displaying a ruler, a pencil, and a protractor, indicates that clicking the button will switch the display to the Design view of the table. This button will change depending on the current view to allow you to switch back and forth between ***Design view*** and ***Datasheet view***.

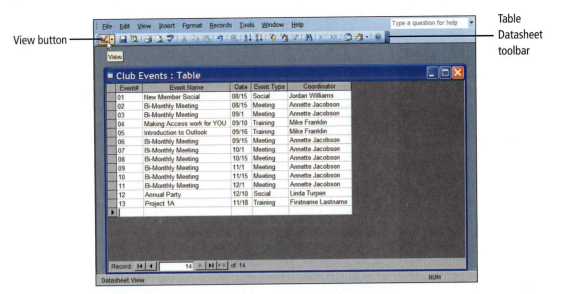

Figure 1.21

2. Click the **View** button .

The Design view of the table displays. Notice that in Design view, you do not see the names of the club events—or other information contained in the records. You see only the names of the fields, such as *Event Name* and *Coordinator*. In this view, you can change the design of the table—that is, the way each field displays its associated data.

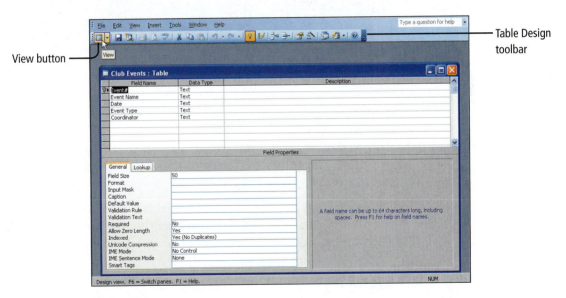

Figure 1.22

3. On the Table Design toolbar, locate the **View** button . See Figure 1.22.

Now the View button displays as a small table—or datasheet. This picture on the View button indicates that clicking the button will return you to the Datasheet (table) view.

Project 1A: Computer Club | **Access** 19

4 Click the **View** button.

The table redisplays in Datasheet view. Recall that the Datasheet view of a table displays the individual records in horizontal rows and the field names at the top of each column. Thus, the View button displays as when you are in the Datasheet view and as when you are in the Design view—indicating which view will be displayed when you click the button.

5 In the upper right corner of the Table window, click the **Close** button to close the table. See Figure 1.23.

The Database window displays.

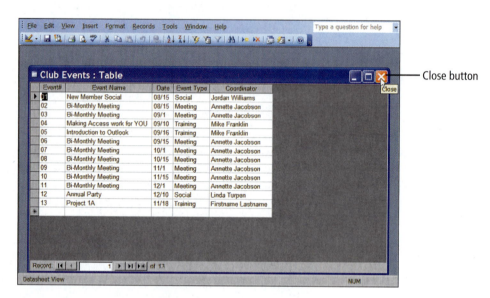

Figure 1.23

Activity 1.6 Viewing a Query

The second object on the Objects bar is *Queries*. To **query** is to ask a question. The Queries object is a tool with which you can ask questions about the data stored in the Tables objects.

For example, you could use the Queries object to ask how many Club Events are social events. Locating specific information in a database, such as the number of social events, is referred to as **extracting** information from the database.

1 On the Objects bar, click **Queries**.

The Database window displays two command icons that can be used to create a new query. They are followed by one query that has been created and saved as part of the Computer Club database. Later, you will create and save your own queries.

■ Double-click the **Social Events Query**. Alternatively, you can right-click the query name, and then click Open on the displayed shortcut menu, or click once to select the query and then click the Open button [Open] in the Database window.

When a query is opened, Access *runs*—processes—the query and displays the results. The results of the query will display only selected information from the table.

■ Look at the records that display as a result of this query.

The number of records in the query result is less that the number of records in the original table because certain **criteria**—specifications that determine what records will be displayed—were entered as part of the query. For example, this query was created to locate the names of all the events in the table that are Social Events. Notice that two records display—New Member Social and Annual Party. See Figure 1.24.

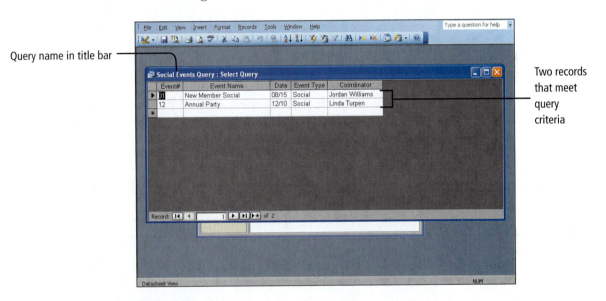

Figure 1.24

■ In the upper right corner of the query window, click the **Close** button [X].

The Database window displays.

Activity 1.7 Viewing a Form

Forms, the third object on the Objects bar, provides an alternative method to both enter and display data in the Tables object. The records that display in a form are the same records that are in the table, with one difference: forms can be designed to display only one record at a time.

■ On the Objects bar, click **Forms**.

To the right of the Objects bar, two command icons for creating a new form display, followed by a form that has been created and saved as part of the Computer Club database. Thus far, only one form, the Club Events form, has been created for this database.

2 Double-click the **Club Events** form.

The Club Events form displays with fields filled in with the data representing the first record in the database. See Figure 1.25.

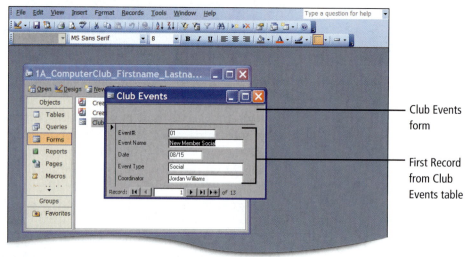

Figure 1.25

3 At the lower edge of the form, click the **Next Record** button until you see the 12th record—the Annual Party event—displayed in the form. See Figure 1.26.

As you click the Next Record button, notice how each individual record in the table of Club Events displays in the window.

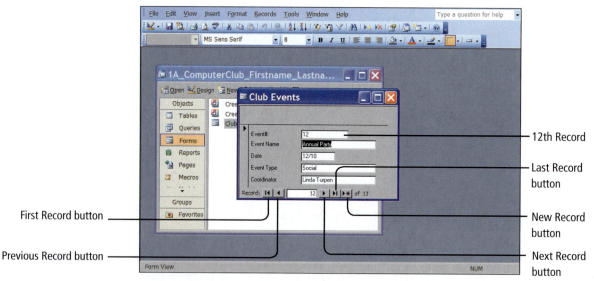

Figure 1.26

4 In the upper right corner of the Club Events form window, click the **Close** button to close the form. The Database window displays.

Activity 1.8 Viewing and Printing a Report

The fourth button on the Objects bar is *Reports*. A **report** is a database object that displays the fields and records from the table (or query) in an easy-to-read format suitable for printing. Reports are created to summarize information in a database in a professional-looking manner.

1 On the Objects bar, click **Reports**. See Figure 1.27.

To the right of the Objects bar, command icons for creating a new report display, followed by a report that has been created and saved as part of the Computer Club database. Thus far, only one report, the Club Events report, has been created for this database.

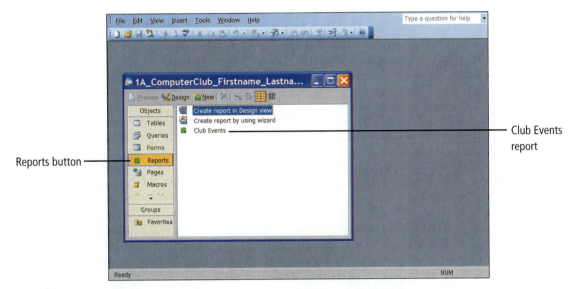

Figure 1.27

2 Double-click the **Club Events** report.

The Club Events report displays, as shown in Figure 1.28.

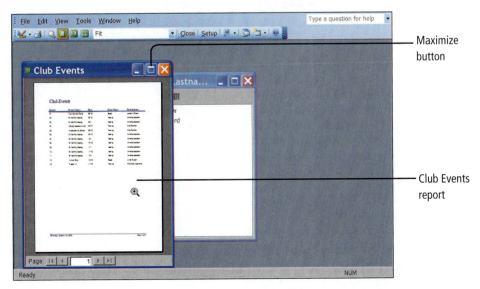

Figure 1.28

Project 1A: Computer Club | **Access** | 23

3 In the upper right corner of the Club Events report window, click the **Maximize** button.

The window is maximized on your screen.

4 On the toolbar, pause the mouse pointer over the word *Fit* and see the ScreenTip *Zoom*.

To **zoom** means to make the page view larger or smaller. **Fit** means that an entire page of the report will display on your screen at one time giving you an overall view of what the printed pages will look like.

5 On the toolbar, click the **Zoom arrow** and then, from the displayed list, click **100%**. See Figure 1.29.

Zooming to 100% displays the report in the approximate size it will be when it is printed.

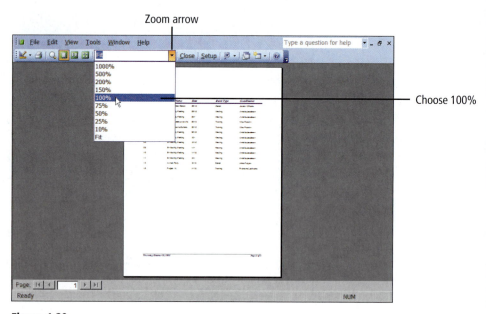

Figure 1.29

6 In the displayed report page, locate the record **Project 1A**. You may need to use the vertical scroll bar in the window to see this record. See Figure 1.30.

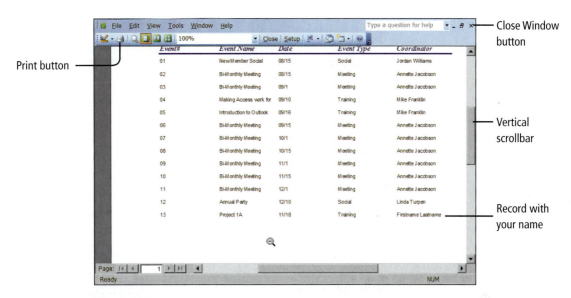

Figure 1.30

Notice that on your screen, the report displays as if it were printed on a piece of paper. A report is designed to be a professional-looking document that you can print.

A report is generated each time you open it and displays up-to-date information. For example, this report was created before you opened the database, but the record you added with your name now displays in the report.

7 On the toolbar, click the **Print** button 🖨. See Figure 1.30.

The Club Events report prints.

8 In the upper right corner of the report window, click the **Close Window** button ⊠ to close the report.

The Database window displays.

9 To the right of the **Type a question for help** box, click the small **Restore Window** button to restore the Database window to its previous size. See Figure 1.31.

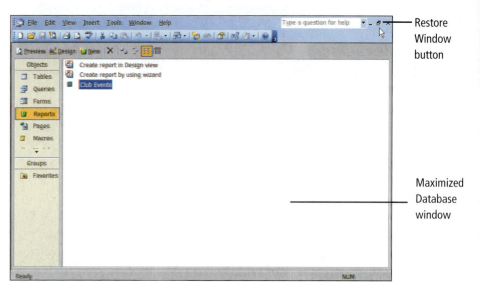

Figure 1.31

10 In the Database window, click the **Close** button to close the Computer Club database. See Figure 1.32.

The Computer Club database closes. The Access program remains open. As you advance in your studies of Access, you will learn about the remaining objects on the Objects bar: Pages, Macros, and Modules.

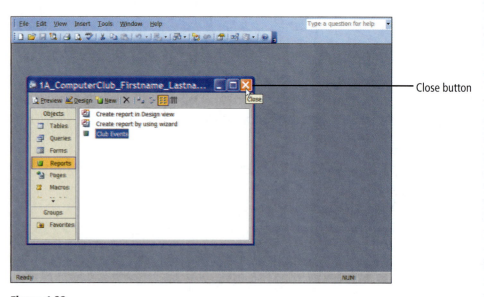

Figure 1.32

End You have completed Project 1A

Project 1B School

In the previous project, you opened an existing database. The Tables object and some of the other object tools used for viewing and manipulating the database were already created. In this project, you will begin a new database and create the table yourself.

In Activities 1.9 through 1.27 you will create a new database for the Distance Learning Department at Lake Michigan City College. The database will have one table that will store student records. Your student table object will look like Figure 1.33. You will save the database as *1B_School_Firstname_Lastname*.

Student#	Last Name	First Name	Address	City	Postal Code	Balance	First Term Atten
23895	Jackson	Robert	2320 Aldrich Circle	Chicago	60605	$46.00	SP01
45689	Jackson	Laura	1967 Arizona St.	Chicago	60605	$65.00	FA02
54783	Williams	Pat	62 Cockatiel Lane	Chicago	60605	$42.00	SP03
63257	Apodaca	Allen	679 Martinique Pl.	Chicago	60605	$32.00	SU03
64589	Metheny	Elizabeth	10225 Fairview	Chicago	60605	$15.00	FA02
95140	Vaughn	Sydney	2105 Waldo Ave.	Chicago	60605	$56.00	FA03
95874	Van Wegan	Michaela	100 Quantico Ave.	Chicago	60605	$25.00	FA99
96312	Berstein	Krista	136 South Street	Chicago	60605	$12.00	FA00

Figure 1.33

Objective 3
Create a New Database

Activity 1.9 Creating a New Database

In this activity you will create a new database. There are two methods to create a new Access database:

- Create a new database using a wizard (an Access tool that walks you step-by-step through a process).
- Create a new blank database—which is more flexible because you can add each object separately.

Regardless of which method you use, you will have to name and save the database before you can create any objects such as tables, queries, forms, or reports. Think of a database file as a container that stores the database objects—tables, queries, forms, reports, and so forth—that you create and add to the database.

1 If necessary, start Access and close any open databases.

2 On the Database toolbar, click the **New** button.

The New File task pane displays on the right. See Figure 1.34. Recall that the task pane is a window within a Microsoft Office application that provides commonly used commands related to the current task.

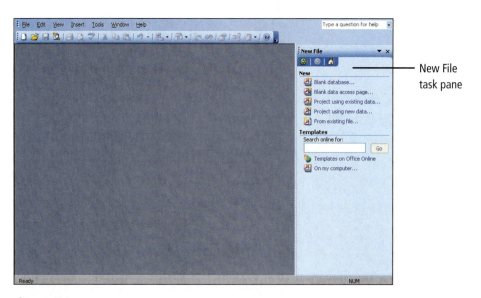

Figure 1.34

3 In the task pane, under **New**, click **Blank database**.

The File New Database dialog box displays.

4 In the **Save in** box, click the **Save in arrow** (the arrow at the right edge of the Save in box) to view a list of the drives available to you.

5 If necessary, navigate to your Chapter 1 folder where you are storing your projects.

6 Clear any text in the **File name** box and then, using your own information, type **1B_School_Firstname_Lastname**

7 In the lower right corner of the dialog box, click **Create**.

The School database is created and the Database window displays with the new database name indicated in the title bar of the Database window.

Objective 4
Create a New Table

When you buy a new address book, it is not very useful until you fill it with names, addresses, and phone numbers. Likewise, a new database is not useful until you *populate*, or fill, a table with data.

In the next activity, you will create a table in Design view and then add the table's fields.

Activity 1.10 Adding Fields to a Table

Recall that fields, located in columns, contain the information that describes each record in your database. The columnar fields describe the records in a table. For example, in the Club Events table you viewed earlier in Project 1A, there were fields for the *Event Name*, *Event Type*, and so forth. These fields provided information about the records in the table.

1 In the Database window, double-click the command icon **Create table in Design view**. See Figure 1.35. Alternatively, right-click the command icon and click Open on the displayed shortcut menu.

The Design view of the new table displays and the title bar indicates *Table1*: Because you have not yet named or saved this table, it has the default name *Table1*. The word *Table* after the colon indicates that this database object is a table. The insertion point is blinking in the first Field Name box, indicating that Access is ready for you to type the first field name. See Figure 1.36.

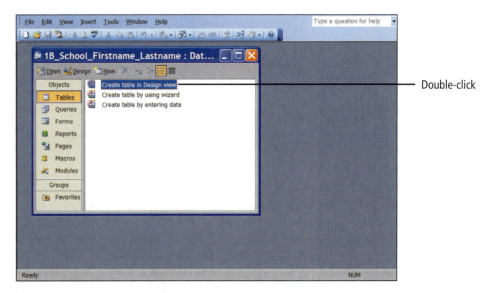

Figure 1.35

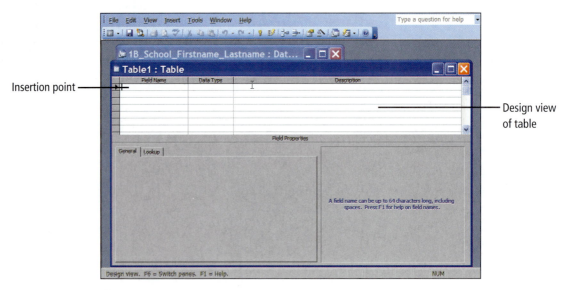

Figure 1.36

2 In the first **Field Name** box, refer to Figure 1.37 and then type **Student#**

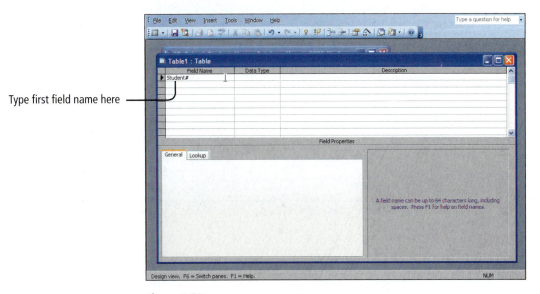

Type first field name here

Figure 1.37

3 Press Tab to move the insertion point to the **Data Type** column.

The insertion point is blinking in the Data Type column and *Text* displays and is selected. At the right end of the box, an arrow displays. Notice that this arrow does not display until you click in this box. Some Access features become available in this manner—when a specific location is selected.

Data type specifies how Access organizes and stores data in a field. For example, if you define a field's data type as *Text*, any character can be typed as data in the field. If you define a field's data type as *Number*, only numbers can be typed as data in the field.

4 Click the **Data Type arrow** to display a list of data types. From the displayed list, click **Text** to accept the default data type. See Figure 1.38.

This field will contain a student number for each individual record. Although the student number contains only numbers—no letters or characters—it is customary to define such a number as *Text* rather than *Number*. Because the numbers are used only as a way to identify students—and not used for mathematical calculations—they function more like text.

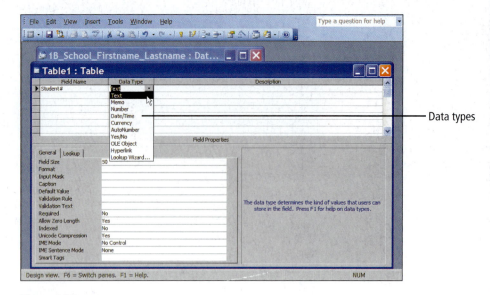

Figure 1.38

5 Press Tab to move the insertion point to the **Description** column.

Descriptions for fields in a table are not required. Include a description if the Field Name does not provide an obvious description of the field. In this instance, the field name *Student#* is self-explanatory, so no additional description is necessary.

6 Press Tab again to move the insertion point down and prepare to enter the next field name.

7 Using the technique you just practiced, add the fields shown in the Figure 1.39.

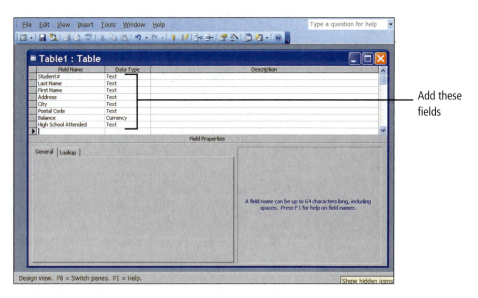

Figure 1.39

Another Way

Creating a New Table in a Database

There are three ways to create a new table in a database:

- Create a table in Design view by creating and naming the fields (columns).
- Create a table using a wizard, a process that helps you, step-by-step, to create the table.
- Create a table by typing data directly into an empty table in the Datasheet view, creating the column (field) names as you do so.

Activity 1.11 Switching Between Views

By naming and defining the data types for the fields, you have determined the number and type of pieces of information that you will have for each student's record in your database. In this activity, you will add the student records to the database. You will use the method of typing records directly into the Datasheet view of the table. You will learn other ways to enter records as your study of Access progresses.

1 On the Table Design toolbar, click the **View** button, as shown in Figure 1.40.

A message displays indicating that you must save the table before this action can be completed. See Figure 1.41.

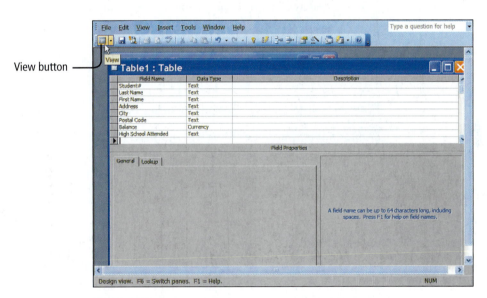

Figure 1.40

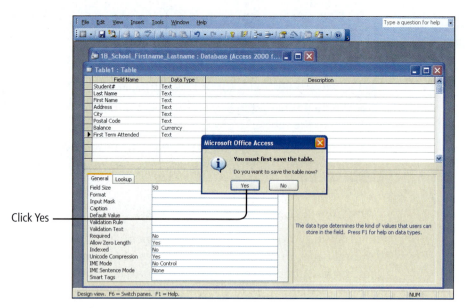

Click Yes

Figure 1.41

2 Click **Yes**.

3 In the displayed **Save As** dialog box, in the **Table Name** box, use your own first and last name and type **1B Students Firstname Lastname** and then click **OK**.

The message *There is no primary key defined* displays.

4 Click **No**.

The Datasheet view displays. You will add a primary key to the table in the next activity.

> **Note** — Varying Toolbar Names
>
> *Toolbar name changes depending on view.*
>
> In Access, the name used to refer to the toolbar changes, depending on the current view of the database object. When a table is displayed in the Design view, the toolbar below the menu bar is referred to as the Table Design toolbar.

Objective 5
Create a Primary Key and Add Records to a Table

A *primary key* is a field that uniquely identifies a record in a table. For example, in a college registration system, your student number uniquely identifies you—no other student at the college has your exact student number. Two students at your college could have the exact same name, for example, *David Michaels*, but each would have a different and unique student number. Designating a field as a primary key ensures that you do not enter the same record more than once, because primary keys do not permit duplicate entries within the database.

Activity 1.12 Creating a Primary Key in a Table

If Access creates a primary key for you, as it prompted you to do in the previous activity, Access will add an additional field with a Data Type of

AutoNumber. AutoNumber assigns a number to each record as it is entered into the database. AutoNumber fields are convenient as a primary key for a database where the records have no unique field—such as the CDs in your CD collection. When each record in your table already has a unique number, such as a Student#, you will want to define that as your primary key.

1. On the Table Datasheet toolbar, click the **View** button to switch to the Design view of your Students table.

   When a table is displayed in the Datasheet view, the toolbar is referred to as the *Table Datasheet toolbar*.

2. Click to position the insertion point anywhere in the Field Name for **Student#**.

3. On the toolbar, click the **Primary Key** button, as shown in Figure 1.42.

   The Primary Key image displays to the left of the Student# field.

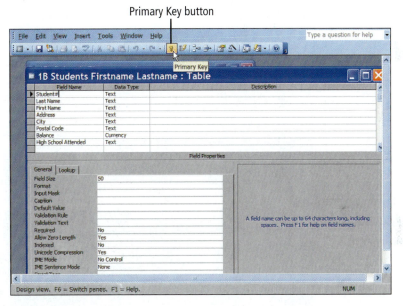

Figure 1.42

Alert! — **Does Your Screen Differ?**
If you attached the Primary Key to the wrong Field Name, move to the toolbar and then click the Primary Key button again. The Primary Key image will be removed and you can click the correct field name.

4. On the toolbar, click the **View** button to switch back to the Datasheet view. When prompted, click **Yes** to save the change you have made to the table.

Activity 1.13 Adding Records to a Table

1 With your table in Datasheet view, make sure your insertion point is in the **Student#** column and then type **54783**

2 Press [Tab] to move to the **Last Name** column and then type **Williams**

3 Press [Tab], and then, in the **First Name** column, type **Pat**

4 Continue in this manner until the remainder of the information for Pat Williams is entered as the first record in the Students table shown in Figure 1.43. Press [Tab] after you enter the information for each column.

> **Note — Entering Currency Data**
>
> *Type only the whole number.*
>
> When you enter the information in the Balance column, you only need to type in the whole number, for example, 42, for the Balance in the Pat Williams record. After you press [Tab], Access will add the dollar sign, decimal point, and two decimal places to the entry in that column. The reason for this is that the Balance field has a data type of Currency.

As you type, do not be alarmed if it appears that your entries will not fit into the columns in the table. The widths of the columns in the figure have been adjusted so that you can view the data that is to be entered.

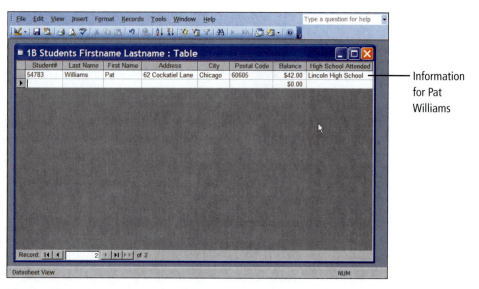

Information for Pat Williams

Figure 1.43

5 Continue entering the remaining seven records shown in Figure 1.44.

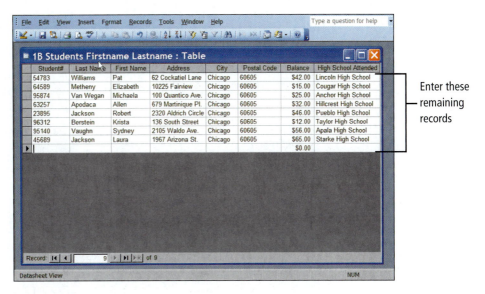

Figure 1.44

Objective 6
Close and Save a Table

When you close a table object, Access saves any additions or changes you made to the records or fields. You do not have to initiate a Save operation.

Activity 1.14 Closing and Saving a Table

1 In the upper right corner of the Table window, click the **Close** button. See Figure 1.45.

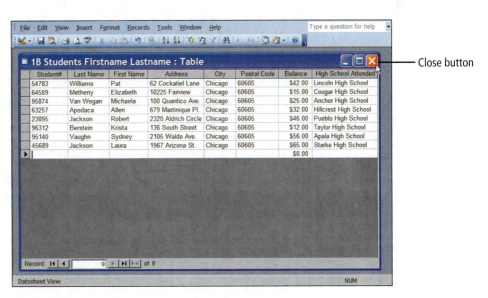

Figure 1.45

The table is closed and the records you entered are saved. Your Students table displays in the Database window. See Figure 1.46.

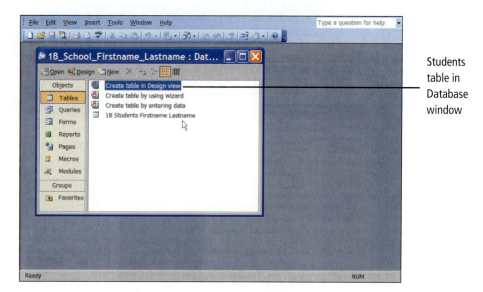

Students table in Database window

Figure 1.46

Objective 7
Open a Table

There are multiple ways to perform tasks in Access. You can open a table in Design view or Datasheet view, depending on what action you want to perform on the table. For example, if you want to view, add, delete, or modify records, use the Datasheet view. If you want to view, add, delete, or modify the field information (such as field name), use the Design view.

Activity 1.15 Opening a Table

1. In the Database window, double-click your **1B Students** table.

   The table opens in Datasheet view, but the records do not display in the same order in which you entered them. Rather, Access has placed the records in sequential order according to the Primary key field.

2. Click the **Close** button ⊠ in the upper right corner of the table window to close the table.

   The Database window displays.

3. If necessary, click your **1B Students** table once to select it, and then just above the Objects bar, click the **Open** button in the Database window.

   The table opens again in Datasheet view. This is another method to open a table in the Datasheet view.

4. In the upper right corner of the table window, click the **Close** button ⊠ to close the table and display the Database window.

5 Open the table in Design view by clicking your **1B Students** table once (it may already be selected), and then clicking the **Design** button in the area above the Objects bar. See Figure 1.47. Alternatively, you can right-click the table name and then click Design View from the displayed shortcut menu.

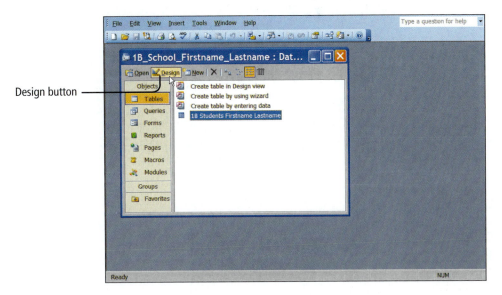

Figure 1.47

6 Leave the table open in Design view for the next activity.

Objective 8
Modify the Table Design

An early consideration when creating a new table is the number and content of the fields in the table. This is referred to as the table's ***design***. For example, when setting up an address book database, you will want to have fields for name, address, home phone number, and so forth. After you begin entering records, you might realize that you should have included a field for a cell phone number, too. Fortunately, Access lets you add or delete fields at any time.

Activity 1.16 Deleting Fields

If you decide that a field in your database is no longer useful to you, you can delete that field from the table.

1 In the Design view of your **1B Students** table, position your mouse pointer in the row selector at the far left, next to **High School Attended** field.

The pointer changes to a right-pointing arrow. See Figure 1.48.

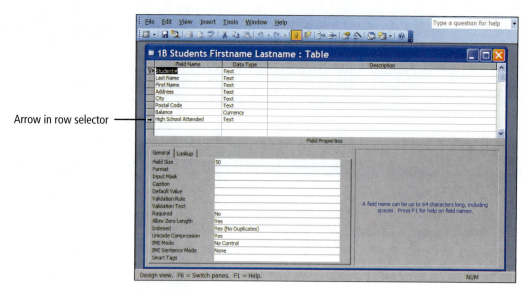

Figure 1.48

[2] Click to select the row **High School Attended** and then press Delete.

A message displays asking whether or not you want to permanently delete the field. See Figure 1.49.

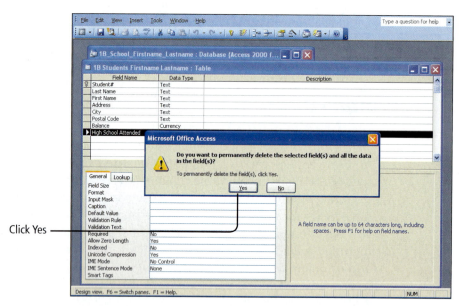

Figure 1.49

[3] Click **Yes** to delete the field.

The High School Attended field is deleted. Deleting the field also deletes any data in the field of each record. Later, you could add the field back if you decide to do so, but you would have to re-enter the field's data for each record.

4 Pause your mouse pointer in the title bar area of the table and right-click. On the displayed shortcut menu, click **Datasheet view**, and when prompted, click **Yes** to save the table. This is another way to switch back to Datasheet view.

The High School Attended field no longer displays in the Datasheet view of the table.

5 On the toolbar, click the **View** button to switch back to Design view.

Activity 1.17 Adding Fields

If you decide to add a field to the table, you can add the field and then, for each record, enter data into the field.

1 At the bottom of the list of fields, click in the next available **Field Name** box, type **First Term Attended** and then press Tab two times.

The default text data type is accepted and the description column is left empty.

2 Use any method to switch back to Datasheet view, and when prompted, click **Yes** to save the table. Notice the new column for the field you just added.

3 For each record, enter the information shown in Figure 1.50 for the **First Term Attended** field.

> **Note** — Using Long Column Headings
>
> *Adjust them later.*
>
> The column heading for the First Term Attended field may not display entirely. You will adjust this in a later step.

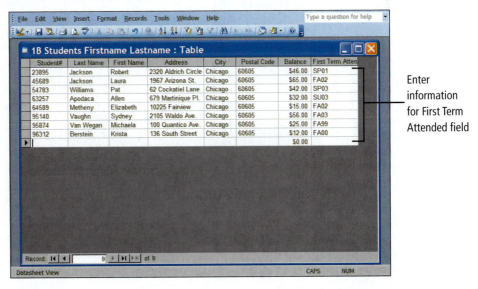

Figure 1.50

Objective 9
Print a Table

There are multiple ways to print objects in Access. The quickest way to print a database table is to click the Print button on the Database toolbar. This will print one complete copy of the table on the default printer. If you want to print anything other than one complete copy, for example, multiple copies or only selected pages, or to select a different printer, you must initiate the Print command from the File menu.

Activity 1.18 Printing a Table

Although a printed table is not as professional or formal looking as a report, there are times when you may want to print your table in this manner as a quick reference or for proofreading.

1 If necessary, open your **1B Students** table in the Datasheet view.

2 On the toolbar, locate but do not click the **Print** button.

You could print the table without opening the table by selecting the table from the Database window, and then clicking the Print button on the toolbar. This method does not offer you an opportunity to change anything about the way the table prints.

3 With your **1B Students** table still open, display the **File** menu and then click **Print**.

The Print dialog box displays. Here you can make changes to your print settings. See Figure 1.51.

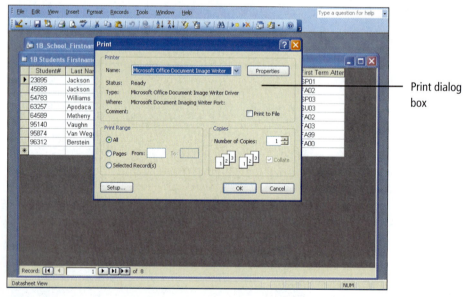

Figure 1.51

4 In the upper right corner next to the printer name, click the **Properties** button.

The Properties dialog box displays. See Figure 1.52. Because the settings for printer models vary, your Properties box may display differently than that shown in the figure.

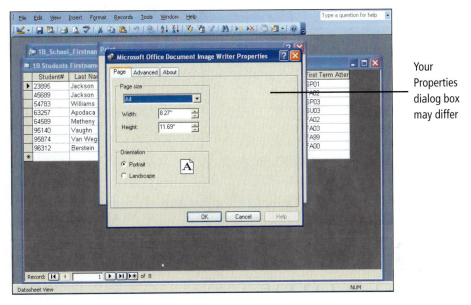

Your Properties dialog box may differ

Figure 1.52

By default, Access prints in **Portrait orientation**—the printed page is taller than it is high. An alternate orientation is **Landscape orientation**—the printed page is wider than it is tall.

5 Locate and then click **Landscape**. See Figure 1.53. The properties for printer models vary somewhat. You may have to locate the Landscape orientation on a different tab of your printer Properties dialog box, and thus your screen will differ from the figure shown.

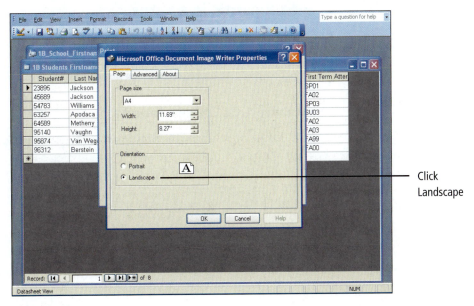

Click Landscape

Figure 1.53

Project 1B: School | **Access** 43

6 Click the **OK** button.

7 In the lower left corner of the **Print** dialog box, click the **Setup** button.

The Page Setup dialog box displays with margins set to 1 inch on the Top, Bottom, Left, and Right of the page. See Figure 1.54.

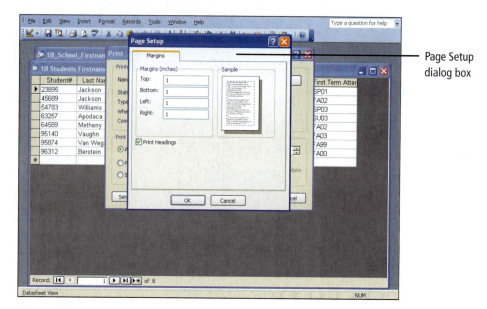

Figure 1.54

8 Click **OK** to accept the default settings.

9 In the Print dialog box, click **OK**.

Your table prints, and your name is printed at the top of the page in the table name.

Objective 10
Edit Records in a Table

When necessary, you will edit (change) the information in a record. For example, you may realize that you made an error when you entered the information in the table, or the information has changed.

Activity 1.19 Editing a Record

1 Make sure your **1B Students** table is open in Datasheet view.

2 Locate the record for **Pat Williams**. In the **Address** field, click to position the insertion point to the right of *62*. See Figure 1.55.

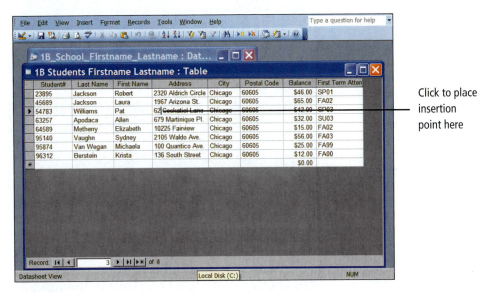

Click to place insertion point here

Figure 1.55

3 Type **5** and then press Tab.

The address for Pat Williams is changed to *625 Cockatiel Lane*. Leave the Students table open.

Activity 1.20 Deleting a Record

Keeping a database up to date means that you may have to delete records when they are no longer needed. In this activity, you will delete the record for Sydney Vaughn, which was mistakenly included in the Students table—she is not a student.

1 Be sure your **1B Students** table is open in Datasheet view.

2 Locate the record for **Sydney Vaughn**, position the mouse pointer in the row selector for Sydney Vaughn's record until it takes the shape of a right-pointing arrow, and then click to select the row.

The entire record is selected. See Figure 1.56.

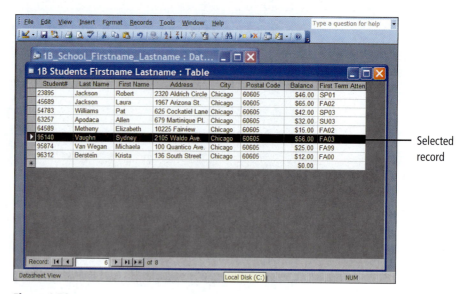

Figure 1.56

3 On the toolbar click the **Delete Record** button . Alternatively, you could press Delete on the keyboard.

A message displays alerting you that you are about to delete a record. If you click Yes and delete the record, you cannot use the Undo button to reverse the action. If you delete a record by mistake, you will have to re-create the record.

4 Click **Yes** to delete the record.

The record is deleted from the 1B Students table.

Activity 1.21 Resizing Columns and Rows

You can adjust the size of columns and rows in a table. Sometimes this is necessary to get a better view of the data. Column widths and row heights are adjusted by dragging the borders between the columns or rows. Reducing the column width allows you to display more fields on your screen at one time. Increasing the width of a column allows you to view data that is too long to display in the column.

Adjusting the size of columns and rows does not change the data contained in the table's records. It changes only your *view* of the data.

1 Be sure your **1B Students** table is open in Datasheet view.

2 In the gray row of column headings, pause your mouse pointer over the vertical line between the **Address** column and the **City** column until it becomes a double-headed arrow, as shown in Figure 1.57.

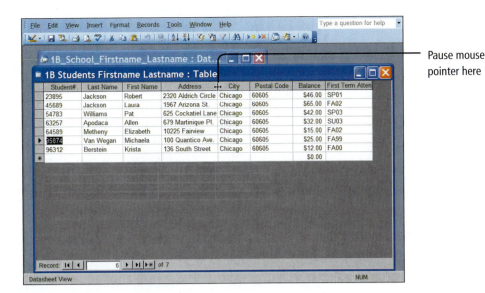

Figure 1.57

[3] Press and hold the left mouse button and drag the line in between the columns to the right approximately 0.5 inch. The measurement need not be precise; use your eye to judge this. Release the mouse button.

The column's width is increased.

[4] In the gray column headings, point to the vertical bar between the **Address** column heading and the **City** column heading until the double-headed arrow displays, and then double-click.

Access adjusts the width of the Address column to accommodate the widest entry in the column. Use this as a quick method to adjust columns to accommodate the widest entry in a column.

[5] In the row of column headings, pause the mouse pointer over the **Student#** column heading until the mouse pointer becomes a downward-pointing black arrow. Then drag to the right until all of the columns are selected. See Figure 1.58.

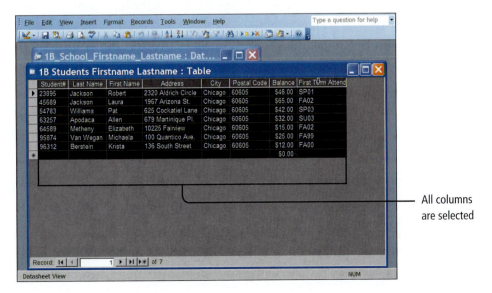

Figure 1.58

Project 1B: School | **Access** 47

6 With the columns selected, pause your mouse pointer over the vertical line between any of the column headings until the mouse pointer takes the shape of a double-headed arrow, and then double-click.

All of the columns are resized to accommodate the widest entry in each column. In some instances, the widest entry is the column heading, for example, *First Term Attended*. Use this method as a quick way to adjust the widths of several columns at once.

7 Click anywhere in the table to deselect the table.

8 To adjust row height, point to the horizontal line between the second and third record until the double-headed arrow displays. See Figure 1.59.

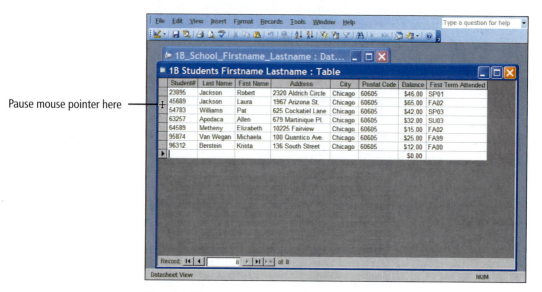

Pause mouse pointer here

Figure 1.59

9 Drag the horizontal line down approximately 0.5 inch. The exact measurement is not important. Use your eye to judge the distance. Release the mouse button.

The height of all of the rows is increased by the same amount. Adjusting the row height enables you to see long names that may have wrapped to two lines in a column—and still have many columns visible on the screen.

10 On the menu bar, click **Format** and then click **Row Height**.

The Row Height dialog box displays. Here you can return row heights to their default setting or enter a precise number for the height of the row.

11 Select the **Standard Height** check box and then click **OK**. See Figure 1.60.

The height of all rows is restored to the default setting. Use this dialog box to set the rows to any height.

Standard Height check box

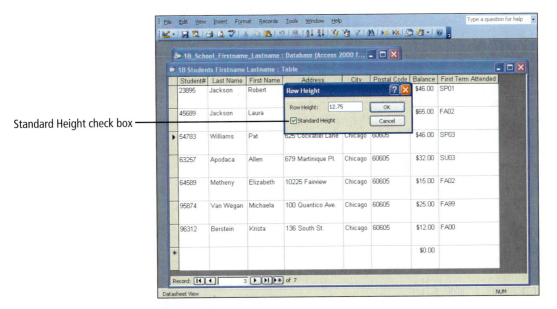

Figure 1.60

Activity 1.22 Hiding Columns

When a table contains many fields (columns), you can temporarily hide one or more columns so that you can get a better view of other columns.

1 Click to position your insertion point anywhere in the **City** column, display the **Format** menu, and then click **Hide Columns**.

The City column is hidden from view, and the columns to the right of the City column shift to the left. Hidden columns and the data that they contain are not deleted—they are merely hidden from view.

2 From the **Format** menu, click **Unhide Columns**. See Figure 1.61.

The Unhide Columns dialog box displays. All of the columns except the City column are checked, indicating that they are in view.

Unhide Columns option on Format menu

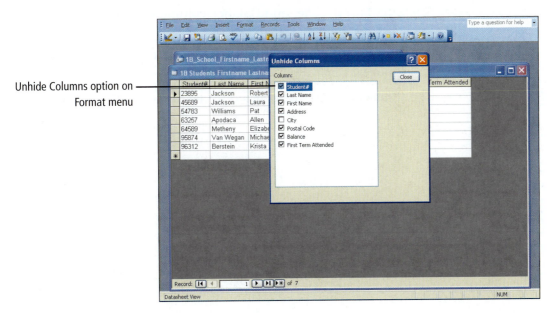

Figure 1.61

3 Select the **City** check box and then click the **Close** button.

The City column returns to view.

4 Click the column heading **City**, press and hold Shift, and then click the column heading **Balance**.

The City, Postal Code, and Balance columns are selected.

You can hide two or more *adjacent* columns (columns that are next to each other) at one time. If you select a column and then select another column while holding Shift, those columns are selected in addition to any columns between them.

5 With the three columns selected, display the **Format** menu, and then click **Hide Columns**. See Figure 1.62.

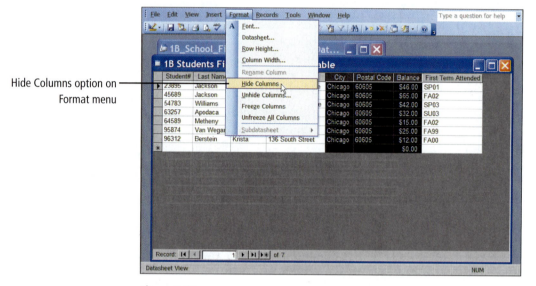

Hide Columns option on Format menu

Figure 1.62

The City, Postal Code, and Balance columns are hidden.

6 To unhide the columns, display the **Format** menu, click **Unhide Columns**, and then select the **City**, **Postal Code**, and the **Balance** check boxes. Click the **Close** button.

The three columns are returned to view in your 1B Students table.

Objective 11
Sort Records

Sorting records in a table is the process of rearranging records in a specific order. For example, you could sort the names in your address book database alphabetically by each person's last name, or you could sort your CD collection database by the date of purchase.

Activity 1.23 Sorting Records in a Table

Information stored in an Access table can be sorted in either **ascending order** or **descending order**. Ascending order sorts text alphabetically (A to Z) and sorts numbers from the lowest number to the highest number. Descending order sorts text in reverse alphabetic order (Z to A) and sorts numbers from the highest number to the lowest.

1. Be sure your **1B Students** table is open in the Datasheet view.

2. Click anywhere in the **Last Name** column and then on the toolbar click the **Sort Ascending** button. See Figure 1.63.

   The records are sorted in ascending order according to each Student's Last Name.

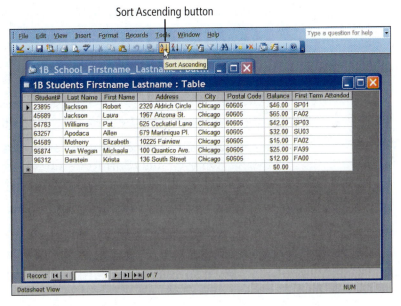

Figure 1.63

3 Click anywhere in the **First Name** column and then on the toolbar click the **Sort Ascending** button.

The records are sorted in ascending order according to each student's First Name.

4 Click the column heading **Last Name**, press and hold Shift, and then click the column heading **First Name**.

Both the Last Name column and the First Name column are selected.

Information in an Access table can be sorted using more than one field. For example, data can be sorted by the *primary sort field*—the field that Access sorts by initially—and then, for any records having an identical primary sort field, records are sorted further by the *secondary sort field*—the field that Access uses to sort records that have matching primary sort fields.

5 On the toolbar, click the **Sort Ascending** button.

The records are sorted alphabetically by Last Name. Within records that have identical last names, for example, *Jackson*, the records are sorted alphabetically by First Name.

Access sorts the records consecutively from left to right, meaning any fields that you want to sort *must* be adjacent to each other, and your primary sort field (*Last Name* in this example) must be to the left of the secondary sort field (*First Name* in this example).

6 Look at the two records for which the last name is **Jackson**.

Notice that those two records are also sorted alphabetically by First Name—Laura comes before Robert.

7 On the menu bar, click **Records** and then click **Remove Filter/Sort**.

You can return your records to the original sort order at any time by selecting Remove Filter/Sort from the Records menu. In this instance, the original sort order is by primary key.

8 Leave your **1B Students** table open for the next activity.

Objective 12
Navigate to Records in a Table

The Students table that you created has only seven records, and you can see all of them on the screen. Most Access tables, however, contain many records—more than you can see on the screen at one time. Access provides several tools to help you navigate (move) among records in a table. For example, you can move the insertion point to the last record in a table or to the first record in a table, or move up one record at a time or down one record at a time.

Activity 1.24 Navigating Among Records Using the Navigation Area

Figure 1.64 illustrates the navigation functions in the navigation area of a table.

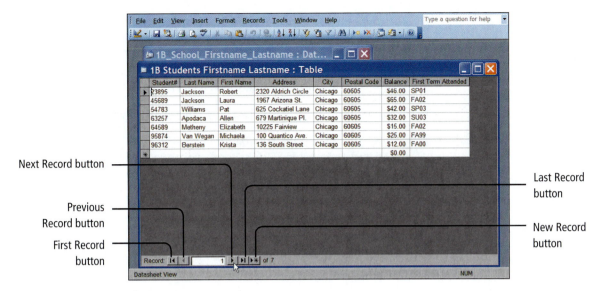

Figure 1.64

1. If necessary, open your **1B Students** table in Datasheet view.

2. Click anywhere in the first record of the table.

3. In the navigation area, click the **Next Record** button.
   See Figure 1.64.

   Depending on the field in which your insertion point was located, the next record in the table is selected, in the same field.

4. In the navigation area, click the **Last Record** button.
   See Figure 1.64.

   The last record in the table is selected.

5. Experiment with the different navigation buttons as shown in Figure 1.64.

Activity 1.25 Navigating Among Records Using the Keyboard

You can also navigate among records in a table using the keyboard. Figure 1.65 lists the keystrokes and the resulting movement.

Key Combinations for Navigating a Table

Keystroke	Movement
↑	Moves the selection up one record at a time.
↓	Moves the selection down one record at a time.
Page Up	Moves the selection up one screen at a time.
PageDown	Moves the selection down one screen at a time.
Ctrl + Home	Moves the selection to the first field in the table.
Ctrl + End	Moves the selection to the last field in the table.

Figure 1.65

1 If necessary, open your **1B Students** table in Datasheet view and click anywhere in any record except the last record.

2 Press ⬇.

The selection moves down one record.

3 Experiment with the different navigation keystrokes.

4 Click the **Close** button ☒ in the table window to close the **1B Students** table. Click **Yes** if you are prompted to save changes to the design of your table.

The Database window displays.

Objective 13
Close and Save a Database

When you close an Access table, any changes are saved automatically. At the end of your Access session, close your database and then close Access.

Activity 1.26 Closing and Saving a Database

1 In the smaller Database window, click the **Close** button ☒.

The database closes. The Access program remains open. See Figure 1.66.

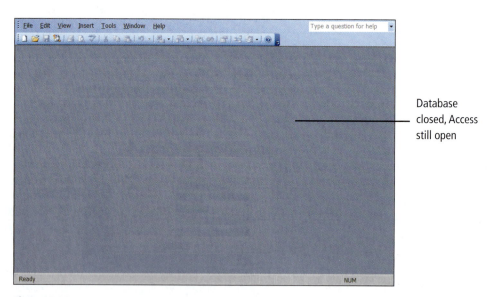

Database closed, Access still open

Figure 1.66

2 On the title bar of the Access window, click the **Close** button ☒ to close the Access program.

Objective 14
Use the Access Help System

Access contains a Help feature designed to assist you when performing a task in Access or if you would like more information about a particular topic in Access. There are multiple ways to use the Help feature in Access, including the Office Assistant, and the Type a question for help box.

Activity 1.27 Using the Access Help System

The Office Assistant is an animated figure that displays to assist you with a task.

1 Start Access. On the menu bar, click **Help** and then click **Show the Office Assistant**.

The Office Assistant character displays. The animated character may be a paperclip, or some other character.

2 Double-click the Office Assistant to display the **What would you like to do?** box.

3 With *Type your question here and then click Search* highlighted, type **How do I get help?** and then click **Search**.

4 In the **Search Results** task pane, click **About getting help while you work**. You may have to use the vertical scroll bar to see this topic.

The Microsoft Access Help window displays with hyperlinks (usually in blue text) listed. Clicking on these hyperlinks will link you to additional information about the topic.

5 Click on the links that display and you will see the description of each of these expanded in the area below the link. For example, click **Microsoft Press** to expand the topic and then click it again to collapse it.

6 After viewing the Help topics, click the **Close** button ☒ to close the Help window. See Figure 1.67.

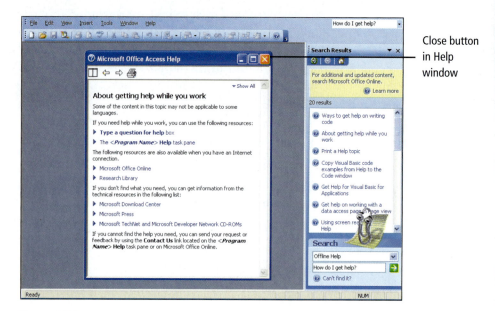

Figure 1.67

7 In the upper right corner of the Access window, locate the **Type a question for help** box and click it. See Figure 1.68.

The text in the box is selected.

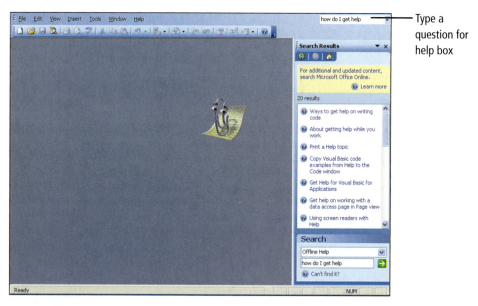

Figure 1.68

8 In the **Type a question for help** box, type **table**

9 Press Enter and click **About creating a table (MDB)**.

A window containing information about creating a table displays. See Figure 1.69. Keywords, identified in a different color, display additional information when they are clicked.

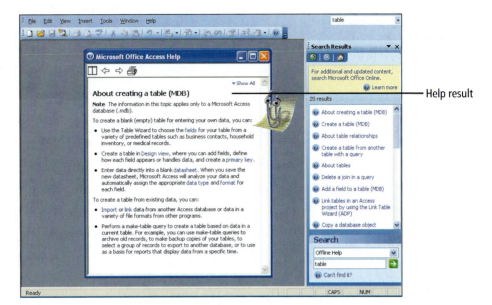

Help result

Figure 1.69

10 In the second bullet, click on the words **Design view**. Scroll down if necessary to view this description.

An explanation of Design View displays in green within the paragraph.

11 In the Microsoft Access Help window, on the toolbar, click the **Print** button . See Figure 1.70.

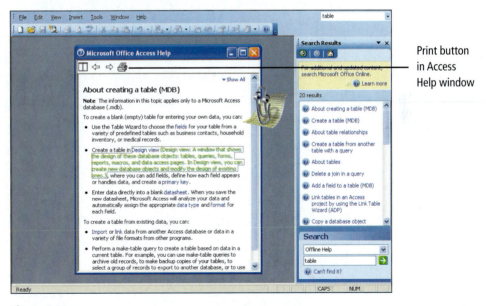

Print button in Access Help window

Figure 1.70

12 In the **Print** dialog box, click **Print** (or **OK**).

The Help topic you have displayed is printed. Keep this document for your reference.

13 Close the Microsoft Access Help window.

14 On the title bar of the Access window, click the **Close** button to close Access.

End You have completed Project 1B

Project 1B: School | **Access** 57

Summary

Microsoft Access 2003 is a database management system. Databases help you organize information, such as the names and addresses in your address book, a CD collection, or a list of students at a college.

In an existing database, you can either view the information in the database or edit the information. Access contains tools, called objects, which enable you to enter information into a database, and then organize, manipulate, and analyze the information. Information in a database is stored in tables. The data in a table is organized by rows, called records, and columns, called fields. Each record in a table stores information about one database item.

Queries extract information from a table according to the criteria set for the query. Forms are another tool that you can use to either enter or view records—one record at a time. Reports are professional-looking documents that summarize the information in a table.

Information stored in a table can be edited and sorted. Access contains navigation tools to assist you in locating specific records.

In This Chapter You Practiced How To

- Rename a Database
- Start Access, Open an Existing Database, and View Database Objects
- Create a New Database
- Create a New Table
- Create a Primary Key and Add Records to a Table
- Close and Save a Table
- Open a Table
- Modify the Table Design
- Print a Table
- Edit Records in a Table
- Sort Records
- Navigate to Records in a Table
- Close and Save a Database
- Use the Access Help System

Concepts Assessments

Matching Match each term in the second column with its correct definition in the first column by writing the letter of the term on the blank line in front of the correct definition.

____ 1. A printing orientation in which the printed page is taller than it is high.

____ 2. The field that serves as a unique identifier for records in a table.

____ 3. The Access object that stores the information in a database.

____ 4. The process of rearranging items in a specific order.

____ 5. The Access object that displays records one at a time.

____ 6. A sorting order in which records are sorted alphabetically from A to Z.

____ 7. The process of pulling out information from a database according to specified criteria.

____ 8. The Access object that displays selected fields and records in an easy-to-read format.

____ 9. A printing orientation in which the printed page is wider than it is tall.

____ 10. A window within a Microsoft Office application that provides commonly used commands.

____ 11. The Access object that assists you in asking a question about the data.

____ 12. A sorting order in which records are sorted alphabetically from Z to A.

____ 13. Data that has been organized in a useful manner.

____ 14. A collection of data related to a particular topic.

____ 15. The collection of tools in Access used to enter and manipulate the data in a database.

A Ascending

B Database

C Descending

D Extracting

E Form

F Information

G Landscape

H Objects

I Portrait

J Primary key

K Query

L Report

M Sorting

N Table

O Task pane

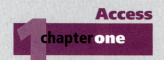

Concepts Assessments (continued)

Fill in the Blank Write the correct answer in the space provided.

1. Tables are the foundation of an Access database, because that is where the data is _____.

2. Each table in an Access database stores data about only _____ subject.

3. The _____ window displays when a database is open.

4. Each horizontal _____ of a table stores all the information about one database record.

5. Each vertical _____ of a table has a name that describes one category of information contained within each record.

6. The small gray box at the left end of a row in a table is the _____.

7. In the _____ view of a table, only the names of the fields, and not the records, display.

8. Specifications that determine what records will be displayed as a result of a query are called _____.

9. Filling a table with data is referred to as _____ the table.

10. A rule that you define for data within a field is referred to as the _____.

Skill Assessments

Project 1C — Departments

Objectives: *Rename a Database; Start Access, Open an Existing Database, and View Database Objects; Close and Save a Table; Open a Table; Print a Table; Sort Records; and Close and Save a Database.*

In the following Skill Assessment, you will open an existing database, view the database objects, and add two records to the database table. This database is used by the administration offices at Lake Michigan City College to store information regarding the various departments at the College. Your completed database objects will look like the ones shown in Figures 1.71 and 1.72. You will rename and save the database as *1C_LMccDept_Firstname_Lastname*.

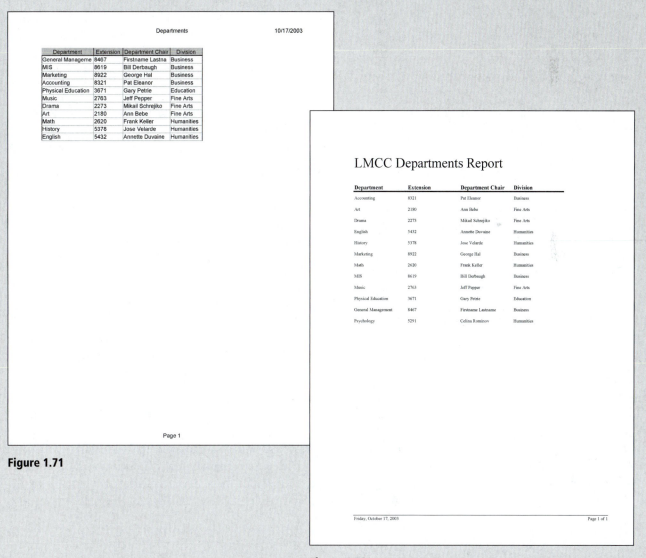

Figure 1.71

Figure 1.72

(Project 1C–Departments continues on the next page)

Skill Assessments (continued)

(Project 1C–Departments continued)

1. On your Windows desktop, open **My Computer** and navigate to the student files that accompany this textbook. Locate and then click once to select the file **a01C_LMccDept**.

2. Move the mouse pointer over the selected file name and then right-click to display a shortcut menu. On the displayed shortcut menu, click **Copy**. Navigate to the drive and folder where you are storing your projects for this chapter. On the menu bar, click **Edit** and then click **Paste**. The database file is copied to your folder and is selected (highlighted).

3. Move your mouse pointer over the selected file name, right-click to display the shortcut menu, and then on the shortcut menu, click **Rename**. In the **File name** box, clear any existing text. Using your own first and last name, type **1C_LMccDept_Firstname_Lastname** and then press Enter to save the new file name. If the **Confirm File Rename** dialog box displays, click **Yes**. Be sure that the file name is still selected (highlighted) and then right-click to display the shortcut menu.

4. On the displayed shortcut menu, click **Properties**. At the lower part of the displayed dialog box, click to clear the check mark next to **Read-only**, and then click **OK** to close the dialog box. Close **My Computer**.

5. Start Access. On the menu bar, click **File** and then click **Open**. Click the **Look in arrow** and then navigate to the location where you are storing your projects for this chapter. Locate the database file that you renamed and saved with your name in Step 3. Click the database file once to select it, and then, in the lower right corner, click the **Open** button. Alternatively, you can double-click the name of the database, and it will open. If the security warning message displays, click **Yes and/or Open**.

6. In the Database window, on the Objects bar, click **Tables** once to display a list of tables in this database. To the right of the Objects bar, double-click the **Departments** table to open the table in Datasheet view. Notice that the table includes fields for Department, Extension, Department Chair, and Division.

7. In the **Department** column, click in the blank record at the bottom of the table and type **General Management** as the department name for the new record. Press Tab once. In the **Extension** field type **8467** and press Tab once. In the **Department Chair** field and using your own information, type your **Firstname Lastname** and press Tab once. In the **Division** field, type **Business** and then press Enter to complete the record.

(Project 1C–Departments continues on the next page)

Skill Assessments (continued)

(Project 1C–Departments continued)

8. On the Table Datasheet toolbar, click the **View** button to switch to the Design view and notice that the **Department** field is the primary key. Recall that one field in a table is designated as the primary key so that each record has a unique identifier. In this case, each department has a different name—no two departments at the college have the same name.

9. On the Table Design toolbar, click the **View** button to return to the Datasheet view. Click anywhere in the **Division** column, and then, on the Table Datasheet toolbar, click the **Sort Ascending** button. Notice that the records are now sorted in alphabetical order by Division.

10. On the Table Datasheet toolbar, click the **Print** button. In the upper right corner of the table window, click the **Close** button to close the table. A copy of the table is printed, and your name is printed as the Chair of the General Management Department. Save any changes if prompted to do so.

11. On the Objects bar, click **Queries** to display a list of available queries in the database. Double-click the **Business Division** query to open the query. Notice that each entry in the *Business Division* query has *Business* in the **Division** field. Recall that a query locates records from a table that meet specific criteria and then displays the result. In this case, the Business Division query was designed to locate all of the records that have *Business* as the Division. You can see that there are four Departments within the Business Division. In the upper right corner of the table window, click the **Close** button to close the query.

12. On the Objects bar, click **Forms** to display a list of available forms in the database. Recall that forms are another database object, in addition to tables, that allow you to view and enter new records into a table—one record at a time. To the right of the Objects bar, double-click the **Departments Form** to open the form. The Departments Form opens and the first record in the table displays.

13. At the bottom of the Department Form, locate the **New Record** button (the button at the bottom of the form with the *) and click it. With the insertion point blinking in the **Department** box, type **Psychology** and then press Tab once. Use the information below to fill in the remaining information for this record.

Department	Extension	Department Chair	Division
Psychology	5291	Celina Rominov	Humanities

14. In the Form window, click the **Close** button to close the form.

(Project 1C–Departments continues on the next page)

Skill Assessments (continued)

(Project 1C–Departments continued)

15. On the Objects bar, click **Reports** to display a list of available reports that have been created for this database. Recall that a report is a professional-looking document that summarizes information from a table in an easy-to-read format. To the right of the Objects bar, double-click the **LMCC Departments Report** to open the report in Print Preview.

16. In the upper right corner of the report title bar, click the **Maximize** button and then on the Print Preview toolbar, click the **Zoom arrow**. Zoom to **100%**. On the Print Preview toolbar, click the **Print** button to print the report. On the Print Preview toolbar, click the **Close** button to close the report. In the Access window, click the **Close** button to close Access.

End You have completed Project 1C

Project 1D — Office Supplies

Objectives: *Create a New Database, Create a New Table, Create a Primary Key and Add Records to a Table, Close and Save a Table, Modify the Table Design, Print a Table, and Close and Save a Database.*

In the following Skill Assessment, you will create a new database to track office supplies for the Distance Learning Department at Lake Michigan City College. The database table will look like the one shown in Figure 1.73. You will save your database as *1D_Office_Supplies_Firstname_Lastname*.

1. Start Access. From the **File** menu, click **New**. In the **New File** task pane, under **New**, click **Blank database**.

2. In the displayed **File New Database** dialog box, click the **Save in arrow**, and then navigate to the folder in which you are storing your projects for this chapter. In the **File name** box, delete any existing text, type **1D_Office_Supplies_Firstname_Lastname** and then in the lower right corner click **Create**. The Office Supplies database is created and the Database window displays with the new database name indicated in the title bar.

3. In the Database window, double-click the command icon **Create table in Design view**. Because you have not yet named or saved this table, the title bar indicates the default name of *Table1*. The insertion point is blinking in the first **Field Name** box.

4. In the first **Field Name** box, type **Inventory #** and then press to move the insertion point to the **Data Type** column. Recall that Data Type refers to the rules that you can define for data within a field.

5. Press to accept the default Data Type of **Text**. Press again to move to the next **Field Name** box.

(Project 1D–Office Supplies continues on the next page)

Skill Assessments (continued)

(**Project 1D**–Office Supplies continued)

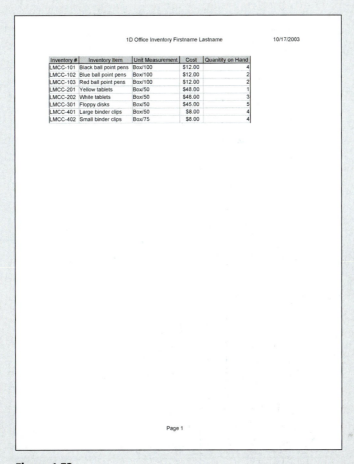

Figure 1.73

6. Use the following information to add the remaining fields to your table. Recall that a description for a field is optional. The descriptions for this table describe the purpose of the corresponding field.

Field Name	Data Type	Description
Inventory Item	Text	
Unit Measurement	Text	Identifies the number of items in a unit
Cost	Currency	Cost per unit
Quantity on Hand	Number	Current number of items available

7. Click in the field name for **Inventory #**. On the toolbar, click the **Primary Key** button to set the **Inventory #** field as the primary key for this table. Within this table, no two items will have the same Inventory number—the Inventory number is a unique identifier. On the Table Design toolbar, click the **View** button to switch to the Datasheet view. When prompted, click **Yes** to save the table.

(**Project 1D**–Office Supplies continues on the next page)

Skill Assessments (continued)

(Project 1D–Office Supplies continued)

8. In the displayed **Save As** dialog box, in the **Table Name** box, use your own first and last name to type **1D Office Inventory Firstname Lastname** and then click **OK**. The table displays and you can begin to enter records into it.

9. With the table in Datasheet view, be sure your insertion point is in the **Inventory #** column. Type **LMCC-101** and press Tab. Type **Black ball point pens** and press Tab. Type **Box/100** and press Tab. Type **12** in the **Cost** column and press Tab. The dollar sign and the decimal point are inserted for you because a data type of Currency was specified for the Cost field. Type **4** in the Quantity on Hand column and press Enter.

10. Use the following information to add the remaining records to the Inventory table. Press Enter after entering the last record.

Inventory #	Inventory Item	Unit Measurement	Cost	Quantity on Hand
LMCC-102	Blue ball point pens	Box /100	12.00	2
LMCC-103	Red ball point pens	Box/100	12.00	2
LMCC-201	Yellow tablets	Box/50	48.00	1
LMCC-202	White tablets	Box/50	48.00	3
LMCC-301	Floppy disks	Box/50	45.00	5
LMCC-401	Large binder clips	Box/50	8.00	4
LMCC-402	Small binder clips	Box/75	8.00	4

11. Pause the mouse pointer over the gray **Inventory #** column heading, and then click and hold the left mouse button while dragging to the right until all of the columns are selected. With the columns selected, pause your mouse pointer over the vertical line between any of the column headings until the mouse takes the shape of a double-headed arrow, and then double-click. All of the columns are resized to accommodate the widest entry in each column. Recall that you can use this method as a quick way to adjust the widths of several columns at once. Recall also that adjusting the size of columns and rows does not change the data contained in the table's records. It changes only your *view* of the data.

12. Click anywhere in the table to deselect the table. On the Table Datasheet toolbar, click the **Print** button. Because you inserted your name in the table name, it prints in the heading. In the upper right corner of the table window, click the **Close** button to close the table. Click **Yes** to save changes to the layout of the table.

(Project 1D–Office Supplies continues on the next page)

Skill Assessments (continued)

(Project 1D–Office Supplies continued)

13. In the Database window, click the **Close** button to close the Office Supplies database. In the Access window, click the **Close** button to close Access.

 You have completed Project 1D

Project 1E—Recipes

Objectives: *Rename a Database; Start Access, Open an Existing Database, and View Database Objects; Open a Table; Print a Table; Edit Records in a Table; Navigate to Records in a Table; and Close and Save a Database.*

In the following Skill Assessment, you will open and edit an existing database that stores information about the recipes that the Computer Club at Lake Michigan City College prepares for social events. Your completed database objects will look like the ones shown in Figure 1.74. You will save the database as *1E_Recipes_Firstname_Lastname* in the folder designated for this chapter.

Figure 1.74

(**Project 1E**–Recipes continues on the next page)

Skill Assessments (continued)

(Project 1E–Recipes continued)

1. Open **My Computer** and navigate to the student files that accompany this textbook. Click once to select the file **a01E_recipes**. Move the mouse pointer over the selected file name, right-click, and on the displayed shortcut menu, click **Copy**.

2. Navigate to the drive and folder where you will be storing your projects for this chapter. On the menu bar, click **Edit** and then click **Paste**. The database file is copied to your folder and is selected. Move your mouse pointer over the selected file name, right-click to display the shortcut menu, and then click **Rename**. Using your own first and last name, type **1E_Recipes_Firstname_Lastname**

3. Press Enter to save the new file name. If the Confirm File Rename message displays, click **Yes**. Be sure that the file name is still selected (highlighted), point to the file name, and right-click to display the shortcut menu. On the displayed shortcut menu, click **Properties**.

4. In the lower portion of the displayed dialog box, click to clear the check mark from the **Read-only** check box. Click **OK** to close the dialog box. Close **My Computer** and start Access.

5. On the menu bar, click **File** and then click **Open**. In the displayed dialog box, click the **Look in arrow**, and then navigate to the location where you are storing your projects for this chapter. Locate the database file that you saved and renamed with your name in Step 2. Click the database file once to select it, and then, in the lower right corner, click the **Open** button. Alternatively, you can double-click the name of the database, and it will open.

6. If necessary, in the Database window on the Objects bar, click **Tables** to display a list of tables in this database. To the right of the Objects bar, double-click the **Recipes** table to open the table in Datasheet view.

7. In **record #5**, click in the **Type** field and delete the existing text. Type **Beverage** and then press Enter. In **record #11**, click to place the insertion point in front of *Potato*. Use your own information to type **Firstname Lastname's** and then press Spacebar once.

8. On the Table Datasheet toolbar, click the **Print** button. In the upper right corner of the table window, click the **Close** button to close the table. On the title bar of the Access window, click the **Close** button to close Access.

End You have completed Project 1E

Performance Assessments

Project 1F — CD Log

Objectives: *Create a New Database, Create a New Table, Create a Primary Key and Add Records to a Table, Close and Save a Table, Sort Records, Print a Table, and Close and Save a Database.*

In the following Performance Assessment, you will create a new database and a new table to store information about the CD collection for the Music Department at Lake Michigan City College. Your completed table will look like the one shown in Figure 1.75. You will save your database as *1F_CDlog_Firstname_Lastname*.

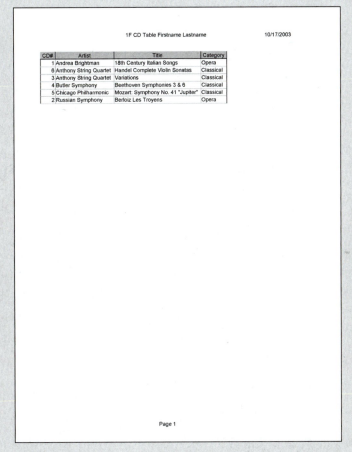

Figure 1.75

(Project 1F–CD Log continues on the next page)

Performance Assessments (continued)

(Project 1F–CD Log continued)

1. Start Access. Display the **New File** task pane and click **Blank database**. In the **File New Database** dialog box, navigate to the drive and folder where you are storing your projects for this chapter. Name the file **1F_CDlog_Firstname_Lastname**

2. In the Database window, double-click the command icon **Create table in Design view**. Use the following information to create the fields for the table.

Field Name	Data Type	Description
CD#	AutoNumber	
Artist	Text	
Title	Text	
Category	Text	Music Classification

3. Because two CDs could have the same title, you will use the **AutoNumber** field that you created as the primary key. Click in the field name for **CD#** and then click the **Primary Key** button. Click the **View** button to switch to the Datasheet view of the table.

4. When prompted, save the table by typing **1F CD Table Firstname Lastname** in the **Save As** dialog box and then click **OK**.

5. With the table open in the Datasheet view, press [Tab] to move to the **Artist** field and type the first artist in the following table. As you type in the **Artist** field, Access fills in the AutoNumber to assign a unique number to each CD. You do not need to type the numbers. Use the following information to create the records.

CD#	Artist	Title	Category
1	Andrea Brightman	18th Century Italian Songs	Opera
2	Russian Symphony	Berlioz Les Troyens	Opera
3	Anthony String Quartet	Variations	Classical
4	Butler Symphony	Beethoven Symphonies 3 & 6	Classical
5	Chicago Philharmonic	Mozart: Symphony No. 41 "Jupiter"	Classical
6	Anthony String Quartet	Handel Complete Violin Sonatas	Classical

(Project 1F–CD Log continues on the next page)

Performance Assessments (continued)

(Project 1F–CD Log continued)

6. Select all of the columns in the table. Display the **Format** menu, click **Column Width**, and in the displayed **Column Width** dialog box, click **Best Fit**. All of the columns are resized to accommodate the widest entry in each column.

7. Click anywhere in the table to deselect it. Click the **Artist** column heading to select the column, press and hold , and then click the **Title** column heading. On the toolbar, click the **Sort Ascending** button. The table is sorted by Artist, and within Artist, it is further sorted by title.

8. On the Table Datasheet toolbar, click the **Print** button. Close the table, save any changes, and then close Access.

End You have completed Project 1F

Project 1G—Employees

Objectives: *Rename a Database; Start Access, Open an Existing Database, and View Database Objects; Create a Primary Key and Add Records to a Table; Close and Save a Table; Open a Table; Modify the Table Design; and Print a Table.*

In the following Performance Assessment, you will open an existing database that stores employee information for Lake Michigan City College, add a record, and then work with other objects in the database. The first page of your completed database object will look similar to Figure 1.76. You will rename the database as *1G_Employees_Firstname_Lastname*.

1. Use the Windows My Computer tool to navigate to your student files and then select the file **a01G_Employees**. Copy the file to the drive and folder where you are storing your projects for this chapter. Using your own information, rename the file **1G_Employees_Firstname_Lastname**

2. Remove the Read-only attribute from the renamed file so that you can make changes to the database. Start Access.

3. Open your **1G_Employees** database that you renamed in Step 1. Open the **Employees** table and switch to Design view. Set the primary key for this table to **ID**. This is the employee ID number, which uniquely identifies each employee.

(Project 1G–Employees continues on the next page)

Performance Assessments (continued)

(Project 1G–Employees continued)

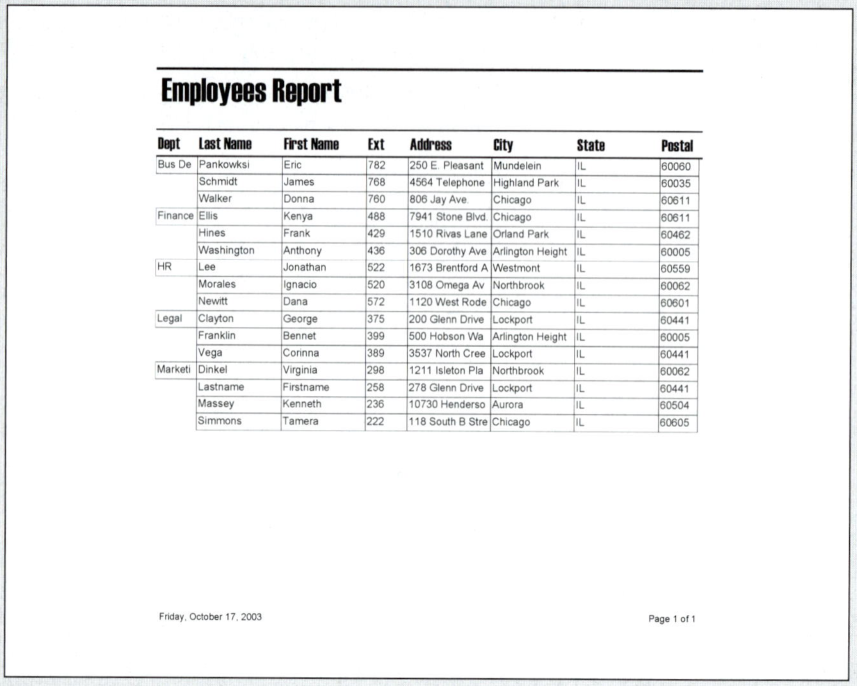

Employees Report

Dept	Last Name	First Name	Ext	Address	City	State	Postal
Bus De	Pankowksi	Eric	782	250 E. Pleasant	Mundelein	IL	60060
	Schmidt	James	768	4564 Telephone	Highland Park	IL	60035
	Walker	Donna	760	806 Jay Ave.	Chicago	IL	60611
Finance	Ellis	Kenya	488	7941 Stone Blvd.	Chicago	IL	60611
	Hines	Frank	429	1510 Rivas Lane	Orland Park	IL	60462
	Washington	Anthony	436	306 Dorothy Ave	Arlington Height	IL	60005
HR	Lee	Jonathan	522	1673 Brentford A	Westmont	IL	60559
	Morales	Ignacio	520	3108 Omega Av	Northbrook	IL	60062
	Newitt	Dana	572	1120 West Rode	Chicago	IL	60601
Legal	Clayton	George	375	200 Glenn Drive	Lockport	IL	60441
	Franklin	Bennet	399	500 Hobson Wa	Arlington Height	IL	60005
	Vega	Corinna	389	3537 North Cree	Lockport	IL	60441
Marketi	Dinkel	Virginia	298	1211 Isleton Pla	Northbrook	IL	60062
	Lastname	Firstname	258	278 Glenn Drive	Lockport	IL	60441
	Massey	Kenneth	236	10730 Henderso	Aurora	IL	60504
	Simmons	Tamera	222	118 South B Stre	Chicago	IL	60605

Friday, October 17, 2003   Page 1 of 1

Figure 1.76

4. Switch to the Datasheet view of the table and save changes to the table when prompted to do so. Add the following record to the table, using your own first and last name.

ID	5588
First Name	Your First Name
Last Name	Your Last Name
Dept	Marketing
Ext	258
Address	278 Glenn Drive
City	Lockport
State	IL
Postal Code	60441
Phone	815-555-0365

5. Use any method to resize all of the columns to accommodate their data and then close the table. On the Objects bar, click **Queries** and open the **Marketing Query**. Because you added your name as a member of the Marketing Department, you should see your record among the other employees in the Marketing Department.

(Project 1G–Employees continues on the next page)

Performance Assessments (continued)

(Project 1G–Employees continued)

6. Close the query. On the Objects bar, click the **Reports** button and open the **Employees Report**. Display the **File** menu, and then click **Page Setup**. In the **Page Setup** dialog box, click the **Page tab**, and then click the **Landscape** option button so that the report prints in Landscape orientation. Print the report. Notice that your name will print as one of the employees in the Marketing Department. Close the report and then close the database. Close Access.

End You have completed Project 1G

Project 1H — DL Courses

Objectives: *Create a New Database, Create a New Table, Create a Primary Key and Add Records to a Table, Modify the Table Design, Close and Save a Table, Print a Table, and Close and Save a Database.*

In the following Performance Assessment, you will create a new database and a new table to store information about Distance Learning courses at Lake Michigan City College. Your completed table will look similar to the one shown in Figure 1.77. You will save your database as 1H_DLcourses_Firstname_Lastname.

1. Start Access and display the **New File** task pane. Click **Blank database**. Navigate to the drive and folder where you are storing your projects for this chapter. In the **File name** box, type **1H_DLcourses_Firstname_Lastname** as the name for your database, and then click **Create**.

2. Use the following information to create a table in Design view and to add fields to the table.

Field Name	Data Type	Description
Course Number	Text	
Course Name	Text	
Credit Hours	Number	Credit hours for this course

3. Switch to the Datasheet view of the table. Using your own first and last name, save the table as **1H DLcourses Firstname Lastname** and then click **OK**. When prompted if you would like to add a primary key now, click **No**.

(**Project 1H**–DL Courses continues on the next page)

Performance Assessments (continued)

(**Project 1H**–DL Courses continued)

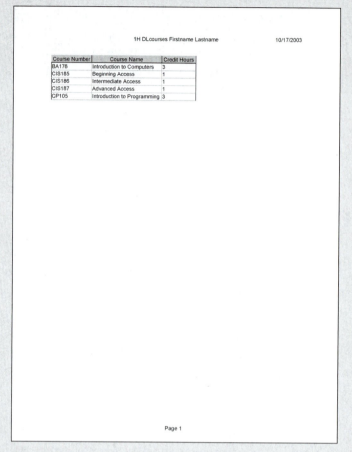

Figure 1.77

4. Using the following information, fill in the records for the DLcourses table.

Course Number	Course Name	Credit Hours
BA176	Introduction to Computers	3
CP105	Introduction to Programming	3
CIS185	Beginning Access	1
CIS186	Intermediate Access	1
CIS187	Advanced Access	1

5. Switch to the Design view of the table. Set the **Course Number** field as the primary key for this table. Click the **View** button to switch to the Datasheet view of the table. Save the table when prompted. Verify that the records are sorted by the primary key.

6. Use any method to resize the column widths to accommodate their data. Print and then close the table, saving any changes if prompted to do so. Close the database and close Access.

End You have completed Project 1H

Mastery Assessments

Project 1I — Suppliers

Objectives: *Create a New Database, Create a New Table, Create a Primary Key and Add Records to a Table, Close and Save a Table, Modify the Table Design, Sort Records, Navigate to Records in a Table, and Close and Save a Database.*

In the following Mastery Assessment, you will create a new database and a new table to store supplier information for Lake Michigan City College. Your completed table will look like the one shown in Figure 1.78. You will save your database as *1I_LMCCsuppliers_Firstname_Lastname*.

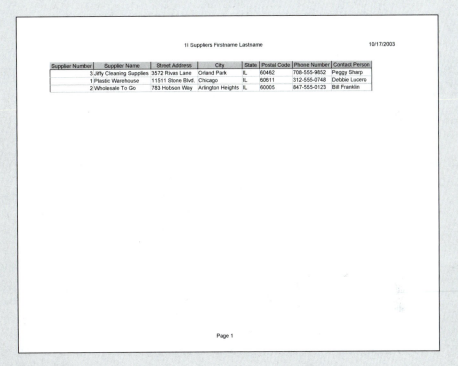

Figure 1.78

(**Project 1I**–Suppliers continues on the next page)

Mastery Assessments (continued)

Project 1I–Suppliers continued)

1. Start Access. In your Project folder, create a new database and name it **1I_LMCCsuppliers_Firstname_Lastname**

2. Use the following information to create a new table.

Field Name	Data Type	Description
Supplier Number	AutoNumber	
Supplier Name	Text	
Street Address	Text	
City	Text	
State	Text	
Postal Code	Text	
Phone Number	Text	
Contact Person	Text	Main contact

3. Choose the **Supplier Number** as the primary key for this table. Switch to Datasheet view, and then, using your own information, save the table as **1I Suppliers Firstname Lastname** and then add the following records to the table.

Supplier Number	Supplier Name	Street Address	City	State	Postal Code	Phone Number	Contact Person
1	Plastic Warehouse	11511 Stone Blvd.	Chicago	IL	60611	312-555-0748	Debbie Lucero
2	Wholesale To Go	783 Hobson Way	Arlington Heights	IL	60005	847-555-0123	Bill Franklin
3	Jiffy Cleaning Supplies	3572 Rivas Lane	Orland Park	IL	60462	708-555-9852	Peggy Sharp

4. Resize all of the columns to accommodate their data. Sort the table alphabetically by Supplier Name. Display the **Page Setup** dialog box and change the page orientation to **Landscape**. Print and then close the table. Close the database and then close Access.

End You have completed Project 1I

Mastery Assessments (continued)

Project 1J — Expenses

Objectives: *Rename a Database; Start Access, Open an Existing Database, and View Database Objects; Modify the Table Design; Print a Table; Edit Records in a Table; Navigate to Records in a Table; and Close and Save a Database.*

In the following Mastery Assessment, you will open an existing database and modify items in the database that stores information about the expenses of the Computer Club at Lake Michigan City College. Your completed database object will look similar to the one shown in Figure 1.79. You will rename the database as *1J_Expenses_Firstname_Lastname*.

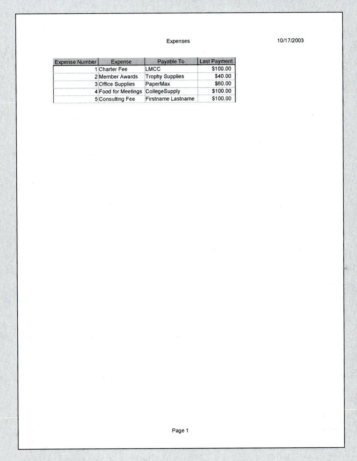

Figure 1.79

(**Project 1J**–Expenses continues on the next page)

Mastery Assessments (continued)

Project 1J–Expenses continued)

1. Copy the student file **a01J_Expenses** to the drive and folder where you are storing your projects for this chapter. Rename the database as **1J_Expenses_Firstname_Lastname** and remove the Read-only attribute.

2. Start Access and open the database you renamed in Step 1. Open the **Expenses** table and make the following changes to the table:

   Change the *Expense ID* field to **Expense Number**

   Change the primary key for the table to **Expense Number**

   For the *Member Awards* expense record, change the information in the Payable To column from *LMCC* to **Trophy Supplies**

3. Add the following record using your own name:

Expense Number	Expense	Payable To	Last Payment
AutoNumber	Consulting Fee	Firstname Lastname	100

4. Resize the fields in the table to accommodate their data. Print and then close the table, saving any changes if prompted to do so. Close the database and close Access.

End You have completed Project 1J

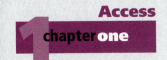

Problem Solving

Project 1K — Video Store

Objectives: *Create a New Database, Create a New Table, Create a Primary Key and Add Records to a Table, Modify the Table Design, Close and Save a Table, Print a Table, and Close and Save a Database.*

Lake Michigan City College has a small video rental shop on campus that rents videos and DVDs to students, staff, and faculty of the college. Create a database that will store information about the movie rentals such as customer names and the names of movies in the inventory. This database should have at least two tables: one for customers and another for the inventory of videos that are available to rent. Create a new database with an appropriate name for the video rental store and add two tables as described above to the database. In each of the tables, add the fields that you think should be included in each of these tables. Designate one field in each table as the primary key. Print your tables.

 You have completed Project 1K

Project 1L — Fix It

Objectives: *Rename a Database; Start Access, Open an Existing Database, and View Database Objects; Create a Primary Key and Add Records to a Table; Open a Table; Modify the Table Design; and Close and Save a Database.*

The Business Division at Lake Michigan City College needs to correct some errors in a student database. Copy the student file a01L_FixIt to your storage location and rename it **1L_FixIt_Firstname_Lastname**. Clear the Read-only property and then open the database. View the FixIt table in this database. Think about the way the data is arranged in the table. Based on the databases you have worked with in this chapter, identify at least four ways this table could be improved. Then make your suggested changes to this database.

 You have completed Project 1L

On the Internet

Databases and Today's Industries

Most of the world's information is stored in some type of database. Databases play a large role in industries today. Their expansive applications have made databases an integral part of business in the current marketplace.

Go online and perform a search to identify the current trends involving databases and the different career paths that include database training as part of their job descriptions.

GO! with Help

Searching Access Help

The Access Help system is extensive and can help you as you work. In this exercise, you will view information about getting help as you work in Access.

1. Start Access. In the **Type a question for help** box, type **Printing a table** and then press Enter.

2. In the displayed **Search Results** task pane, click the result—**Print a record, datasheet, or database object**. Maximize the displayed window, and at the top of the window, click the **Show All** button. Scroll through and read about printing database objects in Access.

3. If you want, print a copy of the information by clicking the printer button at the top of the window.

4. Close the Microsoft Access Help window, then close Access.

Access 2003

chapter two

Forms and Reports

In this chapter you will: complete these projects and **practice these skills.**

Project 2A
Creating Forms

Objectives
- View and Navigate to Records with a Form
- Create an AutoForm
- Save and Close an AutoForm
- Use a Form to Add Records to and Delete Records from a Table

Project 2B
Creating Forms and Reports

Objectives
- Create a Form with the Form Wizard
- Modify a Form
- Create a Report with the Report Wizard
- Save a Report
- Modify the Design of a Report
- Print a Report

Lake Michigan City College

Lake Michigan City College is located along the lakefront of Chicago—one of the nation's most exciting cities. The college serves its large and diverse student body and makes positive contributions to the community through relevant curricula, partnerships with businesses and nonprofit organizations, and learning experiences that allow students to be full participants in the global community. The college offers three associate degrees in 20 academic areas, adult education programs, and continuing education offerings on campus, at satellite locations, and online.

© Getty Images, Inc.

Forms and Reports

You can both enter and view database information in the database table itself. However, for entering and viewing information, it is usually easier to use an Access form.

Think about having to enter the information from hundreds of paper forms into a database. If the form on the screen matches the pattern of information on the paper form, it will be much easier to enter the new information. Additionally, when using a form, only one record is visible at a time, making data entry easier.

When viewing information, it is also easier to view just one record at a time. For example, your college counselor can look at your college transcript in a nicely laid out form on the screen without seeing the records for dozens of other students at the same time.

Reports in Access summarize the data in a database in a professional-looking manner suitable for printing. The design of a report can be modified so that the final report is laid out in a format that is useful for the person reading it.

In this chapter, you will create and modify both forms and reports for Access databases.

Project 2A Computer Club

In Chapter 1, you saw that two database objects can be used to enter data into a database. You can type data directly into a table in Datasheet view. Recall that tables are the place where the data is stored. You can also type data into a form. A *form* is an organized view of the fields in one or more database tables or queries laid out in a visually appealing format on the screen. For the purpose of entering new records or viewing existing records, forms are generally easier to use than the table itself.

The Computer Club at Lake Michigan City College maintains a database with two tables—the Members table and the Club Events table. In Activities 2.1 through 2.5 you will use an Access form to view and navigate to the records in the Members table. Then, using AutoForm, you will create and save a new form to view and navigate to the records in the Club Events table. Your completed database objects will look similar to Figure 2.1. In addition, you will use the new form to add and delete records in the Club Events table.

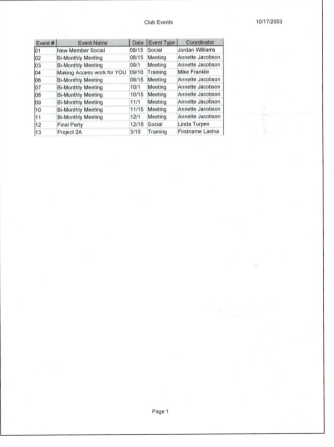

Figure 2.1
Project 2A—Computer Club

Project 2A: Computer Club | **Access** 83

Objective 1
View and Navigate to Records with a Form

Your personal address book would not be useful to you if the addresses or phone numbers in it contained errors. Likewise, a database is useful only if the data in it is accurate. You can see that the process of getting the information into a database is an important one. The individual who performs the *data entry*—typing in the actual data—has a better chance of entering the data accurately if he or she is provided with a data entry tool that assists in preventing data entry errors. Access forms are an example of such a tool.

Because a form can be set to display only one record in the database at a time, a form is also useful to anyone who has the job of viewing information in a database. For example, when you visit the Records office at your college to obtain a transcript, someone displays your record on a screen. For the viewer, it is much easier to look at one record at a time, using a form, than to look at all the student records in the database table.

Activity 2.1 Viewing and Navigating to Records Using a Form

1 Using the skills you practiced in Chapter 1, and using either My Computer or Windows Explorer, create a new folder named Chapter 2 in the location where you will be storing your projects for this chapter.

2 Locate the file **a02A_ComputerClub** from the student files that accompany this text. Copy and paste the file to the Chapter 2 folder you created in Step 1.

3 Using the technique you practiced in Activity 1.1 of Chapter 1, rename the file as **2A_ComputerClub_Firstname_Lastname** and remove the Read-only property from the file if necessary.

4 Close the Windows accessory you are using, either My Computer or Windows Explorer. Start Access and open your **2A_ComputerClub** database.

5 On the Objects bar, click **Forms**.

To the right of the Objects bar, two command icons for creating a new form display, followed by the Members form that has been created and saved as part of the Computer Club database.

6 Click to select the **Members** form if necessary, and then on the toolbar above the Objects bar, click the **Open** button [Open]. Alternatively, double-click the Members form to open it.

The Members form, in *Form view*, displays the first record in the Members table—the record for *Annette Jacobson*. In Form view, you can modify the information in a record or add a new record, one record at a time.

7 At the lower edge of the form, in the navigation area, click the **Last Record** button . See Figure 2.2.

Record 15—*Ceara Thibodeaux*—displays.

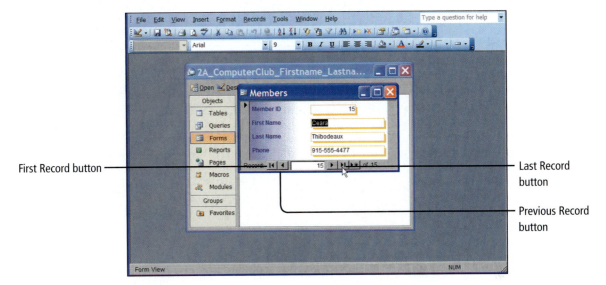

First Record button

Last Record button

Previous Record button

Figure 2.2

8 In the navigation area, click the **Previous Record** button once.

Record 14, the previous record—*Debbie Greggs*—displays.

9 In the navigation area, click the **First Record** button .

Record 1—*Annette Jacobson*—displays.

10 Position your mouse pointer in the navigation area over the number of the current record until the pointer takes the shape of an I-beam. See Figure 2.3.

First Record button

I-beam in navigation area

Figure 2.3

Project 2A: Computer Club | **Access** 85

11 Drag your mouse over the number **1** to select it. See Figure 2.4.

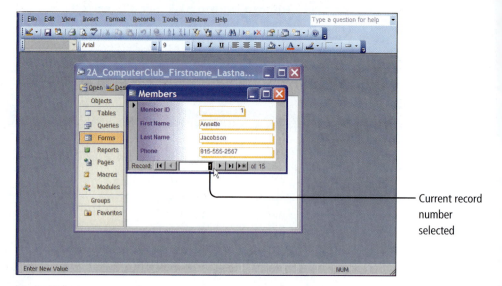

Figure 2.4

12 With the number 1 selected, type **8** and then press Enter.

Record 8 in the Members table—*Kathleen Lightfoot*—displays, as shown in Figure 2.5.

Assuming you know the exact number of the record you want to view, this is a useful method of navigating to a record when there is a large number of records to navigate through.

Use the navigation buttons—Next Record, Last Record, Previous Record, First Record—to jump to specific records in a database table. Use the New Record button to move to the end of the database table for the purpose of entering a new record. You will do this in a later activity.

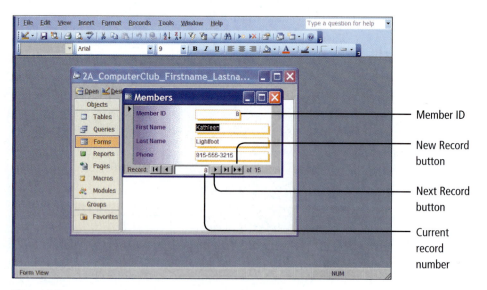

Figure 2.5

13 In the upper right corner of the **Members** form, click the **Close** button to close the form.

Objective 2
Create an AutoForm

AutoForm is a feature that creates a form for an existing database table. AutoForm incorporates all the information, both the field names and the individual records, from an existing table and then creates the form for you.

Activity 2.2 Creating an AutoForm

1 On the Objects bar, verify that **Forms** is selected. Above the Objects bar, locate and then click the **New** button.

The New Form dialog box displays as shown in Figure 2.6. The dialog box lists a variety of form types that can be created with a ***wizard***, an Access feature that walks you step by step through a process by having you answer questions.

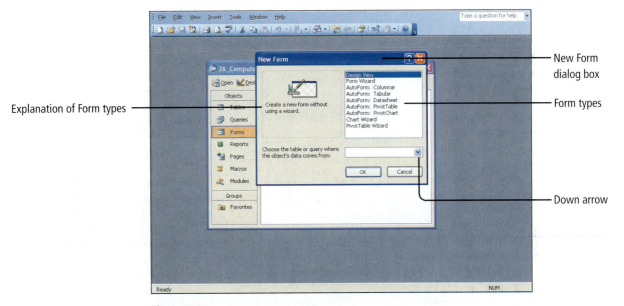

Figure 2.6

2 On the right side of the displayed dialog box, click **AutoForm: Datasheet** and then read the explanation in the box to the left. Then, on the displayed list, click **Chart Wizard** and read the explanation in the box to the left.

As you progress in your study of Access, you will use many of the New Form wizards, and you can see that Access provides explanations for each one.

3 On the displayed list, click **AutoForm: Columnar** and then read the explanation to the left.

The Columnar format displays records in a form one at a time in a column format.

4 In the text box to the right of *Choose the table or query where the object's data comes from:* click the **down arrow**.

A list of available tables and queries for this database displays. An AutoForm can be created using the information in either a table or a query. Recall that a query contains only those records that meet specified criteria.

5 From the displayed list, click **Club Events** and then click **OK**. Compare your screen to Figure 2.7.

A new form, based on the fields and records in the Club Events table, is created and displays on your screen. Notice that all five field names in the table are shown and the first record, Event #01, is displayed.

Depending on previous use of the computer at which you are working, your form may have a different background color. The various Form Wizards apply different backgrounds, and Access will apply the most recently used background. The background color will not affect the way the form works.

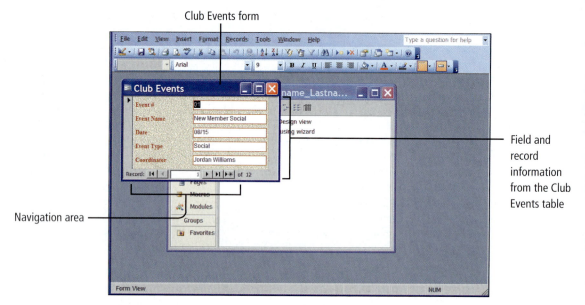

Figure 2.7

6 Click several of the navigation buttons to view the records in the form. All of the records in the Club Events table are available for viewing.

Objective 3
Save and Close an AutoForm

Because this form will be convenient for people who need to enter new data into the Club Events table, and for people who need to look up information about various club events, you will want to save the form for future use. When you close a form, you will be asked to save the changes.

Activity 2.3 Saving and Closing an AutoForm

1 In the upper right corner of the **Club Events** form, click the **Close** button ⊠.

Because you have not previously named or saved this form, a message displays asking you if you want to save the changes to the design of form "Form1."

2 Click **Yes**.

The Save As dialog box displays.

3 In the **Form Name** box, accept the default form name of *Club Events* by clicking **OK**.

The form is saved and closed. The new form name, *Club Events*, displays in the Database window. See Figure 2.8. The default name of a form created in this manner is the name of the table upon which the form was based.

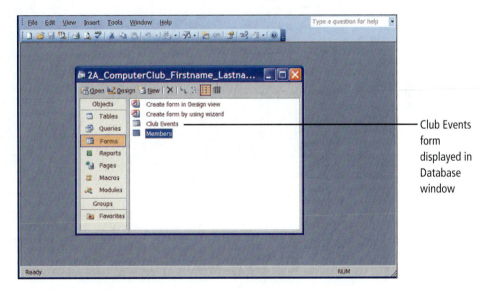

Figure 2.8

Another Way

Using the Database Toolbar to Create an AutoForm

Use the New Object: AutoForm button.

Access can create an AutoForm directly from the Database toolbar. On the Objects bar, click Tables. Click once on the table that contains the fields and records you would like in your form, then click the New Object: AutoForm button on the Database toolbar.

Objective 4
Use a Form to Add Records to and Delete Records from a Table

Forms and tables are interactive objects in an Access database. That is, when a record is added to a table using a form, the new record is inserted into the corresponding table. The reverse is also true—when a record is added to a table, the new record can be viewed in the corresponding form.

Activity 2.4 Adding Records to a Table Using a Form

1 On the Objects bar, verify that **Forms** is selected and then open the **Club Events** form.

The Club Events form opens in the Form view.

2 In the navigation area of the form, click the **New Record** button.

The fields are cleared and ready to accept a new entry. The record number advances to 13, indicating that this will be the 13th record. See Figure 2.9.

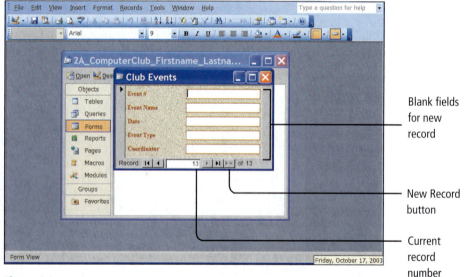

Figure 2.9

3 With the insertion point blinking in the **Event #** box, type **13** and then press Tab. After you start typing, notice that the pencil image displays in the gray bar to the left.

4 In the **Event Name** box, type **Project 2A** and then press Tab.

5 In the **Date** box type **3/10** and then press Tab.

6 In the **Event Type** box, type **Training** and then press Tab.

7 In the **Coordinator** box, using your own information, type **Firstname Lastname**

90 Access | Chapter 2: Forms and Reports

8 On the title bar of the **Club Events** form, click the **Close** button ![X].

The form closes and the new record is saved and added to the Club Events table.

9 On the Objects bar, click **Tables** and then double-click the **Club Events** table to open it in Datasheet view. Alternatively, select the table name and click the Open button ![Open] just above the Objects bar.

10 Verify that record 13, the record you just added using the form, displays in the table and that your name is listed as the coordinator.

Recall that tables and forms are interactive objects—the record you added by using the Club Events *form* displays in the Club Events *table*.

11 On the title bar of the table, click the **Close** button ![X] to close the table.

12 On the Objects bar, click **Forms**. Right-click the **Club Events** form and then click **Open**.

13 Using the navigation method of your choice (the **Next Record** button ![▶], the **Last Record** button ![▶|], or by typing the record number in the Record box), navigate to record **13**.

Record 13 displays and your name displays in the Coordinator field.

Activity 2.5 Deleting Records from a Table Using a Form

Using a form, you can also delete records from a database table. You should delete records when they are no longer needed in your database. In this activity, you will delete a record in the Club Events table—the record for the Introduction to Outlook event.

1 With the **Club Events** form displayed, navigate to **Event #5**, *Introduction to Outlook*. Then, on the left side of the form, locate the gray bar that contains a right-pointing arrow, as shown in Figure 2.10.

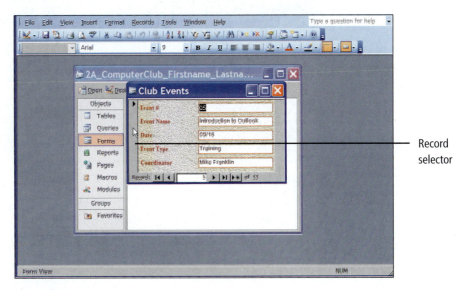

Record selector

Figure 2.10

2 Click anywhere in the gray bar area.

The gray bar is selected; this area is known as the ***record selector***. The record selector in the form is similar to the record selector in a table. The record selector selects an entire record in a form, just as the record selector in a table allows you to select the entire row (record) in the table. When the record selector is highlighted in black—selected—all the fields in the displayed record are selected.

3 On the Form View toolbar, click the **Delete Record** button . Alternatively, press Delete on the keyboard.

A message displays alerting you that you are about to delete a record. If you click Yes and delete the record, you cannot use the Undo button to reverse the action. If you delete a record by mistake, you will have to re-create the record.

4 Click **Yes** to delete the record.

The record is deleted from the Club Events table, reducing the number of records in the table to 12.

5 On the title bar of the **Club Events** form, click the **Close** button to close the form.

6 Be sure the **Club Events** form is selected in the Database window. Display the **File** menu, click **Page Setup**, and in the displayed **Page Setup** dialog box, click the **Columns tab**. See Figure 2.11.

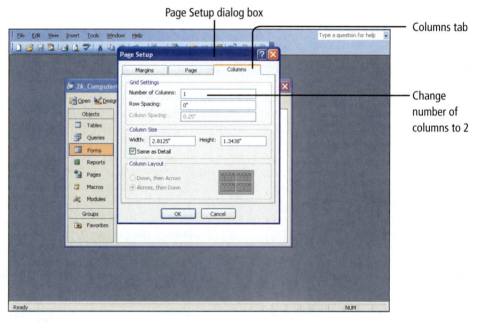

Figure 2.11

7 Under **Grid Settings**, change the **Number of Columns** to **2** and then click **OK**. On the Database toolbar, click the **Print** button .

Each record in the table will print in a newspaper column format. By selecting 2 columns, all the records will print on a single sheet. Recall that record 13 contains your name and that record 5 was deleted. Depending upon previous usage of your computer, your printed format may vary slightly from the one shown in Figure 2.1.

8 On the Objects bar, click **Tables** and then click the **Club Events** table. On the Database toolbar, click the **Print** button . Compare this printout to your forms printout.

You can see that all of the records are contained within both printouts. In the printed table, each record occupies a single row. In the Forms view, each record displays in its own individual form. The current date will print on the table printout.

9 On the title bar of the Database window, click the **Close** button to close the database. On the title bar of the Access window, click the **Close** button to close Access.

End You have completed Project 2A

Project 2B School

In Project 2A, you used AutoForm to create a form that incorporated all the fields from the table on which it was based. AutoForm creates a form in a simple top-to-bottom layout, with all the fields lined up in a single column. For the individual who is typing in the records, this layout is efficient and easy to use. Whereas AutoForm creates a form using all the fields in the table, and lays them out in a simple column, the **Form Wizard** creates a form in a manner that gives you much more flexibility in the design, layout, and number of fields included.

In Activities 2.6 through 2.15, you will use the Form Wizard to create a form for the Students database at Lake Michigan City College. Then you will modify the form and add a Page Footer to the form. You will also create a report for the Students database. See Figure 2.12.

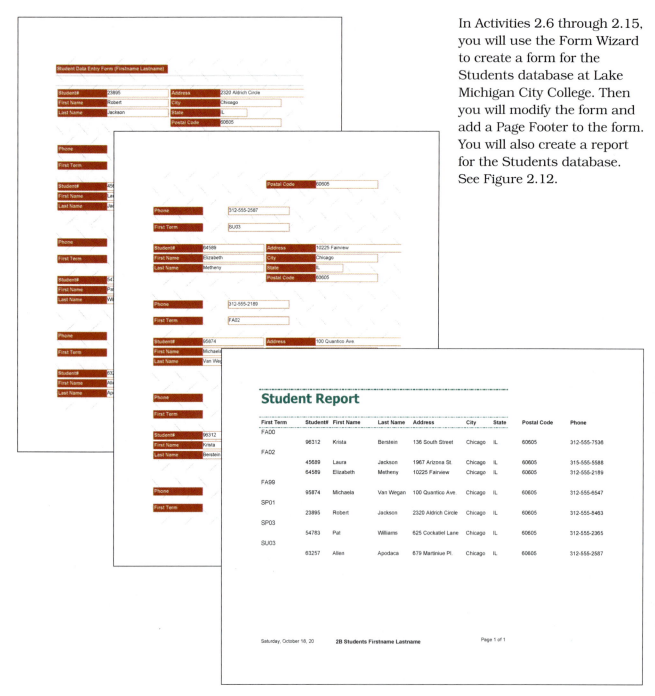

Figure 2.12
Project 2B—School

Objective 5
Create a Form with the Form Wizard

Different form layouts are useful for individuals who both view database information with a form and enter information into a database using a form. For example, when the admissions representative at your college displays your information to answer a question for you, it is easier to view the information spread out in a logical pattern across the screen rather than in one long column.

Activity 2.6 Creating a Form Using the Form Wizard

Recall that a wizard is an Access feature that walks you step by step through a process by asking you questions.

1. Using either **My Computer** or **Windows Explorer**, locate the file **a02B_School** from your student files. Copy the file and then paste it into your Chapter 2 folder. Rename the file as **2B_School_Firstname_Lastname** and remove the Read-only attribute. Close the Windows accessory you are using.

2. Start Access and open your **2B_School** database. On the Objects bar, click **Forms**.

3. To the right of the Objects bar, double-click the command icon **Create form by using wizard**. Alternatively, right-click the command icon and click Open on the displayed shortcut menu.

   The Form Wizard dialog box displays, as shown in Figure 2.13. The first step is to indicate the table for which you want the wizard to design a form, and then indicate what fields from the table that you want to include in the form.

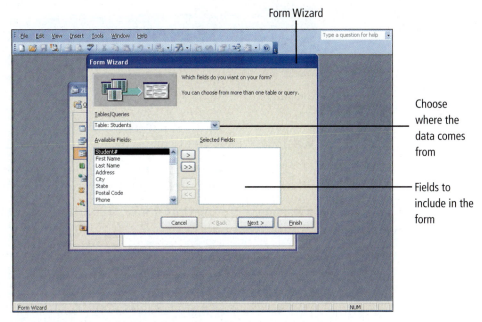

Figure 2.13

4 Under **Tables/Queries**, click the **down arrow**.

A list of tables and queries available for this database displays. Currently, only one object, the Students table, has been created in this database.

5 Click **Table: Students**.

Under Available Fields, a list of the fields in the Students table displays.

6 To the right of the **Available Fields** list, click the **All Fields** button [>>] to select all of the fields from the Students table and move them into the Selected Fields column. See Figure 2.14.

This action will place *all* of the fields from the table into the new form. It is also possible to use the **One Field** button [>] to select fields one at a time so that you can select only those fields you want to include in the form.

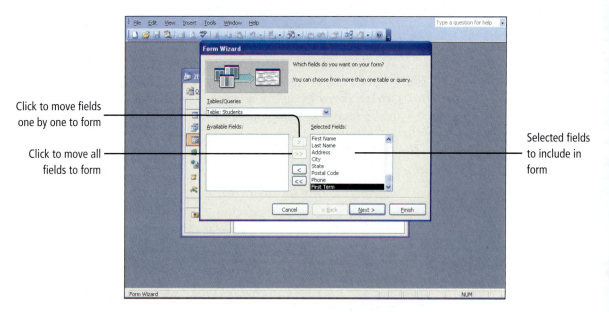

Figure 2.14

7 In the lower right corner of the dialog box, click the **Next** button.

The next step in the Form Wizard displays requesting information about the desired layout of your form.

8 Make sure the **Columnar** option button is selected and then click the **Next** button.

The next step in the Form Wizard displays requesting information about the desired style of your form, similar to Figure 2.15. Depending on previous use of your computer, a different style might be highlighted. Styles are combinations of attractive colors and graphics that are applied to the form to make it more visually appealing.

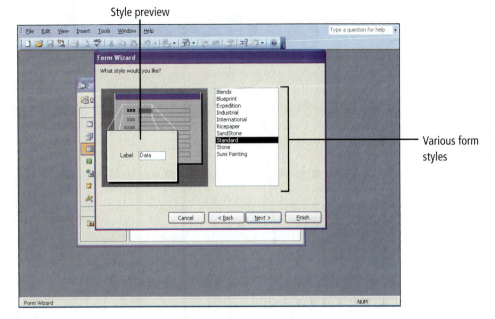

Figure 2.15

9. Click the **Industrial** style, notice the small preview of the style on the left, and then click the **Next** button.

   The final step in the Form Wizard displays, and the default name for the form—*Students*—displays and is highlighted. Access always uses the table name as the default name for the form.

10. With the default name highlighted, press Delete and then, using your own first and last name, type **Students Firstname Lastname**

11. Click the **Finish** button.

    Access creates the form using the responses you provided in the Wizard. The completed form displays in Form view. See Figure 2.16. Leave the form open for the next activity.

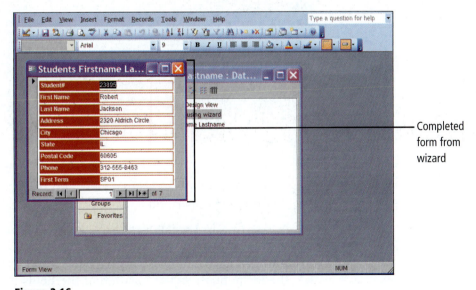

Figure 2.16

Objective 6
Modify a Form

You have seen that it is a quick and easy process to create a form using either the AutoForm method or the Form Wizard. After you have created a form, you may want to change the placement of the fields on the form for easier viewing or more efficient data entry. In the following activities, you will modify a form.

Activity 2.7 Switching Between Views in a Form and Adding a Form Header

Access provides tools that you can use to modify the layout of a form. These tools are available by displaying the form in its Design view. You can open a form in Design view or Form view, depending on what action you want to perform on the form. For example, if you want to view, add, delete, or modify records using a form, use the Form view. If you want to view, add, delete, or modify the field information (such as the placement of the fields on the form), use the Design view.

1 With your **Students** form displayed, on the Form View toolbar, click the **View** button. See Figure 2.17. In a manner similar to viewing tables, the View button will change depending on the current view to allow you to switch back and forth between *Design view* and *Form view*.

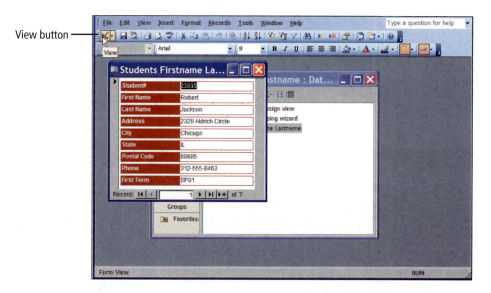

Figure 2.17

The form displays in Design view and the Toolbox toolbar displays, floating on your screen.

Notice that in Design view, you do not see the names of the students—or other information contained in the records. You see only the names of the fields. In this view, you can change the design of the form, such as the location of the fields on the form.

2 If necessary, drag the Toolbox by its title bar into the gray area of your screen. On the form's title bar, click the **Maximize** button.

The Design view of the form is maximized on your screen. This larger view is helpful to view the various sections of the form. See Figure 2.18.

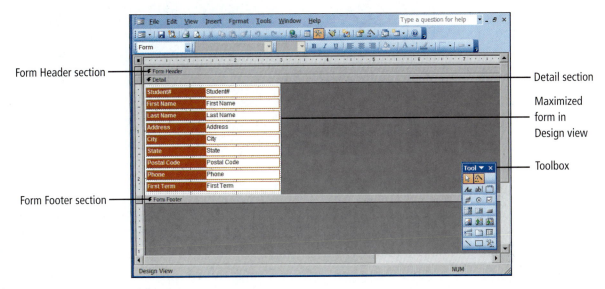

Figure 2.18

3 On your screen, locate the following three sections of the form, as shown in Figure 2.18: the Form Header section, the Detail section, and the Form Footer section.

Information typed into the **Form Header** or **Form Footer** sections displays at the top (header) or bottom (footer) of the form when it is viewed in Form view or when the form is printed. For example, on a form that displays transcript information for students, the form header could indicate *Official Transcript* and the form footer could indicate the name of the college. The **Detail** section contains the fields and records that display in the form. The small dots behind the Detail section create a grid to guide your eye in rearranging the layout of the form if you decide to do so.

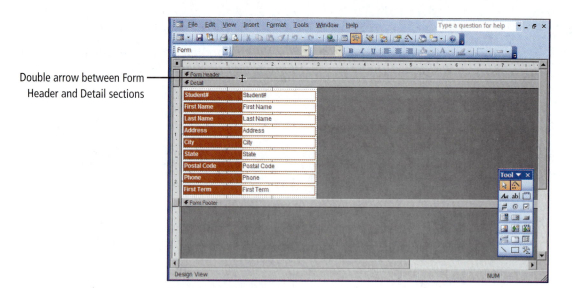

Double arrow between Form Header and Detail sections

Figure 2.19

4 Position your pointer on the horizontal line between the **Form Header** section and the **Detail** section until the pointer changes to a large double arrow, as shown in Figure 2.19.

5 Drag downward approximately 0.5 inch. Use your eye or the vertical ruler to determine this distance; it need not be exact. Release the mouse button.

The Form Header section expands and a grid pattern of dots displays.

6 On the Toolbox toolbar floating on your screen, click the **Label** button , as shown in Figure 2.20.

The **Toolbox** toolbar has various **controls** that can be added to forms in Access. Controls are the objects in a form, such as the brown labels and white text boxes currently displayed on your screen, with which you view or manipulate information stored in tables or queries.

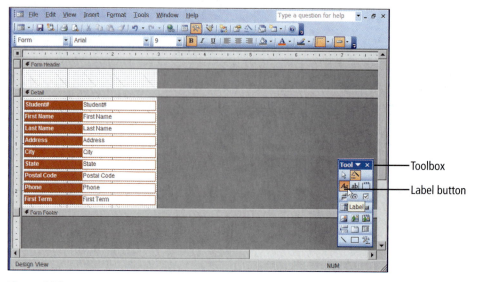

Toolbox
Label button

Figure 2.20

Alert! — **Is your Toolbox missing?**
If the toolbox is not displayed, click the Toolbox button on the Form Design toolbar. Alternatively, from the View menu, click Toolbox.

7 Move your pointer into the **Form Header section** and notice that the pointer shape is a plus sign and the letter A. See Figure 2.21.

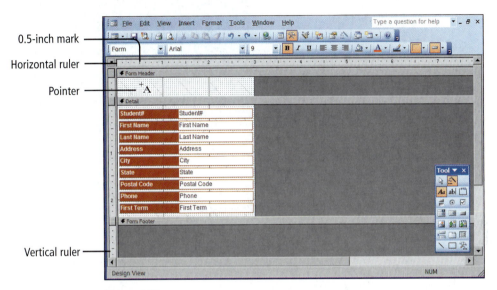

0.5-inch mark
Horizontal ruler
Pointer
Vertical ruler

Figure 2.21

8 On your screen, locate the horizontal and vertical rulers as shown in Figure 2.21 and then locate the 0.5-inch mark on the horizontal ruler.

Note — **Displaying Rulers in Form Design View**

Click Ruler on the View menu.

If the rulers are not displayed in the Design view of your form, display the View menu and then click Ruler.

9 With the plus sign of your mouse pointer positioned at the left edge of the **Form Header section**, drag down about 0.25 of an inch and to the right to **2.5 inches on the horizontal ruler**. Release the mouse button and compare your result to Figure 2.22.

If you are not satisfied with your result, click the Undo button and begin again. A new label control is created in the Form Header section and the insertion point is blinking in the control.

Project 2B: School | **Access** 101

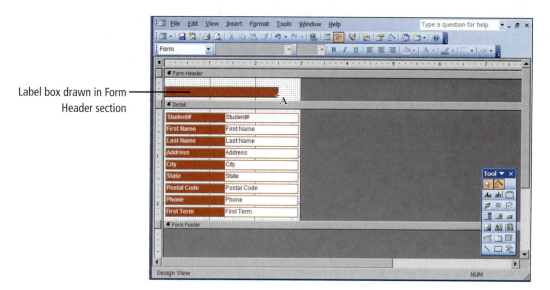

Label box drawn in Form Header section

Figure 2.22

10. In the label control that you just created, using your own first and last name, type **Student Data Entry Form (Firstname Lastname)**

    The label expands to accommodate your typing.

11. Press [Enter] and then notice that the label is surrounded by small squares.

    The small squares surrounding the label are ***sizing handles*** that indicate that the label control is selected.

12. On the Form View toolbar, click the **View** button to switch to the Form view.

    The form header displays with the information you inserted. See Figure 2.23. By placing a form header on the form, you have created information that will display at the top of the form when it is viewed, and also print at the top of the form when it is printed.

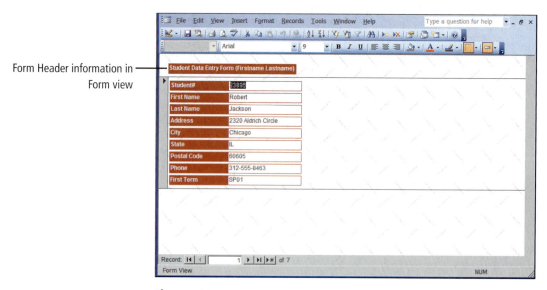

Form Header information in Form view

Figure 2.23

13 Click the **View** button again to return to the Design view of the form for the next activity.

Activity 2.8 Moving and Resizing Fields in a Form

The Design view of any database object is the view that is used to change the layout—the design—of the object. The reason for changing the layout of a form is usually to make it easier for the people using it to view and enter data. Sometimes forms are modified to match an existing paper form already in use by an organization. For example, the Student Registration Department at your college may have an existing paper form that you fill out when registering for courses. Transferring or entering this information from the paper form is easier if the Access form on the screen matches the pattern on the paper form.

1 With your form displayed in Design view, locate the horizontal and vertical rulers on your screen. Notice that the form is 3 inches wide.

2 As shown in Figure 2.24, position your mouse pointer on the right edge of the form until your pointer changes to a large, double arrow. Then, drag the right edge of the form to **6.5 inches on the horizontal ruler**.

By increasing the width of the form area, you have more space in which to rearrange the various form controls.

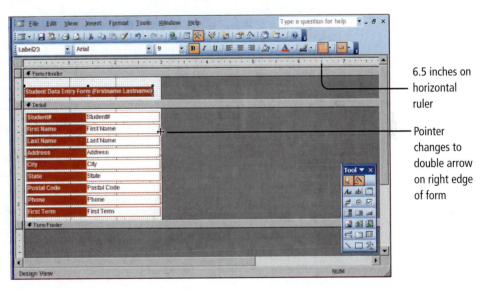

Figure 2.24

3 Click once in the white **Address text box control**. See Figure 2.25.

The Address **text box control** is selected and handles surround the selected object. A text box control on a form is where data from the corresponding table is displayed when the form is viewed.

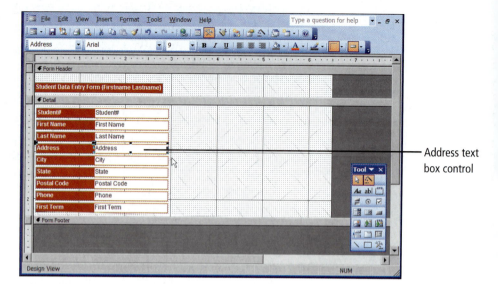

Figure 2.25

4 Position your mouse pointer over any border of the selected text box control until the **hand** pointer displays. See Figure 2.26. The hand pointer displays when the mouse pointer is positioned on the border of a control.

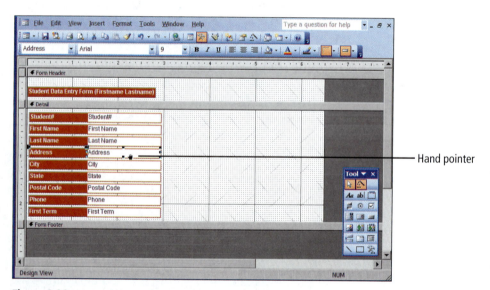

Figure 2.26

5 With the **hand** pointer displayed, drag the text box up and to the right of the Student# field as shown in Figure 2.27. Make sure that the left edge is positioned at approximately **3 inches on the horizontal ruler**.

Notice that both the *label* control—the brown box that, when viewed in Form view, contains the field name—and the *text box* control—the white box that, when viewed in Form view, contains the actual data—move together to the new location. Dragging with the hand pointer on the border of a control allows you to reposition both the label control and the text box control as one unit.

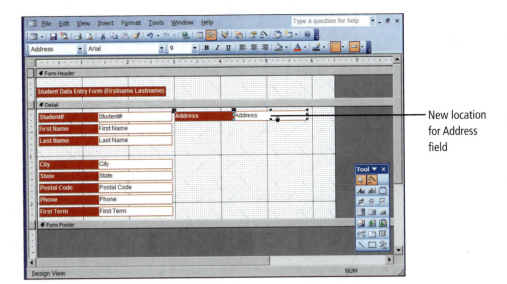

Figure 2.27

6 Click once in the white **City text box control** to select it, then position your pointer over any border of the text box to display the **hand pointer**.

7 Drag to position the **City controls** directly under the **Address controls**, to the right of the First Name controls, as shown in Figure 2.28.

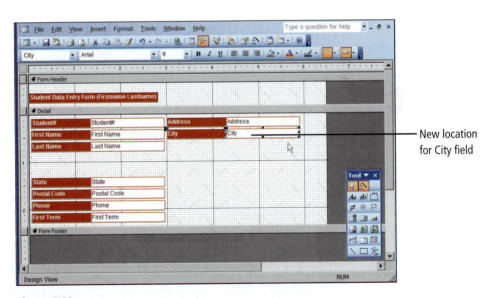

Figure 2.28

8 Using the technique you just practiced, move the **State controls** and the **Postal Code controls**, as shown in Figure 2.29.

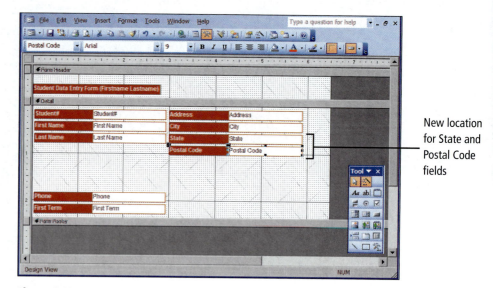

Figure 2.29

[9] Click once in the **Phone text box control** to select it. Position your pointer over the large black handle that is between the Phone label control and the Phone text box control until the **pointing hand** pointer displays. See Figure 2.30.

The pointing hand displays when your mouse pointer is positioned on the larger, upper left handle. With this pointer shape, you can move the text box control separately from the label control.

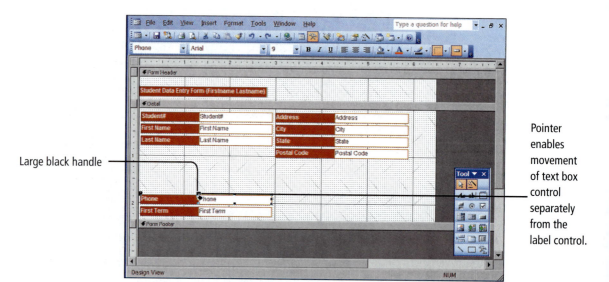

Figure 2.30

10 With the **pointing hand** pointer displayed, drag the white **Phone text box control** to the position shown in Figure 2.31—positioning its left edge at **2 inches on the horizontal ruler** and its top edge at **1.5 inches on the vertical ruler**.

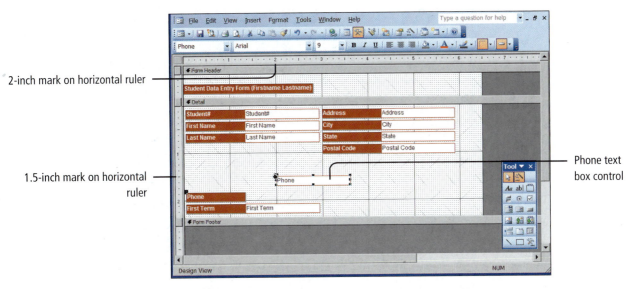

Figure 2.31

11 Select the brown **Phone label control**, point to the large black handle at the upper left corner to display the **pointing hand** pointer, and then drag to position it as shown in Figure 2.32.

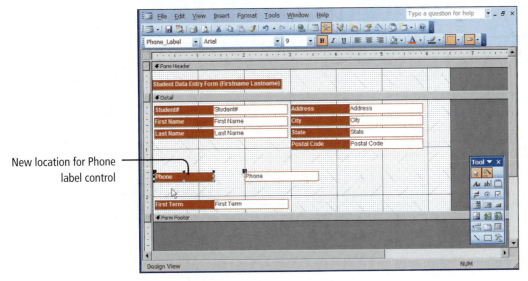

Figure 2.32

12. Move the white **First Term text box control** directly under the Phone text box control aligning its left edge at **2 inches on the horizontal ruler** and its top edge **at 1⅞ inches on the vertical ruler**, as shown in Figure 2.33.

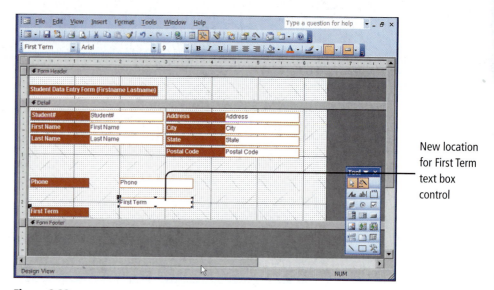

Figure 2.33

13. Move the brown **First Term label control** as shown in Figure 2.34.

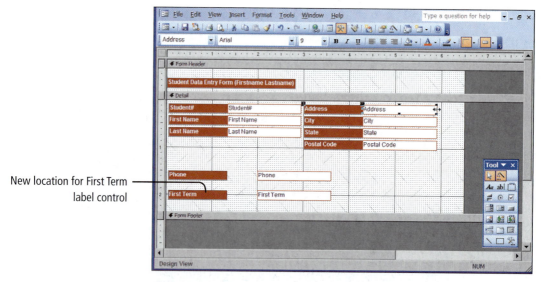

Figure 2.34

14. Click to select the white **Address text box control**, then position your pointer over the right center handle until the pointer changes to a horizontal double arrow, as shown in Figure 2.35.

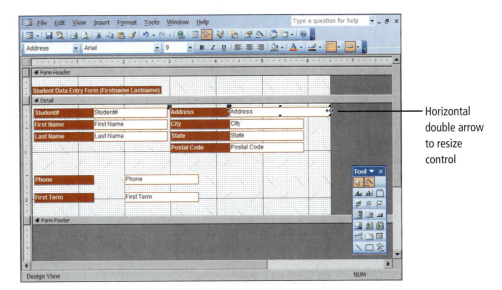

Figure 2.35

15. Drag the center right handle to **6.5 inches on the horizontal ruler**.

    The width of the Address text box control is increased. This is a good idea because addresses are typically longer than the data in a City or State field.

16. Use the technique you just practiced to *decrease* the width of the **State text box control**, as shown in Figure 2.36.

    You can see how the grid pattern provides a visual guide in placing the controls exactly where you want them.

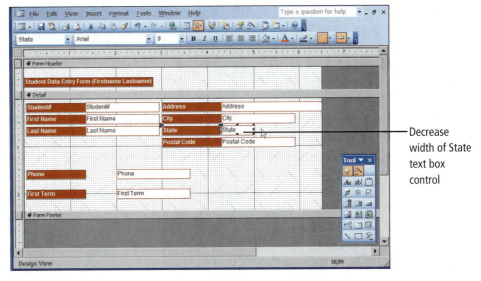

Figure 2.36

17. On the Form Design toolbar, click the **View** button to switch to the Form view and notice the changes you have made to the layout of the form.

18. Click the **View** button again to return to the Design view of the form for the next activity.

Project 2B: School | **Access** 109

Activity 2.9 Adding a Page Footer to a Form

A *Page Header* or *Page Footer* contains information that displays on every page of a form when it is printed. Header information displays at the top of a printed page and footer information displays at the bottom of a printed page.

1 On the menu bar, click **View** and then click **Page Header/Footer**.

Page Header and Page Footer sections are added to your form, as shown in Figure 2.37.

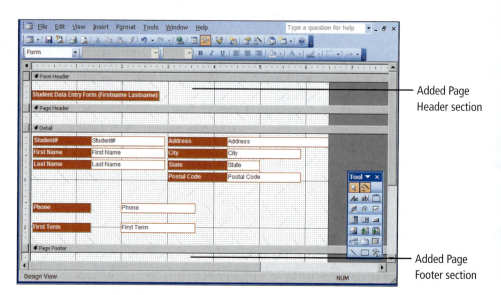

Figure 2.37

2 Locate the Toolbox toolbar floating on your screen. If it is not visible, display the View menu and click **Toolbox**. On the Toolbox, click the **Label** button.

3 Position the plus sign of your pointer just below the Page Footer separator at **2 inches on the horizontal ruler**, and then drag down to the lower separator and to the right to **4.5 inches on the horizontal ruler**, as shown in Figure 2.38.

If you are not satisfied with your result, recall that you can click the Undo button and begin again. An insertion point is blinking at the left edge of the control.

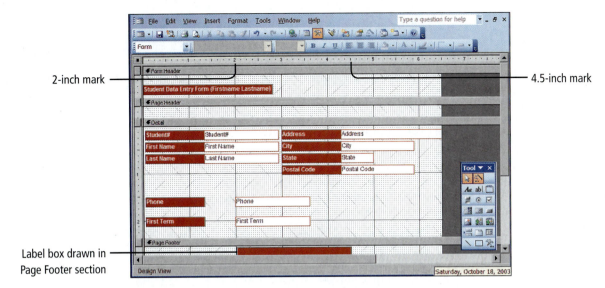

2-inch mark

4.5-inch mark

Label box drawn in Page Footer section

Figure 2.38

4 In the label control you just created, using your own first and last name, type **2B Students Firstname Lastname** and then press Enter.

Label controls, when placed in headers or footers, function as descriptors to either clarify the contents of a text box control, or to add additional information—such as a title or your name—to a form.

5 Click the **View** button to switch to the Form view.

Notice that the Page footer you created does *not* display in the Form view of the form. Page Headers and Footers only display when the form is printed.

6 On the Form View toolbar, click the **Print Preview** button. Locate your name in the Page footer at the lower edge of the page in Print Preview.

7 On the Print Preview toolbar, click the **Print** button to print the form.

Three pages will print; the last page will contain only the page footer.

8 To the right of *Type a question for help*, click the small **Close Window** button.

9 Click **Yes** when prompted to save changes to the design of the form.

The Database window, maximized, displays.

Project 2B: School | **Access** 111

Objective 7
Create a Report with the Report Wizard

Recall that a report is a database object that displays the fields and records from a table in an easy-to-read format suitable for printing. Reports are created to summarize information in a database in a professional-looking manner.

The **Report Wizard** assists you in creating a professionally designed report. The Report Wizard asks you a series of questions and then creates a report based on your answers.

Activity 2.10 Creating a Report Using the Report Wizard

1 If desired, to the right of the *Type a question for help box*, click the small **Restore Window** button. On the Objects bar, click **Reports**.

2 To the right of the Objects bar, double-click the command icon **Create report by using wizard**.

The Report Wizard displays with its first question. See Figure 2.39. Here you will select the table from which you want to get information, and then select the fields that you want to include in the report.

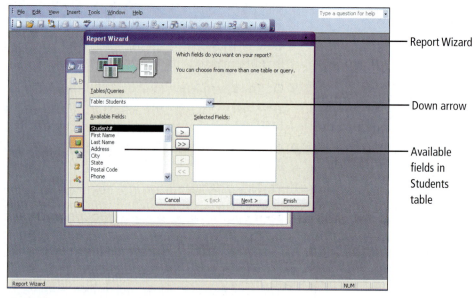

Figure 2.39

3 Under **Tables/Queries**, click the **down arrow**.

A list of tables and queries available for this database displays. Currently, only one object, the Students table, has been created in this database.

4 Click **Table: Students**.

Under Available Fields, a list of the fields in the Students table displays.

Access | Chapter 2: Forms and Reports

5 To the right of the list of available fields, click the **All Fields** button to move all of the fields from the Students table to the Selected Fields column on the far right.

This action will cause all of the fields to be included in the report.

6 Click the **Next** button.

7 Under **Do you want to add any grouping levels?** click **State** and then to the right, click the **One Field** button.

The preview on the right displays the State field as the field by which to group the records in the report. Grouping data helps you organize and summarize the data in your report. Grouping data in a report places all of the records within the same group field together.

8 In the center column, click the **One Field Back** button.

The State field is removed as the field by which to group the data. Because each of the records in the Students table has the same State information, it would not be useful to group the records by State.

9 Click **First Term** and then click the **One Field** button.

This action will cause the data in the report to be grouped by the First Term field.

10 Click the **Next** button.

11 In the **1** box on the right, click the **down arrow** to select a sort order for the records in the report. See Figure 2.40.

A list of fields in the report displays.

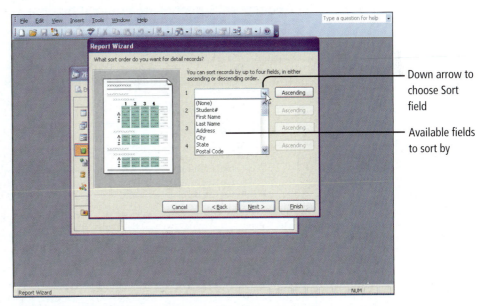

Figure 2.40

12 Click **Student#** and leave the default order as **Ascending**.

This action will cause the records in the report to be sorted numerically by each Student's Student# *within* the grouping option specified, which was First Term. Sorting records in a report presents a more organized report.

13 Click the **Next** button.

14 Under **Layout**, click the **Block** option button and notice the preview on the left. Click the **Outline 1** option button and notice the preview on the left.

15 Click the remaining **Layout** option buttons and view the preview.

The layout you choose for a report determines the arrangement of the data on the printed pages of your report.

16 After you are finished viewing the layout options, click the **Stepped** option button to select it as the layout option for the report.

17 On the right side of the dialog box, under **Orientation**, be sure that **Portrait** is selected, and keep the check mark next to *Adjust the field width so all fields fit on a page*.

18 Click the **Next** button. In the displayed list of styles, click **Soft Gray**.

19 Notice the preview to the left and then click **Compact** to view its preview. Click to view each of the remaining styles and then click **Casual**.

20 Click the **Next** button. In the **What title do you want for your report?** box type **Student Report** and then click the **Finish** button.

The report displays in Print Preview.

21 Maximize the window if necessary. On the toolbar, click the **Zoom arrow** and then click **75%**.

22 If necessary, use the vertical scroll bar to examine the data in the report. Notice that each of the specifications you defined for the report in the Report Wizard is reflected in the Print Preview of the report. Students are grouped by First Term. See Figure 2.41.

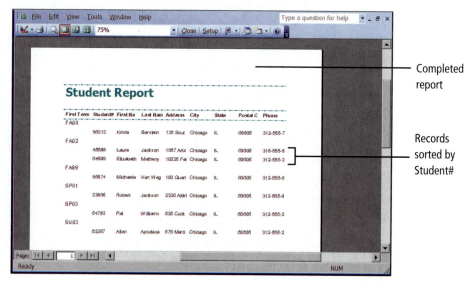

Figure 2.41

Objective 8
Save a Report

You do not need to create a new report each time data in the corresponding table is modified. Once you have created a report and laid it out in a format that is useful to you, you can save the report for future use. Each time the report is opened, any changes made to the table will be automatically reflected in the report.

Activity 2.11 Saving a Report

1 Click the **Close Window** button ✗ to close the report.

The report name, *Student Report*, displays in the Database window. Reports created with the Report Wizard are named in the final step of the wizard. When the report is closed, it is automatically saved.

2 Double-click the **Student Report**.

The report opens in Print Preview.

3 Adjust the zoom to **75%** so you can view the records in the report, and if necessary, maximize the window.

In the displayed report, notice that some of the field names are not completely displayed; they are cut off. For example, the *First Name*, *Last Name*, and *Postal Code* field names are not fully displayed.

4 Leave the report displayed in Print Preview for the next activity.

Objective 9
Modify the Design of a Report

After a report is created, you can still make modifications to its design by opening the report in Design view.

Activity 2.12 Switching Between Report View and Design View

1 On the Print Preview toolbar, click the **View** button to switch to the Design view of the report.

2 In the Design view of the report, examine the sections of the report, and notice that the report contains a Page Header and a Page Footer section. See Figure 2.42.

Design view for a report is similar to the Design view of a form. You can make modifications, and the dotted grid pattern assists you with alignment. Reports created with the Report Wizard contain a Page Header and Page Footer. You do not need to manually add these as you did with the form created with the Form Wizard.

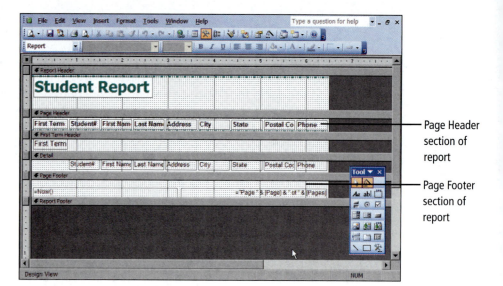

Figure 2.42

3. On the Report Design toolbar, click the **View** button.

The report displays in Print Preview..

4. On the Print Preview toolbar, click the **Setup** button. Alternatively, click File, Page Setup.

5. In the displayed **Page Setup** dialog box, click the **Page tab**. See Figure 2.43.

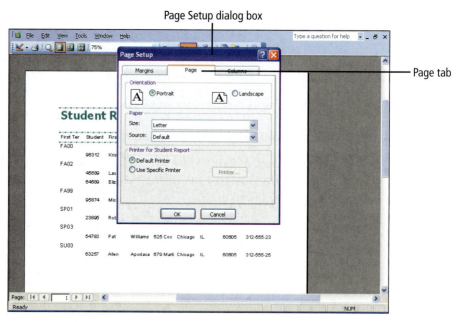

Figure 2.43

6. Under **Orientation**, click the **Landscape** option button and then click **OK**.

The report displays in landscape orientation. Changing the report to landscape orientation will allow more information to print across the page.

7 On the Print Preview toolbar, click the **View** button to switch to Design view, and leave the report open in Design view for the next activity.

Now that you have adjusted the page orientation, you can move to Design view to make additional modifications to the report.

Activity 2.13 Moving and Resizing Fields in a Report

Moving and resizing fields in the Design view of a report is accomplished with the same techniques you practiced when you moved and resized controls in a form in Design view.

1 If necessary, use the horizontal scroll bar to scroll the report to the right so that you can see the 9-inch mark on the horizontal ruler.

2 Position your pointer on the right edge of the report until your pointer changes to a large double arrow, and then drag the right edge of the report to the right to **9 inches on the horizontal ruler**. See Figure 2.44.

The width of the report is increased. By increasing the width of a report, you create more working space to move and reposition fields on the report.

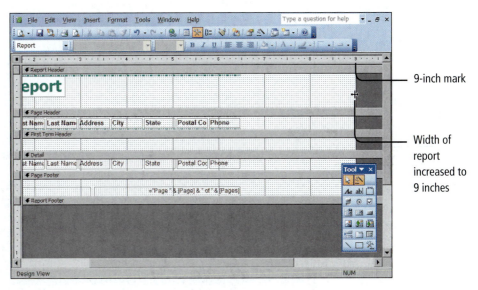

Figure 2.44

3 In the **Detail section**, click to select the **Phone text box control**. See Figure 2.45.

The Phone text box control is selected and handles surround the selected object.

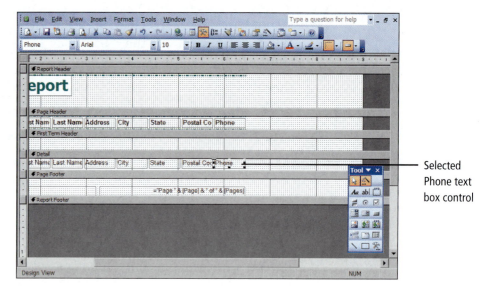

Figure 2.45

4 Press and hold down Shift. In the **Page Header section**, click the **Phone label control**. Then release the Shift key.

Both the Phone text box control and the Phone label control are selected, as shown in Figure 2.46.

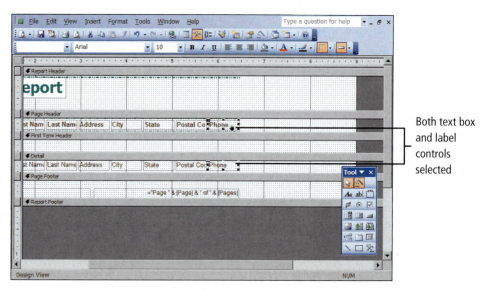

Figure 2.46

5 In the **Page Header section**, position your pointer in the **Phone label control** until the **hand** pointer displays, and then drag to position the right edge of the two objects, which will move together, at **8.75 inches on the horizontal ruler**.

Both controls are repositioned. Because the text box control and corresponding label control are in different sections of the report, you must use Shift to select both of the controls and then move them together.

6 With both controls still selected, resize the controls by dragging the center right handle of either control so that the right edge of the controls is stretched to **9 inches on the horizontal ruler**. See Figure 2.47.

The width of both controls is increased.

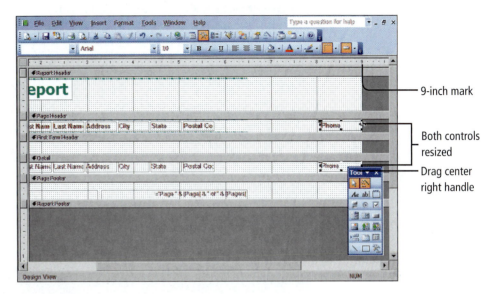

Figure 2.47

7 In the **Detail section**, click the **Postal Code text box control** to select it. Hold down Shift, and then in the **Page Header section**, click the **Postal Code label control**. Release Shift and then point to one of the controls to display the **hand** pointer. Drag to reposition the right edge of the two controls at **7.5 inches on the horizontal ruler**.

8 In the **Detail section**, resize the controls by dragging the center right handle of the **Postal Code text box control** so that the right edge of the control is stretched to **7.75 inches on the horizontal ruler**. See Figure 2.48.

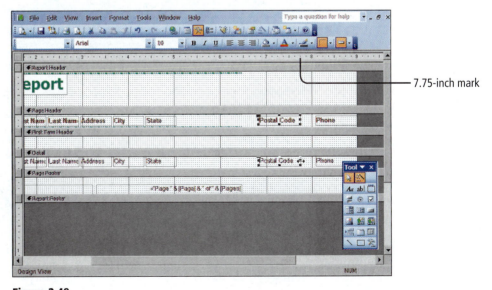

Figure 2.48

9 In the **Detail section**, click the **City text box control**, hold down Shift, and then click the **State text box control**. Continue to hold down Shift, and in the **Page Header section**, click the **City label control** and the **State label control**. Release Shift.

Four controls are selected—the City and State label controls in the Page Header section and the City and State text box controls in the Detail section, as shown in Figure 2.49.

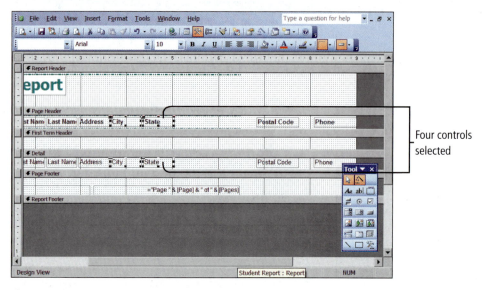

Figure 2.49

10 Position your pointer over any of the selected controls until the **hand** pointer displays. Move the grouped controls to the right until the right edge of the State controls are positioned at **6.75 inches on the horizontal ruler**. See Figure 2.50.

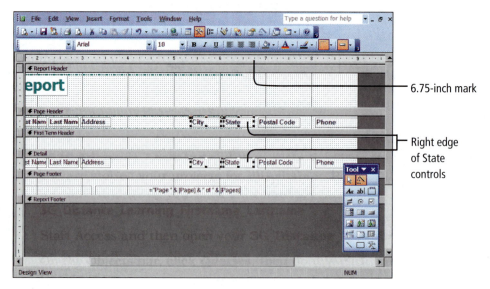

Figure 2.50

11 In the **Detail section**, click the **Address text box control**. Hold down Shift, and in the Page Header section, click the **Address label control**.

12 Position your pointer over the center right handle of the **Address label control** until the pointer changes to a double horizontal arrow, and then resize the controls by stretching the right edge to **4.25 inches on the horizontal ruler**. See Figure 2.51.

The width of the two controls is increased.

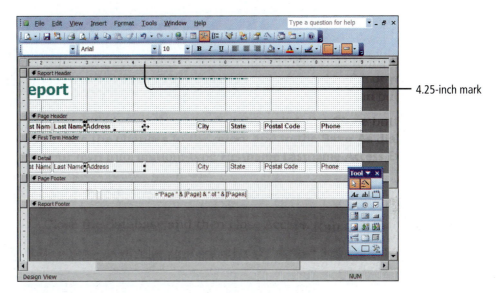

4.25-inch mark

Figure 2.51

13 With the two objects still selected, position the pointer over one of the objects until the **hand** pointer displays, then move the two controls until their right edges are at **5.25 inches on the horizontal ruler**.

The two controls are moved one inch to the right.

14 With the two controls still selected, hold down Ctrl and press →.

The two objects are **nudged**—moved slightly—to the right. Nudging is a useful technique to move controls with precision.

15 Using the Ctrl + → technique, nudge the selected controls to the right two more times.

16 Using the techniques you have just practiced, select, as a group, the **Last Name text box control** and the **Last Name label control**. Then move the selected objects to the right so that their right edge is at **3.75 inches on the horizontal ruler**. See Figure 2.52.

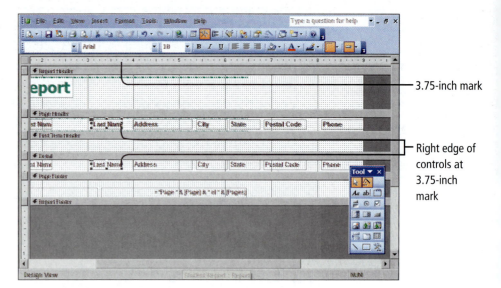

Figure 2.52

[17] With the objects still selected, lengthen the controls by dragging their right edge to match Figure 2.53.

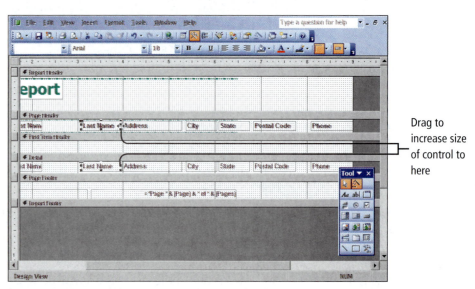

Figure 2.53

[18] If necessary, use the horizontal scroll bar to scroll the report so you can see the remainder of the fields to the left. Using the techniques you have practiced to resize the controls, select, then resize the **First Name controls** so their right edge is at **2⅜ inches on the horizontal ruler,** as shown in Figure 2.54.

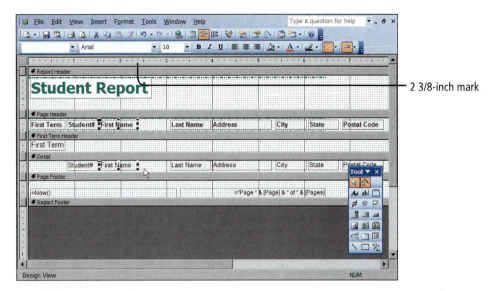

Figure 2.54

19. With the First Name controls still selected, hold [Shift] and select the **Student# text box control** and the **Student # label control**. Move the fields as a group until the right edge of the First Name field is positioned at **2.75 inches on the horizontal ruler**.

20. On the Report Design toolbar, click the **View** button to switch to the Print Preview of the report. Verify that the changes you made to the report are reflected in the Print Preview of the report, and then compare your screen to Figure 2.55.

> **Note** — Using Graphic Elements on Reports
>
> *Graphic lines can be lengthened.*
>
> The aqua graphic line on the report does not continue across the length of the report. As you progress in your study of Access, you will learn about graphic elements on reports.

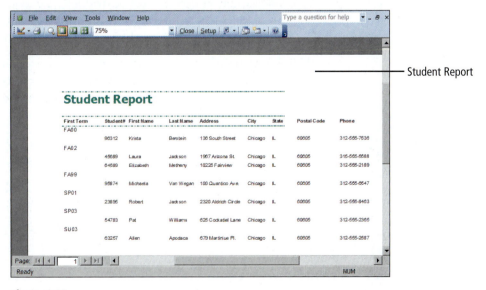

Figure 2.55

21 On the Print Preview toolbar, click the **View** button to switch to the Design view of the report. Leave the report open in Design view for the next activity.

Activity 2.14 Adding a Page Footer and a Report Footer to a Report

1 Locate the **Page Footer** section of the report. Notice that there are two controls in this section. See Figure 2.56.

The control on the left, identified as =*Now( )*, will insert the current date each time the report is opened. The control on the right, identified as =*"Page " & [Page] & " of " & [Pages]*, will insert the page numbers of the pages in the report when the report is displayed in Print Preview or when the report is printed.

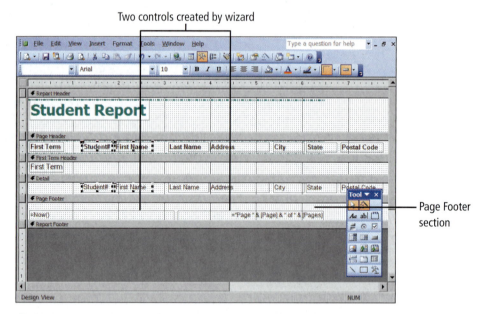

Figure 2.56

2 Click once in the control on the left, the control containing =*Now ( )*, to select it. Shorten this control by dragging its right center handle to the left to **1.5 inches on the horizontal ruler**.

3 Select the control on the right, the control that contains the =*"Page " & [Page] & " of " & [Pages]*. Shorten this control by dragging the left center handle of that control to **4.5 inches on the horizontal ruler**.

4 In the Toolbox, click the **Label** button.

5 Beginning at **2 inches on the horizontal ruler** and aligned with the top of the other two controls, drag down and to the right to **4.25 inches on the horizontal ruler** to draw a new label control, as shown in Figure 2.57.

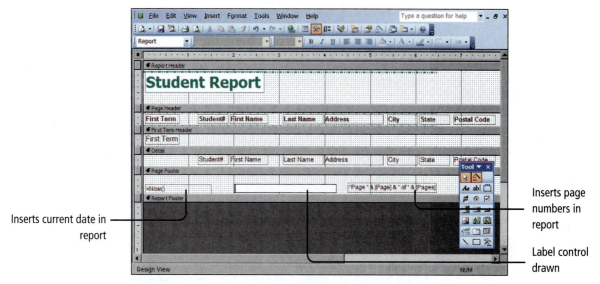

Figure 2.57

6 In the label box you just created, and using your own information, type **2B Students Firstname Lastname** and then press Enter.

An Alert button may display, which when pointed to, indicates *This is a new label and is not associated with a control.*

7 Switch to the Print Preview of the report and verify that your name displays at the lower edge of the report. If you are not satisfied with the positioning of the label control containing your name, return to Design view and use the Nudge feature (Ctrl + any arrow key) to nudge the control into a precise position.

Objective 10
Print a Report

An attractively formatted report printed on paper is much easier to view than looking at the database table on the screen or viewing one record at a time in a form on the screen. Reports are routinely printed for management, staff, or customers who need to look at information. For example, when you visit the Records Office of your college, you probably request a printed copy of your transcript. This is easier than viewing your records on the screen.

Activity 2.15 Printing a Report

1 On the Print Preview toolbar, click the **Print** button.

The report prints on one page.

2 To the right of *Type a question for help*, click the small **Close Window** button to close the report. Click **Yes** to save your changes.

3 Close the database and then click the **Close** button to close Access.

End You have completed Project 2B

Summary

A form is a tool for either entering or viewing information in a database. Although you can both enter and view database information in the database table itself, the use of a form is usually preferable for two reasons.

First, for entering data, a form is convenient and time saving, because the person entering the data using a form is not distracted by seeing the entire database table on the screen. He or she sees only the record being entered. Additionally, the fields on the form can be laid out in a manner that is easy for the person entering information to navigate.

Second, for viewing data, a form is easier to view than an entire table of information, because only the record needed is displayed. This is much easier for the person whose job it is to look up information in a database. For example, your college counselor can look at your college transcript in a nicely laid out form on the screen without seeing the records for hundreds of other students at the same time.

Two methods for creating forms in Access are through an AutoForm or through the Form Wizard. Once created, a form can be opened in Design View and further modified to make data entry or viewing even easier. Page headers and footers can be added that will display on each page of the form.

Reports in Access summarize the data in a database in a professional-looking manner suitable for printing. The design of a report can be modified so that the final report is laid out in a format that is useful for the person reading it.

In This Chapter You Practiced How To

- View and Navigate to Records with a Form
- Create an AutoForm
- Save and Close an AutoForm
- Use a Form to Add Records to and Delete Records from a Table
- Create a Form with the Form Wizard
- Modify a Form
- Create a Report with the Report Wizard
- Save a Report
- Modify the Design of a Report
- Print a Report

Concepts Assessments

Matching Match each term in the second column with its correct definition in the first column by writing the letter of the term on the blank line in front of the correct definition.

____ 1. Information that displays at the top of the form when the form is viewed in Form view or is printed.

____ 2. A bar that is used to select an entire record in a form or a table.

____ 3. An object such as a label or text box in a form or report that allows you to view or manipulate information stored in tables or queries.

____ 4. Information that displays at the lower edge of each page of a form or report.

____ 5. An Access feature that guides you step by step to create a form.

____ 6. A toolbar from which you can add various types of controls to forms and reports in Access.

____ 7. A feature in Access that quickly creates a form using the information from one table.

____ 8. A control on a form or report where data from the corresponding table is displayed

____ 9. A feature in Access used to create a professionally designed report.

____ 10. Using a form, the view in which you can enter and modify the information in a record.

____ 11. In the Design view of a form or report, the section that contains the fields and records that display in the form or report.

____ 12. The small squares that surround a selected object.

____ 13. The database object that provides an organized view of the fields in one or more tables or queries.

____ 14. The database object that displays the fields and records from a table in a format suitable for printing.

____ 15. A useful technique to move controls in Design view with precision.

A AutoForm
B Control
C Detail
D Form
E Form header
F Form view
G Form Wizard
H Nudge
I Page footer
J Record selector
K Report
L Report Wizard
M Sizing handles
N Text box
O Toolbox

Concepts Assessments (continued)

Fill in the Blank Write the correct answer in the space provided.

1. Using a form simplifies the data entry process because forms display only _____ record at a time.

2. The navigation buttons on a form include methods to go directly to the next record, last record, first record, and the _____ record in a table, as well as a button to create a new record.

3. Forms and tables are _____ database objects, meaning information entered into one will be automatically entered in the other.

4. A bar in Access used to select an entire record in a form or a table is the _____.

5. Creating a form using the Form Wizard offers more flexibility in the design of the form than creating a form using a(n) _____.

6. To change the layout and arrangement of fields on a form or report you must use the _____ view of the form or report.

7. Two visual aids that guide your placement of controls on a report or form in Design view are the dotted grid pattern and the _____ at the top and left of the screen.

8. Access reports are printed so individuals can view the information in the report without _____ the database itself.

9. To select more than one field simultaneously in the Design view of a form or report, you must hold down the _____ key on the keyboard.

10. The layout that you choose for a report in the Report Wizard determines the _____ of the data in the report.

Access chapter two
Skill Assessments

Project 2C—LMccDepts

Objectives: *View and Navigate to Records with a Form, Create an AutoForm, Save and Close an AutoForm, and Use a Form to Add Records to and Delete Records from a Table.*

In the following Skill Assessment, you will create an AutoForm for use with the database of Department names at Lake Michigan City College. You will use the new form to add records to and delete records from the database. Your completed form will look like the one shown in Figure 2.58. You will rename the database as *2C_LMccDepts_Firstname_Lastname* in the folder you have created for this chapter.

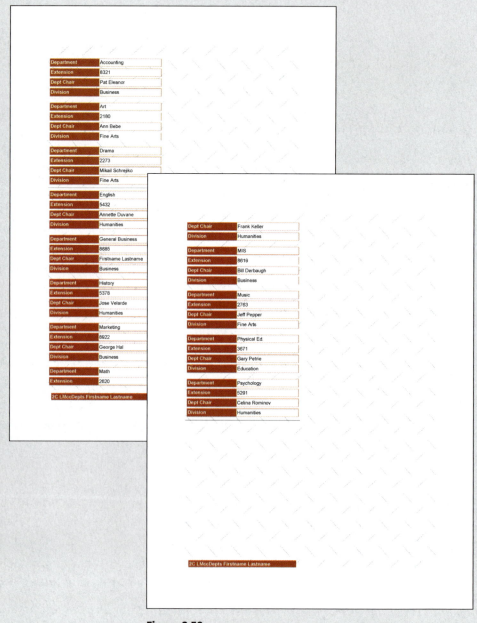

Figure 2.58

(**Project 2C**–LMccDepts continues on the next page)

Skill Assessments (continued)

(Project 2C–LMccDepts continued)

1. Open **My Computer** or **Windows Explorer** and navigate to the location where the student files that accompany this textbook are located. Click once to select the file **a02C_LMccDepts**.

2. Copy and paste the **a02C_LMccDepts** file to the folder where you are storing your projects for this chapter.

3. Rename the file **2C_LMccDepts_Firstname_Lastname**

4. Right-click the file you just renamed and click **Properties**. On the displayed **Properties** dialog box, remove the Read-only property from the file and then click **OK**.

5. Close the Windows accessory you are using—either My Computer or Windows Explorer.

6. Start Access and open your **2C_LMccDepts** database. On the Objects bar, click **Forms**.

7. Above the Objects bar, locate and then click the **New** button. On the displayed **New Form** dialog box, click **AutoForm: Columnar**.

8. In the text box to the right of *Choose the table or query where the object's data comes from:*, click the **downward pointing arrow**. There is only one table for this database. Click **Departments** and then click **OK**. A new form based on the information in the Departments table is created and displays on your screen.

   Recall that AutoForm places all of the table's fields into the form. Access will apply the most recently used form formatting; thus, the format displayed on your screen will depend on previous use of the computer at which you are working.

9. At the lower edge of the form, in the navigation area, click the **Last Record** button. The last record in the table, for the Psychology Department, displays.

10. In the navigation area, click the **Previous Record** button once. The previous record, for the Physical Ed. Department, displays. In the navigation area, click the **First Record** button. The first record, for the Accounting Department, displays.

11. Position your mouse pointer in the navigation area over the number of the current record until the pointer turns into an I-beam. Then, drag to select the number. Type **9** and then press [Enter]. The record for the MIS Department displays.

    Recall that if you know the exact number of the record you want to view, this method of navigating to a record in a form is quicker than moving through the records one by one with the navigation buttons.

(Project 2C–LMccDepts continues on the next page)

Skill Assessments (continued)

(Project 2C–LMccDepts continued)

12. On the title bar of the **Departments** form, click the **Close** button. Because you have not previously named or saved this form, a message displays asking you if you want to save the changes to the design of form "*Form1*." Click **Yes**.

13. In the displayed **Save As** dialog box, in the **Form Name** box, accept the default form name of *Departments* by clicking **OK**. For this database, you now have a convenient form with which you can view or enter records, rather than viewing or entering records in the database table itself. Notice that the name of the form displays in the Database window.

14. Click to select the **Departments** form, and then above the Objects bar, click **Design**. The **Departments** form that you created opens in Design view. On the form's title bar, click the **Maximize** button. Maximizing a form in Design view allows you to view the different sections of the form and provides space to make changes to the layout of the form.

15. From the **View** menu, click **Page Header/Footer**. Page Header and Page Footer sections are added to your form.

16. Locate the Toolbox floating on your screen. If necessary, open the Toolbox by displaying the View menu and clicking Toolbox. Recall that the Toolbox is a toolbar that is used to add various types of controls to forms and reports in Access. On the Toolbox, click the **Label** button.

17. Move your pointer into the **Page Footer** section and create a label control approximately **2.75 inches wide**, centered vertically and horizontally in the available space. If you are not satisfied with your result, click the Undo button and begin again. Recall that you can use the Nudge feature (Ctrl + any arrow key) to position the object precisely. In the label, using your own information, type **2C LMccDepts Firstname Lastname** and then press Enter.

18. Switch to Form view. In the navigation area of the form, click the **New Record** button. The fields are cleared and ready to accept a new entry. The record number advances by one to 13.

19. In the blank **Department** field, where the insertion point is blinking, type **General Business** and then press Tab.

20. In **Extension** field, type **8885** and then press Tab. In the **Dept Chair** field, using your own information, type **Firstname Lastname** and then press Tab.

21. In the **Division** field, type **Business**

22. Navigate to record 5, the Department of General Mgt. On the left side of the form, locate the record selector bar that contains a right-pointing arrow. Click once in the record selector. The entire record is selected.

(Project 2C–LMccDepts continues on the next page)

Skill Assessments (continued)

(Project 2C–LMccDepts continued)

23. On the Form View toolbar, click the **Delete Record** button, or press . In the displayed alert, click **Yes**. The record is deleted from the Departments table.

24. To the right of *Type a question for help*, click the **Close Window** button. Click **Yes** if prompted to save your changes. The form closes and your changes are saved.

25. On the Objects bar, click **Tables**, and then double-click the **Departments** table to open it in Datasheet view. Examine the table and notice that the changes you made using the form are updated in the corresponding table. The Department of General Business has been added, and the Department of General Mgt. has been deleted. Notice that the records in the table have been sorted by the primary key.

26. To the right of *Type a question for help*, click the **Close Window** button to close the table. On the Objects bar, click **Forms**, and then, if necessary, click the **Departments** form once to select it.

27. On the Database toolbar, click the **Print** button to print the form. Two pages will print, and your name will print in the page footer on each page. Recall that depending on previous use of your computer, the format applied to your form may differ from the one shown in Figure 2.58. To the right of *Type a question for help*, click the **Close Window** button to close the database and then close Access.

End You have completed Project 2C

Project 2D — Office Supplies

Objectives: *Create a Form with the Form Wizard and Modify a Form.*

In the following Skill Assessment, you will use the Form Wizard to create a form for the Office Supplies database at Lake Michigan City College, and then make modifications to the layout of the form. Your completed database objects will look similar to Figure 2.59. You will rename and save your database as *2D_Office_Supplies_Firstname_Lastname*.

1. Open **My Computer** or **Windows Explorer** and navigate to the location where the student files that accompany this textbook are located. Click once to select the file **a02D_Office_Supplies**.

2. Copy and paste the **a02D_Office_Supplies** file to the folder where you are storing your projects for this chapter. Rename the file **2D_Office_Supplies_Firstname_Lastname**

3. Right-click the file you just renamed and click **Properties**. From the displayed **Properties** dialog box, remove the Read-only property from the file, and then click **OK**.

(Project 2D–Office Supplies continues on the next page)

Skill Assessments (continued)

(Project 2D–Office Supplies continued)

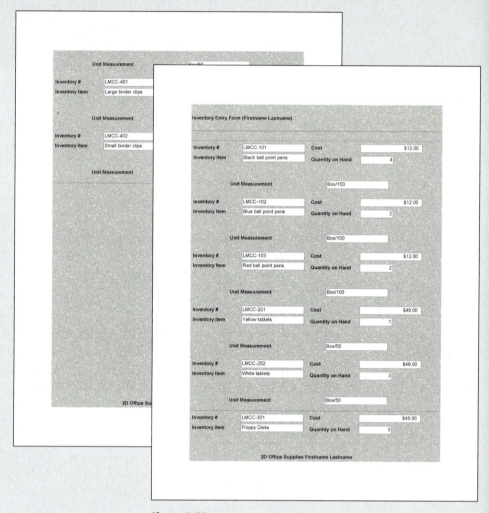

Figure 2.59

4. Close the Windows accessory you are using—either My Computer or Windows Explorer. Start Access and open your **2D_Office_Supplies** database. On the Objects bar, click **Forms**.

5. To the right of the Objects bar, double-click the command icon **Create form by using wizard**. The Form Wizard opens requesting information about the table (or query) upon which the form will be based, and the fields from the table to include on the form.

6. Under **Tables/Queries**, click the **down arrow**. A list of tables and queries available for this database displays. Currently only one object, the **Office Inventory** table, has been created in this database. Click **Table: Office Inventory**.

7. To the right of the list of available fields, click the **All Fields** button to move all of the fields from the **Office Inventory** table to the **Selected Fields** column on the right.

(Project 2D–Office Supplies continues on the next page)

Skill Assessments (continued)

(Project 2D–Office Supplies continued)

8. Click the **Next** button. For the layout of the form, make sure the **Columnar** option button is selected, and then click the **Next** button. For the style of the form, click **SandStone**. A preview of the SandStone style displays on the left. Click the **Next** button.

9. With *Office Inventory* highlighted, press [Delete] to delete the default text. Then, using your own information type **Inventory Firstname Lastname**

10. Click the **Finish** button. Access creates the form using the information you specified in the Wizard screens. The completed form displays in Form view. On the Form View toolbar, click the **View** button to switch to Design view, and then on the form's title bar, click the **Maximize** button.

11. Position your pointer on the horizontal line between the **Form Header section** and the **Detail section** until the pointer changes to a large double arrow. Drag down approximately 0.5 inch. Use your eye and the vertical ruler to determine this distance. The **Form Header** section expands and grid dots display in this area.

12. Locate the **Toolbox** on your screen. (If necessary, display the View menu and click Toolbox.) On the Toolbox, click the **Label** button.

13. Move your pointer into the **Form Header section**, and position the pointer's plus sign at the **left edge of the Form Header area** and centered vertically (use your eye to approximate this distance) in the **Form Header section**. Drag down **about 0.25 inch and to the right to 3.0 inches on the horizontal ruler**. If you are not satisfied with your result, click the Undo button and begin again. In the label box you just created, use your own information to type **Inventory Entry Form (Firstname Lastname)** and then press [Enter].

14. On the Form Design toolbar, click the **View** button to switch to the Form view, and notice the Form Header information you added with your name. On the Form View toolbar, click the **View** button to return to Design view. By placing a Form Header on the form, you have created an informative title that will print at the beginning of the form. Someone who reads the printed form will have an indication as to the contents of the form.

15. Position your pointer on the right edge of the form until your pointer changes to a large double arrow. Drag the right edge of the form to the right to **6.5 inches on the horizontal ruler**. The width of the form is expanded. By increasing the dimensions of a form, you create more working space to move and reposition the controls on the form.

16. Click once in the white text box control **Cost**. The Cost text box control is selected and handles surround the selected object. Recall that a text box control on a form is where data from the corresponding table is displayed, or where new data for the table is entered.

(Project 2D–Office Supplies continues on the next page)

Skill Assessments (continued)

(Project 2D–Office Supplies continued)

17. Position your pointer over any border of the text box until the **hand** pointer displays. Using the grid dots and the horizontal ruler as a guide, drag the **Cost controls** up and to the right of the Inventory# controls—until the right edge of the Cost controls are positioned at approximately **6.0 inches on the horizontal ruler** and aligned with the Inventory# controls, as shown in Figure 2.59.

18. Click once on the white **Quantity on Hand** text box control to select it. Position your pointer over any border of the text box until the **hand** pointer displays. Drag the **Quantity on Hand** controls up and position them directly under the Cost controls—and to the right of the Inventory Item controls. See Figure 2.59.

19. Click once in the white **Unit Measurement** text box control to select it. Position your pointer over the large black handle that is between the **Unit Measurement text box control** and the **Unit Measurement label control** until the **pointing hand** pointer displays. Recall that with this pointer, you can move the text box control independently of the label control. Drag only the **Unit Measurement text box control** to the right, so that its left edge is positioned at **3.5 inches on the horizontal ruler** and its top edge is positioned at **1.0 inch on the vertical ruler**. See Figure 2.59.

20. Position your pointer over the large black handle in the **Unit Measurement label control** until the **pointing hand** pointer displays. Drag the label control until it left edge is positioned at **1.0 inch on the horizontal ruler** and its top edge is positioned at **1.0 inch on the vertical ruler**.

21. Display the **View** menu and click **Page Header/Footer**. On the Toolbox, click the **Label** button. Move your pointer into the **Page Footer** section and create a label control approximately 3 inches wide, centered vertically and horizontally in the available space. Recall that you can use the Nudge feature (Ctrl + any arrow key) to position the object precisely. In the label, using your own information, type **2D Office Supplies Firstname Lastname** and then press Enter.

22. On the Form Design toolbar, click the **View** button to switch to the Form view and then view the changes to your form. The Form Header displays; recall that Page Footers display only when printed or in Print Preview. Then, on the Form View toolbar, click the **Print** button to print the form. Two pages will print.

23. To the right of *Type a question for help*, click the **Restore Window** button. The form is restored to its original size. On the title bar of the form, click the **Close** button. Click **Yes** to save your changes. Close the database and then close Access.

End You have completed Project 2D

136 Access | Chapter 2: Forms and Reports

Skill Assessments (continued)

Project 2E—Inventory

Objectives: *Create a Report with the Report Wizard, Save a Report, Modify the Design of a Report, and Print a Report.*

The Computer Club at Lake Michigan City College has an inventory of hardware, software, and other equipment that it uses for training and various club events. The club maintains a database of this inventory. In the following Skill Assessment, you will use the Report Wizard to create a report listing the information from a table in the Inventory database. After creating the report, you will modify its design. Your completed report will look like the one shown in Figure 2.60. You will rename and save your database as *2E_Inventory_Firstname_Lastname.*

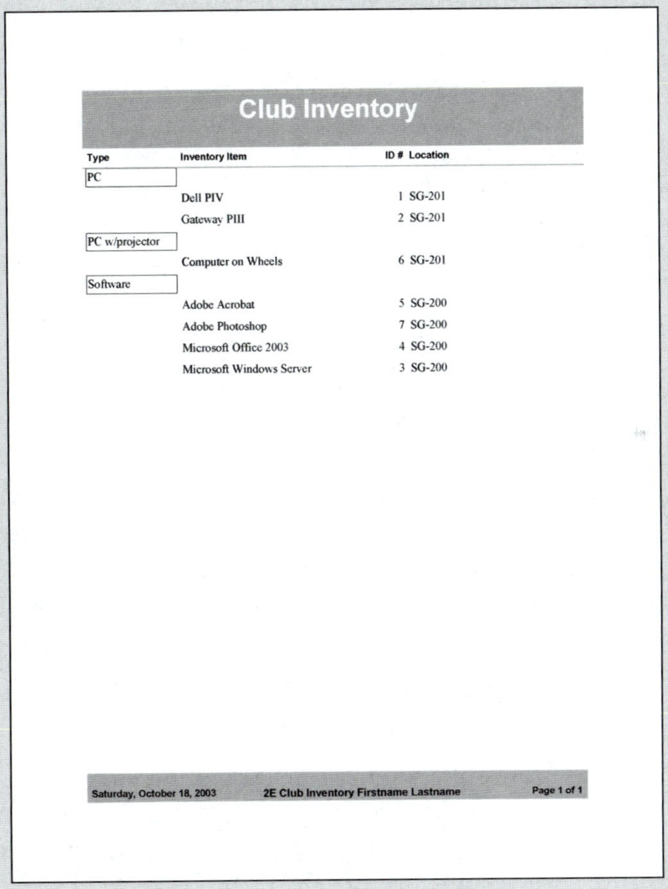
Club Inventory

Type	Inventory Item	ID #	Location
PC			
	Dell PIV	1	SG-201
	Gateway PIII	2	SG-201
PC w/projector			
	Computer on Wheels	6	SG-201
Software			
	Adobe Acrobat	5	SG-200
	Adobe Photoshop	7	SG-200
	Microsoft Office 2003	4	SG-200
	Microsoft Windows Server	3	SG-200

Saturday, October 18, 2003 2E Club Inventory Firstname Lastname Page 1 of 1

Figure 2.60

1. Open **My Computer** or **Windows Explorer** and navigate to the location where the student files that accompany this textbook are located. Click once to select the file **a02E_Inventory**.
2. Copy and paste the **a02E_Inventory** file to the folder where you are storing your projects for this chapter. Rename the file **2E_Inventory_Firstname_Lastname**

(Project 2E–Inventory continues on the next page)

Skill Assessments (continued)

(Project 2E–Inventory continued)

3. Right-click the file you just renamed and click **Properties**. From the displayed **Properties** dialog box, remove the Read-only property from the file and then click **OK**.

4. Close the Windows accessory you are using—either My Computer or Windows Explorer. Start Access and open your **2E_Inventory** database. On the Objects bar, click **Reports**.

5. To the right of the Objects bar, double-click **Create report by using wizard**. The Report Wizard opens. The first step in the Report Wizard is to determine from which table (or query) information for the report will be taken, and also what fields from the table to include in the report. Under **Tables/Queries**, click the **down arrow**. A list of tables and queries available for this database displays. Currently only one object, the Inventory table, has been created in this database.

6. Click **Table: Inventory**. A list of the fields in the Inventory table displays in the Available Fields column on the left. To the right of the list of available fields, click the **All Fields** button to move all of the fields from the Inventory table to the Selected Fields column on the far right. All of the fields that were listed under Available Fields display in the Selected Fields list. Click the **Next** button.

7. Recall that it is often useful to group information on a printed report by one or more of the fields in the table. In the displayed list of field names, click **Type**, and then click the **One Field** button. The preview on the right displays the **Type** field, indicating that on the finished report, records will be grouped by type. Click the **Next** button.

8. In this step of the Report Wizard, you can designate an order by which records in the table will be sorted. To the right of the **1** text box, **click** the **down arrow**. In the list of available fields, click **Inventory Item**. Leave the default order as **Ascending**. Click the **Next** button.

9. Under **Layout**, make sure the **Stepped** option button is selected. Under **Orientation**, make sure the **Portrait** option button is selected. Click the **Next** button.

10. From the list of styles that can be applied to the report, click **Soft Gray** and then click the **Next** button. With *Inventory* highlighted, press Delete. Type **Club Inventory** and then click the **Finish** button. The report displays in Print Preview.

11. If necessary, on the Club Inventory title bar, click the **Maximize** button. On the Print Preview toolbar, click the **Zoom arrow** and then click **75%**. Notice that the specifications you defined for the report in the Report Wizard are reflected in the Print Preview of the report. For example, the inventory items are grouped by Type—PC, PC w/projector, and Software. Within each type, the equipment is alphabetized by Inventory Item name.

(Project 2E–Inventory continues on the next page)

Skill Assessments (continued)

(Project 2E–Inventory continued)

12. To the right of *Type a question for help*, click the **Close Window** button. The report closes and the report name displays in the Database window. Reports created with the Report Wizard are named in the final step of the wizard. When the report is closed, it is automatically saved.

13. Double-click the **Club Inventory** report to open the report in Print Preview. On the Print Preview toolbar, click the **View** button to switch to the Design view of the report. If necessary, on the title bar of the report, click the **Maximize** button. The Design view of the report fills the working area.

14. In the **Report Header section**, click the label **Club Inventory**. The label is selected and handles surround the selected object. Position your pointer over a border of the selected object to display the **hand pointer**. Drag the label to the right, until the left edge is positioned at **2.0 inches on the horizontal ruler**, maintaining its vertical placement.

15. In the **Page Footer section** of the report, notice the two controls. The control on the left causes the current date to display in this section each time the report is opened. The control on the right causes the page numbers, as well as the total number of pages, to display in the report.

16. Click to select the **date** control on the left. Drag the center right handle to the left to **2 inches on the horizontal ruler**. Select the page number control on the right. Drag the center left handle to the right to **5.25 inches on the horizontal ruler**.

17. Locate the **Toolbox** floating on your screen. (If necessary, display the View menu and click Toolbox to display it.) Click the **Label** button. In the **Page Footer section**, position the pointer's plus sign near the upper edge of the existing controls at **2.25 inches on the horizontal ruler**. Drag down about **0.25 inch** and to the right to **5.0 inches on the horizontal ruler**.

18. In this label, using your own information, type **2E Club Inventory Firstname Lastname** and then press Enter.

19. On the Report Design toolbar, click the **Print Preview** button to verify that your information displays at the lower edge of the report. If you are not satisfied with the placement of your information, return to Design view, select the label, and use the Nudge feature (Ctrl + any arrow key) to reposition the label.

20. If necessary, return to **Print Preview**. On the Print Preview toolbar, click the **Print** button. One page will print. To the right of *Type a question for help*, click the **Close Window** button. Click **Yes** to save your changes. Close the database and close Access.

End You have completed Project 2E

Access chapter two
Performance Assessments

Project 2F — Music Dept

Objectives: *Create an AutoForm, Save and Close an AutoForm, and Create a Form with the Form Wizard.*

In the following Performance Assessment, you will create two new forms for the Music Department at Lake Michigan City College: one by using the Form Wizard and another by creating an AutoForm. Your completed forms will look similar to Figure 2.61. You will rename and save your database as *2F_Music_Dept_Firstname_Lastname*.

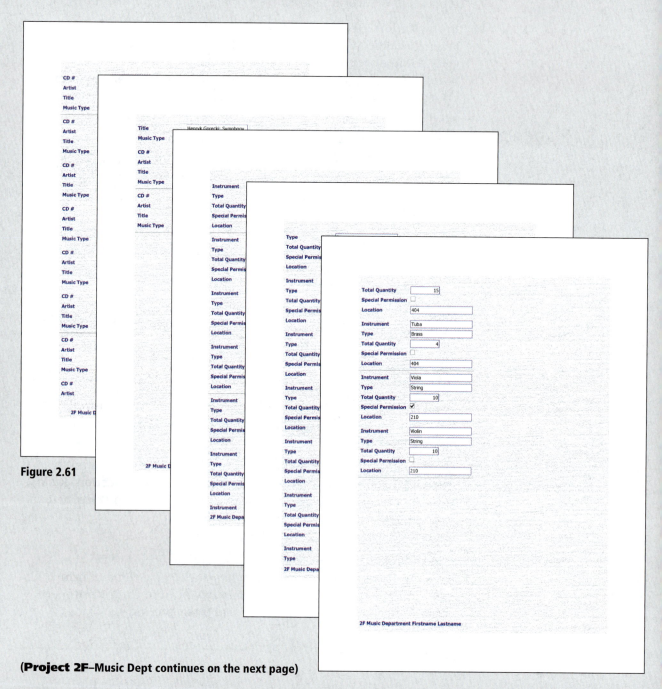

Figure 2.61

(**Project 2F**—Music Dept continues on the next page)

Performance Assessments (continued)

(Project 2F–Music Dept continued)

1. Open **My Computer** or **Windows Explorer** and navigate to the student files for this textbook. Copy and paste the file **a02F_Music_Dept** to the folder where you are storing your projects for this chapter. Rename the file, using your own information, **2F_Music_Dept_Firstname_Lastname** and remove the Read-only property. Close My Computer or Windows Explorer.

2. Start Access and open your **2F_Music_Dept** database. On the Objects bar, click **Forms** and then start the Form Wizard. Under **Tables/Queries**, click the **down arrow**, and then click **Table: CD Collection**. Include all of the fields from the table in the form. Click the **Next** button.

3. Select the **Columnar** layout, click **Next**, and then click the **Sumi Painting** style for the form. Click **Next**. As the title for the form, type **CD Collection Firstname Lastname** and then click **Finish**.

4. Maximize the form and switch to the Design view of the form. Display the **View** menu and then click **Page Header/Footer**.

5. On the Toolbox, click the **Label** button and then move the pointer into the **Page Footer section**. Position the pointer plus sign just below the Page Footer separator at **0.25 inch on the horizontal ruler**. Drag down to the lower edge and to the right to **3 inches on the horizontal ruler**. In the label, and using your own information, type **2F Music Dept Firstname Lastname** and then press [Enter].

6. Switch to the Form view and print the form. Two pages will print. Click the **Close Window** button and save your changes.

7. Make sure **Forms** is selected on the Objects bar and then click the **New** button. In the displayed **New Form** dialog box, click **AutoForm: Columnar**. To the right of *Choose the table or query where the object's data comes from*, click the **down arrow**, and then from the displayed list, click **Rental Instruments**. Click **OK**. Click the **Close Window** button and save the form using the default name of *Rental Instruments*.

8. Open the **Rental Instruments** form, switch to the Design View, display the **View** menu, and then click **Page Header/Footer**. In the Toolbox, click the **Label** button. In the **Page Footer** section, just below the Page Footer separator, create a label within the space beginning at the **left edge of the form** and ending at **3.0 inches on the horizontal ruler**. In the label box, use your own information and type **2F Music Dept Firstname Lastname** and then press [Enter].

9. Switch to Form view and print the form. Three pages will print. Click the **Close Window** button, save your changes, close the database, and then close Access.

 You have completed Project 2F

Performance Assessments (continued)

Project 2G — Music

Objectives: *Create a Report with the Report Wizard and Save a Report.*

In the following Performance Assessment, you will use the Report Wizard to create a report for the Music Department at Lake Michigan City College. Your completed report will look similar to Figure 2.62. You will save your database as 2*G_Music_Firstname_Lastname*.

Rental Instruments Report

Type	*Instrument*	*Quantity*	*Location*
Brass			
	Tuba	4	404
	Trumpet	15	404
	Trombone	10	404
Percussion			
	Snare Drum	8	302
	Drum Pad	12	302
String			
	Violin	10	210
	Viola	10	210
	Cello	8	210
	Bass	8	210
Woodwind			
	Piccolo	10	SB-106
	Oboe	7	SB-106
	Flute	14	SB-106
	Clarinet	15	SB-106
	Bassoon	3	SB-106
	Bass Clarinet	5	SB-106
	Alto Clarinet	5	SB-106

Saturday, October 18, 2003 *2G Music Firstname Lastname* *Page 1 of 1*

Figure 2.62

1. Open **My Computer** or **Windows Explorer** and navigate to the student files for this textbook. Copy and paste the file **a02G_Music** to the folder where you are storing your projects for this chapter. Rename the file, using your own information, **2G_Music_Firstname_Lastname** and remove the Read-only property. Close My Computer or Windows Explorer.
2. Start Access and open your **2G_Music** database. On the Objects bar, click **Reports** and then start the Report Wizard. Under **Tables/Queries**, click the **down arrow** and then click **Table: Rental Instruments**. Include all of the fields from the **Rental Instruments** table in the report. Click the **Next** button.

(Project 2G–Music continues on the next page)

Performance Assessments (continued)

(Project 2G–Music continued)

3. Group the records by **Type** and click **OneField** button to display Type in the Preview. Click the **Next** button. Sort the records by **Instrument** in **Ascending** order. Click the **Next** button. Select the **Stepped** layout and the **Portrait** orientation. Click the **Next** button. As the style for the report, click **Corporate** and then click the **Next** button. For the name of the report, type **Rental Instruments Report** and then click the **Finish** button.

4. If necessary, maximize the displayed **Print Preview** and then zoom to **75%**. After examining the report, click the **View** button to switch to Design view.

5. In the **Page Footer** section of the report, click the **date control** on the left to select it and then drag the center right handle to the left until the right edge of the control is positioned at **2.0 inches on the horizontal ruler**. Select the **page number control** on the right, and drag its left center handle to **5.25 inches on the horizontal ruler**.

6. In the Toolbox, click the **Label** button. In the **Page Footer** section, starting at approximately the **2.0-inch mark on the horizontal ruler** and vertically aligned with the other controls, drag down and to the right to **5.25 inches on the horizontal ruler**. In the **Label** box, using your own information, type **2G Music Firstname Lastname** and press [Enter].

7. Switch to the **Print Preview** of the report and verify that your information displays in the footer. **Print** the report. Click the **Close Window** button and save your changes. Close the database and then close Access.

 You have completed Project 2G

Project 2H — DL Courses

Objectives: *View and Navigate to Records with a Form, Use a Form to Add Records to and Delete Records from a Table, Modify the Design of a Report, and Print a Report.*

In the following Performance Assessment, you will open an existing form for the Distance Learning Courses database at Lake Michigan City College. You will add and delete records using the form. Additionally, you will open an existing report and make changes to the design of the report. Your completed database objects will look similar to Figure 2.63. You will rename and save your database as *2H_DL_Courses_Firstname_Lastname*.

(Project 2H–DL Courses continues on the next page)

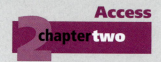

Performance Assessments (continued)

(Project 2H–DL Courses continued)

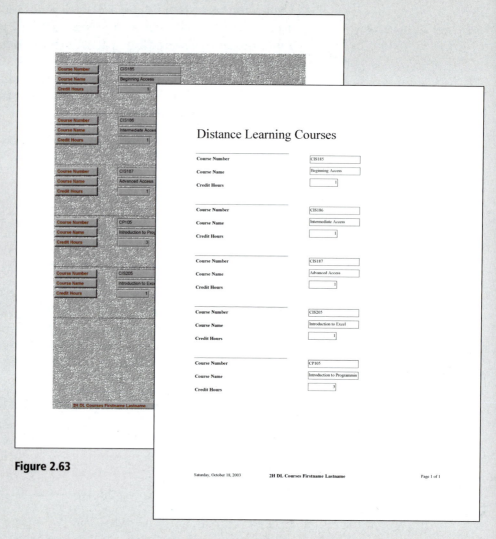

Figure 2.63

1. Open **My Computer** or **Windows Explorer** and navigate to the student files for this textbook. Copy and paste the file a02H_DL_Courses to the folder where you are storing your projects for this chapter. Rename the file, using your own information, **2H_DL_Courses_Firstname_Lastname** and remove the Read-only property. Close My Computer or Windows Explorer.

2. Start Access and open your **2H_DL_Courses** database. On the Objects bar, click **Forms** and then open the **Distance Learning Courses** form. Click the **New Record** button. In the **Course Number** field, type **CIS205** and press Tab. In the **Course Name** field type **Introduction to Excel** and in the **Credit Hours** field type **1**

3. Navigate to record 1, which has the course name *Introduction to Computers.* Use the record selector bar to select the entire record and then delete the record.

(Project 2H–DL Courses continues on the next page)

Performance Assessments (continued)

(Project 2H–DL Courses continued)

4. Switch to Design view and maximize the form window. Display the **View** menu and then click **Page Header/Footer**. On the Toolbox, click the **Label** button. In the **Page Footer section**, just below the Page Footer separator at **0.5 inch on the horizontal ruler**, drag down to the lower separator and to the right to **3 inches on the horizontal ruler**. In the label box, using your own information, type **2H DL Courses Firstname Lastname** and press (Enter).

5. Switch to Form view and print the form. Close the form and save your changes.

6. On the Objects bar, click **Reports** and then open the **Distance Learning Courses** report in Print Preview. If necessary, maximize the window and then zoom to 100%. View the report and notice that the labels and their corresponding text boxes are formatted in a manner that is difficult to read. Switch to Design view. Using the techniques you practiced in this chapter, arrange the label and text box controls to match Figure 2.64.

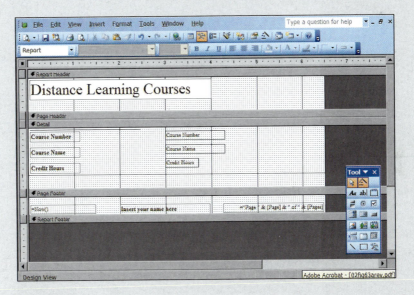

Figure 2.64

7. In the **Page Footer section** of the report, in the control *Insert your name here*, click the control once to select it, and then delete the text in the control. Using your own information, type **2H DL Courses Firstname Lastname** and then press (Enter).

8. Switch to the **Print Preview** of the report. Verify that your information is at the lower edge of the report and then print the report. Close the report, save your changes, close the database, and then close Access.

End You have completed Project 2H

Mastery Assessments

Project 2I — Employees

Objectives: *Create an AutoForm, Save and Close an AutoForm, Create a Report with the Report Wizard, Save a Report, and Print a Report.*

In the following Mastery Assessment, you will create an AutoForm and a report that corresponds to the Employees table for Lake Michigan City College. Your completed database objects will look similar to Figure 2.65. You will save your database as *2I_Employees_Firstname_Lastname*.

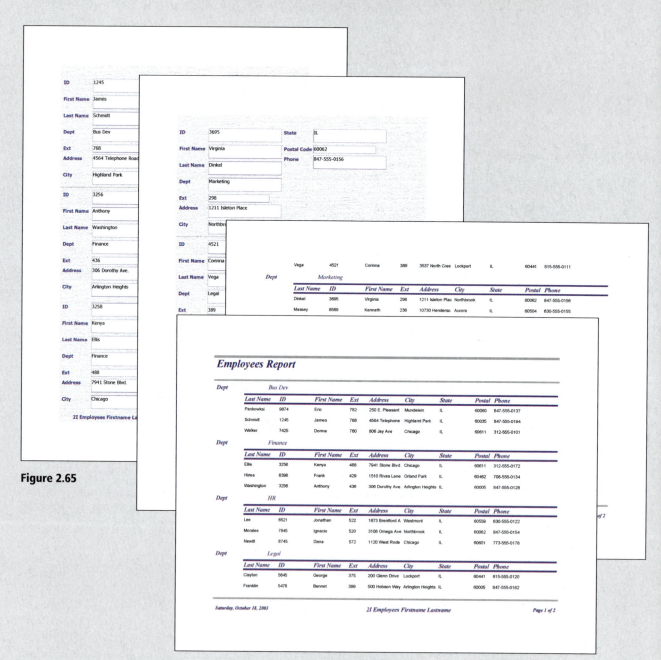

Figure 2.65

(Project 2I–Employees continues on the next page)

Mastery Assessments (continued)

(Project 2I–Employees continued)

1. From the student files that accompany this textbook, copy the file **a02I_Employees** and then paste the file to the folder where you are storing your projects for this chapter. Using your own information, rename this file to **2I_Employees_Firstname_Lastname** and remove the Read-only attribute.

2. Start Access and then open your **2I_Employees** database.

3. Create an AutoForm based on the **Employees** table. Use the **Columnar** format for the form. Add a Page Footer to the form and in it type **2I Employees Firstname Lastname** and then save the AutoForm as **Employees Form** Print the form. Five pages will print.

4. Use the Report wizard to create a report based on the **Employees** table. As you proceed through the wizard, use the following specifications for your report:

   Include all of the fields from the Employees table
   Group the records by Dept
   Sort the records alphabetically by Last Name
   Use the Outline 1 layout for the report in Landscape orientation
   Use the Corporate style for the report
   Save the report as Employees Report

5. In the **Page Footer** section, decrease the width of the control on the right by dragging its left edge to **7.5 inches on the horizontal ruler**. Create a label in the **Page Footer** section, and in it type **2I Employees Firstname Lastname**

6. Print the report. Two pages will print. Close any open database objects, the database, and then close Access.

 End You have completed Project 2I

Project 2J — Suppliers

Objectives: *Use a Form to Add Records to and Delete Records from a Table, Create a Form with the Form Wizard, and Modify a Form.*

In the following Mastery Assessment, you will use the Form Wizard to create a new form for the Suppliers database at Lake Michigan City College. Your completed form will look similar to Figure 2.66. You will save your database as *2J_Suppliers_Firstname_Lastname*.

1. From the student files that accompany this textbook, copy the file a02J_Suppliers and then paste the file to the folder where you are storing your projects for this chapter. Using your own information, rename this file as **2J_Suppliers_Firstname_Lastname** and remove the Read-only attribute.

(Project 2J–Suppliers continues on the next page)

Mastery Assessments (continued)

(**Project 2J**–Suppliers continued)

Figure 2.66

2. Start Access and then open your **2J_Suppliers** database.

3. Create a form using the Form Wizard based on the **Suppliers** table. Use the following specifications in your form:

   Include all of the fields from the Suppliers table
   Apply the Columnar layout to the form
   Apply the Expedition style to the form
   Accept the default name for the form

(**Project 2J**–Suppliers continues on the next page)

Mastery Assessments (continued)

(Project 2J–Suppliers continued)

4. Add a **Page Footer** to the form and in it type **2J Suppliers Firstname Lastname**

5. Delete the record for **Jiffy Cleaning Supplies**. Edit the record for **Plastic Warehouse** by changing the name of the contact person from **Debbie Lucero** to **Beau Gellard**.

6. Modify the design of the form by widening it to **6 inches on the horizontal ruler**. Then, instead of one column of eight fields, create two columns of four fields. Begin the second column with the **State** controls, aligning them at **3 inches on the horizontal ruler**. Refer to Figure 2.67. Print and close the form. Two pages will print. Close the database and then close Access.

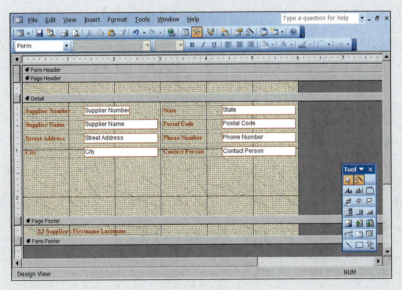

Figure 2.67

End You have completed Project 2J

Access Chapter 2

Problem Solving

Project 2K — Employees

Objectives: *Create an AutoForm* or *Create a Form with the Form Wizard* and *Modify a Form.*

In this Problem Solving assessment, you will create a form for entering data into the Employees database at Lake Michigan City College.

1. From the student files that accompany this textbook, copy the file *a02K_Employees* and then paste the file to the folder where you are storing your projects for this chapter. Using your own information, rename this file as **2K_Employees_Firstname_Lastname** and remove the Read-only attribute.

2. New employees fill out a paper form similar to the one shown in Figure 2.68. Then, the data entry clerk uses the paper forms to enter the new employees into the database. Create a form, using any method you choose, and then modify the layout of the form so that it closely resembles the layout of the paper form. This will make it much easier and faster to enter new employees into the database.

```
                    Lake Michigan City College
                    Employee Information Form


        First Name                        ID
        _____          _____

        Last Name                         Dept
        _____          _____

        Address                           Ext
        _____          _____

        City
        _____

        State              Postal Code
        _____   _____
```

Figure 2.68

3. Add your name and the project name in a Page Footer on the form and print the form.

 You have completed Project 2K

Problem Solving (continued)

Project 2L — Depts

Objectives: *Create a Report with the Report Wizard, Save a Report, Modify the Design of a Report, and Print a Report.*

In this Problem Solving assessment, you will create a report that faculty and staff members at Lake Michigan City College can consult to obtain information about the departments at the college.

1. From the student files that accompany this textbook, copy the file *a02L_Depts* and then paste the file to the folder where you are storing your projects for this chapter. Using your own information, rename this file as **2L_Depts_Firstname_Lastname** and remove the Read-only attribute.

2. Use the Report Wizard to create a report that includes all the fields in alphabetical order by department name. Arrange the fields on the report in an attractive, easy-to-ready layout. In Design view, create a label in the footer area with the project name and your name. Print the report.

End You have completed Project 2L

On the Internet

Discovering What's New in Access

Working with current database software is an important part of your database training.

Go to **www.microsoft.com** and perform a search to identify the changes from Access 2002 Access 2003.

GO! with Help

Creating a Form in Design View

Besides using the Form Wizard to create a form, you can also create a form from the Design view. Use the Access Help system to find out how to create a form using Design view.

1. Start Access. if necessary, from the **View** menu, click **Task Pane** to display the **Getting Started** task pane. On the task pane, to the right of *Getting Started*, click the **down arrow**. From the displayed list of available task panes, click **Help**.

2. Click in the **Search for** box and type **Create a form**

3. Press [Enter], scroll the displayed list as necessary, and then click **Create a form**.

4. At the lower part of the pane, locate the text *On your own in Design view*, and under this result, click **How?**

5. If you would like to keep a copy of this information, click the **Print** button. One page will print.

6. Click the **Close** button in the top right corner of the Help window to close the Help window and then close Access.

Access 2003

chapter three
Queries

In this chapter, you will: complete these projects and practice these skills.

Project 3A
Creating Queries

Objectives
- Create a New Select Query
- Run, Save, and Close a Query
- Open and Edit an Existing Query
- Specify Text Criteria in a Query

Project 3B
Defining Queries

Objectives
- Use Wildcards in a Query
- Specify Numeric Criteria in a Query
- Use Compound Criteria
- Sort Data in a Query

Project 3C
Using Calculated Fields and Calculating Statistics in a Query

Objectives
- Use Calculated Fields in a Query
- Group Data and Calculate Statistics in a Query

Lake Michigan City College

Lake Michigan City College is located along the lakefront of Chicago—one of the nation's most exciting cities. The college serves its large and diverse student body and makes positive contributions to the community through relevant curricula, partnerships with businesses and nonprofit organizations, and learning experiences that allow students to be full participants in the global community. The college offers three associate degrees in 20 academic areas, adult education programs, and continuing education offerings on campus, at satellite locations, and online.

© Getty Images, Inc.

Queries

Access queries allow you to isolate specific data in a database by asking questions and setting conditions that Access can interpret. The conditions, known as criteria, can be either text or numeric in nature. Wildcard characters can be used when a portion of what you are looking for is unknown.

Access provides comparison operators that, combined with numeric criteria, can further refine the query search. Logical operators such as AND and OR, as well as statistical functions, can be used in queries. In this chapter, you will create and modify queries for an Access database.

Project 3A School

Just like tables, forms, and reports, queries are also database objects. Queries can be used to locate information in an Access database based on certain *criteria* that you specify as part of the query. Criteria are conditions that identify the specific records you are looking for. Queries can also be created to view only certain fields from a table.

Lake Michigan City College uses queries to locate information about the data in their databases that meet certain criteria. In Activities 3.1 through 3.6 you will use queries to locate information about the records in the Students table. Your query result will look similar to Figure 3.1.

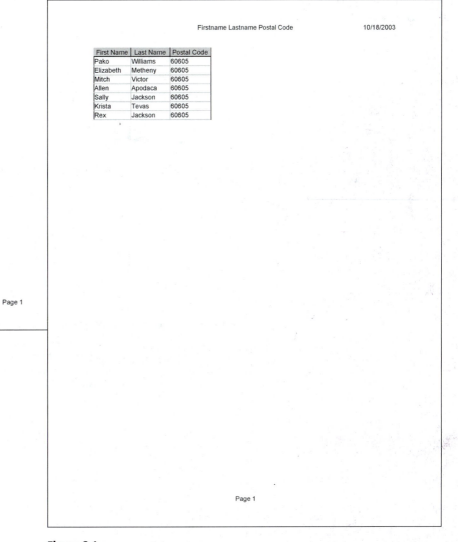

Figure 3.1
Project 3A—School

Objective 1
Create a New Select Query

A ***query*** is a question formed in a manner that Access can interpret. The question that is asked may be simple or complex. For example, you might want to ask, "Which students are Business Majors?" Unless a query has already been set up to ask this question, you must create a new one. A query that retrieves data from one or more tables and then displays the results is called a ***select query***. In the following activity, you will create a simple select query with no criteria specified.

Activity 3.1 Creating a New Query, Using the Select Query Window, and Adding Fields to the Design Grid

1 Using the skills you practiced in Chapter 1, and using either My Computer or Windows Explorer, create a new folder named *Chapter 3* in the location where you will be storing your projects for this chapter.

2 Locate the file **a03A_School** from the student files that accompany this text. Copy and paste the file to the Chapter 3 folder you created in Step 1.

3 Using the technique you practiced in Activity 1.1 of Chapter 1, remove the Read-only property from the file and rename the file as **3A_School_Firstname_Lastname**

4 Close the Windows accessory you are using—either My Computer or Windows Explorer. Start Access and open your **3A_School** database.

5 On the Objects bar, click **Queries**.

To the right of the Objects bar, two command icons for creating a new query display.

6 Double-click **Create query in Design view**.

A new Select Query window opens and the **Show Table** dialog box displays. See Figure 3.2. The **Show Table** dialog box lists all of the tables in the database.

> **Note** — Creating Queries in Design View
>
> *Queries in Design view.*
>
> In this chapter, you will create queries only in Design view. Creating queries using the wizard will be addressed as you progress in your study of Access.

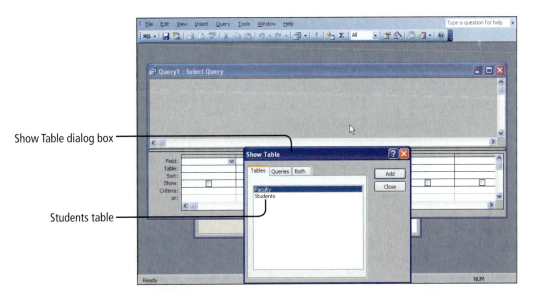

Figure 3.2

7 In the **Show Table** dialog box, click **Students**, click the **Add** button, and then click the **Close** button. See Figure 3.3. Alternatively, you can double-click Students and then click Close.

A list of the fields in the Students table displays in the upper pane of the Select Query window. The **Student#** field is bold, unlike the other fields in the list, because the **Student#** field is the primary key in the Students table.

The Select Query window has two parts: the *table area* (upper pane) and the *design grid* (lower pane). After a table has been selected from the **Show Table** dialog box, it displays in the table area, as shown in Figure 3.4.

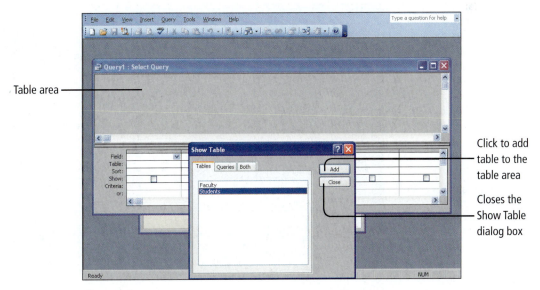

Figure 3.3

Project 3A: School | **Access** 157

8 In the **Students** field list, double-click **Student#**.

The **Student#** field displays in the design grid. See Figure 3.4. The design grid of the Select Query window is where you specify the fields and other criteria to be used in the query.

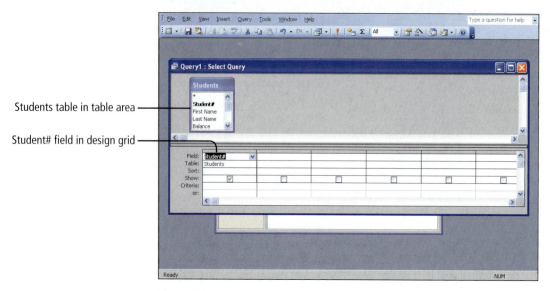

Figure 3.4

9 In the **Students** field list, double-click **First Name**. Repeat this action for all the remaining fields in the field list. Use the vertical scroll bar in the field list window to view the fields toward the end of the list.

As you double-click each field, notice the fields display one by one to the right of the previous field in the design grid. See Figure 3.5.

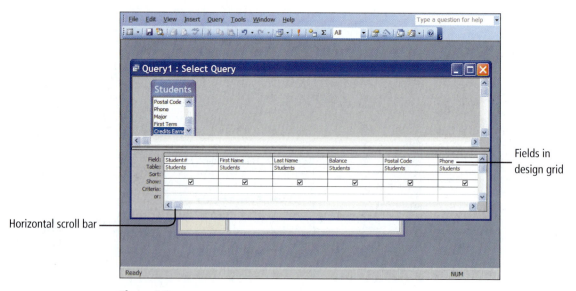

Figure 3.5

10 Use the horizontal scroll bar to scroll to the right to view all the fields in the design grid. Verify that all of the fields from the field list are displayed in the design grid.

Another Way

Adding All Fields to a Query

Double-click the *.

You can add all the fields to a query by double-clicking the * at the top of the field list. The field row will display the name of the table followed by .* indicating that all of the fields in the table have been added to the design grid. You will see each field displayed in the datasheet when you run the query.

11 Maximize the Select Query window.

The Select Query window is maximized. The Select Query window can be manipulated like any other window.

12 Position your mouse pointer over the thin gray line in between the table area and the design grid until the pointer changes to a vertical double arrow. See Figure 3.6. Drag the line separating the table area and the design grid down about one inch. See Figure 3.7.

The table area size is increased.

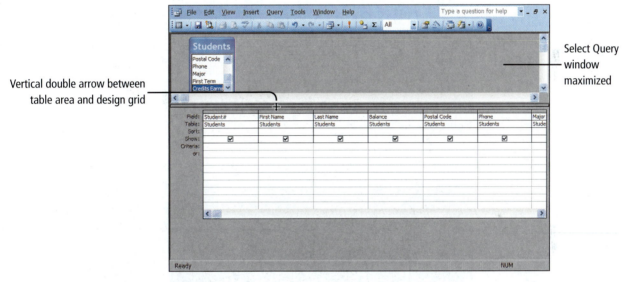

Figure 3.6

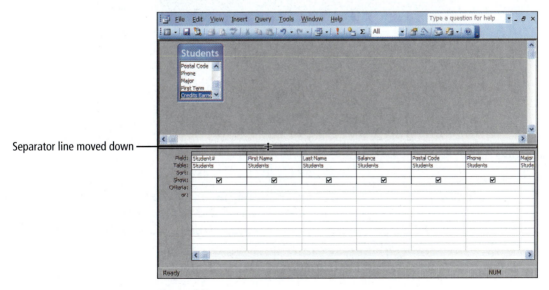

Figure 3.7

Project 3A: School | **Access** 159

13 In the table area, position your mouse pointer on the lower edge of the field list until it displays as a black double arrow, as shown in Figure 3.8. Drag the lower edge of the field list down until all of the fields in the Students table are visible. See Figure 3.9.

The field list displays all of the fields in the table. Use the techniques you just practiced whenever you need to enlarge the upper or lower panes of the Select Query window to gain a better working view.

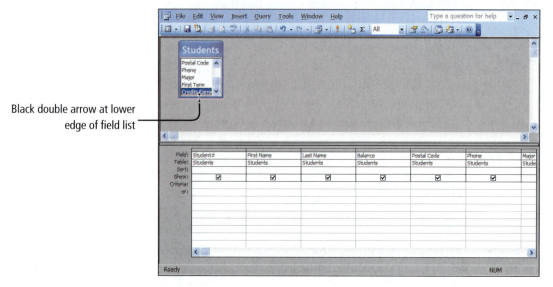

Figure 3.8

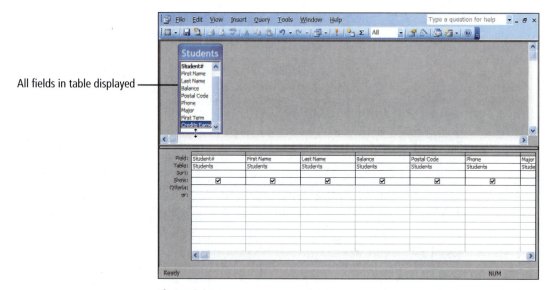

Figure 3.9

14 If desired, resize the elements that you adjusted in Steps 11 through 13 and restore the Select Query window. The following figures show the Select Query window resized to the previous sizes. Leave the query window open for the next activity.

Objective 2
Run, Save, and Close a Query

When you run a query, Access looks at the records in the table (or tables) you have defined, finds the records that match the specified criteria (if any), and displays those records in a table.

Activity 3.2 Running, Saving, and Closing a Query

1 On the Query Design toolbar, click the **Run** button. See Figure 3.10.

The results of the query display in a table in Datasheet view. The fields display in columns, the records display in rows, and a Navigation area displays at the lower edge, in the same manner as in a table. See Figure 3.11. Because no criteria were specified in the design grid of the query, the query results are the same as the data in the Students table.

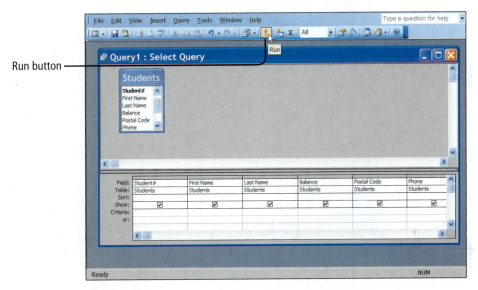

Figure 3.10

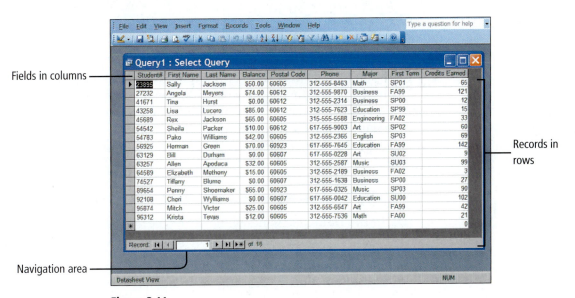

Figure 3.11

2 In the title bar of the query result, click the **Close** button ☒.

Because you have not previously named or saved this query, a message displays asking you if you want to save the changes to the design of query "Query1." The default name of a query created in this manner is "Query" followed by a number, such as "Query1."

3 Click **Yes**.

The Save As dialog box displays. Once created, a query can be run multiple times; thus, queries are frequently saved for future use.

4 In the **Save As** dialog box, in the **Query Name** box, delete the highlighted text. Then using your own information, type **Firstname Lastname Query1** and click **OK**.

The query is saved and closed. The new query name displays in the Database window. See Figure 3.12.

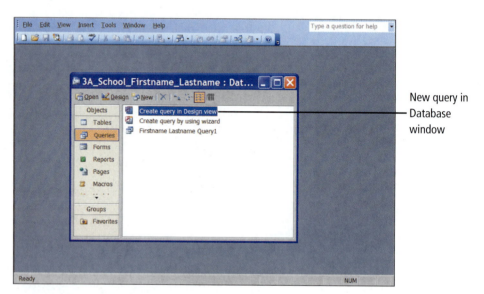

New query in Database window

Figure 3.12

Objective 3
Open and Edit an Existing Query

After you have created and saved a query, you can open the query. Opening an existing query will cause the query to run and the results display in Datasheet view. You do not need to create a new query each time data in the corresponding table is modified. Each time the query is run, any changes made to the table will be automatically reflected in the query results.

Activity 3.3 Opening an Existing Query and Switching Between Views

1 In the Database window, be sure **Queries** is selected on the Objects bar and then double-click your **Query1** saved in Activity 3.2.

The query opens in the Datasheet view. If you want to view the records in a query result, use Datasheet view.

2 On the Query Datasheet toolbar, click the **View** button.

The query displays in Design view.

3 On the title bar of the Query window, click the **Close** button to close the query.

The query closes.

4 With your **Query1** selected in the Database window, above the Objects bar, click the **Design** button, as shown in Figure 3.13.

Your Query1 query opens directly in Design view. This is another way to display the query in Design view. From the Design view of a query you can make changes to the structure of the query. You can open a query in Design view or Datasheet view, depending on what you want to do with the query. If you want to modify the design of the query, such as the fields included in the query, use Design view.

Leave your query open in Design view for the next activity.

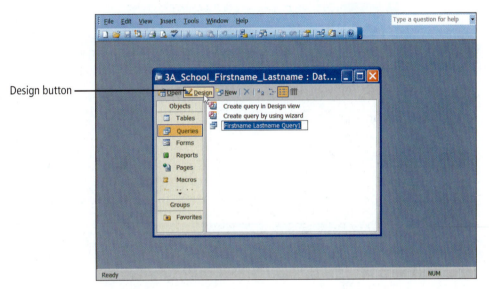

Figure 3.13

Activity 3.4 Editing a Query

A query does not have to contain all the fields from the table.

1 If necessary, open your **Query1** in Design view. In the design grid, move your pointer above the **Balance** field until it displays as a black downward-pointing arrow and click. See Figure 3.14.

The Balance column is selected (highlighted), as shown in Figure 3.15.

Downward-pointing arrow

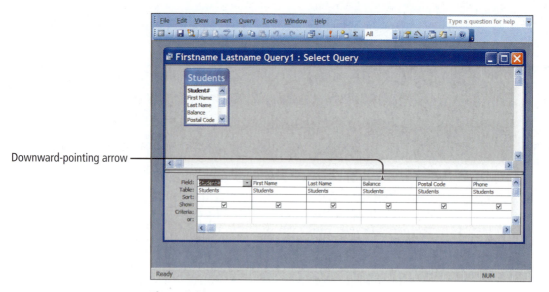

Figure 3.14

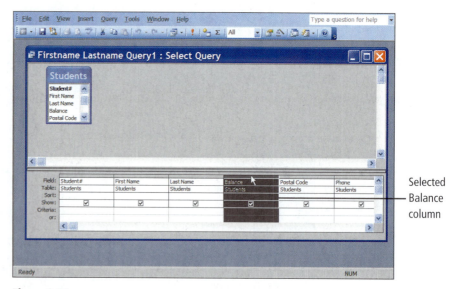

Selected Balance column

Figure 3.15

2 Press Delete.

The Balance field is removed from the design grid, and the remaining fields shift to the left. Removing a field from the design grid of a query does *not* affect the field in its corresponding table.

3 In the design grid, move your pointer above the **Postal Code** field until it displays as a black downward-pointing arrow and click to select the **Postal Code** field.

The Postal Code field is selected (highlighted). See Figure 3.16.

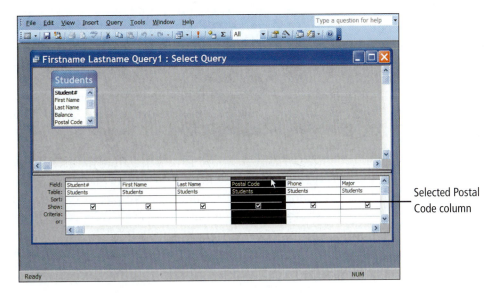

Figure 3.16

4 Press Delete to remove the **Postal Code** field from the design grid.

5 Repeat the technique you have just practiced to remove the **Phone**, **First Term**, and **Credits Earned** fields from the design grid.

The Student#, First Name, Last Name, and Major fields remain in the design grid. See Figure 3.17.

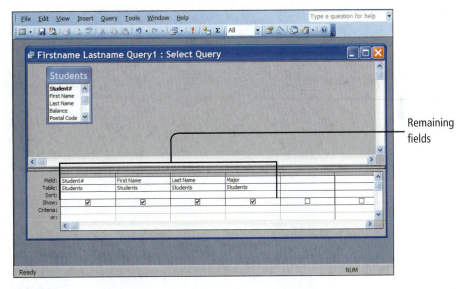

Figure 3.17

6 On the Query Design toolbar, click the **Run** button.

The results of the query display in a table with only the four specified fields displayed. This is a convenient method to use when you want to see only some of the fields from the table.

7 On the Query Datasheet toolbar, click the **View** button to return to Design view. Leave your query open in Design view for the next activity.

Objective 4
Specify Text Criteria in a Query

Specifying criteria in a query will limit the records that display in the query result. Up to this point, the query you created and ran did not limit the number of records displayed by specifying specific criteria; thus all of the records from the corresponding table displayed in the result.

Recall that to query is to ask a question. When criteria is specified in a query, you are asking a more specific question, and therefore you will get a more specific result. For example, suppose you want to find out which students live in a particular area. You could specify a specific Postal Code in the query criteria and only records that match the specified Postal Code will display. Keep in mind that queries do not have to contain all of the fields from a table in order to locate the requested information.

Activity 3.5 Specifying Text Criteria in a Query

In this activity, you will specify the criteria in the query so that only records in the Students table that have *Business* in the Major field display. Records that indicate a major other than Business will not display. You will save the query with a new name.

1 If necessary, open your **Query1** query in Design view. In the design grid, locate the **Criteria** row as indicated in Figure 3.18.

The Criteria row is where you will specify the criteria that will limit the results of the query to your exact specifications.

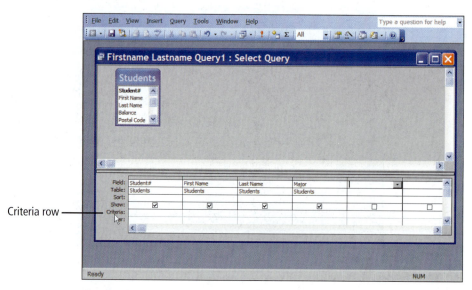

Figure 3.18

2 In the **Criteria** row, under the **Major** field, click and then type **Business** See Figure 3.19.

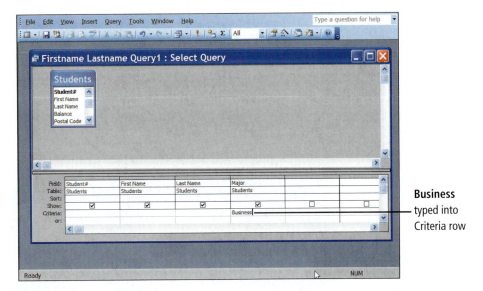

Figure 3.19

3 On the Query Design toolbar, click the **Run** button.

The query runs and the query results display in a table in Datasheet view. See Figure 3.20. Clicking the Run button causes Access to look at all the records in the Students table and locate those records that meet the specified criteria—records that have *Business* in the Major field.

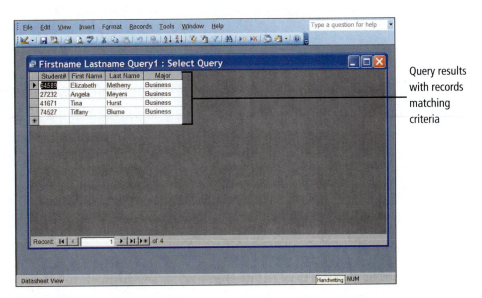

Figure 3.20

4 Examine the records in the query result and verify that the records that display have been limited to those students that have Business as their major.

5 On the **File** menu, click **Save As**.

The Save As dialog box displays. Here you can give this query a different name from the first query and thus have both as saved queries.

Project 3A: School | **Access** 167

6 Under **Save Query 'Firstname Lastname Query1' To:**, and using your own information, type **FirstName LastName Business Major** and click **OK**.

The query with the criteria you specified is saved with the new name and the new name displays in the title bar of the query window. See Figure 3.21.

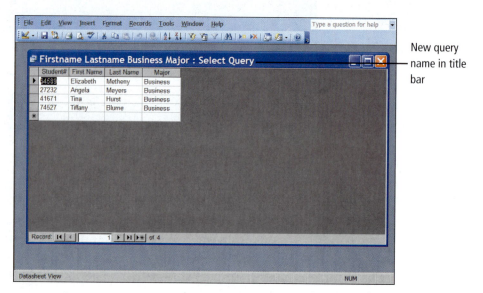

Figure 3.21

7 On the title bar of the query window, click the **Close** button to close the query.

The name of your new query displays in the Database window.

8 If necessary, click **Queries** on the Objects bar and then double-click **Create query in Design view**.

A new query window displays and the Show Table dialog box lists the tables in the database.

9 In the **Show Table** dialog box, click the **Queries tab** shown in Figure 3.22.

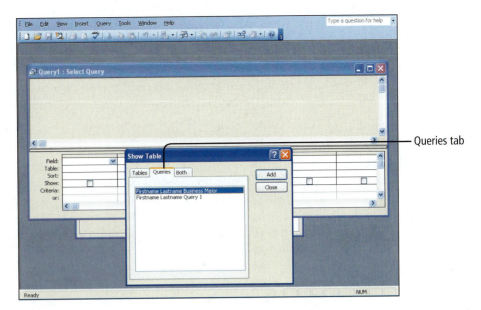

Figure 3.22

10 On the **Queries tab**, notice that the names of the two queries you have created thus far display. Click the **Both tab** and notice that the names of the two tables in the database as well as the names of the two queries you created display. See Figure 3.23.

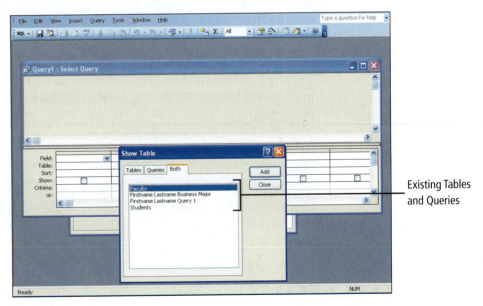

Figure 3.23

11 Click the **Tables tab**, double-click the **Students** table, and then click **Close**.

The field list for the Students table is added to the table area of the query and the Show Table dialog box closes. Next, you will add criteria to the query that will find the records that have a particular Postal Code.

12 In the **Students** field list, double-click the **First Name**, **Last Name**, and **Postal Code** fields to add them to the design grid. If necessary, use the vertical scroll bar to view the **Postal Code** field.

Recall that queries do not have to contain all of the fields from a table in order to locate the requested information.

> **Another Way**
>
> **Adding Fields to the Design Grid**
>
> *Drag fields from the field list or click in the Field row.*
>
> You can also add fields to the design grid by dragging the field from the field list and dropping it into the desired location in the design grid. Or, you can click in the field row and then choose the field from the drop-down list.

13 In the **Criteria** row, under **Postal Code**, type **60605** See Figure 3.24.

Although fields such as Postal Code contain numbers, they are considered text because mathematical calculations are not performed on them.

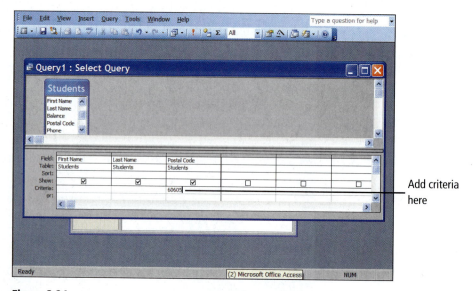

Figure 3.24

14 On the Query Design toolbar, click the **Run** button.

The query results display only the First Name, Last Name, and Postal Code fields for those records in the Students table that have a Postal Code of 60605. See Figure 3.25.

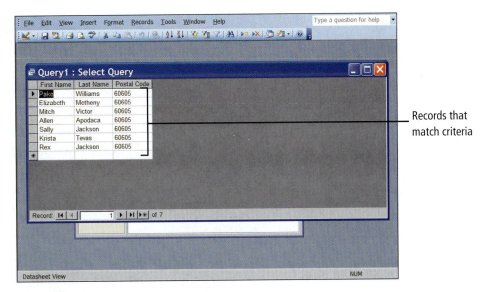

Figure 3.25

15 On the title bar of the query window, click the **Close** button ⊠.

16 When prompted to save the changes to the design of query "Query1", click **Yes**. For the query name, using your own information, type **Firstname_Lastname Postal Code** and click **OK**.

The name of the Postal Code query you created displays in the Database window as shown in Figure 3.26.

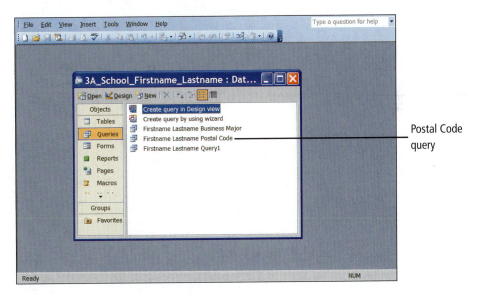

Figure 3.26

Activity 3.6 Printing a Query

Query results in Datasheet view can be printed similar to other database objects.

1 If necessary, on the Objects bar, click **Queries** and then click your **Business Major** query to select it.

2 On the Database toolbar, click the **Print** button . Alternatively, you could display the File menu and click Print.

The query results print with *your* name in the query name at the top of the page.

3 In the Database window, click your **Postal Code** query once to select it.

4 On the Database toolbar, click the **Print** button .

The query results of the Postal Code query print with your name at the top of the page in the query name.

5 Close your **School** database and then close Access.

End You have completed Project 3A

Project 3B Students

In this project you will explore new ways to refine queries with more specific information.

In Activities 3.7 through 3.15 you will continue to create new queries and specify criteria in more detail. Your queries will look similar to Figure 3.27.

Figure 3.27
Project 3B—Students

Objective 5
Use Wildcards in a Query

Wildcard characters in a query serve as a placeholder for an unknown character or characters in your criteria. When you are unsure of the particular character or set of characters to include in your criteria, you can use wildcard characters in place of the characters in the criteria of the query.

Activity 3.7 Using the * Wildcard in a Query

The asterisk, *, is used to represent any group of characters. For example, if you use the * wildcard in the criteria *Fo**, the results would return *Foster, Forrester, Forrest, Fossil,* and so forth. In this activity, you will use the * wildcard and specify the criteria in the query so that only records that have a postal code beginning with 606 will display.

1 Locate the file **a03B _School** from the student files that accompany this text. Copy and paste the file to the Chapter 3 folder you created in Project 3A.

2 Using the technique you practiced in Activity 1.1 of Chapter 1, remove the Read-only property from the file and rename the file as **3B_School_Firstname_Lastname**

3 Close the Windows accessory you are using—either My Computer or Windows Explorer. Start Access and open your **3B_School** database.

4 Click **Queries** on the Objects bar and then double-click **Create query in Design view**.

A new query window displays and the Show Table dialog box lists the tables in the database.

5 In the **Show Table** dialog box, double-click **Students** and then click **Close**.

6 Add the following fields to the design grid by double-clicking the fields in the **Students** field list: **Student#**, **First Name**, **Last Name**, **Postal Code**.

Four fields are added to the design grid, as shown in Figure 3.28.

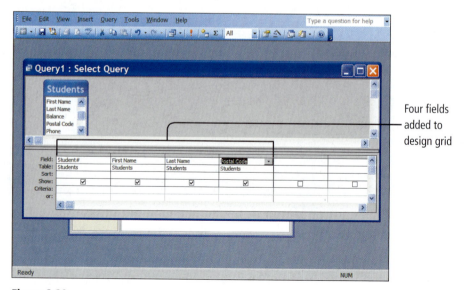

Four fields added to design grid

Figure 3.28

7 In the **Criteria** row, under **Postal Code**, type **606*** as shown in Figure 3.29 and then click the **Run** button .

The query results display 14 records.

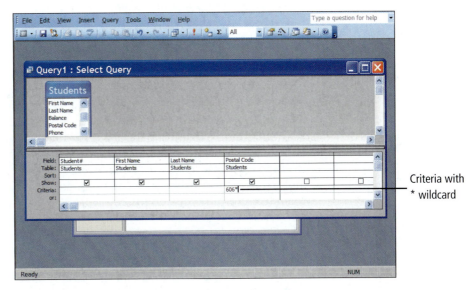

Criteria with
* wildcard

Figure 3.29

8 Examine the entries in the **Postal Code** field and notice that each entry begins with *606* but that the last digits vary, as illustrated in Figure 3.30.

The wildcard character, *, is used as a placeholder to match any number of characters.

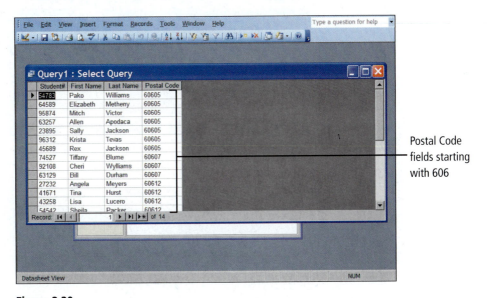

Postal Code fields starting with 606

Figure 3.30

9 On the Query Datasheet toolbar, click the **View** button to return to Design view.

Notice that Access has inserted the criteria *Like "606*"* in the Criteria row under Postal Code. *Like* is used by Access to compare a sequence of characters and test whether or not the text matches a pattern. Access will automatically insert expressions similar to this when creating queries.

> **More Knowledge** — Structured Query Language
>
> *SQL: Structured Query Language.*
>
> SQL (Structured Query Language) is a language used in querying, updating, and managing relational databases. The term *Like* is used in SQL to compare string expressions. In Access, the term *expression* is the same thing as a formula. A *string expression* looks at a sequence of characters and compares them to the criteria in a query. You will learn more about SQL as you advance in your studies of Access.

10 In the **Criteria** row under **Postal Code**, select and then delete the existing text *Like "606*"*.

11 In the **Criteria** row under **Last Name**, type **m*** as shown in Figure 3.31 and then click the **Run** button.

The query results display two records, both with Last Names that begin with M. This search was not case sensitive; that is, lowercase *m*** will find text beginning with either *m* or *M*.

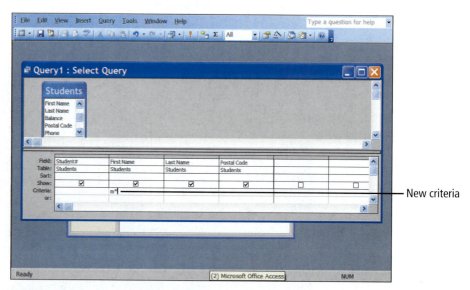

Figure 3.31

12 Notice that *Metheny* and *Meyers* have a different number of characters; *Metheny* contains seven characters and *Meyers* contains six.

The * wildcard can be used to find entries that have a any number of characters.

13 On the Query Datasheet toolbar, click the **View** button to return to Design view. In the **Criteria** row under **Last Name**, select and then delete the existing text *Like "m*"*.

14 In the **Criteria** row under **Student#**, type ***5** as shown in Figure 3.32 and then click the **Run** button.

Two records display, both with Student# entries ending in 5. See Figure 3.33. Wildcard characters can be used either at the beginning or at the end of the criteria.

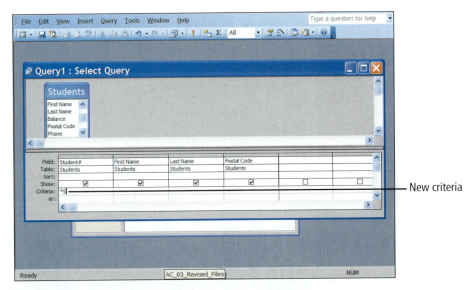

Figure 3.32

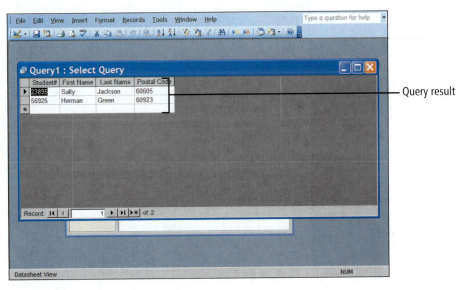

Figure 3.33

15 In the title bar of the query window, click the **Close** button. Click **Yes** to save changes to the query, and then in the **Save As** dialog box and using your own information, type **Firstname Lastname Wildcard 1** as the query name. Click **OK**.

16 In the Database window, select your **Wildcard 1** query and then on the Database toolbar, click the **Print** button .

The query results print.

Activity 3.8 Using the ? Wildcard in a Query

The ? wildcard is a placeholder for only one character in a query. For example, if you use the ? wildcard in the criteria *"l?ne"*, the results could be *lane*, *line*, or *lone*. In this activity, you will use the ? wildcard and specify the criteria in the query so that only those records with either spelling of the last name of *Williams* or *Wylliams* will display.

1 Be sure **Queries** is selected on the Objects bar, then double-click **Create query in Design view**.

A new query window displays and the Show Table dialog box lists the tables in the database.

2 In the **Show Table** dialog box, double-click **Students** and then click **Close**.

3 Add the following fields to the design grid by double-clicking the fields in the **Students** field list: **Student#**, **First Name**, **Last Name**.

Three fields are added to the design grid, as shown in Figure 3.34.

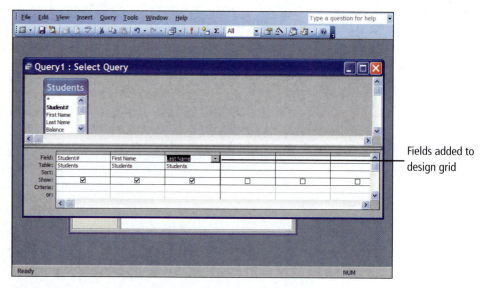

Figure 3.34

4 In the **Criteria** row under **Last Name**, type **w?lliams** as shown in Figure 3.35 and then click the **Run** button .

Two results display with the Last Names of *Williams* and *Wylliams*. See Figure 3.36.

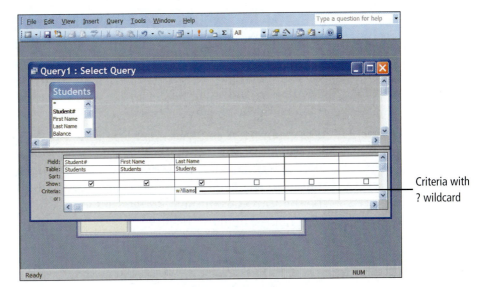

Figure 3.35

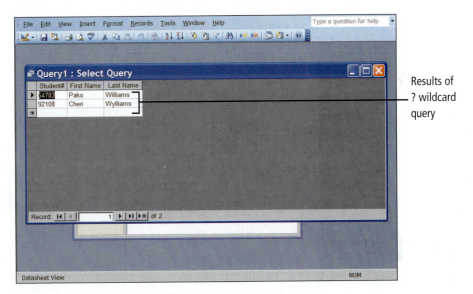

Figure 3.36

[5] In the title bar of the query window, click the **Close** button. Click **Yes** to save changes to the query and in the **Save As** dialog box, using your own information, type **Firstname Lastname Wildcard 2** as the query name. Click **OK**.

The Database window displays.

[6] Be sure your **Wildcard 2** query is selected and then on the Database toolbar, click the **Print** button.

The query results print.

Activity 3.9 Specifying Criteria Using a Field Not Displayed in the Query Result

In the queries you have created thus far, all of the fields that you included in the query design have also been included in the query result. It is not required, however, that every field in the query also display in the result, and there will be times when you will not want all the fields to display in the result.

For example, if you were querying your CD Collection database to find out what records in the CD table were performed by a particular artist, you would need the CD Artist field in the query design, but you would not need the field to display in the query result because the artist would be the same for all the records. Including the field would be redundant and not particularly useful.

1 Be sure **Queries** is selected on the Objects bar, then double-click **Create query in Design view**.

A new query window displays and the Show Table dialog box lists the tables in the database.

2 In the **Show Table** dialog box, double-click **Students** and then click **Close**.

3 Add the following fields to the design grid by double-clicking the fields in the **Students** field list: **Student#**, **First Name**, **Last Name**, and **Major**.

Four fields are added to the design grid, as shown in Figure 3.37.

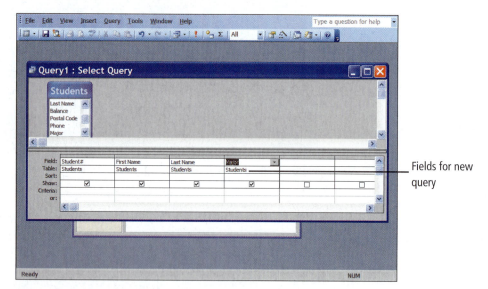

Figure 3.37

4 In the **Criteria** row under **Major**, type **Music** as shown in Figure 3.38 and then click the **Run** button.

The query results display the two records in the Students table that have Music as entries in the Major field.

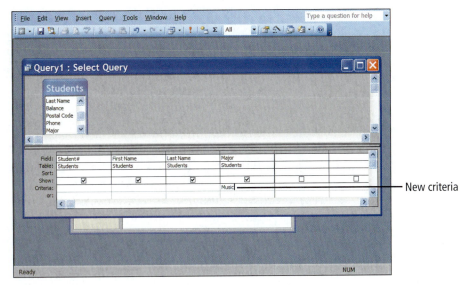

Figure 3.38

5 On the Query Datasheet toolbar, click the **View** button to return to Design view.

6 Directly above the **Criteria** row, in the **Show** row, under **Major**, notice the **Show** check box with a check mark in it. See Figure 3.39.

Fields where the Show check box is checked in the design grid display in the query results.

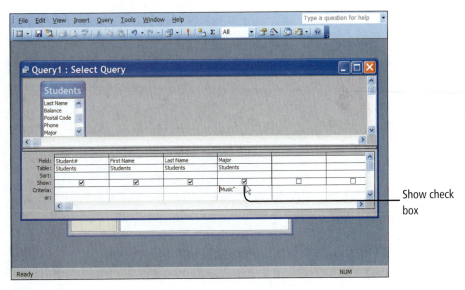

Figure 3.39

7 In the **Show** check box under **Major**, click to clear the **check mark**, as shown in Figure 3.40.

Project 3B: Students | **Access** 181

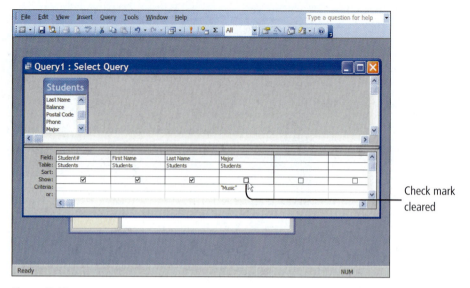

Figure 3.40

8 On the Query Design toolbar, click the **Run** button.

The query results display the same two records but the Major field does not display. See Figure 3.41. Although the Major field was still included in the query criteria for the purpose of identifying specific records, it is not necessary to display the field in the result.

Clear the Show check box when necessary to avoid cluttering the query results with redundant data.

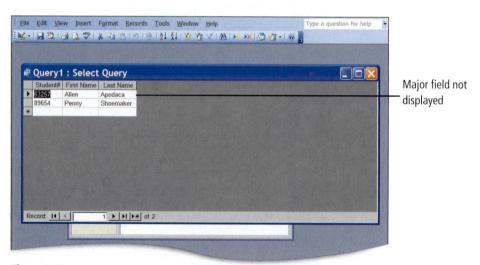

Figure 3.41

9 On the Query Datasheet toolbar, click the **View** button to return to Design view.

10 On the Menu bar, click **Edit**, **Clear Grid**.

The fields are cleared in the design grid. Use this method to quickly clear the design grid to begin a new query. Leave the query open in Design view for the next activity.

Objective 6
Specify Numeric Criteria in a Query

Criteria can be set for fields that contain numeric data as well as text data. Numeric data types are set for fields that will contain numbers on which mathematical calculations will be performed. Because the data is numeric, you can use mathematical symbols to further specify the criteria and locate the desired records.

Activity 3.10 Specifying Numeric Criteria in a Query

In this activity, you will specify the criteria in the query so that only records in the Students table that have a balance of zero will display.

1 With your cleared query window from the previous activity open in Design view, add the following fields to the design grid by double-clicking the fields in the **Students** field list: **Student#**, **First Name**, **Last Name**, and **Balance**.

Four fields are added to the design grid.

2 In the **Criteria** row under **Balance**, type **0** as shown in Figure 3.42 and then click the **Run** button.

Four records display in the query results; each has a balance of $0.00.

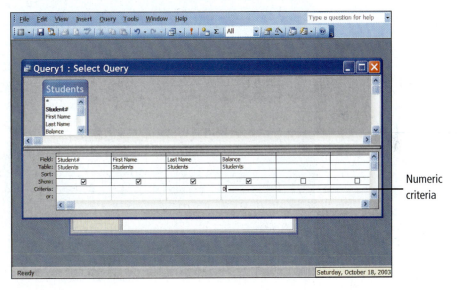

Figure 3.42

3 On the Query Datasheet toolbar, click the **View** button. Leave the query open in Design view for the next activity.

Activity 3.11 Using Comparison Operators

In Activity 3.10, you created a query to display those records where the student's balance was equal to zero. The equal sign, =, is a comparison operator that, when used in query criteria, causes Access to display those records that have entries equal to the number specified (zero in the previous activity). Other comparison operators can be used in query criteria to cause Access to display a different set of records based on the numeric criteria specified. The most common comparison operators include the < (less than), > (greater than), and the = (equal) signs.

In this activity, you will specify the criteria in the query so that the records in the Students table that have a balance that is greater than $50.00 will display.

1 Be sure your query from the last activity is displayed in Design view.

2 In the **Criteria** row, under **Balance**, select the existing text, *0*, type **>50** as illustrated in Figure 3.43, and then click the **Run** button.

Five records display and each of these has a Balance greater than (but not equal to) $50.00. See Figure 3.44.

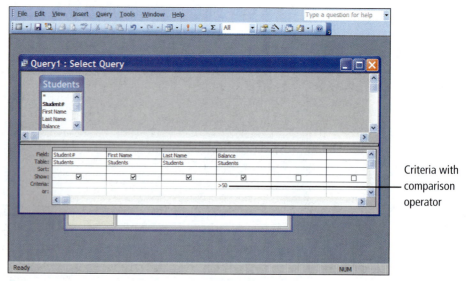

Criteria with comparison operator

Figure 3.43

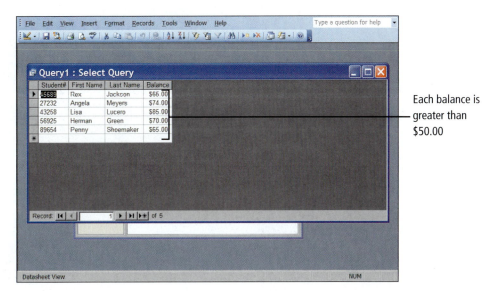

Each balance is greater than $50.00

Figure 3.44

3. On the Query Datasheet toolbar, click the **View** button.

4. In the **Criteria** row, under **Balance**, change the greater than sign (>) to the less than sign (<) and then click the **Run** button.

   Ten records display and each has a balance less than $50.00. Notice that the results show those records for which the Balance is less than $50.00, but not equal to $50.00. See Figure 3.45.

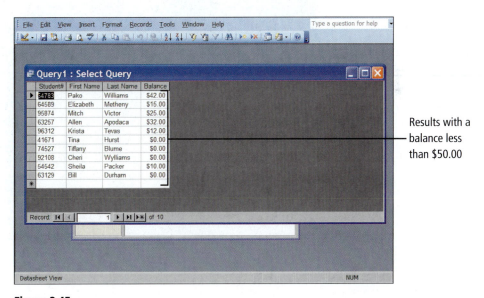

Results with a balance less than $50.00

Figure 3.45

5. On the Query Datasheet toolbar, click the **View** button.

6. In the **Criteria** row, under **Balance** and to the right of the less than sign <, type the equal sign, = but do not replace the less than, < sign. See Figure 3.46.

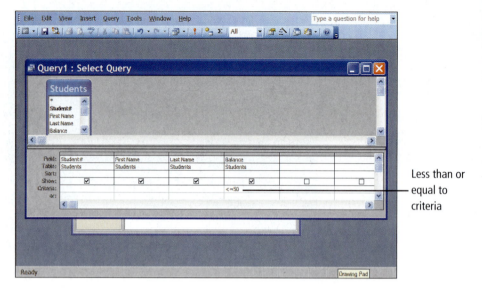

Figure 3.46

7 On the Query Design toolbar, click the **Run** button.

Eleven records display, including the record for Sally Jackson, who has a balance of exactly $50.00. See Figure 3.47. Comparison operators can be combined to form operators, such as the less than or equal to <= symbol.

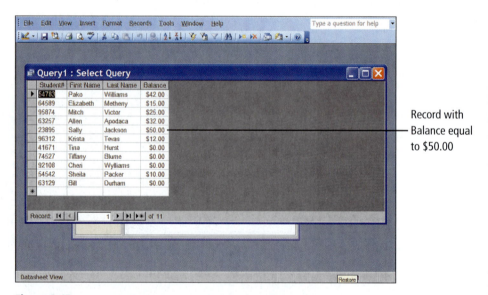

Figure 3.47

8 In the title bar of the query window, click the **Close** button. Click **Yes** to save changes to the query. Then in the **Save As** dialog box and using your own information, type **Firstname Lastname Balance Query** as the query name. Click **OK**.

The Database window displays.

9 Be sure your **Balance Query** is selected and then on the Database toolbar, click the **Print** button.

The query results print.

Objective 7
Use Compound Criteria

You may find that you need to specify more than one condition—criteria—in a query. Two or more criteria are called ***compound criteria***. Compound criteria are used to create more specific criteria and thus further limit the query results. Two types of compound criteria used in queries are AND and OR. Both of these are ***logical operators***. Logical operators allow you to enter criteria for the same field or different fields. For example, suppose you wanted to find those students who have a balance greater than $100.00 *and* who have earned more than 120 credits. You could specify both of those conditions in the same query using AND. Compound criteria that create an AND condition will return those records in the query result that meet *both* parts of the specified criteria.

Activity 3.12 Using AND in a Query

In this activity, you will specify the criteria in the query so that the records in the Students table that have a postal code of 60612 *and* a Business major will display.

1 With **Queries** selected on the Objects bar, double-click **Create query in Design view**.

A new query window displays and the Show Table dialog box lists the tables in the database.

2 In the **Show Table** dialog box, double-click **Students** and then click **Close**.

3 Add the following fields to the design grid by double-clicking the fields in the **Students** field list: **First Name**, **Last Name**, **Postal Code**, and **Major**.

Four fields are added to the design grid.

4 In the **Criteria** row under **Postal Code**, type **60612**

5 In the **Criteria** row under **Major**, type **Business** as shown in Figure 3.48 and then click the **Run** button.

The query results show two records, Angela Meyers and Tina Hurst. These records have *both* the specified Postal Code (60612) *and* the specified Major (Business). The criteria in the above query has two parts: the Postal Code part and the Major part. Criteria specifying an AND condition is always on the same line in the Criteria row.

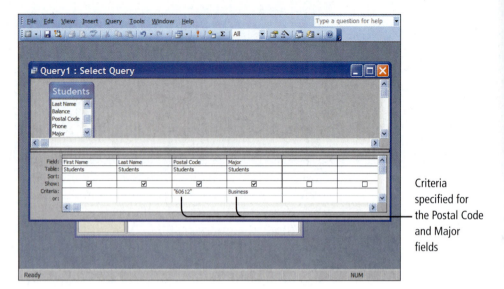

Figure 3.48

[6] In the title bar of the query window, click the **Close** button ⊠. Click **Yes** to save changes to the query and in the **Save As** dialog box and using your own information, type **Firstname Lastname AND Query** as the query name. Click **OK**.

The Database window displays.

[7] Be sure your **AND Query** is selected and then, on the Database toolbar, click the **Print** button.

Activity 3.13 Using OR in a Query

[1] With **Queries** selected on the Objects bar, double-click **Create query in Design view**. In the **Show Table** dialog box, double-click **Students** and then click **Close**.

[2] Add the following fields to the design grid by double-clicking the fields in the **Students** field list: **First Name**, **Last Name**, and **Major**.

Three fields are added to the design grid.

[3] In the **Criteria** row under **Major**, type **Music**

[4] Under **Major**, below the **Criteria** row, in the **or** row, type **Art** See Figure 3.49.

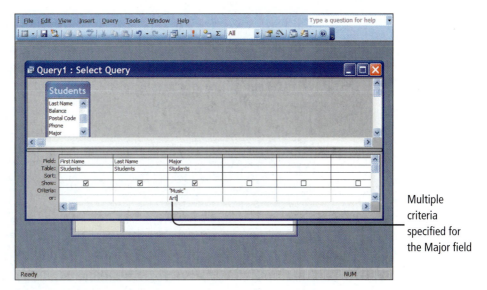

Figure 3.49

5. On the Query Design toolbar, click the **Run** button.

   The query results display those records whose Major has an entry that is either Music *or* Art. Use the OR condition to specify multiple criteria for a single field.

6. In the title bar of the query window, click the **Close** button. Click **Yes** to save changes to the query and in the **Save As** dialog box and using your own information, type **Firstname Lastname OR Query** as the query name. Click **OK**.

   The Database window displays.

7. Be sure your **OR Query** is selected and then, on the Database toolbar, click the **Print** button. Leave the database open for the next activity.

Objective 8
Sort Data in a Query

To better organize your data, you will find it useful to sort query results. Sorting results in a query is similar to sorting in a table. Records can be sorted in either ascending or descending order. Data in a query can be sorted either from the Datasheet view or from the Design view.

Activity 3.14 Sorting Data in a Query

In this activity, you will sort the results of the Balance Query you created in an earlier activity.

1. With **Queries** selected on the Objects bar, right-click the **Balance Query** that you created in an earlier activity, and then from the displayed shortcut menu, click **Open**.

   The query opens in Datasheet view.

2. Click anywhere in the **Last Name column** and then on the Query Datasheet toolbar click the **Sort Ascending** button.

   The records are sorted alphabetically by Last Name.

3 Click anywhere in the **Balance column** and then on the Query Datasheet toolbar, click the **Sort Descending** button.

The records are sorted by the entries in the Balance column from the largest to the smallest balance. See Figure 3.50.

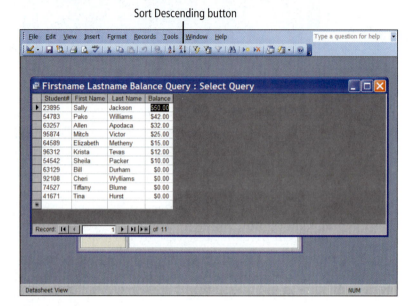

Figure 3.50

4 Switch to the Design view of the query for the next activity.

Activity 3.15 Modifying the Query Design and Sorting Data Using Multiple Fields in a Query

Sorting data in a query using more than one field allows you to further organize your query results. In this activity, you will sort the records in your Balance Query first by balance and then by last name.

1 In the design grid, move your pointer just above the **Balance** column until the pointer displays as a black downward-pointing arrow. See Figure 3.51.

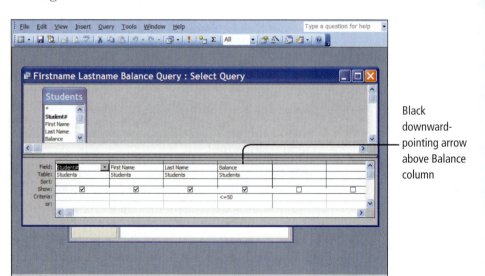

Figure 3.51

2 With the black downward-pointing arrow displayed, click once to select the **Balance** column.

The Balance column in the design grid is selected.

3 With the **Balance** column selected and your mouse pointer displayed as an arrow and positioned in the black bar above the **Balance** column, click and hold the left mouse button and then drag the **Balance** column to the left until you see a black vertical line between the **Student#** column and the **First Name** column. See Figure 3.52. Release the mouse button.

The Balance column is repositioned in between the Student# field and the First Name field. Recall from Chapter 1 that the field that is to be sorted first (Balance) must be to the left of the field that is sorted next (Last Name).

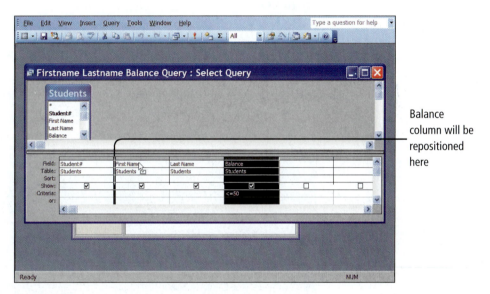

Balance column will be repositioned here

Figure 3.52

4 Repeat this action for the **Last Name** field by moving your pointer just above the **Last Name** column until the pointer displays as a black downward-pointing arrow.

5 With the black downward-pointing arrow displayed, click once to select the **Last Name** column.

The Last Name column in the design grid is selected.

6 With the **Last Name** column selected, click and hold the left mouse button and then drag the **Last Name** column to the left until you see a black vertical line between the **Balance** column and the **First Name** column. Release the mouse button.

The Last Name column is repositioned between the Balance field and the First Name field. See Figure 3.53.

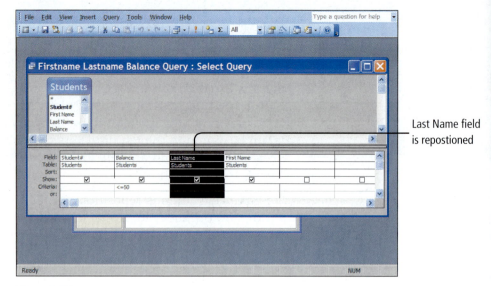

Figure 3.53

7 In the design grid, in the **Sort** row, under **Balance**, click once. See Figure 3.54.

The insertion point is blinking in the Sort row in the Balance field and a downward-pointing arrow displays.

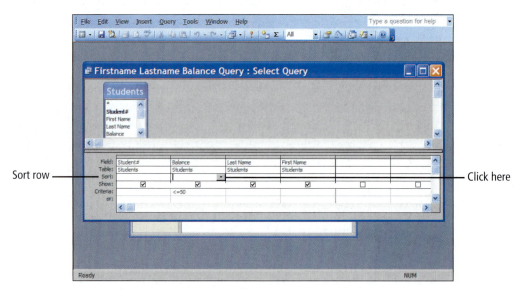

Figure 3.54

8 Click the **downward-pointing arrow** and then from the displayed list, click **Descending**. See Figure 3.55.

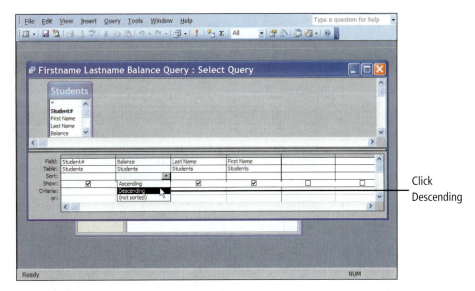

Figure 3.55

9. In the **Sort** row, under **Last Name**, click once.

   The insertion point is blinking in the Sort row in the Last Name field and a downward-pointing arrow displays.

10. Click the **downward-pointing arrow** and then click **Ascending**. See Figure 3.56.

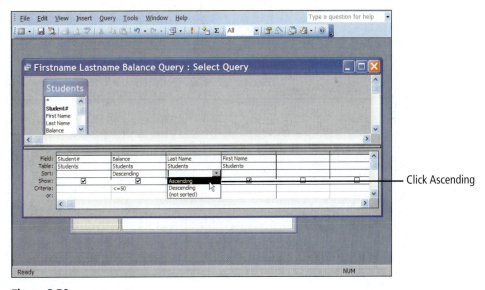

Figure 3.56

11. On the Query Design toolbar, click the **Run** button.

    The query results display with the records sorted first by the Balance field in descending order and then, for those records who have the same balances, the records are further sorted alphabetically by Last Name. See Figure 3.57.

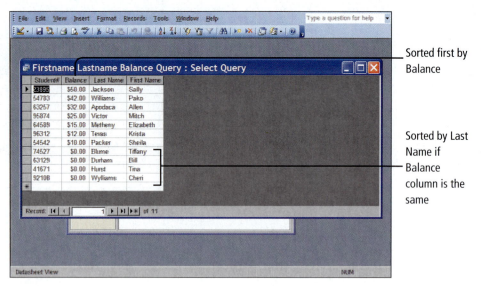

Figure 3.57

12 From the **File** menu, click **Save As**. In the **Save As** dialog box and using your own information, type **Firstname Lastname Sorted Balance Query** and then click **OK**.

The query displays in Datasheet view. The original sorted query remains and now there is a new sorted query.

13 On the Database toolbar, click the **Print** button.

The query results print.

14 Close the query. Close the database and then close Access.

End You have completed Project 3B

Project 3C Faculty

Using calculated fields, statistics, and group data in queries allows you to calculate additional information beyond what is contained in the fields.

In Activities 3.16 through 3.18 you will create queries using calculated fields and statistical functions. Your queries will look like Figure 3.58.

Figure 3.58
Project 3C—Faculty

Objective 9
Use Calculated Fields in a Query

As an example of using calculated fields in queries, you could multiply two fields together, such as Inventory Quantity and Cost per Item and get a Total Cost amount for each Inventory item. Or, as illustrated in the following activity, you could calculate a raise amount for Faculty Salaries by multiplying the salary amount by the raise percentage.

There are two steps to produce a calculated field in a query. First, you must provide a new name for the field that will store the calculated values. Second, you must specify the expression that will perform the calculation. Any field names used in the calculation must be enclosed within square brackets, [ ].

Activity 3.16 Using Calculated Fields in a Query

1. Locate the file **a03C_School** from the student files that accompany this text. Copy and paste the file to the Chapter 3 folder you created in Project 3A of this chapter.

2. Using the technique you practiced in Activity 1.1 of Chapter 1, remove the Read-only property from the file and rename the file as **3C_School_Firstname_Lastname**

3. Close the Windows accessory you are using—either My Computer or Windows Explorer. Start Access and open your **3C_School** database.

4. On the Objects bar, select **Queries** and then double-click **Create query in Design view**. In the **Show Table** dialog box, double-click **Faculty** and then click **Close**.

5. Add the following fields to the design grid by double-clicking the fields in the **Faculty** field list: **First Name**, **Last Name**, and **Salary**.

   Three fields are added to the design grid.

6. In the design grid, in the **Field** row, click in the first empty column on the right, right-click to display a shortcut menu, and then click **Zoom**.

7. In the **Zoom** dialog box, type **Raise Amount: [Salary]*.08** as shown in Figure 3.59.

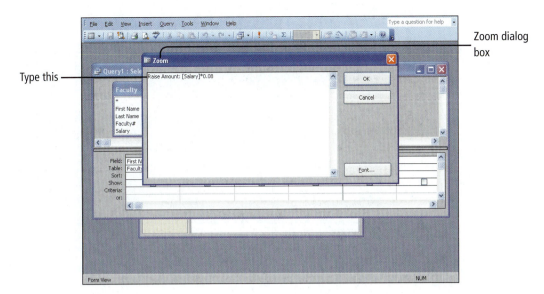

Figure 3.59

8 Look at the expression you have just typed.

The first element, *Raise Amount*, is the name of the new field where the calculated amounts will display. Following that is a colon (:). A colon in a calculated field separates the new field name from the expression. *Salary* is in square brackets because it is an existing field name from the Faculty table. It contains the information on which the calculation will be performed. Following the square brackets is an asterisk (*), which in math calculations signifies multiplication. Finally, the percentage (8% or .08) is indicated.

Alert! — **Does Your Screen Differ?**
If your calculations in a query do not work, carefully check the expression you typed. Spelling or syntax errors will prevent calculated fields from working properly.

9 In the **Zoom** dialog box, click **OK**, and then click the **Run** button.

The query results display the three fields from the Faculty table plus a fourth field—*Raise Amount*—in which a calculated amount displays. Each calculated amount equals the amount in Salary field multiplied by .08. See Figure 3.60.

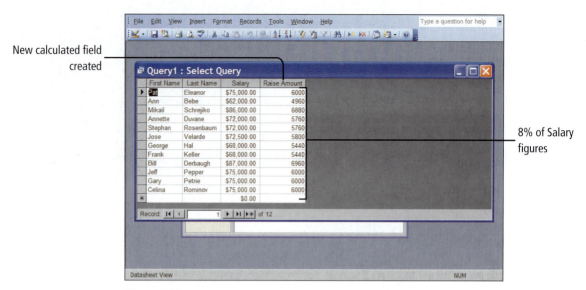

Figure 3.60

10. Notice the formatting of the **Raise Amount** field. There are no dollar signs, commas, or decimal places. You will change this formatting in a later step. Switch to **Design view**. In the **Field** row, in the first empty column, right-click and then click **Zoom**.

   The Zoom dialog box displays. Although you can type directly into the Field box in the column, it is easier to use the Zoom dialog box for a better view of the calculations you want to type.

11. In the **Zoom** dialog box, type **New Salary: [Salary]+[Raise Amount]** and then click **OK**.

12. Click the **Run** button to run the query.

   Access has calculated the New Salary amount by adding together the Salary field and the Raise Amount field. The New Salary column includes dollar signs, commas, and decimal points because the Salary field, on which the calculation was based, uses a format that includes them.

13. Switch to **Design view**. In the **Raise Amount** column, right-click and then click **Properties**. See Figure 3.61.

   The Field Properties dialog box displays. In the Field Properties dialog box, you can customize fields in a query, for example, the format of numbers in the field. As you progress in your study of Access, you will learn more about the Field Properties dialog box.

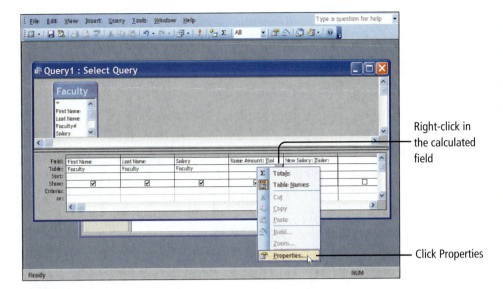

Figure 3.61

14 In the **Field Properties** dialog box, to the right of **Format**, click in the white box and then click the **downward-pointing arrow** that displays. See Figure 3.62.

A list of possible formatting options for this field displays.

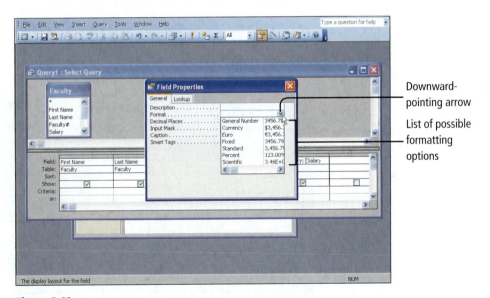

Figure 3.62

15 In the list of formatting options, click **Currency**. Then on the title bar of the **Field Properties** dialog box, click the **Close** button ⊠. See Figure 3.63.

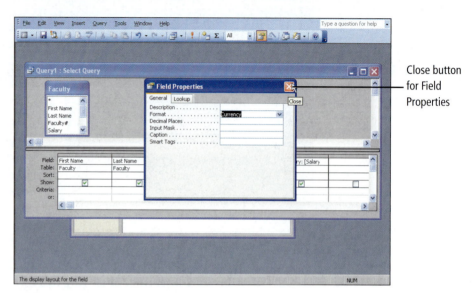

Figure 3.63

16 Click the **Run** button to run the query.

The Raise Amount column displays with Currency formatting—a dollar sign, thousands comma separators, and two decimal places. See Figure 3.64.

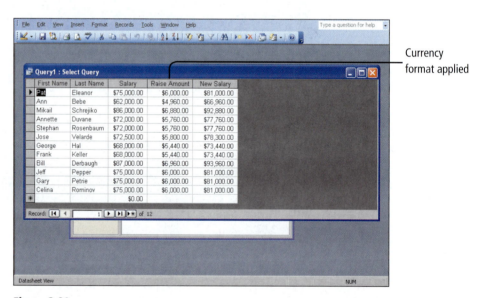

Figure 3.64

17 In the title bar of the query window, click the **Close** button ⊠. Click **Yes** to save changes to the query and in the **Save As** dialog box and using your own information, type **Firstname Lastname Faculty Raise** as the query name. Click **OK**.

The Database window displays.

18 Be sure your **Faculty Raise** query is selected and on the Database toolbar, click the **Print** button. Leave the database open for the next activity.

Objective 10
Group Data and Calculate Statistics in a Query

In Access queries, you can perform statistical calculations on a group of records. Statistics that are performed on a group of records are called *aggregate functions*. Access supports the aggregate functions summarized in the table shown in Figure 3.65.

Aggregate Functions

Function Name	What It Does
SUM	Totals the values in a field
AVG	Averages the values in a field
MAX	Locates the largest value in a field
MIN	Locates the smallest value in a field
STDEV	Calculates the Standard Deviation on the values in a field
VAR	Calculates the Variance on the values in a field
FIRST	Displays the First value in a field
LAST	Displays the Last value in a field

Figure 3.65

In the activities that follow, you will use the first four functions in Figure 3.65: SUM, AVG, MAX, and MIN. As you progress in your study of Access, you will use the remaining functions.

Activity 3.17 Grouping Data in a Query

When you want to group records in a query by a specific field, include only that field in the query. For example, if you wanted to group (summarize) the CDs in your CD Collection database by the type of music, you would include only the Type field in your query. To group data in a query, you must insert a Total row in the query design. The Total row does not appear by default. In this activity, you will create a query and group the records by Division.

1 Be sure **Queries** is selected on the Objects bar and then double-click **Create query in Design view**. In the **Show Table** dialog box, double-click **Faculty** and then click **Close**.

2 From the list of fields for the Faculty table, double-click the **Division** field to add it to the design grid.

3 On the Query Design toolbar, click the **Totals** button ∑. See Figure 3.66.

A Total row is inserted as the third row of the design grid. See Figure 3.66.

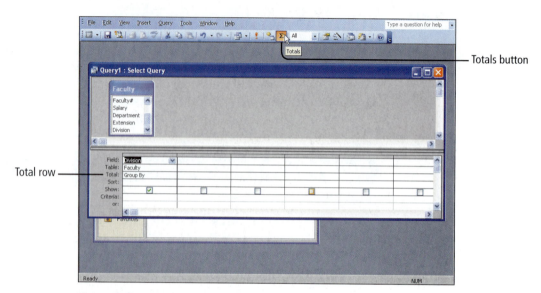

Figure 3.66

4 In the **Total** row, under **Division**, click and then click the arrow that displays to the right of *Group By*.

The list of aggregate functions displays.

5 Click **Group By** and then click the **Run** button to run the query.

The query results display summarized by the entries in the Division field: Business, Education, Fine Arts, and Humanities. See Figure 3.67.

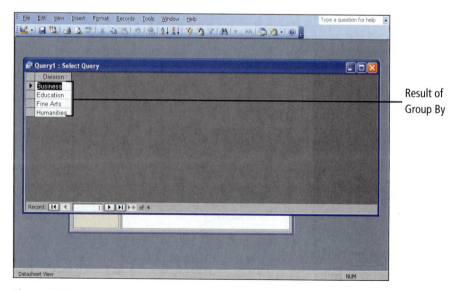

Figure 3.67

Activity 3.18 Using the AVG, SUM, MAX, and MIN Functions in a Query

In this activity, you will create a query that will display the Faculty salary amounts grouped by Division.

1 Switch to **Design view** and then add the **Salary** field to the design grid.

2 Click the **Run** button to run the query.

The query results contain the individual salary amounts, grouped together by division, as shown in Figure 3.68.

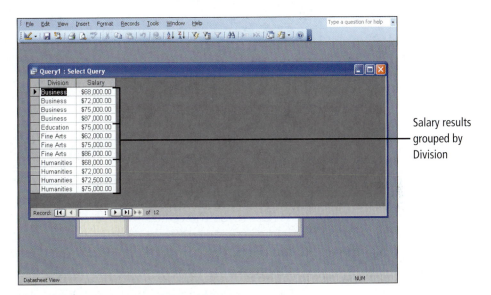

Salary results grouped by Division

Figure 3.68

3 Switch to **Design view**. In the **Total** row, under **Salary**, click and then click the arrow that displays.

4 From the list of functions, click **Avg** as shown in Figure 3.69 and then click the **Run** button.

Access calculates an average salary for each of the four divisions. Notice the field name, *AvgOfSalary*, for the calculation. This query answers the question, "What is the average faculty salary within each division?"

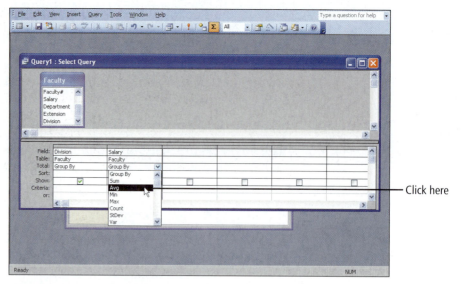

Figure 3.69

[5] Switch to **Design view**. In the **Total** row under **Salary**, click and then click the arrow that displays. From the list of functions, click **Sum**.

[6] Run the query.

Access sums the Salaries for each of the four Divisions. Notice the field name, *SumOfSalary*, for the calculation. Thus, the total annual salary amount for all of the faculty members in the Business Division is $302,000.00.

[7] Switch to **Design view**. In the **Total** row, under **Salary**, click and then click the arrow that displays. From the list of functions, click **Min**.

[8] Run the query.

Access locates the smallest value in each of the Divisions and displays the results. Thus, the lowest paid faculty member in the Fine Arts Division earns an annual salary of $62,000.00.

[9] Switch to **Design view**. In the **Total** row, under **Salary**, click and then click the arrow that displays. From the list of functions, click **Max**.

[10] Run the query.

Access locates the largest value in each of the Divisions and displays the results. See Figure 3.70. Thus, the highest paid faculty member in the Humanities Division earns $75,000.00.

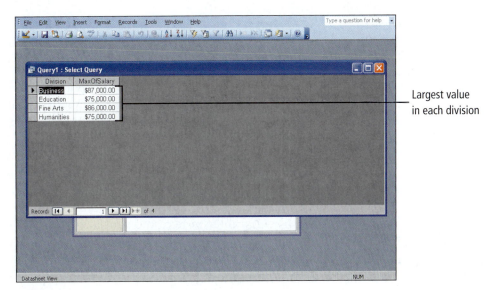

Figure 3.70

11 In the title bar of the query window, click the **Close** button. Click **Yes** to save changes to the query and in the **Save As** dialog box and using your own information, type **Firstname Lastname Max Salary** as the query name. Click **OK**.

The Database window displays.

12 Print your **Max Salary** query.

13 Close your **School** database and then close Access.

End You have completed Project 3C

Summary

Queries allow you to ask questions about the data in a database in a manner that Access can interpret. Queries are useful for locating data that matches the criteria, or conditions, that you specify.

Text is one type of criteria that can be specified. Wildcard characters such as the *, which serves as a placeholder for a group of characters, are included as part of the criteria when a portion of what you are looking for is unknown. The wildcard character ? serves as a placeholder for a single character in textual criteria.

Numeric criteria can also be specified in a query. Specifying numeric criteria allows you to use comparison operators, such as less than (<), greater than (>), and equal to (=).

Queries can also have more than one criteria, known as compound criteria, to assist you in locating specific data. There are two types of compound criteria, AND and OR.

Calculations can be performed in a query. Statistical calculations such as SUM, AVG, MAX, and MIN can be used on grouped data in a query.

In This Chapter You Practiced How To

- Create a New Select Query
- Run, Save, and Close a Query
- Open and Edit an Existing Query
- Specify Text Criteria in a Query
- Use Wildcards in a Query
- Specify Numeric Criteria in a Query
- Use Compound Criteria
- Sort Data in a Query
- Use Calculated Fields in a Query
- Group Data and Calculate Statistics in a Query

Concepts Assessments

Matching Match each term in the second column with its correct definition in the first column by writing the letter of the term on the blank line in front of the correct definition.

____ 1. The symbols < (less than) > (greater than) and = (equal).

____ 2. The upper portion of the query design grid where selected tables used in the query display.

____ 3. The category that includes AND and OR operators.

____ 4. Statistics performed on a group of records.

____ 5. Two or more conditions in a query.

____ 6. A question formed in a manner that Access can interpret.

____ 7. The conditions that identify the specific records you are looking for.

____ 8. The lower pane of the query window where the fields are added to the query.

____ 9. Characters that serve as a placeholder for an unknown character or characters in a query.

____ 10. Displays the tables available for use in a query.

____ 11. Language used in querying, updating, and managing relational databases.

____ 12. Term used to compare expressions.

____ 13. Examines a sequence of characters and compares them to the criteria in a query.

____ 14. Wildcard character used as a placeholder to match any number of characters.

____ 15. Wildcard character used as a placeholder to match one character.

A Aggregate functions
B Asterisk (*)
C Comparison operators
D Compound criteria
E Criteria
F Design grid
G "Like"
H Logical operators
I Query
J Question mark (?)
K Show Table dialog box
L SQL
M String expression
N Table area
O Wildcard characters

Concepts Assessments (continued)

Fill in the Blank Write the correct answer in the space provided.

1. When a query is run, the results display in a(n) _____.

2. To include, but not display, a field in query results, clear the _____ box in the design grid.

3. In an _____ condition, both parts of the query must be met.

4. In an _____ condition, either part of the query may be met.

5. If sorting records by multiple fields, the field that is to be sorted first must be positioned to the _____ of the field that is sorted next.

6. Use the _____ to better view the calculations entered into a calculated field in a query.

7. To locate the largest value in a group of records, use the _____ function.

8. To display the row in the design grid where you can specify statistical functions, such as Sum or Avg, click the _____ button.

9. To locate the smallest value in a group of records, use the _____ function.

10. To save an existing query with a new name, use the _____ command.

Skill Assessments

Project 3D — Rental Instruments

Objectives: *Create a New Select Query; Run, Save, and Close a Query; and Specify Text Criteria in a Query.*

In the following Skill Assessment, you will create a query that will locate specific information for rental instruments at the Lake Michigan City College Music Department. Your completed query will look similar to the one shown in Figure 3.71. You will rename the database as *3D_Rental_Instruments_Firstname_Lastname* in the folder you have created for this chapter.

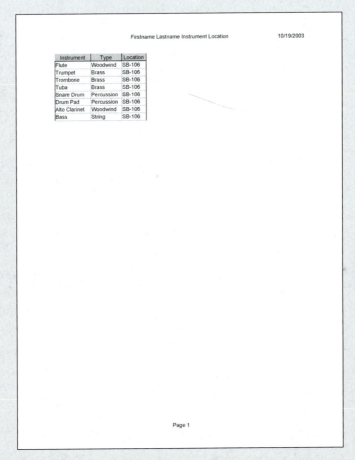

Figure 3.71

1. Locate the file **a03D_Rental_Instruments** from the student files that accompany this text. Copy and paste the file to the Chapter 3 folder you created earlier in this chapter.

2. Using the technique you practiced in Activity 1.1 of Chapter 1, remove the Read-only property from the file and rename the file as **3D_Rental_Instruments_Firstname_Lastname**

(**Project 3D**–Rental Instruments continues on the next page)

Skill Assessments (continued)

(Project 3D–Rental Instruments continued)

3. Close the Windows accessory you are using—either My Computer or Windows Explorer. Start Access and open your **3D_Rental_Instruments** database.

4. On the Objects bar, click **Queries**.

5. Double-click **Create query in Design view**. A new Select Query window opens and the **Show Table** dialog box displays. The Show Table dialog box lists all of the tables in the database.

6. In the **Show Table** dialog box, click **Rental Instruments**, click the **Add** button, and then click the **Close** button. Alternatively, you can double-click Rental Instruments and then click Close.

7. In the **Rental Instruments** field list, double-click **Instrument**. The **Instrument** field displays in the design grid.

8. In the **Rental Instruments** field list, double-click **Type**. Repeat this action for the **Location** field. As you double-click each field, notice the fields display one by one in the design grid.

9. In the **Criteria** row, under the **Location** field, type **SB-106**

10. On the Query Design toolbar, click the **Run** button. The query runs and the query results display in a table in Datasheet view. Clicking the Run button causes Access to look at all the records in the Rental Instruments table and locate only the records that meet the specified criteria, which, in this case, are the records that have SB-106 in the Location field.

11. In the title bar of the query window, click the **Close** button. Click **Yes** to save changes to the query and, in the **Save As** dialog box using your own information, type **Firstname Lastname Instrument Location** as the query name. Click **OK**.

12. Be sure your **Instrument Location** query is selected. Then on the Database toolbar, click the **Print** button.

13. Close the database and then close Access.

 You have completed Project 3D

Project 3E—Inventory

Objectives: *Create a New Select Query; Run, Save, and Close a Query; Specify Numeric Criteria in a Query; and Use Compound Criteria.*

In the following Skill Assessment, you will create a new query to locate information about the inventory at LMCC. Your completed query will look similar to Figure 3.72. You will rename and save your database as *3E_Inventory_Firstname_Lastname*.

(Project 3E–Inventory continues on the next page)

Skill Assessments (continued)

(Project 3E–Inventory continued)

Inventory #	Inventory Item	Cost	Quantity on Hand
LMCC-301	Floppy Disks	$45.00	5

Firstname Lastname Cost Quantity — 10/19/2003

Page 1

Figure 3.72

1. Locate the file **a03E_Inventory** from the student files that accompany this text. Copy and paste the file to the Chapter 3 folder you created earlier in this chapter.

2. Using the technique you practiced in Activity 1.1 of Chapter 1, remove the Read-only property from the file and rename the file as **3E_Inventory_Firstname_Lastname**

3. Close the Windows accessory you are using—either My Computer or Window Explorer. Start Access and open your **3E_Inventory** database.

4. On the Objects bar, click **Queries**. To the right of the Objects bar, two command icons for creating a new query display.

5. Double-click **Create query in Design view**. A new **Select Query** window opens and the **Show Table** dialog box displays. The Show Table dialog box lists all of the tables in the database.

(Project 3E–Inventory continues on the next page)

Skill Assessments (continued)

(Project 3E–Inventory continued)

6. In the **Show Table** dialog box, double-click **Office Inventory** and then click the **Close** button. A list of the fields in the Office Inventory table displays in the upper pane of the Select Query window. The **Inventory #** field is bold, unlike the other fields in the list, because the Inventory # field is the primary key in the Office Inventory table.

7. In the **Office Inventory** field list, double-click **Inventory #**. The Inventory # field displays in the design grid. The design grid of the Select Query window is where you specify the fields and other criteria to be used in the query.

8. In the **Office Inventory** field list, double-click **Inventory Item**. Repeat this action for the **Cost** and **Quantity on Hand** fields in the field list. Use the vertical scroll bar in the field list window to view the fields toward the end of the list. As you double-click each field, notice the fields display one by one in the design grid.

9. In the **Criteria** row, under **Cost**, type **>40** and then click the **Run** button. Three records display in the query results; each has a Cost greater than $40.00. On the Query Datasheet toolbar, click the **View** button to switch to Design view.

10. In the **Criteria** row, under **Quantity on Hand**, type **>=5** and then click the **Run** button. One record displays for Floppy Disks. This record meets the criteria of a Cost that is greater than $40.00 AND a Quantity on Hand that is greater than or equal to 5.

11. In the title bar of the query window, click the **Close** button. Click **Yes** to save changes to the query and in the **Save As** dialog box using your own information, type **Firstname Lastname Cost Quantity** as the query name. Click **OK**.

12. Be sure your **Cost Quantity** query is selected, then on the Database toolbar, click the **Print** button.

13. Close the database and then close Access.

 You have completed Project 3E

Project 3F—Computer Inventory

Objectives: *Create a New Select Query; Run, Save, and Close a Query; Use Calculated Fields in a Query; and Group Data and Calculate Statistics in a Query.*

In the following Skill Assessment you will create two queries for the Computer Inventory database at LMCC. Your completed queries will look similar to Figure 3.73. You will rename and save your database as *3F_Computer_Inventory_Firstname_Lastname*.

(Project 3F–Computer Inventory continues on the next page)

Skill Assessments (continued)

(Project 3F–Computer Inventory continued)

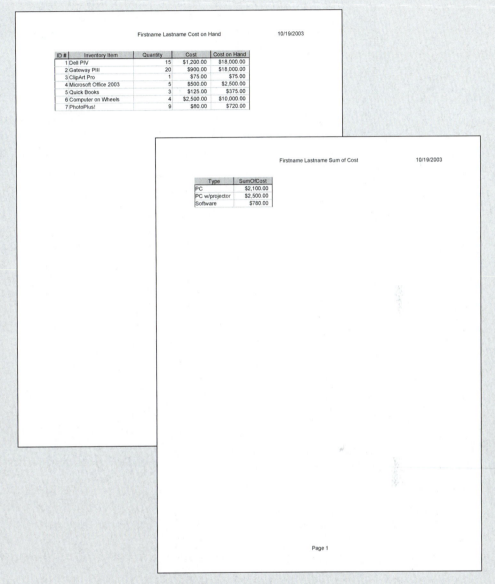

Figure 3.73

1. Locate the file **a03F_Computer_Inventory** from the student files that accompany this text. Copy and paste the file to the Chapter 3 folder you created earlier in this chapter.

2. Using the technique you practiced in Activity 1.1 of Chapter 1, remove the Read-only property from the file and rename the file as **3F_ComputerInventory_Firstname_Lastname**

3. Close the Windows accessory you are using—either My Computer or Windows Explorer. Start Access and open your **3F_ComputerInventory** database.

(Project 3F–Computer Inventory continues on the next page)

Skill Assessments (continued)

(Project 3F–Computer Inventory continued)

4. On the Objects bar, click **Queries**. To the right of the Objects bar, two command icons for creating a new query display.

5. Double-click **Create query in Design view**. A new Select Query window opens and the **Show Table** dialog box displays. The **Show Table** dialog box lists all of the tables in the database.

6. In the **Show Table** dialog box, double-click **Inventory** and then click the **Close** button. A list of the fields in the Inventory table displays in the upper pane of the Select Query window. The ID # field is bold, unlike the other fields in the list, because the ID # field is the primary key in the Inventory table.

7. In the **Inventory** field list, double-click **ID #**. The ID # field displays in the design grid. The design grid of the Select Query window is where you specify the fields and other criteria to be used in the query.

8. In the **Inventory** field list, double-click **Inventory Item**. Repeat this action for the **Quantity** and **Cost** fields in the field list. Use the vertical scroll bar in the field list window to view the fields toward the end of the list. As you double-click each field, notice the fields display one by one in the design grid.

9. In the design grid, in the **Field** row, click in the first empty column on the right, right-click to display the shortcut menu, and then click **Zoom**.

10. In the Zoom dialog box, type **Cost on Hand:[Quantity]*[Cost]**

11. Look at the expression you have just typed. The first element, *Cost on Hand*, is the name of the new field where the calculated amounts will display. Following that is a colon (:). A colon in a calculated field separates the new field name from the equation. *Quantity* and *Cost* are in square brackets because they are existing fields from the Inventory table. In between the fields is an asterisk (*), which in mathematical calculations signifies multiplication.

12. In the **Zoom** dialog box, click **OK** and then click the **Run** button. The query results display the four specified fields from the Inventory table plus a fifth field, *Cost on Hand*, that, for each record, displays a calculated amount that results from multiplying the figure in the *Quantity* field by the figure in the *Cost* field.

13. In the title bar of the query window, click the **Close** button. Click **Yes** to save changes to the query and in the **Save As** dialog box and using your own information, type **Firstname Lastname Cost on Hand** as the query name. Click **OK**. The Database window displays.

14. In the Database window, be sure your **Cost on Hand** query is selected and then on the Database toolbar, click the **Print** button.

(Project 3F–Computer Inventory continues on the next page)

Skill Assessments (continued)

(Project 3F–Computer Inventory continued)

15. If necessary, on the Objects bar, click **Queries**, then double-click **Create query in Design view**.

16. In the **Show Table** dialog box, double-click **Inventory** and then click the **Close** button.

17. In the **Inventory** field list, double-click **Type** and **Cost** to add these fields to the design grid.

18. On the Query Design toolbar, click the **Totals** button. The **Total** row displays in the design grid.

19. In the **Total** row, under **Cost**, click and then click the **arrow** that displays to the right of *Group By*. The list of aggregate functions displays.

20. From the list of functions, click **Sum** and then click the **Run** button to run the query. Access calculates a total cost amount for each type of inventory.

21. In the title bar of the query window, click the **Close** button. Click **Yes** to save changes to the query and in the **Save As** dialog box using your own information, type **Firstname Lastname Sum of Cost** as the query name. Click **OK**. The Database window displays.

22. Be sure your **Sum of Cost** query is selected and on the Database toolbar, click the **Print** button.

23. Close the database. Close Access.

End You have completed Project 3F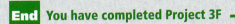

Access
chapter three
Performance Assessments

Project 3G—Distance Learning

Objectives: *Create a New Select Query; Run, Save, and Close a Query; and Use Wildcards in a Query.*

In the following Performance Assessment, you will create queries to locate information about Distance Learning courses at Lake Michigan City College. Your completed query will look similar to Figure 3.74. You will rename and save your database as *3G_Distance_Learning_Firstname Lastname*.

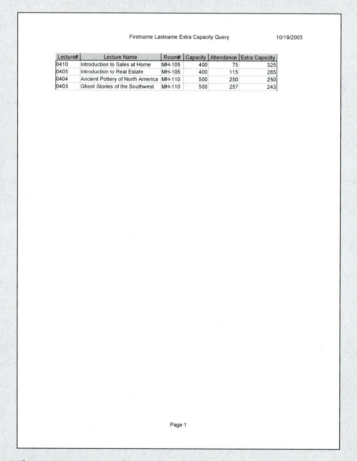

Figure 3.74

1. From the student files that accompany this textbook copy the file **a03G_Distance_Learning** and then paste the file to the folder where you are storing your projects for this chapter. Remove the Read-only attribute and using your own information, rename this file as **3G_Distance_Learning_Firstname_Lastname**

2. Start Access and then open your **3G_Distance_Learning** database.

3. On the Objects bar, click **Queries**, then double-click **Create query in Design view**.

(Project 3G–Distance Learning continues on the next page)

216 Access | Chapter 3: Queries

Access chapter three

Performance Assessments (continued)

(Project 3G–Distance Learning continued)

4. In the **Show Table** dialog box, double-click **Distance Learning Courses** and then click the **Close** button.

5. In the **Distance Learning Courses** field list, double-click the following fields to add them to the design grid: **Course Number**, **Course Name**, and **Credit Hours**.

6. Enter the criteria to search for the records whose Course Name contains either Access or Excel by performing the following: In the **Criteria** row, under the **Course Name** field, type *Access and in the **or** row, under the **Course Name** field, type *Excel and then click the **Run** button.

7. In the title bar of the query window, click the **Close** button. Click **Yes** to save the changes to the query and in the **Save As** dialog box using your own information, type Firstname Lastname Access Excel Query as the query name. Click **OK**.

8. Print your Access Excel query.

9. Close the database and then close Access.

End You have completed Project 3G

Project 3H—Lecture Series

Objectives: *Open and Edit an Existing Query, Specify Numeric Criteria in a Query, Sort Data in a Query, and Use Calculated Fields in a Query.*

In the following Performance Assessment, you will create a query to locate information about the lectures in the college's new Lecture Series. Your completed query will look similar to Figure 3.75. You will rename and save your database as *3H_Lecture_Series_Firstname_Lastname.*

1. From the student files that accompany this textbook copy the file **a03H_Lecture_Series** and then paste the file to the folder where you are storing your projects for this chapter. Remove the Read-only attribute and using your own information, rename this file as 3H_Lecture_Series_Firstname_Lastname

2. Start Access and then open your **3H_Lecture_Series** database.

3. Open the **Extra Capacity Query** in Design view.

4. Create a calculated field, called *Extra Capacity*, that will subtract the figures in the **Attendance** field from the figures in the **Capacity** field. (Hint: Capacity—Attendance.) Run the query.

5. Switch to the **Design view**. Add criteria to the query that will limit the query results to those records that have an Extra Capacity that is greater than 200. Sort the records by the **Extra Capacity** field in **Descending** order. Run the query.

(Project 3H–Lecture Series continues on the next page)

Performance Assessments (continued)

(Project 3H–Lecture Series continued)

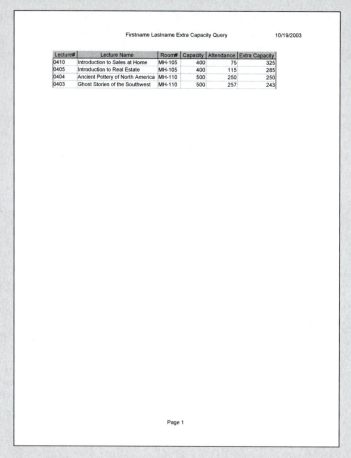

Figure 3.75

6. Using **File**, **Save As**, save the query as **Firstname Lastname Extra Capacity Query**

7. Print your Extra Capacity Query query. Close the database and then close Access.

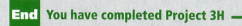

You have completed Project 3H

Project 3I—Lecture Hall

Objectives: *Create a New Select Query; Run, Save, and Close a Query; and Group Data and Calculate Statistics in a Query.*

In the following Performance Assessment, you will create a query to locate information about the lectures in LMCC's new Lecture Series. Your completed query will look similar to Figure 3.76. You will rename and save your database as *3I_Lecture_Hall_Firstname_Lastname*.

(Project 3I–Lecture Hall continues on the next page)

Performance Assessments (continued)

(Project 3I–Lecture Hall continued)

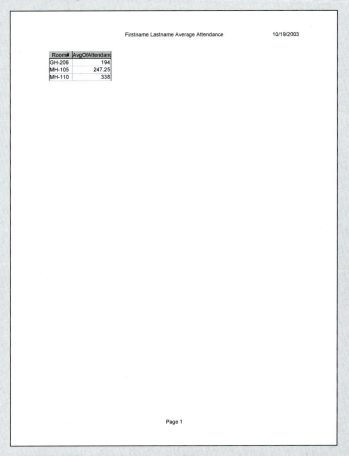

Figure 3.76

1. From the student files that accompany this textbook copy the file **a03I_Lecture_Hall** and then paste the file to the folder where you are storing your projects for this chapter. Remove the Read-only attribute and using your own information, rename this file as **3I_Lecture_Hall_Firstname_Lastname**

2. Start Access and then open your **3I Lecture_Hall** database.

3. Open the **Average Attendance** query in Design view. Click the **Totals** button to display the **Total** row. In the **Total** row, under **Attendance**, click the **arrow** that displays and then click **Avg**. Group the query results by Room#.

4. Run the query. Using **File**, **Save As**, save the query using your own information, as **Firstname Lastname Average Attendance**

5. Print the query you created. Close the database and then close Access.

End You have completed Project 3I

Mastery Assessments

Project 3J—Employees

Objectives: *Create a New Select Query, Run, Save, and Close a Query, Open and Edit an Existing Query, Specify Numeric Criteria in a Query, and Use Calculated Fields in a Query.*

In the following Mastery Assessment, you will create a new query for the Employees database at LMCC. Your completed query will look like Figure 3.77. You will rename and save your database as *3J_Employees_Firstname_Lastname*.

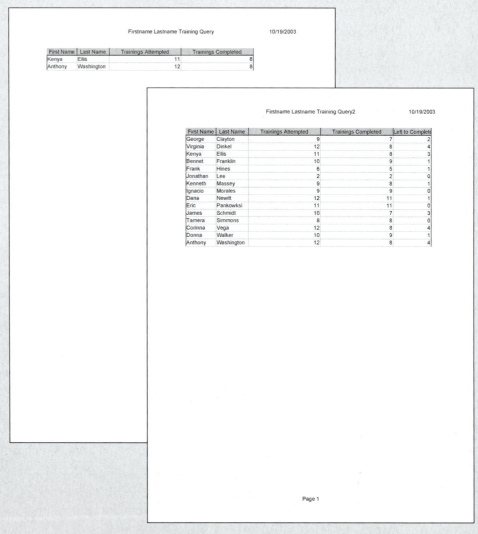

Figure 3.77

1. From the student files that accompany this textbook copy the file **a03J_Employees** and then paste the file to the folder where you are storing your projects for this chapter. Remove the Read-only attribute and using your own information, rename this file as **3J_Employees_Firstname_Lastname** Open your **3J_Employees** database.

(*Project* 3J–Employees continues on the next page)

Mastery Assessments (continued)

(Project 3J–Employees continued)

2. Create a query based on the **Employees** table that will locate the records of the employees in the Finance Department that have completed seven or more trainings. Include the **Trainings Attempted** field in the design grid. (Hint: Trainings Completed is greater than or equal to 7.)

3. Clear the **Show** box for the **Dept** field so it will not display in the query result. Sort the Query alphabetically by the employee's last name. Run the query.

4. Using your own information, save the query as **Firstname Lastname Training Query**

5. Open the **Training** query you just created in Design view. Delete the existing criteria and then remove the **Dept** field from the design grid. Using **File**, **Save As**, save the query with the name **Firstname Lastname Training Query2**

6. Create a calculated field, called *Left to Complete*, which will subtract the figures in the **Trainings Completed** field from the figures in the **Trainings Attempted** field. Run the query. Close the query and save changes.

7. Print both queries. Close the database and then close Access.

End You have completed Project 3J

Project 3K — Employee Training

Objectives: *Open and Edit an Existing Query; Group Data and Calculate Statistics in a Query.*

In the following Mastery Assessment, you will modify an existing query for the Employee Training database at LMCC. Your completed query will look similar to Figure 3.78. You will rename and save your database as *3K_Employee_Training_Firstname_Lastname*.

1. From the student files that accompany this textbook copy the file **a03K_Employee_Training** and then paste the file to the folder where you are storing your projects for this chapter. Remove the Read-only attribute and using your own information, rename this file as **3K_Employee_Training_Firstname_Lastname** Open your **3K Employee Training** database.

2. Open the **Average Trainings** query in Design view. Add a Totals row and calculate an average number of **Trainings Completed** and group them by **Dept**. (Hint: Delete all the fields except Dept and Trainings Completed.)

3. Run the query. Use **File**, **Save As** to save the query with the name (using your own information) **Firstname Lastname Average Trainings** and then close the query.

(Project 3K–Employee Training continues on the next page)

Mastery Assessments (continued)

(Project 3K–Employee Training continued)

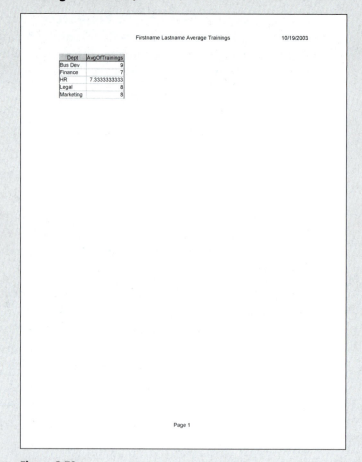

Figure 3.78

4. Print your **Average Trainings** query. Close the database and then close Access.

 You have completed Project 3K

Access chapter three | Problem Solving

Project 3L — Bookstore

Objectives: *Open and Edit an Existing Query, Use Calculated Fields in a Query, and Group Data and Calculate Statistics in a Query.*

In the following Problem Solving exercise, you will modify an existing query for the Bookstore database at LMCC.

1. From the student files that accompany this textbook copy the file **a03L_Bookstore** and then paste the file to the folder where you are storing your projects for this chapter. Remove the Read-only attribute and using your own information, rename this file as **3L_Bookstore_FirstName_LastName** Open your **3L Bookstore** database.

2. Modify the **Bookstore Balance** query so that a total sum of all student balances displays in the query result. Run and then save your query as **Firstname Lastname Bookstore Balance** Print the query.

3. Modify the **New Balance Query** using the following information: The manager of the bookstore has decided to give all students a 15% reduction in their bookstore balances. Create the calculated fields in the manner you choose to determine, first, the 15% discount and then to calculate what the students' new balances will be. Run and then save your query as **Firstname Lastname New Balance Query** Print the query.

End You have completed Project 3L

Project 3M — LMCC

Objectives: *Create a New Select Query; Run, Save, and Close a Query; and Specify Text Criteria in a Query.*

In the following Problem Solving exercise, you will modify an existing query for the Bookstore database at LMCC.

1. From the student files that accompany this textbook copy the file **a03M_LMCC** and then paste the file to the folder where you are storing your projects for this chapter. Remove the Read-only attribute and using your own information, rename this file as **3M_LMCC_Firstname_Lastname** Open your **3M_LMCC** database.

2. Create a query that will locate those students who began attending Lake Michigan City College in the FA02 term. Save your query as **Firstname_Lastname_First Term** Print the query.

End You have completed Project 3M

On the Internet

Microsoft Certification Exam

As you progress with your study of Access, you will learn skills necessary to complete the Microsoft certification test for Access 2003. Go to the Microsoft Web site at **www.microsoft.com** and then search the site to locate information regarding the certification exam. Print the core objectives for the Microsoft Access user certification and any additional information about taking the test.

GO! with Help

Getting Help Using Wildcards

There are many types of wildcards that you can use in your queries. Use the Access Help system to find out more about wildcards in Access.

1. Start Access. If necessary, from the **View** menu, click **Task Pane** to display the **Getting Started** task pane. On the task pane, to the right of *Getting Started*, click the **downward-pointing arrow**. From the displayed list of available task panes, click **Help**.

2. Click in the **Search For** box, then type **wildcards**

3. Press [Enter], scroll the displayed list as necessary, and then click **About using wildcard characters**.

4. If you would like to keep a copy of this information, click the **Print** button.

5. Click the **Close** button in the top right corner of the Help window to close the Help window and then close Access.

Access 2003

chapter four

Customizing Tables, Data Access Pages, and Converting a Database

In this chapter, you will: **complete these projects** and **practice these skills.**

Project 4A
Restricting Data in a Table

Objectives
- Customize a Field
- Specify a Field Format
- Create Input Masks Using the Input Mask Wizard
- Create Input Masks Using the Input Mask Properties Box
- Specify a Required Field
- Validate Data Entry

Project 4B
Finding Data in a Table

Objectives
- Create a Lookup Wizard Field
- Find a Record
- Display Specific Records

Project 4C
Creating Data Access Pages and Converting a Database

Objectives
- Create and Use a Data Access Page
- Convert a Database from a Previous Version of Access

Jefferson Country Inn

About 2 hours outside Washington, DC, the Jefferson Country Inn is located in Charlottesville, Virginia. The Inn's proximity to Washington, DC, and Richmond, VA, make it a popular weekend getaway for locals and a convenient base for out-of-town vacationers. The Inn offers 12 rooms, all individually decorated. A fresh country breakfast and afternoon tea are included each day.

Meeting rooms offering the latest high-tech amenities like high-speed Internet connections have made the Inn an increasingly popular location for day-long meetings and events.

© Getty Images, Inc.

Customizing Tables, Data Access Pages, and Converting a Database

Access provides tools for customizing tables and improving data accuracy and data entry. In this chapter, you will use information from the Jefferson Country Inn to find specific information in a table without using a query, apply special formatting to records that meet specified conditions, and discover how Access can create Web pages containing table data. You will customize the fields in a table, create a data access page, and convert a database that was created in an older version of Access to the current version of Microsoft Access.

Project 4A Jefferson Inn Employees

You have practiced creating fields and indicating the type of data that could be entered by specifying the field's data type, for example, Text, Currency, or Number. This sets restrictions on the data entered in the field. You can further restrict the data by modifying the field's ***properties***. A field's property determines its content and appearance. Restrict data in fields to keep the database organized, and also to help eliminate errors during the data entry process. You can also set a specific field size and create a default value for a field.

In Activities 4.1 through 4.10, you will modify the properties and customize the fields in a table that stores information about the Jefferson Country Inn. Specifically, you will add features to the tables that will help to accomplish two things: reduce errors in the data and make data entry easier. Your completed table will look similar to Figure 4.1. You will save your database as *4A_Jefferson_Inn_Employees_Firstname_Lastname*.

Figure 4.1
Project 4A—Jefferson Inn Employees

Objective 1
Customize a Field

Activity 4.1 Changing a Data Type

In this activity you will change some of the data types for fields in the Jefferson Employees table to restrict the data entered and to make it more useful.

1. Using the skills you practiced earlier, create a new folder named Chapter 4 in the location where you will be storing your projects for this chapter. Locate the file **a04A_Jefferson_Inn_Employees** from your student files and copy and paste the file to the Chapter 4 folder you created. Remove the Read-only property from the file and rename the file as **4A_Jefferson_Inn_Employees_Firstname_Lastname** Start Access and open the database you just renamed.

2. On the Objects bar, click **Tables** if necessary, right-click the **Jefferson Employees** table, and then click **Rename**.

3. In the box that displays, and using your own information, type **Jefferson Employees Firstname Lastname** and then press Enter.

   The table is renamed to include your name.

4. Open your **Jefferson Employees** table in **Datasheet view** and examine the data in the table. In particular, notice that the data in the Email column is employee Email addresses. Currently, this data is not formatted as hyperlinks; they will not open a Web page nor invoke an e-mail program when clicked.

   The Jefferson Employees table contains information about the employees at Jefferson Country Inn, including an employee ID#, First Name, Last Name, Email, Address, and Hire Date information.

5. Switch to **Design view**.

6. In the **Email** row, click in the **Data Type** column, and then click the **downward-pointing arrow** that displays. See Figure 4.2.

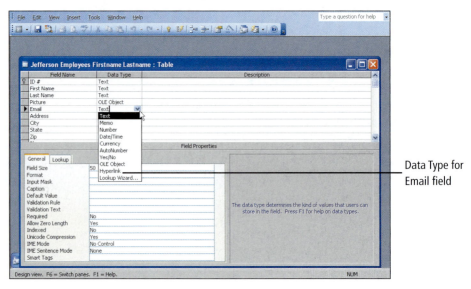

Data Type for Email field

Figure 4.2

7 From the displayed list of data types, click **Hyperlink**.

A Hyperlink field stores a hyperlink address. Selecting the Hyperlink data type will convert the data in the field to a Web hyperlink provided the data is in a recognizable hyperlink format. This Email field contains data entered in a format suitable for hyperlinks, for example, rdoggett@jeffinn.com.

8 Switch to **Datasheet view** and save the table when prompted. Examine the data in the Email column and notice that the data displays as hyperlinked Email addresses.

The text is a different color and underlined. Additionally, the Link Select pointer displays when the mouse pointer is paused over one of the Email addresses. See Figure 4.3. Restricting data with a Hyperlink data type reduces errors in the table by ensuring that items like Email addresses have the proper format.

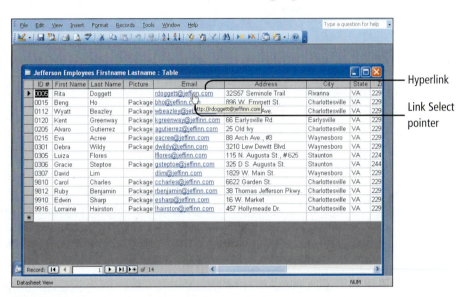

Figure 4.3

9 Switch to **Design view**. Under **Data Type**, scroll down as necessary, click in the **Hire Date** row, and then click the **downward-pointing arrow** that displays.

10 From the displayed list of data types, click **Date/Time**.

11 Switch to **Datasheet view**, save the table when prompted, and then examine the data in the **Hire Date** column.

Although the data in this column does not display differently than it did with the data type of *Text*, now there is a difference in the way the data will be interpreted when new data is entered.

12 In the first record—**Rita Doggett**—scroll as necessary to view the **Hire Date** field, delete the existing text, type **2222** and then press [Enter].

The error message shown in Figure 4.4 displays, indicating that the value entered is not valid for this field. Restricting data with the Date/Time data type reduces errors in the table by ensuring that only entries that are entered as a date format are accepted.

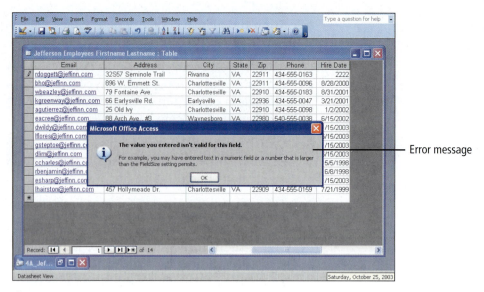

Figure 4.4

13 In the displayed message box, click **OK**, and then on the Table Datasheet toolbar, click the **Undo** button twice.

The original date of 6/15/2003 displays in the field.

14 Switch to **Design view**. Notice the Data Type for the **Picture** field is *OLE Object*.

OLE stands for Object Linking and Embedding. Linking and embedding are the two methods by which external items can be contained in an Access database. **Embedded** objects are placed into the database object. **Linked** objects have only a link in the database object to the address or location of the external item, such as a picture or Word document. Thus, linked objects do not reside directly in the database.

15 Switch to **Datasheet view** and save the table if necessary. In the **Picture** column for **Kent Greenway's** record, point to and then double-click **Package**. See Figure 4.5. Alternatively, right-click, point to Package Object, and then click Activate Contents.

A program such as Windows Picture and Fax Viewer opens and a photo of Kent Greenway, an employee at Jefferson Inn, displays. A data type of OLE is suitable for this field because it allows database users to view pictures of the employees at Jefferson Country Inn. Three employees do not yet have pictures in their records.

Double-click here.

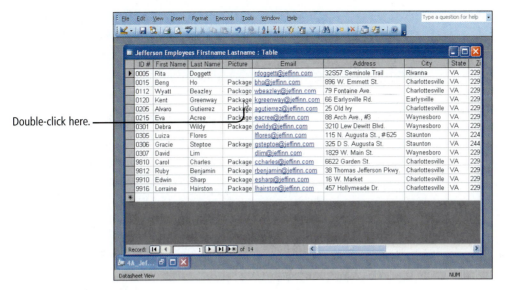

Figure 4.5

16 On the title bar of the window where the picture displays, click the **Close** button ⊠. In the first record, the one for **Rita Doggett**, click in the **Picture** field, and then right-click to display the shortcut menu.

17 On the displayed shortcut menu, click **Insert Object**.

The dialog box to insert an object displays. OLE objects can be sounds, graphics, movies, documents, spreadsheets, or other objects that can be created within a Windows-based application. From this dialog box, you can create a new object or insert an existing object, assuming you know the location of the object.

18 On the left side of the dialog box, click the **Create from File** option button. Under **File**, click the **Browse** button, and then navigate to the location where the student files that accompany this textbook are stored. Double-click the file **a04A_RitaDoggett**, and then in the displayed dialog box, click **OK**.

After a few seconds, *Package* displays in the Picture field for Rita Doggett.

19 In the **Picture** field for **Rita Doggett**, double-click the word **Package**.

A photo of this employee displays.

20 On the title bar of the window where the picture displays, click the **Close** button ⊠.

21 Using the techniques you have just practiced to insert an object into a field, insert the picture files for the two remaining employees who do not yet have their pictures in the table—**Luiza Flores** and **David Lim**.

Every record now has an associated picture file for each employee. Take a moment to study the table in Figure 4.6, which describes the data types available in Access.

Project 4A: Jefferson Inn Employees | **Access** 231

Data Types Supported by Access

Data Type	Description
Text	Text data including numbers that do not require calculations. Can be up to 255 characters in length.
Memo	Text data. Use for longer text fields; up to 65,536 characters.
Number	Numeric data that may be used in calculations.
Date/Time	Dates and/or times.
Currency	Currency or monetary values; dollar sign and two decimal places inserted by default.
AutoNumber	Numeric data in either sequential numbering in increments of 1 or random ID numbers.
Yes/No	True or False values.
OLE Object	OLE objects such as Word documents, Excel worksheets, and graphic files.
Hyperlink	Hyperlinks; either URLs or UNC paths.
Lookup Wizard	Not an actual data type, but listed under Data Types. Allows you to select a value for a field from another table or a list of values.

Figure 4.6

22 Switch to **Design view** for the next activity.

Activity 4.2 Changing a Field Size

In this activity, you will set a field size to restrict the size of the data that can be entered in a field.

1 In the upper portion of the table window, in the **Field Name** column, click anywhere in the **State** field. In the lower area of the screen, under **Field Properties**, notice that the field size is set to 255 characters, which is the default field size. See Figure 4.7.

The Field Properties area displays the properties—specifications—for a selected field.

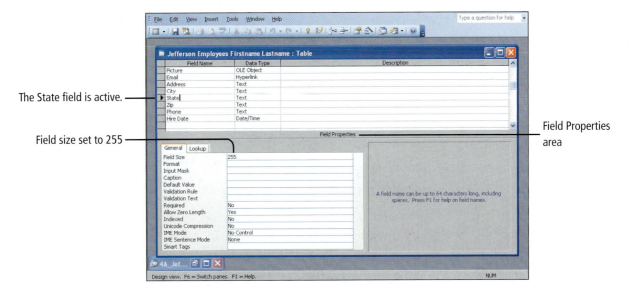

The State field is active.

Field size set to 255

Field Properties area

Figure 4.7

2 Under **Field Properties**, click in the **Field Size** box, select the existing text of **255**, and then type **2**

The Field Size property limits the number of characters that can be entered in a field and can be set for data types of Text, Number, and AutoNumber. The Field Size property can be set to any number between 0 and 255.

3 Switch to **Datasheet view** and save your changes.

Access displays a message as shown in Figure 4.8, indicating that some data may be lost because of the change in the field size.

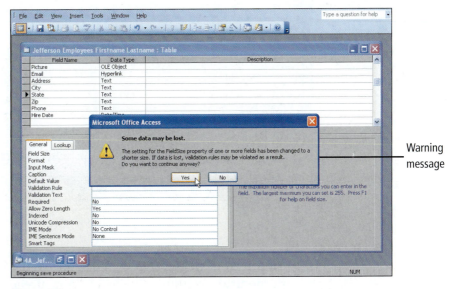

Warning message

Figure 4.8

Project 4A: Jefferson Inn Employees | **Access** 233

4 In the displayed warning message box, click **Yes**. In the record for **Wyatt Beazley**, under the **State** column, select the existing text, and then try to type **Virginia**

Access will not allow more than two characters in this field because of the limitations you set in the field properties. Specifying a field size prevents a user from entering some types of invalid data, such as an entry that is too long.

5 Enter **VA** for the **State** field for **Wyatt Beazley**.

Activity 4.3 Entering a Default Value

Most employees who work for Jefferson Country Inn live in Virginia. Specifying a default value for this field will save time in data entry.

1 Switch to **Design view**. In the upper portion of the Table window, click in the **State** field if necessary to make it the active field.

2 Under **Field Properties**, in the **Default Value** box, type **VA** See Figure 4.9.

Notice to the right that a description of this field property displays. Also, to the right of the Default Value box, a small button with three dots, called the **Build button**, displays. The Build button displays after you click in a field property box so you can further define the property. You will use the Build button in a field property in a later activity.

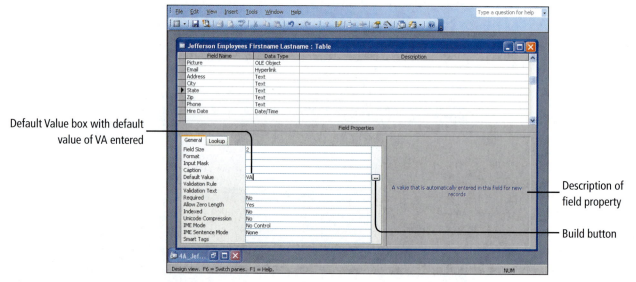

Figure 4.9

3 Switch to **Datasheet view** and save. Notice under the last record, in the **State** column, a value of VA is already entered, ready for the next record.

Specifying a default value for a field saves data entry time and also reduces the possibility of typographical errors.

4 Switch to **Design view**. Under **Field Properties**, notice that quotation marks surround *VA*.

Quotation marks indicate that the entry will be treated as a string. For further information on strings, see the discussion in Chapter 3 or refer to Access Help.

Objective 2
Specify a Field Format

Specifying a field format allows you to affect how data in a field will display. For example, the date 9-10-67 can be displayed as September 10, 1967, or 10-Sept-67, or 09-10-1967. Access allows you to choose the format to display data in a field.

Activity 4.4 Specifying a Field Format

In this activity, you will specify a date format for the Hire Date field that will affect how the date in this field displays.

1 In the upper portion of the Table window, click in the **Hire Date** field to make it the active field. Under **Field Properties**, click in the **Format** box, and then click the **downward-pointing arrow** that displays. See Figure 4.10.

A list of available formats for the Date/Time data type displays.

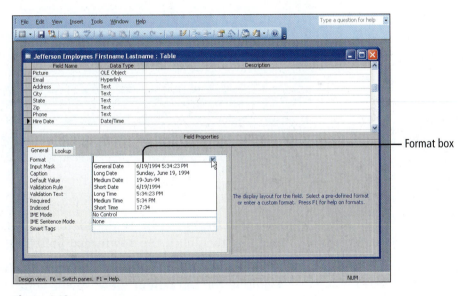

Figure 4.10

2 From the list of available formats, click **Long Date**.

The Property Update Options smart tag displays.

> **More Knowledge** — Smart Tags in Access
>
> *Smart tags added to Access!*
>
> Smart tags, first introduced in some applications in Office XP, provide a submenu of options in the context of a user's actions. In Microsoft Office 2003, smart tags have been extended to Access. The *Property Update Options* smart tag provides a means for users to update a formatting change to a property everywhere that field occurs.

3 Switch to the **Datasheet view**, saving your changes. If necessary, use the horizontal scroll bar to scroll to the right so you can view the **Hire Date** field, and then adjust the column width so the entire contents of the **Hire Date** field display.

4 Notice the additional information—day of the week, month spelled, year in four digits—that displays in the **Hire Date** field as a result of the specified Date format. See Figure 4.11.

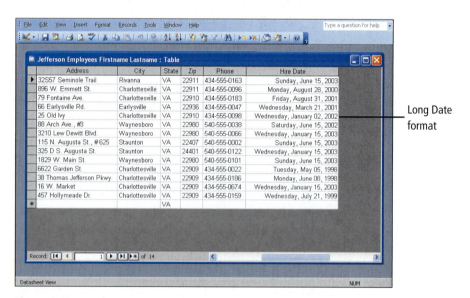

Figure 4.11

5 Switch to **Design view**. Under **Field Properties**, click in the **Format** box, and then click the **downward-pointing arrow**.

6 From the list of available formats, click **Medium Date**, and then switch to the **Datasheet view**, saving your changes.

7 If necessary, scroll to the right to view the **Hire Date** field and notice the display of the dates. See Figure 4.12.

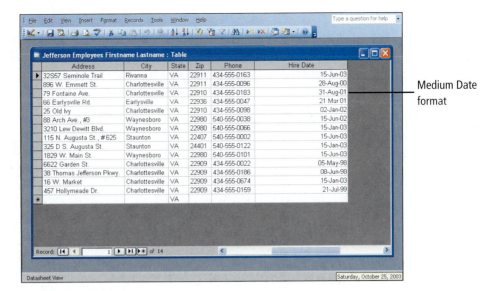

Medium Date format

Figure 4.12

8 Double-click the column border to the right of the **Hire Date** field to adjust the column width to accommodate the widest entry.

9 Using the technique you just practiced, switch to **Design view**, change the format of the **Hire Date** field to **Short Date**, and then leave your table open in **Design view** for the next activity.

Objective 3
Create Input Masks Using the Input Mask Wizard

An *input mask* is a field property that determines the data that can be entered, how the data displays, and how the data is stored. There are two methods of adding an input mask to your table—using the Input Mask Wizard or using the Input Mask properties box.

Activity 4.5 Creating Input Masks Using the Input Mask Wizard

Regardless of which method you use for creating an input mask, the wizard or the properties box, an input mask displays a template for the data that is being entered, and it will not permit the entry of data that does not fit the template. Because postal zip codes require at least five digits, in this activity, you will create an input mask for the zip field that will require the entry of at least five digits.

1 In the upper portion of the Table window, click in the **Zip** field to make it the active field. Under **Field Properties**, click in the **Input Mask** box, and then click the **Build** button that displays. See Figure 4.13. If prompted, save the table.

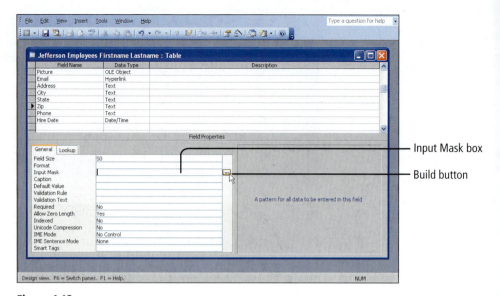

Figure 4.13

The Input Mask Wizard starts. The Input Mask Wizard allows you to create an input mask using one of several standard masks that Access has already built for you—such as Phone Number, Social Security Number, and Zip Code—for text and data fields.

2 In the first screen of the Input Mask Wizard, under **Input Mask**, click **Zip Code**, as shown in Figure 4.14. Click **Next**.

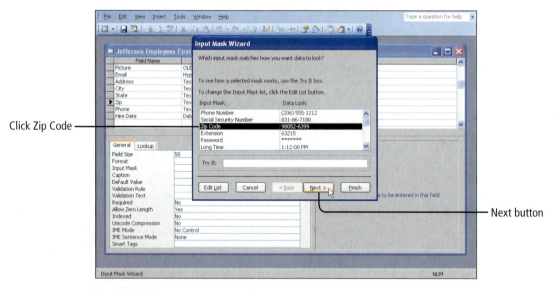

Figure 4.14

3 In the next screen of the wizard, notice the entry to the right of **Input Mask**.

A *0* indicates a required digit, and a *9* indicates an optional digit or space. The hyphen in between is a character that Access will insert in the specified place. See Figure 4.15. Most zip codes (postal codes) follow the format of five digits followed by a hyphen (-) and four optional digits.

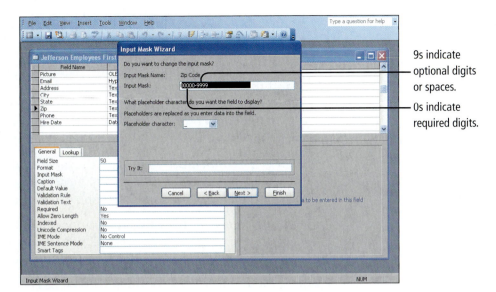

9s indicate optional digits or spaces.

0s indicate required digits.

Figure 4.15

4 Leave all the settings at their defaults and click **Next**.

5 The third screen of the wizard asks how you want to store the data. Be sure that the **Without the symbols in the mask, like this** option button is selected, as shown in Figure 4.16. Click **Next**.

This third screen allows you to specify whether you want to store the data with the symbols, which takes up more space in the database, or without the symbols to save some space.

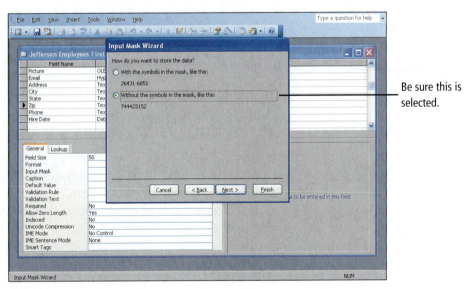

Be sure this is selected.

Figure 4.16

6 In the final screen of the wizard, click **Finish**.

The wizard closes and Access displays the mask in the **Input Mask** box. Notice the 0s indicating the required digits for the postal code and the 9s that represent optional digits or spaces. The semicolons that follow separate the mask into three sections. This mask, however, has data only in the first section, the one containing the 0s and 9s. The other two sections are optional and not needed at this time.

7 Switch to **Datasheet view**, save the table, and scroll to the right to view the **Zip** field. Widen the **Zip** field if necessary to see the contents of the field. Notice the hyphens that display to the right of the five digits.

8 In the record for **Rita Doggett**, under **Zip**, delete the existing text and try to type **aaaaa** Access will not allow a letter entry because the input mask you just created requires numbers only in this field.

9 In the **Zip** field for Rita Doggett, type **22911**

10 Switch to **Design view** for the next activity.

Objective 4
Create Input Masks Using the Input Mask Properties Box

In addition to using the wizard, input masks can also be created directly in the Input Mask box. The advantage in doing this is that you can customize the mask for a particular field.

Activity 4.6 Specifying Uppercase and Lowercase Text

In this activity, you will use the **Input Mask Properties** box to create a mask that will ensure that an entry begins with a capital letter and that the remaining text in the field displays in lowercase letters.

1 With your **Jefferson Employees** table displayed in **Design view**, click in the **First Name** field to make it the active field.

2 Under **Field Properties**, in the **Input Mask** box, type **>L<???????????????** (There are 15 question marks.) See Figure 4.17.

The greater than (>) sign converts any text following it to uppercase. The *L* indicates that a letter (not a number) is required (first names begin with a letter), the less than (<) sign converts any text following it to lowercase, and the question marks (?) indicate optional letters.

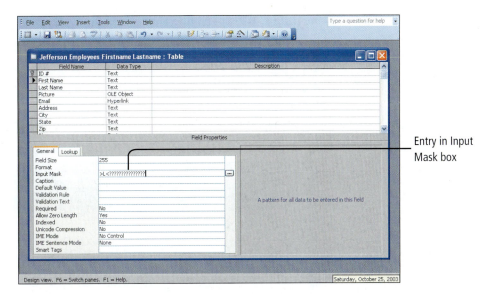

Figure 4.17

3. In the upper portion of the Table window, click in the **Last Name** field to make it the active field.

4. Under **Field Properties**, in the **Input Mask** box, type >L<??????????????? (There are 15 question marks.)

5. In the upper portion of the Table window, click in the **City** field to make it the active field.

6. Under **Field Properties**, in the **Input Mask** box, type >L<?????????????????? (There are 18 question marks to allow for longer city names.)

7. Switch to **Datasheet view** and save. Type the following information as the next record in the table being careful *not* to capitalize the first letter of the First Name, Last Name, and City fields, so that you can see how Access handles such errors. Because you set the **State** field to always display VA, you do not have to enter the state. There is no picture file available for this employee.

ID #	0405
First Name	shelby
Last Name	rincon
Picture	
Email	srincon@jeffinn.com
Address	63 W. Eden
City	rivanna
State	
Zip	22911
Phone	434-555-2736
Hire Date	5/6/1998

   As you typed in the data, Access capitalized the first letter in the First Name, Last Name, and City fields. Additionally, Access entered a value of VA in the State field from the default value you gave it in an earlier activity.

8. Switch to **Design view** for the next activity.

Activity 4.7 Specifying Numeric Input Masks

In this activity, you will create an input mask that will require four digits in the ID # field in the Employee table.

1 In the upper portion of the Table window, click in the **ID #** field to make it the active field. Under **Field Properties**, click in the **Input Mask** box, and then type **0000** See Figure 4.18.

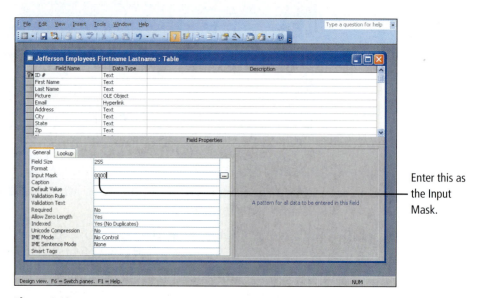

Enter this as the Input Mask.

Figure 4.18

> ### More Knowledge — Do I Use Input Masks or Field Formats?
>
> *Input masks affect how data looks and is stored.*
>
> The characters that are used in input masks are similar to the ones you used earlier in the chapter when you specified a field format. The difference between specifying a field format and creating an input mask is that input masks affect how data looks and how it is stored. Field formats affect only how the data looks.

2 Switch to **Datasheet view** and save the table when prompted. Under the last record, click at the beginning of the **ID #** field.

Notice that Access has inserted a template that is four spaces long.

3 In the **ID #** field for this new record, try to type **abcd**

Access will not allow this entry because the input mask requires four digits and will not allow letters.

4 In the **ID #** field type **9999** and then click the **row selector** for this record. See Figure 4.19.

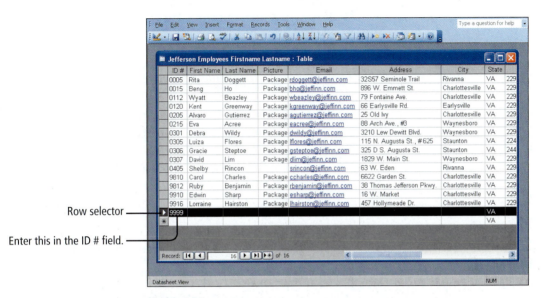

Figure 4.19

5 Press Delete to delete this record, and then click **Yes**.

Because the ID # is the primary key in this table and a primary key field cannot be blank, Access requires that you type in an entry before you can delete the record. Custom input masks can be created to match your field requirements using the characters shown in the table in Figure 4.20. Use this table as a reference.

Another Way — Removing a Record

Use the Escape key

You can use Esc to remove a record you are currently entering. Upon creating a new record, pressing Esc once will remove the entry in the current field. Pressing Esc two times will remove the entire record.

Most Common Input Mask Characters	
Character	Description
0	Required digit (0 through 9).
9	Optional digit or space.
#	Optional digit or space; blank positions are converted to spaces; plus and minus signs are allowed.
L	Required letter (A through Z).
?	Optional letter (A through Z).
A	Required letter or digit.
a	Optional letter or digit.
&	Required character (any kind) or a space.
C	Optional character (any kind) or a space.
<	All characters that follow are converted to lowercase.
>	All characters that follow are converted to uppercase.
!	Characters typed into the mask fill it from left to right. The exclamation point can be included anywhere in the input mask.
\	Character that follows is displayed as a literal character.
Password	Creates a password entry box where any character that is typed is stored as the character entered but displays as an *.

Figure 4.20

6 Switch to **Design view** for the next activity.

Objective 5
Specify a Required Field

Recall that if a table has a field designated as the primary key, an entry for this field is required; it cannot be left empty. You can set this requirement on other fields, and you may find it necessary to make an entry required for a field that is not the primary key. For example, in the following activity, you will specify that the employee name fields cannot be left empty for an employee at Jefferson Country Inn.

Activity 4.8 Specifying a Required Field

1 In the upper portion of the Table window, click in the **First Name** field to make it the active field. Under **Field Properties**, click in the **Required** box, and then click the **downward-pointing arrow** that displays. See Figure 4.21.

Only Yes and No appear in the list that displays.

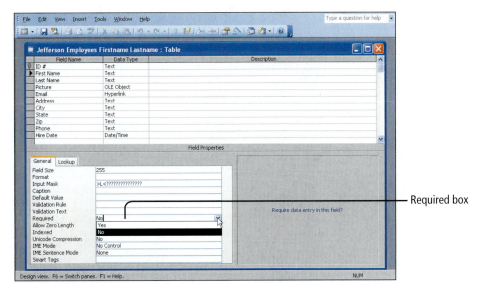

Figure 4.21

> **2** Click **Yes**.
>
> Clicking Yes in the Required box will require a user to enter a first name for each record.
>
> **3** In the upper portion of the Table window, click in the **Last Name** field to make it the active field. In the **Field Properties** section, click in the **Required** box, and then click the **downward-pointing arrow** that displays.
>
> **4** Click **Yes**.
>
> This action will require the person typing data into the database to enter a last name for each record.
>
> **5** Switch to **Datasheet view**, saving your changes when prompted. In the warning message that displays, click **Yes**. See Figure 4.22.
>
> Access displays a message warning you that data integrity rules have been changed and asks you if you want the existing data to be tested with the new rules.

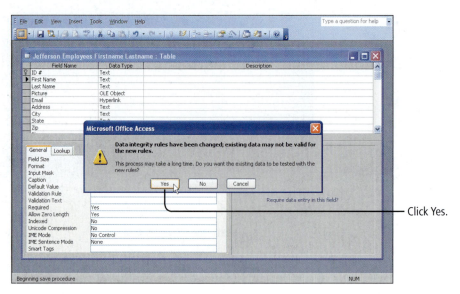

Figure 4.22

6 Switch to **Design view** for the next activity.

Objective 6
Validate Data Entry

You can further restrict data entry by adding a validation rule to a field in your table. A *validation rule* is an expression that precisely defines the information that will be accepted in a field. An *expression* is a combination of functions, field values, constants, and operators that brings about a result. In the following activity, you will create a validation rule to restrict entries in the Hire Date field of your table.

Activity 4.9 Using the Expression Builder to Create Validation Rules

1 In the upper portion of the Table window, click in the **Hire Date** field to make it the active field. Under **Field Properties**, click in the **Validation Rule** box, and then click the **Build** button that displays. See Figure 4.23.

The *Expression Builder* dialog box displays. The Expression Builder is a feature used to create formulas (expressions) in query criteria, form and report properties, and table validation rules.

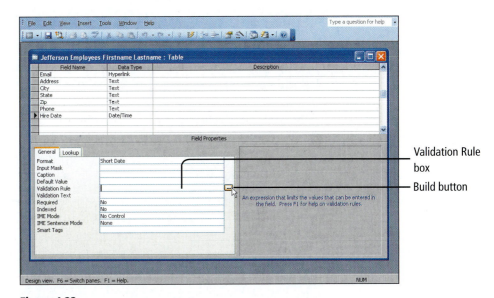

Figure 4.23

2 In the upper white area of the **Expression Builder** dialog box type **>=1/1/1998**

Jefferson Country Inn began operations on January 1, 1998; therefore, no hire dates should be prior to this one.

> **Another Way**
>
> **Using the Expression Builder**
>
> *Type expressions or use the existing toolbar buttons*
>
> When creating an expression in the Expression Builder, you can either type in the entire expression, or, on the small toolbar within the dialog box, click an existing button, such as the > button, to insert the characters you need in your expression.

3 In the **Expression Builder** dialog box, click **OK**, and then switch to **Datasheet view**, saving your changes. Click **Yes** in the warning message.

4 In the **Hire Date** field for **Luiza Flores**, change the year to **1997** and then press Tab.

A message displays that the value you entered violates a validation rule set for this field.

5 In the message box, click **OK**, change the year back to **2003** for **Luiza Flores**, and then press Tab.

Access allows this entry because the validation rule you set is not violated.

6 Switch to **Design view** for the next activity.

Activity 4.10 Creating Validation Text

Setting a validation rule will prevent the entry of data that may violate the rule; but, what if the person entering the data is unaware of the rule? For this reason, it is a good practice to add *validation text* that will display the correct format in the event someone attempts to enter invalid data. In this activity, you will add validation text to accompany the validation rule you created for the **Hire Date** field.

1 In the upper portion of the Table window, be sure the **Hire Date** field is the active field.

2 Under **Field Properties**, click in the **Validation Text** box, and then type **Year must be 1998 or later** as shown in Figure 4.24.

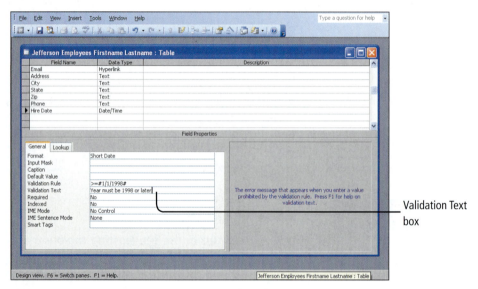

Figure 4.24

3 Switch to **Datasheet view** and save changes to the table. In the **Hire Date** field for **Rita Doggett**, change the year to **1997** and press Tab.

A message displays with the validation text you created for the Hire Date validation rule.

4 Click **OK**, and then click the **Undo** button two times.

5 From the **File** menu, click **Page Setup**. Click the **Margins** tab, and change the **Left** margin to **0.5** and change the **Right** margin to **0.5**. Click the **Page tab**, and under **Orientation**, click the **Landscape** button. Click **OK**.

6 Print the Jefferson Employees table. Close the table, save changes, close the database, and then close Access.

End You have completed Project 4A

Project 4B Jefferson Inn Guests

People sometimes spell things differently. To represent the state of Colorado, someone creating a mailing list might use *CO*, *Colo.*, or *Colorado*. These different spellings may not confuse the person who is looking at a printout of the mailing list because most people would understand that each of those three spellings indicates the state of Colorado. A computer, however, interprets data literally. For example, if you queried Access to create a mailing list of guests of Jefferson Country Inn from CO, it would not include those from Colo. or Colorado.

In Activities 4.11 through 4.15, you will create a Lookup Wizard field and practice skills that will assist you in finding data in the Guests table for Jefferson Country Inn. Additionally, you will apply conditional formatting to a field in the Guests table. Your completed table will look similar to Figure 4.25. You will save the database as *4B_Jefferson_Inn_Guests_Firstname_Lastname.*

Guests Firstname Lastname 10/26/2003

Visit Date	Nights	First Name	Last Name	# in Party	Address	City	State	Zip	Phone
6/15/2003	2	Brandon	Smith	2	2745 Sherwin Ave.	Washington	DC	20017	202-555-0110
5/25/2003	2	Catrina	Johnson	3	3532 Preble St.	Richmond	VA	23222	804-555-0178
5/23/2003	2	Bill	Kukielka	2	1357 Nathan Lane, #D	Charlottesville	VA	22907	434-555-0098
7/21/2003	3	Zachary	Juras	2	15 Aspen Blvd.	Denver	CO	80202	303-555-0122
6/18/2003	1	Elaine	Broderick	1	1611 Lakehurst	Chicago	IL	60611	312-555-0129
5/15/2003	2	Julio	Ferrer	4	892 Cactus Ave.	Scottsdale	AZ	85259	480-555-0199
5/15/2003	1	Kelvin	McNeely	3	5188 S. University St.	Simi Valley	CA	93065	805-555-0154
6/15/2003	1	Theodora	Lanham	2	1849 Burleson Ave.	Naples	FL	34102	239-555-0173
6/15/2003	1	Ethan	Stowe	2	288 S. Orange Grove Blvd. #23	Orlando	FL	32825	407-555-0192
7/21/2003	3	Javier	Nye	2	2 West California St.	Clovis	CA	93613	559-555-0148
5/1/2003	4	Sharon	Cousins	1	333 S. Washington Blvd. #1215	Washington	DC	20011	240-555-0126
5/2/2003	4	Neel	Singh	4	76 Chesapeake Way	Baltimore	MD	21224	410-555-0182
5/30/2003	2	Leane	Wang	3	2444 Cortez Way	Richmond	VA	23222	804-555-0002
6/1/2003	3	Sacha	Federov	4	3318 Allegheny Court	Charlotte	NC	28210	704-555-0107
6/10/2003	4	Sirvat	Torosian	2	7982 Paseo Margarita	Austin	TX	78710	512-555-0082
5/12/2003	1	Brandon	Smith	1	9315 Orchard Ave.	Albuquerque	NM	87110	505-555-2749

Page 1

Figure 4.25
Project 4B—Jefferson Inn Guests

Objective 7
Create a Lookup Wizard Field

Creating a Lookup field restricts the data entered in a field because the person entering the data must choose from a predefined list. A ***Lookup field*** allows you to create and then display a list of values from a field in another table.

Activity 4.11 Creating a Lookup Wizard Field

In this activity you will create a Lookup Wizard field for the State field in the Guests table at Jefferson Country Inn.

1 Locate the file **a04B_Jefferson_Inn_Guests** from your student files and copy and paste the file to your Chapter 4 folder. Remove the Read-only property from the file and rename the file as **4B_Jefferson_Inn_Guests_Firstname_Lastname** Start Access and open the database you just renamed.

2 On the Objects bar, click **Tables** if necessary, right-click the **Jefferson Guests** table, and then click **Rename**.

3 In the box that displays and using your own information, type **Guests Firstname Lastname** and then press [Enter].

4 Open your **Guests** table in **Datasheet view**. Examine the fields and records in the table and notice that the last four records do not have entries for the **State** field.

These entries could be typed, but to ensure consistent entries for items in the State field, a Lookup field will be more efficient.

5 Switch to **Design view**. In the upper portion of the Table window, in the **Data Type** column, click in the **State** field under **Data Type**, and then click the **downward-pointing arrow** that displays.

6 From the list of data types, click **Lookup Wizard**. See Figure 4.26.

The Lookup Wizard starts.

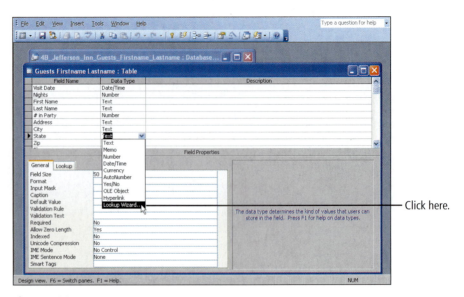

Figure 4.26

7 In the first screen of the wizard, be sure *I want the lookup column to look up the value in a table or query.* is selected.

The first screen of the Lookup Wizard allows you to choose whether you want Access to find the information from another table or whether you would like to type the information yourself.

8 Click **Next**. In the next screen of the wizard, under *Which table or query should provide the values for your lookup column?*, click **Table: States** as shown in Figure 4.27, and then click **Next**.

This database contains a table called States that includes the information you need for this field.

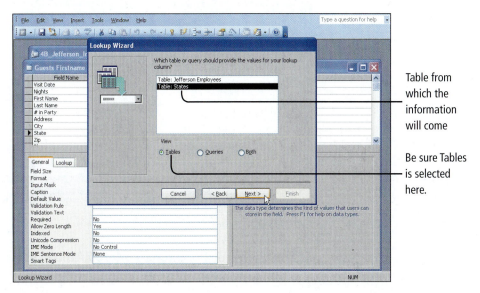

Figure 4.27

9 In the next screen, under **Available Fields**, click **Abbreviation**, and then click the **One Field** button to move the **Abbreviation** field under **Selected Fields**. Click **Next**.

10 In the **1** box, click the **downward-pointing arrow**, and then click **Abbreviation**. Leave the order as **Ascending**.

This screen allows you to choose a Sort order for the data in this field.

11 Click **Next**, and then at the next screen, click **Next** again.

12 Under *What label would you like for your lookup column?*, leave the default of **State**, and then click the **Finish** button.

13 Click **Yes** to save the table, and then switch to **Datasheet view**.

14 In the record for **Leane Wang**, under **State**, click once.

A downward-pointing arrow displays.

15 Click the **downward-pointing arrow**. From the list of states, scroll down, and then click **VA**, as shown in Figure 4.28.

VA displays in the State field for Leane Wang.

Another Way — **Locate Items in a List Quickly**

Type the first letter

You can find an entry in a long list faster if you type the first letter of what you are looking for. The selection will move down to the first entry that begins with that letter. For example, typing V will quickly locate the first entry in the list that begins with the letter V.

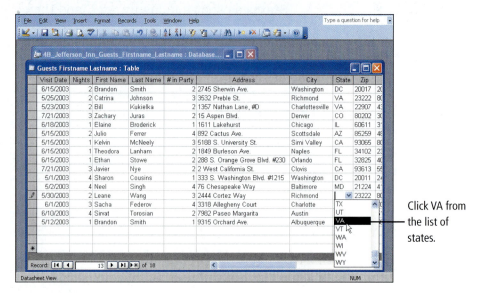

Figure 4.28

16 In the record of **Sacha Federov**, under **State**, click once, and then click the **downward-pointing arrow**.

17 From the list of states, click **NC**.

18 Repeat this technique to add **TX** as the state for **Sirvat Torosian** and **NM** as the state for **Brandon Smith**.

19 Stay in **Datasheet view** for the next activity.

Objective 8
Find a Record

Queries can locate information, but for a quick search to simply locate a record in a table, for example, the record of a specific guest, use the Find button on the Table Datasheet toolbar. Performing a search using this method is similar to using Find and Replace in other Microsoft Office applications.

Activity 4.12 Finding a Record by Searching a Single Field

In this activity you will use the Find button to locate a specific guest in the Guests table for Jefferson Country Inn.

1 In the **Datasheet view** of your **Guests** table, click anywhere in the **Last Name** column.

To search for a record using the Find button, you must first select the field where you want Access to look for your information.

2 On the Table Datasheet toolbar, click the **Find** button.
See Figure 4.29.

The Find and Replace dialog box displays.

Figure 4.29

3 In the **Find What** box, type **nye** and then click **Find Next**.

Access has located the record with *nye* as a last name as indicated by the highlighted last name and the row selector. See Figure 4.30.

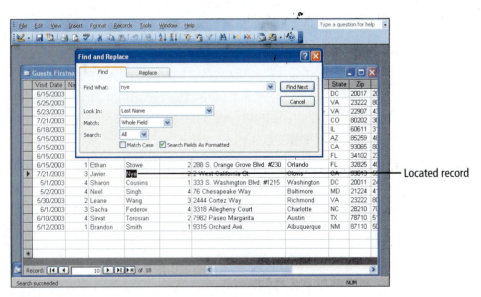

Figure 4.30

4 If necessary, move the **Find and Replace** dialog box out of your way by clicking and dragging its title bar up and to the right so you can view the record Access has located.

This method is particularly useful to quickly locate a record and view the information. For example, at the Jefferson Inn, employees might want to quickly find information such as a guest reservation.

5 In the **Find and Replace** dialog box, click **Cancel** to close the dialog box.

6 Leave your table open in **Datasheet view** for the next activity.

Activity 4.13 Finding a Record by Searching the Table

It is faster to search for a particular record by having Access search only one field, as you just practiced in the last activity. However, you can perform a search and have Access search all the fields in the table.

1 Click anywhere in the first record of the table, and then on the Table Datasheet toolbar, click the **Find** button.

The Find and Replace dialog box displays.

2 In the **Find What** box, type **Washington**

3 In the **Look In** box, click the **arrow**, and then from the displayed list, click **Guests Firstname Lastname: Table**.

Searching the entire table is useful if you do not know in what field the information is located.

4 In the **Match** box, click the **arrow**, and then from the displayed list, click **Any Part of Field**.

Clicking Any Part of Field directs Access to locate an instance of *Washington* even if it is not the entire entry in a field.

5 Click **Find Next**.

Access locates the record for Brandon Smith, who lives in the City of *Washington*.

6 Click **Find Next**.

Access locates the record for Sharon Cousins, who has *Washington* in her address.

7 Click **Find Next**.

Access highlights *Washington* in the City field for Sharon Cousins.

8 Click **Find Next**.

A message displays indicating that the searching of the records is finished. Access displays a message indicating that the item was not found. This means that after it found the three occurrences, it did not find any more.

9 Click **OK**, and then click **Cancel** in the **Find and Replace** dialog box.

10 Leave the table open in **Datasheet view** for the next activity.

Objective 9
Display Specific Records

Sorting records organizes a table in a logical manner; but viewing the entire table can be difficult. To locate and display only the records you would like to see, you can create a filter. You can apply a simple filter while viewing a table (or form). Creating a filter to quickly view desired information while hiding unwanted records is quicker than creating a query, but it does not allow you to specify criteria as precisely as a query does.

Activity 4.14 Displaying Specific Records Using Filter By Selection

In this activity, you will create a Filter By Selection to locate those records that have *VA* as the state. ***Filter By Selection*** allows you to locate records based on data in a field.

1 In the **Datasheet view** of your **Guests** table, in the **State** column, click in the record for **Catrina Johnson**. (For this example, you could click in any record where the state is VA.)

2 On the Table Datasheet toolbar, click the **Filter By Selection** button. See Figure 4.31.

Three records display; each has VA in the State field.

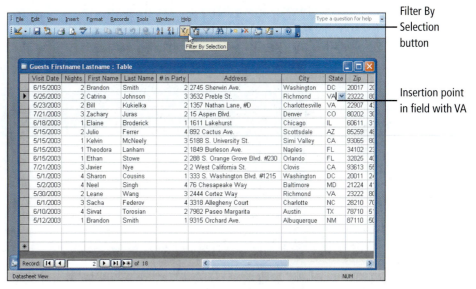

Figure 4.31

Note — Filter By Selection

Unmatched fields are not deleted.

When you filter a table, the records that do not match are not deleted from your table; they are only hidden from view.

3 On the Table Datasheet toolbar, click the **Remove Filter** button ▼. See Figure 4.32.

The filter is removed and all the records display.

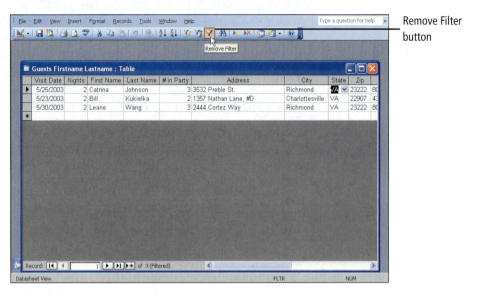

Figure 4.32

4 In the **Last Name** column, in the record for **Ethan Stowe**, select the **S** in *Stowe*. See Figure 4.33.

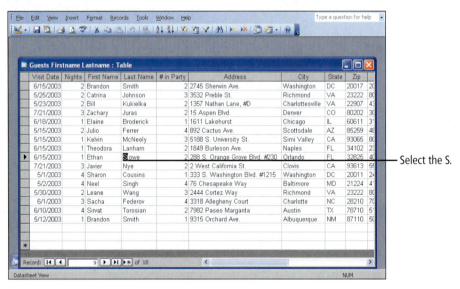

Figure 4.33

5 On the Table Datasheet toolbar, click the **Filter By Selection** button ▼.

Four records display; each has a last name beginning with S.

6 On the Table Datasheet toolbar, click the **Remove Filter** button.

The filter is removed and all the records display.

7 Leave your table open in **Datasheet view** for the next activity.

Activity 4.15 Displaying Specific Records Using Filter By Form

Suppose you are looking for information based on more than one field in a table. For example, you may need to find a guest at Jefferson Inn whose name, you think, begins with a K and you think he or she is from Virginia. For a search such as this, you could not use Filter By Selection; instead you would use **Filter By Form**. This is a technique for filtering data that uses a version of the current form or datasheet with empty fields in which you can type the values that you want the filtered records to contain.

1 On the Table Datasheet toolbar, click **Filter By Form**.
See Figure 4.34.

Filter By Form button

Figure 4.34

2 In the **Last Name** column, delete any existing text and then type **k***

The asterisk (*) is a wildcard that serves as a placeholder for any number of characters.

3 Click in the **State** column, click the **arrow** that displays, scroll down to the bottom of the list, and then click **VA**. See Figure 4.35.

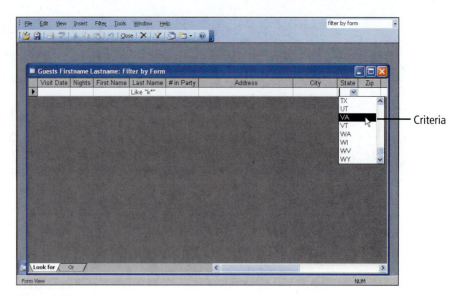

Figure 4.35

[4] On the Table Datasheet toolbar, click the **Apply Filter** button .

The record for Bill Kukielka in VA displays.

[5] On the Table Datasheet toolbar, click the **Remove Filter** button .

[6] From the **File** menu, click **Page Setup**. Click the **Margins tab**, and then change the **Left** and **Right** margins to **0.5**. Be sure the **Print Headings** check box is selected. Click the **Page tab**, and under **Orientation**, click the **Landscape** option button. Click **OK**. On the Standard toolbar, click the **Print** button .

[7] Close the table, click **Yes** if prompted to save any changes, close the database, and then close Access.

End You have completed Project 4B

Project 4C Jefferson Inn Library

Pages, the fifth object on the Objects bar, enables you to view information contained in a database from the Internet or a company intranet. An ***intranet*** is a privately owned Web-based network used by companies and organizations to share information by using Web technology, but without publishing their private information on the public Internet. Access pages are viewed by users through a ***browser***—a program such as Microsoft Internet Explorer—that enables you to view Web pages.

In Activities 4.16 through 4.18, you will create a data access page for Jefferson Country Inn so guests can view listings of books, videos, and DVDs that are available for them to check out from the Inn's library. Your data access page will look like Figure 4.36. You will save the database as *4C_Jefferson_Inn_Library_Firstname_Lastname*. Additionally, in Activity 4.19, you will convert a database containing older records for the Inn from a previous version of Access to the current version.

Figure 4.36
Project 4C—Jefferson Inn Library

Objective 10
Create and Use a Data Access Page

Activity 4.16 Creating a Data Access Page

In this activity you will create a data access page so that guests of the Jefferson Country Inn can view a list of library items that are available to check out from the Jefferson Inn's library.

1. Locate the file **a04C_Jefferson_Inn_Library** from your student files and copy and paste the file to the Chapter 4 folder you created. Remove the Read-only property from the file and rename the file as **4C_Jefferson_Inn_Library_Firstname_Lastname** Start Access and open the database you just renamed.

2. Open the **Jefferson Library** table in **Datasheet view** and examine the records in the table.

   The table contains a list of items such as books, CDs, DVDs, and videos that guests of Jefferson Country Inn can check out from the Inn's library.

3. **Close** the table.

4. On the Objects bar, click **Pages**.

   Three command icons for creating or editing data access pages display.

5. In the Database window, double-click **Create data access page by using wizard**.

   The Page Wizard begins and is similar to other wizards you have used in Access to create a new object.

6. Under **Tables/Queries** verify that **Table: Jefferson Library** displays. This is the table that contains the information to display in the data access page.

7. To the right of the list of available fields, click the **All Fields** button [>>]. See Figure 4.37.

   All of the fields from the Jefferson Library table will be used in the corresponding data access page.

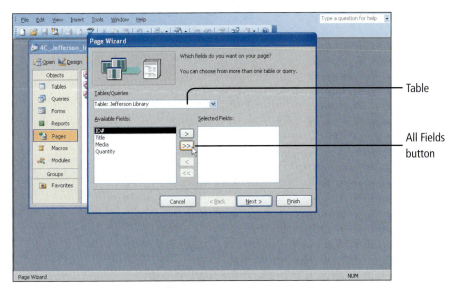

Figure 4.37

8 Click **Next**. Under **Do you want to add any grouping levels?**, accept the default ID# and click **Next** again.

9 On the page regarding sort order, click **Next**.

10 Under **What title do you want for your page?**, and using your own information, type the title as shown in Figure 4.38.

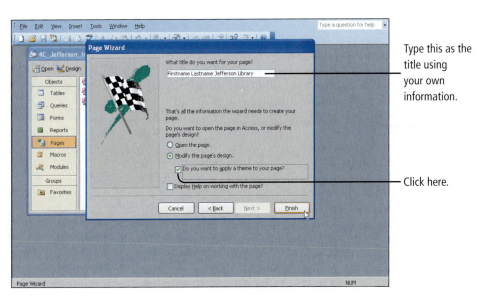

Figure 4.38

11 In the same screen where you added the title, select (click to place a check mark in) the *Do you want to apply a theme to your page?* check box, and then click **Finish**. See Figure 4.38.

The page is created and the Theme dialog box displays.

12 Under **Choose a Theme**, click **Iris**, and then click **OK**.

The data access page displays in Design view with the theme you selected. This view of a data access page is similar to the Design view of a form or report.

Project 4C: Jefferson Inn Library | **Access** 261

13 Maximize the data access page. If necessary, close the Field List task pane and the Toolbox toolbar.

14 At the top of the page, click anywhere in the area *Click here and type title text*. Then, using your own information, type **Firstname Lastname Library Page** as the name of the page.

The page title displays across the top of the page. See Figure 4.39.

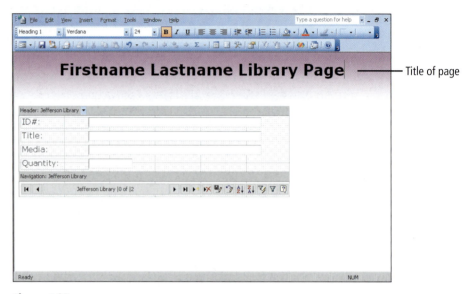

Figure 4.39

15 To the right of the *Type a question for help* box, locate the small **Close Window** button ⊠ and click it to close the data access page. Click **Yes** to save changes to the design of *data access page 'Page1'*.

The Save As Data Access Page dialog box displays.

16 In the **Save As Data Access Page** dialog box, verify that the location where the page will be saved is your Chapter 4 folder and the file name is as shown in Figure 4.40, with your own information.

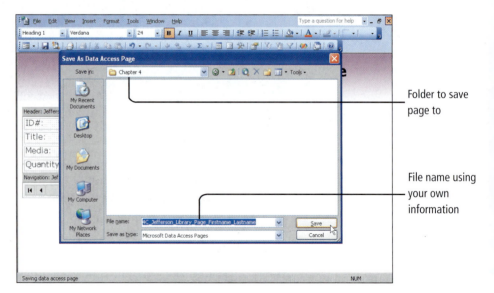

Figure 4.40

17 Click **Save**, and then click **OK** in the message that displays.

You are not using a UNC path for this page; therefore, it is OK to click OK. A shortcut to your data access page displays in the Database window, indicated by the small icon with a curved arrow.

18 Click the **Restore Window** button to restore the Database window to its original size.

19 Leave the database open for the next activity.

Activity 4.17 Viewing the Data Access Page with a Browser

Data access pages can be viewed directly in Access or in browser software.

1 On the Objects bar, be sure that **Pages** is selected. In the Database window, double-click the **shortcut** to your **Jefferson Library Page**. See Figure 4.41.

The page opens in Page view. Data access pages are not contained in the database itself. Rather, a shortcut to the page displays in the Database window and the actual page is stored in another location as specified when the page was created.

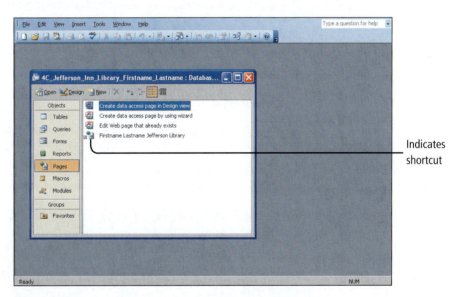

Figure 4.41

2 On the Page View toolbar, click the **Design View** button.

The page displays in Design view. Use Design view to make changes to the layout of the page.

3 On the Page Design toolbar, click the **Page View** button.

The page redisplays in Page view. Page view is useful to see how the page will display in the browser without actually connecting to the Internet or the organization's intranet. You can think of this as a Web page preview.

4 In the lower portion of the data access page, locate the **Navigation bar**, as shown in Figure 4.42.

The navigation buttons in a data access page function in the same manner as the navigation buttons in a table or form.

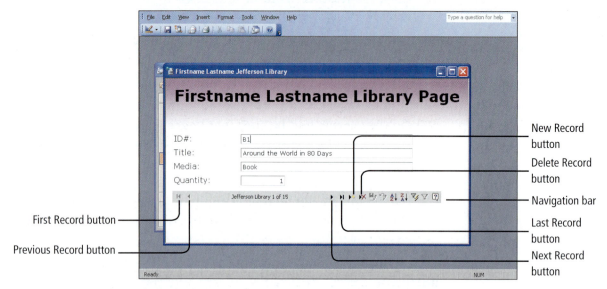

Figure 4.42

5 Practice clicking the various navigation buttons and view the records that display.

6 On the Page View toolbar, click the **View button arrow**, and then from the list of views, click **Web Page Preview**. See Figure 4.43.

The page opens in the default browser.

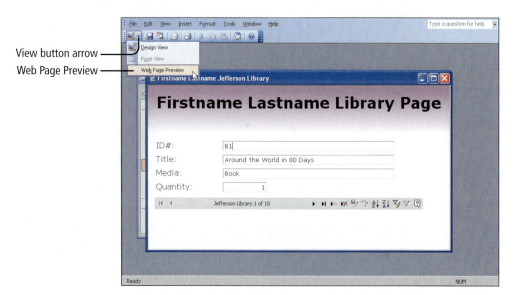

Figure 4.43

7 Examine the page and notice that it looks like it did in Page view.

The page will function in Web Page Preview as it did in Page view.

8 If necessary, click to position the insertion point in the **ID#** field.

On the Navigation bar, click the **Sort Ascending** button.

The records are sorted alphabetically by ID#; the first record displays.

9 On the Navigation bar, click the **Sort Descending** button.

The records are sorted in reverse alphabetical order; the last record displays.

10 Use the navigation buttons to navigate to the record titled *Big Band Jazz*, and then click in the **Media** field so the insertion point is blinking in the field.

11 On the **Navigation bar**, click the **Filter by Selection** button.

Five records are filtered and each has a Media of CD, as shown on the Navigation bar. See Figure 4.44.

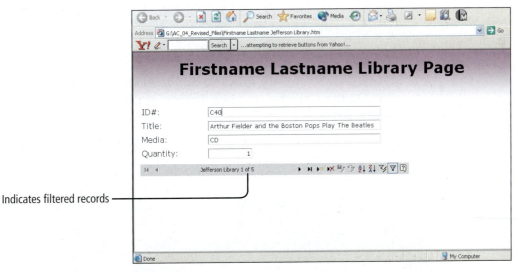

Indicates filtered records

Figure 4.44

12 Click the **Next Record** button to view the next CD in the table.

You can see that the Filter by Selection feature is useful to display only specific records.

13 On the **Navigation bar**, click the **Filter Toggle Button** located to the right of the Filter by Selection button.

The filter is removed and the Navigation bar indicates 15 records.

14 Leave the data access page open in Web Page Preview for the next activity.

Activity 4.18 Using a Data Access Page

1 On the **Navigation bar**, click the **New** button.

Data access pages can be used to add records to the data in a table.

2 Complete the information in the fields, as shown in Figure 4.45.

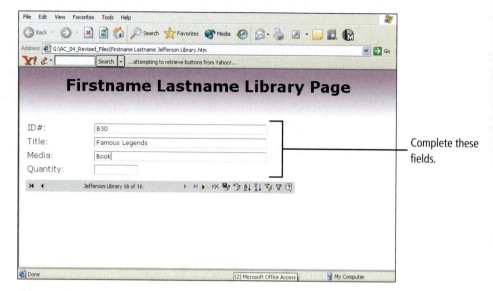

Figure 4.45

3. After you have filled in the information, on the **Navigation bar**, click the **Save** button.

   The record is saved as part of the table.

4. **Close** the Web Page Preview, and then **close** the data access page. On the Objects bar, click **Tables**, and then open the **Jefferson Library** table.

   The record you entered in the data access page displays in the table. See Figure 4.46.

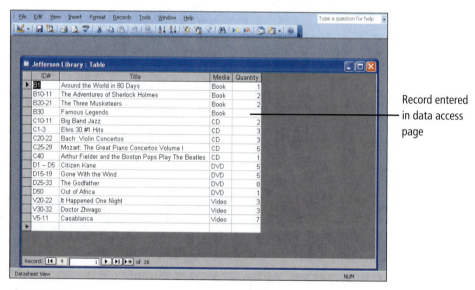

Figure 4.46

5 **Close** ✕ the table.

6 On the Objects bar, click **Pages**, open the **Jefferson Library** data access page, and then print it.

7 Close the page, close the database, and then close Access.

Objective 11
Convert a Database from a Previous Version of Access

As you work with Access, occasionally you will likely need to convert a database created in a prior version of Access to the current version. Perhaps the company you work for created all of its databases in Access 97 (or Access 2000) and now they would like to use the information in those databases in Microsoft Access 2003. To achieve full functionality of the latest version of Access, those older databases will need to be converted to the new version.

Activity 4.19 Converting a Database from a Previous Version of Access

1 Locate the file **a04C_Jefferson_Suppliers1999** from your student files and copy and paste the file to the Chapter 4 folder you created. Remove the Read-only property from the file.

2 Start Access and open this database.

You will see the message in Figure 4.47 indicating that this database was created in an earlier version of Access and you will not be able to make changes to it.

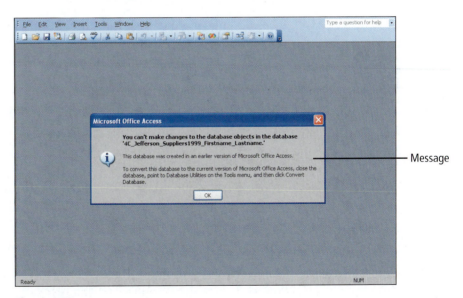

Figure 4.47

3 Click **OK**.

The database opens.

4 Drag the right edge of the Database window to view the full name in the title bar. Notice that it indicates that this database is in Access 97 file format. See Figure 4.48.

Project 4C: Jefferson Inn Library | **Access** 267

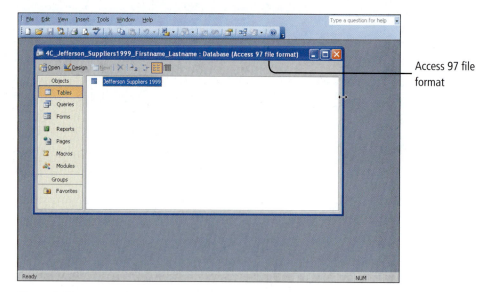

Figure 4.48

5 From the **Tools** menu, point to **Database Utilities**, point to **Convert Database**, and then click **To Access 2002 – 2003 File Format**.

The Convert Database Into dialog box displays.

6 Click the **Save in arrow**, and then navigate to the Chapter 4 folder where you are saving your projects for this chapter.

7 In the **File name** box, select the existing text and, using your own information, type **4C_Jefferson_Converted_Suppliers_Firstname_ Lastname** and then click **Save**.

Access displays a message that after you have converted the database, you can no longer share information with Access 2000 users or Access 97 users.

8 Click **OK**.

The old database remains open in the Database window.

9 Close the **a04C_Jefferson_Suppliers1999** database.

Access remains open.

10 On the Database toolbar, click the **Open** button and, if necessary, navigate to the location where you just saved the converted database (your Chapter 4 folder).

11 Double-click your **4C_Jefferson_Converted_Suppliers** file.

12 The converted database opens. Drag the right edge of the database window to see the full name in the title bar.

Notice in the title bar of the database window that the Access 2002-2003 File Format displays.

13 Close the database, and then close Access.

End You have completed Project 4C

Summary

Using Microsoft Access 2003 you can set several properties that enable you to limit the data that users can enter into a database. In this chapter you practiced customizing fields by using several data types, such as Hyperlink and OLE. Additionally, you practiced specifying formats such as date formats. You created an input mask to control data entry and added a validation rule that allows a user to enter only data that meets certain criteria. You constructed a lookup field that allows the user to select data from another table.

In this chapter you also practiced locating specific data directly from a table by using several tools. You used the Find button to search either one field or the entire table for a particular entry. The Filter By Selection and Filter By Form methods are useful for locating records in a table.

Data access pages are a new database object you created in this chapter that allow you to view information contained in a table from either the Internet or a company intranet using a browser. You created a data access page, observed the page in Design view, Page view, and Web Page Preview. You practiced using the data access page to add a new record to its corresponding table.

Finally, you practiced converting a database created in an earlier version of Access to the current version of Access.

In This Chapter You Practiced How To

- Customize a Field
- Specify a Field Format
- Create Input Masks Using the Input Mask Wizard
- Create Input Masks Using the Input Mask Properties Box
- Specify a Required Field
- Validate Data Entry
- Create a Lookup Wizard Field
- Find a Record
- Display Specific Records
- Create and Use a Data Access Page
- Convert a Database from a Previous Version of Access

Concepts Assessments

Matching Match each term in the second column with its correct definition in the first column by writing the letter of the term on the blank line in front of the correct definition.

____ 1. The feature that allows you to locate records based on data in more than one field.

____ 2. The field property that determines the data that can be entered, how the data displays, and how the data is stored.

____ 3. A feature that allows you to display a list of values from a field in another table in order to restrict data entry.

____ 4. The data type that allows you to insert graphics, spreadsheets, and other objects in a table.

____ 5. The text that displays if a user attempts to enter data in a field that violates a validation rule.

____ 6. A program such as Internet Explorer that enables you to view Web pages.

____ 7. A feature of Access that is used to create formulas in query criteria, form and report properties, and table validation rules.

____ 8. Allows you to locate records based on data in one field.

____ 9. When working with OLE fields, these objects are actually placed into the database object.

____ 10. A privately owned network that uses Web technology to share information within an organization.

____ 11. When working with OLE fields, these objects are not contained in the database; only their address or location is contained in the database.

____ 12. Expression that defines the information that will be accepted in a field.

____ 13. The database object that allows users to manipulate data in a database via the Internet.

____ 14. A combination of functions, field values, constants, and operators that brings about a result.

____ 15. The field setting that determines the content and appearance of that field.

A Browser
B Embedded
C Expression
D Expression Builder
E Filter By Form
F Filter By Selection
G Input Mask
H Intranet
I Linked
J Lookup field
K OLE
L Pages
M Property
N Validation rule
O Validation text

Concepts Assessments (continued)

Fill in the Blank Write the correct answer in the space provided.

1. One method of keeping a database organized and useful is to _____, or limit, the data that can be entered in the database.

2. The data type that allows the entry of additional text, up to 65,536 characters, is _____.

3. The data type that permits the entry of a URL is _____.

4. If a field will have the same entry most of the time, you can assign a _____ to the field to save data entry time and ensure consistency.

5. In an input mask, the _____ sign causes the letters that follow to be capitalized.

6. The lower portion of the table window is called the _____.

7. After a filter has been applied to a table, in order to view all the records in the table, you must _____ the filter.

8. The view of a data access page that displays the page in a browser is the _____.

9. To gain full functionality of an older database, you must _____ the database to the most current version of Access.

10. Commands for Database Utilities, which contain the option to convert a database, are located on the _____ menu.

Skill Assessments

Project 4D—Guests1

Objectives: *Customize a Field, Specify a Field Format, and Create Input Masks Using the Input Mask Wizard.*

In the following Skill Assessment, you will customize fields in the database and create an input mask for a field using the wizard. This database is used by the Jefferson Country Inn to store information about the guests that stay at the Inn. Your completed table will look like the one shown in Figure 4.49. You will rename and save the database as *4D_Guests1_Firstname_Lastname*.

Jefferson Guests Firstname Lastname 10/26/2003

Visit Date	Nights	First Name	Last Name	# in Party	Address	City	State	Zip	Phone
6/15/2003	2	Brandon	Smith	2	2745 Sherwin Ave.	Washington	DC	20017	202-555-0110
5/25/2003	2	Catrina	Johnson	3	3532 Preble St.	Richmond	VA	23222	804-555-0178
5/23/2003	2	Bill	Kukielka	2	1357 Nathan Lane, #D	Charlottesville	VA	22907	434-555-0098
7/21/2003	3	Zachary	Juras	2	15 Aspen Blvd.	Denver	CO	80202	303-555-0122
6/18/2003	1	Elaine	Broderick	1	1611 Lakehurst	Chicago	IL	60611	312-555-0129
5/15/2003	2	Julio	Ferrer	4	892 Cactus Ave.	Scottsdale	AZ	85259	480-555-0199
5/15/2003	1	Kelvin	McNeely	3	5188 S. University St.	Simi valley	CA	93065	805-555-0154
6/15/2003	1	Theodora	Lanham	2	1849 Burleson Ave.	Naples	FL	34102	239-555-0173
6/15/2003	1	Ethan	Stowe	2	288 S. Orange Grove Blvd. #23	Orlando	FL	32825	407-555-0192
7/21/2003	3	Javier	Nye	2	2 West California St.	Clovis	CA	93613	559-555-0148
5/1/2003	4	Sharon	Cousins	1	333 S. Washington Blvd. #1215	Washington	DC	20011	240-555-0126
5/2/2003	4	Neel	Singh	4	76 Chesapeake Way	Baltimore	MD	21224	410-555-0182
5/30/2003	2	Leane	Wang	3	2444 Cortez Way	Richmond	VA	23222	804-555-0002
6/1/2003	3	Sacha	Federov	4	3318 Allegheny Court	Charlotte	NC	28210	704-555-0107
6/10/2003	4	Sirvat	Torosian	2	7982 Paseo Margarita	Austin	TX	78710	512-555-0082
5/12/2003	1	Brandon	Smith	1	9315 Orchard Ave.	Albuquerque	NM	87110	505-555-2749
9/6/2003	2	Devon	Albrey	2	306 Skyward	Sedona	AZ	86339	(928) 555-444

Page 1

Figure 4.49

1. Locate the file **a04D_Guests1** from your student files and copy and paste the file to the Chapter 4 folder where you are storing your projects for this chapter. Remove the Read-only property from the file and rename the file as **4D_Guests1_Firstname_Lastname** Start Access and open the database you just renamed.
2. On the Objects bar, click **Tables** if necessary, right-click the **Jefferson Guests** table, and then click **Rename**.
3. In the box that displays and using your own information, type **Jefferson Guests Firstname Lastname** and then press Enter.
4. Open your **Jefferson Guests** table in **Datasheet view** and examine the data in the table. Switch to **Design view**. In the upper portion of the Table window, click in the **# in Party** field to make it the active field.

(Project 4D–Guests1 continues on the next page)

Skill Assessments (continued)

(Project 4D–Guests1 continued)

5. Under **Field Properties**, in the **Default Value** box, type **2**

6. Switch to **Datasheet view** and save the table. Notice under the last record, in the **# in Party** column, a value of 2 is already entered, ready for the next record. Specifying a default value for a field saves data entry time and also reduces the possibility of typographical errors.

7. Switch to **Design view** and click in the **City** field to make it the active field. Under **Field Properties**, in the **Input Mask** box, type **>L<????????????????????** (There are 20 question marks.) The greater than (>) sign forces the following text to display in uppercase. The L requires a letter entry (first names begin with a letter), the less than (<) sign forces the following text to display in lowercase, and the question mark (?) allows either a letter or no letter to be entered.

8. Click in the **Visit Date** field to make it the active field. Under **Field Properties**, click in the **Format** box, click the **arrow**, and from the list of date formats, click **Short Date**.

9. Switch to **Datasheet view** and save the table. Click in the first column of the last row of the table. Type the following information as the next record in the table paying careful attention not to capitalize the first letter of the **City** field. Notice that you do not have to type in an entry for the **# in Party** field. Note: Do not enter a phone number for this record. You will do that in a later step.

Visit Date	9/6/2003
Nights	2
First Name	Devon
Last Name	Albrey
# in Party	2
Address	306 Skyward
City	sedona
State	AZ
Zip	86339
Phone	

   As you typed in the data, Access capitalized the first letter in the City field. Additionally, Access entered a value of 2 in the # in Party field from the default value you defined.

10. Switch to **Design view** and in the upper portion of the Table window, click in the **Phone** field to make it the active field. Under **Field Properties**, click in the **Input Mask** box, and then click the **Build** button that displays.

11. In the first screen of the Input Mask Wizard, click **Phone Number**, if necessary, and then click **Next**.

(Project 4D–Guests1 continues on the next page)

Skill Assessments (continued)

(Project 4D–Guests1 continued)

12. Leave all the default settings and click **Next**.

13. On the third screen of the wizard that asks you how you want to store the data, be sure *Without the symbols in the mask, like this* is selected, and then click **Next**.

14. In the final screen of the wizard click **Finish**. Access creates an input mask for a typical phone number.

15. Switch to **Datasheet view**, save, and if necessary, scroll to the right to view the **Phone** field. In the last record, click in the **Phone** field and notice the parentheses and hyphen that display.

16. Click in the **Zip** field for this record, press [Tab], and then type **9285554444** as the phone number. Press [Tab], and then scroll to the right to view the entry. Now that you have defined the field as a phone number, Access inserts the parentheses and hyphens commonly used as the format for a phone number. You did not have to type them.

17. From the **File** menu, click **Page Setup**. Click the **Page tab**, and then under **Orientation**, click the **Landscape** option button. Click **OK**, and then click **Print** to print the Guests table. Close the database and then close Access.

End You have completed Project 4D

Project 4E—Guests2

Objectives: *Specify a Required Field, Validate Data Entry, and Create a Lookup Wizard Field.*

In the following Skill Assessment, you will add a required field and create validation rules and text for fields in the Guests table for Jefferson Country Inn. Additionally, you will add a Lookup field to the table. The table will look similar to the one shown in Figure 4.50. You will save your database as *4E_Guests2_Firstname_Lastname*.

1. Locate the file **a04E_Guests2** from your student files and copy and paste the file to the Chapter 4 folder where you are storing your projects for this chapter. Remove the Read-only property from the file and rename the file as **4E_Guests2_Firstname_Lastname** Start Access and open the database you just renamed.

2. On the Objects bar, click **Tables** if necessary, right-click the **Jefferson Guests** table, and then click **Rename**.

3. In the box that displays and using your own information, type **Guests2 Firstname Lastname** and then press .

(Project 4E–Guests2 continues on the next page)

274 Access | Chapter 4: Customizing Tables, Data Access Pages, and Converting a Database

Skill Assessments (continued)

(Project 4E–Guests2 continued)

Guests2 Firstname Lastname 10/26/2003

Visit Date	Nights	First Name	Last Name	# in Party	Address	City	State	Zip	Phone
6/15/2003	2	Brandon	Smith	2	2745 Sherwin Ave.	Washington	DC	20017	202-555-0110
5/25/2003	2	Catrina	Johnson	3	3532 Preble St.	Richmond	VA	23222	804-555-0178
5/23/2003	2	Bill	Kukielka	2	1357 Nathan Lane, #D	Charlottesville	VA	22907	434-555-0098
7/21/2003	3	Zachary	Juras	2	15 Aspen Blvd.	Denver	CO	80202	303-555-0122
6/18/2003	1	Elaine	Broderick	1	1611 Lakehurst	Chicago	IL	60611	312-555-0129
5/15/2003	2	Julio	Ferrer	4	892 Cactus Ave.	Scottsdale	AZ	85259	480-555-0199
5/15/2003	1	Kelvin	McNeely	3	5188 S. University St.	Simi Valley	CA	93065	805-555-0154
6/15/2003	1	Theodora	Lanham	2	1849 Burleson Ave.	Naples	FL	34102	239-555-0173
6/15/2003	1	Ethan	Stowe	2	288 S. Orange Grove Blvd. #23	Orlando	FL	32825	407-555-0192
7/21/2003	3	Javier	Nye	2	2 West Califomia St.	Clovis	CA	93613	559-555-0148
5/1/2003	4	Sharon	Cousins	1	333 S. Washington Blvd. #1215	Washington	DC	20011	240-555-0126
5/2/2003	7	Neel	Singh	4	76 Chesapeake Way	Baltimore	MD	21224	410-555-0182
5/30/2003	2	Leane	Wang	3	2444 Cortez Way	Richmond	VA	23222	804-555-0002
6/1/2003	3	Sacha	Federov	4	3318 Allegheny Court	Charlotte	NC	28210	704-555-0107
6/10/2003	4	Sirvat	Torosian	2	7982 Paseo Margarita	Austin	TX	78710	512-555-0082
5/12/2003	1	Brandon	Smith	1	9315 Orchard Ave.	Albuquerque	NM	87110	505-555-2749

Page 1

Figure 4.50

4. Open your **Guests2** table in **Datasheet view** and examine the data in the table.
5. Switch to **Design view**. In the upper portion of the Table window, click in the **Visit Date** field to make it the active field. Under **Field Properties**, click in the **Required** box, click the **arrow**, and then click **Yes**. Clicking Yes in the Required box will require the person entering the data to enter a visit date for each record.
6. In the upper portion of the Table window, click in the **Last Name** field to make it the active field. Under **Field Properties**, click in the **Required** box, click the **arrow**, and then click **Yes**.
7. In the upper portion of the Table window, click in the **# in Party** field to make it the active field. Under **Field Properties**, click in the **Validation Rule** box, and then click the **Build** button that displays.
8. In the upper white area of the Expression Builder, type **>0** The entry in the **# in Party** field should be greater than zero. In the **Expression Builder** dialog box, click **OK**.
9. Verify that the **# in Party** is still the active field and under **Field Properties**, in the **Validation Text** box, click, and then type **The number of people in the party must be greater than 0**

(Project 4E–Guests2 continues on the next page)

Skill Assessments (continued)

(Project 4E–Guests2 continued)

10. In the upper portion of the Table window, in the **Nights** field, click in the **Data Type** column, and then click the **arrow**. From the list of data types, click **Lookup Wizard**.

11. In the first screen of the wizard, be sure *I want the lookup column to look up the value in a table or query* option button is selected. The first screen of the Lookup Wizard allows you to choose whether you want Access to find the information from another table or whether you would like to type in the information yourself.

12. Click **Next**. In the next screen of the wizard, under **Which table or query should provide the values for your lookup column?**, verify that **Table: Nights** is selected, and then click **Next**.

13. In the next screen, under **Available Fields**, click **# of Nights** if necessary, and then click the **One Field** button to move the **# of Nights** field under **Selected Fields**. Click **Next**.

14. In the **1** box, click the **arrow**, and then click **# of Nights**. Leave the order as **Ascending**. Click **Next**, and then at the next screen, click **Next** again.

15. Under **What label would you like for your lookup column?**, accept the default of **Nights**, and then click the **Finish** button. Click **Yes** to save the table, and click **Yes** in any messages that display.

16. Switch to **Datasheet view** and save the table if prompted. In the **Visit Date** field for **Elaine Broderick**, delete the date, and then press [Tab]. A message displays that this field cannot be empty.

17. In the message box, click **OK**, change the date back to **6/18/2003** for **Elaine Broderick**, and then press [Tab].

18. Click in the **Nights** field for **Neel Singh**, and then click the **downward-pointing arrow** that displays. From the list that displays, click **7** to change the number of nights for this record.

19. Click in the **# in Party** field for **Zachary Juras**, delete the existing text, type **0** and then press [Tab]. A message displays indicating that the number in the party must be greater than 0.

20. Click **OK**, and then type **2** to change the **# in Party** back to its original entry.

21. From the **File** menu, click **Page Setup**. Click the **Page tab**, click **Landscape**, and then click **OK**. On the toolbar, click the **Print** button to print the Guests table. Close the table, close the database, and then close Access.

 End You have completed Project 4E

Skill Assessments (continued)

Project 4F — Employees

Objectives: *Find a Record, Display Specific Records, and Create and Use a Data Access Page.*

In the following Skill Assessment, you will practice finding specific records in the Employees table for Jefferson Country Inn. Additionally, you will create a data access page for the database and then convert a database created in an older version of Access to the current version. Your completed database objects will look similar to the ones shown in Figure 4.51. You will save the database as *4F_Employees_Firstname_Lastname* in the folder designated for this chapter.

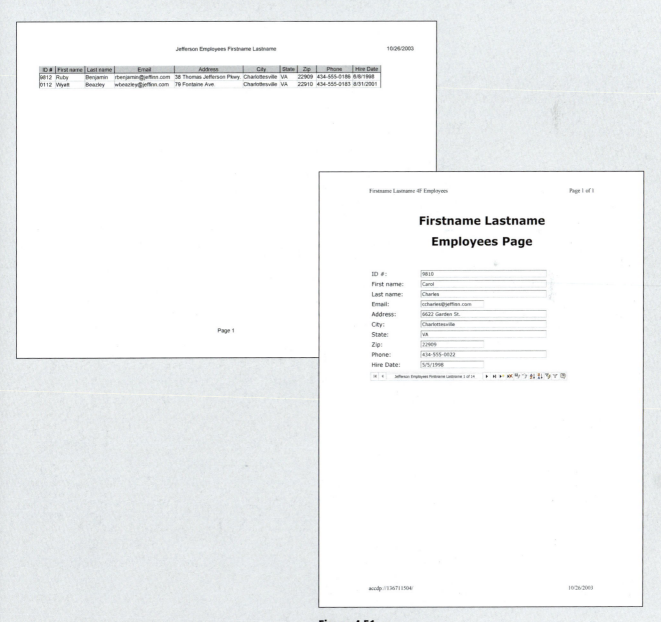

Figure 4.51

(**Project 4F**–Employees continues on the next page)

Skill Assessments (continued)

(Project 4F–Employees continued)

1. Locate the file **a04F_Employees** from your student files and copy and paste the file to the Chapter 4 folder where you are storing your assignments for this chapter. Remove the Read-only property from the file and rename the file as **4F_Employees_Firstname_Lastname** Start Access and open the database you just renamed.

2. On the Objects bar, click **Tables** if necessary, right-click the **Jefferson Employees** table, and then click **Rename**.

3. In the box that displays and using your own information, type **4F Employees Firstname Lastname** and then press Enter.

4. Open your **Employees** table in **Datasheet view** and examine the data in the table.

5. Click anywhere in the **City** column. To search for a record using the **Find** button, you must first select the field where you want Access to look for the information.

6. On the **Table Datasheet** toolbar, click the **Find** button. In the **Find What** box, type **Waynesboro** and then click **Find Next**. Move the dialog box as necessary, and notice that Access locates a record with Waynesboro as the City, as indicated by the highlighted City and the row selector.

7. In the **Find and Replace** dialog box, click **Find Next** (move the **Find and Replace** dialog box out of your way if necessary). Access locates another record with a City of Waynesboro.

8. In the **Find and Replace** dialog box, click **Find Next** two more times. Access displays a message that it has finished searching the records and the search item was not found. Click **OK**, and then in the **Find and Replace** dialog box, click **Cancel** to close the dialog box.

9. In the **Zip** column, click in the record for **Beng Ho**. On the Table Datasheet toolbar, click the **Filter By Selection** button. Three records display; each has a Zip of 22910, the same as the Zip for Beng Ho.

10. On the **Table Datasheet** toolbar, click the **Remove Filter** button.

11. In the **Last name** column, in the record for **Wyatt Beazley**, select the **B** in *Beazley*. On the Table Datasheet toolbar, click the **Filter By Selection** button. Two records display, each with a Last name beginning with the letter B.

12. From the **File** menu, display the **Page Setup** dialog box, click **Page**, click **Landscape**, and then click **OK**. On the **Table Datasheet** toolbar, click the **Print** button.

(Project 4F–Employees continues on the next page)

Skill Assessments (continued)

(Project 4F–Employees continued)

13. On the **Table Datasheet** toolbar, click the **Remove Filter** button. Close the table and save your changes.

14. On the Objects bar, click **Pages** and in the Database window, double-click **Create data access page by using wizard**.

15. Under **Tables/Queries** verify that *Table: 4F Employees Firstname Lastname* displays—this is the table that contains the information to display in the data access page. To the right of the list of available fields, click the **All Fields** button.

16. Click **Next** and in the following screen, under *Do you want to add any grouping levels?*, click **Next** again.

17. In the next screen click **Next**. Under **What title do you want for your page?**, and using your own information, type **4F_Employees_Page_Firstname Lastname** In this same screen, select *Do you want to apply a theme to your page?* check box, and then click **Finish**.

18. In the displayed **Theme** dialog box, under **Choose a Theme**, click **Axis**, and then click **OK**.

19. If necessary, close the task pane and any floating toolbars. Click anywhere in *Click here and type title text*, and using your own information, type **Firstname Lastname** and then press Enter. Then type **Employees Page** If necessary, select the text you just typed and format it as bold, 24 point, to match your name.

20. **Close** the data access page and click **Yes** to save changes to the design of *data access page 'Page1.'* In the **Save As** dialog box, verify that the location where the page will be saved is your Chapter 4 folder and the file name is *4F_Employees_Page_Firstname_Lastname*. Click **Save**, and then click **OK** in the message that displays. A shortcut to the data access page displays in the database window.

21. In the Database window, double-click the data access page you just created. On the Page View toolbar, click the **Print** button.

22. Close the page, close the database, and then close Access.

End You have completed Project 4F

Performance Assessments

Project 4G—Library1

Objectives: *Customize a Field, Specify a Field Format, Specify a Required Field, and Validate Data Entry.*

In the following Performance Assessment, you will customize the fields in the Library database for Jefferson Country Inn. The Inn uses the database to store information about library items that are available for guests to use. Your completed table will look like the one shown in Figure 4.52. You will save your database as *4G_Library1_Firstname_Lastname*.

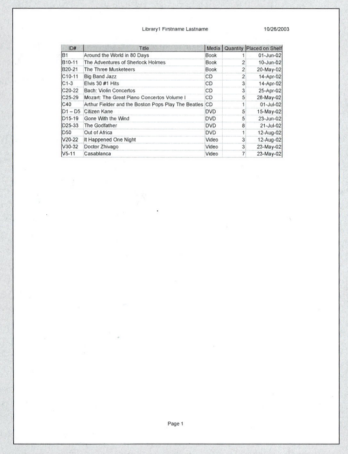

Figure 4.52

1. Locate the file **a04G_Library1** from your student files and copy and paste the file to the Chapter 4 folder where you are storing your assignments for this chapter. Remove the Read-only property from the file and rename the file as **4G_Library1_Firstname_Lastname** Start Access and open the database you just renamed.

2. On the Objects bar, click **Tables** if necessary, right-click the **Jefferson Library** table, and then rename the table as **Library1 Firstname Lastname**

(**Project 4G**–Library1 continues on the next page)

Performance Assessments (continued)

(Project 4G–Library1 continued)

3. Open your **Library1** table in **Datasheet view**, examine the data in the table, and then switch to **Design view**.

4. Click anywhere in the **Media** field. Under **Field Properties**, notice the default **Field Size** of **255**. Change the field size for the **Media** field to **7**.

5. Click in the **Placed on Shelf** field name to make it the active field, and then under **Field Properties**, in the **Format** box, change the format to **Medium Date**.

6. Click in the **Title** field to make it the active field, and then under **Field Properties**, in the **Required** box, click **Yes**.

7. Click in the **Placed on Shelf** field to make it the active field, and then under **Field Properties**, in the **Validation Rule** box, open the **Expression Builder**. Type **>4/1/02** Close the **Expression Builder** dialog box.

8. Verify that the **Placed on Shelf** field is still the active field and in the **Validation Text** box, type **The Date must be later than 4/1/02**

9. Switch to **Datasheet view**, save changes, and accept any warnings that display.

10. Print the **Library** table. Close the table. Close the database, and then close Access.

 End You have completed Project 4G

Project 4H—Library2

Objectives: *Create Input Masks Using the Input Mask Wizard, Create a Lookup Wizard Field, and Find a Record.*

In the following Performance Assessment, you will create an input mask and a lookup field for the Library database at Jefferson Country Inn. Additionally, you will locate specific records within the Library table. Your completed table will look similar to Figure 4.53. You will rename the database as *4H_Library2_Firstname_Lastname*.

1. Locate the file **a04H_Library2** from your student files and copy and paste the file to the Chapter 4 folder where you are storing your assignments for this chapter. Remove the Read-only property from the file and rename the file as **4H_Library2_Firstname_Lastname** Start Access and open the database you just renamed.

(Project 4H–Library2 continues on the next page)

Performance Assessments (continued)

(Project 4H–Library2 continued)

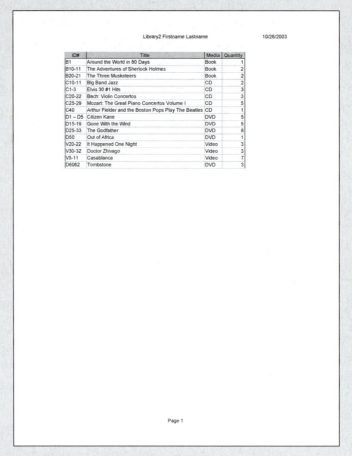

Figure 4.53

2. On the Objects bar, click **Tables** if necessary, right-click the **Jefferson Library** table, and then rename the table as **Library2 Firstname Lastname**

3. Open your **Library2** table in **Datasheet view**, examine the data in the table, and then switch to **Design view**.

4. Click in the **ID#** field to make it the active field, and then in the **Input Mask** box, type **L0aaaaa** (be sure to type a zero, not the uppercase O).

5. In the **Quantity** field under **Data Type**, change the data type to **Lookup Wizard**. Specify that you want to look up the values in a table or query.

6. In the next screen of the wizard, verify that **Table: Quantity** is selected, and then click **Next**. In the next screen, click **Number List** if necessary, and then move the **Number List** field under **Selected Fields**, and then click **Next**.

(Project 4H–Library2 continues on the next page)

Performance Assessments (continued)

(Project 4H–Library2 continued)

7. Specify that the **sort** order is by **Number List**, **Ascending**. Click **Next** two more times. Accept the default label, click the **Finish** button, and then save the table.

8. Switch to **Datasheet view**. Verify that the specifications that you created for this table have taken effect by adding the following record to the table:

ID#	Title	Media	Quantity
D6062	**Tombstone**	**DVD**	**3**

9. Click anywhere in the **Quantity** column. Click the **Find** button. In the **Find What** box, type **1** and then click **Find Next**. Access has located a record with a Quantity of 1. Click **Find Next** again. Access locates another record with a Quantity of 1. Continue this until Access notifies you that it has finished searching the records. Click **OK** and then close the **Find and Replace** dialog box.

10. Print the Library table. Close the table. Close the database, and then close Access.

End You have completed Project 4H

Project 4I—Recipes

Objectives: *Display Specific Records, Create and Use a Data Access Page, and Convert a Database from a Previous Version of Access.*

In the following Performance Assessment, you will practice filtering a table in the Recipes database for Jefferson Country Inn. In addition, you will create a data access page for the Recipes table. Finally, you will convert a database from an older version of Access to the current version. Your completed database objects will look similar to the ones shown in Figure 4.54. You will save your database as *4I_Recipes_Firstname_Lastname*.

1. Locate the file **a04I_Recipes** from your student files and copy and paste the file to the Chapter 4 folder where you are storing your assignments for this chapter. Remove the Read-only property from the file and rename the file as **4I_Recipes_Firstname_Lastname** Start Access and open the database you just renamed.

2. On the Objects bar, click **Tables** if necessary, right-click the **Jefferson Dishes** table, and then rename the table as **Jefferson Dishes Firstname Lastname**

3. Open your **Jefferson Dishes** table in **Datasheet view** and examine the data in the table.

(Project 4I–Recipes continues on the next page)

Performance Assessments (continued)

(Project 4I–Recipes continued)

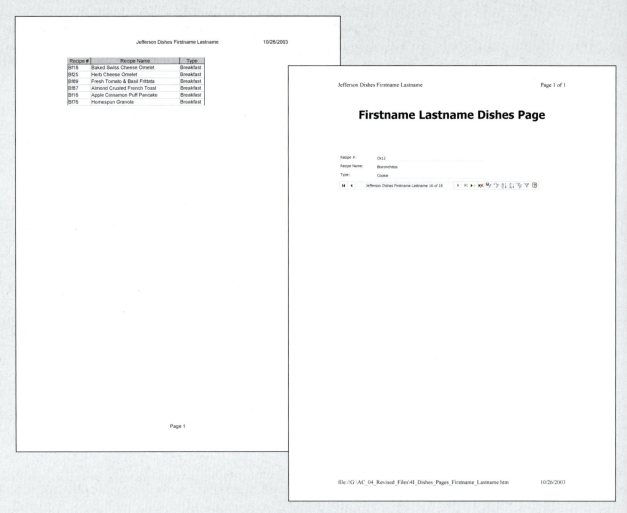

Figure 4.54

4. On the Table Datasheet toolbar, click **Filter By Form**. In the **Type** column, click the **downward-pointing arrow**, and then click **Breakfast**. On the Table Datasheet toolbar, click the **Apply Filter** button.

5. Print the filtered table. On the Table Datasheet toolbar, click the **Remove Filter** button. Close the table and save changes.

6. On the Objects bar, click **Pages**, and then create a data access page by using the wizard. Base the page on your **Jefferson Dishes** table, include all fields from the table, and then accept all remaining defaults in the wizard. In the page's **Design view**, add a title as follows: **Firstname Lastname Dishes Page**

(Project 4I–Recipes continues on the next page)

Performance Assessments (continued)

(Project 4I–Recipes continued)

7. Switch to the **Web Page Preview**, save your changes and name the file **4I_Dishes_Page_Firstname Lastname** and then add the following record by using the Web Page Preview:

Recipe #	Recipe Name	Type
Ck12	**Bisconchitos**	**Cookie**

8. Save the new record, and then with the new record displayed in the Web Page Preview, print the page.

9. Close the Web Page Preview, and then close any remaining windows in the database. Close the database, and then close Access.

10. Locate the file **a04I_Expenses2000** from your student files and copy and paste the file to the Chapter 4 folder you created. Remove the Read-only property from the file.

11. Start Access and open the database you just copied. From the **Tools** menu, point to **Database Utilities**, point to **Convert Database**, and then click **To Access 2002 – 2003 File Format**.

12. In the **Save in** box, navigate to the Chapter 4 folder where you are saving your projects for this chapter and in the **File name** box, select the existing text and type **4I_Converted_Expenses_Firstname_Lastname** and then click **Save**. Click **OK** in the warning message.

13. Close the database, and then close Access.

End **You have completed Project 4I**

Mastery Assessments

Project 4J—Inventory

Objectives: *Customize a Field, Specify a Field Format, Create Input Masks Using the Input Mask Wizard, Specify a Required Field, Validate Data Entry, Create a Lookup Wizard Field, and Find a Record.*

In the following Mastery Assessment, you will customize a table for the Jefferson Country Inn. Your completed table will look similar to the one shown in Figure 4.55. You will save your database as *4J_Inventory_Firstname_Lastname*.

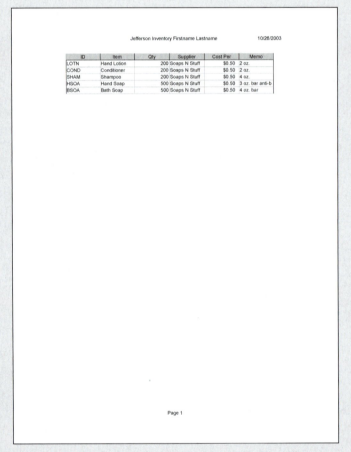

Figure 4.55

1. Locate the file **a04J_Inventory** from your student files and copy and paste the file to the Chapter 4 folder where you are storing your projects for this chapter. Remove the Read-only property from the file and rename the file as **4J_Inventory_Firstname_Lastname** Start Access and open the database you just renamed.

2. Rename the **Jefferson Inventory** table as **Jefferson Inventory Firstname Lastname**

(**Project 4J**–Inventory continues on the next page)

Mastery Assessments (continued)

(Project 4J–Inventory continued)

3. Open your **Jefferson Inventory** table in **Datasheet view**, examine the data in the table, and then switch to **Design view** and make the following changes to the table:

   Make the **Supplier** field required.

   Change the data type for the **Memo** field to **Memo**.

   Change the data type for the **Cost Per** field to **Currency**.

   Change the data type for the **Qty** field to **Number**.

   Add an input mask for the **ID** field that requires four capital letters (Hint: >LLLL)

   Create a validation rule for the **Qty** field to ensure that the quantity is greater than or equal to 0.

   Add validation text to support the validation rule you just created.

   Add a lookup field between the **Supplier** field and the **Supplier List** table.

4. Create a **Filter By Selection** to locate the records that have **Soaps N Stuff** as the **Supplier**. Print the filtered table, and then remove the filter.

5. Close the table. Close the database, and then close Access.

 You have completed Project 4J

Project 4K — Guests Web Page

Objectives: *Display Specific Records and Create and Use a Data Access Page.*

In the following Mastery Assessment, you will create a data access page for the Jefferson Country Inn. Your completed page will look similar to the one shown in Figure 4.56. You will rename the database as *4K_Guests_Web_Page_Firstname_Lastname.*

1. Locate the file **a04K_Guests_Web_Page** from your student files and copy and paste the file to the Chapter 4 folder where you are storing your projects for this chapter. Remove the Read-only property from the file and rename the file as **4K_Guests_Web_Page_Firstname_ Lastname** Start Access and open the database you just renamed.

2. Rename the **Jefferson Guests** table as **4K Jefferson Guests Firstname Lastname** and then open your **Jefferson Guests** table and examine the data in the table.

(Project 4K–Guests Web Page continues on the next page)

Mastery Assessments (continued)

(Project 4K–Guests Web Page continued)

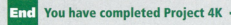

Figure 4.56

3. Close the table, and then create a data access page by using the wizard based on the information in your **Jefferson Guests** table. Include all of the fields from the table, and then accept all remaining defaults in the wizard until the last screen, and then apply the Papyrus theme to the page.

4. Add a title to the page, using your own information, that reads **Firstname Lastname Guests**

5. From the File menu, display the **Web Page Preview**, save the page as **4K_Guests_Firstname_Lastname** and then print the page.

6. Close the Web Page Preview, close the data access page, close the database, and then close Access.

End You have completed Project 4K

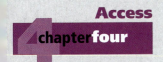

Problem Solving

Project 4L—Suppliers

Objectives: *Customize a Field, Specify a Field Format, Create Input Masks Using the Input Mask Wizard, Specify a Required Field, and Create a Lookup Wizard Field.*

1. Locate the file **a04L_Suppliers** from your student files and copy and paste the file to the Chapter 4 folder where you are storing your assignments for this chapter. Remove the Read-only property from the file and rename the file as **4L_Suppliers_Firstname_Lastname** Start Access and open the database you just renamed.

2. Rename the Suppliers table as **4L_Suppliers_Firstname Lastname**

3. Using the skills you have practiced in this chapter, customize the fields in the table where appropriate. You should change data types, add input masks, require fields, and create a lookup field for the **Name** field.

4. Make a list of the changes you have made to the table, and then print your table.

End You have completed Project 4L

Project 4M—Jefferson Meeting Rooms

Objective: *Create and Use a Data Access Page.*

The owners of Jefferson Country Inn would like a Web page that contains information about their guest rooms. Guest rooms at the Jefferson Inn are named after the flowers and trees that Thomas Jefferson grew in his gardens at Monticello. Copy the student file a04M_Guest_Rooms to your storage location, clear the Read-only property, rename it **4M_Guest_Rooms_Firstname_Lastname** and then open the database.

Create a data access page from the Jefferson Guest Rooms table in this database. Include a theme of your choice and an appropriate title for the Web page. Save all files to the folder where you are storing your projects for this chapter.

End You have completed Project 4M

On the Internet

How Do Databases and Web Applications Relate?

The power of the Internet combined with the strengths of database applications has changed the way businesses manage their information.

Go online and perform a search to identify the relationship between databases and Web applications.

GO! with Help

Viewing Information About Data Types

Working with data types is an important part of working with Access databases. In this exercise, you will view information about data types in Access.

1. Start Access. In the **Type a question for help** box, type **data types** then press Enter.

2. In the displayed **Search Results** task pane, click the result **Field data types available in Access (MDB)**. Maximize the displayed window, and at the top of the window, click **Show All**. Scroll through and read about data types in Access.

3. If you want, print a copy of the information by clicking the **Print** button at the top of the window.

4. Close the Microsoft Office Access Help window, and then close Access.

Access 2003

chapter five

Building and Maintaining a Relational Database

In this chapter, you will: complete these projects and practice these skills.

Project 5A
Building a Relational Database

Objectives
- Index Fields in a Table
- View Relationships in a Database
- Establish Relationships Between Tables
- Create a Query from Joined Tables

Project 5B
Maintaining a Relational Database

Objectives
- Identify and Correct Design Errors in Tables
- Protect and Maintain a Database

Southland Gardens

With gardening booming as a hobby, Southland Media, a TV production company headquartered in Irvine, California, saw a need for practical and entertaining information on the subject.

"Southland Gardens" was developed especially for the year-round gardeners in Southern California. The show features experts on vegetable and flower gardening, landscape design, projects for kids, and tours of historical and notable gardens. The company also offers a companion Web site where viewers can get more information about show segments, purchase supplies, and e-mail guests of the show.

Building and Maintaining a Relational Database

Access databases are relational databases—the tables in a database can relate, or connect, to other tables through common fields. Advantages of relational databases are a reduction in data redundancy and improved data accuracy. Access includes features to establish relationships between tables. Additionally, Access includes many features to help you maintain and protect your databases, such as checking for duplicate data and adding security features to a database.

Project 5A Southland Gardens

Access allows you to create relational databases where relationships can be established between tables that have related information. Relational databases reduce data redundancy and promote data accuracy and data integrity. Data redundancy occurs when the same data is stored in more than one location.

In Activities 5.1 through 5.8, you will create indexes and establish relationships for the tables in the database for Southland Gardens. Additionally, you will create a query from joined tables. Your relationships window will look similar to Figure 5.1. You will save your database as 5A_SouthlandGardens_Firstname_Lastname.

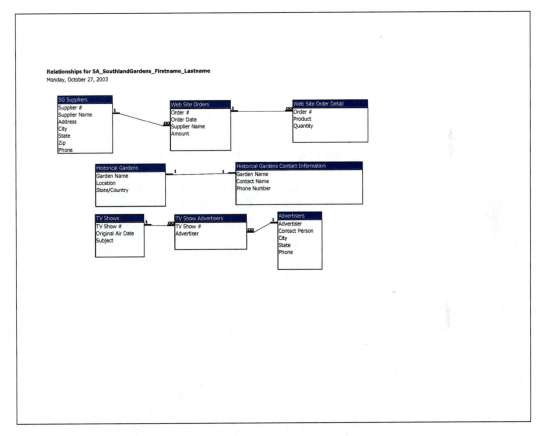

Figure 5.1
Project 5A—Southland Gardens

Objective 1
Index Fields in a Table

You have practiced setting primary keys and sorting fields in database objects. Adding a primary key to a field automatically creates an ***index*** for that field. An index is a special list that is created in Access to speed up searches and sorting—like the index at the back of a book. The index is visible only to Access, and not to you, but it helps Access find items much faster. Indexes can be added to fields that are not set as a primary key. Additionally, indexes can be created for multiple fields in a table.

Activity 5.1 Indexing Fields Without Duplicates

When you add an index to a field, you have the option of allowing duplicate values in that field or not allowing them. When a primary key is created, the field is always indexed without duplicates because primary keys, by their definition, cannot contain duplicate values. You can, however, add an index without duplicates to a field that is not the primary key. In this activity you will add an index to a field that will not allow duplicates.

1. Using the skills you practiced earlier, create a new folder named **Chapter 5** in the location where you will be storing your projects for this chapter. Locate the file **a05A_SouthlandGardens** from your student files and copy and paste the file to the Chapter 5 folder you created. Remove the Read-only property from the file and rename the file as **5A_SouthlandGardens_Firstname_Lastname** Start Access and open the database you just renamed.

2. Open the **TV Shows** table in **Datasheet view** and examine the data in the table.

3. Switch to **Design view** and click once in the **Original Air Date** field to make it the active field.

4. Under **Field Properties**, click once in the **Indexed** box, and then click the **downward-pointing arrow** that displays. See Figure 5.2.

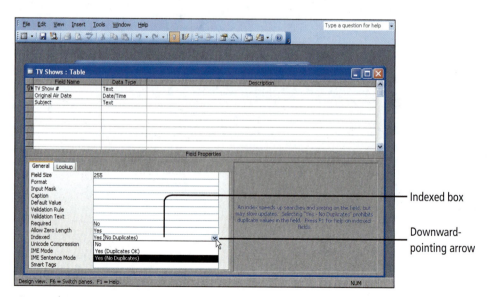

Figure 5.2

5 From the displayed list, click **Yes (No Duplicates)**.

By adding an index without duplicates to the Original Air Date field, you are assured that Access will add an index to speed searching and sorting and not allow duplicate data in this field. Each TV show for Southland Gardens has only one original air date. Recall that in large Access tables, adding an index to one or more fields will speed your searches.

6 Close the **TV Shows** table and save changes when prompted.

Activity 5.2 Indexing Fields with Duplicates

You can also create an index for a field where duplicate data *is* appropriate. For example, you may want to create an index for a Last Name field to speed searching and sorting on this field. Such a field, of course, frequently contains duplicate last names. In this activity you will add an index to a field that will allow duplicates.

1 Open the **SG Employees** table and switch to **Design view**.

2 Click once in the **Last Name** field to make it the active field.

3 Under **Field Properties**, click once in the **Indexed** box, and then click the **downward-pointing arrow** that displays.

4 From the displayed list, click **Yes (Duplicates OK)**.

By adding an index to a field and allowing duplicates, you create faster searches and sorts on this field, while still allowing duplicate data.

5 Close the **SG Employees** table and save changes when prompted.

Another Way

Displaying Indexes

Display the Indexes Dialog Box

Display the Indexes dialog box by clicking the Indexes button while in Design view. A list of indexes for the table will display.

Objective 2
View Relationships in a Database

A database created using Microsoft Access 2003 is a **relational database**, which is a database that can contain multiple tables that are related (or connected) to each other by common fields. Typically, data about an item is stored only once in a relational database thus reducing or eliminating redundant data. Relational databases store data about different topics in different tables and allow you to connect the data together in a meaningful way. **Flat file databases** store different types of information in one table and usually contain data about one particular item in multiple places. This creates redundant information and increases the likelihood of data entry errors.

Activity 5.3 Viewing Relationships in a Database

The connection between two fields in separate tables within a relational database is called a **relationship**. Relationships between tables allow you to bring related information together. For example, Southland Gardens sells various garden tools on their companion Web site. Thus, the database for Southland Gardens includes a Web Site Orders table that lists the Order #, Order Date, Supplier, and the Amount of the Order. There is also a Web Site Order Detail table that lists the individual items in each order. The Order # field exists in both tables, thus relating the two tables to each other.

1 Open the **Web Site Orders** table in **Datasheet view**. Examine the data in the table.

2 At the left side of the table, notice the column containing **expand indicators** (plus signs) next to the Order # for each record. See Figure 5.3.

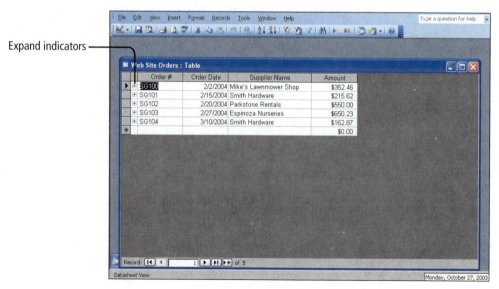

Expand indicators

Figure 5.3

3 In the row for Order # **SG100**, click the **expand indicator**. See Figure 5.3.

The expand indicator changes to the *collapse indicator* (a minus sign) and additional information about the order—the product description and the quantity ordered for each product—displays. See Figure 5.4. This information is gathered from the Web Site Order Detail table, because a relationship has been created between a field in the Web Site Orders table and a field in the Web Site Order Detail table.

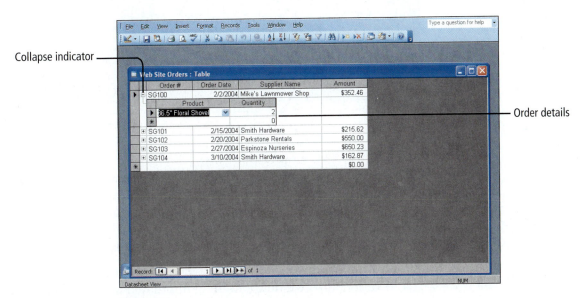

Figure 5.4

4 Click the **collapse indicator** (minus sign) for this record.

The details of the order are removed from view.

5 In the row for Order # **SG101**, click the **expand indicator**.

The order details for this order display indicating that three products—12' Hose, Border Rake, and Front Tine Rototiller—were included in this order.

6 Click the **collapse indicator** for this record.

7 Close the **Web Site Orders** table and open the **Web Site Order Detail** table in **Datasheet view**.

8 Examine the data in this table and notice the order information for the orders **SG100** and **SG101**. This information matches the information that displayed in the Web Site Orders table. Close the **Web Site Order Detail** table.

9 On the Database toolbar, click the **Relationships** button. See Figure 5.5.

The *Relationships window* displays. Here you can view, create, and modify relationships between tables and also between queries. Currently, four tables display in the Relationships window.

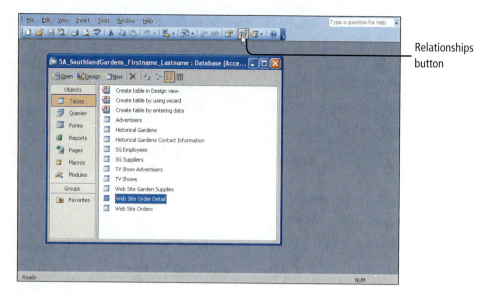

Figure 5.5

10 Position the pointer over the right edge of the **Web Site Order Detail** table, and then with the double arrow displayed, drag the right edge of the **Web Site Order Detail** table to the right until the entire title of the table is displayed. See Figure 5.6.

Use this technique to display the content of a table in the Relationships window. The sides and lower corners of a table in the Relationships window can be manipulated in a manner similar to that for any other window in the Windows operating system.

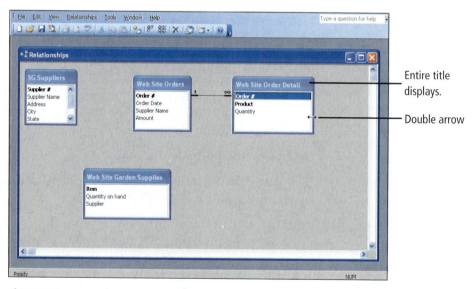

Figure 5.6

11 On the Relationship toolbar, click the **Show All Relationships** button .

Any existing relationships between tables are displayed. Currently there is one established relationship—the relationship between the Web Site Orders table and the Web Site Order Detail table. Because of this relationship, you were able to expand an order in the Web Site Orders table to see data contained within the Web Site Order Detail table. See Figure 5.7.

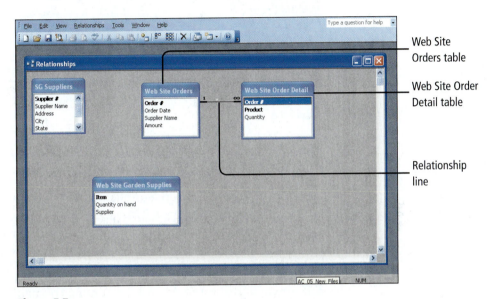

Figure 5.7

12 Locate the line connecting the two tables.

The line connecting the two tables is the **Relationship line**. There is a *1* next to the Web Site Orders table and an infinity (∞) sign next to the Web Site Order Detail table. This indicates a **one-to-many relationship** between these tables. One-to-many relationships occur when one record in the first table (the Web Site Orders table) corresponds to many records in the second table (the Web Site Order Detail table).

13 In the Relationships window, drag the title bar of the **Web Site Order Detail** table to the right about 0.5 of an inch. The exact distance need not be precise.

The line connecting the two tables stretches and moves. The tables that display in the Relationships window can be moved by dragging their title bars without breaking the line that indicates existing relationships.

14 In the Relationships window, locate the **Web Site Garden Supplies** table, and if necessary, move and expand the table so its list of fields is in full view. See Figure 5.8.

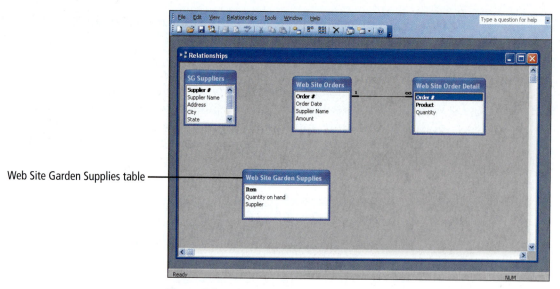

Figure 5.8

15 Point to any field in the **Web Site Garden Supplies** table and right-click. From the shortcut menu that displays, click **Hide Table**.

The Web Site Garden Supplies table is removed from view in the Relationships window. This action does not delete the table; it simply allows more space to view and create relationships among tables, and removes from view those tables whose relationships you are not concerned with at this time.

16 In each of the table windows, notice the fields that are in bold text. See Figure 5.9.

Bold text indicates the primary key for the table. Recall that the primary key in a table serves as a unique identifier for each record in a table.

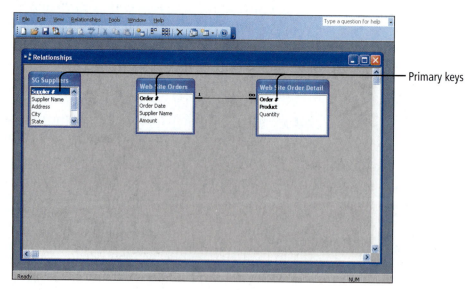

Figure 5.9

17 Keep the Relationships window open for the next activity.

Objective 3
Establish Relationships Between Tables

Relationships between tables allow you to relate the information in one table to the information in another table, as you saw between the Web Site Orders table and the Web Site Order Detail table. Three types of relationships are possible: one-to-many, one-to-one, and many-to-many. When two tables are related, or *linked*, a **foreign key** is created in the second table. A foreign key is the field in the second table that identifies the linked records. In the example of the Web Site Orders table and the Web Site Order Detail table, the Order # field is the primary key in the Web Site Orders table and the foreign key in the Web Site Order Detail table.

Activity 5.4 Establishing a One-to-Many Relationship and Enforcing Referential Integrity

In the previous activity, the relationship between the Web Site Orders table and the Web Site Order Detail table was a **one-to-many** relationship, which can be indicated as *1:∞*. This means that for each record in the Web Site Orders table, there can be many records in the Web Site Order Detail table—one order, many products in the order. However, for each record in the Web Site Order Detail table, there can be only one record in the Web Site Orders table—each product ordered is associated with only one order. One-to-many relationships are the most common type of relationship between two database tables. In this activity, you will establish a one-to-many relationship between the SG Suppliers table and the Web Site Orders table.

1 Be sure the Relationships window is open.

2 Locate the **SG Suppliers** table, point to the **Supplier Name** field in that table, and click so that it is highlighted. Drag the highlighted name to the **Web Site Orders** table, positioning your pointer directly over the **Supplier Name** field in the **Web Site Orders** table, and then release the mouse button. See Figure 5.10.

The Edit Relationships dialog box displays. See Figure 5.11.

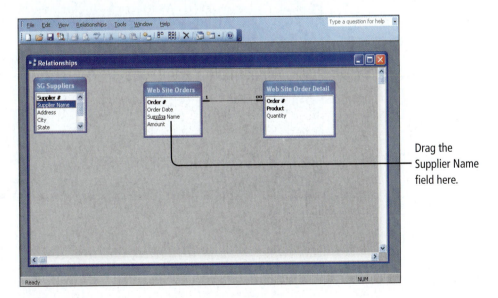

Drag the Supplier Name field here.

Figure 5.10

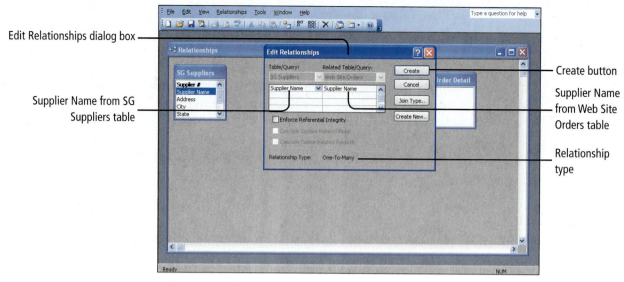

Figure 5.11

3 In the **Edit Relationships** dialog box, notice that *Supplier Name* is indicated in both columns—from both the **SG Suppliers** table and the **Web Site Orders** table. Refer to Figure 5.11.

4 At the bottom of the **Edit Relationships** dialog box, to the right of *Relationship Type*, notice that *One-To-Many* displays.

5 In the **Edit Relationships** dialog box, click **Create**. See Figure 5.11.

A relationship line is drawn between the Supplier Name fields in both the SG Suppliers table and the Web Site Orders table. See Figure 5.12.

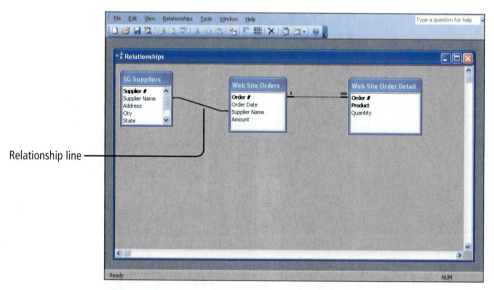

Figure 5.12

6 Examine the line and notice that there is no one-to-many indication as there is in the existing relationship between the Web Site Orders table and the Web Site Order Detail table.

7 Right-click on the **relationship line** that you just created, and from the displayed shortcut menu, click **Edit Relationship**.

The Edit Relationships window displays. Alternatively, you can double-click the Relationship line to display the Edit Relationships dialog box.

8 In the Edit Relationships window, select (click to place a check mark in) the **Enforce Referential Integrity** check box. See Figure 5.13.

Referential integrity is a set of rules that Access uses to ensure that the data between related fields is valid. Enforcing referential integrity between the two Supplier Name fields ensures that no supplier name can exist in the Web Site Orders table unless that supplier name is a valid supplier name in the SG Suppliers table.

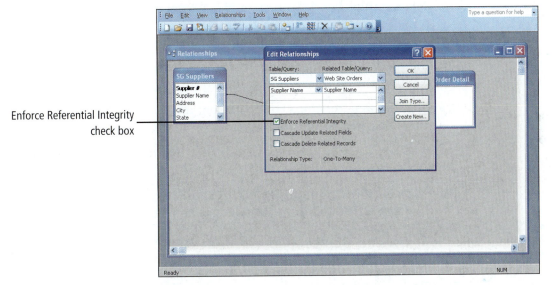

Enforce Referential Integrity check box

Figure 5.13

9 Click **OK**.

The relationship line now indicates a one-to-many relationship.

10 Right-click the **relationship line** between the **Supplier Name** fields again, and then click **Edit Relationship** to display the **Edit Relationships** dialog box.

11 In the lower portion of the **Edit Relationships** dialog box, select the **Cascade Update Related Fields** check box.

When the Cascade Update Related Fields check box is selected, any changes you make to the primary key in the first table—the SG Suppliers table—will automatically update the foreign key in the second table—the Web Site Orders table. For example, if a supplier changes the name of his or her company, changing the name in the SG Suppliers table will automatically change the supplier's name in the Web Site Orders table too.

Project 5A: Southland Gardens | **Access** 303

12 Select the **Cascade Delete Related Records** check box.

The result of this action will be that when a record with a primary key is deleted, the matching foreign key record(s) will be deleted in the related table. There can be more than one record deleted in the related table.

> **Note** — Cascade
>
> The word *cascade* refers to things arranged in a series so that action on one produces an action on the next.

13 In the upper right corner of the dialog box, click **OK**. Leave the Relationships window open for the next activity.

Activity 5.5 Printing the Relationships Window

Printing the Relationships window creates a report that displays the relationships for the database. You can save this report for future reference.

1 With the Relationships window open, display the **File** menu, and then click **Print Relationships**.

Access displays a report with a header *Relationships for* and the database name.

2 From the **File** menu, display the **Page Setup** dialog box, change the **Page Orientation** to **Landscape**, and then click **OK**. On the Print Preview toolbar, click the **Print** button.

The Relationships report prints.

3 **Close** the Relationships report and click **Yes** when prompted to save your changes to the report. Verify that the default name for the report is **Relationships for 5A SouthlandGardens Firstname Lastname** and click **OK** to save the report.

4 **Close** the Relationships window. In the Database window, on the Objects bar, click **Reports**, and then verify that the Relationships report you created is listed. Leave the database open for the next activity.

Activity 5.6 Establishing a One-to-One Relationship

One-to-one relationships require that for every record in one table, there can be only one matching record in the other table. This kind of relationship is much less common than one-to-many relationships.

1 On the Objects bar, click **Tables**, open the **Historical Gardens** table in **Datasheet view**, and then examine the data in the table.

Recall that the Southland Gardens TV show frequently features famous historical gardens.

2 **Close** ⊠ the **Historical Gardens** table, open the **Historical Gardens Contact Information** table in **Datasheet view**, and then examine the data in the table.

These two tables both contain the Garden Name field. This table contains the name and phone number of the person to contact regarding a particular historical garden.

3 **Close** ⊠ the **Historical Gardens Contact Information** table, and then on the Database toolbar, click the **Relationships** button.

4 In the gray area of the displayed Relationships window, right-click to display a shortcut menu. See Figure 5.14.

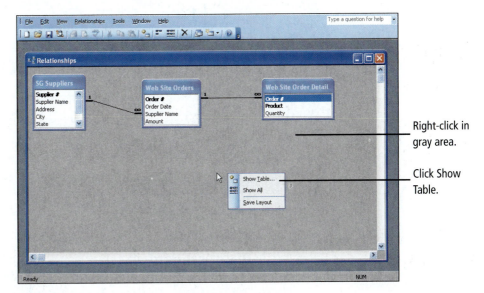

Right-click in gray area.

Click Show Table.

Figure 5.14

5 From the shortcut menu, click **Show Table**. Refer to Figure 5.14.

The Show Table dialog box displays.

Another Way — Displaying Tables in the Relationships Window

Alternatively, you can click the Show Table button on the Relationships toolbar.

6 In the **Show Table** dialog box, click **Historical Gardens**, and then click **Add**. Alternatively, you can double-click a table to add it to the Relationships window.

Project 5A: Southland Gardens | **Access** 305

7 In the **Show Table** dialog box, double-click the **Historical Gardens Contact Information** table to add it to the Relationships window, and then click **Close**.

The Historical Gardens table and the Historical Gardens Contact Information table have been added to the Relationships window.

8 Move and resize the table windows in the Relationships window to match, approximately, Figure 5.15.

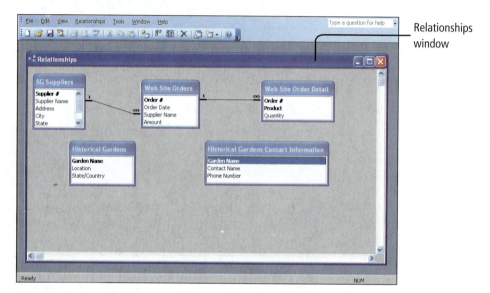

Figure 5.15

9 In the **Historical Gardens** table, point to the **Garden Name** field, and then drag and drop it on top of the **Garden Name** field in the **Historical Gardens Contact Information** table.

The Edit Relationships dialog box displays.

10 In the lower portion of the **Edit Relationships** dialog box, notice that the **Relationship Type** is *One-To-One*.

For each record in the Historical Gardens table, there is only one record in the Historical Gardens Contact Information table.

More Knowledge — One-to-One Relationships

How do you know it should be a one-to-one relationship?

How do you know if you should create a one-to-one relationship? If you could add the data from the second table to the first table without creating redundant records, then a one-to-one relationship can exist between the two tables.

11 In the **Edit Relationships** dialog box, select the **Enforce Referential Integrity** check box, select the **Cascade Update Related Fields** check box, select the **Cascade Delete Related Records** check box, and then click **Create**. Leave the Relationships window open for the next activity.

A relationship line between the Historical Gardens table and the Historical Gardens Contact Information table indicates a one-to-one relationship. See Figure 5.16.

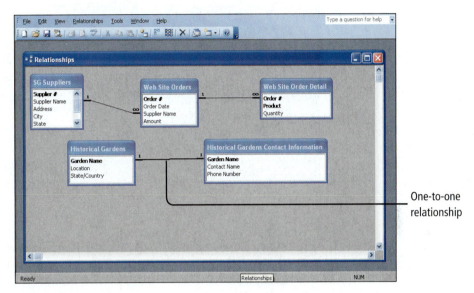

Figure 5.16

Activity 5.7 Establishing a Many-to-Many Relationship

Another relationship, although not a common one, is the ***many-to-many relationship***. Many-to-many relationships involve two tables that each have a one-to-many relationship to a third table, called a ***junction table***. The primary keys of the junction table are composed of the primary keys of each of the other tables. For example, in the Southland Gardens database, each episode of the TV show (TV Shows table) can have many advertisers (Advertisers table) and each advertiser can appear on many shows.

1 Right-click in a gray area of the Relationships window, and then from the shortcut menu, click **Show Table**. From the **Show Table** dialog box, add the **TV Shows** table, the **TV Show Advertisers** table, and the **Advertisers** table to the Relationships window. Close the **Show Table** dialog box.

The TV Shows table contains information about Southland Garden TV shows that have aired. The Advertisers table contains the name and address and contact information for the sponsors that pay Southland to show their ads on a TV show. The TV Show Advertisers table contains a list of the aired shows and the advertisers who had an ad on each show.

2 Move and resize the tables in the Relationships window to match Figure 5.17.

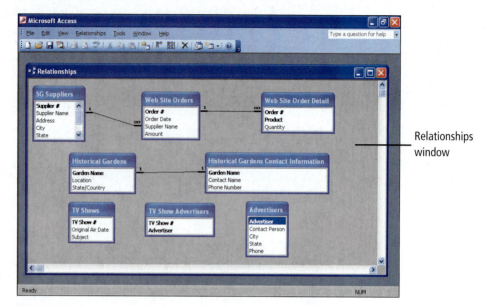

Figure 5.17

3 In the **TV Shows** table, point to the **TV Show #** field, and then drag and drop it on top of the **TV Show #** field in the **TV Show Advertisers** table.

4 In the **Edit Relationships** dialog box, select the **Enforce Referential Integrity** check box, the **Cascade Update Related Fields** check box, and the **Cascade Delete Related Records** check box, and then click **Create**.

5 In the **TV Show Advertisers** table, point to the **Advertiser** field, and then drag and drop it on top of the **Advertiser** field in the **Advertisers** table.

6 In the **Edit Relationships** dialog box, select the **Enforce Referential Integrity** check box, the **Cascade Update Related Fields** check box, and the **Cascade Delete Related Records** check box, and then click **Create**.

7 Examine the Relationships window. Notice the one-to-many relationships you established. These one-to-many relationships create a many-to-many relationship. See Figure 5.18.

By creating the one-to-many relationship between the TV Shows table and the TV Show Advertisers table, and then creating another one-to-many relationship between the Advertisers table and the TV Show Advertisers table, you created a many-to-many relationship between the TV Shows table and the Advertisers table, with the TV Show Advertisers table serving as the junction table.

In both the TV Shows table and the TV Show Advertisers table, the primary key is the TV Show # field. The primary keys of the junction table—the TV Show Advertisers table—is a combination of the two primary keys of the other two tables. You can see that in the TV Show Advertisers table, both fields are in bold, indicating that they are primary keys.

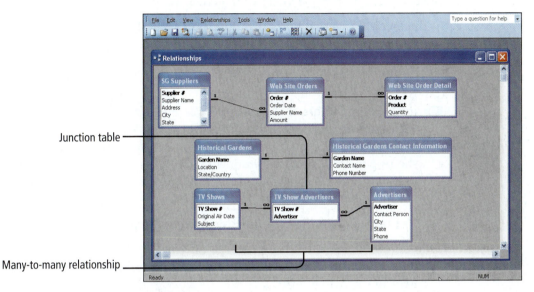

Figure 5.18

> **Note** — **Deleting a Relationship**
>
> To delete an existing relationship between tables, right-click the Relationship line and then click Delete.

8 From the **File** menu, click **Print Relationships**. Display the **File** menu again, click **Page Setup**, and on the **Page tab**, click **Landscape**. Click **OK**. Click the **Print** button to print the Relationships report.

9 **Close** the Relationships report and click **Yes** to save the changes to the design of the report. In the **Save As** dialog box, save the report as **Relationships for 5A SouthlandGardens Firstname Lastname** (delete *1* from the end of the proposed name), click **OK**, and then click **Yes** to replace the existing report.

10 Close the Relationships window. Leave the database open for the next activity.

Objective 4
Create a Query from Joined Tables

When a query is created from related tables, the relationships between the tables automatically display in the query design grid.

Activity 5.8 Creating a Query from Joined Tables

In this activity, you will create a query that will display the orders for a particular supplier.

1 On the Objects bar, click **Queries**, and then double-click **Create query in Design view**.

2 In the **Show Table** dialog box, double-click the **SG Suppliers**, **Web Site Orders**, and **Web Site Order Detail** tables to add them to the table area, and then click **Close**. As shown in Figure 5.19, enlarge the upper portion of the window by dragging the upper edge of the title bar, and enlarge each of the table windows to get a complete view of each table's name and list of fields.

The tables are added to the table area of the query window, and their relationship lines display.

3 In the **SG Suppliers** table, double-click **Supplier Name** to add the field to the design grid.

4 In the **Web Site Orders** table, double-click **Order #** to add the field to the design grid.

5 In the **Web Site Order Detail** table, add the **Product** and **Quantity** fields to the design grid.

6 In the design grid, under **Supplier Name**, in the **Criteria** row, type **Smith Hardware** and then click the **Run** button. See Figure 5.19.

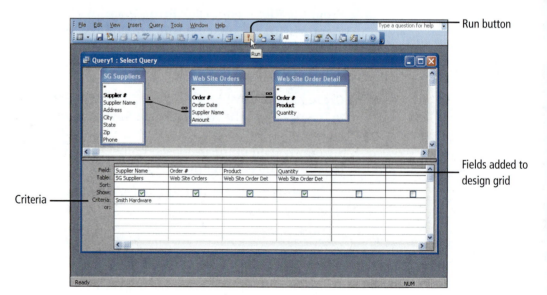

Figure 5.19

7 Examine the query results. Smith Hardware is one of the suppliers that supplies items that are offered for sale on Southland Gardens' companion Web site. See Figure 5.20.

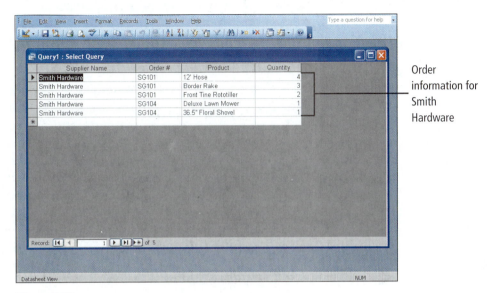

Order information for Smith Hardware

Figure 5.20

8 Close the query, click **Yes** to save it, and then, using your own information, save the query as **Smith Hardware Query Firstname Lastname**

9 Close the database, and then close Access.

End You have completed Project 5A

Project 5B Southland Gardens Maintenance

You have practiced using Access features that help to reduce or eliminate errors and redundant information. It is impossible to eliminate all errors and redundancy, but there are Access tools to assist with identifying, or getting rid of, unnecessary data.

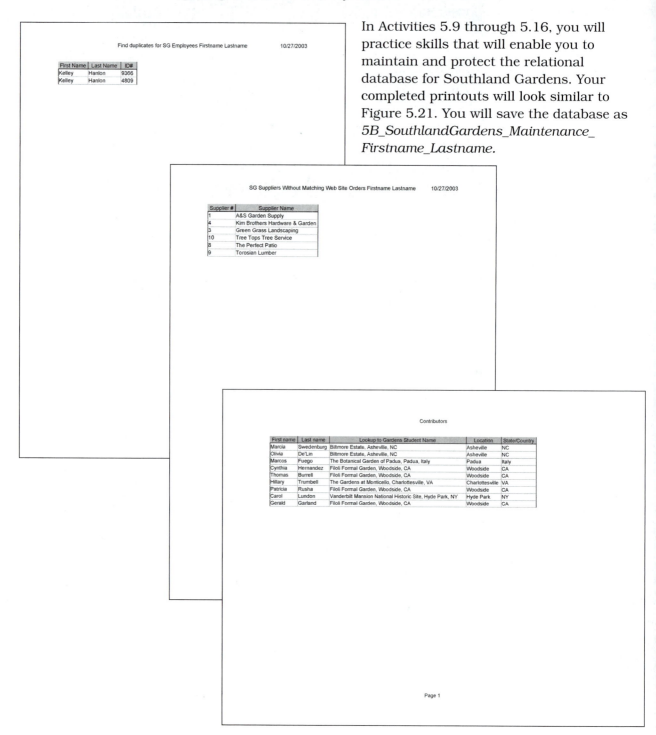

In Activities 5.9 through 5.16, you will practice skills that will enable you to maintain and protect the relational database for Southland Gardens. Your completed printouts will look similar to Figure 5.21. You will save the database as *5B_SouthlandGardens_Maintenance_Firstname_Lastname*.

Figure 5.21
Project 5B—Southland Gardens Maintenance

Objective 5
Identify and Correct Design Errors in Tables

Activity 5.9 Finding Duplicate Records

Even when a table contains a primary key, it is still possible to have duplicate records in a table. For example, the same employee could be entered into a table twice but with different ID#s. In this activity, you will use the Find Duplicates Query Wizard to create a query that will locate duplicate records in a table for Southland Gardens.

1 Locate the file **a05B_SouthlandGardens_Maintenance** from your student files, and then copy and paste the file to the Chapter 5 folder you created earlier. Remove the Read-only property from the file and rename the file as **5B_SouthlandGardens_Maintenance_Firstname_Lastname** Start Access and open the database you just renamed.

2 On the Database toolbar, click the **New Object button arrow**. From the list that displays, click **Query** as shown in Figure 5.22.

The New Query dialog box displays a list of query types.

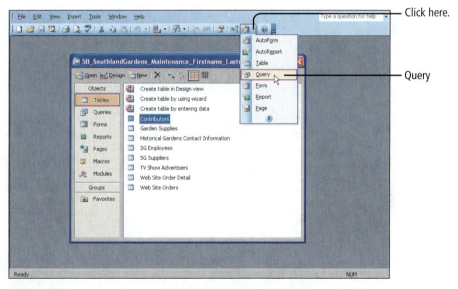

Figure 5.22

3 From the list of query types, click **Find Duplicates Query Wizard** as shown in Figure 5.23, and then click **OK**.

The Find Duplicates Query Wizard starts.

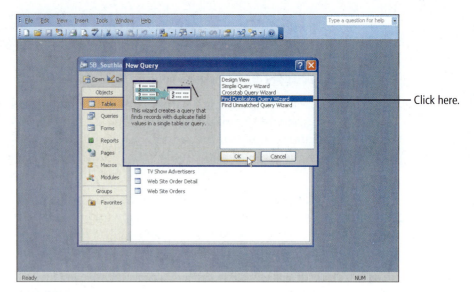

Figure 5.23

4. From the list of tables, click **Table: SG Employees**, and then click **Next**.

5. In the screen that indicates *Which fields might contain duplicate information?*, click **First Name**, and then click the **One Field** button .

6. Click **Last Name**, click the **One Field** button , and then click **Next**.

7. Read the information at the top of this screen, click the **ID#** field, and then click the **One Field** button . See Figure 5.24.

   The field that you select in this screen will display in the query results.

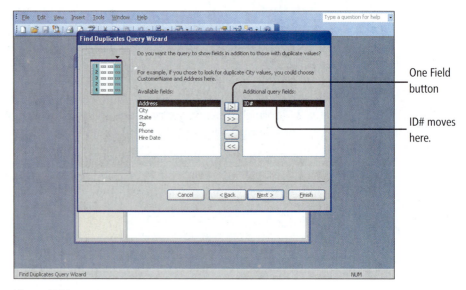

Figure 5.24

8 Click **Next** and in this final screen of the wizard, using your own information, add your name to the default query name so the name of the query is **Find duplicates for SG Employees Firstname Lastname** and then click **Finish**.

The query results display with two records that have the same first name and last name, *Kelley Hanlon*, but with different ID#s.

9 Print the query, and then close the query. Leave the database open for the next activity.

Access has limitations on what it can determine for you. In this instance, further investigation would be necessary to determine if this is one employee that was entered into the database twice with different ID#s, or if this is two different employees with the same name.

Activity 5.10 Finding Unmatched Records

You can use the Find Unmatched Query Wizard to create a query that will locate unmatched records in related tables. For example, in the SG Suppliers table, you could locate individual suppliers with whom no orders have been placed and then delete them from the table. It makes sense to delete unneeded records.

1 On the Database toolbar, click the **New Object button arrow**. From the list that displays, click **Query**.

The New Query dialog box displays a list of query types.

2 From the list of query types, click **Find Unmatched Query Wizard**, and then click **OK**.

The Find Unmatched Query Wizard starts. The first screen of the wizard asks you to identify the first table in which you want Access to compare records.

3 From the list of tables, click **Table: SG Suppliers**, and then click **Next**.

The next screen of the wizard displays. Here you identify the table that you would like Access to compare to the first table for the purpose of locating unmatched records.

4 From the list of tables, click **Table: Web Site Orders**, and then click **Next**.

The next screen of the wizard asks you to identify which field is in both tables.

5 From the list of fields, click **Supplier Name** in both lists, click the **double-headed arrow** button, and then compare your dialog box with Figure 5.25.

At the bottom of the dialog box, Access indicates that the matching fields are Supplier Name.

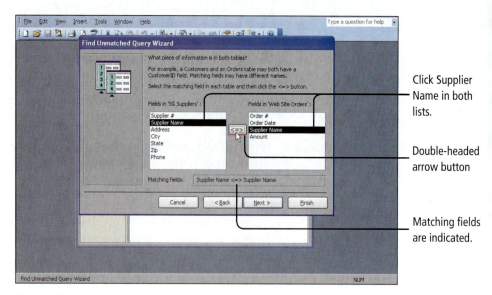

Figure 5.25

6. Click **Next**. In this screen of the wizard, click **Supplier #**, and then click the **One Field** button.

7. Click **Supplier Name**, click the **One Field** button, and then click **Next**.

8. In the last screen of the wizard, using your own information, add your name to the default query name so the name of the query is **SG Suppliers Without Matching Web Site Orders Firstname Lastname** and then click **Finish**.

   The query results display six supplier names with whom no orders have been placed. See Figure 5.26.

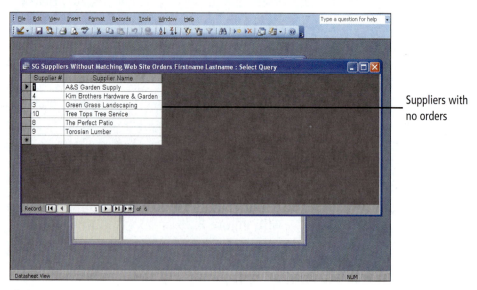

Figure 5.26

9. Print the query, and then close the query. Leave the database open for the next activity.

Activity 5.11 Examining Tables to Check for Design Errors

A challenging task for new database users is to build accurate tables using an efficient design and without typographical errors and redundant fields. Access analyzing features examine a table or database and look for errors in the table or the database design. In this activity, you will use the Table Analyzer to check for design errors in a table.

In this database, if a featured historical garden is fortunate enough to have a contributing sponsor—someone who donates funds to the garden—the sponsor receives mention on the TV episode that features the garden. The information about contributing sponsors is contained in the Contributors table.

1 Be sure your database is open from the previous activity.

2 On the menu bar, click **Tools**, point to **Analyze**, and then click **Table**.

The first two screens of the Table Analyzer wizard are introductory explanatory screens that describe how the Table Analyzer functions and provide examples for you.

3 Read the information in the first screen, and then click **Next**.

4 Read the information in the second screen, and then click **Next**.

The third screen of the wizard asks you to identify which table contains fields with values that are repeated in many records.

5 From the list of tables, click **Contributors** as shown in Figure 5.27. Click **Next**.

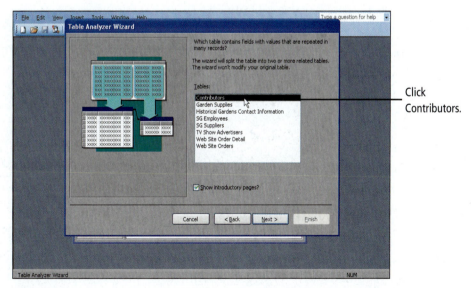

Figure 5.27

6 In this screen of the wizard, verify that the **Yes, let the wizard decide** option button is selected, and then click **Next**.

7 In this screen of the wizard, examine the suggestion that Access makes, which is to split the **Contributors** table. See Figure 5.28.

Access suggests splitting the Contributors table into two tables—one table that will list the Contributors and a lookup field to another table that lists the Garden information that pertains to each contributor.

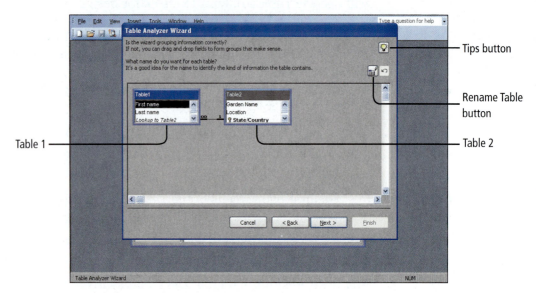

Figure 5.28

8 In the upper right corner of the wizard screen, click the **Tips** button. Refer to Figure 5.28.

A list of helpful tips for splitting these tables displays. See Figure 5.29.

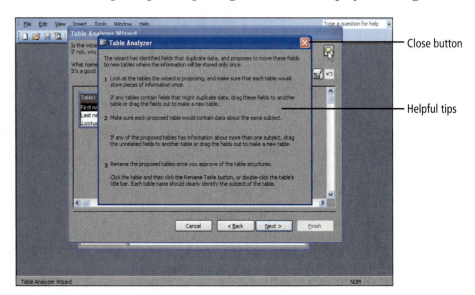

Figure 5.29

9 Read these important tips carefully; they will assist in your understanding of good database design. When you are finished, click the **Close** button ✖ in the Table Analyzer window that lists these tips.

10 Click the **title bar** of **Table1** so that it is selected, and then in the upper right corner, click the **Rename Table** button. Refer to Figure 5.28.

11 In the dialog box that displays, and using your own information, type **Garden Contributors Firstname Lastname** and then click **OK**.

12 Click the title bar of **Table2** to select it, and then click the **Rename Table** button.

13 In the dialog box, and using your own information, type **Gardens Firstname Lastname** and then click **OK**.

14 Click **Next**.

The next screen of the wizard displays as shown in Figure 5.30.

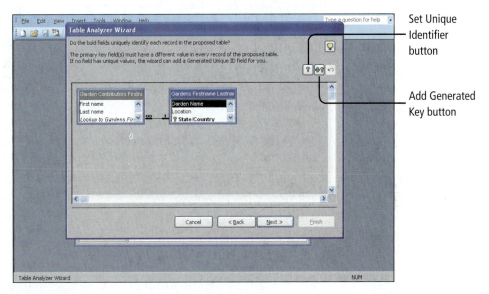

Figure 5.30

15 In this screen, in the **Gardens** table on the right, click the **Garden Name** field, and then click the **Set Unique Identifier** button. Refer to Figure 5.30.

The primary key for this table is changed to Garden Name. Garden Name is a unique field in this table.

16 Click **Next**, and in this final screen of the wizard, accept the default settings, and then click **Finish**.

A Help topic on the Table Analyzer may display, and a Select Query displays based on the information you entered in the wizard.

17 Examine the information in the displayed Help window, and print this window if you would like to use the information for future reference. Then click the Help window's **Close** button ⊠.

18 Print the Contributors query, and then close the query. On the Objects bar, click **Tables**.

Access created a Contributors query that contains the information from the old Contributors table and a Lookup field. The database window displays with the names of the two tables Access created and the word OLD attached to the old Contributors table. See Figure 5.31. Leave the database open for the next activity.

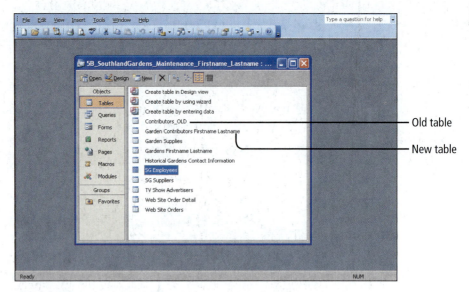

Figure 5.31

Activity 5.12 Testing the Design of a Database

The Performance Analyzer feature examines the objects in a database and makes recommendations to *optimize* (improve performance by increasing efficiency) the database. In this activity, you will use the Performance Analyzer to test the design of the database for Southland Gardens.

1 On the menu bar, click **Tools**, point to **Analyze**, and then click **Performance**.

The Performance Analyzer dialog box displays.

2 Click the **Tables tab** if necessary. Notice that a list of all the tables in the database displays. On the right side, click **Select All**. See Figure 5.32.

A small check mark displays to the left of each table name, indicating that the Performance Analyzer will examine all of the table objects in the database.

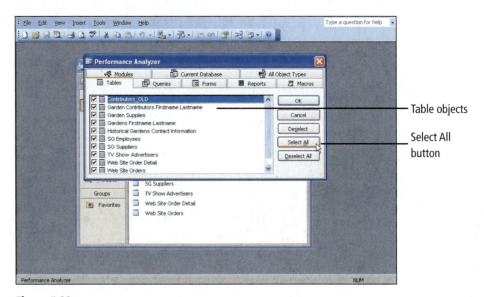

Figure 5.32

3 Click **OK**.

Access displays suggestions for increasing the efficiency of this database. Access categorizes the results of the Performance Analyzer into three categories: Recommendation, Suggestion, and Idea. The Fixed category within the Key area will display next to a suggestion if you choose to have Access optimize the suggestion and implement the recommendation. See the Key area in Figure 5.33. The Performance Analyzer found three items for which it suggests ideas as shown in Figure 5.33.

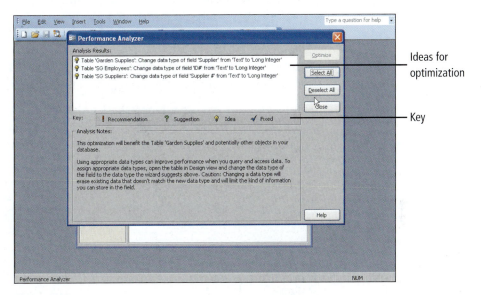

Figure 5.33

4 Click the **Close** button to close the Performance Analyzer.

Your database will function properly without implementing any of these ideas. However, in large databases, you will likely want to implement Recommendations. To do so, you would click on the Recommendation you would like to implement, and then click the Optimize button.

5 Close the database, and then close Access.

Objective 6
Protect and Maintain a Database

Controlling who has access to your database is part of protecting and maintaining a database. Frequently, databases contain sensitive data that should only be accessed by authorized users. For example, think of the database of student grades at your college. Access has several features that allow you to control who can open a database, and within various Access features, control different degrees of security.

Activity 5.13 Protecting a Database with a Password

Protecting database files with a password is a common method for protecting a database from unauthorized users. When trying to open a file that is password protected, the user is prompted to enter the password in order to gain access to the file. In this activity, you will create a password for your database.

1 Locate the file **a05B_Password** from your student files and copy and paste the file to the Chapter 5 folder you created earlier. Remove the Read-only property from the file and rename the file as **5B_Password_Firstname_Lastname** Start Access and open the database you just renamed.

2 On the **Tools** menu, point to **Security**, and then click **Set Database Password**.

A message displays indicating that you need to open the database for *exclusive use*. Exclusive use means that nobody else can have the database open at that time.

3 Click **OK**, and then close the database.

4 On the **File** menu, click **Open**, and then navigate to the location where you are storing your projects for this chapter.

5 Click your **5B_Password** file (the one that you just renamed) once, and then in the lower right corner, locate the **Open button arrow** and click it to display a menu. See Figure 5.34.

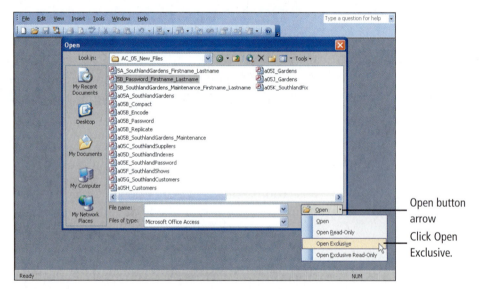

Figure 5.34

6 From the displayed menu, click **Open Exclusive**. When the database opens, display the **Tools** menu, point to **Security**, and then click **Set Database Password**.

The Set Database Password dialog box displays as shown in Figure 5.35.

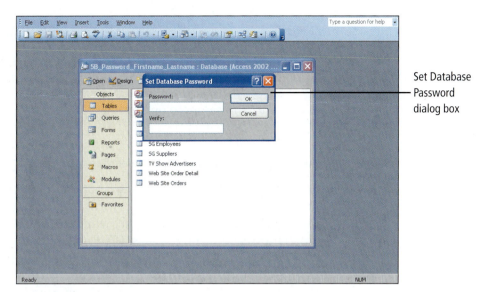

Set Database Password dialog box

Figure 5.35

7 In the **Password** box, type **Bstudent007** (as you type, only * characters display) and press Tab.

The insertion point moves to the Verify box.

Note — Passwords display as *****

When you type a password in the Password box, each character that you type will display as an asterisk (*). This ensures that someone looking over your shoulder at your screen cannot learn your password as you type it.

8 In the **Verify** box, type **Bstudent007** and then click **OK** to assign the password to the database.

When creating a password, you must enter the password twice to ensure that you entered it correctly.

Note — Passwords are case sensitive

Passwords in Access are case sensitive, meaning that Access will interpret *B* differently than *b*. Take care when typing a password to only capitalize letters that were initially entered as uppercase letters.

9 Close the database, and then reopen it.

The Password Required dialog box displays.

10 Under **Enter database password** type **student** and then click **OK**.

Access warns you that the password is not valid.

11 Click **OK** to close the message, and then type the correct password that you created, **Bstudent007** and then click **OK**.

The database opens.

12 Close the database.

Project 5B: Southland Gardens Maintenance | **Access**

Note — Removing a Password from Your Database

To remove a password from a database, open the database with the password. Then, on the Tools menu, point to Security and click Unset Database Password. Type the password that you have added to the database, and then press Enter. The password is removed.

Activity 5.14 Encoding and Decoding a Database

Sometimes security measures are not enough to keep unwanted users from viewing the information in your databases. A database created with Microsoft Access is a **binary** file, which means that it is constructed of mostly unreadable characters. If an Access database is opened in a word processor, Microsoft Word for example, the file will appear to most people to be completely unreadable. If, however, you continue looking through the file, you will notice some readable characters as shown in Figure 5.36.

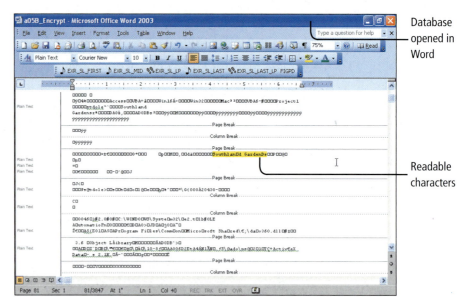

Figure 5.36

1. Locate the file **a05B_Encode** from your student files and copy and paste the file to the Chapter 5 folder you created earlier. Remove the Read-only property from the file and rename the file as **5B_Encode_Firstname_Lastname** Start Access and open the database you just renamed.

2. From the **Tools** menu, point to **Security**, and then click **Encode/Decode Database**.

The Encode Database As dialog box displays. To prevent unauthorized users from opening your database in a word processing program and scanning the file for information, you can **encode** the database. Encoding a file scrambles the file so it is unreadable.

3 Use the **Save in** arrow to navigate to the folder where you are storing your projects for this chapter, and then in the **File name** box, delete the existing text and type **5B_Southland_Encode_Firstname_Lastname** as the file you want to create, and then click **Save**.

Access creates an encoded version of the database in the location you specified but leaves the original database open.

4 **Close** ☒ the **5B_Encode** database (you can leave Access open) and then open a word processing program such as Microsoft Word or Notepad.

5 In the word processing program, open the encoded file you just created. You will likely need to click the **Files of type arrow**, and then click **All Files**. In the dialog box that displays, click **OK**.

The original database file was difficult to read in a word processor (see Figure 5.36), but the encoded version is even more difficult to read. The file that displays in the word processing program will be many pages long (approximately 3850 pages!). Encoding a file does not prevent a user from opening the file in Access or provide any password protection. Encoding a file prevents someone who does not have a copy of Access from being able to read the data in the file.

6 Close the word processing program.

7 Start Access, if necessary, and then open your **5B_Southland_Encode** database.

The encoded database looks like the original. You can tell the files apart by the different file names you specified. In this example your original file was the 5B_Encode_Firstname_Lastname file and the file name you specified for the encoded file was 5B_Southland_Encode_Firstname_Lastname. When working with an encoded file in Access, you may notice that some tasks take longer to complete.

8 Close the **5B_Southland_Encode** database but leave Access open. On the **Tools** menu, point to **Security** and click **Encode/Decode Database**.

9 In the **Encode/Decode Database** dialog box, browse to the folder where you are storing your projects for this chapter, click the **5B_Southland_Encode** file with your name in it, and then click **OK**.

The Decode Database As dialog box opens.

10 In the **File name** box, using your own information, type **5B_Southland_Decode_Firstname_Lastname** and then click **Save**.

Decoding a database unscrambles it back to the format the database was originally.

11 Close Access.

Activity 5.15 Compacting and Repairing Database Files

After you work with a database for a period of time, the file may become quite large. Even if you delete objects from the database, Access does not really delete them; it only *marks* them for deletion. As a consequence, database files can grow quite large even though the data in the file appears to be small. **Compacting** a database will remove these deleted objects from the database.

1 Locate the file **a05B_Compact** from your student files and copy and paste the file to the Chapter 5 folder you created earlier. Remove the Read-only property from the file and rename the file as **5B_Compact_Firstname_Lastname**

Before you compact a database, you should create a backup of the database. You have done this by copying the database to your folder.

2 Start Access, but do not open the database yet. On the **Tools** menu, point to **Database Utilities**, and then click **Compact and Repair Database**.

The Database to Compact From dialog box opens.

3 Navigate to the folder where you are storing your projects for this chapter, and then click your file **5B_Compact_Firstname_Lastname** file to select it. With the file still selected, in the lower right corner of the dialog box, click **Compact**.

4 In the displayed **Compact Database Into** dialog box, click the **5B_Compact_Firstname_Lastname** file with your name, and then click **Save**.

Because you are saving the compacted database using the same name, Access displays the message shown in Figure 5.37.

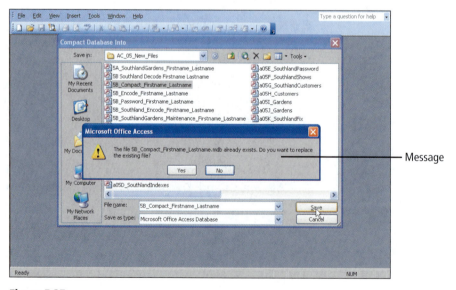

Figure 5.37

5 Click **Yes**.

The Access window displays. You will not see a visual indication of compacting, but compacting has taken place.

Activity 5.16 Making Backup Copies of a Database and Replicating a Database

It is common to have individuals seated at different computers working on the same database. This will create several different versions of the same database. In order to bring the different versions into one, cohesive version, the database should be replicated. **Replicating** a database is the process of creating copies, or **replicas**, of the database so that multiple users can edit the database.

1 Locate the file **a05B_Replicate** from your student files and copy and paste the file to the Chapter 5 folder you created earlier. Remove the Read-only property from the file and rename the file as **5B_Replicate_Firstname_Lastname** Start Access and open the database you just renamed.

2 On the **Tools** menu, point to **Replication**, and then click **Create Replica**.

The message in Figure 5.38 displays. When you click Yes, the 5B Replicate database becomes the **Design Master**. The Design Master is a copy of the original database and is the only database in the **replica set** to which you can make structural changes—such as adding new tables or adding new fields to existing tables. The replica set consists of the Design Master and any replicas, or copies, that you create.

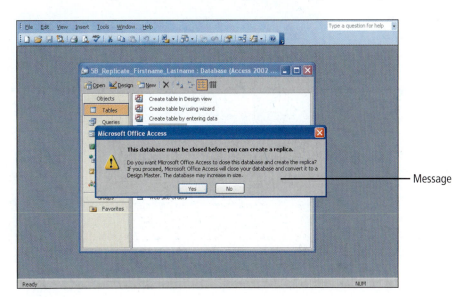

Figure 5.38

3 Click **Yes**.

After a moment, another message displays, recommending that you create a backup copy of the file.

4 Click **Yes**.

The Location of New Replica dialog box displays. See Figure 5.39.

Location of New Replica dialog box

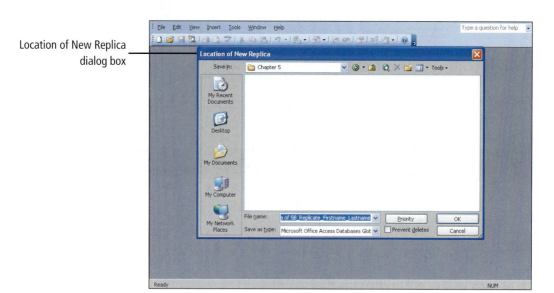

Figure 5.39

5 If necessary, navigate to the location where you are storing your projects for this chapter, keep the default file name, and then click **OK**.

The new Design Master database displays along with a message box similar to the one shown in Figure 5.40.

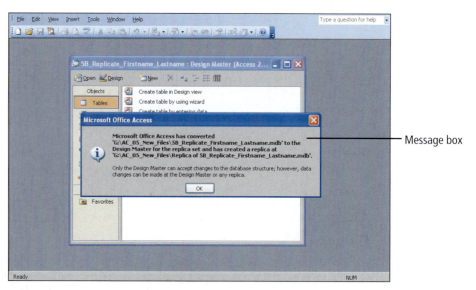

Message box

Figure 5.40

6 In the message box, click **OK**.

The Database window displays and indicates *Design Master*. See Figure 5.41.

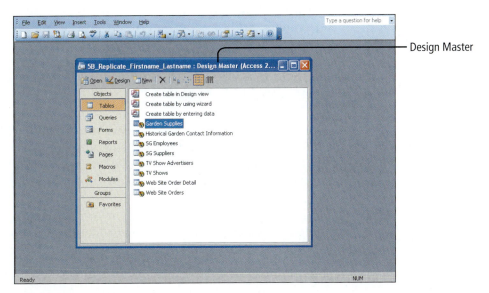

Figure 5.41

7 Close the Design Master database, and then close Access.

Replicating a database and managing the replicas is a complex process. The steps above showed you how to replicate a database. To learn more about this process, refer to the replication topic in Access Help.

End You have completed Project 5B

Summary

In this chapter you practiced techniques for building and maintaining a relational database. You created indexes to speed searching and sorting on fields. Additionally, you practiced viewing the relationships in a database and created three types of relationships: one-to-many, one-to-one, and many-to-many. Relationships in a database help to reduce data redundancy and increase data accuracy. You also created a query from tables that were joined.

Additionally, you practiced techniques for maintaining a database by identifying and correcting tables and using the Find Duplicates Query Wizard and the Find Unmatched Query Wizard. You used features of Access that analyzed both the database and tables within the database.

You practiced applying various security measures to a database, including password protection, and encoding and decoding a database. You practiced compacting a database by using the Compact and Repair feature of Access. Finally, you practiced replicating a database.

In This Chapter You Practiced How To

- Index Fields in a Table
- View Relationships in a Database
- Establish Relationships Between Tables
- Create a Query from Joined Tables
- Identify and Correct Design Errors in Tables
- Protect and Maintain a Database

Concepts Assessments

Matching Match each term in the second column with its correct definition in the first column by writing the letter of the term on the blank line in front of the correct definition.

____ 1. A special list that is created in Access to speed up searches and sorting.

____ 2. A type of database that can contain two or more tables that are related (connected) to each other by common fields.

____ 3. The third table in a many-to-many relationship.

____ 4. An association among tables in which a record in Table A can have many matching records in Table B, and a record in Table B can have many matching records in Table A—made possible by defining one-to-one relationships to a third table.

____ 5. A database type that stores different types of information in one table—usually contains data about one particular item in multiple places.

____ 6. The method used to locate records that do not have corresponding records in a related table.

____ 7. Copies of a database that are distributed to multiple users for editing.

____ 8. An association between two tables in which each record in Table A can have only one matching record in Table B, and each record in Table B can have only one matching record in Table A.

____ 9. The type of file created with Microsoft Access that is composed mostly of unreadable characters.

____ 10. A set of rules that Access uses to ensure that the data between related fields is valid.

____ 11. An association between two tables in which a record in Table A can have many matching records in Table B, but a record in Table B has only one matching record in Table A.

____ 12. Between two linked tables, the field in the second table that identifies the linked records.

____ 13. A process that removes deleted objects from a database and thus increases available space.

____ 14. The Design Master and any replicas of a database.

____ 15. Opening a database in a manner where no other users can open the database at the same time.

A Binary
B Compacting
C Exclusive use
D Find Unmatched Query Wizard
E Flat file database
F Foreign key
G Index
H Junction table
I Many-to-many relationship
J One-to-many relationship
K One-to-one relationship
L Referential integrity
M Relational database
N Replicas
O Replica set

Concepts Assessments (continued)

Fill in the Blank Write the correct answer in the space provided.

1. The line that Access draws to indicate a link between fields is the _____.

2. The connection between fields in a relational database is called a(n) _____.

3. The option when creating relationships that will cause Access to automatically change the data in a linked table to reflect a change in the first table is called _____.

4. _____ is the manner in which a database must first be opened in order to set a password for the database.

5. _____ a file, or scrambling it so that it is unreadable, will prevent users who do not have a copy of Access from opening a database and gathering information contained in the database.

6. Creating copies of a database so multiple users can edit the database is called _____.

7. The option when creating relationships that will cause Access to delete a record in a linked table if it is deleted in the first table is called _____.

8. The window where you can view, create, and modify relationships between tables and queries is the _____ window.

9. The process of updating and merging replicas with the Design Master is called _____.

10. Unscrambling a database that has been previously scrambled is called _____.

Skill Assessments

Project 5C—Southland Suppliers

Objectives: *View Relationships in a Database, Establish Relationships Between Tables, and Create a Query from Joined Tables.*

In the following Skill Assessment, you will view and create relationships for the Southland Suppliers database. Additionally, you will create a query from the joined tables that will identify the supplies that Southland Gardens features and sells on its Web site from Parkstone Rentals. Your completed query will look similar to the one shown in Figure 5.42. Your completed Relationships report will look similar to the one shown in Figure 5.42. You will rename and save the database as 5C_SouthlandSuppliers_Firstname_Lastname.

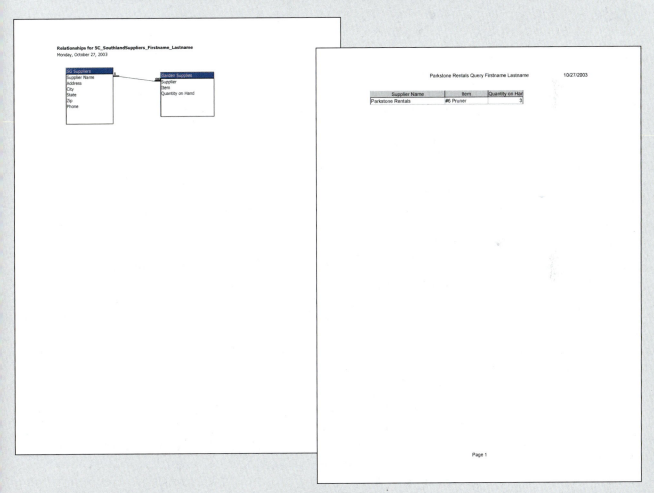

Figure 5.42

1. Locate the file **a05C_SouthlandSuppliers** from your student files and copy and paste the file to the Chapter 5 folder where you are storing your projects for this chapter. Remove the Read-only property from the file and rename the file as **5C_SouthlandSuppliers_Firstname_Lastname** Start Access and open the database you just renamed.

(**Project 5C**–Southland Suppliers continues on the next page)

Skill Assessments (continued)

(Project 5C–Southland Suppliers continued)

2. Open the **SG Suppliers** table in **Datasheet view** and examine the data in the table. Close the **SG Suppliers** table, and then open the **Garden Supplies** table in **Datasheet view** and examine the data in the table.

3. Close the **Garden Supplies** table. On the Database toolbar, click the **Relationships** button.

4. Right-click in the gray area of the Relationships window, and from the displayed shortcut menu, click **Show Table**.

5. In the **Show Table** dialog box, click **SG Suppliers**, click **Add**, click **Garden Supplies**, click **Add**, and then click **Close**.

6. Move and enlarge the tables so that you can see the entire title of the tables and all of the fields in the table. In the **SG Suppliers** table, point to the **Supplier Name** field, and then drag and drop it on top of the **Supplier** field in the **Garden Supplies** table.

7. In the **Edit Relationships** dialog box, select the **Enforce Referential Integrity** check box, select both the **Cascade Update Related Fields** and **Cascade Delete Related Records** check boxes, and then click **Create**.

8. With the Relationships window open, display the **File** menu, and then click **Print Relationships**. On the Print Preview toolbar, click the **Print** button.

9. Close the Relationships report and click **Yes** when prompted to save your changes to the report. Click **OK** to save the report using the default report name. Close the Relationships window, and then in the Database window, on the Objects bar, click **Reports**. Verify that the **Relationships** report you created is listed.

10. On the Objects bar, click **Queries**, and then double-click **Create query in Design view**.

11. In the **Show Table** dialog box, double-click the **SG Suppliers** and **Garden Supplies** tables to add them to the table area, and then click **Close**.

12. If necessary, enlarge the parts of the Select Query window and the tables so that you can see the entire title bar of each table and all the fields in each table. In the **SG Suppliers** table, double-click **Supplier Name** to add the field to the design grid. In the **Garden Supplies** table, double-click **Item** and **Quantity on Hand** to add the two fields to the design grid.

13. Under **Supplier Name**, in the **Criteria** row, type **Parkstone Rentals** and then on the toolbar click the **Run** button.

    The query results display one item from Parkstone Rentals.

(Project 5C–Southland Suppliers continues on the next page)

Skill Assessments (continued)

(Project 5C–Southland Suppliers continued)

14. Close the query, click **Yes** to save it, and then, using your own information, save it as **Parkstone Rentals Query Firstname Lastname** Print the query.

15. Close the database, and then close Access.

End You have completed Project 5C

Project 5D—Southland Indexes

Objectives: *Index Fields in a Table, and Identify and Correct Design Errors in Tables.*

In the following Skill Assessment, you will create an index for the Historical Gardens table in the Southland Gardens database. Additionally, you will create a query that will locate duplicate records in the Customers table. The query will look similar to the one shown in Figure 5.43. You will save your database as *5D_SouthlandIndexes_Firstname_Lastname*.

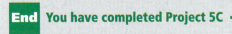

Figure 5.43

(Project 5D–Southland Indexes continues on the next page)

Skill Assessments (continued)

(Project 5D–Southland Indexes continued)

1. Locate the file **a05D_SouthlandIndexes** from your student files and copy and paste the file to the Chapter 5 folder where you are storing your projects for this chapter. Remove the Read-only property from the file and rename the file as **5D_SouthlandIndexes_Firstname_Lastname** Start Access and open the database you just renamed.

2. Open the **Historical Gardens** table in **Datasheet view** and examine the data in the table.

3. Switch to **Design view** and click once in the **Location** field to make it the active field.

4. Under **Field Properties**, click once in the **Indexed** box, click the **arrow**, and from the displayed list, click **Yes (Duplicates OK)**. This creates an index that will not only speed searches and sorting on this field, but will also allow duplicate entries in the field.

5. Close the **Historical Gardens** table and save changes when prompted.

6. On the Database toolbar, click the **New Object button arrow**, and from the displayed list, click **Query**.

7. In the displayed **New Query** dialog box, from the list of query types, click **Find Duplicates Query Wizard**, and then click **OK**.

8. In the first Wizard screen, from the list of tables, click **Table: Customers**, and then click **Next**.

9. In this screen, which indicates *Which fields might contain duplicate information?*, click **Last Name**, click the **One Field** button, and then click **Next**.

10. In this screen, which indicates *Do you want the query to show fields in addition to those with duplicate values?*, click the **First Name** field, and then click the **One Field** button. Click **Next**.

11. In this final screen of the wizard, using your own information, add your name to the default query name so the name of the query is **Find duplicates for Customers Firstname Lastname** and then click **Finish**.

    Query results display with two duplicate records that have the same First Name and Last Name, *Virginia Dinkel* and *Frank Hines*. Further investigation at this point would be necessary to determine if the duplicates for Virginia Dinkel and Frank Hines were truly employees entered into the table twice with different ID#s, or if each Virginia Dinkel and each Frank Hines is a different person.

12. Print and then close the query. Close the database, and then close Access.

End You have completed Project 5D

Skill Assessments (continued)

Project 5E—Southland Password

Objectives: *Identify and Correct Design Errors in Tables and Protect and Maintain a Database.*

In the following Skill Assessment, you will add a password for the Southland Gardens database. Additionally, you will create a query to find unmatched records in the Web Site Orders table for Southland Gardens. Your completed query will look similar to the one shown in Figure 5.44. You will save the database as *5E_SouthlandPassword_Firstname_Lastname* in the folder designated for this chapter.

Figure 5.44

1. Locate the file **a05E_SouthlandPassword** from your student files and copy and paste the file to the Chapter 5 folder you created earlier. Remove the Read-only property from the file and rename the file as **5E_SouthlandPassword_Firstname_Lastname** Start Access but DO NOT OPEN THE DATABASE you just renamed.

(**Project 5E**–Southland Password continues on the next page)

Skill Assessments (continued)

(Project 5E–Southland Password continued)

2. Be sure that no databases are open. On the **File** menu, click **Open**, and then navigate to the location where you are storing your projects for this chapter.

3. Click your **5E_SouthlandPassword_Firstname_Lastname** file once to select it. In the lower right corner, locate and then click the **Open button arrow**, and from the displayed list, click **Open Exclusive**. Recall that opening a database for Exclusive use will ensure that no one else can open the database at this time.

4. On the **Tools** menu, point to **Security**, and then click **Set Database Password**.

5. In the **Password** box, type **Keyboard2** and press Tab.

6. In the **Verify** box, type **Keyboard2** and then click **OK** to assign the password to the database. Close the database, and then reopen it.

7. Type the correct password you created, **Keyboard2** and then click **OK**.

8. On the Database toolbar, click the **New Object button arrow**. From the displayed list, click **Query**.

9. In the **New Query** dialog box, from the list of query types, click **Find Unmatched Query Wizard**, and then click **OK**.

10. In the screen that indicates *Which table or query contains records you want in the query results?*, from the list of tables, click **Table: Web Site Order Detail**, and then click **Next**.

11. In the screen that indicates *Which table or query contains the related records?*, click **Table: Web Site Orders**, and then click **Next**.

12. In the screen that indicates *What piece of information is in both tables?*, from the list of fields, click **Order #** in both lists, and then click the **double-headed arrow** button. The matching fields are indicated in the lower portion of the dialog box. Click **Next**.

13. In the screen that indicates *What fields do you want to see in the query results?*, click the **All Fields** button to move all three fields to the **Selected fields** list, and then click **Next**.

14. In the last screen of the wizard, using your own information, delete the existing text and type **Order Detail Without Matching Orders Firstname Lastname** and then click **Finish**.

    The query results display one unmatched record, that with an Order # of SG103.

15. Print the query. Close the query, close the database, and then close Access.

 You have completed Project 5E

Access chapter five

Performance Assessments

Project 5F — Southland TV Shows

Objectives: *Index Fields in a Table and Create a Query from Joined Tables.*

In the following Performance Assessment, you will create an index in a table and create a query to find unmatched records for Southland Gardens. Your completed table will look similar to the one shown in Figure 5.45. You will save your database as *5F_SouthlandTV_Shows_Firstname_Lastname*.

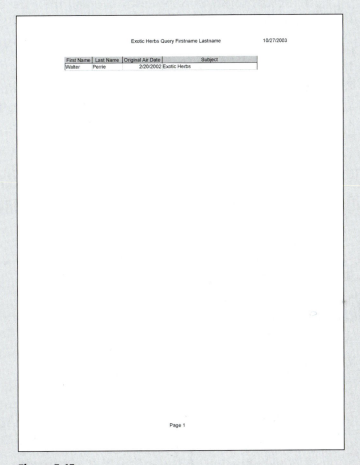

Figure 5.45

1. Locate the file **a05F_SouthlandTV_Shows** from your student files and copy and paste the file to the Chapter 5 folder you created earlier. Remove the Read-only property from the file and rename the file as **5F_SouthlandTV_Shows_Firstname_Lastname** Start Access and open the database you just renamed.

2. Open the **TV Shows** table and examine the data in the table.

3. Switch to **Design view**, click once in the **Producer** field, and then under **Field Properties**, click once in the **Indexed** box. Click the **arrow**, and from the displayed list, click **Yes (Duplicates OK)**.

(**Project 5F**–Southland TV Shows continues on the next page)

Performance Assessments (continued)

(Project 5F–Southland TV Shows continued)

4. Close the **TV Shows** table and save changes when prompted.

5. On the Objects bar, click **Queries**, and then double-click **Create query in Design view**.

6. Add both tables to the Select Query window, and then click **Close**. Adjust the size of the window and tables as necessary.

7. From the **SG Employees** table, add the **First Name** and **Last Name** to the design grid.

8. From the **TV Shows** table, add the **Original Air Date** and **Subject** fields to the design grid.

9. Under **Subject**, in the **Criteria** row, type **Exotic Herbs** and then click the **Run** button. In the query result, one record that has a subject of Exotic Herbs displays, indicating that one show had a subject of Exotic Herbs.

10. Close the query, click **Yes** to save it, and then, using your own information, save it as **Exotic Herbs Query Firstname Lastname**

11. Print the Exotic Herbs query. Close the database, and then close Access.

End You have completed Project 5F

Project 5G — Customers

Objectives: *View Relationships in a Database and Establish Relationships Between Tables.*

In the following Performance Assessment, you will establish one-to-many relationships and view those relationships for Southland Gardens. Your relationships report will look similar to Figure 5.46. You will rename the database as *5G_SouthlandCustomers_Firstname_Lastname*.

1. Locate the file **a05G_SouthlandCustomers** from your student files and copy and paste the file to the Chapter 5 folder you created earlier. Remove the Read-only property from the file and rename the file as **5G_SouthlandCustomers_Firstname_Lastname** Start Access and open the database you just renamed.

2. Open the **Customers** table in **Datasheet view**. Examine the data in the table.

3. Close the **Customers** table, and then open the remaining tables in the database and view the data in them. Close all the tables.

4. On the Database toolbar, click the **Relationships** button.

(Project 5G–Customers continues on the next page)

Performance Assessments (continued)

(Project 5G–Customers continued)

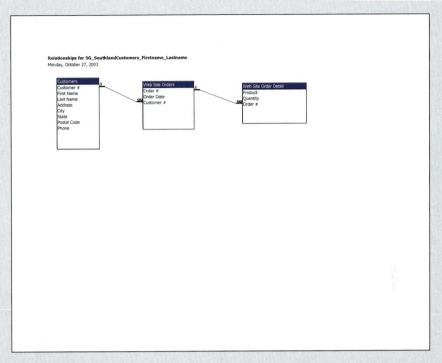

Figure 5.46

5. Right-click in the gray area, click **Show Table**, and then add the **Customers**, **Web Site Orders**, and **Web Site Order Detail** tables to the Relationships window. Resize and move the tables as necessary so that you can view the title bar and complete field list for each table.

6. In the **Customers** table, point to the **Customer #** field, and then drag and drop it on top of the **Customer #** field in the **Web Site Orders** table.

7. In the displayed **Edit Relationships** dialog box, select the **Enforce Referential Integrity** check box, and then click **Create**. A one-to-many relationship is created.

8. In the **Web Site Orders** table, point to the **Order #** field, and then drag and drop it on top of the **Order #** field in the **Web Site Order Detail** table.

9. In the **Edit Relationships** dialog box, select the **Enforce Referential Integrity** check box, and then click **Create**. A one-to-many relationship is created.

10. With the Relationships window open, display the **File** menu, and then click **Print Relationships**. Display the **Page Setup** dialog box and change the page orientation to **Landscape**. On the Print Preview toolbar, click the **Print** button.

(Project 5G–Customers continues on the next page)

Performance Assessments (continued)

(Project 5G–Customers continued)

11. Close the Relationships report and click **Yes** when prompted to save your changes to the report. Using your own information, save the report as **Relationships for 5G_SouthlandCustomers_Firstname Lastname**

12. Close the Relationships window, close the database, and then close Access.

End You have completed Project 5G

Project 5H—Customer Web Site Orders

Objectives: *Identify and Correct Design Errors in Tables and Protect and Maintain a Database.*

In the following Performance Assessment, you will attempt to establish a relationship in a database but will find that you first need to use an Access feature to identify and correct errors in a table. You will correct the errors by locating unmatched records between tables. After locating the unmatched records, you will delete the unmatched records and then establish the relationship. Your completed Relationships report and query results will look similar to the ones shown in Figure 5.47. Additionally, you will encode a database for security purposes. You will save your database as *5H_Customers_Firstname_Lastname*.

1. Locate the file **a05H_Customers** from your student files and copy and paste the file to the Chapter 5 folder you created earlier. Remove the Read-only property from the file and rename the file as **5H_Customers_Firstname_Lastname** Start Access and open the database you just renamed.

2. Open the Relationships window and add the **Web Site Orders** table and the **Web Site Order Detail** table. Move and size the tables so that you can see the entire table title and all the fields. In the **Web Site Orders** table, point to the **Order #** field, and then drag and drop it on the **Order #** field in the **Web Site Order Detail** table. In the **Edit Relationships** dialog box, select the **Enforce Referential Integrity** check box, and then click **Create**. Access displays a message stating referential integrity cannot be enforced.

3. In the message box, click **OK**, close the **Edit Relationships** dialog box, and then close the Relationships window. Click **Yes** to save changes to the layout of the Relationships window.

4. On the Database toolbar, click the **New Object button arrow**. From the displayed list, click **Query**, and from the list of query types, click **Find Unmatched Query Wizard**. Click **OK**.

(Project 5H–Customer Web Site Orders continues on the next page)

Performance Assessments (continued)

(Project 5H–Customer Web Site Orders continued)

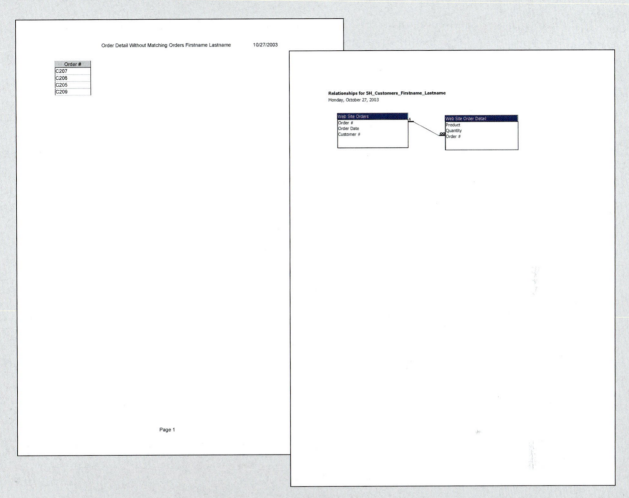

Figure 5.47

5. From the list of tables, click **Table: Web Site Order Detail** and then click **Next**. In this screen, from the list of tables, click **Table: Web Site Orders**, and then click **Next**.

6. From the list of fields, click **Order #** in both lists and then click the **double-headed arrow** button. Click **Next**. Under **Available fields**, click **Order #**, click the **One Field** button, and then click **Next**.

7. In the last screen of the wizard, using your own information, name the query **Order Detail Without Matching Orders Firstname Lastname** and then click **Finish**.

8. Print the query results, and then close the query window.

9. Open the **Web Site Order Detail** table in **Datasheet view**, and then, using your printed query as a reference, delete the records that have the same Order # as in the query results—Order #s **C205**, **C206**, **C207**, and **C209**. Close the table and save if prompted.

(Project 5H–Customer Web Site Orders continues on the next page)

Performance Assessments (continued)

(Project 5H–Customer Web Site Orders continued)

10. Open the Relationships window and create a one-to-many relationship between the **Order #** field in the **Web Site Orders** table and **Order #** field in the **Web Site Order Detail** table. Select the **Enforce Referential Integrity** check box. Print the Relationships report. Close the report and save it as **Relationships for 5H_Customers Firstname_Lastname** Close the Relationships window.

11. On the **Tools** menu, point to **Security**, and then click **Encode/Decode Database**. In the **Encode Database As** dialog box, use the **Save in arrow** to navigate to the folder where you are storing your projects for this chapter and then, in the **File name** box, type **5H_Customer_Encode_Firstname_Lastname** as the file you want to create. Click **Save**.

12. Close the 5H_Customers database and then open the encoded file in a word processing program. View the file, and then close the word processing program. Close Access.

 You have completed Project 5H

Mastery Assessments

Project 5I—Gardens

Objectives: *Index Fields in a Table, View Relationships in a Database, Establish Relationships Between Tables, and Identify and Correct Design Errors in Tables.*

In the following Mastery Assessment, you will perform several operations on the Garden database for Southland Gardens to help improve data accuracy and data integrity. You will also create an index to speed searching and sorting. Your printed Relationships report will look similar to the one shown in Figure 5.48. You will save your database as *5I_Gardens_Firstname_Lastname*.

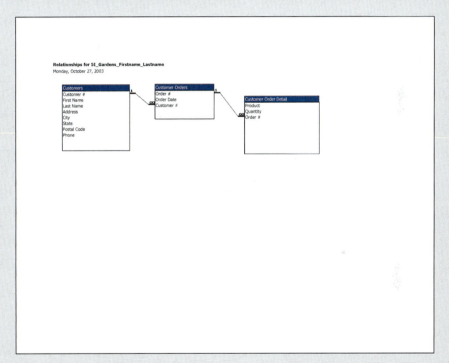

Figure 5.48

1. Locate the file **a05I_Gardens** from your student files and copy and paste the file to the Chapter 5 folder where you are storing your projects for this chapter. Remove the Read-only property from the file and rename the file as **5I_Gardens_Firstname_Lastname** Start Access and open the database you just renamed.

2. In the **States** table, create an index that will not allow duplicate records in the **Abbreviation** field.

3. Create a one-to-many relationship between the **Customers** table and the **Customer Orders** table using the **Customer #** field and enforce referential integrity. Select both the **Cascade Update Related Fields** and **Cascade Delete Related Records** check boxes.

(**Project 5I**–Gardens continues on the next page)

Mastery Assessments (continued)

(Project 5I–Gardens continued)

4. Create a one-to-many relationship between the **Customer Orders** table and the **Customer Order Detail** table using the **Order #** field and enforce referential integrity. You will not be able to enforce referential integrity in this relationship because there are unmatched records between the tables. To correct this, create a query using the **Find Unmatched Query Wizard** to locate the unmatched records between the **Customer Order Detail** table and the **Customer Orders** table. In the query, specify the **Customer Order Detail** table first. Use the **Order #** field as the piece of information that is in both tables. Specify the **Order #** field to display in the query result. Save the query with the default name. Make a note of the Order #s displayed in the query result.

5. Delete any unmatched records from the **Customer Order Detail** table that were displayed in the unmatched records query result you just created, and then establish the relationship between the **Customer Orders** and **Customer Order Detail** table and enforce referential integrity. Select both the **Cascade Update Related Fields** and **Cascade Delete Related Records** check boxes.

6. Change the page orientation of the Relationships report to **Landscape**, print the Relationships report, and be sure your name is in the report name. Close the Relationships report, saving any changes. Close the database and then close Access.

 End You have completed Project 5I

Project 5J — Compact Gardens

Objectives: *Create a Query from Joined Tables and Protect and Maintain a Database.*

In the following Mastery Assessment, you will create a query from joined tables. Your completed query will look similar to the one shown in Figure 5.49. Additionally, you will compact the database. You will rename the database as *5J_Gardens_Firstname_Lastname*.

1. Locate the file **a05J_Gardens** from your student files and copy and paste the file to the Chapter 5 folder where you are storing your projects for this chapter. Remove the Read-only property from the file and rename the file as **5J_Gardens_Firstname_Lastname** Start Access and open the database you just renamed.

2. Create a query that will locate all of the customers in the **Customers** table that have a **Customer Representative** with an **ID#** of **1637**. In your query results, include the **ID#** field from the **SG Employees** table and the **Customer #**, **First Name**, and **Last Name** fields from the **Customers** table.

(Project 5J–Compact Gardens continues on the next page)

Mastery Assessments (continued)

(Project 5J–Compact Gardens continued)

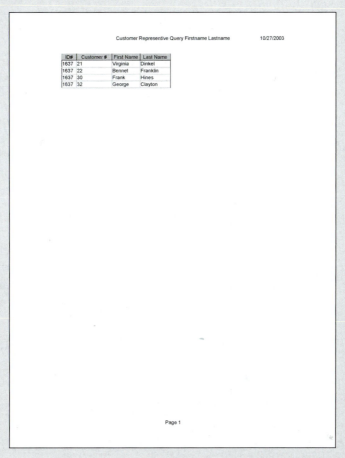

Figure 5.49

3. Save the query as **Customer Representative Query Firstname Lastname** and then print the query.

4. Close the **5J Gardens** database. Compact the **5J_Gardens** database. Save the compacted file as **5J_Gardens_Compacted_Firstname_Lastname** and then close Access.

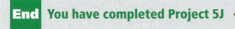 You have completed Project 5J

Access chapter five

Problem Solving

Project 5K—Historical Contacts

Objective: *Create a Query Using the Simple Query Wizard.*

The Simple Query Wizard will not limit data, but it will retrieve data. It is ideal, for example, to create a simple phone list of the contacts in a database.

1. Locate the file **a05K_Historical_Gardens** from your student files and copy and paste the file to the Chapter 5 folder where you are storing your assignments for this chapter. Remove the Read-only property from the file and rename the file as **5K_Historical_Gardens_Firstname_Lastname** Start Access and open the database you just renamed.

2. On the Objects bar, click **Queries**, and then on the Database window toolbar, click **New**. From the displayed list, click **Simple Query Wizard**, and then click **OK**. In the first screen of the Wizard, under **Tables/Queries**, click the arrow, and from the displayed list, click **Table: Historical Gardens Contact Information**. Use the **One Field** button to add the fields **Contact Name** and **Phone Number**, and then click **Next**.

3. Type **Gardens Phone List Firstname Lastname** as the title for the query, and then click **Finish**. Print the query, close the database, and then close Access.

End You have completed Project 5K

Project 5L—SG Income

Objective: *Create and Modify a Crosstab Query.*

Sales of products on the TV show's companion Web site have been growing. The owners of Southland Gardens would like to compare income from each product by state. A special type of query, called a crosstab query, can calculate a sum, average, count, or other type of total for data that is grouped by two types of information—in this case by product and by state. The products will be listed down the left side of the query result, and the states will be listed across the top. Recall that you can run a query based on an existing query. A query containing the product, state, and amount has already been created.

1. Locate the file **a05L_SG_Income** from your student files and copy and paste the file to the Chapter 5 folder where you are storing your assignments for this chapter. Remove the Read-only property from the file and rename the file as **5L_SG_Income_Firstname_Lastname** Start Access and open the database you just renamed.

(**Project 5L**–SG Income continues on the next page)

Problem Solving (continued)

(Project 5L–SG Income continued)

2. On the Objects bar, click **Queries**, and then on the Database window toolbar, click **New**. From the displayed list, click **Crosstab Query Wizard**, and then click **OK**. Under **View**, click the **Queries** option button. At the top of the dialog box, click **Query: Customers Query**, and then click **Next**.

3. Here you select which fields' values (you can pick more than one field) that you want to use as row headings. Under **Available Fields**, click **Product**, and then click the **One Field** button to move this field to the **Selected Fields** list. Click **Next**. Here you select which field's values (you can pick only one field) that you want to use as column headings. Click **StateOrProvince**, and then click **Next**.

4. Here you decide what number you want calculated for each column and row intersection. Under **Fields**, click **Amount**. Under **Functions**, click **Sum**. Click **Next**. Under **What do you want to name your query?**, type **Crosstab Firstname Lastname** and then click **Finish**. Change the **Page Setup** to **Landscape**, and then print your crosstab query. Close the query, close the database, and close Access.

 You have completed Project 5L

On the Internet

Databases and Normalization

The power of relational databases depends on the relationships that are established between the tables in the database. The process of identifying and eliminating the problems associated with data redundancy and a lack of data integrity is called normalization.

Go online and perform a search to learn more about databases and normalization.

GO! with Help

Exporting Data from Access

You can export data from Access to other Microsoft Office 2003 programs. For example, information in a table can be exported into an Excel spreadsheet.

1. Start Access. In the **Type a question for help** box, type **export data** and then press Enter.

2. In the displayed **Search Results** task pane, click the result **Export data or database objects**. Maximize the displayed window. Locate and then click the link **To a Microsoft Excel or other spreadsheet**. Then, click **Save an object's output as a Microsoft Excel file.** Print the Help information. Close the Help window.

3. Open any of the databases that you used in this chapter and, using the printed information, export one of the tables to an Excel spreadsheet. Save the spreadsheet in your chapter folder with a name of your choice.

4. Close the database, and then close Access.

Access 2003

chaptersix

Advanced Forms and Subforms

In this chapter, you will: complete these projects and practice these skills.

Project 6A **Customizing a Form**	**Objectives** • Add Fields to a Form • Use Toolbar Buttons to Enhance a Form • Use Form Control Properties • Make a Form User-Friendly
Project 6B **Creating a Form and Subform**	**Objectives** • Create a Form in Design View • Create a Subform

The Perfect Party

The Perfect Party store, owned by two partners, provides a wide variety of party accessories including invitations, favors, banners and flags, balloons, piñatas, etc. Party planning services include both custom parties with prefilled custom "goodie bags" and "parties in a box" that include everything needed to throw a theme party. Big sellers in this category are the Football and Luau themes. The owners are planning to open a second store and expand their party planning services to include catering.

© Getty Images, Inc.

Advanced Forms and Subforms

Access forms provide you with a way to enter, edit, and display data. You have created forms by using an AutoForm and by using the Form Wizard. Forms can also be created directly in Design view. Access provides tools with which you can enhance the visual appeal of forms, for example, by adding color, backgrounds, borders, user instructions, and ControlTips to the form. In this chapter, you will use advanced techniques to customize forms in Access.

Forms can be used to manipulate data from multiple tables if a relationship exists between the tables. You have practiced creating relationships between tables and have seen that information from multiple objects can be presented in one object, such as a query that located data from multiple tables. Similarly, you can use a form to view information from multiple tables when a one-to-many relationship exists between the tables; this is accomplished by using a form and a subform. A form that is embedded within another form (the main form) is called a *subform*. Subforms are used to view, enter, and edit detailed information that is related to the data in the main form. In this chapter, you will create a subform.

Project 6A New Customers

The Perfect Party uses forms in Access to enter data about their customers into a database. Forms can be customized by adding font colors, backgrounds, borders, and visual cues. Customizing a form in this manner makes the form easier to use for the person who is entering the data.

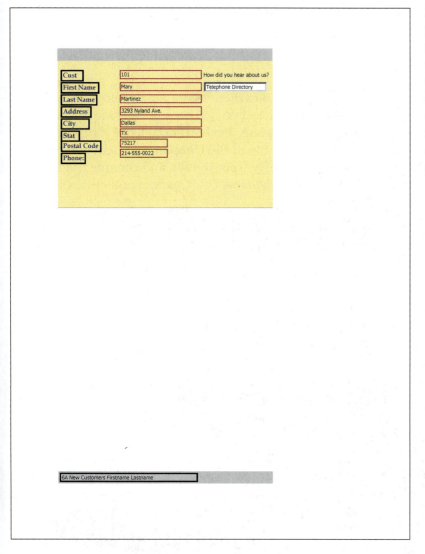

In Activities 6.1 through 6.10, you will modify and enhance the form that The Perfect Party uses to gather data about new customers. Additionally, you will customize the form using many of the features Access provides to make forms easy to use. Your completed form will look similar to Figure 6.1.

Figure 6.1
Project 6A—New Customers

Objective 1
Add Fields to a Form

Using either AutoForm or the Form Wizard, you have practiced creating a form in which you included all of the fields from the underlying table in the form. Fields can also be added to the form after the form is created.

Activity 6.1 Adding Fields to a Form

In this activity, you will add two fields to the Customer Information form, which is used to enter customer information into The Perfect Party customer database.

1 Using the skills you practiced earlier, create a new folder named Chapter 6 in the location where you will be storing your projects for this chapter. Locate the file **a06A_PerfectParty** from your student files and copy and paste the file to the Chapter 6 folder you created. Remove the Read-only property from the file and rename the file as **6A_PerfectParty_Firstname_Lastname** Start Access and open the database you just renamed.

2 On the Objects bar, click **Forms**. Open the **Customer Information** form in **Form view** and examine the layout and fields in the form.

The underlying table for the Customer Information form is the PP Customers table. This form is **bound**—linked to—the PP Customers table. The PP Customers table is the **record source** for the Customer Information form. Between two bound objects, the record source is the object from which the actual data comes.

3 Switch to **Design view** and maximize the window. View the controls in the form, and then resize the right edge of the form to approximately **4.5 inches on the horizontal ruler** and the bottom edge to approximately **3 inches on the vertical ruler**. See Figure 6.2. This will give you more space to work with the form.

Recall that the Design view of a form displays **text box controls**—where the actual data from the corresponding table is displayed—and **label controls**—the field names from the corresponding table. See Figure 6.2. Each text box is bound (linked to) a specific field in the table. A **control** is a graphical user interface object, such as a text box, a check box, scroll bar, or command button, which provides user control for a program.

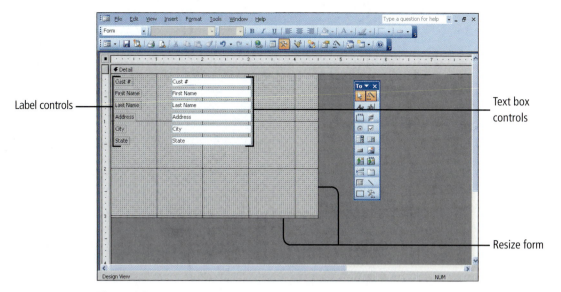

Figure 6.2

4. From the **View** menu, click **Page Header/Footer**. If necessary, display the Toolbox toolbar, and then click the **Label** button. In the **Page Footer section**, draw a label control as shown in Figure 6.3, and then, using your own information, type **6A New Customers Firstname Lastname**

5. If necessary, on the Form Design toolbar, click the **Field List** button to display the field list. Alternatively, display the View menu, and then click Field List.

   The field list displays a list of the fields from the corresponding table—PP Customers.

6. Point to the lower edge of the field list, drag to expand the list so that you can view all the field names, and then drag the list to the right side of your screen. In the **Field List**, click the **Postal Code** field, and then drag it into the **Detail section** of the form, positioning the small white box attached to your mouse pointer directly under the left edge of the white **State** text box control. Compare your screen with Figure 6.3. If you are not satisfied with your result, click **Undo** and begin again. Notice that the point at which you drop the small box attached to the pointer is where the white text box control will be created, and the label control will be positioned to the left.

   The Postal Code control is added to the Customer Information form.

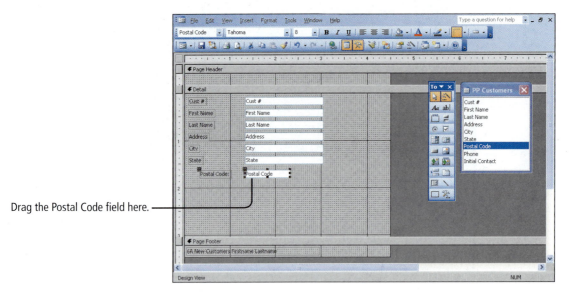

Drag the Postal Code field here.

Figure 6.3

> ### Note — Positioning the Fields You Add to a Form
>
> *Position the field where you want the text box control to be*
>
> When adding fields to a form in Design view by dragging from the Field List, the position is determined by the text box control. Drag and drop the field from the field list in the location where you want the text box control to be and the label control will be positioned to the left of the text box control. Then, select the label control, display the pointing hand pointer, and adjust its position as desired.

7 Point to the large selection handle in the upper left corner of the **Postal Code label control** until the pointing hand mouse pointer displays. Then, using the techniques you have practiced in previous chapters, adjust the position of the **Postal Code label control** and text box control as shown in Figure 6.4. (Hint: Recall that you can use the arrow keys on your keyboard to nudge the controls in small increments.)

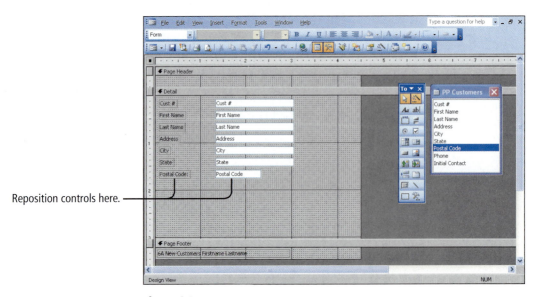

Reposition controls here.

Figure 6.4

356   **Access** | Chapter 6: Advanced Forms and Subforms

8 Use the technique you just practiced to add the **Phone** field to the **Customer Information** form, and then adjust the position of the controls, as shown in Figure 6.5.

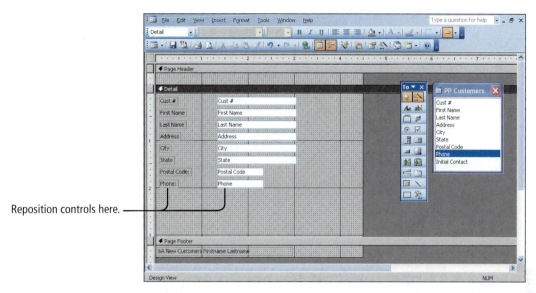

Reposition controls here.

Figure 6.5

9 Save the form and switch to **Form view** to view the changes to the form.

10 Switch to **Design view** and leave the **Customer Information** form open in Design view for the next activity.

Objective 2
Use Toolbar Buttons to Enhance a Form

Many of the Access features for enhancing the appearance of a form are available from the Formatting toolbar. For example, from the Formatting toolbar, you can modify font colors that make the form more attractive.

Activity 6.2 Modifying Font Color

In this activity, you will modify the font color in the fields for the Customer Information form.

1 With the **Customer Information** form open in Design view, click once in the **Cust # label control**. See Figure 6.6.

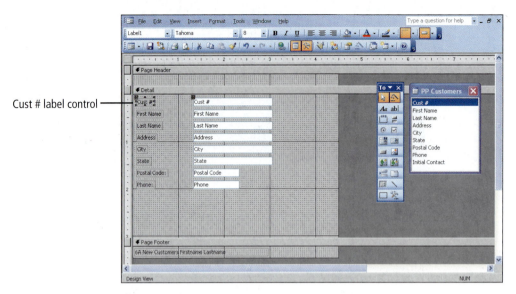

Cust # label control

Figure 6.6

2 On the Formatting toolbar, click the **Font/Fore Color button arrow**, and from the color palette, in the first row, click the seventh color—**dark blue**. See Figure 6.7.

The color of the text changes from black to blue.

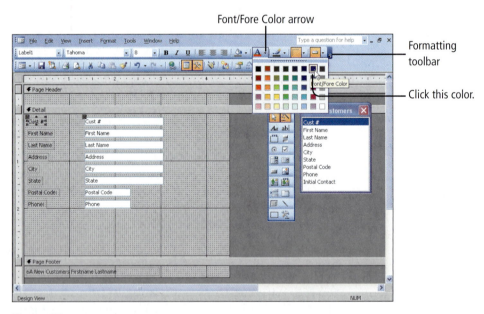

Figure 6.7

3 Hold down Shift and click each of the remaining label controls to select them. On the Formatting toolbar, click the **Font/Fore Color** button. Notice that you do not need to display the color palette—the button retains the color most recently used.

Another Way — To Select Controls on a Form

Use the rulers!

Controls on a form can be selected by using either the horizontal ruler or the vertical ruler in Design view. Clicking on a location on the horizontal ruler will select all of the controls on the form that are located directly beneath the location on the ruler where you clicked. Clicking a location on the vertical ruler will select the controls that are located directly to the right in the form.

4 Deselect the label controls, and then switch to **Form view** to view the changes to the form. See Figure 6.8.

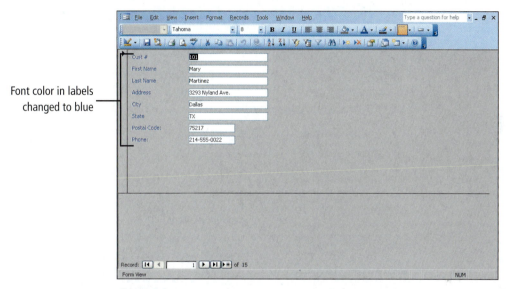

Font color in labels changed to blue

Figure 6.8

5 Switch to **Design view** and leave the form open in Design view for the next activity.

Activity 6.3 Adding a Background Color to a Form

Color can also be added to the background of a form. In this activity, you will modify the background color for the Customer Information form.

1 With the **Customer Information** form open in Design view, locate the **Section Selector** for the **Detail** section, as shown in Figure 6.9.

Section selectors are used to select entire sections of a form to perform section-level operations, such as adding background colors.

2 Click once on the **Section Selector** for the **Detail** section. See Figure 6.9.

The darkened bar, as shown in Figure 6.9, indicates that the entire Detail section of the form is selected.

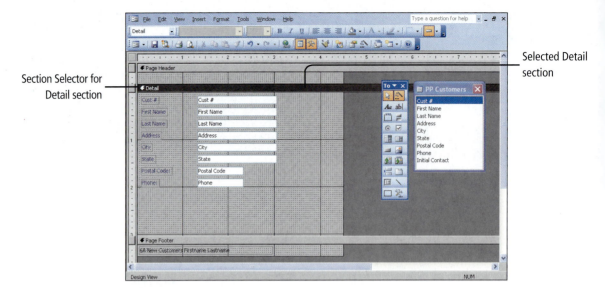

Figure 6.9

3. On the Formatting Toolbar, click the **Fill/Back Color button arrow**, and from the displayed palette, in the fifth row, click the second color—**pale peach**. See Figure 6.10.

The background color for the form changes to a peach color.

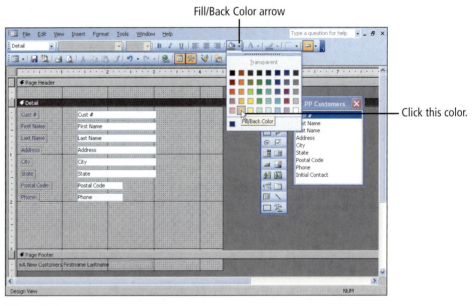

Figure 6.10

4 Switch to **Form view** and view the background color that has been added to the form.

5 Switch to **Design view**, display the **Fill/Back Color** palette again, and then in the fifth row, click the third color—**pale yellow**.

The background color for the form changes to yellow.

6 Save the form, and then switch to **Form view** and view the background color for the form. See Figure 6.11.

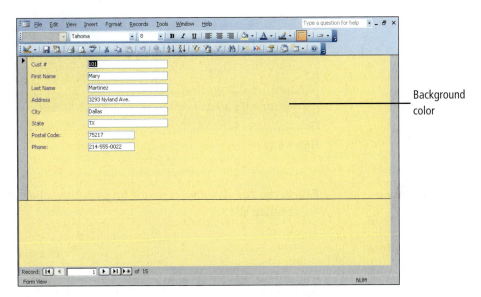

Background color

Figure 6.11

7 Switch to **Design view** and leave the form open in Design view for the next activity.

More Knowledge — Adding a Background Color to Text boxes

Apply a background color to a text box

Background colors can also be added to the background of text box controls. First, click the text box control to which you want to add a background color. Then, on the Formatting toolbar, click the Fill/Back Color arrow, and click the background color you want to apply.

Activity 6.4 Applying a Border to a Control in a Form

In this activity, you will add a border to controls in the Customer Information form.

1 With the **Customer Information** form open in Design view, click once in the **Cust # label control**.

2 On the Formatting toolbar, click the **Line/Border Width button arrow**. See Figure 6.12.

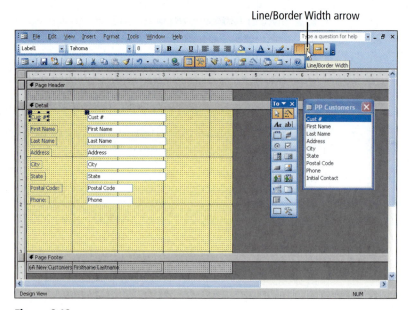

Figure 6.12

3 From the displayed set of line widths, click **3** as shown in Figure 6.13.

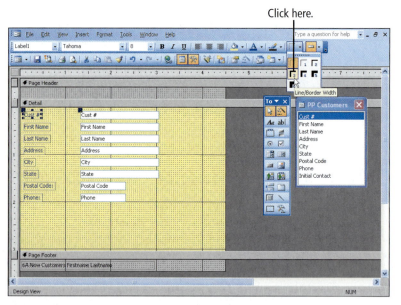

Figure 6.13

4 Switch to **Form view** and view the border that surrounds the **Cust # label**.

This border is too wide to be visually appealing on this form.

5 Switch to **Design View**, be sure the **Cust # control** is still selected, and then change the **Line/Border Width** to **2**.

6 On the **Edit** menu, click **Select All** to select all of the controls on the form, and then apply a **Line/Border Width** of **2** to all of the controls. You need only click the button, because it has retained its most recent selection of 2. See Figure 6.14.

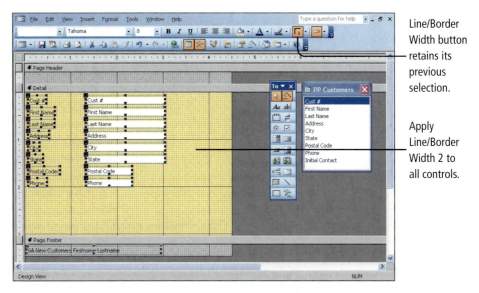

Line/Border Width button retains its previous selection.

Apply Line/Border Width 2 to all controls.

Figure 6.14

More Knowledge — Applying Formats

Use the Format Painter

Once you apply formatting to a control, you can apply the same formatting to a control by using the Format Painter located on the Formatting toolbar. Select the control that has the formatting that you want to apply to other controls, click the Format Painter button on the Formatting toolbar, and then click the control to which you want the formatting applied.

7 Deselect the controls, save the form, and then switch to **Form view** and view the changes made to the form. See Figure 6.15.

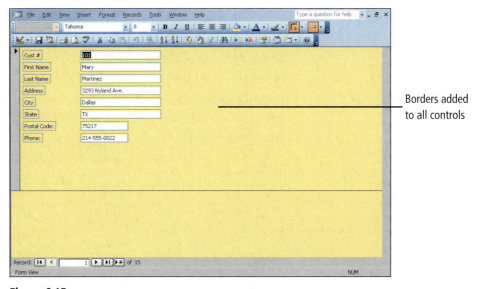

Borders added to all controls

Figure 6.15

Project 6A: New Customers | **Access** 363

8 Switch to **Design view** and leave the form open in Design view for the next activity.

Objective 3
Use Form Control Properties

There are multiple methods you can use to modify a form's appearance. Each control on a form has **properties**—characteristics that determine not only the appearance, but also the structure and behavior of the control, as well as the characteristics of the text or data it contains. You can view a control's properties on its associated **property sheet**. The color and border width of a control are examples of control properties. They can be changed from the Formatting toolbar, as you did in the previous activity, and are also available in each control's associated property sheet, along with numerous other control properties.

Activity 6.5 Changing Text Properties on a Form Using the Property Sheet

In this activity, you will modify text properties for the Customer Information form using the property sheet associated with a control.

1 With the **Customer Information** form open in Design view, click once in the **Cust # label control**.

2 On the Form Design toolbar, click the **Properties** button to display the property sheet.

The property sheet for the Cust # label control displays. Both the title bar and the box at the top of the property sheet indicate *Label1*.

Another Way

To Display the Property Sheet

Click the Properties button

You can also display a control's property sheet by right-clicking a control, and then clicking Properties from the shortcut menu. Alternatively, you can double-click the control.

---

3 Click the **Format tab**, and then, if necessary, move the property sheet to the top of the screen and drag the lower edge of the property sheet down so that all properties can be viewed. See Figure 6.16.

Related properties for the control can be displayed by clicking on the appropriate tab. The Format tab displays properties related to how the control displays.

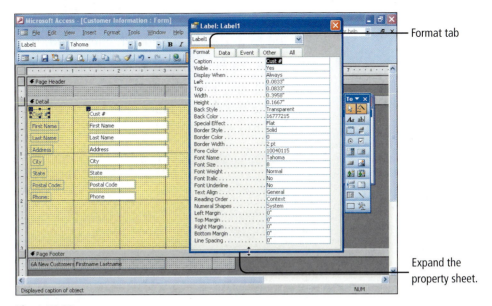

Figure 6.16

4 About halfway down the list, locate and click in the **Font Name** box, and then click the **down arrow** that displays. See Figure 6.17.

A list of available fonts displays.

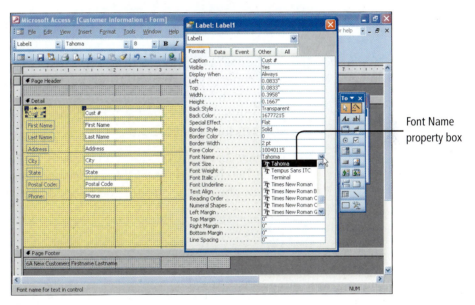

Figure 6.17

5 From the list of available fonts, scroll as necessary, and then click **Book Antiqua**.

6 Click in the **Font Size** box, click the **down arrow** that displays, and from the list of font sizes, click **10**.

7 Click in the **Font Weight** box, click the **down arrow** that displays, and from the displayed list, click **Bold**.

8 Close the property sheet by clicking the **Close** button ☒ in the title bar of the property sheet.

9 Resize the **Cust # label control** to accommodate the increased font size and weight. See Figure 6.18.

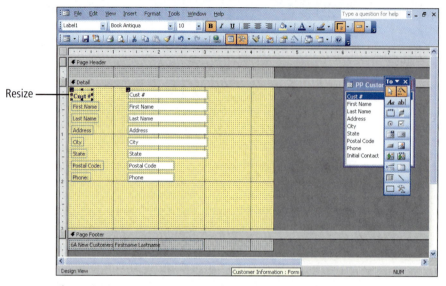

Figure 6.18

10 Hold down Shift and select all the remaining label controls. Display the Properties sheet, and then use the techniques you just practiced to apply the same modifications to the remaining label controls as you applied to the **Cust # label control** (**Book Antiqua** font, font size **10**, font weight **Bold**).

11 Deselect the controls and adjust each control slightly to accommodate the enlarged text. Then, save the form and switch to **Form view** to view the changes to the form. See Figure 6.19.

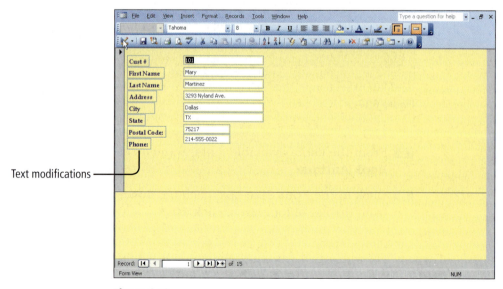

Figure 6.19

12 Switch to **Design view** and leave the form open in Design view for the next activity.

Activity 6.6 Refining Additional Properties on a Form Using the Properties Box

In this activity, you will modify more properties for the Customer Information form using the property sheet.

1 With the **Customer Information** form open in Design view, click the **Cust # text box control**, display the **Properties sheet**, click once in the **Back Style** box, and then click the **down arrow** that displays. See Figure 6.20.

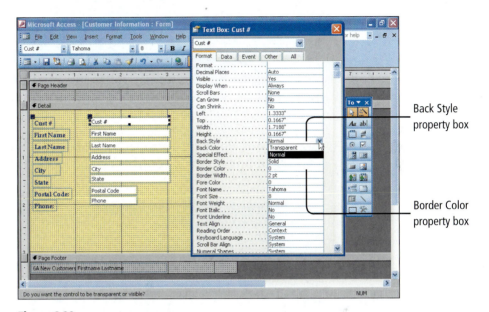

Figure 6.20

2 Click **Transparent**.

The background of the control is now transparent and will allow the background color of the form to show through.

3 Click once in the **Border Width** box, click the **down arrow**, and in the list of widths, click **1 pt**.

4 Click once in the **Border Color** box, click the **Build** button (the button with the three small dots), and from the displayed **Color** dialog box, in the third row, click the seventh color—**burgundy**. Compare your property sheet with Figure 6.21, and then click **OK**.

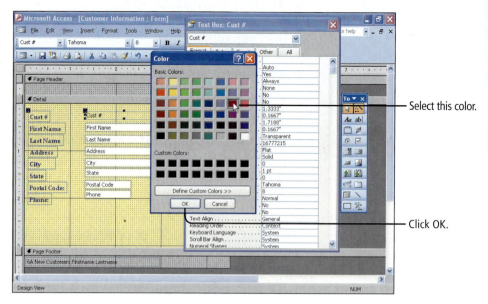

Figure 6.21

5 Without closing the property sheet, hold down Shift and select the remaining text box controls on the form. See Figure 6.22.

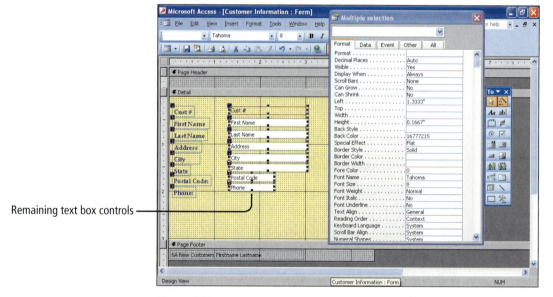

Figure 6.22

6 To the remaining text box controls, apply the same **Back Style**, **Border Width**, and **Border Color** as you applied to the **Cust # text box control**.

7 Close the property sheet, save the form, deselect the controls, and then switch to **Form view** to view the changes you have made to the form. See Figure 6.23.

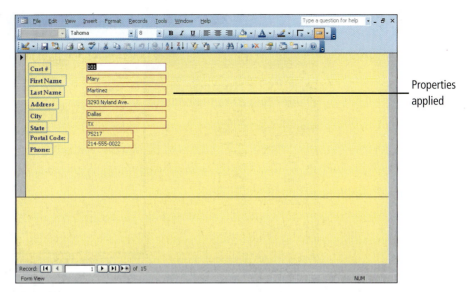

Figure 6.23

8 Switch to **Design view** and leave the form open in Design view for the next activity.

Objective 4
Make a Form User-Friendly

To make Access forms easy to use, you can also add instructions for a user that display on the status bar while data is being entered and custom ControlTips that display within the form. Additionally, you can change the **tab order** of the fields on a form and add controls such as a **combo box** to a form. Tab order refers to the order in which fields are selected when the Tab key is pressed—the order does not necessarily have to be in the exact order that the controls display on the screen. A combo box allows the person entering data into the form to either type the information or choose information from a predefined list.

Activity 6.7 Adding Instructions to the Status Bar of a Form

One way to make data entry easier is to provide instructions relating to the field that will display on the **status bar**. The status bar is the horizontal bar at the bottom of the screen directly above the taskbar. Its function is to display information about the current condition of the program, such as the status of items in the window and the progress of the current task, or information about the selected item. In this activity, you will use features of Access to add user instructions to the status bar in the Customer Information form.

1 With the **Customer Information** form open in Design view, click the **First Name text box control** to select it, and then click the **Properties** button to display the property sheet.

2 In the Properties sheet, click the **Other tab**. See Figure 6.24.

Figure 6.24

3 In the **Status Bar Text** box, type **Enter customer's First Name**

4 Click in the **Last Name text box control** to select it.

5 In the property sheet, in the **Status Bar Text** box, type **Enter customer's Last Name**

6 Close the Properties sheet, switch to **Form view**, click once in the **First Name** field in the form, and view the status bar. See Figure 6.25.

The instructions that you specified display in the status bar.

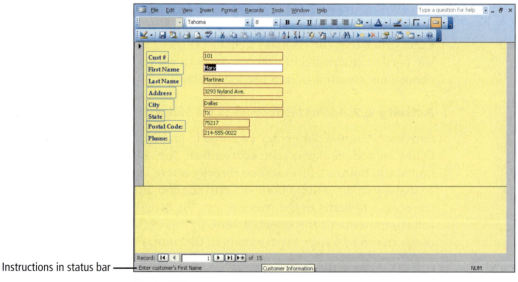

Figure 6.25

7 Click in the **Last Name** field and view the instruction that displays in the status bar.

8 Switch to **Design view** and leave the form open in Design view for the next activity.

Activity 6.8 Creating Custom ControlTips

Another way to make a form easier to use is to add custom **ControlTips** that display when a user pauses the mouse pointer over a control in a form. A ControlTip, similar to a Windows ScreenTip, temporarily displays descriptive text while the mouse pointer is paused over the control. This method is somewhat limited, because most users use the Tab key to move from field to field, and thus do not see the ControlTip. However, adding ControlTips is a useful technique, particularly in a training situation when a user is new to the data entry form.

1 With the **Customer Information** form open in Design view, click the **Cust # label control** to select it.

2 Display the **Properties sheet** and click the **Other tab**.

3 In the **ControlTip Text** box, type **Customer #** as shown in Figure 6.26.

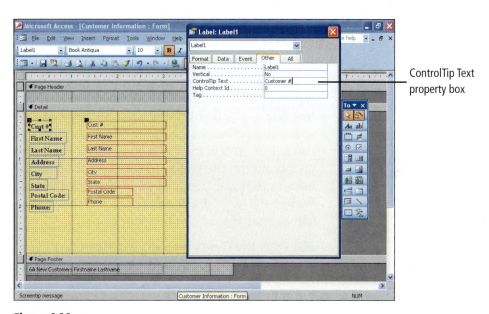

Figure 6.26

4 Without closing the Properties sheet, click the **Address label control** once to select it.

5 In the **Properties sheet**, in the **ControlTip Text** box, type **Customer Address**

6 Close the **Properties sheet**, save the form, switch to **Form view**, and position your mouse pointer over the **Cust # label**. See Figure 6.27.

The ControlTip you specified displays.

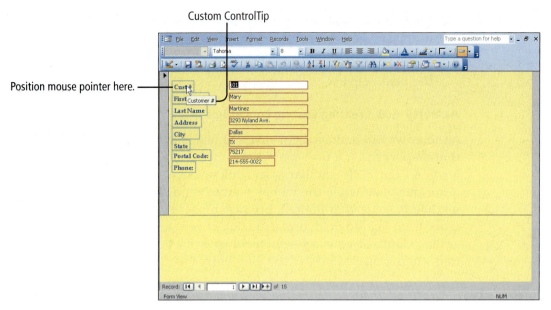

Figure 6.27

▣ Switch to **Design view** and leave the form open in Design view for the next activity.

Activity 6.9 Adding a Combo Box to a Form

A **combo box** is another control that can be added to a form. A combo box combines the features of a text box and a list box—you can either type text into the control or choose a selection from a predefined list. A **list box** is a control that displays a scrollable list of selections. You can add a combo box to a form to display a list of values from which a user can select. The values in a combo box can either come from a table or the user can type the value. In this activity, you will add a combo box to the form to indicate the form of advertising that brought the customer to The Perfect Party. You will create the list that the user will see by typing the values that the combo box will display.

▣ With the **Customer Information** form open in Design view, if necessary, click the Toolbox button 🛠 to display the Toolbox toolbar.

▣ On the Toolbox toolbar, click the **Combo Box** button 📇, and then position your mouse pointer in the form as shown in Figure 6.28.

372 **Access** | Chapter 6: Advanced Forms and Subforms

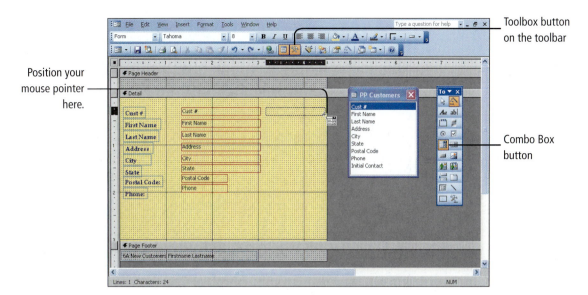

Figure 6.28

3 Draw a rectangle as shown in Figure 6.29, and then release the mouse button.

The Combo Box Wizard displays.

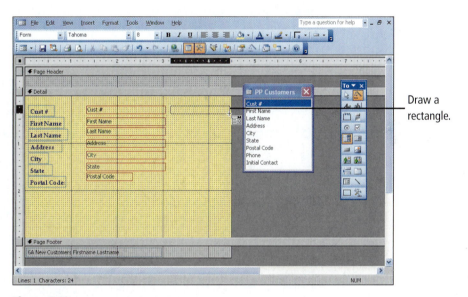

Figure 6.29

4 In the first screen of the wizard, click the **I will type in the values that I want** option button, and then click **Next**.

5 In this screen of the wizard, click under **Col1**, type **Telephone Directory** and then widen the column slightly so that you can see your typing as shown in Figure 6.30.

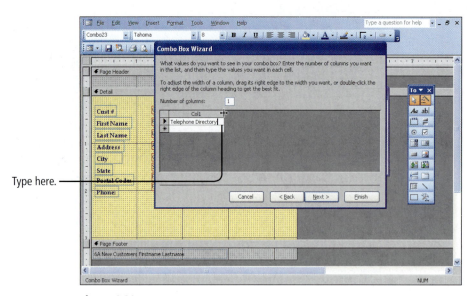

Figure 6.30

[6] Press Tab and type **Internet**

[7] Press Tab and type **Newspaper Ad**

[8] Press Tab and type **Friend**

[9] Press Tab and type **Other** as shown in Figure 6.31, and then click **Next**.

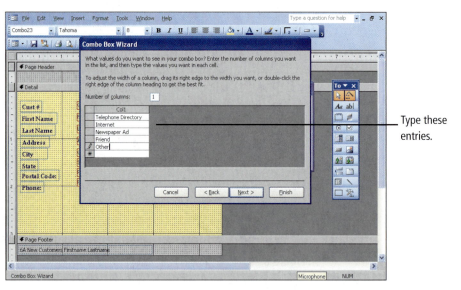

Figure 6.31

[10] In this screen, be sure that the **Remember the value for later use** option button is selected.

This screen allows you to choose how you want Access to store the values you typed for the combo box.

11 Click **Next**, and in this screen of the wizard, under *What label would you like for your combo box?*, type **How did you hear about us?** and then click **Finish**.

12 Reposition the control below its label control as shown in Figure 6.32 (move the white box down and the label control to the right). This control is an **unbound** object, meaning that the data in this field is not derived from data that is contained in a table; rather, the data is derived from the list you created within the wizard.

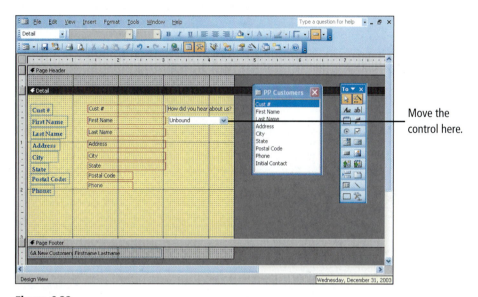

Move the control here.

Figure 6.32

13 Be sure the white **combo box text box control** you added is selected, and then click the **Properties** button to display the Properties sheet.

14 Click the **Data tab** and then in the **Control Source** box, click the **down arrow**. See Figure 6.33.

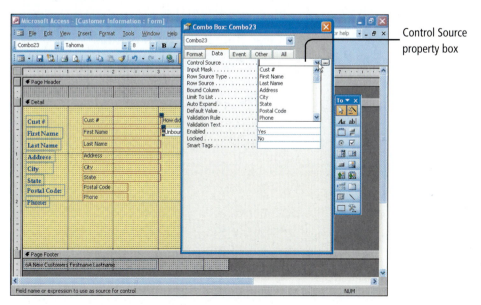

Control Source property box

Figure 6.33

Project 6A: New Customers | **Access** 375

15 From the displayed list, scroll down and click **Initial Contact**.

Specifying this field as the control source will insert the information entered in the combo box into the Initial Contact field for this customer in the PP Customers table. In this manner, the table will be updated with the information about how the customer learned about The Perfect Party.

16 Close the **Properties sheet**, switch to **Form view**, and while viewing the record for Cust # 101, click the **down arrow** that displays in the **combo box control** you added to the form.

The list of choices that you specified displays.

17 Click **Telephone Directory** as shown in Figure 6.34.

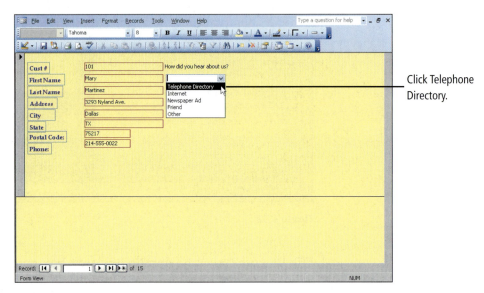

Figure 6.34

18 Close the form, save your changes, and open the **PP Customers** table in Datasheet View. Locate the information for Cust # 101, and notice that under Initial Contact, the new information has been inserted.

19 Close the **PP Customers** table.

Activity 6.10 Changing the Tab Order on a Form

You can customize the order in which you enter data on a form by customizing the tab order on a form. Tab order refers to the order in which the fields will be selected each time the Tab key is pressed.

1 Open the **Customer Information** form in **Form view**, and watch the form as you press Tab eight times.

Notice that the insertion point moves from field to field starting with the Cust # and ending with the combo box control.

2 Switch to **Design view**, display the **View** menu, and then click **Tab Order**. Alternatively, right-click the control and click Tab Order from the displayed shortcut menu.

The Tab Order dialog box displays.

3 Click the **selector** that is to the left of the **Combo** field. See Figure 6.35. (Note: You will see a number, such as *19*, next to your combo box. This is a number automatically assigned by Access and will differ from the number shown in the figure, depending on what controls have been created previously on your computer.)

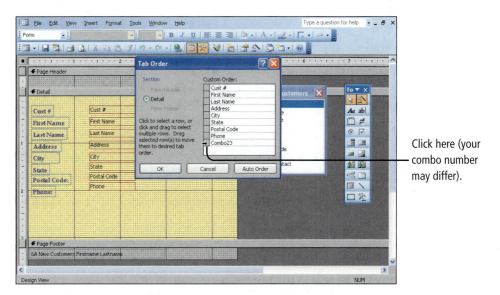

Click here (your combo number may differ).

Figure 6.35

4 Drag this field up under the **Cust #** field, as shown in Figure 6.36, and then click **OK**.

The order of fields that displays in this list is the order in which fields will be selected as the Tab key is pressed.

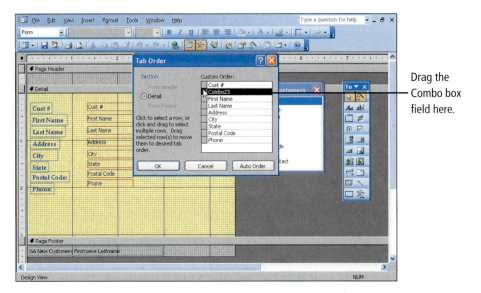

Drag the Combo box field here.

Figure 6.36

5 Switch to **Form view** and press Tab.

Notice that the insertion point moves from the Cust # field to the combo box, because this is the tab order you specified.

6 On the **File** menu, click **Print**. In the **Print** dialog box, under **Print Range**, click the **Selected Record(s)** option button, and then click **OK**.

The form containing record #101 will print, with your name in the page footer.

7 Close the form and save your changes. Close the database and close Access.

End You have completed Project 6A

Project 6B Existing Customers

As you have seen and practiced, forms can be created using a variety of methods. Another method by which a form can be created is by creating the form entirely in Design view.

In Activities 6.11 through 6.15, you will create a form in Design view and then modify the form. Additionally, you will add a subform to an existing form. Your completed form will look similar to Figure 6.37.

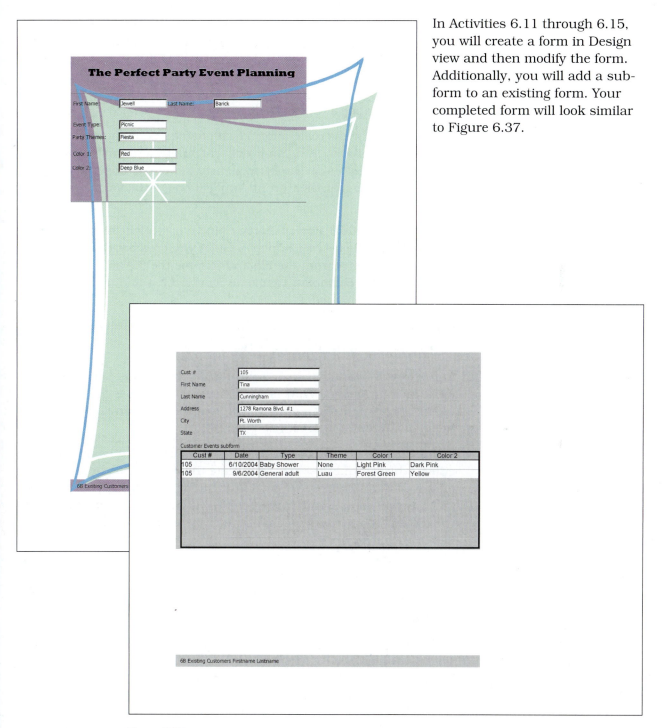

Figure 6.37
Project 6B—Existing Customers

Objective 5
Create a Form in Design View

Usually when you create a form, you will use either AutoForm or the Form Wizard and then modify the form in Design view to suit your needs. When the selections in AutoForm or the Form Wizard do not provide a good match with the specifications for your form, you can create a form entirely in Design view. Creating a form in Design view is a common technique when additional controls, such as combo boxes or subforms, need to be added to the form.

Activity 6.11 Creating a Form in Design View

In this activity, you will create a form that customers of The Perfect Party fill out when they are planning an event. The information in this form will assist the employees at The Perfect Party in helping customers choose party supplies for their event. You will create the form entirely in Design view.

1 Locate the file **a06B_PerfectParty** from your student files and copy and paste the file to the Chapter 6 folder you created. Remove the Read-only property from the file and rename the file as **6B_PerfectParty_Firstname_Lastname** Start Access and open the database you just renamed.

2 On the Objects bar, click **Forms**, and then on the database window toolbar, click the **New** button.

3 In the **New Form** dialog box, from the list of methods to create a form, be sure **Design View** is selected. Next to *Choose the table or query where the object's data comes from*, click the **down arrow**, and then click **Event Choices**. See Figure 6.38.

Event Choices is a query in this database. Forms can be based on either tables or queries. You will create this form using fields that exist in multiple tables. When creating a form in Design View where the data will come from multiple tables, it is easier to use a query as the record source for the form because the tables were already specified in the query.

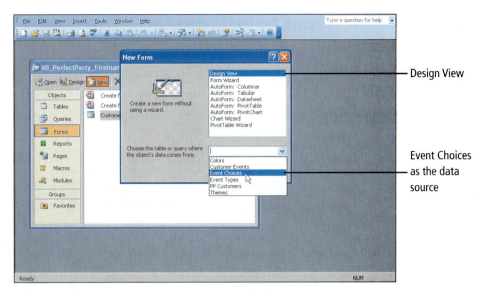

Figure 6.38

4 Click **OK**.

A blank form displays in Design view and the field list for the Event Choices query displays. Additionally, the Toolbox toolbar displays floating on your screen. See Figure 6.39.

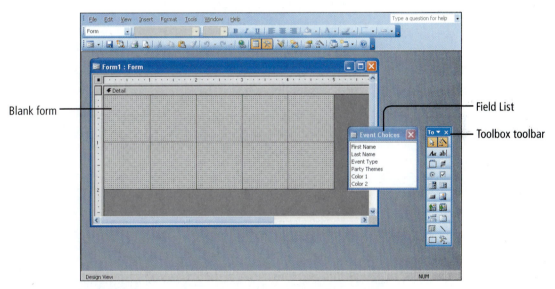

Figure 6.39

5 Display the **File** menu, click **Save As** and then, in the **Save As** dialog box, under **Save Form 'Form 1' To** type **Event Planning** Click **OK**.

The name displays in the title bar of the form.

6 Using the techniques you practiced in Project 6A, add the fields from the field list to the form and reposition them approximately as shown in Figure 6.40. (Hint: Align the left edge of the small white box attached to the pointer, which represents the white label control, with the vertical grid line. Use [Ctrl] plus the arrow keys to move in small increments.)

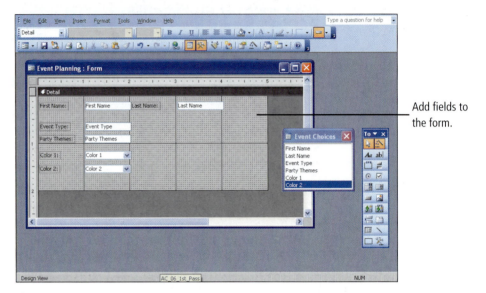

Add fields to the form.

Figure 6.40

7 Click the **Color 1 text box control**, hold down [Shift], and then click the **Color 2 text box control**.

Both controls are selected.

8 Resize the controls by dragging a right center sizing handle to approximately **2.25 inches on the horizontal ruler**, so that they display as shown in Figure 6.41.

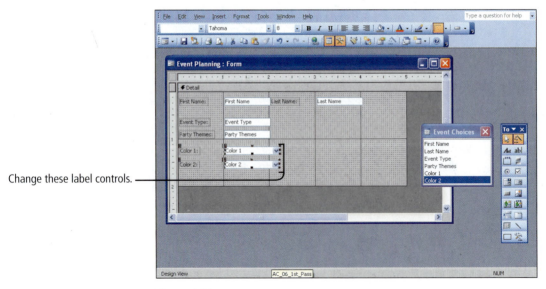

Change these label controls.

Figure 6.41

382   **Access** | Chapter 6: Advanced Forms and Subforms

9 Deselect the controls.

10 Using the technique you practiced in Project 6A, click the **Section Selector** for the **Detail section**, click the **Fill/Back Color button arrow**, and in the fifth row, click the seventh color—**lavender**.

11 On the Form Design toolbar, click the **Save** button to save the form.

12 Leave the form open in Design view for the next activity.

Activity 6.12 Specifying a Picture Background

Forms can be customized to reflect the intention of the designer, whether it be fun, serious, or professional. In this activity, you will add a picture to the background of the form.

1 Be sure your **Event Planning** form is open in **Design view**, and locate the **Form selector** as shown in Figure 6.42.

The **Form selector** is the box where the rulers meet, in the upper left corner of a form in Design view. Use the Form selector to perform form-level operations, such as selecting the form.

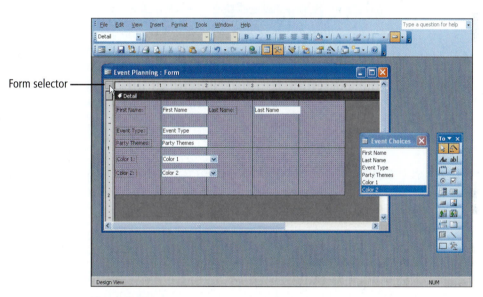

Figure 6.42

Another Way

To Select the Entire Form

Use the Edit menu

Another way to select the entire form is to display the Edit menu and then click Select Form.

2 Double-click the **Form selector**.

The Properties sheet for the form displays.

3 Click the **Format tab**, click in the **Picture** box, and then click the **Build** button (the button with the three small dots).

4 In the displayed **Insert Picture** dialog box, navigate to the location where your student files are stored, and then double-click the file **a06B_ppbackground**.

The ppbackground graphic displays in the background of the form. (In this file name, *pp* stands for Perfect Party.)

5 Click in the **Picture Size Mode** box, click the **down arrow**, and then click **Stretch**.

The Stretch mode sizes the picture to fit the Form window.

6 **Close** the Properties sheet, **Save** the form, switch to **Form view**, and then view the changes you have made to the form.

More Knowledge — Other Picture Properties

Picture Type, Picture Alignment, Picture Tiling

From the property sheet, you can modify additional properties related to a graphic inserted into the form. Picture Type allows you to choose whether the picture will be embedded or linked. Picture Alignment allows you to modify the alignment of the picture. If you want the picture to be repeated across the form's background, choose the Yes option for Picture Tiling.

---

7 Switch to **Design view** and leave the form open for the next activity.

Activity 6.13 Adding a Title to the Form

A title on a form informs the user about the purpose of a form. In this activity, you will add a title to the Event Planning form.

1 Be sure your **Event Planning** form is open in **Design view**, maximize the form, display the **View** menu, and then click **Form Header/Footer**.

Form Header and Footer sections display in the form.

2 Expand the **Form Header section** down to approximately **0.5 inches on the vertical ruler** by positioning your pointer on the horizontal line between the **Form Header section** and the **Detail section** until the pointer changes to a large double arrow, then drag downward to approximately **0.5 inch on the vertical ruler**. (Hint: Drag past the 0.5 inch mark to view it, and then drag up again for precise positioning.)

3 If necessary, display the Toolbox, and then on the Toolbox toolbar, click the **Label** button. Draw a label control in the **Form Header section** as shown in Figure 6.43.

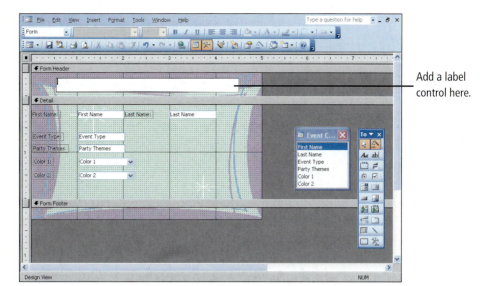

Figure 6.43

4. In the label box, type **The Perfect Party Event Planning**

5. Click in a blank area of the form to deselect the **Form Header label control**, and then click it again to select it.

6. On the Formatting toolbar, click the **Center** button.

   The text in the label control is centered horizontally within the label.

7. With the label still selected, change the font for the text in the label to **Rockwell Extra Bold**, and then change the font size to **16**.

8. If necessary, drag the left and right center resize handles to accommodate the text, and then compare your screen with Figure 6.44.

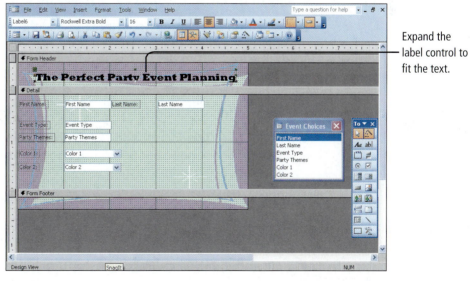

Figure 6.44

Project 6B: Existing Customers | **Access** 385

9 Display the **View** menu, and then click **Page Header/Footer**. Add a label control in the **Page Footer section** and, using your own information, type **6B Existing Customers Firstname Lastname**

10 Switch to **Form view** and view the changes you have made to the form. Navigate to record **6**, the record for Jewell Barick.

11 On the **File** menu, click **Print**. In the **Print** dialog box, under **Print Range**, click the **Selected Record(s)** option button, and then click **OK**.

12 Close the form and save your changes.

Objective 6
Create a Subform

A *subform* is a form contained within another form. The form that contains the subform is the *main form*. Subforms are especially useful when you want to display data between two tables that have a one-to-many relationship. To create a form that will display data from two tables, a relationship must exist between the tables. The main form contains the data that is the *one* side of the relationship and the subform contains the data that is the *many* side of the relationship.

Activity 6.14 Creating a Subform

The Customer Information form you modified in Project 6A contains contact information about customers of The Perfect Party. The owners of The Perfect Party want to view the information in the Customer Information form and, at the same time, view information about the events that each customer has coordinated through The Perfect Party. This is accomplished by creating a subform within a main form. In this activity, you will add a subform that contains information about customer events to the main form—the Customer Information form.

1 Open the **Customer Information** form in **Design view**. If necessary, close the **Field List**.

2 **Maximize** the form if necessary, and then expand the width of the form to **6.5 inches on the horizontal ruler**.

Expanding the form will provide space for you to place the subform.

3 From the **View** menu, add the **Page Header/Footer sections** to your form. Then, create a label in the **Page Footer** and type **6B Existing Customers Firstname Lastname**

4 In the **Toolbox**, locate the **Subform/Subreport** button.

Recall that the Toolbox contains controls that can be added to database objects.

5 Click the **Subform/Subreport** button, draw a control in the lower part of the form as shown in Figure 6.45, and then release the mouse button.

The SubForm Wizard displays.

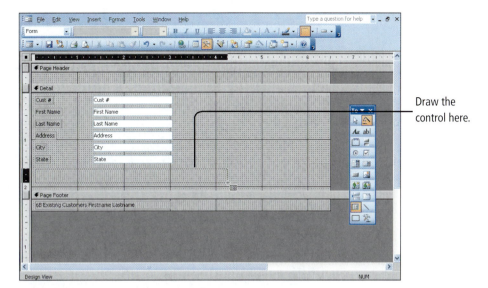

Figure 6.45

6 In the first screen of the wizard, accept the default selection *Use existing Tables and Queries* by clicking **Next**.

7 Under **Table/Queries**, click the **down arrow**, and then click **Table: Customer Events**.

The Customer Events table contains the information that will display in the subform.

8 Click the **All Fields** button , and then click **Next**.

Clicking the All Fields button will cause all of the fields in the Customer Events table to display in the subform.

9 This screen allows you to define which fields link the main form to the subform. In other words, this is where you choose which field(s) are common to both tables. Be sure that the **Choose from a list** option button is selected, and then click **Next**.

10 In the final screen of the wizard, accept the default subform name and click **Finish**.

A subform is created in the Customer Information form. The form may display much smaller than it did before you created the subform.

11 **Maximize** the form, close the **Field List**, and close the **Toolbox**. The subform will display too small to be useful; therefore, expand the subform by dragging the right edge of the subform to **6.5 inches on the horizontal ruler**. Then, if necessary, hold down Ctrl and click ↓ ten to twelve times to nudge the subform down so that the subform label control is not touching the **State control**.

12 Switch to **Form view** and view the subform.

The record with Cust # 101 displays in the main form and below the main form, notice the subform that displays any events that are related to this customer. See Figure 6.46.

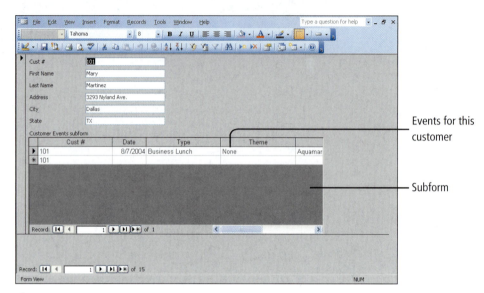

Figure 6.46

13 Leave the form open in **Form view** for the next activity.

Activity 6.15 Adding Records Using the Subform

Records that are added in a subform will also be added to and display in the corresponding table. In this activity, you will add a record using the subform in the Customer Information form, and that will update information in the Customer Events table.

1 Be sure your **Customer Information** form is open in **Form view**. Resize the field widths in the subform so that all of the fields display in the subform, and then at the bottom of your screen, use the navigation area in the main form to navigate to the record that has **Cust # 105**. See Figure 6.47.

Both the form and the subform have their own navigation areas to assist you in locating specific records.

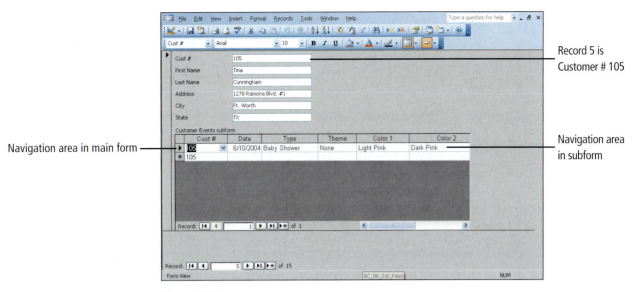

Figure 6.47

2 In the subform, enter the data as shown in Figure 6.48 using the down arrows to select from a list.

A relationship between the PP Customers table and the Customer Events table exists. The field that ties the two tables together is the Cust # field.

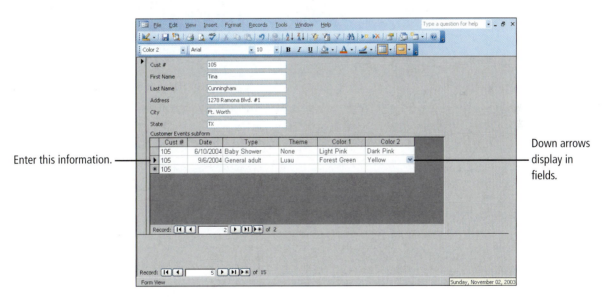

Figure 6.48

3 Display the **Page Setup** dialog box, click the **Page tab**, click **Landscape**, and then click **OK**. On the **File** menu, click **Print**, and in the **Print** dialog box, under **Print Range**, click **Selected Record(s)**. Click **OK**. Close the form and save your changes to the form and subform.

The subform name displays in the Database window. You can view the information contained in the subform either by opening the subform directly from the Database window or by opening the main form.

4 On the Objects bar, click **Tables**, and then open the **Customer Events** table and locate the information you just entered. See Figure 6.49.

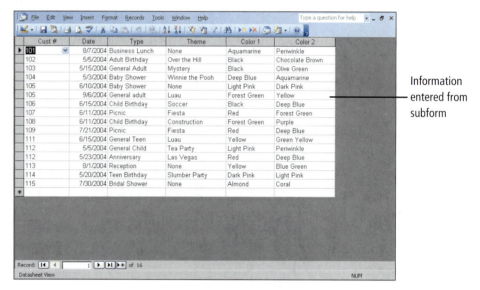

Information entered from subform

Figure 6.49

5 Close the **Customer Events** table. Close the database, and then close Access.

End You have completed Project 6B

Summary

In this chapter, you practiced creating and modifying forms in Access using advanced techniques. You added fields to a form in Design view. You modified a form's properties using both the Formatting toolbar and the form's property sheet. You modified properties such as font properties, backgrounds, colors, and record sources. Additionally, you added user-friendly qualities to a form such as custom ControlTips, added status bar instructions, and customized the tab order.

You created a form in Design view and then modified its properties. Finally, you created a subform and added it to a main form. You practiced adding a record to the subform and viewed the updated record in the corresponding table.

In This Chapter You Practiced How To

- Add Fields to a Form
- Use Toolbar Buttons to Enhance a Form
- Use Form Control Properties
- Make a Form User-Friendly
- Create a Form in Design View
- Create a Subform

Concepts Assessments

Matching Match each term in the second column with its correct definition in the first column by writing the letter of the term on the blank line in front of the correct definition.

____ 1. The toolbar that contains buttons that allow you to change the way a control displays.

____ 2. The location that provides access to the properties of the controls on a form.

____ 3. The term used to describe two objects that are linked to each other.

____ 4. The control that contains the actual data from the corresponding table.

____ 5. The object where the data comes from between two linked objects.

____ 6. The horizontal bar at the bottom of the screen that displays information about the current condition of the program.

____ 7. The property sheet tab that contains properties for a control related to the manner in which the property displays.

____ 8. Descriptive text that temporarily displays when the mouse is pointed to a control in the form.

____ 9. The type of control that displays the field names.

____ 10. A graphical user interface object such as a text box or a check box that provides user control for a program.

____ 11. The characteristics that determine the appearance, structure, and behavior of a control.

____ 12. A form that is embedded within a main form.

____ 13. Used to select a portion of a form in order to perform section-level operations, such as adding background colors.

____ 14. Data in this kind of field is not derived from data contained in a table.

____ 15. In a one-to-many relationship, the form that contains the data from the table that corresponds to the *one* side of the relationship.

A Bound
B Control
C ControlTip
D Format
E Formatting
F Label control
G Main form
H Properties
I Property sheet
J Record source
K Section selector
L Status bar
M Subform
N Text box control
O Unbound

Concepts Assessments (continued)

Fill in the Blank Write the correct answer in the space provided.

1. The control that lets you either type in text or choose from a list selection is a _____.

2. The properties for a control can be accessed by right-clicking the control, clicking the Properties button on the Formatting toolbar, or by _____ the control.

3. Each text box control on a form is bound, or linked to, a field in a _____.

4. In the property sheet, related properties are grouped together and can be accessed by clicking the appropriate _____.

5. The sequence in which fields are selected when the Tab key is pressed is referred to as the _____.

6. The Control Source property box is available in the property sheet on the _____ tab.

7. The control that contains a scrollable list of selections is a _____.

8. Creating a form using _____ provides additional flexibility in the form's construction over other methods of creating a form.

9. When adding a title to a form in the Form Header section, you should use a _____ control.

10. The small gray box located in a form's Design View where the two rulers meet is the _____.

Skill Assessments

Project 6C—Questionnaire

Objectives: *Add Fields to a Form and Use Toolbar buttons to Enhance a Form.*

In the following Skill Assessment, you will modify a form that is an interview questionnaire that customers of The Perfect Party fill out. You will add fields to the form and modify form properties. Your completed form will look similar to the one shown in Figure 6.50. You will rename the database as *6C_Questionnaire_Firstname_Lastname* in the folder you have created for this chapter.

Figure 6.50

1. Locate the file **a06C_Questionnaire** from your student files, and copy and paste the file to the Chapter 6 folder you created. Remove the Read-only property from the file and rename the file as **6C_Questionnaire_Firstname_Lastname** Start Access and open the database you just renamed.

2. Open the **Customer Questionnaire** form in **Form view** and examine the form structure.

(**Project 6C**–Questionnaire continues on the next page)

Skill Assessments (continued)

(Project 6C–Questionnaire continued)

3. Switch to **Design view**, maximize the window, and then view the controls in the form.

4. Display the **Toolbox** toolbar, click the **Label** button, draw a label control in the **Page Footer section**, and then using your own information, type **6C Questionnaire Firstname Lastname** into the **Page Footer control**.

5. On the Form Design toolbar, click the **Field List** button to display the list of fields in the **Customer Questionnaire** table. Alternatively, display the View menu and then click Field List.

6. If necessary, drag the field list to the right of your screen and expand it so that you can view all the fields in the list. Click the **Consultation?** field, drag into the form, position the small box under the left side of *What one special event do you plan this year?* and then release the mouse button.

7. If necessary, adjust the position of the **Consultation? text box control** and label control as shown in Figure 6.51.

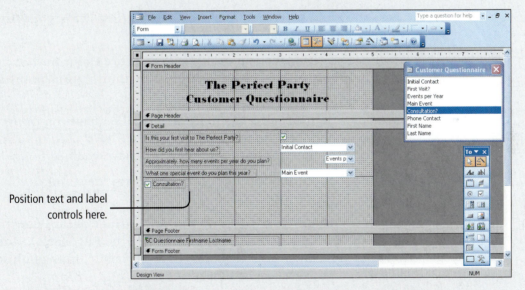

Position text and label controls here.

Figure 6.51

8. Select the **Events per Year** control and drag its left center sizing handle to the left to **3 inches on the horizontal ruler**. Then, using the technique you just practiced, add the **Phone Contact**, **First Name**, and **Last Name** fields to the **Customer Questionnaire** form and position them as shown in Figure 6.52. (Recall that the white box attached to the pointer indicates where the white label control will be placed, and that after you drop the field into the form, you can use Ctrl plus the arrow keys on your keyboard to nudge the control in small increments.)

(Project 6C–Questionnaire continues on the next page)

Skill Assessments (continued)

(Project 6C–Questionnaire continued)

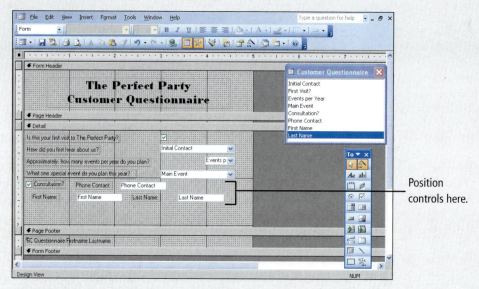

Figure 6.52

9. Close the **Field List**, and then click once in the **Is this your first visit to The Perfect Party? label control**.

10. On the Formatting toolbar, click the **Font/Fore Color button arrow** and from the displayed color palette, in the third row, click the seventh color—**dark purple**.

11. Hold down Shift and select the remaining **label controls** on the form. Change the font color to the same dark purple color used in the previous step—the **Font/Fore Color** button will have retained this color.

12. Deselect the controls and then switch to **Form view** and view the changes to the form.

13. Switch to **Design view**. Click once in the **Initial Contact control** to select it. On the Formatting toolbar, click the **Fill/Back Color button arrow** and from the displayed color palette, in the fifth row, click the sixth color—**light blue**.

14. Hold down Shift and select the **five remaining controls** (Events per Year, Main Event, Phone Contact, First Name, Last Name), and apply the same blue color to those controls as you applied in Step 13.

15. Click to deselect all the controls, and then click once in the **Initial Contact control** to select it. On the Formatting toolbar, click the **Line/Border Color button arrow** and from the displayed palette, in the second row, click the seventh color—**blue**. The applied color is not immediately visible in Design view.

(Project 6C–Questionnaire continues on the next page)

Skill Assessments (continued)

(Project 6C–Questionnaire continued)

16. Select the **five remaining controls** (Events per Year, Main Event, Phone Contact, First Name, Last Name), and apply the same blue border color to those controls as you applied to the Initial Contact control in Step 15.

17. Switch to **Form view** and view the changes made to the form.

18. On the Formatting toolbar, click the **Print Preview** button to view your form as it will print, and then, on the Print Preview toolbar, click **Close**. On the **File** menu, click **Print**, and then click **OK**.

19. Close the form and save your changes. Close the database, and then close Access.

 You have completed Project 6C

Project 6D — Perfect Party Customers

Objectives: *Use Form Control Properties and Create a Form in Design View.*

In the following Skill Assessment, you will create a new form in Design view for customers of The Perfect Party. Additionally, you will modify properties for the form. Your completed form will look similar to Figure 6.53. You will rename and save your database as 6D_*PerfectPartyCustomers_Firstname_Lastname*.

1. Locate the file **a06D_PerfectPartyCustomers** from your student files and copy and paste the file to the Chapter 6 folder you created. Remove the Read-only property from the file and rename the file as **6D_PerfectPartyCustomers_Firstname_Lastname** Start Access and open the database you just renamed.

2. On the Objects bar, click **Forms**, and then on the Database window toolbar, click the **New** button.

3. From the list of methods to create a form, be sure **Design View** is selected. To the right of *Choose the table or query where the object's data comes from*, click the **down arrow**, and then click **Perfect Party Customers**. Click **OK**.

4. **Maximize** the form. Display the **File** menu, click **Save As**, and in the **Save As** dialog box, under **Save Form 'Form1' To** type **Perfect Party Customers** and then click **OK**.

(**Project 6D**–Perfect Party Customers continues on the next page)

Skill Assessments (continued)

(Project 6D–Perfect Party Customers continued)

Figure 6.53

5. From the **View** menu, click **Page Header/Footer**. If necessary, display the Toolbox toolbar, click the **Label** button, and then draw a label control in the **Page Footer section** beginning at the upper left corner and extending down and to **3.5 inches on the horizontal ruler**. Using your own information, type **6D Perfect Party Customers Firstname Lastname** into the **Page Footer control**.

6. Expand the form to **6.5 inches on the horizontal ruler,** and then add all of the fields from the **Field List** to the form as shown in Figure 6.54.

(Project 6D–Perfect Party Customers continues on the next page)

Skill Assessments (continued)

(Project 6D–Perfect Party Customers continued)

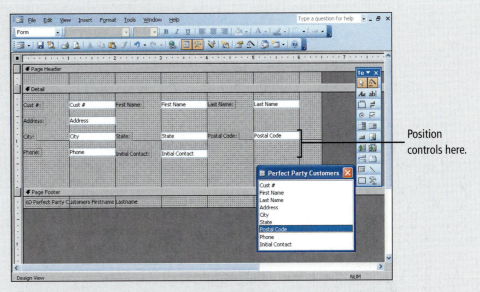

Figure 6.54

7. Display the **Edit** menu, click **Select All**, and then click the **Properties** button to display the Properties sheet.

8. Be sure the **Format tab** is selected, click in the **Font Name** property box, and then click the **down arrow** that displays.

9. From the list of available fonts, scroll as necessary, and then click **Lucida Sans**. Close the Properties sheet. Click in a blank area of the form to deselect the controls.

10. Hold down Shift, and then select all of the *label* controls. With all of the label controls selected, display the **Properties** sheet, and then click the **Format tab**. Click in the **Font Underline** property box, click the **down arrow** that displays, and then click **Yes**.

11. Close the Properties sheet. With all of the label controls still selected, right-click any *label* control, on the displayed shortcut menu, point to **Font/Fore Color**, and from the color palette, in the fifth row, click the last color—**white**.

12. Deselect the label controls by clicking a blank area of the form. Click the **Detail section selector**, and on the Formatting toolbar, click the **Fill/Back Color button arrow**. From the color palette, in the first row, click the seventh color—**dark blue**. Apply this same background color to the **Page Header section** and the **Page Footer section**.

13. Select the **Initial Contact label control**, and then stretch the right edge of this control slightly to the right so that the entire label displays. Select the **Page Footer control**, and then click the **Font/Fore Color** button, which should be white, to change the footer text to white.

(Project 6D–Perfect Party Customers continues on the next page)

Skill Assessments (continued)

(Project 6D–Perfect Party Customers continued)

14. From the **View** menu, click **Form Header/Footer,** and then expand the **Form Header section** down to approximately **0.5 inches on the vertical ruler**.

15. On the Toolbox toolbar, click the **Label** button, and then draw a label control in the **Form Header section** beginning at **1 inch on the horizontal ruler** to **6 inches on the horizontal ruler**, and in the label box, type **The Perfect Party Customers**

16. Click in a blank area of the form to deselect the label control and then click the **Form Header control** again to select it. Click the **Font/Fore Color** button to change the font color to **white**. On the Formatting toolbar, click the **Center** button.

17. On the Formatting toolbar, click the **Font Size button arrow**, and then click **14**.

18. Select the **Cust # text box control**. On the Form Design toolbar, click the **Properties** button, and then click the **Other tab**.

19. In the **Status Bar Text** property box, type **Enter the Customer #** and then close the Properties sheet.

20. Switch to **Form view**, and view the modifications you have made to the form.

21. Click once in the **Cust #** field in the form, and view the instruction in the status bar.

22. On the **File** menu, click **Print**, and in the **Print** dialog box, under **Print Range**, click **Selected Record(s)**, and then click **OK**.

23. Close the form and save your changes. Close the database, and then close Access.

 You have completed Project 6D

Skill Assessments (continued)

Project 6E — Special Orders

Objectives: *Make a Form User-Friendly and Create a Subform.*

In the following Skill Assessment, you will modify the properties of an existing form and add a subform. Your completed form will look similar to Figure 6.55. You will rename and save your database as *6E_SpecialOrders_Firstname_Lastname.*

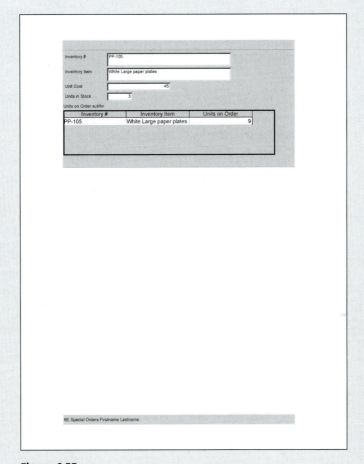

Figure 6.55

1. Locate the file **a06E_SpecialOrders** from your student files and copy and paste the file to the Chapter 6 folder you created. Remove the Read-only property from the file and rename the file as **6E_SpecialOrders_Firstname_Lastname** Start Access and open the database you just renamed.

2. On the Objects bar, click **Forms**. Open the **Inventory** form in **Form view** and examine the layout and data in the form. Switch to **Design view**, and then **maximize** the form on your screen.

(Project 6E–Special Orders continues on the next page)

Skill Assessments (continued)

(Project 6E–Special Orders continued)

3. From the **View** menu, click **Page Header/Footer**. If necessary, display the Toolbox toolbar, click the **Label** button, and then, beginning in the upper left corner of the **Page Footer section**, draw a control down and over to **3.5 inches on the horizontal ruler**. Using your own information, type **6E Special Orders Firstname Lastname** into the **Page Footer control** you just created.

4. Select the **Unit Cost label control**.

5. On the Formatting toolbar, click the **Properties** button, and then click the **Other tab**.

6. In the **ControlTip Text** property box, type **Cost for each inventory unit**

7. Leave the Properties sheet open, select the **Units in Stock label control**, and then in the **ControlTip Text** property box, type **Number of units currently in stock**

8. Close the Properties sheet. In the Toolbox, click the **Subform/Subreport** button. Starting at the left edge of the form at **1.5 inches on the vertical ruler**, draw a rectangle approximately one inch tall and four inches wide. Use the horizontal and vertical rulers to guide you, but do not be concerned about getting this measurement exact, because you will resize the subform in a later step.

9. In the first screen of the wizard, leave the default selection as *Use existing Tables and Queries*, and then click **Next**.

10. Under **Tables/Queries**, click the **down arrow**, and then click **Table: Units on Order**.

11. Click the **All Fields** button, and then click **Next**

12. Accept the default settings in this screen of the wizard, and then click **Next**.

13. In the final screen of the wizard, accept the default subform name and click **Finish**.

(Project 6E–Special Orders continues on the next page)

Skill Assessments (continued)

(Project 6E–Special Orders continued)

14. Maximize the form if necessary. As shown in Figure 6.56, resize the form and position the subform. Expand the right edge of the form as shown in Figure 6.56, and then expand the right edge of the subform.

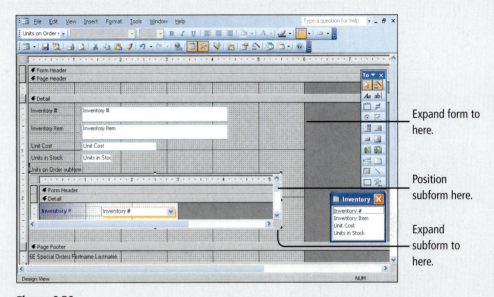

Figure 6.56

15. Switch to **Form view**. Navigate to record **PP-105**, examine the data in the subform and verify that there are 9 units on order for this record.

16. On the **File** menu, click **Print**, and in the **Print** dialog box, under **Print Range**, click **Selected Record(s)**, and then click **OK**.

17. Close the form and save your changes to the form and subform. Close the database, and then close Access.

You have completed Project 6E

Access chapter six

Performance Assessments

Project 6F—Customer Events

Objectives: *Make a Form User-Friendly and Create a Form in Design View.*

In the following Performance Assessment, you will create a form in Design view for The Perfect Party Customer Events. Your completed form will look similar to Figure 6.57. You will rename and save your database as *6F_CustomerEvents_Firstname_Lastname*.

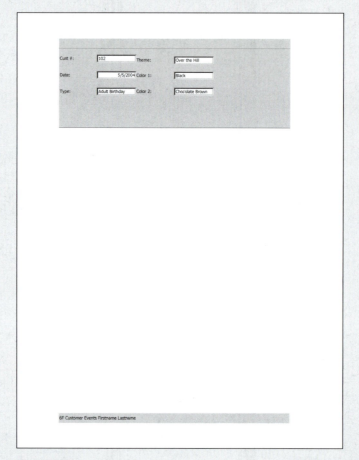

Figure 6.57

1. Locate the file **a06F_CustomerEvents** from your student files and copy and paste the file to the Chapter 6 folder you created. Remove the Read-only property from the file and rename the file as **6F_CustomerEvents_Firstname_Lastname** Start Access and open the database you just renamed.

2. On the Objects bar, click **Forms**, and then on the database window toolbar, click **New**. From the list of methods to create a form, be sure **Design View** is selected and select **Customer Events** as the table where the object's data comes from. Click **OK**.

(**Project 6F**–Customer Events continues on the next page)

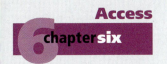

Performance Assessments (continued)

(Project 6F–Customer Events continued)

3. **Maximize** the form on your screen, and then save the form as **The Perfect Party Customer Events**

4. Add the **Page Header/Footer sections** to your form, draw a label control in the **Page Footer section**, and using your own information, type **6F Customer Events Firstname Lastname** into the form's **Page Footer section**.

5. Expand the right edge of the form to **6 inches on the horizontal ruler**. Expand the **Field List** as necessary to view all of the field names. Add all of the fields from the **Field List** to the form, dropping the text box controls on the vertical lines and positioning them as shown in Figure 6.58.

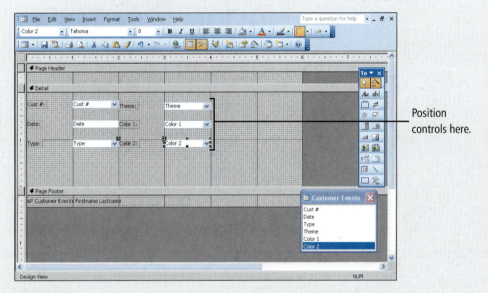

Figure 6.58

6. Right-click anywhere in a blank area of the **Detail section**, and from the displayed shortcut menu, click **Tab Order**.

7. In the **Tab Order** dialog box, position the pointer in the **selector** to the left of the **Theme** field until a black right-pointing arrow displays and then click. Point to the small selector box, and then drag up slightly to position this field as the first one in the list. Click **OK**.

8. Switch to **Form view** and notice that the **Theme** field is selected, because you made it first in the Tab order. Press [Tab] until you have moved through each field.

9. Be sure record 2 for Cust #102 is displayed. On the **File** menu, click **Print**, and in the **Print** dialog box, under **Print Range**, click **Selected Record(s)**, and then click **OK**.

10. Close the form and save your changes. Close the database, and then close Access.

End You have completed Project 6F

Access chapter six

Performance Assessments (continued)

Project 6G—Customer Questionnaire

Objectives: *Use Toolbar Buttons to Enhance a Form and Use Form Control Properties.*

In the following Performance Assessment, you will modify an existing questionnaire form for new customers of The Perfect Party. Your completed form will look similar to Figure 6.59. You will rename and save your database as *6G_CustomerQuestionnaire_Firstname_Lastname*.

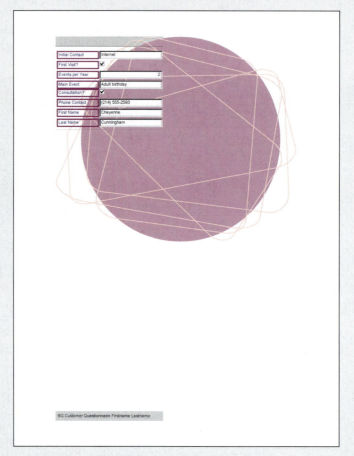

Figure 6.59

1. Locate the file **a06G_CustomerQuestionnaire** from your student files and copy and paste the file to the Chapter 6 folder you created. Remove the Read-only property from the file and rename the file as **6G_CustomerQuestionnaire_Firstname_Lastname** Start Access and open the database you just renamed.

2. Open the **Customer Questionnaire** form in **Design view** and **maximize** the form. Right-click a blank area of the form and from the **Fill/Back Color** palette, in the fifth row, click the last color—**white**.

(**Project 6G**–Customer Questionnaire continues on the next page)

Performance Assessments (continued)

(Project 6G–Customer Questionnaire continued)

3. Select all of the **label controls** on the form. On the Formatting toolbar, click the **Font/Fore Color button arrow** and from the displayed palette, in the first row, click the seventh color—**blue**.

4. With the label controls still selected, click the **Properties** button. On the **Format tab**, change the **Border Color** to **purple** (fourth row, seventh color). Change the **Border Width** to **2 pt**.

5. Leave the Properties sheet open. Click the **Form Selector** button (at the left end of the horizontal ruler), be sure the **Format tab** is displayed, click the **Picture** property box, and then click the **Build** button that displays. From the displayed **Insert Picture** dialog box, navigate to your student files and insert the file **a06G_ppbackground** as the background for this form.

6. In the Properties sheet, change the **Picture Size Mode** to **Zoom**, change the **Picture Alignment** to **Top Left**, and then close the Properties sheet.

7. Create a **Page Footer control** the approximate width of the form, and type **6G Customer Questionnaire Firstname Lastname** Switch to **Form view**.

8. On the **File** menu, click **Print**, and in the **Print** dialog box, under **Print Range**, click **Selected Record(s)**, and then click **OK**.

9. Close the form and save your changes. Close the database, and then close Access.

 You have completed Project 6G

Project 6H—Customer Orders

Objectives: *Add Fields to a Form and Create a Subform.*

In the following Performance Assessment, you will create a subform for the Customers Form that will include information about customer orders at The Perfect Party. Your completed form will look similar to Figure 6.60. You will rename and save your database as *6H_CustomerOrders_Firstname_Lastname*.

1. Locate the file **a06H_CustomerOrders** from your student files and copy and paste the file to the Chapter 6 folder you created. Remove the Read-only property from the file and rename the file as **6H_CustomerOrders Firstname_Lastname** Start Access and open the database you just renamed.

2. Open the **Customers Form** in **Design view**, and then **maximize** the form on your screen.

(Project 6H–Customer Orders continues on the next page)

Performance Assessments (continued)

(Project 6H–Customer Orders continued)

[Figure: Customer Order Form screenshot]

Figure 6.60

3. In the **Toolbox**, click the **Subform/Subreport** button, and then draw a rectangle in the form approximately the width of the form beginning at **1.75 inches on the vertical ruler** down to **2.75 inches on the vertical ruler**, positioned directly under the **City**, **State**, and **Postal code controls**. In the Subform Wizard, use existing tables and queries, and then use all of the fields from the **Customer Orders** table in the subform. Accept the remaining defaults in the wizard.

4. The subform will display too small to use; therefore, **maximize** the form, and expand the subform to approximately the width of the main form.

5. Create a label control in the **Page Footer section** of the form, type **6H Customer Orders Firstname Lastname** and then switch to **Form view**. Resize the fields in the subform so that they fit in the viewable area of the subform. In the **main form**, navigate to **Cust # 104** and view the order information in the subform.

6. On the **File** menu, click **Page Setup**, and change the **Page Orientation** to **Landscape**. On the **File** menu, click **Print**, and in the **Print** dialog box, under **Print Range**, click **Selected Record(s)**, and then click **OK.**

7. Close the form and save your changes to the form and subform. Close the database, and then close Access.

Mastery Assessments

Project 6I — Inventory

Objectives: *Use Toolbar Buttons to Enhance a Form, Use Form Control Properties, Make a Form User-Friendly, and Create a Form in Design View.*

In the following Mastery Assessment, you will create a form in Design view for inventory at The Perfect Party. Your completed form will look like Figure 6.61. You will rename and save your database as *6I_Inventory_Firstname_Lastname*.

Figure 6.61

1. Locate the file **a06I_Inventory** from your student files and copy and paste the file to the Chapter 6 folder you created. Remove the Read-only property from the file and rename the file as **6I_Inventory_Firstname_Lastname** Start Access and open the database you just renamed.

(**Project 6I**—Inventory continues on the next page)

Project 6I: Inventory | **Access** 409

Mastery Assessments (continued)

(Project 6I–Inventory continued)

2. On the Objects bar, click **Forms**. Using Figure 6.62 as your guide, from the database window toolbar, click **New** and create a new form in **Design View** using the data in the **Inventory** table. Save the form as **Inventory Form** and then add all four of the fields from the table to the form. Position the fields as shown in Figure 6.62. Recall that as you drag the field into the form, the white text box control will be positioned at the point where you drop the small box, and the gray label control box will be positioned to its left.

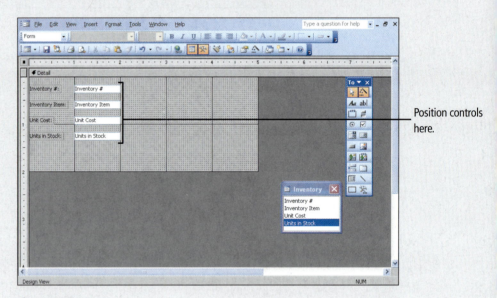

Figure 6.62

3. Change the font for the four **label controls** to **Times New Roman** and change the font size to **12**. Resize the label controls appropriately to accommodate the enlarged text.

4. Change the **background color** for the **label controls** to **white** and add a **1 pt. dark blue border** to the **label controls**. Change the **background color** for the **form** to **white**.

5. Add **ControlTip Text** to the **Unit Cost textbox control** that reads Enter Cost per Unit

(Project 6I–Inventory continues on the next page)

Mastery Assessments (continued)

(Project 6I–Inventory continued)

6. Add a **Form Header section**, add a label that reads **Inventory Form** and then center the text in the control and change the font size to **14**. Apply **Bold** to the text in the Form Header. (Hint: Recall that you must deselect and then reselect the form header label for the purpose of applying formatting.)

7. Create a control the **Page Footer section** and type **6I Inventory Firstname Lastname**

8. Print only the first record of the form.

9. Close the form and save your changes. Close the database, and then close Access.

 You have completed Project 6I

Project 6J — Orders and Events

Objectives: *Make a Form User-Friendly and Create a Subform.*

In the following Mastery Assessment, you will add a subform to an existing form. Your completed form will look similar to Figure 6.63. You will rename and save your database as *6J_OrdersEvents_Firstname_Lastname*.

1. Locate the file **a06J_OrdersEvents** from your student files and copy and paste the file to the Chapter 6 folder you created. Remove the Read-only property from the file and rename the file as **6J_OrdersEvents_Firstname_Lastname** Start Access and open the database you just renamed.

2. Using the **Customer Orders** form as the main form, add a **subform** using the **Customer Events** table. Include all of the fields from the table and accept the remaining defaults in the wizard.

3. The subform will display too small to use; therefore, expand the subform so that its left edge begins at the left edge of the main form and its right edge reaches to **7 inches on the horizontal ruler**.

4. In the **Page Footer section** of the main form, create a label control and type **6J OrdersEvents Firstname Lastname**

(Project 6J–Orders and Events continues on the next page)

Mastery Assessments (continued)

(Project 6J–Orders and Events continued)

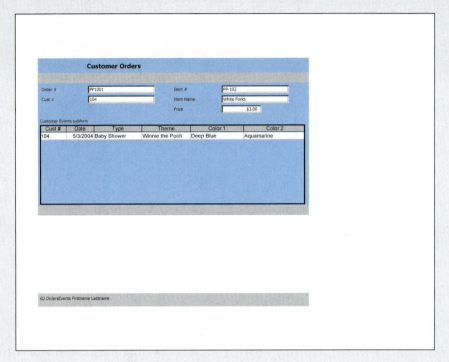

Figure 6.63

5. Switch to **Form view**. Resize the fields in the subform so that they display in the viewable area of the subform. In the **Page Setup** dialog box, change the page orientation to **Landscape**, and then print only the first record of the form.

6. Close the form and save your changes. Close the database, and then close Access.

End You have completed Project 6J

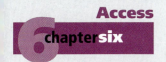

Problem Solving

Project 6K — Calculated Control

Objective: *Add a Calculated Control to a Report Section.*

The owners of The Perfect Party want to know the value of their inventory. They have a report that lists each inventory item, its unit cost, and the number of units in stock. In the following Problem Solving exercise, you will add a calculated control to a report section to provide a total value of the inventory.

1. Locate the file **a06K_Calculated_Control** from your student files and copy and paste the file to the Chapter 6 folder you created. Remove the Read-only property from the file and rename the file as **6K_Calculated_Control_Firstname_Lastname** Start Access and open the database you just renamed.

2. On the Objects bar, click **Reports**, and then open the **Inventory** report in Report view. **Maximize** the window. Use the navigation bar at the bottom of the window to scroll to **page 2**, click the **Zoom** arrow, and then click **100%**. Scroll to view the bottom of the page, and notice that there is no total for the value of the inventory. Click the **View** button to open the **Design view** of the report and, if necessary, maximize the window.

3. On the Toolbox, click the **Text Box** button. At the bottom of the form, in the **Report Footer section**, create a text box the full height of the area beginning at **3 inches on the horizontal ruler** and dragging to **6 inches on the horizontal ruler**. Click in the box that indicates *Text* followed by a number, select and delete the text, and type **Total Value** Click in the **Unbound** box and type the formula **=Sum([Unit Cost]*[Units in Stock])**

4. Click in a blank area of the form, and then click to select the text box where you typed the formula. Right-click, click **Properties**, click the **Format tab**, click in the **Format** box, display the list, and then scroll the list and click **Currency**. Close the property sheet.

5. Expand the **Page Footer** area, create a label, and type **6K Calculated Control Firstname Lastname**

6. Switch to **Print Preview** and navigate to the second page. Scroll to view the bottom of the second page. The inventory value is totaled. Close the report, saving any changes. Close the database, and then close Access.

End You have completed Project 6K

Problem Solving (continued)

Project 6L—Customers

Objectives: *Import Structured Data Into a Table and Format a Query.*

In the following Problem Solving exercise, you will import data from an Excel spreadsheet into a table, create a query, and then format the query.

1. Locate the file **a06L_Import** from your student files and copy and paste the file to the Chapter 6 folder you created. Remove the Read-only property from the file and rename the file as **6L_Import Firstname_Lastname** Start Access and open the database you just renamed.

2. From the **File** menu, point to **Get External Data**, and then click **Import**. In the displayed **Import** dialog box, navigate to your student files, change the **Files of type** at the bottom to **Microsoft Excel**, and then click the file **a06L_Excel_Data**. Click **Import**.

3. In the displayed wizard screen, select the **First Row Contains Column Headings** check box, and then click **Next**. Be sure the **In a New Table** option button is selected, and then click **Next**. Click **Next** two more times, and then under **Import to Table**, type New Customers Click **Finish**, and then click **OK**.

4. Open the **New Customers** table, and be sure that the data from the Excel spreadsheet was successfully imported. Close the table. On the Objects bar, click **Queries**, and then double-click **Create query in Design view**. Using the **New Customers** table, create a query that displays the **First Name**, **Last Name**, and **Phone** of all customers in **Dallas**. Do not display the **City** field. Save the query as Dallas Customers Firstname Lastname

5. Open your **Dallas Customers** query. Make the **Last Name** column the first column. From the **Format** menu, click **Font**, and then change the **Font** to **Bell MT**, the **Font style** to **Bold Italic**, and the **Size** to **12**. Resize the columns as necessary to display all the data. Sort the query alphabetically by **Last Name**.

6. Print the query, close and save your changes, close the database, and close Access.

End You have completed Project 6L

On the Internet

Locating Templates Online

Microsoft provides several templates that you can download and use to assist you in creating new databases, such as Order Management and Inventory Control. Go to **www.microsoft.com** and search for *templates*. Try to find some templates that would be helpful in a business that you have worked for, or the business of someone you know.

GO! with Help

Getting Help with PivotChart View

PivotChart view is a view that shows a graphical analysis of data in a datasheet or form. In PivotChart view, you can see different levels of detail or specify the layout by dragging fields and items or by showing and hiding items in the drop-down lists for fields.

1. Start Access. If necessary, from the **View** menu, click **Task Pane** to display the **Getting Started** task pane. On the task pane, to the right of *Getting Started*, click the **down arrow**. From the displayed list of available task panes, click **Help**.

2. Click in the **Search for** box, type **PivotChart view**

3. Press [Enter], scroll the displayed list as necessary, and then click **Elements of a PivotTable or PivotChart view**. Maximize the Help screen. At the upper right, click Show All, and then scroll down to view the section beginning Elements of a PivotChart view.

(**GO! with Help**—Continues on the next page)

GO! with Help (continued)

4. Read through each of the elements, and see if you can locate the various elements on the PivotChart view shown in Figure 6.64. If you would like to keep a copy of this information, click the **Print** button.

5. Click the **Close** button in the top right corner of the Help window to close the Help window, and then close Access.

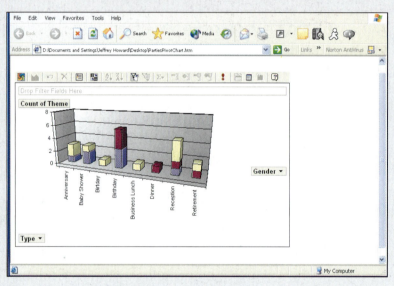

Figure 6.64

Access 2003

chapter seven

Advanced Reports and Queries

In this chapter, you will: complete these projects and practice these skills.

Project 7A
Customizing a Report

Objectives
- Create a Subreport
- Group Data in a Report
- Create Calculated Fields in a Report
- Set Report and Report Section Properties
- Create a Crosstab Report

Project 7B
Creating Queries

Objectives
- Create an Update Query
- Create a Delete Query
- Create Special Purpose Queries
- Create Action Queries
- View Queries in SQL

Greater Atlanta Job Fair

The Greater Atlanta Job Fair is a nonprofit organization supported by the Atlanta Chamber of Commerce and Atlanta City Colleges. The organization holds several targeted job fairs in the Atlanta area each year. Candidate registration is free and open to area residents and students enrolled in certificate or degree programs at any of the City Colleges. Employers pay a nominal fee to participate in the fairs. When candidates register for a fair, their resumes are scanned into an interactive, searchable database that is provided to the employers.

© Getty Images, Inc.

Advanced Reports and Queries

After you have entered data into the tables of your database, Access provides you with the tools to search, sort, update, and display your data in a variety of ways. You can display formatted information from one or more tables of a database in report form. You can also group information in a report and calculate results in a report. In this chapter, you will use advanced techniques to customize reports in Access.

Queries are usually thought of as a way to extract specific data from a database by asking questions and setting certain conditions. However, Access queries are also useful to add, update, or delete records from your database. In this chapter, you will create multiple types of queries.

Project 7A Job Fair

The Greater Atlanta Job Fair maintains a database to keep track of all the employers and candidates registered for the fair. The number of employers who exhibit at the fairs, and the number of candidates that attend, continues to grow. Thus, creating custom reports will be helpful in viewing the information in the database in a meaningful way.

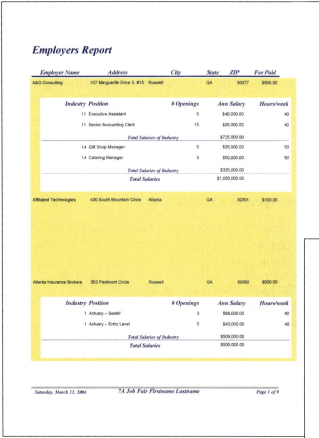

In Activities 7.1 through 7.6, you will create and modify a report for Michael Augustino, Executive Director of the Greater Atlanta Job Fair, to view information from the Employers table and the Candidates table. You will customize the report using features available in Access. Your completed reports will look similar to Figure 7.1. You will save your database as *7A_Job_Fair_Firstname_Lastname*.

Figure 7.1
Project 7A—Job Fair

Objective 1
Create a Subreport

Reports can include information from more than one table in the database. For example, the Greater Atlanta Job Fair wants to create a report listing all the employer names (from the Employers table), and then under each employer name, list the job openings for which the employer will be recruiting at the Job Fair (from the Job Openings table). One way to accomplish this is by creating a ***subreport***. A subreport is a report inserted into a control, and the control is then embedded in another report.

To create a subreport, the two tables must contain a one-to-many relationship. In your database, one employer can have many job openings, so a one-to-many relationship has been established between the Employers table and the Job Openings table. The main report will come from the *one* side of the one-to-many relationship—the Employers table—and the subreport will come from the *many* side of the relationship—the Job Openings table.

Activity 7.1 Embedding a Subreport in a Report

Recall that a subreport is a report inserted into a control, and then the control is embedded in another report. In this activity, you will embed a subreport into the existing *Employers Report*.

1 Create a new folder named Chapter 7 in the location where you will be storing your projects for this chapter. Locate the file **a07A_Job_Fair** from your student files, and copy and paste the file to the Chapter 7 folder you created. Remove the Read-only property from the file and rename the file as **7A_Job_Fair_Firstname_Lastname** Start Access and open the database you just renamed.

2 On the Objects bar, if necessary, click **Tables**. Take a moment to open and examine the data in each of the five tables in this database—**Candidates**, **Employers**, **Industries**, **Job Fair Sections**, and **Job Openings**.

3 On the Objects bar, click **Reports**, and then double-click the **Employers Report** to open it in **Print Preview**. If necessary, **maximize** the report window. Click the **Zoom arrow** and zoom to **100%**. Using the page navigation buttons in the lower left corner of the screen, take a moment to scroll through and examine the five pages of data presented in the report.

The Employers Report shows the Employer Name, Address, City, State, ZIP, and Fee Paid. This report was generated from the Employers table.

4 Switch to **Design view** and view the controls in the report. If necessary, maximize the window, and then expand the lower edge of the **Detail section** to slightly below **2 inches on the vertical ruler** as shown in Figure 7.2. This will give you space to work with the report.

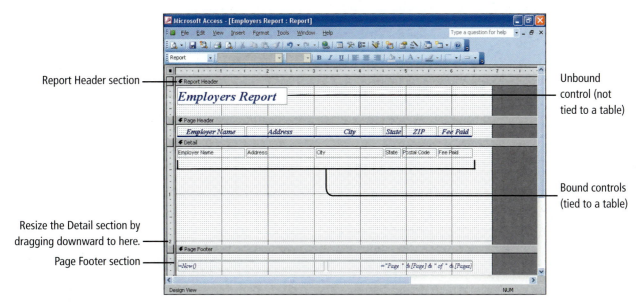

Figure 7.2

5 On your screen locate the **Report Header** and **Report Footer** sections.

This report has a ***Report Header*** section. The Report Header appears only once—at the beginning of a report. Use it for items such as a logo, report title, or print date. This report also has a ***Report Footer*** section. The Report Footer appears only once—at the end of the report. Use it to display items such as report totals. A report is not required to have a report header or a report footer; they are optional.

6 Locate the **Page Header** and **Page Footer** sections.

This report has a ***Page Header*** section. The Page Header appears at the top of every page. Use it for items such as column headings, as has been done in this report. This report also has a ***Page Footer*** section. The Page Footer appears at the bottom of every page. Use it for items such as page numbers. Page headers and footers are optional.

> **Note** — Location of Report Headers and Footers in Relation to Page Headers and Footers
>
> If a Page Header is included in your report, the Report Header prints before the Page Header on the first page of the report. If a Page Footer is included in your report, the Report Footer will print before the Page Footer on the last page of the report.

7 Locate the **Detail section** of the report.

Every report has a ***Detail section***. The Detail section contains the main body of a report's data. This section is repeated for each record in the report's underlying record source. In Design view, you can see that this section usually contains ***bound controls***—controls tied to a field in an underlying table or query, but can also contain ***unbound controls***—controls that have no data source but that display information such as labels that identify a field's contents. See Figure 7.2.

8 In the **Page Footer** section, click to select the **=Now()** control on the left, and then drag its right center sizing handle to the left to approximately **2 inches on the horizontal ruler**. Click the **="Page"** control on the right, and then drag its left center sizing handle to the right to approximately **5.0 inches on the horizontal ruler**.

9 On the Toolbox toolbar, click the **Label** button. Position the plus sign of your pointer just below the light gray bar in the **Page Footer section** at approximately **2.25 inches on the horizontal ruler**, and then drag down about a quarter of an inch and to the right to approximately **4.75 inches on the horizontal ruler**, as shown in Figure 7.3.

If you are not satisfied with your result, click the Undo button and begin again. An insertion point is blinking at the left edge of the label control.

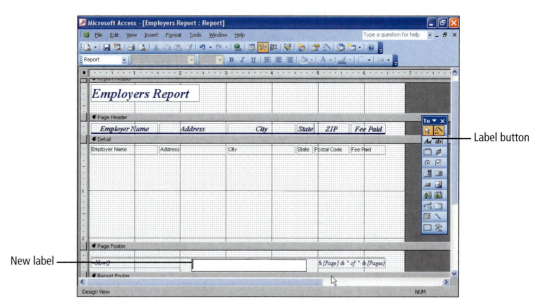

Figure 7.3

10 In the label control you just created, using your own first and last name, type **7A Job Fair Firstname Lastname** Press [Enter]. Press [Ctrl] plus any of the directional arrow keys on your keyboard as necessary to nudge the control into the desired position.

11 On the Toolbox toolbar, click the **Subform/Subreport** button.

12 In the **Detail section** of the report, position the plus sign of your pointer at approximately **0.25 inch on the horizontal ruler** and at **0.5 inch on the vertical ruler** as shown in Figure 7.4.

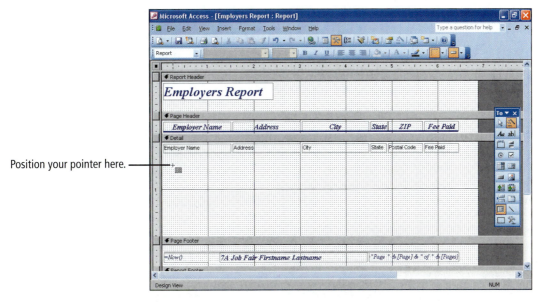

Position your pointer here.

Figure 7.4

13 Click once to launch the SubReport Wizard. Be sure that the **Use existing Tables and Queries** option button is selected, and then click **Next**.

14 Click the **Tables/Queries arrow**, and from the displayed list, click **Table: Job Openings**. Under **Available Fields**, use the **One Field** button to move the fields **Industry**, **Position**, **# Openings**, **Ann Salary**, and **Hours/week** to the **Selected Fields** list as shown in Figure 7.5. Click **Next**.

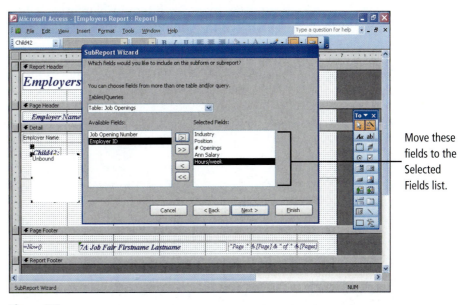

Move these fields to the Selected Fields list.

Figure 7.5

15 Be sure the **Choose from a list** option button is selected and that **Show Job Openings for each record in Employers using Employer ID** is selected.

Because a one-to-many relationship exists between the Employers table and the Job Openings table, you are able to list the current job openings for each employer below each employer name.

16 Click **Next**. Under **What name would you like for your subform or subreport?**, accept the default name *Job Openings subreport* and click **Finish**. If necessary, maximize the report window, and then compare your screen with Figure 7.6.

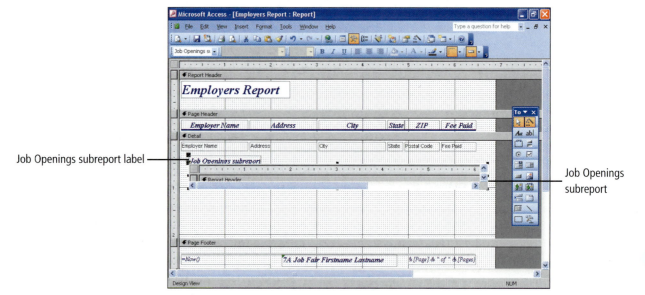

Figure 7.6

17 In the selected embedded report, position the mouse pointer over the lower center sizing handle to display the **Vertical Resize** pointer, and then drag down to approximately **2 inches on the vertical ruler**, as shown in Figure 7.7 (your fonts may differ from the figure).

This gives you a clear indication that another complete report is embedded in the main report, and will print below each employer's name in the main report.

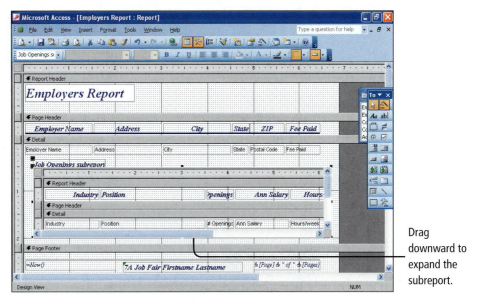

Figure 7.7

18. Switch to **Print preview** to view the **Employers Report** with the Job Openings subreport embedded in it. With the magnifying glass pointer positioned over the report, click to enlarge the report as necessary. Notice that the label *Job Openings subreport* repeats under each employer name. Notice also that the heading *# Openings* is slightly cut off at the beginning. Switch back to **Design view**.

19. In the **Detail section** of the main report, click the **Job Openings subreport label** to select it, and then press Delete.

   Deleting the label will prevent it from printing above every subreport within the main report, which would be repetitious and unnecessary.

20. In the subreport, select the **Position label**, locate the horizontal ruler within the subreport, and then drag its right center sizing handle to **3 inches on the horizontal ruler**. Then, lengthen the left side of the **# Openings label** by approximately one-half inch, so that the *# Openings* is not cut off. Switch to **Print preview**, and then compare your screen with Figure 7.8.

 # Openings not cut off —

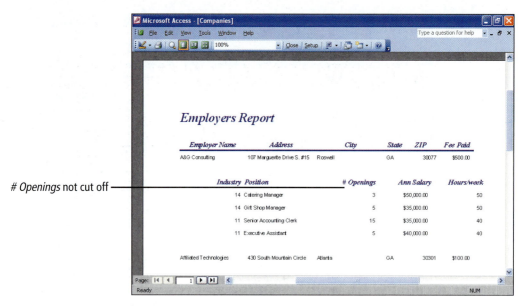

Figure 7.8

21 Using the Page navigation buttons at the lower left corner of the screen, view each of the pages in the report, noticing the subreport inserted below each employer's name.

You can see that many employers have more than one opening, and some employers currently have no openings.

22 In the upper right corner of your screen, click the small **Close Window** button ⊠ to close the **Employers Report**, and save your changes to the two objects. In the upper right corner of your screen, click the small **Restore Window** button. Notice that on the list of reports, a new report is listed—**Job Openings subreport**—as shown in Figure 7.9.

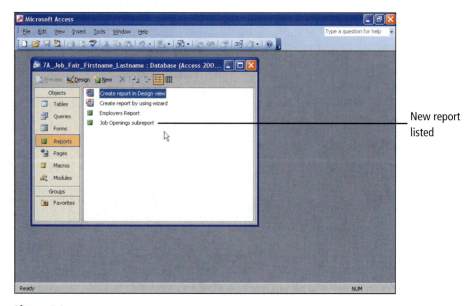

New report listed

Figure 7.9

23 Open the **Job Openings subreport**. Maximize and zoom as necessary to view the report.

The Job Openings subreport was generated by your responses in the Subreport Wizard. It contains a listing of all Job Openings.

24 Close ⊠ the window, and then in the upper right corner, click the small **Restore Window** button to return the database window to a smaller size. Leave the database open for the next activity.

Objective 2
Group Data in a Report

When creating a report, you may need to group information and/or sort information to display the data in a specific format. Or, you may need to group the information before you can calculate a formula in your report. For example, Michael Augustino wants to calculate the total potential yearly income of all the jobs at the fair. This number is useful for advertising purposes, because it demonstrates how large an event the Greater Atlanta Job Fair has become.

Activity 7.2 Grouping Data in a Report

In this activity, you will group the fields in the Job Openings subreport so that jobs from the same industry are listed together.

1 Open the **Job Openings subreport**, switch to **Design view**, and maximize the report window.

2 On the Report Design toolbar, click the **Sorting and Grouping** button. See Figure 7.10.

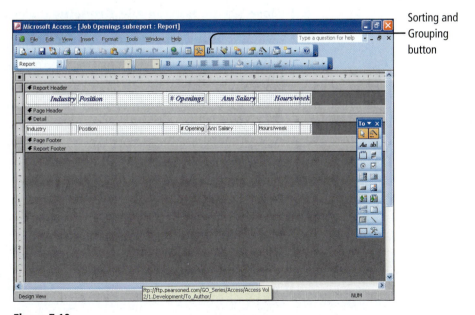

Figure 7.10

3 In the **Sorting and Grouping** dialog box, in the **Field/Expression** column, click the arrow in the first row. From the displayed list, click **Industry** and leave the sort order as **Ascending**. Under **Group Properties**, click the **Group Footer** box, click the arrow, and then click **Yes**. Click the **Keep Together** box, click the arrow, and click **Whole Group**. Compare your screen with Figure 7.11.

Within the Job Openings subreport, the jobs will be grouped by Industry, in Ascending order, and a Group Footer section will be created. You will need the Group Footer section to create a Calculated Field in the next activity.

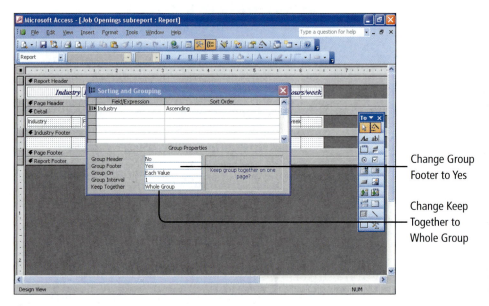

Figure 7.11

4 Close ☒ the **Sorting and Grouping** dialog box.

5 Switch to **Print preview**, and click on the report to zoom in.

Notice that the Job Openings are grouped in ascending order by industry number. See Figure 7.12.

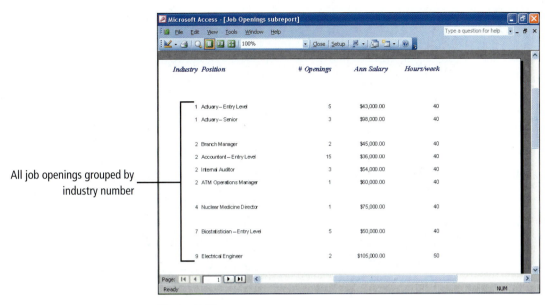

All job openings grouped by industry number

Figure 7.12

6 Switch to **Design view** and leave the report open for the next activity.

Objective 3
Create Calculated Fields in a Report

There are instances when it is useful to perform mathematical calculations and display the results in your report. For example, Michael Augustino wants to calculate the potential annual income of jobs within each industry, and then calculate the potential annual income of all the jobs at the fair. These numbers are useful in advertising the size and strength of the Greater Atlanta Job Fair.

Activity 7.3 Creating a Calculated Field for a Group

In this activity, you will create a calculated field to show the potential income available from all of the job openings within each industry.

1 Be sure the **Job Openings subreport** is open in **Design view**. On the Toolbox toolbar, click the **Text Box** button. Locate the **Industry Footer section** of the report, position the plus sign of your pointer at the upper edge of the Industry Footer and at approximately **4.25 inches on the horizontal ruler**, and click. See Figure 7.13.

Recall that you created the Industry Footer section in a previous activity.

Click to place text box here

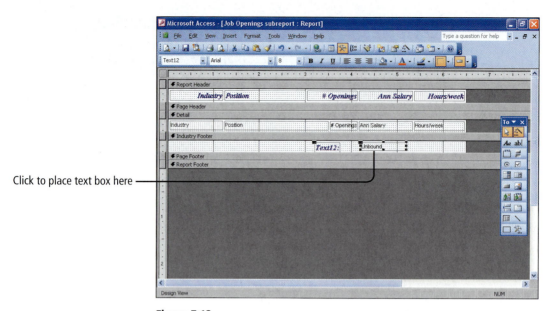

Figure 7.13

② In the **Industry Footer** section, right-click on the **Text Label** you just created. From the shortcut menu, click **Properties**, and then click the **Format tab**. Click in the **Caption** box, delete the text and type **Total Salaries of Industry** See Figure 7.14.

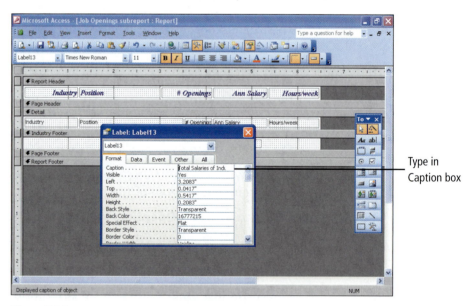

Type in Caption box

Figure 7.14

③ **Close** ☒ the property sheet.

④ With the label still selected, change the **Font Size** to **9**.

⑤ Lengthen the left side of the label to approximately **2.25 inches on the horizontal ruler** as shown in Figure 7.15.

Drag label border to the left —

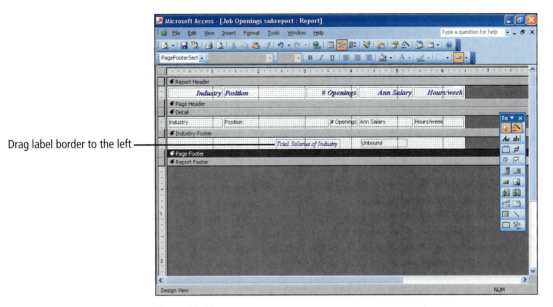

Figure 7.15

6 Right-click the **Unbound control box**, click **Properties**, and then click the **Data tab**. See Figure 7.16.

Data tab selected —

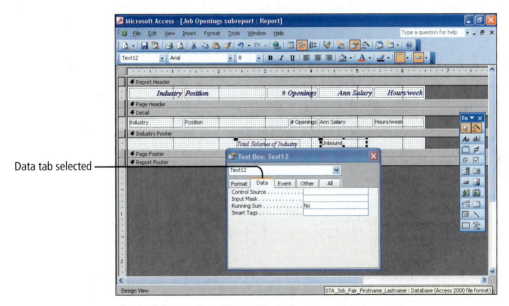

Figure 7.16

7 Click in the **Control Source** box, and then click the **Build** button that displays.

8 In the displayed **Expression Builder** dialog box, at the insertion point type **=sum([# Openings]*[Ann Salary])** Compare your screen with Figure 7.17.

The equal sign indicates the beginning of a formula. First the number of openings for a position is multiplied by the Annual Salary of the position. Then, the formula calculates the sum of these salaries for the industry. When typing field names in a formula, a field name that contains blank spaces must be surrounded by square brackets [ ].

Project 7A: Job Fair | **Access**   431

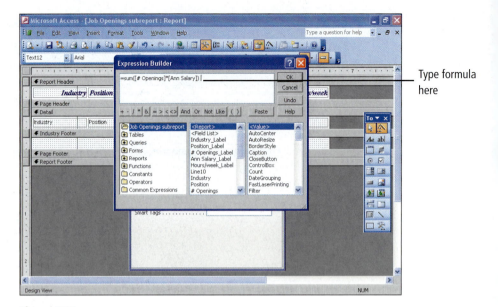

Figure 7.17

Another Way

To Enter a Formula

Instead of typing field names in a formula, you can find the field names under the Report Field List in the expression builder and double-click on the field you want in your formula.

9. Click **OK** to insert the formula in the **Control Source** box. With the **Property sheet** still open, click the **Format tab**. Change the **Format** to **Currency** and the **Decimal Places** to **2**. See Figure 7.18.

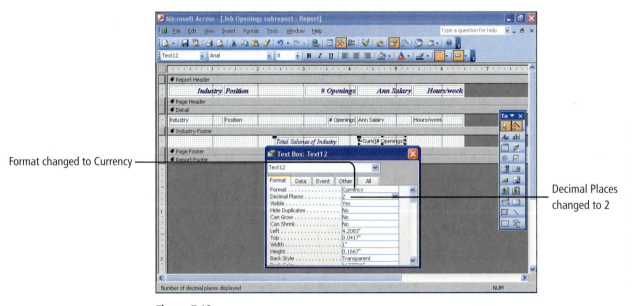

Figure 7.18

10 **Close** ⊠ the **Property sheet**. On the Toolbox toolbar, click the **Line** button. Draw a line along the lower edge of the **Industry Footer** section by positioning the + sign on the left side of the report. Hold down Shift to maintain a straight, not jagged, line and drag the line across to the right side of the report—you will not see the line as you draw it, but after you release the mouse button it will be visible. Compare you screen with Figure 7.19.

The line will provide a visual separation between the different industries in your report.

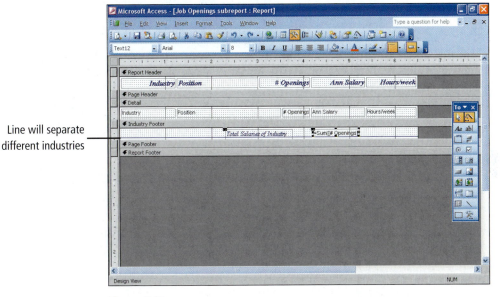

Line will separate different industries

Figure 7.19

11 Switch to **Print preview** to view your updated report. Locate the subtotals of the total salaries by industry. Leave the subreport open for the next activity.

> **Note** — Setting Margins on a Report
>
> A subreport, when created, has margin settings smaller than a regular report so that it can easily fall into the main report at the location you indicate. However, if you decide to print the subreport, adjust the margins from the Page Setup dialog box.

Activity 7.4 Creating a Calculated Field for a Report

In the previous activity, you placed a formula in the Industry Footer section and it summed the total salaries by each industry—within a group. In this activity, you will place the same formula in the Report Footer section, which will sum the total salaries of all the job openings in the report. Recall that this number is useful for advertising how large the fair has become.

1 Switch to **Design view**. Drag the lower edge of the **Report Footer** section to expand its size as shown in Figure 7.20.

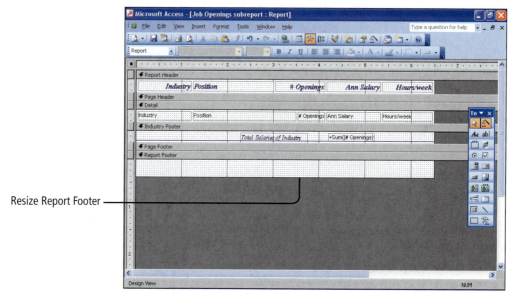

Resize Report Footer

Figure 7.20

2 In the **Industry Footer** section, select the **unbound control box** containing the formula, and then on the Report Design toolbar, click the **Copy** button.

3 Click the **Report Footer section bar** to select the section, and then on the Report Design toolbar, click the **Paste** button to paste the formula in the Report Footer.

4 Drag the label and unbound control box to line up directly under the label and formula you created earlier in the Industry Footer section.

5 Select the text in the label and type **Total Salaries** and change the **Font Size** of the label to **10**. See Figure 7.21.

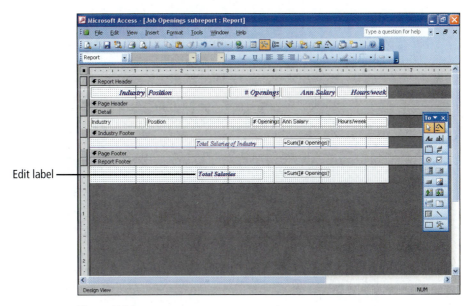

Edit label

Figure 7.21

[6] Switch to **Print preview**. Navigate to the end of the report to see the Total Salaries of $6,441,000.00.

You can see that in advertising, using this large number of potential income would be quite effective.

[7] In the upper right corner of your screen, click the small **Close Window** button ⊠ to close the **Job Openings subreport** and save your changes to the design. Open the **Employers Report**, and click on the report to magnify it.

[8] Examine the **Employers Report** and notice that the embedded **Job Openings subreport** has been modified—the job openings are grouped and totaled by Employer.

[9] Switch to **Design view** and leave the report open for the next exercise.

Objective 4
Set Report and Report Section Properties

In the previous activities, you worked with various sections of a report. Each section of a report has its own Property sheet, and thus each section can be modified separately.

Activity 7.5 Setting Report and Report Section Properties

Some of the most commonly used properties are located on the Format tab of the Property sheet. In this exercise you will change some of the properties on the Format tab to make your report display in a way that is more readable or useful.

[1] With the **Employers Report** open in **Design view**, right-click the **Detail section bar**, and then from the shortcut menu, click **Properties**. Be sure the **Format tab** is selected as shown in Figure 7.22.

2 Click in the **Force New Page** box, click the arrow, and then from the displayed list, click **Before Section**. See Figure 7.22.

By forcing a new page before each section in the Detail section, each Employer and its accompanying list of Job Openings will display on a separate page. Because there are currently 25 employers, the result will be a 25-page report.

Figure 7.22

3 **Close** ☒ the **Property sheet**, and switch to **Print preview**. Use the page navigation buttons in the lower left corner of the screen to scroll through the 25 pages of the report, and verify that each Employer has a separate page.

Notice that many employers do not currently have any job listings.

4 Switch to **Design view**, right-click on the **Detail bar**, and click **Properties**. On the **Format tab**, change the **Force New Page** property back to **None** and be sure the **Keep Together** property is set to **Yes**.

5 Click in the **Back Color** box and click the **Build** button ⊡ that displays. In the displayed **Color** dialog box, in the first row, click the second color—**light yellow**.

6 Click **OK** and close the **Property sheet**.

7 Switch to **Print preview** ⬛ and navigate to **page 1**. Compare your screen with Figure 7.1.

8 From the **File** menu, click **Print**. Under **Print Range**, in the **From** box type **1** and in the **To** box type **1** so that only page 1 will print.

Click **OK**. **Close** ☒ the report, saving the changes to the design.

Click the **Restore Window** button ⬛ to return the Database window to its smaller size. Leave the database open for the next activity.

Objective 5
Create a Crosstab Report

A special type of query, called a **crosstab query**, performs calculations on data that is grouped by *two* types of information. For example, in the Greater Atlanta Job Fair database, if you want to compare a list of the salaries by industry and by state, you could use a crosstab query.

Activity 7.6 Creating a Report from a Crosstab Query

In this activity, you will create a report based on a crosstab query that has already been created.

1 On the Objects bar, click **Queries**, and then open the **Job Openings by Employer_Crosstab** query. Take a moment to study the information in the query. See Figure 7.23.

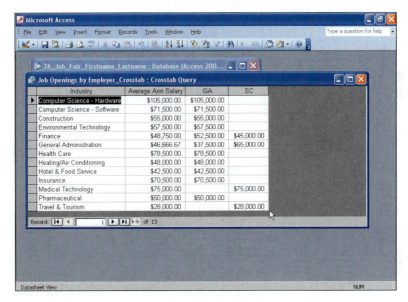

Figure 7.23

2 **Close** ✕ the query.

3 On the Objects bar, click **Reports**. Double-click the command icon **Create report by using wizard**.

4 Click the **Tables/Queries arrow**, and from the displayed list, click **Query: Job Openings by Employer_Crosstab**. Use the **All Fields** button [>>] to move all the fields under **Selected Fields**. See Figure 7.24.

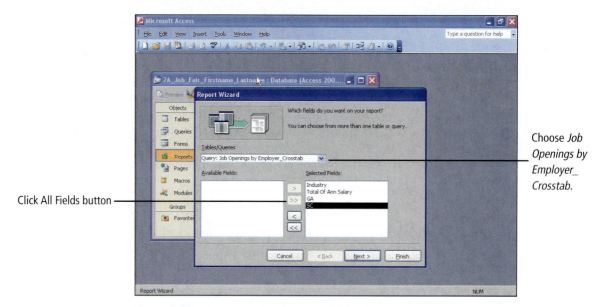

Figure 7.24

5 Click **Next**. No grouping levels will be added, so click **Next** again.

6 To sort the records within the report by Industry, click the arrow next to the **1** box. From the displayed list, click **Industry** and leave the sort order as **Ascending**. Click **Next**.

7 Under **Layout**, be sure the **Tabular** option button is selected, and under **Orientation**, be sure the **Portrait** option button is selected. Click **Next**. Click the **Corporate** style and click **Next**.

8 As the title for your report, accept the default **Job Openings by Employer_Crosstab**

9 Click **Finish** to view the report. Switch to **Design view**, and in the **Page Footer** section, select the **=Now()** control on the left. Drag its right center sizing handle to **2.0 inches on the horizontal ruler**. Select the **="Page"** control on the right, drag its left center sizing handle to **5 inches on the horizontal ruler**. On the Toolbox toolbar, click the **Label** button , and draw a label below the gray bar about one-quarter inch tall, from **2.25 inches on the horizontal ruler** to **4.75 inches on the horizontal ruler**. In the new label, type **7A Crosstab Firstname Lastname** Press Enter, change the **Font Size** to **10**, and then nudge the control as necessary to line it up with the lower edge of the section.

10 Switch to **Print preview**.

11 From the **File** menu, click **Page Setup**. Click the **Margins tab**, and change the **Left margin** to **0.75** and the **Right margin** to **0.75**. From the **File** menu, click **Print**, and then click **OK**. **Close** the report, save your changes, and then close the database.

Project 7B Job Fair Update

As databases grow, you will find that entering new records into your database is only one part of maintaining your database. You will also need to update individual records, and occasionally you will need to update groups of records. Updating your database need not be time consuming. With the use of specific queries, the process of updating your database can be fast and efficient.

In Activities 7.7 through 7.14, you will use multiple queries to update the information in your database. Your results will look similar to those shown in Figure 7.25.

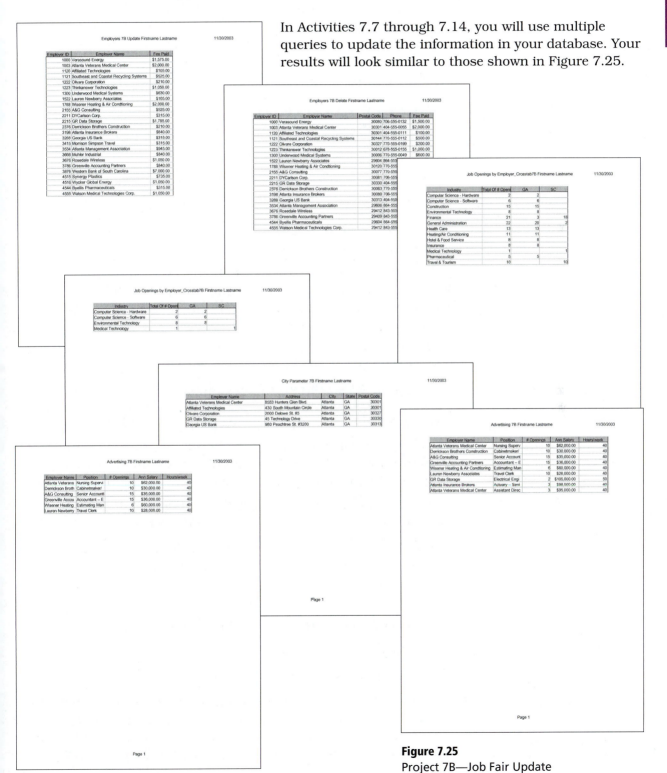

Figure 7.25
Project 7B—Job Fair Update

Objective 6
Create an Update Query

Recall that a **select query** retrieves and displays data from one or more tables based on **criteria** (conditions that identify specific records) that you specify. An **action query**, on the other hand, *changes* data in a table. One type of action query is an **update query**, which updates existing data. When a group of records in a table requires the same update, an update query is an efficient way to accomplish the task, rather than updating each record separately. For example, due to rising costs of conducting the Job Fairs, the Executive Director of the Greater Atlanta Job Fair has indicated that if an employer fee is currently less than $2,000, it should be increased by 5%.

Activity 7.7 Creating an Update Query

In this activity, you will create an update query to update each employer's Fee Paid by 5%—if the fee is currently less than $2,000.

1. Locate the database file **a07B_Job_Fair_Update** from your student files, and copy and paste the file to the Chapter 7 folder you created for this chapter. Remove the Read-only property from the file, and rename the file as **7B_Job_Fair_Update_Firstname_Lastname** Start Access and open the database you just renamed.

2. On the Objects bar, click **Tables**, right-click the **Employers** table, and then click **Copy**. Move your mouse pointer into the white area, right-click, and then click **Paste**. In the displayed **Paste Table As** dialog box, under **Table Name**, type **Employers 7B Update Firstname Lastname** and click **OK**. In this project, you will practice on copies of the original table.

3. Open your **Employers 7B Update** table. Drag across the gray column headings to select the columns **Contact**, **Contact Title**, and **Address**, display the **Format** menu, and then click **Hide Columns**.

4. Examine the numbers in the **Fee Paid** column, and notice that a number of them are less than $2,000. For example, the first Employer, **Verasound Energy**, has a fee of $1,500.00.

5. From the **Format** menu, click **Unhide Columns**. In the displayed **Unhide Columns** dialog box, select the **Contact**, **Contact Title**, and **Address** check boxes, and click **Close**. Close ⊠ the **Employers** table, and click **No** when asked if you want to save changes to the layout of the table.

    Recall that it is sometimes convenient to hide columns temporarily to get a better view of the table, rather than scrolling back and forth.

6. On the Objects bar, click **Queries**, and then on the database window toolbar, click the **New** button.

7. From the list of methods to create a new query, be sure **Design View** is selected, and then click **OK**. In the displayed **Show Table** dialog box, click the **Tables tab**, click to select your **Employers 7B Update** table, and then click **Add**. See Figure 7.26. **Close** the dialog box.

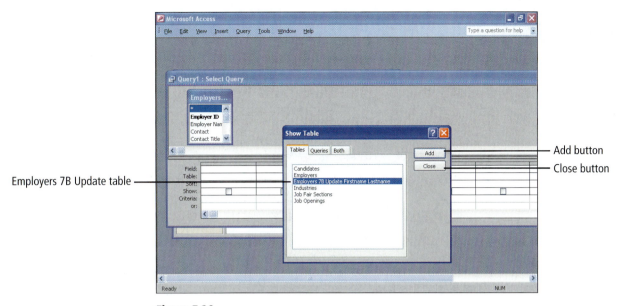

Figure 7.26

8 In the table area, scroll to the bottom of the table's field list and double-click the **Fee Paid** field to place it into to the design grid.

An Update query modifies an existing table or query; thus, you need only select the fields you want to change—in this case, the Fee Paid field. Recall that the query window has two parts: the *table area* (upper pane) and the *design grid* (lower pane).

9 Notice the name in the window's blue title bar—*Select Query*. See Figure 7.27. On the Query Design toolbar, click the **Query Type button arrow**, and then from the displayed list click **Update Query**.

The query type in the blue title bar changes to *Update Query*. When you create a new query, the default type is Select Query. For other types of queries, change the query type, and then set the criteria.

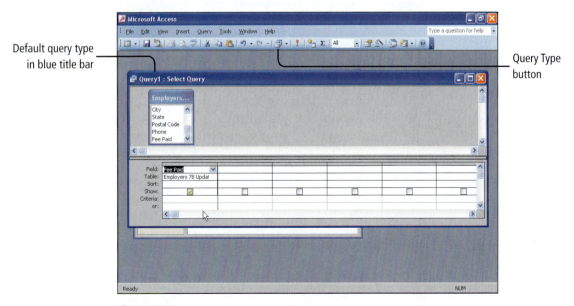

Figure 7.27

Another Way

To Change the Query Type

There are three ways to change the query type in Access. On the Query Design toolbar, click the Query Type button arrow and select from the displayed list, as you did in the previous step. Or, from the menu bar, click Query, and choose from the displayed menu. Finally, in the gray table area, right-click. On the displayed shortcut menu, point to Query Type, and then choose the type of query that you want.

10 In the design grid, in the **Update To** row, click in the first column and type **[Fee Paid]*1.05**

This formula will multiply the amount in the Fee Paid field by 1.05, an increase of 5 percent.

11 In the **Criteria** row, click in the first column and type **<2000**
See Figure 7.28.

Setting this criteria (condition) will apply the formula only to those records where the current value in the Fee Paid field is less than $2,000.

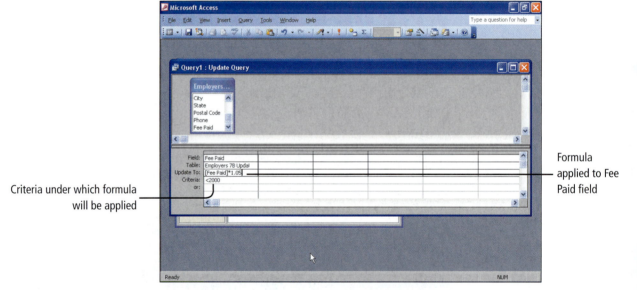

Figure 7.28

442 Access | Chapter 7: Advanced Reports and Queries

12 On the Query Design toolbar, click the **Run** button.

As shown in Figure 7.29, a message displays indicating that this action will update 22 rows, which is 22 records. The Undo command cannot reverse this action. If you update a group of records by mistake, you must correct each record separately.

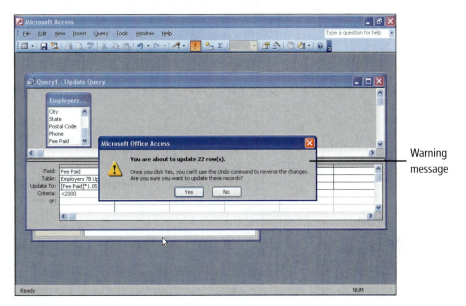

Warning message

Figure 7.29

13 Click **Yes**. **Close** the Update Query window, and then click **No** when asked to save the changes to the query.

The 22 records in the Employers table that met the criteria are updated. Because it is unlikely that you will raise the Employer fees in this manner again, it is not necessary to save the query.

14 On the Objects bar, click the **Tables** button, and then double-click your **Employers 7B Update** table to open it. Scroll all the way to the left, select the **Contact** column, hold down Shift, use the scroll bar to scroll all the way to the right, and select the **Phone** column. All the columns *except* **Employer ID**, **Employer Name**, and **Fee Paid** are selected. Display the **Format** menu and click **Hide Columns**.

Notice the updated fee amounts. For example, the fee for Verasound Energy has been raised to $1,575—an increase of 5 percent.

15 **Print** the table, display the **Format** menu, click **Unhide Columns**, and select the appropriate check boxes to unhide all the columns. Compare your printed table with Figure 7.25.

16 **Close** your **Employers 7B Update** table. Do not save the changes to the layout, so that the columns will not be hidden when you open the table again.

Objective 7
Create a Delete Query

A ***delete query*** is a type of action query that removes records from a table. When information becomes outdated or is no longer needed, the unneeded records should be deleted from your database. Assuming outdated records have a common criterion, perhaps a date, you can gather them together in a delete query, and then delete them all at once. This is much faster than deleting unneeded records one by one. For example, in the Job Fair database, the Executive Director needs to delete all the employers having the Postal Code of 29413 or 29423, because employers in these areas have decided they are not close enough to any of the Job Fair cities to justify exhibiting and paying for a booth.

Activity 7.8 Creating and Running a Delete Query

In this activity, you will create and run a delete query to delete, from the Employers table, employers having the 29413 or 29423 Postal Code. This is accomplished by first creating a select query containing the employers that have the Postal Code criteria, and then changing the query type to a Delete Query.

1 On the Objects bar, click **Tables**. Right-click the **Employers** table, and then click **Copy**. In the white area, right-click again, and then click **Paste**. Name the table **Employers 7B Delete Firstname Lastname** Recall that in this project, you will practice on copies of the original table.

2 On the Objects bar, click the **Queries** button, and then to the right, double-click **Create query in Design view**. Alternatively, on the Database window toolbar, click the New button and click OK.

3 In the **Show Table** dialog box, click the **Tables tab** if necessary, click your **Employers 7B Delete** table, and then click **Add**. Click **Close** to close the dialog box.

4 In the table area, use the vertical scroll bar to view all the fields in the table. Double-click the **Employer Name** field to add it to the first column of the design grid, and then double-click the **Postal Code** field to add it to the second column of the design grid.

5 In the **Criteria** row, click in the second (Postal Code) column and type **29413**

6 In **or** row, in the same column, type **29423** See Figure 7.30.

This action will cause the query to select only those Employers with a Postal Code of 29413 or 29423.

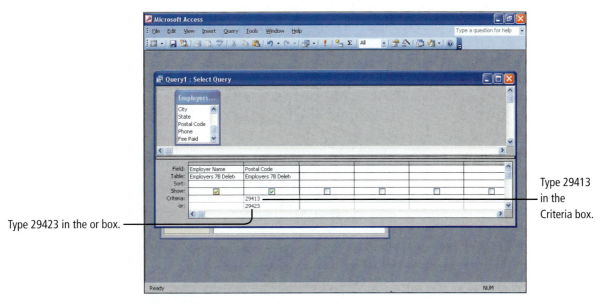

Figure 7.30

7 Click the **Run** button.

The query displays five records that meet the criteria you specified.

8 Switch to **Design view**.

9 In the gray table area, right-click. From the displayed shortcut menu, point to **Query Type** as shown in Figure 7.31, and then click **Delete Query**.

This is another method to display the list of Query Types.

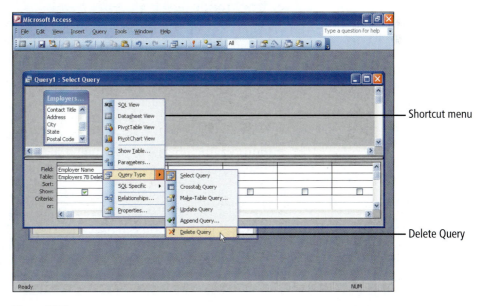

Figure 7.31

Project 7B: Job Fair Update | **Access**   445

10 **Run** the query.

11 A warning message, as shown in Figure 7.32, displays indicating that 5 rows (records) will be deleted from the table.

This action cannot be reversed with the Undo command. If you delete records in error, you must enter each record again.

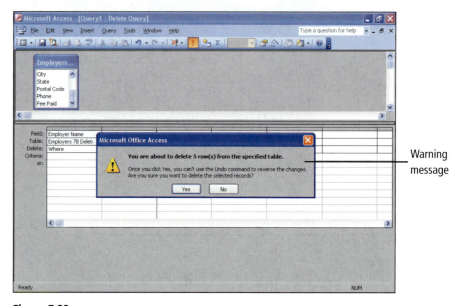

Figure 7.32

Note — Check Your Relationships!

If you have created relationships between tables, running a delete query could also delete records from related tables. Before running a delete query, check the relationships between the table you are modifying and any other table. It is also a good idea to maintain a backup of your database so you can recover from any loss of data.

12 In the displayed warning message, click **Yes**. **Close** the query without saving changes, because it is unlikely that this query will be used again.

13 On the Objects bar, click **Tables**. Open your **Employers 7B Delete** table. Select the columns **Contact**, **Contact Title**, **Address**, **City**, and **State**. Display the **Format** menu and click **Hide Columns**. Notice that there are no records that have the Postal Code of 29413 or 29423. Compare your screen with Figure 7.33.

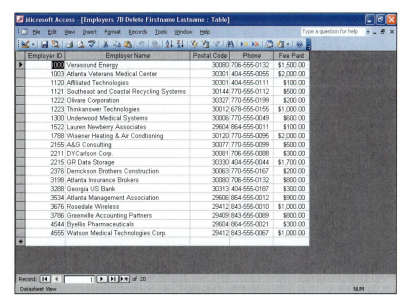

Figure 7.33

14 Print the table. **Close** ⊠ the **Employers** table; do not save the changes to the layout.

Objective 8
Create Special Purpose Queries

A crosstab query is a query that groups summarized data by categories. A crosstab query always has a column heading, a row heading, and a summary field. Use a crosstab query when you want to summarize a large amount of data in a small space that is easy to read. For example, in the Job Fair database, Michael Augustino wants to summarize the number of job openings for each industry by state.

Activity 7.9 Creating a Crosstab Query

In this activity, you will create a crosstab query to summarize, by state, the number of job openings in each industry. Because a crosstab query usually contains information from more than one table in the database, you must first create a select query to include all the tables, and then create the crosstab query. A select query that combines the **Employers**, **Job Openings**, and **Industries** tables has already been created, and is named *Job Openings by Employer*.

1 On the Objects bar, click **Queries**. On the Database window toolbar, click the **New** button . In the **New Query** dialog box, click **Crosstab Query Wizard**. See Figure 7.34. Click **OK**.

Project 7B: Job Fair Update | **Access** 447

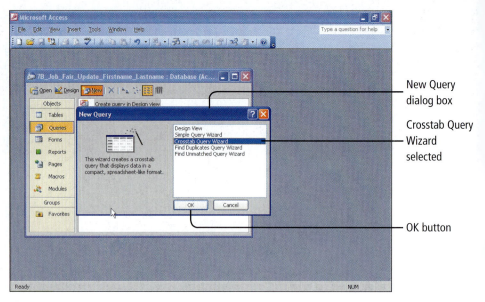

Figure 7.34

▌2▐ In the first screen of the wizard, in which you select the table or query you want to use for your crosstab query, under **View**, click the **Queries** option button.

In the white box, the *Job Openings by Employer* query is selected. See Figure 7.35.

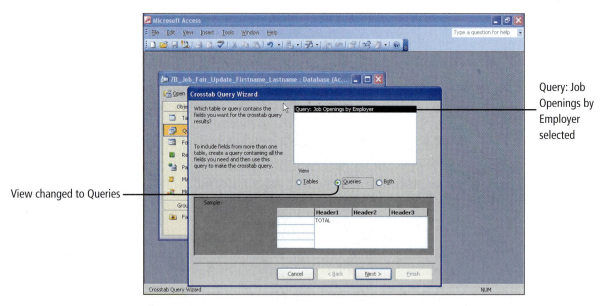

Figure 7.35

▌3▐ Click **Next**. Here you select the fields you want as row headings—up to three can be selected. Under **Available Fields**, use the **One Field** button to move **Industry** under **Selected Fields**. See Figure 7.36.

448 Access | Chapter 7: Advanced Reports and Queries

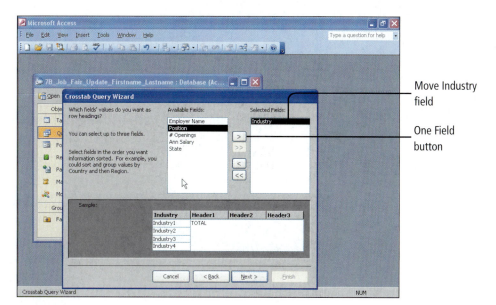

Figure 7.36

4 Click **Next**. Here you select a single field as the column heading. Click **State**.

5 Click **Next**. Here you indicate the number to be calculated for each column and row intersection. Under **Fields**, click **# Openings**, and then under **Functions**, click **Sum**. Under **Do you want to summarize each row?**, be sure that the **Yes, include row sums** check box is selected. See Figure 7.37.

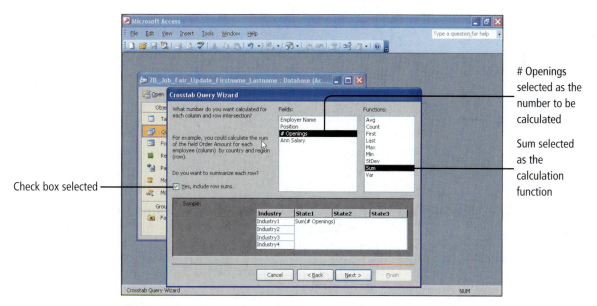

Figure 7.37

6 Click **Next**. In this screen, at the end of the proposed query name, click, and then type **7B Firstname Lastname** to add this to the query name. Click **Finish**. Compare your screen with Figure 7.38.

Recall that the purpose of the crosstab query was to summarize, by State, the number of job openings in each industry. Notice, for example, that in the Finance industry, there are a total of 21 jobs that will be advertised at the job fair—3 in Georgia and 18 in South Carolina.

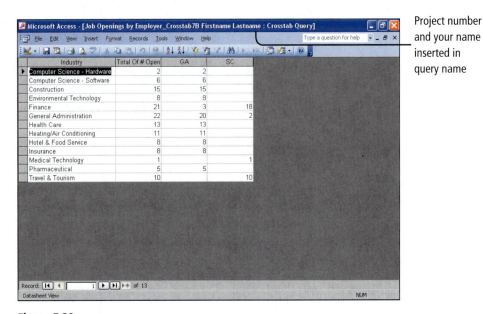

Figure 7.38

7 Print your crosstab query and compare your printed table with the one in Figure 7.25. Switch to **Design view**. Leave your query open in **Design view** for the next activity.

Activity 7.10 Adding Conditions to a Crosstab Query

After you have created a crosstab query, you can break down the information in the query even further. In this activity, you will add additional conditions to your query to display, by State, only the positions in the Computer and Technology industry.

1 Be sure your **Job Openings by Employer_Crosstab 7B** query is open in **Design view**. In the **Criteria** row, click in the **Industry** column and type **Computer*** See Figure 7.39.

The * is a wild card character, which can represent multiple characters, including spaces. Because the * comes after the word *Computer*, any industry starting with *Computer* will satisfy the condition.

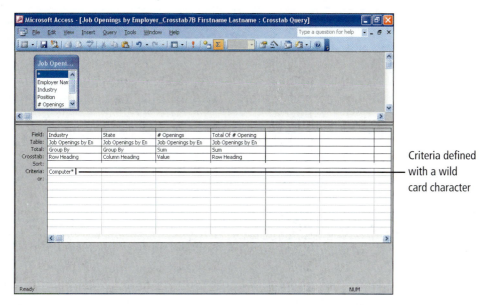

Figure 7.39

2. Switch to **Query view** and compare your screen with Figure 7.40.

   Two industries, both beginning with *Computer*, display.

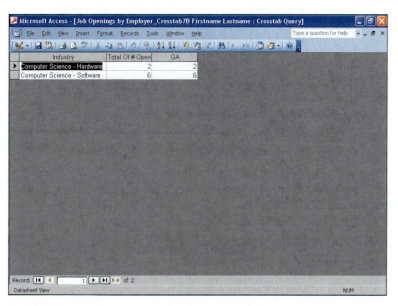

Figure 7.40

3. Switch to **Design view** and notice that the criteria row indicates *Like "Computer*"*.

4. In the **or** row, click in the **Industry** column and type ***Technology** See Figure 7.41.

   This action will select any industry that begins with the word *Computer* or any industry that ends with the word *Technology*.

Project 7B: Job Fair Update | **Access** 451

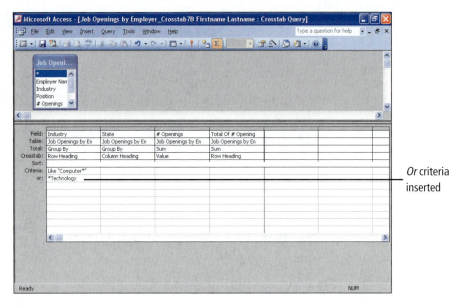

Figure 7.41

5 Switch to **Query view**.

Four different industries display, summarized by the total number of openings in each state. Each industry name either begins with *Computer* or ends with *Technology*.

6 Print, close, and save your query. Compare your printed query to Figure 7.25.

Activity 7.11 Creating a Parameter Query

A *parameter query* is a query that will prompt you for criteria before running the actual query. It can be a select query or an action query. For example, to find Employers in a specific city, you would create a select query and set the criteria to the specific city—creating a separate query for each city. But by using a parameter query, Access will prompt you for the city you want and then display the results based on the given parameter.

In this activity, you will create a parameter query to list Employers by city.

1 On the Objects bar, click **Tables**. Right-click the **Employers** table and click **Copy**. Right-click in the white area, click **Paste**, name the table **Employers 7B Parameter Firstname Lastname** and click **OK**.

2 On the Objects bar, click **Queries**. To the right, double-click the command icon **Create query in Design view**.

3 Add your **Employers 7B Parameter** table to the table area, and then close the **Show Table** dialog box.

4 In the field list, double-click **Employer Name**, **Address**, **City**, **State**, and **Postal Code** to add the fields to the design grid. See Figure 7.42.

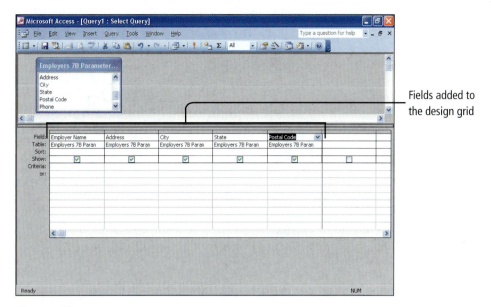

Figure 7.42

5 In the **Criteria** row, in the **City** column, type **[Enter a City]** and then compare your screen with Figure 7.43.

The brackets indicate a *parameter* rather than a specific criteria. When you run the query, the message *Enter a City* will display and allow you to type the name of a city. The city you type will be set as the criterion for the query. In this manner, you can reuse this query over and over without resetting specific criteria.

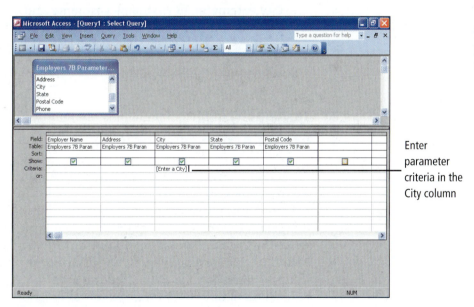

Figure 7.43

6 **Run** the query.

7 In the **Enter Parameter Value** dialog box, type **Greenville** as shown in Figure 7.44.

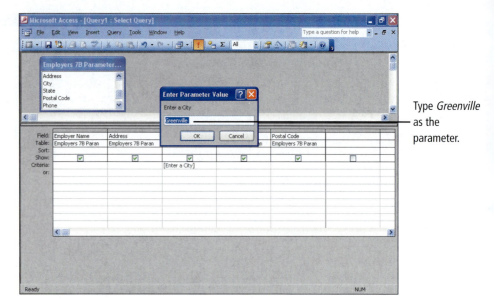

Type *Greenville* as the parameter.

Figure 7.44

8 Click **OK**.

Three employers, all located in Greenville, display.

9 Switch to **Design view** and **Run** the query again.

10 Type **Atlanta** as the parameter value, and then click **OK**.

Five employers, all located in Atlanta, display.

11 From the **File** menu, click **Save As**. In the **Save As** dialog box, type **City Parameter 7B Firstname Lastname** and then click **OK**. Display the **File** menu again, click **Page Setup**, and on the **Page tab**, change the **Orientation** to **Landscape**. Click **OK**, and then print the query.

Close the query. Compare your printed query to Figure 7.25.

Objective 9
Create Action Queries

An action query lets you change data in a table, or create a new table. A ***make-table query*** is an action query that creates a new table based on existing tables. Creating a new table can be useful if you need to back up a table, or if you need to create a custom table for a special purpose. For example, the Executive Director of the Greater Atlanta Job Fair wants to create a table for the purpose of gathering some information to be used in advertising the Job Fair. Creating a new table in this manner will not cause loss of data in or changes to the original table.

Activity 7.12 Creating a Make-Table Query

In this activity, you will use a make-table query to create a table listing all employers that have more than five job openings.

1 On the Objects bar, click **Queries**, and then to the right, double-click the command icon **Create query in Design view**.

2 Add the **Employers** table (the one without your name attached) and the **Job Openings** table to the table area, and then close the **Show Table** dialog box.

Notice that a one-to-many relationship exists between the two tables, because one employer can have many job openings.

3 From the **Employers** table, add the **Employer Name** field to the design grid, and from the **Job Openings** table, add the **Position**, **# Openings**, **Ann Salary**, and **Hours/week** fields to the design grid. See Figure 7.45.

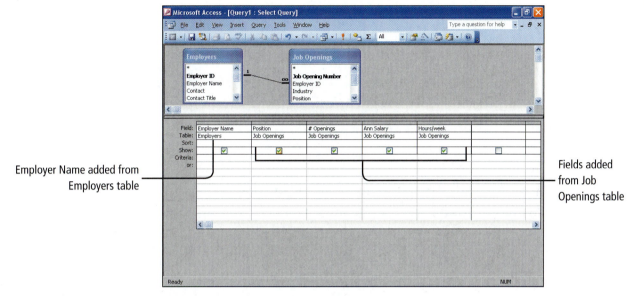

Employer Name added from Employers table

Fields added from Job Openings table

Figure 7.45

4 In the **Criteria** row, click in the **# Openings** column and type **>5**

5 On the menu bar, click **Query**, and then click **Make-Table Query**.

6 In the displayed **Make Table** dialog box, type **Advertising 7B Firstname Lastname** as shown in Figure 7.46.

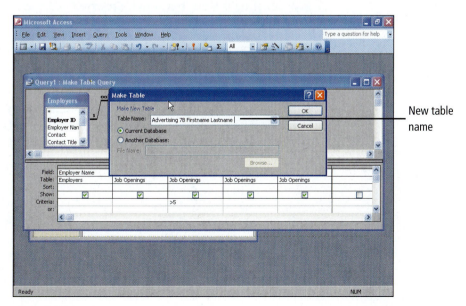

New table name

Figure 7.46

Project 7B: Job Fair Update | **Access**   455

7 Click **OK**, and then **Run** the query. When the message indicating *You are about to paste 6 row(s) into a new table* displays, click **Yes**.

8 **Close** the query and at the prompt, save the query as **Over 5 Openings 7B Firstname Lastname**

9 On the Objects bar, click **Tables**, and then double-click to open your **Advertising 7B** table.

Notice that all employers listed have more than 5 openings.

10 Print and then close your **Advertising** table. Compare your printed table to Figure 7.25.

> **Note** — Using a Make-Table Query
>
> A table created from a make-table query is not automatically updated when information from the original table or tables is modified. To keep the new table up to date, you must run the make-table query periodically to be sure your information is current.

Activity 7.13 Creating an Append Query

In the previous activity, you made a *new* table by copying information from other tables. An **append query** adds new records to an existing table by importing data from another Access database, from another program such as Microsoft Excel, or from a table in the same database. An append query can be limited by criteria.

Michael Augustino wants to add information to the Advertising table by gathering a list of employers that have numerous jobs at very high salaries. He feels that advertising this information will attract many good candidates to the job fairs. In this activity, you will add job openings with high annual salaries to the Advertising table that you created in the last activity by using an append query.

1 On the Objects bar, click **Queries**. To the right of the Objects bar, double-click **Create query in Design view**.

2 Add the **Employers** table (the one without your name) and the **Job Openings** table to the table area, and then close the **Show Table** dialog box.

3 From the **Employers** table, add the **Employer Name** field to the design grid, and from the **Job Openings** table, add **Position**, **# Openings**, **Ann Salary**, and **Hours/week** fields.

4 In the **Criteria** row, in the **Ann Salary** column, type **>=95000** as shown in Figure 7.47.

This criterion will limit the job openings displayed to those with an annual salary greater than or equal to $95,000.

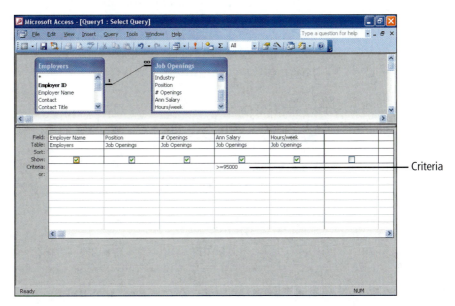

Figure 7.47

5 In the gray table area, right-click, and from the displayed shortcut menu, point to **Query Type** and click **Append Query**.

6 In the displayed **Append** dialog box, click the **Table Name arrow**, and from the displayed list, click your **Advertising 7B** table. Click **OK**.

7 **Run** the query. In the warning message indicating *You are about to append 3 row(s)*, click **Yes**.

8 **Close** the query, and save it as **High Salaries 7B Firstname Lastname**

9 On the Objects bar, click **Tables**, and then open your **Advertising 7B** table. Locate the three records at the bottom of the table. This table now includes employers with more than five openings, and also, employers with job openings with salaries equal to or higher than $95,000.

10 Print and then close your **Advertising 7B** table. Compare your printed table to the one in Figure 7.25.

Objective 10
View Queries in SQL

In this project, you have created various types of queries. As you did so, Access was not directly interacting with your query. To run your query, Access must first translate the query you create in design view into an **SQL statement**. SQL is the commonly used term for **Structured Query Language**, which is a database sublanguage used in querying, updating, and managing relational databases in database programs such as Microsoft Access. Knowing a little about SQL can help you build more powerful queries than you could construct using only the design grid in Access.

Activity 7.14 Viewing Queries in SQL

In the following activity, you will look at a query in SQL view and look at a basic SQL statement.

1 On the Objects bar, click **Queries**, and then open the **Job Openings by Employer** query in **Design view**.

2 In the **Sort** row, under **Employer Name**, click in the box, click the arrow, and from the displayed list, click **Ascending**.

3 In the **Criteria** row, under **Ann Salary**, click in the box and type **<60000** as shown in Figure 7.48.

Two additional criteria are now added to the design grid, which will assist in viewing the four parts of a typical SQL statement.

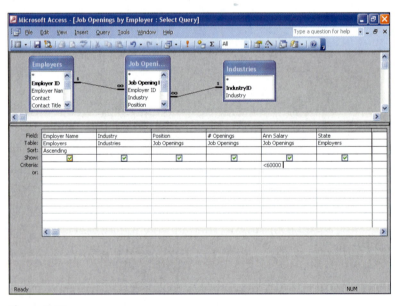

Figure 7.48

4 From the menu bar, click **View**, and then click **SQL View**.

When looking at an SQL statement, you will usually notice four parts: SELECT, FROM, WHERE, and ORDER BY. The SELECT statement lists the fields you want to display. The FROM statement lists the tables used in the query. WHERE indicates the selection criteria, and ORDER BY indicates how the information will be sorted.

While you are designing your queries in Design view, you can see that Access is hard at work translating your work into SQL statements.

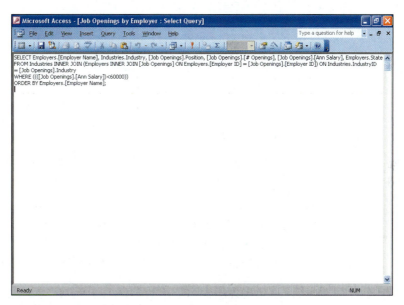

Figure 7.49

5 **Close**  the query and save your changes.

End You have completed Project 7B

Summary

Access provides a variety of ways to search, sort, update, and display data in your database. In this chapter, you practiced advanced techniques to customize reports. You created a subreport, in which a report is inserted into a control, and then the control is embedded in another report. Recall that to create a subreport, the two tables must have a one-to-many relationship established. You practiced how to group data in a report and create calculated fields in a report. Each section of a report has its own properties, and in this chapter you practiced modifying various properties of a report. Another type of advanced report, called a crosstab report, was created based on a crosstab query. A crosstab report displays calculated data grouped by two types of information.

In this chapter, you also conducted advanced queries. Whereas a select query retrieves and displays data from one or more tables based on criteria, action queries actually change data in tables. You practiced creating an update query, which is useful for updating a group of records at the same time. You practiced creating a delete query, which is an action query that removes records from tables. This is an efficient way to remove a group of records at one time. You also practiced creating a crosstab query, which is a query that groups summarized data by categories. A crosstab query always has a column heading, a row heading, and a summary field. Finally, you practiced creating a parameter query, a make-table query, and looked at an SQL statement. A parameter query prompts you for criteria before running the actual query. A make-table query is an action query that creates a new table. You saw that as you develop a query in design view, Access is actually building an SQL statement to carry out your query in structured query language.

In This Chapter You Practiced How To

- Create a Subreport
- Group Data in a Report
- Create Calculated Fields in a Report
- Set Report and Report Section Properties
- Create a Crosstab Report
- Create an Update Query
- Create a Delete Query
- Create Special Purpose Queries
- Create Action Queries
- View Queries in SQL

Concepts Assessments

Matching Match each term in the second column with its correct definition in the first column. Write the letter of the term on the blank line to the left of the correct definition.

____ 1. An optional area in a report frequently used for a logo, report title, or print date, and that appears only once—at the beginning of the report.

____ 2. An action query that creates a new table based on existing tables.

____ 3. A query that adds new records to an existing table by importing data from another Access database, from another program such as Microsoft Excel, or from a table in the same database.

____ 4. A database sublanguage used in querying, updating, and managing relational databases in database programs such as Microsoft Access.

____ 5. A report generated from a crosstab query that displays calculated data grouped by two types of information.

____ 6. An optional area in a report frequently used for column headings, and that appears at the top of every page in a report.

____ 7. A query that changes data in a table.

____ 8. A report inserted into a control, and the control is then embedded in another report.

____ 9. A query that retrieves and displays data from one or more tables based on criteria that you specify.

____ 10. A type of action query that removes records from a table.

____ 11. Controls in a report that are tied to a field in an underlying table or query.

____ 12. The acronym and commonly used term for structured query language.

____ 13. A query that will prompt you for criteria before running the actual query.

____ 14. A special type of query that performs calculations on data that is grouped by two types of information.

____ 15. An optional area in a report useful for displaying report totals, and that appears only once—at the end of the report.

A Action query
B Append query
C Bound controls
D Crosstab query
E Crosstab report
F Delete query
G Make-table query
H Page header
I Parameter query
J Report footer
K Report header
L Select query
M SQL
N Structured Query Language
O Subreport

Concepts Assessments (continued)

Fill in the Blank Write the correct answer in the space provided.

1. To create a subreport, the two tables involved must contain a _____ relationship.

2. In a subreport, the main report comes from the _____ side of the one-to-many relationship.

3. In a subreport, the embedded report comes from the _____ side of the one-to-many relationship.

4. An optional area in a report, frequently used for page numbers, and that appears at the bottom of every page of a report is a page _____.

5. Conditions that identify specific records in a query are called _____.

6. The area of a report that contains the main body of the report's data, and which is repeated for each record in the report's underlying record source is the _____ section.

7. A type of action query that replaces existing data is a(an) _____ query.

8. When you want to summarize a large amount of data in a small space, use a _____ query.

9. To run a query you create in design view, Access must first translate your query into an SQL _____.

10. Controls in a report that have no data source, but that display information such as labels that identify a field's contents are called _____ controls.

Access chapter seven

Skill Assessments

Project 7C — Industries Report

Objectives: *Create a Subreport and Create Calculated Fields in a Report.*

In the following Skill Assessment, you will create a subreport for Michael Augustino, Executive Director of the Greater Atlanta Job Fair, which will list each Industry, and then under each Industry, the number of candidates looking for a job in the industry. You will also calculate the number of candidates looking for jobs in each industry. Your completed report will look similar to the one shown in Figure 7.50. You will rename the database as *7C_Industries_Report_Firstname_Lastname* in the folder you have created for this chapter.

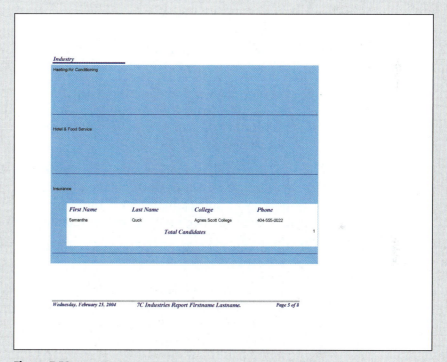

Figure 7.50

1. Locate the database file **a07C_Industries_Report** from your student files, and copy and paste the file to the Chapter 7 folder you created. Remove the Read-only property from the file and rename the file as **7C_Industries_Report_Firstname_Lastname** Start Access and open the database you just renamed.

2. On the Objects bar, click **Reports**, open the **Industries Report** in **Print preview**, **maximize** the report window, adjust the **Zoom** to **100%** so that you can view the data, and then examine the data in the report.

(**Project 7C**–Industries Report continues on the next page)

Skill Assessments (continued)

(Project 7C–Industries Report continued)

3. Switch to **Design view**. In the **Page Footer** section, click the control on the left, and then drag its right center sizing handle to the left to approximately **2 inches on the horizontal ruler**. Click the control on the right, and then drag its left center sizing handle to the right to approximately **5 inches on the horizontal ruler**.

4. On the Toolbox toolbar, click the **Label** button. In the **Page Footer section**, position the plus sign of your pointer just below the gray line at approximately **2.25 inches on the horizontal ruler**, and then drag down about a quarter of an inch and to the right to approximately **4.75 inches on the horizontal ruler**.

5. In the label control you just created, using your own first and last name, type **7C Industries Report Firstname Lastname** Then press Enter. Nudge the control as necessary. (Hint: Holding down Ctrl while pressing a directional key on your keyboard nudges in small precise increments.)

6. Position your mouse pointer at the top of the **Page Footer bar** until the double arrow mouse pointer displays, and then drag down to slightly below **1 inch on the vertical ruler**. This will expand the **Detail section** of the report.

7. On the Toolbox toolbar, click the **Subform/Subreport** button. Within the **Detail section**, position the plus sign attached to the mouse pointer at approximately **0.5 inch on the horizontal ruler** and at **0.5 inch on the vertical ruler** and click once.

8. In the first screen of the Subreport Wizard, be sure the **Use existing Tables and Queries** option button is selected, and then click **Next**.

9. Click the **Tables/Queries arrow**, and from the displayed list, click **Table: Candidates**. Under **Available Fields**, use the **One Field** button to move the **First Name**, **Last Name**, **College**, and **Phone** fields over to the **Selected Fields** list. Click **Next**.

10. Leave **Show Candidates for each record in Industries using IndustryID** selected and click **Next**. In the last screen of the wizard, accept the default report name by clicking **Finish**. **Maximize** the report window.

11. Click in the gray area to cancel any selections, and then click the **Candidates subreport label**. Press Delete. Recall that if this label is not deleted, it will repeat for every record in the report, which is repetitive and unnecessary. On the Toolbox toolbar, click the **Line** button, position the plus sign in the **Detail section** at the left edge and at **1.25 inches on the vertical ruler**, hold down Shift, and drag across to the right edge of the **Detail section**—you may not see the line until you release the mouse button. If you are not satisfied with your result, click **Undo** and begin again.

(Project 7C–Industries Report continues on the next page)

Skill Assessments (continued)

(Project 7C–Industries Report continued)

12. Right-click on the **Detail section bar**, from the shortcut menu point to **Fill/Back Color**, and then in the fifth row, click the sixth color—**light blue**.

13. In the upper right corner of your screen, click the small **Close Window** button to close the report, and then click **Yes** to save the changes to the design. Open the **Candidates subreport** and switch to **Design view**.

14. Drag the lower edge of the **Report Footer** down to **0.5 inch on the vertical ruler**. On the Toolbox toolbar, click the **Text Box** button. Position the plus sign of the pointer in the **Report Footer section** at approximately **4.75 inches on the horizontal ruler**, and then draw a text box approximately the same size as the *Phone* control directly above it.

15. Right-click the **Text Label** you just created and click **Properties**. Click the **Format tab**, and then change the **Caption** to Total Candidates Close the **Property sheet**. With the **Text Label** still selected, drag its left center sizing handle to the left to **2.5 inches on the horizontal ruler**.

16. Right-click the **Unbound control**, click **Properties**, and then click the **Data tab**. Click in the **Control Source** box and click the displayed **Build** button. In the **Expression Builder**, type =count([First Name]) Click **OK** and close the **property sheet**.

17. Click the small **Close Window** button to close the subreport, save your changes, and open the **Industries Report** in **Print preview**. From the **File** menu, click **Page Setup**. Click the **Page tab**, and under **Orientation**, click the **Landscape** option button. Click **OK**. From the **File** menu, click **Print**. Under **Print Range**, click in the **From** box and type **5** and then click in the **To** box and type **5** so that you print only page 5 of this report. Close the database, and then close Access.

 You have completed Project 7C

Access chapter seven

Skill Assessments (continued)

Project 7D — Zip Code

Objective: *Create an Update Query.*

In the following Skill Assessment, you will create an Update Query to update ZIP codes (also known as Postal Codes) in the Candidates table and the Employers table. You will rename and save your database as *7D_Zip_Code_Firstname_Lastname.* Your completed tables will look similar to Figure 7.51.

Figure 7.51

(**Project 7D**–Zip Code continues on the next page)

466 Access | Chapter 7: Advanced Reports and Queries

Skill Assessments (continued)

(Project 7D–Zip Code continued)**

1. Locate the file **7D_Update_Zip_Code** from your student files, and copy and paste the file to the Chapter 7 folder you created. Remove the Read-only property from the file and rename the file **7D_Update_Zip Code_Firstname_Lastname** Start Access and open the database you just renamed.

2. On the Objects bar, click **Queries**, and to the right, double-click the command icon **Create query in Design view**. Add the **Candidates** table to the query, and then close the **Show Table** dialog box.

3. From the **Candidates** field list, double-click the **Postal Code** field to add it to the design grid.

4. On the Query Design toolbar, click the **Query Type button arrow**, and then from the displayed list, click **Update Query**.

5. In the **Criteria** row, under **Postal Code**, type **30301** and then in the **Update To** row in the same column type **30103** This will update any Postal Codes that are currently listed as 30301 to 30103, correcting errors that were made during data entry.

6. **Run** the query, and when the message indicates that you are about to update 2 rows, click **Yes**.

7. Close the query window without saving changes. On the Objects bar, click **Tables**, and then right-click the **Candidates** table. Click **Rename**, and then name the table **Candidates Firstname Lastname** Open the renamed table in **Datasheet view**. Select the first three columns of the table, display the **Format** menu, and then click **Hide Columns**. Use the same process to also hide the **Phone column**. From the **File** menu, click **Page Setup**. Click the **Page tab**, and under **Orientation**, click the **Landscape** option button. Click **OK**, and then on the Standard toolbar, click the **Print** button to print the table. Close the table and save the changes to the layout.

8. Rename the Employers table as **Employers Firstname Lastname** Using the steps above as your guide, update the **Postal Code** on the **Employers table** in the same manner, except that when preparing to print, hide the **Employer ID**, **Contact**, **Contact Title**, **Phone**, and **Fee Paid columns**.

End You have completed Project 7D

Skill Assessments (continued)

Project 7E — Industry Fee

Objective: *Create a Crosstab Report.*

In the following Skill Assessment, you will create a crosstab query to show the fee collected from companies based on the industry type. Then you will create a crosstab report based on the query you created. Your completed report will look similar to Figure 7.52. You will rename and save your database as *7E_Industry_Fee_Firstname_Lastname*.

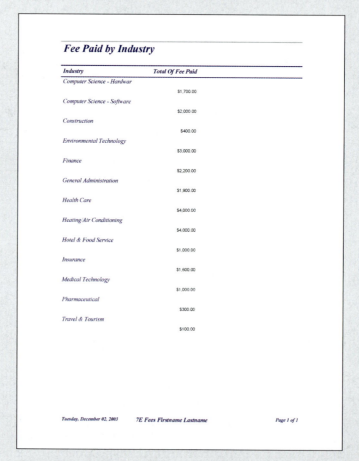

Figure 7.52

1. Locate the file **7E_Industry_Fee** from your student files, and copy and paste the file to the Chapter 7 folder you created. Remove the Read-only property from the file and rename the file as **7E_Industry_Fee_Firstname_Lastname** Start Access and open the database you just renamed.

2. On the Objects bar, click **Queries**. On the Database window toolbar, click the **New** button, and then click **Crosstab Query Wizard**. Click **OK**.

(**Project 7E** – Industry Fee continues on the next page)

Skill Assessments (continued)

(Project 7E–Industry Fee continued)

3. Under **View**, click the **Queries** option button. In the white area, be sure that **Query: Job Openings by Employer** is selected, and then click **Next**.

4. Select **Industry** as the field value to use as the row heading, and move it the **Selected Fields** column. Click **Next**.

5. Select **Employer Name** as the field value to use as the column heading, and then click **Next**.

6. Select **Fee Paid** as the number to be calculated, and **Sum** as the calculation to perform. Click **Next**.

7. As the query name, type **Fee Paid by Industry Crosstab 7E Firstname Lastname** Be sure that the **View the query** option button is selected. Click **Finish**.

8. Examine and then **close** the Query. On the Objects bar, click **Reports**, and then on the Database window toolbar, click the **New** button. In the **New Report** dialog box, click **Report Wizard**. At the bottom of the dialog box, click the **Choose the table or query where the object's data comes from arrow**, and from the displayed list click your **Fee Paid by Industry_Crosstab 7E** query. Click **OK**.

9. Move **Industry** and **Total Of Fee Paid** to the **Selected Fields** list. Click **Next**.

10. For grouping levels, click the **Industry** field, and then click the **One Field** button. Click **Next**. To the right of the **1** box, be sure that **Ascending** displays. Click **Next**.

11. Leave the default setting for **Layout** as **Stepped** and the **Orientation** as **Portrait**. Click **Next**. Be sure the style is **Corporate** and click **Next**. Name the report **Fee Paid by Industry** Click **Finish**.

12. Switch to **Design view**. In the **Page Footer**, select the control on the left, and drag its right center sizing handle to **1.75 inches on the horizontal ruler**. Select the control on the right, and drag its left center sizing handle to **4.5 inches on the horizontal ruler**. On the Toolbox toolbar, click the **Label** button. Position your pointer even with the upper edge of the other controls and at **2 inches on the horizontal ruler**, and drag down about one quarter inch and to the right to **4.25 inches on the horizontal ruler**. Type **7E Fees Firstname Lastname** and then click outside to deselect the control. Select the control again and nudge the control as necessary to be in line with the other controls.

13. Switch to **Print preview**, print the report, close the report and save your changes, and close Access.

End You have completed Project 7E

Performance Assessments

Project 7F—Job Openings

Objectives: *Create a Subreport and Create Calculated Fields in a Report.*

In the following Performance Assessment, you will embed a subreport in the Industry table to list the job openings within each industry. You will also calculate the number of job openings for each industry. Your completed report will look similar to Figure 7.53. You will rename and save your database as *7F_Job_Openings_Firstname_Lastname*.

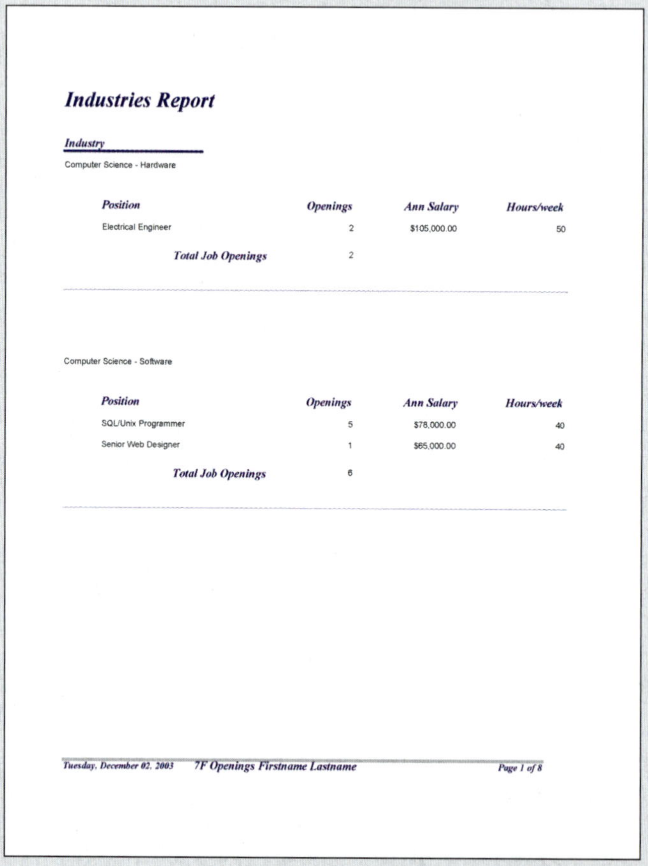

Industries Report

Industry

Computer Science - Hardware

Position	*Openings*	*Ann Salary*	*Hours/week*
Electrical Engineer	2	$105,000.00	50
Total Job Openings	2		

Computer Science - Software

Position	*Openings*	*Ann Salary*	*Hours/week*
SQL/Unix Programmer	5	$78,000.00	40
Senior Web Designer	1	$65,000.00	40
Total Job Openings	6		

Tuesday, December 02, 2003 *7F Openings Firstname Lastname* *Page 1 of 8*

Figure 7.53

1. Locate the database file **a07F_Job_Openings** from your student files, and copy and paste the file to the Chapter 7 folder you created. Remove the Read-only property from the file and rename the file as **7F_Job_Openings_Firstname_Lastname** Start Access and open the database you just renamed.
2. On the Objects bar, click **Reports**, and open the **Industries Report**. **Maximize** the report window, and then switch to **Design view**.
3. Expand the **Detail section** downward to slightly below **1 inch on the vertical ruler**. On the Toolbox toolbar, click the **Subform/Subreport** button, and insert the subreport in the **Detail section** at **0.5 inch on the horizontal ruler** and **0.5 inch on the vertical ruler**.

(**Project 7F**–Job Openings continues on the next page)

Performance Assessments (continued)

(Project 7F–Job Openings continued)

4. In the first screen of the wizard, use existing tables and queries, and in the second screen, select the **Job Openings Table**. Use **Position**, **# Openings**, **Ann Salary**, and **Hours/week** as the selected fields. Leave the name of the subreport as *Job Openings subreport*.

5. If necessary, maximize the report window. Click outside of the report to cancel any selections, and then select and delete the **Job Openings subreport label**. On the Toolbox toolbar, click the **Line** button, and then draw a line under the subreport at **1.25 inches** on the vertical ruler. As you drag across, hold down [Shift] to ensure a straight, not jagged, line. You may not see the line until you release the mouse button. If you are not satisfied with your result, click Undo and begin again.

6. In the **Page Footer** section, select the control on the left, and shorten its right side to **1.75 inches on the horizontal ruler**. Select the control on the right, and shorten its left side to **4.25 inches on the horizontal ruler**. On the Toolbox toolbar, click the **Label** button and create a label in the **Page Footer** section about one-quarter inch tall and from **1.75 inches on the horizontal ruler** to **4.25 inches on the horizontal ruler**. In the label, type **7F Openings Firstname Lastname** Deselect the label, select it again, and then nudge it as necessary to line up with the other controls in the **Page Footer section**. Click the small **Close Window** button, and save changes. Open the **Job Openings subreport** in **Design view**.

7. Expand the **Report Footer** to **0.5 inches on the vertical ruler**. On the Toolbox toolbar, click the **Text Box** button and insert a textbox in the **Report Footer** directly under the *# Openings* text box. Make the new text box the same approximate shape and size as the *# Openings* text box above.

8. Right-click on the **label** control you just inserted, display the **Property sheet**, and on the **Format tab**, change the **Caption** to **Total Job Openings** Close the **Property sheet**, and then drag the left center sizing handle of the label to **1 inch on the horizontal ruler** to accommodate the new caption.

9. Right-click on the **unbound control**, display the **Data tab** of the **Property sheet**, click in the **Control Source** box, and then click the **Build** button. In the Expression Builder, type **=sum([# Openings])** and then click **OK**. Close the **Property sheet**.

10. Click the **Close Window** button to close the subreport and save your changes to the design. Open the **Industries Report** in **Print preview**. From the **File** menu, click **Page Setup**, and change the **Left margin** and the **Right margin** to **0.5**.

11. From the **File** menu, click **Print**, and under **Print Range**, print only **page 1** of the report.

12. Close the report. Close the database, and then close Access.

End You have completed Project 7F

Performance Assessments (continued)

Project 7G — Experienced Candidates

Objectives: *Create a Delete Query and Create Action Queries.*

In the following Performance Assessment, you will create a table using the Make-Table Query, and then use a Delete Query to remove unneeded records. Your completed table will look similar to Figure 7.54. You will rename and save your database as *7G_Experienced_Candidates_Firstname_Lastname*.

Title	First Name	Last Name	Address Line 1	Address Line 2	City	State	Postal Code	Phone
Ms.	Samantha	Quck	124 Whitworth	#352	Atlanta	GA	30301	404-555-0022
Mr.	Walter	Perrie	2495 Sunset Dr		Conyers	GA	30012	678-555-0186
Ms.	Kelley	Bondurant	179 Auburn Co		Cartersville	GA	30120	678-555-0066
Mr.	Taylor	Dunnahoo	189 Ventura St		Atlanta	GA	30330	770-555-0190
Ms.	Lenesha	Barnett	2361 Bluebird	#8	Smyrna	GA	30081	706-555-0183
Mr.	Mauro	Calva	82 E. Ramona		Atlanta	GA	30327	404-555-0096
Mr.	David	Feingold	1821 Alturas St	#1442	Atlanta	GA	30301	404-555-0101
Mr.	Byeong	Chang	2221 Flowers		Roswell	GA	30077	770-555-0066
Ms.	Samira	Ahmed	3418 Longview	#320	Marietta	GA	30063	770-555-0002
Ms.	Jessica	Pyun	1255 Miravista		Kennesaw	GA	30144	770-555-0003

Figure 7.54

1. Locate the database file **a07G_Experienced_Candidates** from your student files, and copy and paste the file to the Chapter 7 folder you created. Remove the Read-only property from the file and rename the file as **7G_Experienced_Candidates_Firstname_Lastname** Start Access and open the database you just renamed.

2. On the Objects bar, click **Queries**. Double-click the **Create query in Design view** command icon. Add the **Candidates** table to the table area, and close the dialog box.

3. In the field list, beginning with the first field, add all of the fields to the design grid.

4. On the Query Design toolbar, click the **Query Type button arrow**, and then click **Make-Table Query**. Name the new table **Candidates with Experience 7G Firstname Lastname** **Run** the query. You will add 14 records to the new table.

(**Project 7G**–Experienced Candidates continues on the next page)

Performance Assessments (continued)

(Project 7G–Experienced Candidates continued)

5. **Close** the query and save it as **Query to Create Candidates Table**

6. To create a table that lists only those candidates with some experience, begin another new query in **Design view**. Add your **Candidates with Experience 7G** table to the table area and close the **Show Table** dialog box. To the design grid, add the fields **Experience?**, **First Name**, and **Last Name**.

7. In the **Criteria** row, under **Experience?** type **No**

8. **Run** the query. Four records will satisfy the criteria. These are the records to delete, because these candidates have no experience. In the Experience column, notice that the records indicate *0*. In Access, 0 means *no* or *false*.

9. Switch to **Design view** and change the **Query Type** to **Delete Query**. **Run** the query and confirm that you will delete 4 records from the table. **Close** the query without saving.

10. On the Objects bar, click **Tables**, and then open your **Candidates with Experience 7G** table in **Datasheet view**. You will see 10 records in your table. Select and hide the first three columns, and then hide the **College** column. From the **File** menu, click **Page Setup**, and change the **Orientation** to **Landscape**. On the **File** menu, click **Print**.

11. Close the table and save your changes. Close the database, and then close Access.

End You have completed Project 7G

Project 7H—Employers by City

Objective: *Create a Parameter Query.*

In the following Performance Assessment, you will create a parameter query for the Employers table for Michael Augustino, the Executive Director of the Greater Atlanta Job Fair. Mr. Augustino wants to be able to type in a city name and have all the employers located in the city display. Your completed query will look similar to Figure 7.55. You will rename and save your database as *7H_EmployersByCity_Firstname_Lastname*.

1. Locate the database file **a07H_EmployersByCity** from your student files, and copy and paste the file to the Chapter 7 folder you created. Remove the Read-only property from the file and rename the file as **7H_EmployersByCity_Firstname_Lastname** Start Access and open the database you just renamed.

(**Project 7H**–Employers by City continues on the next page)

Performance Assessments (continued)

(Project 7H–Employers by City continued)

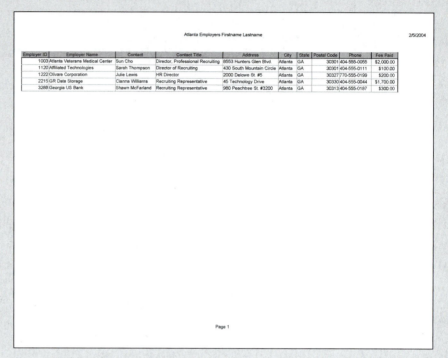

Figure 7.55

2. On the Objects bar, click **Queries**, and then double-click the command icon **Create query in Design view**. Add the **Employers** table to the query.

3. Add all of the fields from the **Employers** table to the design grid.

4. In the **Criteria** row, in the **City** column, type **[Enter the name of the City]**

5. **Run** the query and at the prompt type **Atlanta** as the city. In the resulting query, select all the columns, display the **Format** menu, and then change the **Font Size** to **8**. With the columns still selected, apply **Best Fit**. From the **File** menu, click **Save As**, and save the query as **Atlanta Employers Firstname Lastname** From the **File** menu, click **Page Setup**, and change the **Page Orientation** to **Landscape**. Change the **Left margin** and the **Right margin** to **0.25**. From the **File** menu, click **Print**, and click **OK**.

6. Close the query, close the database, and then close Access.

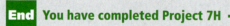

End You have completed Project 7H

Mastery Assessments

Project 7I — Job Fair Sections

Objectives: *Create a Subreport and Create Calculated Fields in a Report.*

The exhibit space at each of the Job Fairs is divided into sections, and each employer is assigned to a specific section. In the following Mastery Assessment, you will embed a subreport in the Job Fair Sections Report to list the employers and the sections they will occupy at the Job Fair. Your completed report will look similar to Figure 7.56. You will rename and save your database as *7I_JobFair_Sections_Firstname_Lastname*.

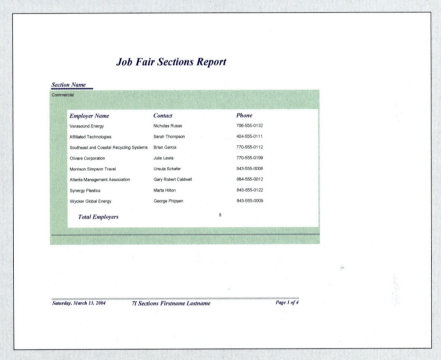

Figure 7.56

1. Locate the file **a07I_JobFair_Sections** from your student files, and copy and paste the file to the Chapter 7 folder you created. Remove the Read-only property from the file and rename the file as **7I_JobFair_Sections_Firstname_Lastname** Start Access and open the database you just renamed.

2. On the Objects bar, click **Reports**, and then open the **Job Fair Sections Report** in **Design view**. Maximize the window.

3. Expand the **Detail section** by dragging its lower edge to slightly below **1 inch on the vertical ruler**. Insert a **Subreport** in the **Detail section** at approximately **0.5 inch on the horizontal and vertical ruler**. Use existing tables, and then select the **Employers** table and use **Employer Name**, **Contact**, **Contact Title**, and **Phone** fields as the **Selected Fields**.

(**Project 7I**–Job Fair Sections continues on the next page)

Mastery Assessments (continued)

(Project 7I–Job Fair Sections continued)

4. Save the Subreport as **Employers Section Subreport**

5. Maximize the window, and then click in the gray area to cancel all selections. Then select and delete the **Employers Section Subreport label**. At **1.25 inches on the vertical ruler**, hold down [Shift] and draw a line across the report. In the **Detail section**, display the **Fill/Back Color** palette, and the fifth row, click the fourth color—**light green**.

6. In the **Page Footer** section, shorten the right side of the control on the left to **2 inches on the horizontal ruler**, and shorten the left side of the control on the right to **5 inches on the horizontal ruler**. Insert a new label control between the two shortened controls, and type **7I Sections Firstname Lastname** Nudge as necessary to align the new label.

7. Close the report, save the changes and open the **Employers Section Subreport** in **Design view**.

8. Expand the **Report Footer** to **0.5 inch on the vertical ruler**. In the **Report Footer** area, insert a **Text Box** at approximately **2 inches on the horizontal ruler** extending to **4 inches on the horizontal ruler**. Right-click the **label control**, display the **Property sheet**, and on the **Format tab**, change the **Caption** to **Total Employers** Select the **label control** and drag the left resizing handle to **0.5 inches** on the **horizontal ruler**. Right-click the **unbound control**, display the **Property sheet**, click the **Data tab**, and in the **Control Source** box, click the **Build** button. Use the count function to calculate the total number of Employers. Hint: =count([Employer Name])

9. Close the subreport and save the changes. Open the **Job Fair Sections Report** in Print preview. From the **File** menu, click **Page Setup**, and change the **Page Orientation** to **Landscape**. Use the page navigation buttons at the lower left of the screen to scroll through the pages of the report, and notice the names of each of the sections. From the **File** menu, click **Print**, and under **Print Range**, print from page **1** to **1** to print only the first page of the report.

10. Close the report, close the database, and then close Access.

 You have completed Project 7I

Mastery Assessments (continued)

Project 7J — Exclusive Job Listings

Objective: *Create Action Queries.*

In the following Mastery Assessment, you will create a table using a Make-Table Query, and then you will add additional records using an Append Query. Your completed table will look similar to Figure 7.57. You will rename and save your database as *7J_Exclusive_JobListings_Firstname_Lastname.*

7J Exclusive Jobs Firstname Lastname 3/13/2004

Employer Name	Industry	Position	# Openings	Ann Salary	City	State
Thinkanswer Technologies	Computer Science - Software	SQL/Unix Programmer	5	$78,000.00	Conyers	GA
Atlanta Insurance Brokers	Insurance	Actuary – Entry Level	5	$43,000.00	Roswell	GA
Atlanta Veterans Medical Center	Health Care	Nursing Supervisor	10	$62,000.00	Atlanta	GA
A&G Consulting	Hotel & Food Service	Gift Shop Manager	5	$35,000.00	Roswell	GA
Derrickson Brothers Construction	Construction	Cabinetmaker/Carpenter	10	$30,000.00	Marietta	GA
Derrickson Brothers Construction	Construction	Civil Engineering Supervisor	5	$80,000.00	Marietta	GA
A&G Consulting	General Administration	Senior Accounting Clerk	15	$35,000.00	Roswell	GA
A&G Consulting	General Administration	Executive Assistant	5	$40,000.00	Roswell	GA
DYCarlson Corp.	Pharmaceutical	Biostatistician – Entry Level	5	$50,000.00	Smyrna	GA
Greenville Accounting Partners	Finance	Accountant – Entry Level	15	$36,000.00	Charleston	SC
Wisener Heating & Air Condtioning	Heating/Air Conditioning	Electrician – Entry Level	5	$36,000.00	Cartersville	GA
Wisener Heating & Air Condtioning	Heating/Air Conditioning	Estimating Manager	6	$60,000.00	Cartersville	GA
Lauren Newberry Associates	Travel & Tourism	Travel Clerk	10	$28,000.00	Greenville	SC
Verasound Energy	Environmental Technology	Petroleum Engineer – Mid Level	5	$70,000.00	Smyrna	GA
Thinkanswer Technologies	Computer Science - Software	SQL/Unix Programmer	5	$78,000.00	Conyers	GA
GR Data Storage	Computer Science - Hardware	Electrical Engineer	2	$105,000.00	Atlanta	GA
Atlanta Insurance Brokers	Insurance	Actuary – Senior	3	$98,000.00	Roswell	GA
Watson Medical Technologies Corp.	Medical Technology	Nuclear Medicine Director	1	$75,000.00	Charleston	SC
Atlanta Veterans Medical Center	Health Care	Assistant Director of Pharmacy	3	$95,000.00	Atlanta	GA
Derrickson Brothers Construction	Construction	Civil Engineering Supervisor	5	$80,000.00	Marietta	GA

Page 1

Figure 7.57

1. Locate the database file **a07J_Exclusive_JobListings** from your student files, and copy and paste the file to the Chapter 7 folder you created. Remove the Read-only property from the file and rename the file as **7J_Exclusive_JobListings_Firstname_Lastname** Start Access and open the database you just renamed.
2. On the Objects bar, click **Queries**, and then double-click the command icon **Create query in Design view**. In the **Show Table** dialog box, click the **Queries tab**, and then add the **Job Openings by Employer** query to the table area.
3. Add all the fields to the design grid. In the **Criteria** row, in the **# Openings** column, type **>=5**

(Project 7J–Exclusive Job Listings continues on the next page)

Mastery Assessments (continued)

(Project 7J–Exclusive Job Listings continued)

4. Change the type of query to a **Make-Table Query**. Name the table **7J Exclusive Jobs Firstname Lastname**

5. **Run** the query, and when the message indicates that 14 row(s) will be added into a new table, click **Yes**.

6. Close the query, and save the query as **Job Listings** On the Objects bar, click **Tables**, and open your **7J Exclusive Jobs** table to view the 14 records. These employers all have 5 or more job openings. Close the table.

7. On the Objects bar, click **Queries**. Point to the **Job Listings** query and right-click. From the displayed shortcut menu, select **Design View**.

8. Delete >=5 from the **# Openings** criteria. In the **Criteria** row, in the **Ann Salary** column, type >=75000 Change the query type to **Append Query**. In the Append dialog box, click **OK**.

9. **Run** the Query. Click **Yes** to append 6 rows to the table.

10. Close the query and save the changes. Open your **7J Exclusive Jobs** table and notice that six records have been appended (added) to the end of the table. These records are for employers who have job openings with annual salaries equal to or greater than $75,000. Select all of the columns and apply **Best Fit**. Hide the **Postal Code**, **Phone**, and **Fee Paid** columns. On the **File** menu, click **Page Setup**, and change the **Page Orientation** to **Landscape**. Change the **Left** and **Right** margins to **0.75**. On the **File** menu, click **Print**. Close your table and save the changes. Close the database, and close Access.

End You have completed Project 7J

Access chapter seven

Problem Solving

Project 7K — Crosstab Choice

Objective: *Create a Crosstab Report.*

In the following Problem Solving exercise, you will create a crosstab query, and then create a new crosstab report for the query.

1. Locate the database file **a07K_CrosstabChoice** from your student files, and copy and paste the file to the Chapter 7 folder you created. Remove the Read-only property from the file and rename the file as **7K_CrosstabChoice_Firstname_Lastname** Start Access and open the database you just renamed.

2. Open the **Job Openings by Employer** query and examine all of the information in the query. Select three fields that would be useful to compare data in a crosstab query.

3. Create the crosstab query based on the fields you selected in the previous step. Be sure the information is displayed in an organized manner. Close the crosstab query you created.

4. Create a new report using the wizard to display the crosstab query in an attractive format.

5. Add your name in the page footer, and print the report.

6. Close the report, saving any changes. Close the database, and then close Access.

End You have completed Project 7K

Project 7L — Fee by Section

Objective: *Create a Subreport.*

In the following Problem Solving exercise, you will create a report with an embedded subreport.

1. Locate the file **a07L_FeeBySection** from your student files, and copy and paste the file to the Chapter 7 folder you created. Remove the Read-only property from the file and rename the file as **7L_FeeBySection_Firstname_Lastname** Start Access and open the database you just renamed.

2. Open the **Job Fair Sections** report and add a subreport based on the **Employers** table. Add the **Employer Name** and **Fee Paid** fields to the subreport.

3. Create a calculated field to sum the **Fees by Section** and also a calculated field to calculate the total amount of fees paid.

4. Add your name in the page footer. Print the report and close the report, saving any changes. Close the database, and then close Access.

End You have completed Project 7L

On the Internet

Getting More Information About Special Queries

The Microsoft Web page contains a variety of information about using special queries in Access. Got to the Microsoft site at www.microsoft.com and click Search. Search for Access queries and examine the information on queries. Print any information that is of interest to you.

GO! with Help

SQL-Specific Queries

In this chapter you viewed queries in SQL, and learned that as you create your queries in design view, Access is working in the background to create SQL statements to run your query. There are some query types, called **SQL-specific queries**, that cannot be created in the design grid; they must be created directly in SQL view. In this Help activity, you will use Help to learn about the four types of queries that are SQL-specific.

1. Start Access. In the *Type a question for help* box, type **SQL queries** and press Enter.

2. In the **Search Results** task pane, click **About SQL queries (MDB)**.

3. At the bottom of the Help window, click the link **SQL-specific queries**. Then click the link for each of the four types of SQL-specific queries—**union**, **pass-through**, **data-definition**, and **subquery**. Read the information for each of the query types.

4. Print the Help information if you want to keep a copy of it. Close the **Help** window, and then close Access.

Access 2003

chapter eight

Integrating Access with Other Office Applications

In this chapter, you will: complete these projects and practice these skills.

| Project 8A
Using Access with Other Office Applications | **Objectives**
• Import Data from a Word Table
• Use Mail Merge to Integrate Access and Word
• Import from Excel
• Add Hyperlinks to Word and Excel Files |

| Project 8B
Linking and Embedding Objects in Access | **Objectives**
• Link Database Objects to Office Files
• Add a Chart to a Form
• Add a Chart to a Report |

University Medical Center

The University Medical Center (UMC) is a premier patient-care and research institution serving the metropolitan area of Orange Beach, Florida. UMC enhances the health and well being of the community through collaborative research and innovations in patient care, medications, and procedures. The center is particularly renowned for its state-of-the-art cancer diagnosis and treatment program and for its South-central Florida Cardiovascular Center. The pediatrics wing specializes in the care of high-risk newborns.

© Photosphere Images Ltd.

Integrating Access with Other Office Applications

When working with Access, information you want to use may be located in a file developed in another application. Fortunately, Access can import or link to the data in other applications so that you do not have to retype the data into your database. You can import data from a large variety of file formats. In this chapter, you will import data from both Microsoft Word and Microsoft Excel.

Rather than importing information from other applications into your database, you may choose to link your database to the original source so that you can view useful information. In this chapter, you will also link to information from an external source.

Project 8A Medical Center

For its popular program of public seminars, the University Medical Center Office of Public Affairs maintains a list of speakers, which is formatted as a Microsoft Word document. They also use Microsoft Excel to track the marketing expenses for the seminars. Finally, they have an Access database with a table containing the scheduled seminars and another table with the names and addresses of media contacts. Mike Martinez, the Director of Public Affairs, thinks it would be useful to bring the information from the Word and Excel files into the Access database.

In Activities 8.1 through 8.5, you will import and link information into an Access database from Word and Excel documents. You will use the information in the Media Contacts table to create a mail merge document in Microsoft Word. You will also create hyperlinks from a form in your database to Word and Excel files. You will save your database as *8A_Medical_Center_Firstname_Lastname*.

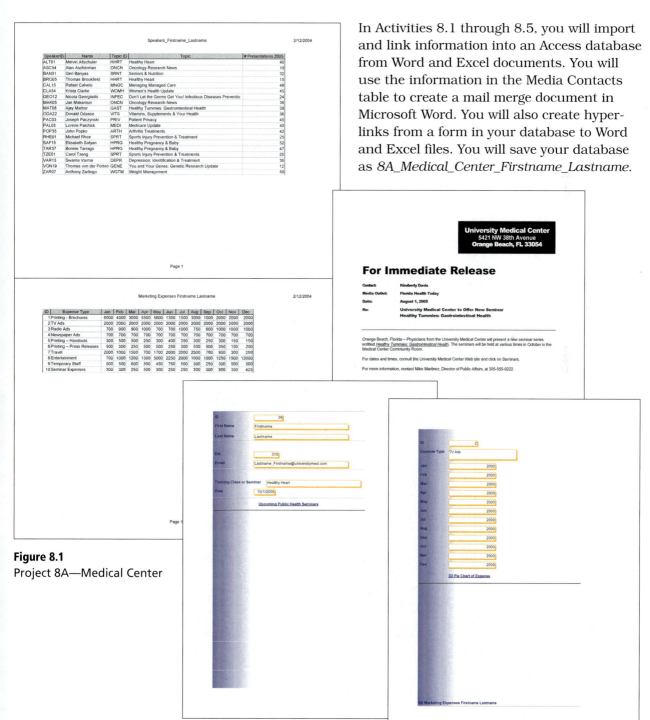

Figure 8.1
Project 8A—Medical Center

Objective 1
Import Data from a Word Table

When you create a database, you can type the records directly into a table. You can also *import* data from a variety of sources. To import means to copy data from a text file like Microsoft Word, a spreadsheet file like Microsoft Excel, or a database table from another Access database, and then insert it into an Access table. For example, the University Medical Center Office of Public Affairs wants to import the information regarding the seminar speakers into their Access database. Currently this information is in a Microsoft Word table.

Activity 8.1 Importing Data from a Word Table

In this activity, you will import information from a Word table and create a new table, named *Speakers*, in your database.

1 Start Microsoft Word. On the Standard toolbar, click **Open**, and from the student files that accompany this textbook, locate and open the Microsoft Word file **a08A_Speakers_Table**.

2 If necessary, click anywhere inside the table. On the menu bar, click **Table**, and then point to **Convert** as shown in Figure 8.2. Click **Table to Text**.

To import data from a Word table into an Access table, the data must first be converted to a *delimited text file*, which is a file containing data where individual field values are separated by a character, such as a comma or a tab. When you import this table into Access, you will choose the same delimiter character so that Access can separate the data into fields.

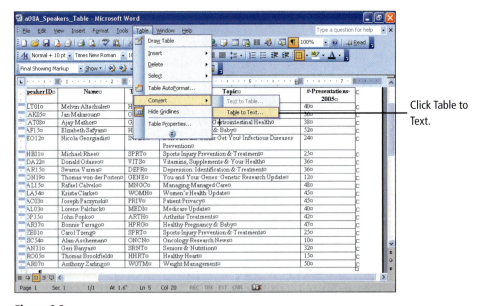

Figure 8.2

3 In the displayed **Convert Table to Text** dialog box, be sure the **Tabs** option button is selected—this is the character you will use to separate the text into fields. Click **OK**. Click anywhere to deselect.

> ### Note — Is the Show/Hide ¶ Button Turned On?
>
> By turning on the Show/Hide ¶ button as shown in Figure 8.3, all of the tabs between the different fields and the extra paragraph mark at the end of the document will be displayed on the screen. If necessary, click the Show/Hide ¶ button to turn it on.

4 Hold down Ctrl and press End to move to the end of the document. Press Bksp once, and then compare your screen with Figure 8.3.

Deleting the extra blank line at the bottom of your file will prevent a blank record from being inserted into your new database table. Notice that Word will flag most proper names as spelling errors because they are not contained within Word's dictionary.

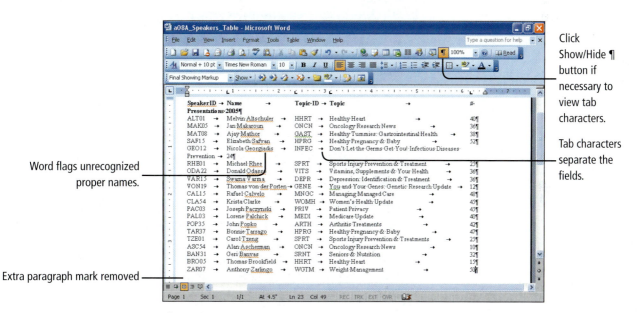

Figure 8.3

5 From the **File** menu, click **Save As**, and then navigate to the location where you are storing your projects for this chapter, creating a new folder for Chapter 8 if you want to do so. At the bottom of the **Save As** dialog box, click the **Save as type arrow**, and from the displayed list, scroll as necessary and click **Plain Text**. In the **File name** box, type **8A_Speakers_Table_Firstname_Lastname** See Figure 8.4.

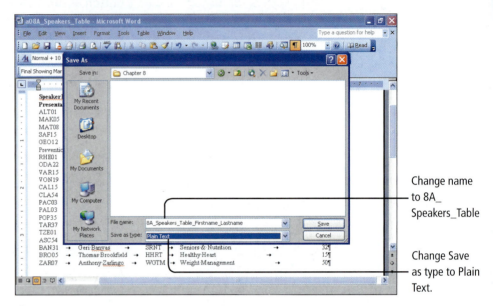

Figure 8.4

6 In the lower right corner of the dialog box, click **Save**. In the displayed **File Conversion** dialog box, accept the default settings and click **OK**. **Close** ⊠ Microsoft Word.

7 Using **My Computer**, navigate to the student files that accompany this textbook and locate the Access database **a08A_Medical_Center**. Copy and paste the file to the Chapter 8 folder you created, and rename the file **8A_Medical_Center_Firstname_Lastname** Remove the Read-only property from the file. **Start** Access and open the database you just renamed.

8 On the Objects bar, click **Tables**. On the menu bar, click **File**, point to **Get External Data**, and on the submenu click **Import**. At the bottom of the displayed **Import** dialog box, click the **Files of type arrow**, and then scroll as necessary and click **Text Files**. Use the **Look in arrow** to navigate to your files for this chapter, and then click your **8A_Speakers_Table** text file as shown in Figure 8.5. In the lower right corner, click **Import**.

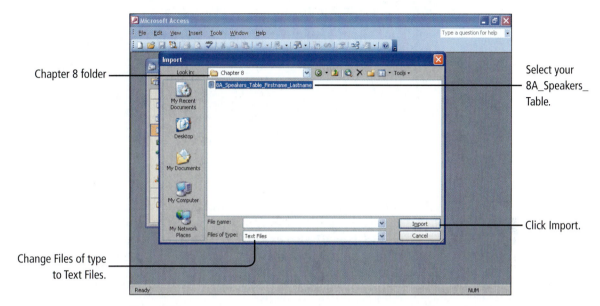

Figure 8.5

9 In the displayed first screen of the **Import Text Wizard**, be sure the **Delimited** option button is selected, and then click **Next**.

Here you indicate which type of character serves as the delimiter to separate the fields.

10 Under **Choose the delimiter that separates your fields**, be sure the **Tab** option button is selected, and then select the **First Row Contains Field Names** check box as shown in Figure 8.6.

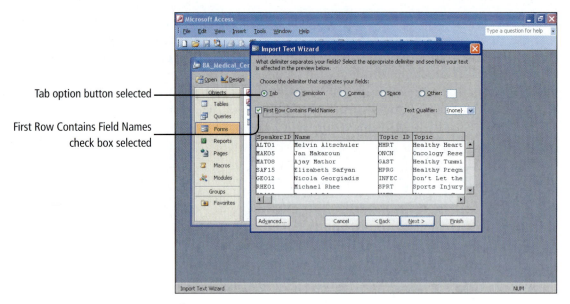

Tab option button selected

First Row Contains Field Names check box selected

Figure 8.6

11 Click **Next**. Here you will indicate where the imported data should be stored—either in a new table or in an existing table. Under **Where would you like to store your data**, be sure the **In a New Table** option button is selected, and then click **Next**.

In this wizard screen, you can specify information about each of the fields you are importing.

More Knowledge — Appending Data in an Existing Table

When importing data into Access, you can also add or update—append—data to the end of an existing table. This process of adding or updating is called *appending*.

12 Under **Field Options**, with **SpeakerID** displayed in the **Field Name** box, click the **Indexed arrow**, and then, as shown in Figure 8.7, click **Yes (No Duplicates)**.

Because the SpeakerID field will be used as the ***primary key*** in this new table, duplicates should *not* be allowed. Recall that a primary key is the field that uniquely identifies a record in a table.

Yes (No Duplicates) selected

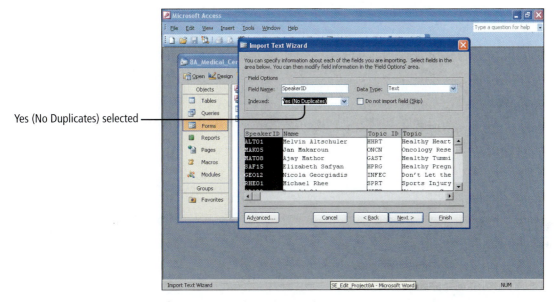

Figure 8.7

13 Click **Next**. Here you will define the field that will serve as the primary key. Click the **Choose my own primary key** option button and be sure that **SpeakerID** displays in the box to the right. Click **Next**. Here you name the new table that will be inserted into your database. In the **Import to Table** box, type **Speakers Firstname Lastname** and click **Finish**. If an error message displays (see the following Alert), click **OK**. In the message indicating that Access has finished importing, click **OK**.

The new table is added to your database.

Alert!

Does an Error Message Display When You Click Finish?

If, when saving your Word document as a text file, you do not delete any extra blank lines at the end, one or more blank records will be inserted into your table and an error message displays after you click Finish. If you see the error message, click OK, and then click OK again. Then, open the new table, delete any empty records, display the table in Design view, and then set the appropriate field as the primary key.

14 Open your **Speakers** table in **Datasheet view**. In the column heading area, drag to select all of the columns, display the **Format** menu, and then click **Column Width**. In the **Column Width** dialog box, click the **Best Fit** button to resize all the columns to fit the data. Click anywhere to deselect, and then compare your completed table with Figure 8.8.

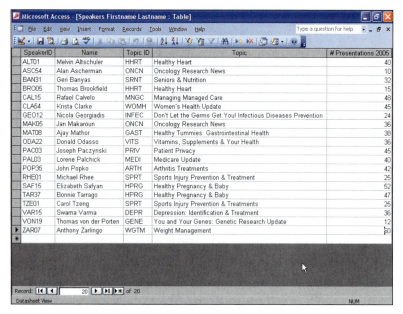

Figure 8.8

> **Another Way**
>
> **To Apply Best Fit to Columns**
>
> You can find the best fit for columns without displaying the Column Width dialog box. Select one or more columns, position the mouse pointer over any of the selected column boundaries in the column heading area to display the two-headed pointer, and then double-click.

15 Display the **File** menu, click **Page Setup**, and then on the **Page tab**, change the **Orientation** to **Landscape**. Click **OK**. On the Database toolbar, click the **Print** button . **Close** your table and save the changes. Leave the database open for the next activity.

Objective 2
Use Mail Merge to Integrate Access and Word

Using Word's ***mail merge*** feature, letters or memos are created by combining (merging) two documents—a ***main document*** and a ***data source***. The main document contains the text of the letter or memo. The data source—an Access table—contains the names and addresses of the individuals to whom the letter, memo, or other document is being sent.

The easiest way to perform a mail merge is to use the Mail Merge Wizard. Recall that a wizard asks you questions and, based on your answers, walks you step by step through a process.

Activity 8.2 Merging an Access Table with a Word Document

In this activity, you will send a Press Release memo to all the media contacts in your database announcing a new seminar that the Medical Center is conducting. You will create the memos by merging the individual names and addresses in the Media Contacts table with a memo created in Microsoft Word.

1 In the Database window, click the **Media Contacts** table to select it.

On the Database toolbar, click the **OfficeLinks button arrow** , and from the displayed list, click **Merge It with Microsoft Office Word**.

Project 8A: Medical Center | **Access**   491

2 In this first screen of the **Microsoft Word Mail Merge Wizard**, click the **Link your data to an existing Microsoft Word document** option button. Click **OK**. In the displayed dialog box, navigate to the student files that accompany this textbook, click the **a08A_Press_Release** Word document, and then click **Open**.

Microsoft Word opens with the memo on the left and the Mail Merge task pane on the right.

3 On the menu bar, click **View**, and then click **Header and Footer**. In the displayed Header and Footer toolbar, click the **Switch Between Header and Footer** button . As shown in Figure 8.9, with your insertion point positioned in the **Footer** box, type **8A Press Release Memo Firstname Lastname**

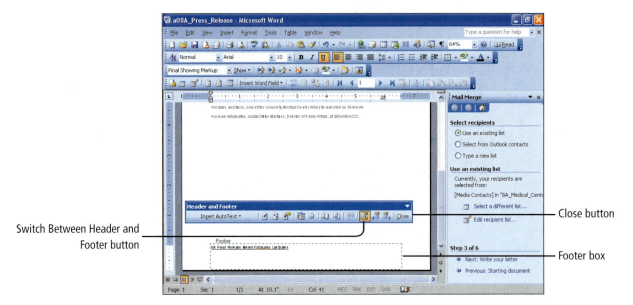

Figure 8.9

4 In the Header and Footer toolbar, click the **Close** button .

5 At the top of the **Mail Merge** task pane, under **Select recipients**, be sure the **Use an existing list** option button is selected. Compare your screen with Figure 8.10.

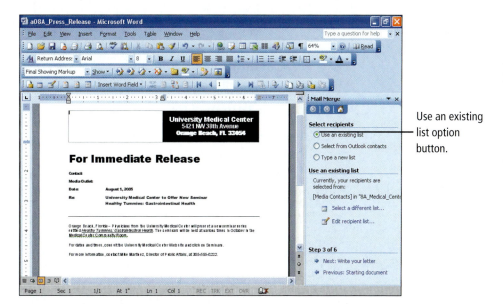

Figure 8.10

6 At the bottom of the task pane, click **Next: Write your letter**. In the displayed Press Release memo, click to move the insertion point to the right of the word *Contact:* and press Tab. In the **Mail Merge** task pane, click the **More items** button. In the displayed **Insert Merge Field** dialog box, under **Fields**, click **Contact**, and then click the **Insert** button. See Figure 8.11.

<<Contact>> displays. By merging the Word document with your Media Contacts table in Access, the field names in the table become available as merge fields in this dialog box.

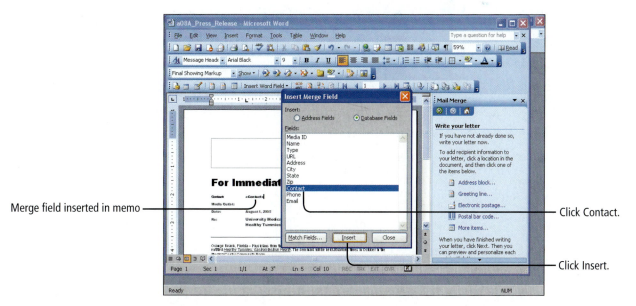

Figure 8.11

Project 8A: Medical Center | **Access** 493

7 At the bottom of the **Insert Merge Field** dialog box, click the **Close** button. In the memo, click to the right of *Media Outlet:* and press Tab. On the task pane, click the **More items** button, click **Name**, click **Insert**, and then click **Close**.

8 At the bottom of the task pane, click **Next: preview your letters**.

9 At the top of the task pane, under **Preview your letters**, click the >> arrows to scroll through and view some of the memos.

You can see that for each record in the table, a memo has been created.

10 At the bottom of the task pane, under **Step 5 of 6**, click **Next: Complete the merge**. In the middle of the task pane, under **Merge**, click **Edit individual letters**. In the **Merge to New Document** dialog box, be sure the **All** option button is selected, and then click **OK**.

11 At the bottom of the Word window, notice that Word created a 20-page document—a one-page memo for each of the 20 media outlets in your Access table. See Figure 8.12.

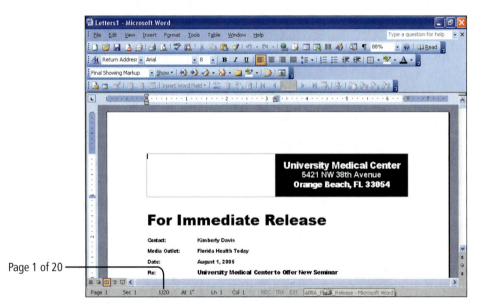

Page 1 of 20

Figure 8.12

12. From the **File** menu, click **Save As**, navigate to the location where you are storing your files for this chapter, and then save the 20-page document as **8A_Press_Release_Memo_Firstname_Lastname**

13. From the **File** menu, click **Print**. Under **Page range**, click the **Pages** option button, and then type **1** as shown in Figure 8.13. Click **OK**. In the upper right corner of your screen, to the right of the *Type a question for help* box, click the small **Close Window** button ⊠. Click the **Close Window** button ⊠ again, and then click **No**. It is not necessary to save the original document. **Close** ⊠ Word. Leave your database open for the next activity.

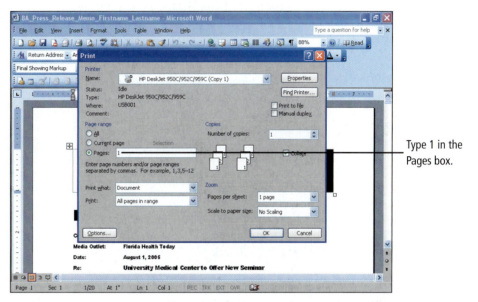

Type 1 in the Pages box.

Figure 8.13

More Knowledge — It's Not Always a "Mail" Merge

Even though the title says mail merge, you can also create form letters, e-mail messages, envelopes, labels, and directories by merging an Access table with Microsoft Word.

Project 8A: Medical Center | **Access**

Objective 3
Import from Excel

The Office of Public Affairs keeps track of marketing expenses in an Excel worksheet. To use this information in an Access report, you can import the Excel spreadsheet data into your database.

Activity 8.3 Importing from Excel

In this activity, you will import an Excel worksheet containing the marketing expenses for the Office of Public Affairs into your database.

1 Be sure the **Tables** object is selected. From the **File** menu, point to **Get External Data**, and then on the submenu, click **Import**. At the bottom of the dialog box, change the **Files of type** to **Microsoft Excel**, navigate to the textbook's student files, and then select the Excel file **a08A_Marketing_Expenses**. See Figure 8.14.

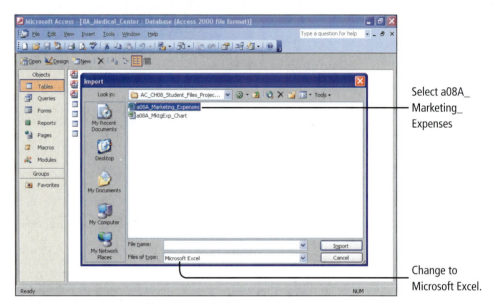

Figure 8.14

2 In the lower right corner of the dialog box, click **Import**. In the **Import Spreadsheet Wizard**, be sure the **First Row Contains Column Headings** check box is selected, and then click **Next**. Be sure the **In a New Table** option button is selected, and then click **Next**. Click **Next** on this screen to accept the default setting. On the next screen, let Access add the primary key and click **Next**.

3 In the **Import to Table** box, type **Marketing Expenses Firstname Lastname** and click **Finish**. Click **OK** to acknowledge the *Finished importing* message.

4 Open your **Marketing Expenses** table in **Datasheet view**. Select all of the columns and apply **Best Fit**—either from the dialog box or by double-clicking on one of the selected column boundaries. Click anywhere in the datasheet to deselect.

5 From the **File** menu, click **Page Setup**, and on the **Page tab**, change the **Orientation** to **Landscape**. Click **OK**. On the Database toolbar, click the **Print** button. Close your table and save the changes.

Objective 4
Add Hyperlinks to Word and Excel Files

In the previous activities, you imported data from Word and Excel into your database. Sometimes you simply want to *view* a Word file or an Excel file while working in Access. For that purpose, you can create a hyperlink to a Word document or an Excel worksheet. A **hyperlink** is a pointer from one object to another. A hyperlink consists of colored or underlined text or a graphic that you click to go to a file, a location in a file, or a Web page. Hyperlinks provide a useful and convenient way to navigate between objects. When you are done viewing the information, you can close the file and return to your database.

Activity 8.4 Adding Hyperlinks from a Form to a Word Document

Employees at the Medical Center are eligible to attend the same seminars that are offered to the public. In this activity, you will enroll employees in seminars using an Access form. You will also create a hyperlink from the form to a Microsoft Word document that lists details about the seminars.

1 In the upper right corner of your screen, on the dark blue title bar, click the **Minimize** button to minimize the Access application to a button on your taskbar.

2 Use **My Computer** to navigate to the student files that accompany this textbook. Locate the Microsoft Word file **a08A_Seminars**, and then copy and paste the file to the folder where you are saving your projects for this chapter. Remove the Read-only property from the file and then rename the file **8A_Seminars_Firstname_Lastname** Double-click your **8A_Seminars** document to open it in Word, and take a moment to examine the list of seminars.

3 Select the title text *Upcoming Public Health Seminars* by triple-clicking anywhere in the title or by dragging over the title, and then on the Standard toolbar, click the **Copy** button. See Figure 8.15 and note that your screen may display the nonprinting Word characters (tabs, paragraph marks, and so forth) if your Word software is set to do so.

Copy button

Select the title.

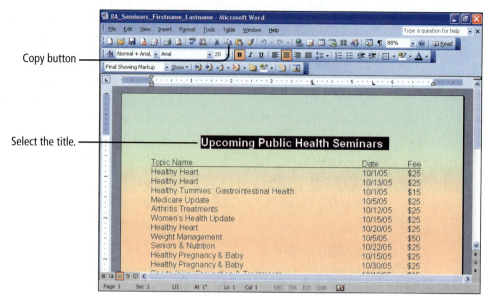

Figure 8.15

4 In the upper right corner of the screen, in the dark blue title bar, click the **Minimize** button to minimize the Word application to a button on your taskbar.

5 On the taskbar, click the button representing your database to maximize it. On the Objects bar, click **Forms**, and then open the **Employee Training and Seminar Enrollments** form. Using the navigation arrows at the bottom of the form, scroll through the 27 records to familiarize yourself with the data.

The table to which this form is bound lists the information for employees who are enrolled in upcoming training courses. The form is also used to enroll employees in seminars.

6 Switch to **Design view** and **Maximize** the form on your screen. From the **Edit** menu, click **Paste as Hyperlink**.

The hyperlink is pasted into the form as a control, but it is pasted into the upper left corner, covering existing form controls.

7 Point to the pasted hyperlink until the Hand pointer displays, and then drag to position the left edge at **1.5 inches on the horizontal ruler** and the bottom edge at **3 inches on the vertical ruler**. Compare your screen with Figure 8.16.

Position hyperlink here.

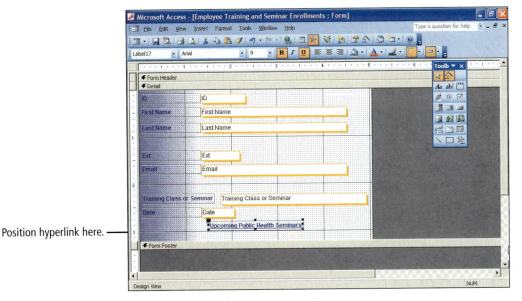

Figure 8.16

8. Switch to **Form view** and examine the updated form. At the bottom of the form, click **Insert New Record**. Using your own information and in the appropriate fields, type **Firstname** and **Lastname** and type **315** as your extension. For the email, use your name and type **Lastname_Firstname@universitymed.com**

9. Click the **Upcoming Public Health Seminars** hyperlink to view the flyer with the upcoming seminars and dates. If a message displays regarding hyperlinks that can be harmful to your computer, click **Yes** to continue.

10. **Minimize** Word and in the form, click in the **Training Class or Seminar** field. Type **Healthy Heart** and press Tab. Type **10/1/05**

11. From the **File** menu, click **Print**. Under **Print Range**, click the **Selected Record(s)** option button, and then click **OK**. Click the **Close Window** button to close the form and save your changes. To the right of the *Type a question for help* box, click the **Restore Window** button. Leave the database open for the next activity.

12. On the taskbar, click the button representing the Word document, and then **Close** Word.

Activity 8.5 Adding Hyperlinks from a Form to an Excel Worksheet

In this activity, you will create a hyperlink from an Access form to a Microsoft Excel file. The Excel file contains a 3-D pie chart indicating the percentage that each type of expense contributes to the total marketing expenses.

1 **Minimize** the Access window to a button on the taskbar. In **My Computer**, navigate to the student files, locate the Microsoft Excel file **a08A_MktgExp_Chart**, and copy and paste the file to the folder where you are storing your projects for this chapter. Remove the Read-only property, and rename the file **8A_MktgExp_Chart_Firstname_Lastname** Open the file and examine the chart. **Close** the workbook and close Excel.

2 From the taskbar, restore the Access window. On the Objects bar, click **Forms**, and double-click **Create form by using wizard**. In the first screen of the wizard, click the **Tables/Queries arrow** and click your **Table: Marketing Expenses Firstname Lastname**. Click the **All Fields** button to move all the fields under **Selected Fields**. See Figure 8.17.

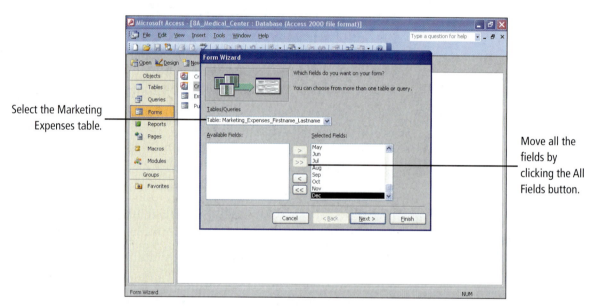

Select the Marketing Expenses table.

Move all the fields by clicking the All Fields button.

Figure 8.17

3 Click **Next**. Be sure the **Columnar** layout is selected and click **Next**. Click **Blends** as the style for the form and click **Next**.

4 Accept the default name **Marketing Expenses Firstname Lastname** and click **Finish**. Use the navigation buttons to scroll through the ten records representing the various types of marketing expenses.

5 Switch to **Design view** and **Maximize** the window. Position your pointer over the upper edge of the **Form Footer bar** to display the double-headed pointer, and then drag toward the lower portion of the screen to **4.75 inches on the vertical ruler**. (Hint: Drag a little further than 4.75 inches and release the mouse button to view the mark, and then drag upward.) See Figure 8.18.

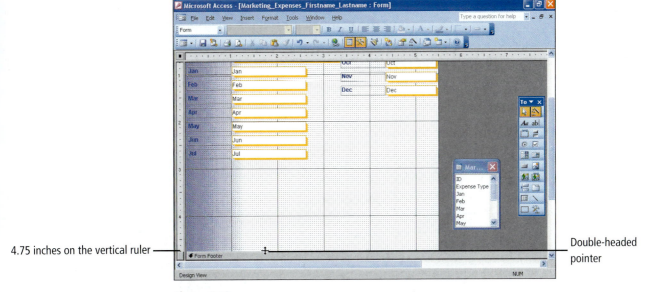

Figure 8.18

6 At the top of the screen in the horizontal ruler, position the pointer over the **4.5-inch mark** to display a small black down arrow, and click once. All of the controls in the second column—**Aug** through **Dec**—are selected. Point to the selected controls until the Hand pointer displays, and then drag the selected controls under the **Jan** through **Jul** labels and bound controls as shown in Figure 8.19. With the controls still selected, point to any of the controls to display the Horizontal Resize pointer and resize the bound controls to match the Jan through Jul bound controls. See Figure 8.19.

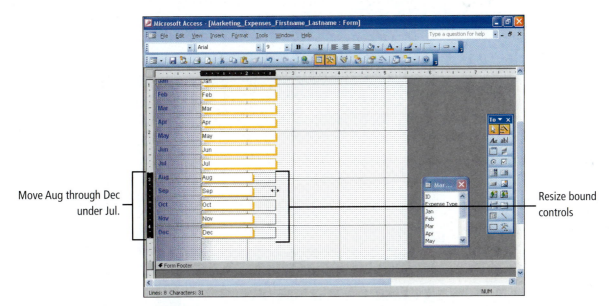

Figure 8.19

7 Click in a blank area of the form to deselect. From the **Insert** menu, click **Hyperlink**. Alternatively, on the Standard toolbar, click the Insert Hyperlink button. In the Link to bar, be sure **Existing File or Web Page** is selected. In the **Text to display** box, type **3D Pie Chart of Expenses** Click the **Look in arrow**, navigate to your chapter files, and then, as shown in Figure 8.20, click your file **8A_MktgExp_Chart_Firstname_Lastname**.

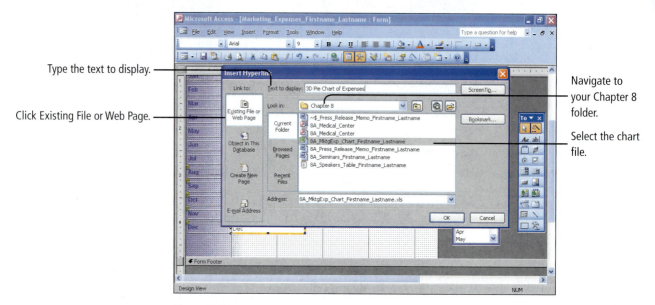

Figure 8.20

8 Click **OK**. Point to the hyperlink to display the Hand pointer and drag the hyperlink to the lower portion of the screen, positioning the left edge at **1 inch on the horizontal ruler** and directly below the December text box control. See Figure 8.21.

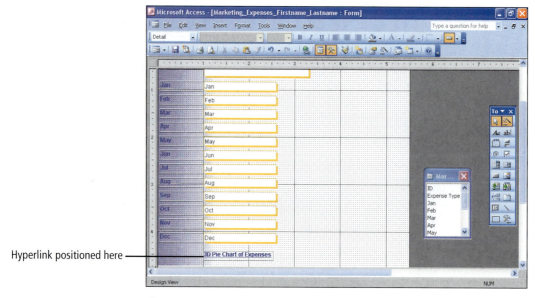

Figure 8.21

9 From the **View** menu, click **Page Header/Footer**. In the **Page Footer** section, draw a label the approximate height of the area from the right edge to **3 inches on the horizontal ruler**. Type **8A Marketing Expenses Firstname Lastname** and click outside the label to deselect the control.

10 Switch to **Form View** and examine your updated form. Navigate to record **2**. At the bottom of the form, click the **3D Pie Chart of Expenses** hyperlink to view the Excel chart. If a warning message displays indicating that hyperlinks can be harmful to your computer, click **Yes** to continue. Notice that TV advertising accounts for 17% of the marketing expenses. **Close** ⊠ Excel.

11 From the **File** menu, click **Print**. Under **Print Range**, click the **Selected Record(s)** option button, and then click **OK**. **Close** ⊠ the form, save your changes, and then close the database and close Access.

End **You have completed Project 8A**

Project 8B Medical Center Update

If you know you will use data only in Microsoft Access, use the import feature that you practiced in Project 8A. If, on the other hand, you want to use a table from another Access database, or information from some other program, and keep both data sources up to date within their own application, use the link feature.

In Activities 8.6 through 8.9, you will continue to import and link information and charts into your database from other sources. Your results will look similar to those shown in Figure 8.22. You will name your database *8B_Medical_Center_Update_Firstname_Lastname*.

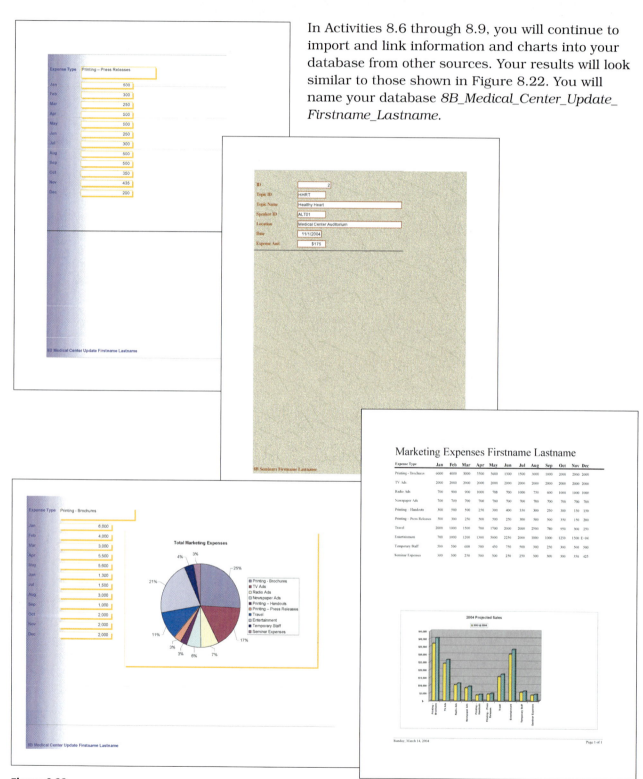

Figure 8.22

Objective 5
Link Database Objects to Office Files

When you *import* data into Access, the data is converted from its original format into an Access table. Changes you make to the data in the table are *not* made to the original file from which the data was imported—there is no connection between the two. Use the import feature when you want to move data into Access and no longer need to use the information in its original program.

There is also a method to connect to data from another program *without* importing it so that you can work with the data in both the original application and in an Access table. For example, when working in an environment where data is shared on a network, it is practical to **link** the data, rather than import it. When information is linked, the Access table will be updated automatically when the information in the original file is changed.

Activity 8.6 Linking a Form and an Excel Worksheet

Linking guarantees that the information in the **external data source**—a file in a program other than Access—and the linked table in Access are always up to date. If you make changes to the linked table in Access, the file in the external data source is also changed. If you make changes to the file in the external data source, the Access table is also changed.

In this activity, you will create a table that is linked to an Excel spreadsheet. Then you will create a form in which changes can be made that are reflected both in the Access table and in the original file in the external data source. The worksheet contains the Marketing Expenses for the Medical Center, and it is important that both the file in the external data source and in the Access table are kept current.

1. Using **My Computer**, from the student files that accompany this textbook, locate the Excel spreadsheet **a08B_Marketing_Expenses**, copy and paste the file to the folder where you are storing your projects for this chapter, remove the Read-only property, and then rename the workbook **8B_Marketing Expenses_Firstname_Lastname** Start Excel, and open the workbook you just renamed.

2. In the Excel worksheet, locate cell **L7**, and notice that the expense amount for printing press releases in November is 150. **Close** Excel.

3 From the student files, locate the Access database **a08B_Medical_Center_Update**, and then copy and paste the file to the folder where you are storing your projects for this chapter. Remove the Read-only property from the file, and rename the file as **8B_Medical_Center_Update_Firstname_Lastname Start** Access and open the database you just renamed.

4 On the Objects bar, be sure **Tables** is selected. From the database window toolbar, click the **New** button [New], and in the **New Table** dialog box, click **Link Table**. See Figure 8.23.

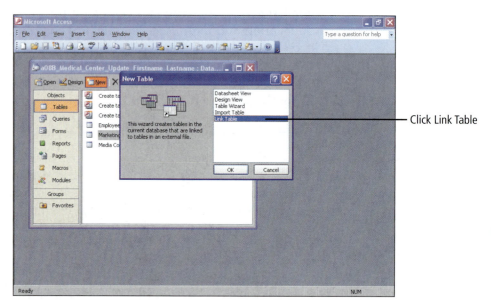

Figure 8.23

5 Click **OK**. In the displayed **Link** dialog box, at the bottom, change the **Files of type** to **Microsoft Excel**, and then use the **Look in arrow** to navigate to your Excel file **8B_Marketing_Expenses_Firstname_Lastname**. Select the file, and then in the lower right corner, click **Link**.

6 In the **Link Spreadsheet Wizard**, be sure the **First Row Contains Column Headings** check box is selected, and then click **Next**. Name the table **2004 Marketing Expenses Firstname Lastname** and click **Finish**. Click **OK** to acknowledge that the linking is finished.

Notice the icon to the left of your new table. The blue arrow indicates that the table is linked, and the Excel icon indicates that the link is to an Excel workbook. See Figure 8.24.

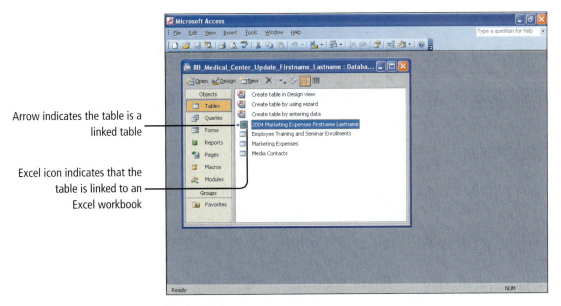

Arrow indicates the table is a linked table

Excel icon indicates that the table is linked to an Excel workbook

Figure 8.24

7 Open the new table in **Datasheet view**. Select all the columns and apply **Best Fit**, either by displaying the Column Width dialog box or by double-clicking a selected column boundary. Click anywhere to deselect. **Close** ⊠ the table and save the changes.

8 On the Objects bar, click **Forms**, and then double-click **Create form by using wizard**. Click the **Tables/Queries arrow**, and then click your **Table: 2004 Marketing Expenses**. Move **all fields** over to the **Selected Fields** column, as shown in Figure 8.25.

2004 Marketing Expenses table selected

Click the All Fields button.

All the fields moved under Selected Fields

Figure 8.25

9 Click **Next**. Click **Columnar** as the layout for the form and click **Next**. Click **Blends** as the style for the form and click **Next**. Leave the form name as **2004 Marketing Expenses Firstname Lastname** and click **Finish**. Maximize the form window and compare your screen with Figure 8.26.

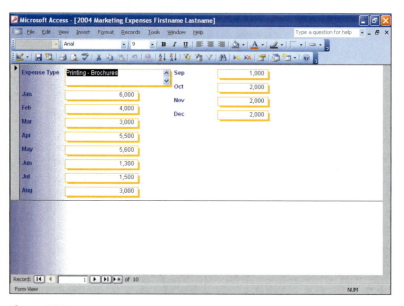

Figure 8.26

10 Switch to **Design view**. Position the pointer on the upper edge of the **Form Footer bar**, and when the double-headed arrow displays, drag downward to expand the **Detail section** to **5 inches on the vertical ruler**. (Hint: Drag a little further than 5 inches to view the mark, and then drag upward.) Position the pointer at approximately the **4.5-inch mark on the horizontal ruler** and click once to select all the controls in the second column. Using the technique you practiced in Project 8A, drag the group of controls under the first column, and widen to match the existing text box controls. See Figure 8.27.

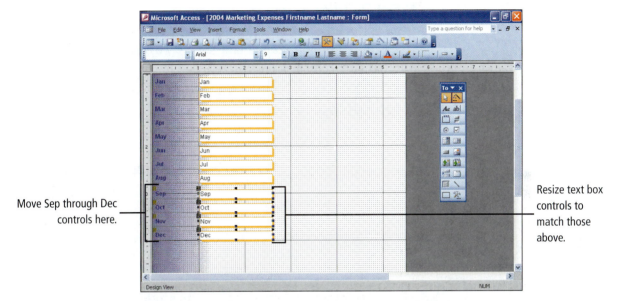

Move Sep through Dec controls here.

Resize text box controls to match those above.

Figure 8.27

11 From the **View** menu, click **Page Header/Footer**. In the **Page Footer section**, create a label the approximate height of the footer area, beginning at the left edge and extending to **3 inches on the horizontal ruler**. Type **8B Medical Center Update Firstname Lastname**

12 Switch to **Form View**. Navigate to record **6**, *Printing–Press Releases*, and change the amount spent in **Nov** from **150** to **435**

13 From the **File** menu, click **Print**. Under **Print Range**, click the **Selected Record(s)** option button, and then click **OK**. Click the **Close Window** button [X] to close the form. Save the changes to the design.

14 Click the **Restore Window** button [□], and then **Minimize** [–] the Access window to a button on the taskbar. In **My Computer**, navigate to your files and open your Excel file **8B_Marketing_Expenses_Firstname_Lastname**. Look at cell **L7**—the *Printing–Press Releases* expense for November—and notice that the amount has been updated to 435.

This is the advantage to linking. Changes made to the table in Access are automatically made to the worksheet in Excel because the two are linked.

15 **Close** [X] Excel. Leave your **8B_Medical_Center_Update** database minimized as a button on the taskbar.

Activity 8.7 Linking Databases

The external data source to which an Access table is linked can be another Access database. After two tables in two separate Access databases are linked, you can update records in one table, and the record in the linked table will be automatically updated at the same time. The reverse is also true. When using the linked table, you may add records or change records, but you cannot change the structure of the table itself. You can change the structure of the table only from the original table.

1 Using **My Computer**, navigate to the student files and locate the Access database **a08B_Seminars**, copy and paste the file to the folder where you are storing your projects, remove the Read-only property from the file, and then rename the file as **8B_Seminars_Firstname_Lastname** Open the database and open the **Seminars** table in **Datasheet view**. Examine record 2. See Figure 8.28.

Close [X] the **Seminars** table, and then close your **8B_Seminars** database.

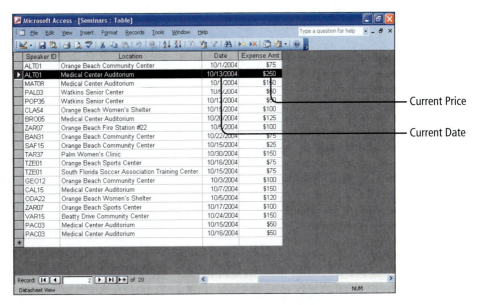

Figure 8.28

2 On the taskbar, click to restore your **8B_Medical_Center_Update** database. On the Objects bar, click **Tables**. On the database window toolbar, click the **New** button and from the **New Table** dialog box, click **Link Table**. Click **OK**.

3 At the bottom of the **Link** dialog box, change the **Files of type** to **Microsoft Office Access**, and then navigate to your projects folder for this chapter. Click your **8B_Seminars_Firstname_Lastname** Access database, and then in the lower right corner, click **Link**.

4 In the **Link Tables** dialog box, click the **Seminars** table, and then click **OK**.

The database window displays with the new table selected. The blue arrow indicates that the table is a linked table, and the Access icon indicates that the table is linked to another Access database.

5 Right-click on the **Seminars** table, click **Rename**, and rename the table **Seminars Firstname Lastname**

Project 8B: Medical Center Update | **Access** 511

6 On the Objects bar, click **Forms**, and then double-click **Create form by using wizard**. Click the **Tables/Queries arrow**, click your **Table: Seminars**, and then move **all fields** over to the **Selected Fields** column as shown in Figure 8.29.

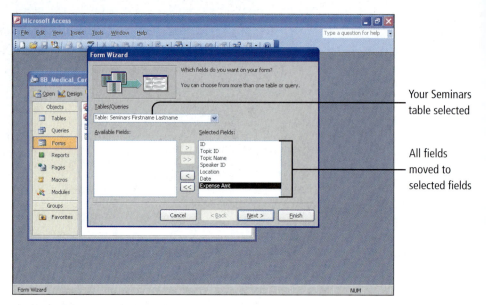

Your Seminars table selected

All fields moved to selected fields

Figure 8.29

7 Click **Next**. For the form layout, click **Columnar** and click **Next**. For the form style, click **Expedition** and click **Next**. Leave the form title as **Seminars Firstname Lastname**. Click **Finish**. When the form displays—this may take several seconds—**Maximize** the form window and compare your screen with Figure 8.30.

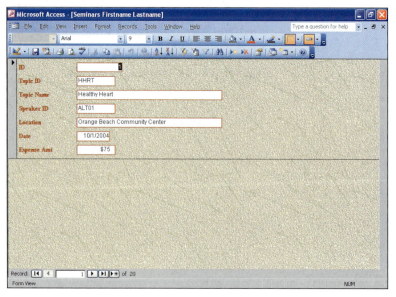

Figure 8.30

8 Switch to **Design view**. From the **View** menu, click **Page Header/Footer**. Create a label in the **Page Footer area**, beginning at the left edge, the approximate height of the footer area, and extending to **3 inches on the horizontal ruler**. Type **8B Seminars Firstname Lastname**

9 Switch back to **Form view**. Navigate to record **2**, change the **Date** to **11/1/2004** and change the **Expense Amt** to **175**

10 From the **File** menu, click **Print**. Under **Print Range**, click the **Selected Record(s)** option button, and then click **OK**. **Close** ☒ the form window and save your changes. Click the **Restore Window** button 🗗, and then **Minimize** ➖ the database to a button on the taskbar.

11 Using **My Computer**, open your Access database **8B_Seminars_Firstname_Lastname**. Open the **Seminars** table in **Datasheet view**. Look at record 2, and notice that the record in this database was automatically updated when you changed the information in the other database.

12 **Close** ☒ the **Seminars** table, close the **8B_Seminars** database, and close Access. Redisplay your **8B_Medical_Center_Update** database, and leave the database open for the next activity.

More Knowledge — Object Linking and Embedding (OLE)

All Microsoft Office programs support *OLE*, which stands for *Object Linking and Embedding* and is pronounced *o-LAY*. OLE is a program-integration technology for sharing information between Office programs. Objects, for example, a Word table or an Excel chart, or some other form of information created in one Office program—the *source file*—can be linked to or *embedded* in another Office program—the *destination file*.

To embed means to insert, using a format that you specify, information from a source file in one program into a destination file in another program. An embedded object maintains the characteristics of the original application, but is not tied to the original file. For example, the object's information in the destination file does not change if you modify the information in the source file.

Objective 6
Add a Chart to a Form

A ***chart*** is a graphic representation of data. Data presented in a chart is easier to understand than a table of numbers. ***Column charts*** show comparisons among related numbers, ***pie charts*** show the contributions of parts to a whole, and ***line charts*** show trends over time.

Activity 8.8 Adding a Chart to a Form

Among the Microsoft Office programs, Excel is the best tool for producing a chart because it has a wide variety of charting types and options available. In this activity, you will insert a Microsoft Excel chart into an Access form—the 2004 Expenses form in your database.

1 On the Objects bar, click **Forms**. Double-click your **2004 Marketing Expenses** form to open it, **Maximize** the form window, and then switch to **Design view**.

2 Resize the form by dragging the right border to **9.0 inches on the horizontal ruler**. At the bottom of the form, position the pointer on the upper edge of the **Page Footer bar**, and when the double-headed arrow displays, drag downward to expand the **Detail section** to **5.75 inches on the vertical ruler**.

3 From the **Insert** menu, click **Object**. On the left side of the dialog box, click the **Create from File** option button as shown in Figure 8.31.

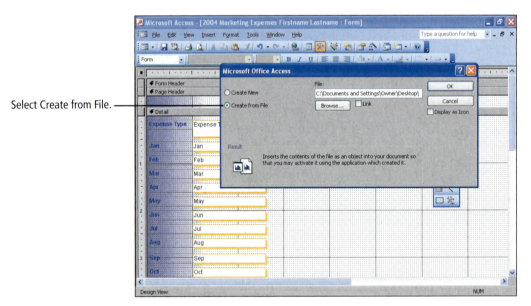

Select Create from File.

Figure 8.31

4 Click the **Browse** button. In the displayed **Browse** dialog box, navigate to the student files that accompany this textbook, select the Excel file **a08B_Pie_Chart_of_Marketing_Expenses**, and click **OK**. Because you will embed this file, *not* link it, in the displayed dialog box, be sure the Link check box is *not* selected. Click **OK**.

A copy of the Excel chart is embedded into your form. The chart is placed in the upper left of your form and will cover the fields in your form. Compare your form with Figure 8.32.

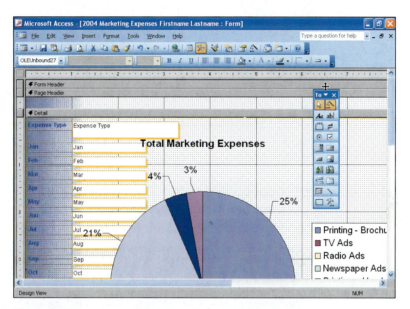

Figure 8.32

5 Scroll down and to the right so that you can see the bottom of the chart and position your mouse pointer over the lower right corner of the selected chart to display the Diagonal Resize pointer as shown in Figure 8.33.

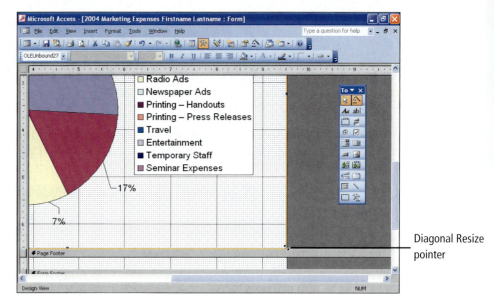

Figure 8.33

6 Drag up and to the left to **6 inches on the horizontal ruler** and **4 inches on the vertical ruler**, as shown in Figure 8.34.

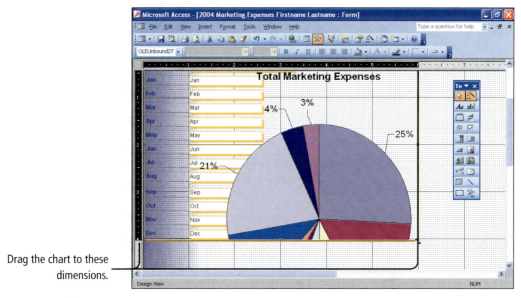

Figure 8.34

7 Point to the chart to display the Hand pointer 🖐 and drag so that the upper left corner of the chart is at the **3-inch mark on the horizontal ruler** and the upper edge is at the **0.75-inch mark on the vertical ruler**. See Figure 8.35.

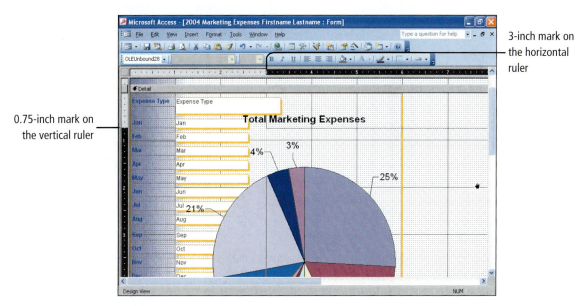

0.75-inch mark on the vertical ruler

3-inch mark on the horizontal ruler

Figure 8.35

8 Release the mouse button to reposition the chart, right-click on the chart, and from the displayed shortcut menu, click **Properties**. Be sure the **Format tab** is selected, click the **Size Mode** arrow, and then click **Zoom**. See Figure 8.36. **Close** ❌ the properties box.

The Zoom setting displays the picture in its entirety after sizing it to fill either the height or width of the area within the control. Using this setting will ensure that the image is not distorted.

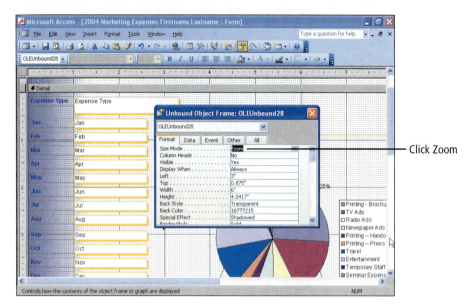

Figure 8.36

9. Click in a blank area of the form to deselect the chart. Switch to **Form view**, and then scroll through all the records and view the embedded chart in each form. Then, navigate to record **1**.

   The embedded chart shows the Total Marketing Expenses for the year by category. The chart can be used to compare the amount spent on each type of marketing expense to the total amount spent on marketing for the year.

10. From the **File** menu, display the **Page Setup** dialog box. On the **Margins tab**, change all four margin settings—**Top**, **Bottom**, **Left**, and **Right**—to **0.5**. On the **Page tab**, change the **Page Orientation** to **Landscape**. From the **File** menu, click **Print**. Under **Print Range**, click the **Selected Record(s)** option button, and then click **OK**.

    Close ⊠ the form and save your changes.

Objective 7
Add a Chart to a Report

Recall that a *report* is a database object that displays the fields and records from a table in an easy-to-read format suitable for printing. Reports are created to summarize information in a database in a professional-looking manner. Adding a chart to a report helps to summarize data by displaying the data in a graphical format.

Activity 8.9 Linking a Chart in a Report

In this activity, you will insert a Microsoft Excel chart into a report.

1 **Minimize** the database and, using **My Computer**, from your student files locate the Excel file **a08B_2004_Projected_Marketing_Expenses** and copy and paste it into your folder for this chapter. Remove the Read-only property, and then rename the file **8B_2004_Projected_Marketing_Expenses_Firstname_Lastname**

2 Close **My Computer** and restore your database. On the Objects bar, click **Reports**. Double-click **Create report by using wizard**. Select **Table: Marketing Expenses**. Move all the available fields over to the **Selected Fields** column. See Figure 8.37.

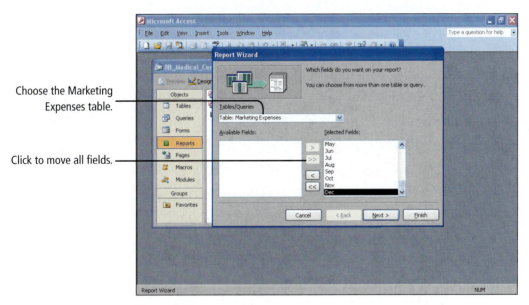

Choose the Marketing Expenses table.

Click to move all fields.

Figure 8.37

3 Click **Next** three times. For the **Layout** of your report, click **Tabular** and then click **Next**. For the **Style** of your report, click **Formal** and then click **Next**. Name the report **Marketing Expenses Firstname Lastname** and click **Finish**. Preview the report.

4 Switch to **Design view** and maximize the window if necessary. In the **Page Header section**, select the **ID label**, hold down Shift, and select the **ID bound control** in the **Detail section**. Press Delete. Hold down Shift and select both the **Expense Type label** and **Expense Type control**. Drag the left center sizing handle to the left edge of the form and the right center sizing handle to **1.25 inches on the horizontal ruler**. With the two controls still selected, change the **Font Size** to **8**. Hold down Shift and in the **Page Header section**, select the **Dec label**, and in the **Detail section**, select the **Dec bound control**. Drag the right center sizing handle of the selected controls to **6 inches on the horizontal ruler**.

5 Resize the **Report Header section** to **0.5 inches on the vertical ruler** by dragging the bottom of the Report Header section up slightly. Resize the **Page Footer section** down to **4 inches on the vertical ruler**. Hold down Shift and at the top of the **Page Footer section**, select the **black line** and then select the **two text boxes**.

With the Hand pointer, drag the selected items to the bottom of the Page Footer section. See Figure 8.38.

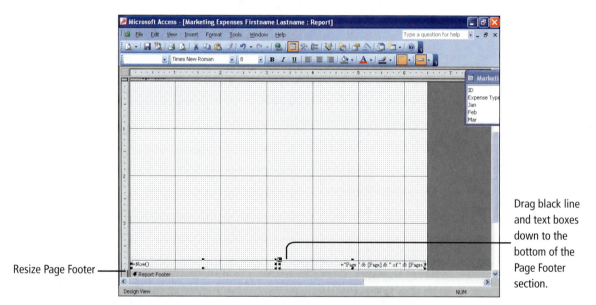

Resize Page Footer

Drag black line and text boxes down to the bottom of the Page Footer section.

Figure 8.38

6 Click the **Page Footer section bar** to select it. From the **Insert menu**, click **Object**. Click the **Create from File** option button. Click the **Browse** button, navigate to your folder for this chapter, select your **8B_2004_Projected_Marketing_Expenses** Excel file, and click **OK**. Because you want to link this file, in the displayed dialog box, select the **Link** check box. Click **OK**.

The chart from the Excel file is inserted into the Page Footer area, and the chart is linked to the Excel file. If, in the Excel spreadsheet, a change is made, that change will be reflected in this chart within the report the next time the report is opened.

7 Scroll down to view the bottom of the chart. In the lower right corner, point to the resizing handle to display the Diagonal Resize pointer and drag up and to the left to approximately **6 inches on the horizontal ruler** and **3.5 inches on the vertical ruler**. Right-click on the chart, and from the displayed shortcut menu, click **Properties**. Be sure the **Format tab** is selected, click the **Size Mode** arrow, and then click **Zoom**. In the **Left** box, type **0.25"** and press Enter. **Close** the property box.

8 Drag the bottom of the **Page Footer** section back up to **4 inches on the vertical ruler**. Drag the right edge of the form to **6.5 inches on the horizontal ruler**. See Figure 8.39.

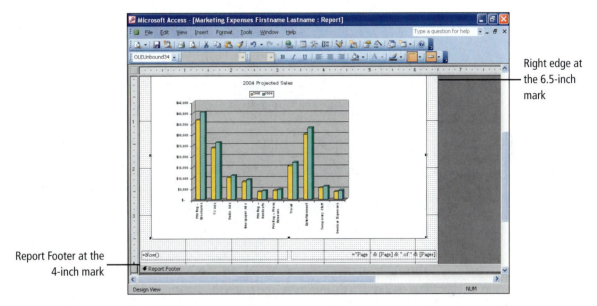

Report Footer at the 4-inch mark

Right edge at the 6.5-inch mark

Figure 8.39

9 Switch to **Report preview** to view your report.

10 From the **File** menu, click **Print**. Close the report, save changes, close the database, and then close Access.

End You have completed Project 8B

Summary

In this chapter, you integrated Access with other Office applications. Because information you want to use may be located in a file developed in another application, Access provides the ability to import or link to data located in other file formats. When you import, you copy data from a text file like Microsoft Word, a spreadsheet file like Microsoft Excel, or a database table from another Access database, and then insert it into an Access table. Importing is particularly convenient, because data does not have to be retyped into Access.

It is also useful to link your database to data in another application in a manner that, when data is updated in one file, it is automatically updated in the other. Linking guarantees that the information in the external data source and the linked table in Access are always up to date. You can also link to another Access database. After two tables in two separate Access databases are linked, you can update records in one table, and the record in the linked table will be automatically updated at the same time.

You practiced creating hyperlinks from Access to files in other applications. A hyperlink is a pointer from one object to another. Inserting a hyperlink provides a useful and convenient way to navigate between objects. When you are done viewing the information in the other application, you can close the file and return quickly to your database.

In this chapter, you practiced merging data from an Access table with Microsoft Word to create form letters. Using Word's mail merge feature, you can combine two documents—a main document created in Word and a data source created in Access—to create a mass mailing.

In This Chapter You Practiced How To

- Import Data from a Word Table
- Use Mail Merge to Integrate Access and Word
- Import from Excel
- Add Hyperlinks to Word and Excel Files
- Link Database Objects to Office Files
- Add a Chart to a Form
- Add a Chart to a Report

Concepts Assessments

Matching Match each term in the second column with its correct definition in the first column by writing the letter of the term on the blank line in front of the correct definition.

____ 1. A graphic representation of data.

____ 2. A file in a program other than Access.

____ 3. A chart that shows trends over time.

____ 4. In a mail merge operation, the Word document that contains the text of the letter or memo.

____ 5. A database object that displays the fields and records from a table in an easy-to-read format suitable for printing. This object is created to summarize information in a database in a professional-looking manner.

____ 6. A chart that shows comparisons among related numbers.

____ 7. A file containing data where individual field values are separated by a character, such as a comma or a tab.

____ 8. To copy data from a text file like Microsoft Word, a spreadsheet file like Microsoft Excel, or a database table from another Access database, and then insert it into an Access table.

____ 9. To create a group of form letters by combining a main document created in Microsoft Word with a data source created in Access.

____ 10. In a database table, the field that uniquely identifies a record in a table.

____ 11. In a mail merge operation, the Access table that contains the names and addresses of the individuals to whom the document is being sent.

____ 12. A pointer from one object to another.

____ 13. The character, such as a comma or a tab, that separates individual field values in a converted text file.

____ 14. A chart that shows the contributions of parts to a whole.

____ 15. To insert information from an external source into an Access table in a way that, when the Access table is updated, the original file is also updated, and vice versa.

A Chart
B Column chart
C Data source
D Delimited text file
E Delimiter character
F External data source
G Hyperlink
H Import
I Line chart
J Link
K Mail merge
L Main document
M Pie chart
N Primary key
O Report

Access Chapter Eight

Concepts Assessments

Fill in the Blank Write the correct answer in the space provided.

1. When saving a Word document as a text file for the purpose of importing the data into an Access table, be sure to delete any extra _____ lines at the end of the document so that empty records are not inserted.

2. To find the best fit for columns in a table without displaying a dialog box, select the columns, and then double-click any of the selected column _____.

3. The easiest way to perform a Mail Merge is to use the _____.

4. If you simply want to view a Word file or an Excel file while working in Access, create a _____ to the file.

5. A hyperlink consists of colored or _____ text or a graphic that you click to go to another location.

6. When you import data into Access, the data is converted from its original format into an Access _____.

7. When you want to move data into Access and no longer need to use the information in its original program, you should _____ rather than link the data.

8. When information is linked, any _____ in the original file are also made automatically in the Access table to which it is linked.

9. When tables from two separate Access databases are linked, you can add and change records in the linked table, but you cannot change the _____ of the table itself.

10. Among the Microsoft Office applications, _____ is probably the best suited for creating complex charts.

Skill Assessments

Access chapter eight

Project 8C—Updated Seminars

Objective: *Import Data from a Word Table.*

In the following Skill Assessment, you will import additional records from a Word table into your Seminars table in Access. Several new seminars, to be conducted in December, have been added to the schedule, and need to be included in the Access database. You will add (append) these records to the bottom of your Seminars table. Your completed table will look similar to Figure 8.40.

Topic ID	Topic Name	Speaker ID	Location	Date	Expense Amt
GAST	Healthy Tummies:Gastrointestinal Health	MAT08	Medical Center Auditorium	10/1/2005	$150
HHRT	Healthy Heart	ALT01	Orange Beach Community Center	10/1/2005	$75
INFEC	Don't Let the Germs Get You! Infectious Diseases Update	GEO12	Orange Beach Community Center	10/3/2005	$100
MEDI	Medicare Update	PAL03	Watkins Senior Center	10/5/2005	$50
WGTM	Weight Management	ZAR07	Orange Beach Fire Station #22	10/5/2005	$100
VITS	Vitamins, Supplements, & Your Health	ODA22	Orange Beach Women's Shelter	10/5/2005	$120
MNGC	Managing Managed Care	CAL15	Medical Center Auditorium	10/7/2005	$150
ARTH	Arthritis Treatments	POP35	Watkins Senior Center	10/12/2005	$50
HHRT	Healthy Heart	ALT01	Medical Center Auditorium	10/13/2005	$250
WOMH	Women's Health Update	CLA54	Orange Beach Women's Shelter	10/15/2005	$100
HPRG	Healthy Pregnancy & Baby	SAF15	Orange Beach Community Center	10/15/2005	$25
SPRT	Sports Injury Prevention & Treatments	TZE01	South Florida Soccer Association Training Center	10/15/2005	$75
PRIV	Patient Privacy	PAC03	Medical Center Auditorium	10/15/2005	$50
PRIV	Patient Privacy	PAC03	Medical Center Auditorium	10/16/2005	$50
SPRT	Sports Injury Prevention & Treatments	TZE01	Orange Beach Sports Center	10/16/2005	$75
WGTM	Weight Management	ZAR07	Orange Beach Sports Center	10/17/2005	$100
HHRT	Healthy Heart	BRO05	Medical Center Auditorium	10/20/2005	$125
SRNT	Seniors & Nutrition	BAN31	Orange Beach Community Center	10/22/2005	$75
DEPR	Depression: Identification & Treatment	VAR15	Beatty Drive Community Center	10/24/2005	$150
HPRG	Healthy Pregnancy & Baby	TAR37	Palm Women's Clinic	10/30/2005	$150
GAST	Healthy Tummies: Gastrointestinal Health	MAT08	Medical Center Auditorium	12/2/2005	$150
VITS	Vitamins, Supplements, & Your Health	ODA22	Kessler Community Center	12/6/2005	$120
MNGC	Managing Managed Care	CAL15	Medical Center Auditorium	12/8/2005	$150
HPRG	Healthy Pregnancy & Baby	SAF15	Midland Avenue Birthing Center	12/13/2005	$25
WOMH	Women's Health Update	CLA54	Orange Beach Women's Shelter	12/30/2005	$100

Figure 8.40

1. Start Microsoft Word, and from the student files that accompany this textbook, locate and then open the Microsoft Word file **a08C_Updated_Seminars**.

2. If necessary, click anywhere inside the table. From the **Table** menu, point to **Convert**, and then click **Table to Text**.

3. In the displayed **Convert Table to Text** dialog box, be sure the **Tabs** option button is selected—this is the character you will use to separate the text into fields. Click **OK**. Click anywhere to deselect.

4. Hold down [Ctrl] and press [End] to move to the end of the document. Press [Bksp] once.

(**Project 8C**–Updated Seminars continues on the next page)

Skill Assessments (continued)

(Project 8C–Updated Seminars continued)

5. From the **File** menu, click **Save As**, and then navigate to the location where you are storing your projects for this chapter. At the bottom of the **Save As** dialog box, click the **Save as type arrow**, and from the displayed list, click **Plain Text**. In the **File name** box, type **8C_Updated_Seminars_Firstname_Lastname**

6. In the lower right corner of the dialog box, click **Save**. In the displayed **File Conversion** dialog box, accept the default settings and click **OK**. **Close** Microsoft Word.

7. From the student files, locate the Access file **a08C_Updated_Seminars**, and copy and paste the file to the Chapter 8 folder you created. Remove the Read-only property from the file and rename the file as **8C_Updated_Seminars_Firstname_Lastname** Start Access and open the database you just renamed.

8. Be sure the **Tables** object button is selected. Right-click on the **Seminars** table and rename the table **Seminars Firstname Lastname**

9. From the **File** menu, point to **Get External Data**, and on the submenu click **Import**. At the bottom of the displayed **Import** dialog box, click the **Files of type arrow**, and then click **Text Files**. Use the **Look in arrow** to navigate to your files for this chapter, click your **8C_Updated_Seminars text file**, and then click **Import**.

10. In this first screen of the **Import Text Wizard**, be sure the **Delimited** option button is selected, and then click **Next**.

11. Under **Choose the delimiter that separates your fields**, be sure the **Tab** option button is selected, and then be sure the **First Row Contains Field Names** check box is *not* selected.

12. Click **Next**. Under **Where would you like to store your data**, click the **In an Existing Table** option button, and then click the arrow to the right. From the displayed list, click your **Seminars Firstname Lastname** table, and then click **Next**. Recall that you are adding—appending—these records to an existing table, and that you must indicate the table to which you want to append the new records. Click **Finish**, and then click **OK** to acknowledge the message.

13. Open your **Seminars** table in **Datasheet view**. In the column heading area, drag to select all of the columns, display the **Format** menu, and then click **Column Width**. In the **Column Width** dialog box, click the **Best Fit** button to resize all the columns to fit the data. Click anywhere to deselect, and then click anywhere in the **Date** column.

(Project 8C–Updated Seminars continues on the next page)

Skill Assessments (continued)

(Project 8C–Updated Seminars continued)

14. On the toolbar, click the **Sort Ascending** button. The records are sorted chronologically by date, and you can see the new December seminars at the bottom of the table.

15. From the **File** menu, click **Page Setup**, and on the **Margins tab**, change the **Top**, **Bottom**, **Left**, and **Right** margins to **0.5 inches**. On the **Page tab**, change the **Orientation** to **Landscape**. Click **OK**. On the Table Datasheet toolbar, click the **Print** button. **Close** your table and save the changes. Close the database.

 You have completed Project 8C

Project 8D—Schedule

Objective: *Use Mail Merge to Integrate Access and Word.*

In the following Skill Assessment, you will create a mail merge document to create a directory of all of the media contacts that lists the contact name, organization, and phone numbers. You will rename and save your database as *8D_Schedule_Firstname_Lastname*. Your completed directory will look similar to Figure 8.41.

Figure 8.41

1. From your student files, locate the database file **a08D_Schedule**, and then copy and paste the file where you are storing your projects for this chapter. Remove the Read-only property from the file and rename the file **8D_Schedule_Firstname_Lastname** Start Access and open the database you just renamed.

(**Project 8D**–Schedule continues on the next page)

Skill Assessments (continued)

(Project 8D–Schedule continued)

2. Be sure the **Tables** object is selected, and then click the **Media Contacts** table to select it. On the database toolbar, click the **OfficeLinks button arrow**, and from the displayed list, click **Merge It with Microsoft Office Word**.

3. In this first screen of the **Microsoft Word Mail Merge Wizard**, click the **Create a new document and then link the data to it** option button. Click **OK**. In the Word **Mail Merge** task pane, under **Select document type**, click the **Directory** option button. Selecting the *Directory* option creates a single document containing a catalog or printed list of addresses by merging your Access table with a specially formatted Word document.

4. At the bottom of the task pane, click **Next: Starting document**. At the top of the task pane, under **Select starting document**, be sure that the **Use the current document** option button is selected. At the bottom of the task pane, click **Next: Select recipients**.

5. At the top of the **Mail Merge** task pane, under **Select recipients**, be sure the **Use an existing list** option button is selected. Note that the term *recipients* is used, even though we are not actually creating letters, but rather a directory list.

6. At the bottom of the task pane, click **Next: Arrange your directory**. In the **horizontal ruler** at the top of the Word window, click directly on the ruler at the **2-inch mark**, and again at the **4.5-inch mark**. This will create a left tab at these two positions.

7. In the **Mail Merge** task pane, click the **More items** button. In the displayed **Insert Merge Field** dialog box, under **Fields**, click **Contact**, and then click the **Insert** button. At the bottom of the **Insert Merge Field** dialog box, click the **Close** button. Press [Tab]. On the task pane, click the **More items** button, click **Name**, click **Insert**, and then click **Close**. Press [Tab]. From the task pane, display the **Insert Merge Field** dialog box one more time, and insert the **Phone** field. Close the dialog box. Press [Enter].

8. At the bottom of the task pane, click **Next: Preview your directory**.

9. At the top of the task pane, under **Preview your directory**, click the >> arrows to scroll through and view the list of names.

10. At the bottom of the task pane, under **Step 5 of 6**, click **Next: Complete the merge**. In the middle of the task pane, under **Merge**, click **To New Document**. In the **Merge to New Document** dialog box, be sure the **All** option button is selected, and then click **OK**.

(Project 8D–Schedule continues on the next page)

Skill Assessments (continued)

(Project 8D–Schedule continued)

11. From the **File** menu, click **Save As**, navigate to the location where you are storing your files for this chapter, and then save the document as **8D_Media_Contacts_Directory_Firstname_Lastname**

12. On the menu bar, click **View**, and then click **Header and Footer**. In the displayed Header and Footer toolbar, click the **Switch Between Header and Footer** button. Then, on the same toolbar, click **Insert AutoText**, and from the displayed list, click **Filename**. This will place the name of your Word file in the footer. On the floating toolbar, click **Close**.

13. From the **File** menu, click **Print**, and then click **OK**. **Close** the document, saving your changes, and **Close** Word. It is not necessary to save the original document. **Close** your database and close Access.

 You have completed Project 8D

Project 8E — Physicians

Objective: *Import from Excel.*

In the following Skill Assessment, you will import an Excel spreadsheet containing a list of the physicians at University Medical Center into your Access database. Your completed table will look similar to Figure 8.42. You will rename and save your database as *8E_Physicians_Firstname_Lastname*.

Phy Num	First Name	Last Name	Dept	Addr1	Addr2	City	State	Postal Code	Phone
PHY539	Sharon	Brougher	Pediatrics	2314 Highland Lake Road		Miami	FL	33145	305-555-0109
PHY148	Annette	Carpenter	Cardiology	28 Fairway Dr.		Miami	FL	33145	305-555-0067
PHY335	Michael	Franklin	Obstetrics	2600 Whisper Lake Lane		Winter Park	FL	32790	407-555-0076
PHY541	Robert	Gaines	Cardiology	200 N. Orlando Ave.	#1650	Coral Springs	FL	33077	954-555-0132
PHY353	Maria	Garcia	Dermatology	30 E. 46th St.		Miami	FL	33174	305-555-0078
PHY145	Jaleel	Hassan	Radiology	2230 Riverside Dr.		Coral Springs	FL	33077	954-555-0012
PHY889	Gregory	Ivanov	General Surgery	7865 Calibre Bend Ln		Hialeah	FL	33013	305-555-0054
PHY130	Nishan	Jibotian	General Surgery	76 Mahogany Key Circle		Miami	FL	33145	305-555-0112
PHY533	Laurene	Kormac	Neurology	1211 NW 87th Ave.		Miami	FL	33150	305-555-0113
PHY342	Paramjeet	Kumar	Radiology	2230 Camino Real	#A	Miami	FL	33143	305-555-0011
PHY451	Wendy	Lee	Psychiatry	2515 Main St.	#300	Hialeah	FL	33018	954-555-0087
PHY641	Vivian	Marsh	Pediatrics	3920 Casa Aloma Way		Miami	FL	33150	305-555-0123
PHY146	Joaquin	Pena	Pediatrics	875 Wood Run Court		Coral Springs	FL	33075	954-555-0122
PHY129	Deepa	Subramani	Geriatrics	1516 NW 67th St.	#1560	Miami	FL	33143	305-555-0111
PHY156	Louise	Tran	Obstetrics	38 111th Terrace	#1600	Coral Springs	FL	33065	954-555-0098
PHY545	Charles	Yang	Geriatrics	1350 Miami Lakeway		Hialeah	FL	33010	305-555-0089

Figure 8.42

1. From your student files, locate the Access database **a8E_Physicians**, and then copy and paste the file to the Chapter 8 folder you created. Remove the Read-only property from the file and rename the file as **8E_Physicians_Firstname_Lastname** Start Access and open the database you just renamed.

2. Be sure the **Tables** object is selected. From the **File** menu, point to **Get External Data**, and then on the submenu click **Import**. At the bottom of the dialog box, change the **Files of type** to **Microsoft Excel**, navigate to the student files that accompany this textbook, and then select the Excel file **a08E_Physicians**. In the lower right corner, click **Import**.

(**Project 8E–Physicians** continues on the next page)

Skill Assessments (continued)

(Project 8E–Physicians continued)

3. In the first screen of the wizard, be sure that the **Show Worksheets** option button is selected and that **Sheet1** is selected, and then click **Next**. Be sure the **First Row Contains Column Headings** check box is selected, and then click **Next**. Store the data **In a New Table**, and then click **Next**. Under **Field Options**, click the **Indexed arrow**, and then click **Yes (No Duplicates)** because you will use the *Phy Num* (Physician Number) as a primary key. Click **Next**. Click **Choose my own primary key** and select **Phy Num** as the field to use for the primary key. Click **Next**.

4. In the **Import to Table** box, type Physicians Firstname Lastname and click **Finish**. Click **OK** to acknowledge the *Finished importing* message.

5. Open your **Physicians** table in **Datasheet view**. Select all of the columns and apply **Best Fit** by double-clicking on one of the selected column boundaries. Click anywhere to deselect. Click anywhere in the **Last Name** column, and then on the toolbar, click the **Sort Ascending** button.

6. From the **File** menu, click **Page Setup**, and on the **Page tab**, change the **Orientation** to **Landscape**. Click **OK**. On the Table Datasheet toolbar, click the **Print** button. Close your table and save the changes. Close the database and close Access.

End You have completed Project 8E

Access chapter eight

Performance Assessments

Project 8F — Physicians with Patients

Objective: *Add Hyperlinks to Word and Excel Files.*

In the following Performance Assessment, you will insert a hyperlink from an Access form to an Excel worksheet that contains a chart. Your completed form will look similar to Figure 8.43. You will rename and save your database as *8F_Physicians_with_Patients_Firstname_Lastname*.

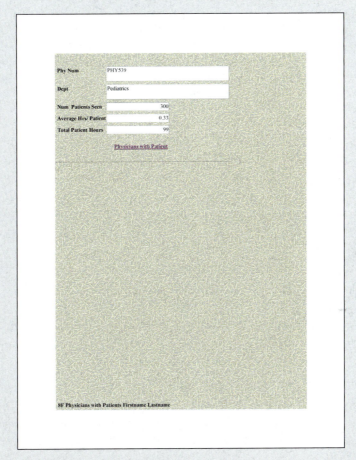

Figure 8.43

1. From your student files, locate the Access file **a08F_Physicians_with_Patients**, and then copy and paste the file to your projects folder for this chapter. Remove the Read-only property from the file and rename the file as **8F_Physicians_with_Patients_Firstname_Lastname** Start Access and open the database you just renamed.

(**Project 8F**—Physicians with Patients continues on the next page)

Performance Assessments (continued)

(Project 8F–Physicians with Patients continued)

2. **Minimize** your database to a button on the taskbar. In **My Computer**, navigate to your student files, locate the Microsoft Excel file **a08F_Physicians_Chart**, and then copy and paste the file to the folder where you are storing your projects for this chapter. Rename the file **8F_Physicians_Chart_Firstname_Lastname** Open the file and examine the chart. The chart compares the number of patients each physician has seen and the number of hours each physician spends with patients. **Close** Excel.

3. From the taskbar, restore your database. On the Objects bar, click **Forms**, and then double-click **Create form by using wizard**. In the first screen of the wizard, click the **Tables/Queries arrow** and click **Table: Physician Activity**. Move all the fields under **Selected Fields**.

4. Click **Next**. Be sure the **Columnar** layout is selected and click **Next**. Click **Ricepaper** as the style for the table and click **Next**. Name the form **Physicians Activity Firstname Lastname** and click **Finish**. Use the navigation buttons to scroll through the six records.

5. Switch to **Design view** and **Maximize** the form window. Resize the height of the **Detail section** to **2.5 inches on the vertical ruler**. From the **Insert** menu, click **Hyperlink**. In the Link to bar, be sure **Existing File or Web Page** is selected. In the **Text to display** box, type **Physicians with Patients** Click the **Look in arrow**, navigate to your files, and then click your Excel file **8F_Physicians_Chart_Firstname_Lastname**. Click **OK**.

6. Move the hyperlink to the lower portion of the screen, positioning the left edge at **1.5 inches on the horizontal ruler** and the top edge at **2 inches on the vertical ruler**.

7. From the **View** menu, click **Page Header/Footer**. In the **Page Footer** section, draw a label the approximate height of the footer area and three inches wide, and then type **8F Physicians with Patients Firstname Lastname** and click outside the label to deselect the control.

8. Switch to **Form View** and examine your updated form. Navigate to record **5**. At the bottom of the form, click the **Physicians with Patients** hyperlink to view the Excel chart. If a warning message displays indicating that hyperlinks can be harmful to your computer, click **Yes** to continue. **Close** Excel.

9. From the **File** menu, click **Print**. Under **Print Range**, click the **Selected Record(s)** option button, and then click **OK**. **Close** the form, save your changes, and then close the database and close Access.

End You have completed Project 8F

Project 8G—Hospital Staff

Objective: *Link Database Objects to Office Files.*

In the following Performance Assessment, you will create a form and link it to an Excel spreadsheet. Your completed form will look similar to Figure 8.44. You will rename and save your database as *8G_Hospital_Staff_Firstname_Lastname.*

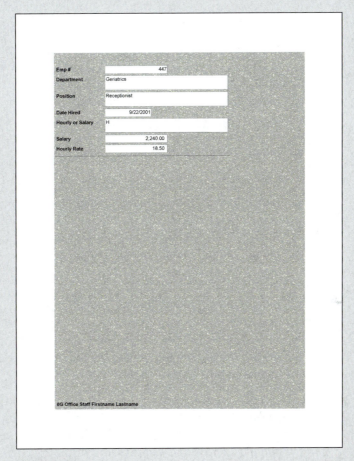

Figure 8.44

1. From the student files that accompany this textbook, locate the Excel spreadsheet **a08G_Office Staff**, copy and paste the file to the folder where you are storing your projects for this chapter, remove the Read-only property, and then rename the workbook **8G_Office_Staff_Firstname_Lastname** Start Excel and open the workbook you just renamed.

2. In the Excel worksheet, locate cell **G9**, and notice that the hourly rate for this staff member is 14.00. **Close** Excel.

(**Project 8G**–Hospital Staff continues on the next page)

Performance Assessments (continued)

(Project 8G–Hospital Staff continued)

3. From the student files, locate the Access database **a08G_Hospital_Staff**, and then copy and paste the file to the folder where you are storing your projects for this chapter. Remove the Read-only property from the file, and rename the file as **8G_Hospital_Staff_Firstname_Lastname** Start Access and open the database you just renamed.

4. On the Objects bar be sure **Tables** is selected. From the Database window toolbar, click the **New** button, and in the **New Table** dialog box, click **Link Table**.

5. Click **OK**. In the displayed **Link** dialog box, at the bottom, change the **Files of type** to **Microsoft Excel**, and then use the **Look in arrow** to navigate to your Excel file **8G_Office_Staff_Firstname_Lastname**. Select the file, and click **Link**.

6. In the **Link Spreadsheet Wizard**, be sure the **First Row Contains Column Headings** check box is selected, and then click **Next**. Name the table **Office Staff Firstname Lastname** and click **Finish**. Click **OK** to acknowledge that the linking is finished.

7. Open the new linked table in **Datasheet view**. Select all the columns and apply **Best Fit**. Click anywhere to deselect. **Close** the table and save the changes.

8. On the Objects bar, click **Forms**, and then double-click **Create form by using wizard**. As the table, use your **Office Staff** table, and then move all the fields over to the **Selected Fields** column.

9. Click **Next**. Click **Columnar** as the layout for the form, and in the next screen, click **SandStone** as the style for the form. On the last screen, accept the default name for the form and click **Finish**. **Maximize** the form window.

10. Switch to **Design view**. From the **View** menu, click **Page Header/Footer**. In the **Page Footer section**, create a label the approximate height of the footer area and three inches wide. Type **8G Office Staff Firstname Lastname**

11. Switch to **Form view**. Navigate to record **8**, *Emp # 447*, and change the hourly rate from 14.00 to **18.50**.

12. From the **File** menu, click **Print**. Under **Print Range**, click the **Selected Record(s)** option button, and then click **OK**. Click the **Close Window** button to close the form. Save the changes to the design. **Close** Access.

13. In **My Computer**, navigate to your files and open your Excel file **8G_Office_Staff_Firstname_Lastname**. Look at cell **G9** and notice that the hourly rate has been updated to 18.50. **Close** Excel, and save any changes.

End You have completed Project 8G

Performance Assessments (continued)

Project 8H—Billing

Objective: *Link a Chart in a Report.*

In the following Performance Assessment, you will insert and link a Microsoft Excel chart in an Access report. Your completed report will look similar to Figure 8.45. You will rename and save your database as 8H_Physicians_Billing_Firstname_Lastname.

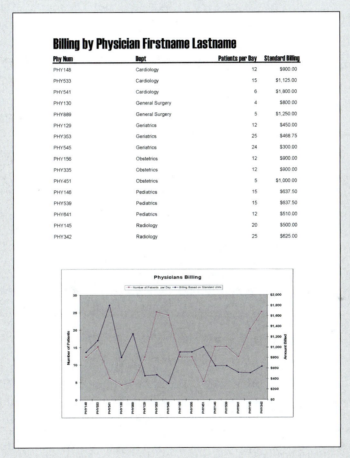

Figure 8.45

1. From the student files that accompany this textbook, locate the Excel file **a08H_Physicians_Billing**, copy and paste it into your chapter folder, and then remove the Read-only property. Rename the file **8H_Physicians_Billing_Firstname_Lastname** Open the file and examine the Excel chart. The chart shows the number of patients each physician had and how much the patients were billed. **Close** Excel.

(**Project 8H**–Billing continues on the next page)

Access chapter eight

Performance Assessments (continued)

(Project 8H–Billing continued)

2. From the student files, locate the Access database **a08H_Billing**, and then copy and paste the file to your chapter folder. Remove the Read-only property from the file, and rename the file as **8H_Billing_Firstname_Lastname** Start Access and open the database you just renamed.

3. On the Objects bar, click **Reports**. Double-click **Create report by using wizard**. Select the **Table: Billing by Physician**. Move the **Phy Num**, **Dept.**, **Patients per Day**, and **Standard Billing** fields over to the **Selected Fields** column and click **Next**. You will not add any grouping levels, so click **Next**, nor will you add a sort order, so click **Next** again. For the layout of your report, click **Tabular**, and for the **Orientation**, click **Portrait**, and then click **Next**.

4. For the report style, click **Compact**, and on the last screen, as the title for the report, type **Billing by Physician Firstname Lastname** and click **Finish**. Preview the report.

5. Switch to **Design view** and **Maximize** the report window. Decrease the size of the **Report Header section** to **0.5 inches on the vertical ruler**. Enlarge the **Page Footer section** to **4 inches on the vertical ruler**. At the top of the **Page Footer** section, hold down [Shift] and select the **line** and the **two text boxes**, and then press [Delete] to delete these three elements.

6. Click the **Page Footer section bar** to select the entire section. From the **Insert** menu, click **Object**. Click the **Create from File** option button. Browse to locate your Excel file **8H_Physicians_Billing_Firstname_Lastname**, select it and click **OK**. Select the **Link** check box and click **OK**.

7. Using the bottom right resize handle, resize the chart to approximately **6 inches wide** and **3.75 inches tall**. Right-click on the chart, click **Properties**, on the **Format tab** click the **Size Mode** arrow, and then click **Stretch**. For the **Left** type **0.25** Close the property box.

8. Reset the bottom of the **Page Footer section** to **4 inches on the vertical ruler**. Decrease the width of the entire form to **6.5 inches on the horizontal ruler**.

9. Switch to **Report preview**. From the **Page Setup** dialog box, change the **Top** and **Bottom margins** to **0.5 inch**. From the **File Menu**, click **Print**. Close the report, save changes, and close the database.

10. Close the database, and then close Access.

End You have completed Project 8H

Mastery Assessments

Project 8I—Updated Staff

Objective: *Import Data from a Word Table.*

In the following Mastery Assessment, you will import records from a Word table in an Access database. The table contains records for members of the Facilities staff. Your completed table will look similar to Figure 8.46. You will rename and save your database as *8I_Updated_Staff_Firstname_Lastname*.

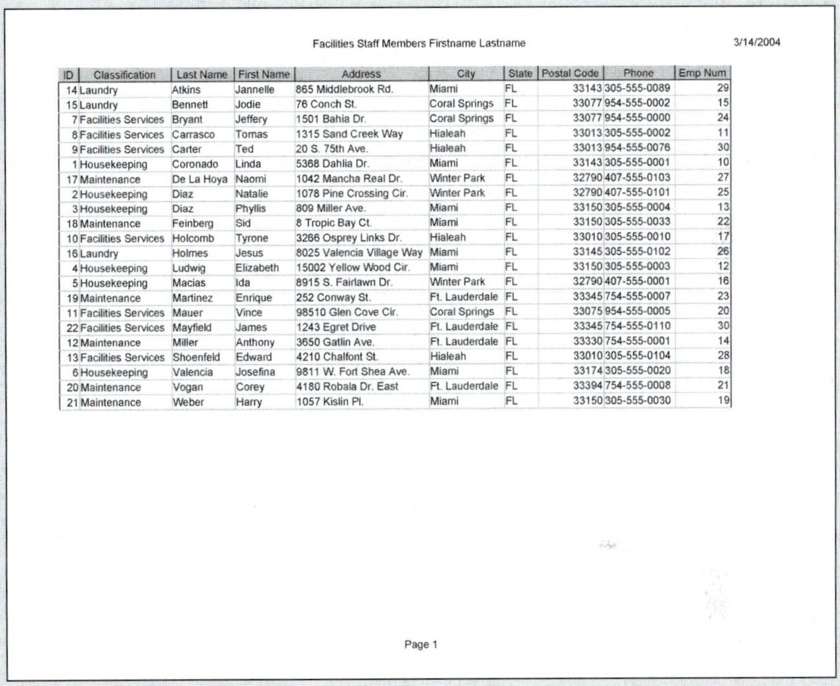
Facilities Staff Members Firstname Lastname 3/14/2004

ID	Classification	Last Name	First Name	Address	City	State	Postal Code	Phone	Emp Num
14	Laundry	Atkins	Jannelle	865 Middlebrook Rd.	Miami	FL	33143	305-555-0089	29
15	Laundry	Bennett	Jodie	76 Conch St.	Coral Springs	FL	33077	954-555-0002	15
7	Facilities Services	Bryant	Jeffery	1501 Bahia Dr.	Coral Springs	FL	33077	954-555-0000	24
8	Facilities Services	Carrasco	Tomas	1315 Sand Creek Way	Hialeah	FL	33013	305-555-0002	11
9	Facilities Services	Carter	Ted	20 S. 75th Ave.	Hialeah	FL	33013	954-555-0076	30
1	Housekeeping	Coronado	Linda	5368 Dahlia Dr.	Miami	FL	33143	305-555-0001	10
17	Maintenance	De La Hoya	Naomi	1042 Mancha Real Dr.	Winter Park	FL	32790	407-555-0103	27
2	Housekeeping	Diaz	Natalie	1078 Pine Crossing Cir.	Winter Park	FL	32790	407-555-0101	25
3	Housekeeping	Diaz	Phyllis	809 Miller Ave.	Miami	FL	33150	305-555-0004	13
18	Maintenance	Feinberg	Sid	8 Tropic Bay Ct.	Miami	FL	33150	305-555-0033	22
10	Facilities Services	Holcomb	Tyrone	3266 Osprey Links Dr.	Hialeah	FL	33010	305-555-0010	17
16	Laundry	Holmes	Jesus	8025 Valencia Village Way	Miami	FL	33145	305-555-0102	26
4	Housekeeping	Ludwig	Elizabeth	15002 Yellow Wood Cir.	Miami	FL	33150	305-555-0003	12
5	Housekeeping	Macias	Ida	8915 S. Fairlawn Dr.	Winter Park	FL	32790	407-555-0001	16
19	Maintenance	Martinez	Enrique	252 Conway St.	Ft. Lauderdale	FL	33345	754-555-0007	23
11	Facilities Services	Mauer	Vince	98510 Glen Cove Cir.	Coral Springs	FL	33075	954-555-0005	20
22	Facilities Services	Mayfield	James	1243 Egret Drive	Ft. Lauderdale	FL	33345	754-555-0110	30
12	Maintenance	Miller	Anthony	3650 Gatlin Ave.	Ft. Lauderdale	FL	33330	754-555-0001	14
13	Facilities Services	Shoenfeld	Edward	4210 Chalfont St.	Hialeah	FL	33010	305-555-0104	28
6	Housekeeping	Valencia	Josefina	9811 W. Fort Shea Ave.	Miami	FL	33174	305-555-0020	18
20	Maintenance	Vogan	Corey	4180 Robala Dr. East	Ft. Lauderdale	FL	33394	754-555-0008	21
21	Maintenance	Weber	Harry	1057 Kislin Pl.	Miami	FL	33150	305-555-0030	19

Page 1

Figure 8.46

1. From the student files, locate and then open the Microsoft Word file **a08I_Facilities_Staff**.
2. Click anywhere in the table. From the **Table** menu, convert the table to text using **Tabs** to separate the text. Press Ctrl + End to move to the end of the document, and press Bksp once to remove the blank line.
3. From the **File** menu, click **Save As**, and then navigate to the location where you are storing your projects for this chapter. Change the **Save as type** to **Plain Text**. In the **File name** box, type **8I_Facilities_Staff_Firstname_Lastname**
4. In the lower right corner of the dialog box, click **Save**. In the displayed **File Conversion** dialog box, accept the default settings and click **OK**. **Close** Microsoft Word.

(Project 8I–Updated Staff continues on the next page)

Mastery Assessments (continued)

(Project 8I–Updated Staff continued)

5. From the student files, locate the database file **a08I_Updated_Staff**, and then copy and paste the file to your chapter folder. Remove the Read-only property from the file and rename the file as **8I_Updated_Staff_Firstname_Lastname** Start Access and open the database you just renamed.

6. On the Objects bar, click **Tables**. Import your text file **8I_Facilities_Staff**.

7. Be sure the **Delimited** option button is selected. Select **Tab** as the delimiter and indicate that the **First Row Contains Field Names**. Store the imported data in a new table. It is not necessary to index any fields; let Access choose the primary key. In the **Import to Table** box, type Facilities Staff Members Firstname Lastname Click **OK** to acknowledge the message box.

8. Open your **Facilities Staff Members** table. Apply **Best Fit** to the columns, and then sort the data alphabetically by **Last Name**.

9. From the **Page Setup** dialog box, change the **Top**, **Botton**, **Left**, and **Right** margins to **0.75 inch** and change the **Page Orientation** to **Landscape**. On the Table Datasheet toolbar, click the **Print** button. Close your table and save the changes. Close your database.

End You have completed Project 8I

Mastery Assessments (continued)

Project 8J — Medical Staff

Objective: *Link Database Objects to Office Files.*

In the following Mastery Assessment, you will create a form for a table, and then link it to an Excel spreadsheet. Your completed form will look similar to Figure 8.47. You will rename and save your database as *8J_Medical_Center_Staff_Firstname_Lastname.*

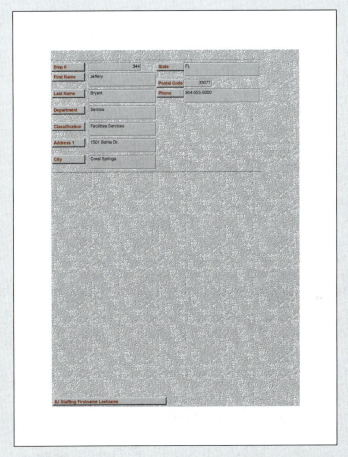

Figure 8.47

1. From the student files that accompany this textbook, locate the Excel file **a08J_Staffing**, copy and paste the file to your chapter folder, remove the Read-only property, and then rename the workbook **8J_Staffing_Firstname_Lastname** Start Excel and open the workbook you just renamed. Take a moment to examine the data, and then close Excel.

(Project 8J–Medical Staff continues on the next page)

Mastery Assessments (continued)

(Project 8J–Medical Staff continued)

2. From the student files, locate the Access database **a08J_Medical_Center_Staff**, and then copy and paste the file to your chapter folder. Remove the Read-only property from the file and rename the file as **8J_Medical_Center_Staff_Firstname_Lastname** Start Access and open the database you just renamed.

3. On the Objects bar, be sure **Tables** is selected. From the Database window toolbar, click the **New** button, and in the **New Table** dialog box, click **Link Table**.

4. Click **OK**. Change the **Files of type** to **Microsoft Excel**, and then navigate to your Excel file **8J_Staffing_Firstname_Lastname**. Select the file, and click **Link**.

5. In the **Link Spreadsheet Wizard**, show the **Staffing** worksheet. Indicate that the **First Row Contains Column Headings**. Name the table **Staffing Firstname Lastname** and click **Finish**. Click **OK** to acknowledge that the linking is finished.

6. Open the new table in **Datasheet view**. Apply **Best Fit** to all the columns. **Close** the table and save the changes.

7. Create a new form using a wizard from your **Table: Staffing**. Move **all fields** over to the **Selected Fields** column. Use a **Columnar** layout for the form, and click **Stone** as the style for the form. Leave the form name as **Staffing Firstname Lastname**. **Maximize** the form window and switch to **Design view**. Shorten the left side of the bound controls in the second column to **1 inch on the horizontal ruler**, and then lengthen the label controls in the first column slightly so that none of the labels are cut off.

8. Insert page headers and footers, and in the **Page Footer section**, create a label the approximate height of the footer area and three inches wide. Type **8J Staffing Firstname Lastname**

9. Switch to **Form view** and navigate to record **42**. From the **File** menu, click **Print**. Under **Print Range**, click the **Selected Record(s)** option button, and then click **OK**. Close the form and save changes. Close the database and close Access.

End You have completed Project 8J

Problem Solving

Project 8K — Friends and Family

Objective: *Import from Excel.*

In the following Problem Solving exercise, you will import an Excel spreadsheet into a new database.

1. Create an Excel spreadsheet with the names of ten of your friends and family members. Create a column for Firstname, Lastname, Address, City, State, ZIP Code, Phone, and E-mail address.

2. Import and Link the Excel worksheet into a new Access table.

3. Change the settings in the table to fit the columns and name the table **Classmates Firstname Lastname Print** the table. Save your database as **8K_Friends_Family_Firstname_Lastname**.

End You have completed Project 8K

Project 8L — Classmates

Objective: *Use Mail Merge to Integrate Access and Word.*

In the following Problem Solving exercise, you will create envelopes in Microsoft Word using the Mail Merge wizard.

1. Open the Access database you created in Project 8K and select the Classmates table you imported from Excel.

2. Use the Mail Merge wizard in Microsoft Word to create an envelope for each of the classmates in the table. Put your name and address as the return address.

3. Print the first envelope. Save the ten envelopes as **8L_Friends_Family_Envelopes**.

End You have completed Project 8L

On the Internet

Getting Information About OLE

The Microsoft Web site contains a variety of information about using OLE in Access. Go to the Microsoft site at www.microsoft.com and click **Search**. Search for **Access OLE** and examine the information. Print any information that would be helpful to you.

GO! with Help

Removing Links

In this chapter you worked with linking tables between databases. Once a link is created, it is possible to remove the link between the tables.

1. Start Access. In the *Type a question for help* box, type **remove links** and press Enter.

2. In the **Search Results** taskbar, click **Delete the link to a linked table in an Access database**.

3. At the top of the Help window, click **Show All** and read the information.

4. Print the Help information if you want to keep a copy of it. Close the **Help** window, and then close Access.

Access 2003

chapter nine

Macros and Switchboards

In this chapter, you will: complete these projects and practice these skills.

Project 9A
Creating and Editing Macros

Objectives
- View the Macro Window
- Create a New Macro
- Run a Macro in Response to an Event
- Create a Macro Group

Project 9B
Creating a Switchboard

Objective
- Create a Switchboard Page

University Medical Center

The University Medical Center is a premier patient-care and research institution serving Orange Beach, Florida. It provides preventive and routine care to the treatment of serious illnesses and traumas and is renowned for its state-of-the-art cardiovascular center. To help promote and maintain the Center's sterling reputation, the Office of Public Affairs (OPA) promotes the services and achievements of the medical staff. The OPA conducts community health seminars, maintains a speakers bureau of health experts, and provides up-to-date information to local and national media.

© Photosphere Images Ltd.

Macros and Switchboards

When working with Access, there are many tasks that you may perform repeatedly. You can automate a task by using a **macro**, a series of commands and instructions grouped together as a single command to accomplish a task—or multiple tasks—automatically. For example, you may create a report or query that you open and print on a weekly basis. You can create a macro that prints the report when the user clicks a command button, or you can create a macro to run multiple queries.

A **switchboard** is a form that displays when you open a database and that provides access to all of the tables, forms, queries, and reports in your database. A switchboard allows you to create a user-friendly interface with which you can control the options the end user has when using the database.

Project 9A Medical Center

The database used by University Medical Center can be improved by adding macros that will allow users to view and edit the information more efficiently.

In Activities 9.1 through 9.7, you will view, create, and edit macros to automate the Medical Center database for Mike Martinez, the Director of Public Affairs. You will save your database as *9A_Medical_Center_Firstname_Lastname*.

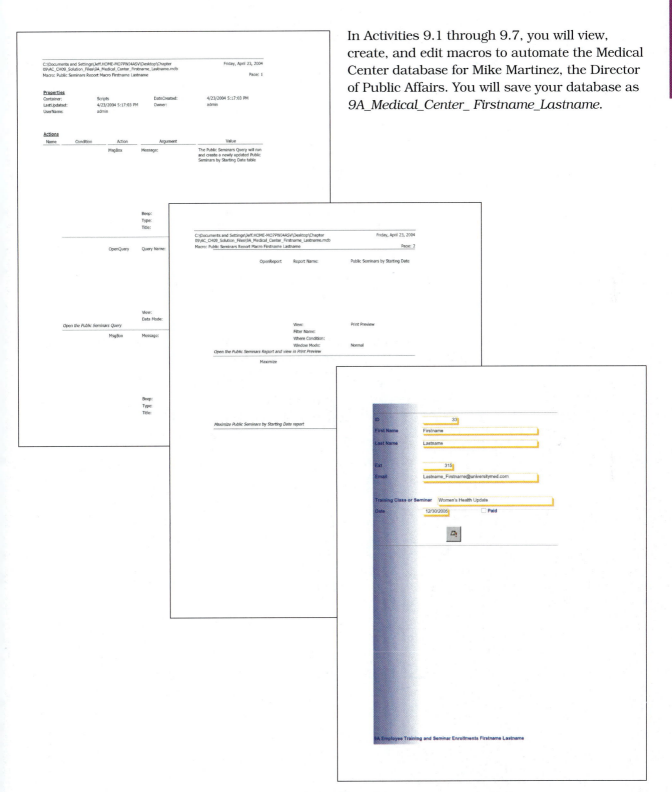

Figure 9.1
Project 9A—Medical Center

Project 9A: Medical Center | **Access** 547

Objective 1
View the Macro Window

A macro improves the efficiency of a database by automating common tasks. Macros are comprised of one or more *actions*, each of which performs a particular operation, such as opening a form or printing a report. An action is a self-contained instruction that can be combined with other actions to automate tasks.

The *Macro window* is the window in which you create and modify macros. In this window, you can add commands in a step-by-step manner until you have completed your macro.

Activity 9.1 Viewing the Macro Window

In this activity, you will open an existing macro in the Macro window and view each macro action.

1 Using **My Computer**, navigate to the student files that accompany this textbook and locate the Access database **a09A_Medical_Center**. Copy and paste the file to your storage location, creating a new folder for Chapter 9 if you want to do so. Rename the file **9A_Medical_Center_Firstname_Lastname** Remove the Read-only property from the file. Start Access and open the database you just renamed.

2 On the Objects bar, click **Macros**. As shown in Figure 9.2, right-click the **Open Training and Seminar Form** and click **Design View** from the shortcut menu to open the Macro window.

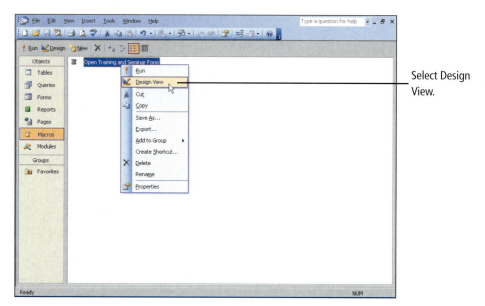

Select Design View.

Figure 9.2

3 Maximize the window, and then locate the three sections of the Macro window: **Action column**, **Comment column**, and **Action Arguments section**. See Figure 9.3.

Each action in the action column is a command that is sequentially executed when the macro is run. Notice that the comment section describes some of the actions. The *action arguments* are additional information required by some macro actions that provide additional instructions on how to execute the action.

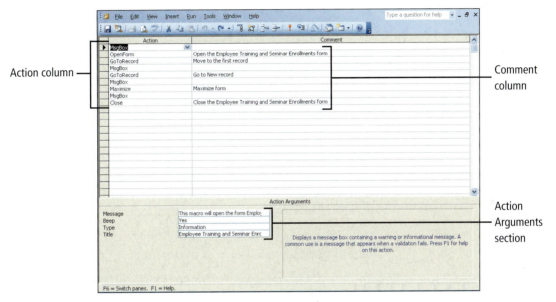

Figure 9.3

4 Read each action and its corresponding comment, noticing that the macro opens the Employee Training and Seminar Enrollments form, and then displays the first record. Then the macro displays a new record, maximizes the form if necessary, and then closes the form.

5 In the **Action** column of the Macro window, click in the **MsgBox** box, and then at the bottom of the window, under **Action Arguments**, locate the four arguments as shown in Figure 9.4.

The MsgBox action displays an information or warning box and waits for the user to click a button, such as OK or Cancel. The action arguments associated with the MsgBox function are message arguments, beep arguments, type arguments, and title arguments. The *Message argument* indicates the message that will be displayed when the macro is started. The *Beep argument*, if selected, sounds a beep when the message box is displayed. The *Type argument* indicates the type of icon that will be displayed when a message box is displayed, and the *Title argument* indicates the text that will be displayed in the title bar of the message box.

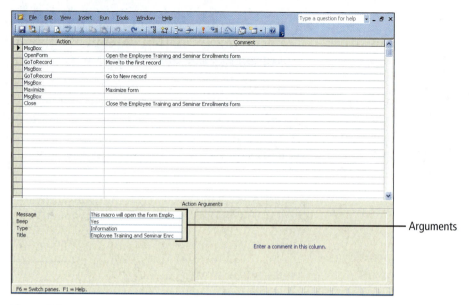

Figure 9.4

6 Click in the **OpenForm** box and observe the Action Arguments at the bottom of the window. Click in the remaining seven Action boxes and observe the Action Arguments that correspond to each action.

Each action performs a separate task, so the Action Arguments will be different for each action performed.

7 To run the macro, on the Macro Design toolbar, click **Run** .

The first message box displays using the Action Arguments from the Macro window. See Figure 9.5.

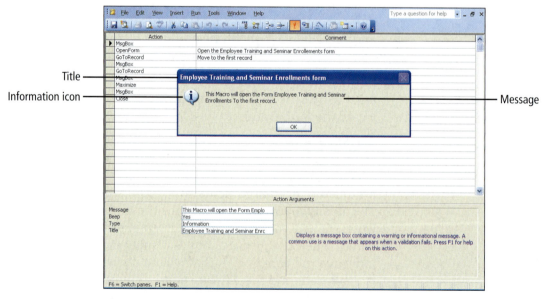

Figure 9.5

550   Access | Chapter 9: Macros and Switchboards

8 Read the message, and then click **OK**.

The Employee Training and Seminar Enrollments form displays and the first record is active. The second message box displays a message indicating that the form will move to a new record allowing you to enter a new participant.

9 Click **OK**.

A blank record is displayed and the third message box displays indicating that the form will now be maximized.

10 Click **OK**.

The form is maximized and the fourth and final message box displays indicating that the form will close.

11 Click **OK**, and then **Close** the Macro window and leave the database open for the next activity.

Objective 2
Create a New Macro

To create a macro, on the Objects bar, click the Macro object, and then on the Database window toolbar, click the New button. Add the desired actions and accompanying arguments.

Activity 9.2 Creating a New Macro

In Activity 9.1, you viewed an existing macro in the Macro window. In this activity, you will open the Macro window and create a new macro. Access has many predefined actions from which you can choose to help you build your macro. When building your macro, you must first decide the order of the steps and then build your macro to follow this order. The actions for the new macro will open the Public Seminars by Starting Date report and then display the report in Print Preview. Because this report is frequently updated and reviewed, it will be useful to have a macro to automatically open and display the report.

1 On the Objects bar, click **Macros**. On the **Database window** menu, click **New**.

A new macro window displays.

2 In the first box of the **Action** column, type **ms** and notice that Access completes the function name *msgBox*. Press F6 to accept the MsgBox function and to move the insertion point to the **Action Arguments** section. In the **Message** box, type **Opening the Public Seminars by Starting Date Report** and then press Tab to move to the **Beep** box. Do not change the default setting—**Yes**. Press Tab again to move to the **Type** box. Click the **Type arrow**, and from the displayed list, click **Information**. Press Tab, and in the **Title** box, type **Public Seminars Report** See Figure 9.6.

The action arguments that you entered instruct Access to display an information message box with the title *Public Seminars Report*. When the information box displays the text that you typed in the Message box, the user's computer will beep.

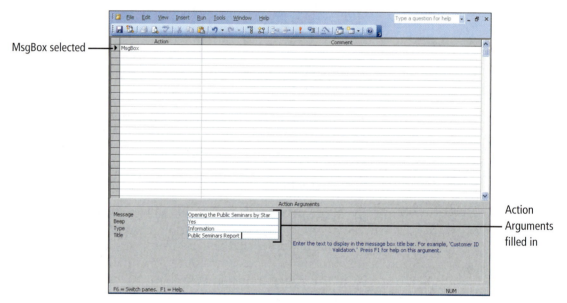

Figure 9.6

3 Press F6 to move back to the **Actions** column in the Macro window. Press Tab twice to move to the next **Action** box. In the second Action box, type **OpenReport** and press Tab.

The OpenReport action allows you to open any of the reports in your database in Print, Print Preview, or Design mode.

4 In the **Comment** column, type **Open the Public Seminars Report and view in Print Preview**

Recall that comments describe each action in your macro. As a macro gets longer, comments provide documentation that can assist you in finding actions that need to be changed or updated.

5 Press F6. Click the **Report Name arrow** to display a list of existing reports, and then click **Public Seminars by Starting Date**. Press Tab, click the **View arrow**, and then click **Print Preview**. See Figure 9.7.

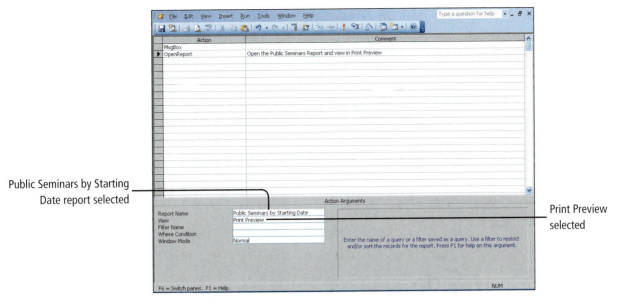

Figure 9.7

6 Press F6 to move back to the upper portion of the window, and then press Tab to move to the next **Action** box. Type **M** and notice that Access completes the word *Maximize*. Press Tab to accept *Maximize* and in the **Comment** box, type **Maximize Public Seminars by Starting Date report**

7 On the Macro Design toolbar, click **Save**, name the macro **Public Seminars Report Macro Firstname Lastname** and then click **OK**. On the Macro Design toolbar, click the **Run** button to start the macro. When the message box displays indicating that the report is being opened, click **OK**.

The Public Seminars by Starting Date report opens and displays in Print Preview, according to the steps you listed in the macro.

8 **Close** the report, and leave the macro open in Design view for the next activity.

Activity 9.3 Adding Actions to a Macro

The report *Public Seminars by Starting Date* is based on a table created from a Make Table query. The Make Table query creates a table of Seminars, by date, starting after the specific date entered by the user. Before creating and viewing the report with your macro, you should run the query to update the report to its most current status. In this activity, you will add additional actions to the macro that will run the Public Seminars Query before opening and previewing the report.

1 Be sure your **Public Seminars Report Macro** is open in Design view.

2 To the left of the **MsgBox** action, click in the selection box to select the first row in the Macro window. Then, on the Macro Design toolbar, click **Insert Rows** two times.

Two blank rows are inserted above the first action.

Project 9A: Medical Center | **Access** 553

3 In the first **Action** box, click the arrow. Scroll the displayed list, and then click **MsgBox**. Press [F6] to move to the **Action Arguments** section. In the **Message** box type **The Public Seminars Query will run and create a newly updated Public Seminars by Starting Date table** Press [Tab] and be sure that the **Beep** box displays **Yes**. Press [Tab], click the **Type arrow**, and then click **Information**. Press [Tab] and type **Creating Public Seminars by Starting Date table** as the **Title** of the message box. See Figure 9.8.

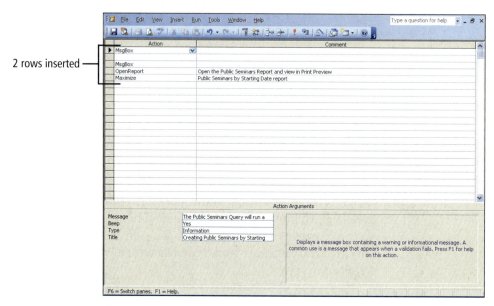

Figure 9.8

4 In the **Action** column, click in the second row. Type **OpenQuery** and then press [F6] to move to the **Action Arguments**. Click the **Query Name arrow** to display a list of existing queries, and then click **Public Seminars Query**. Be sure the **View** is set to **Datasheet** and the **Data Mode** is set to **Edit**. Press [F6] to return to the upper portion of the Macro window, and then press [Tab]. In the **OpenQuery Comment row**, type **Open the Public Seminars Query**

5 On the Macro Design toolbar, click **Save**, and then click **Run**. Click **OK** to close the message box. Click **Yes** to run the make-table query, and then click **Yes** in the warning message that displays regarding information about deleting the table. In the **Please enter a starting date** box, type **11/1/2005** and then click **OK**. When the information box regarding pasting 5 rows displays, click **Yes**. Click **OK** to open the report in Print Preview.

The report lists the seminars starting on or after 11/1/2005.

Another Way

To Run a Macro

To run a macro from the Database window, from the Objects bar click Macros, and then double-click the macro name. Alternatively, from the Tools menu, point to Macro, click Run Macro, and then select the macro from the Macro Name list.

6 Click anywhere in the report to increase the zoom.

Notice that five seminars are listed, all beginning after the date entered of 11/1/2005. See Figure 9.9.

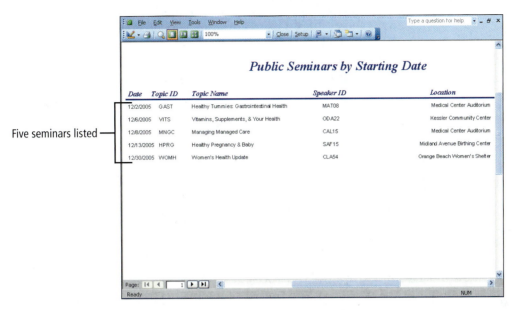

Five seminars listed

Figure 9.9

7 Close ⊠ the report to display the macro in Design view. On the **File** menu, click **Print**. In the **Print Macro Definition** box, click to clear the **Permissions by User and Group** check box. See Figure 9.10, and then click **OK**.

The macro report includes each action and action argument, allowing you to follow each macro step. This process is useful when you try to find errors in your macro.

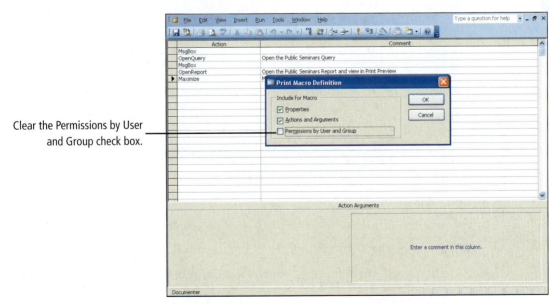

Clear the Permissions by User and Group check box.

Figure 9.10

8 Close ⊠ your macro and leave the database open for the next activity.

Project 9A: Medical Center | **Access** 555

> **More Knowledge** — Debugging a Macro
>
> To test a macro, you can proceed through your macro one step at a time. From the Macro Design toolbar click the *Single Step* button, and then run your macro. By single-stepping through a macro you can see the conditions, actions, and argument values as each action is performed.

Activity 9.4 Attaching a Macro to a Command Button

In the previous activity, you ran your macro from the Macro design window. You may also run your macros from other windows. For example, when you are entering new information into the table from a form, you can run the macro from the form itself. This is accomplished by inserting a command button, which runs the macro directly from the form. In this activity, you will insert a command button in the Employee Training and Seminar Enrollments form so that you can run the macro directly from the form.

1 On the Objects bar, click **Forms**. Right-click the **Employee Training and Seminar Enrollments** form and click **Design View**.

2 **Maximize** the Form design window. Move your mouse pointer to the bottom of the **Detail section** until the resizing handle displays. Drag downward to expand the Detail section to **3.5 inches on the vertical ruler**. (Hint: Drag slightly more than 3.5 inches, and then drag upward.) See Figure 9.11.

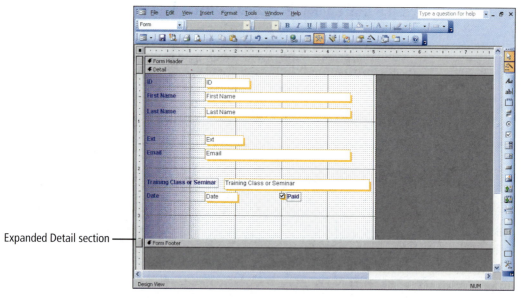

Expanded Detail section

Figure 9.11

3 Be sure the Toolbox toolbar is displayed. If the Toolbox is not displayed, on the Form Design toolbar, click the **Toolbox** button.

4 In the Toolbox, click the **Command Button** button ![icon]. Position the plus sign attached to the pointer at **3 inches on the vertical ruler** and at **2 inches on the horizontal ruler**, and then click to place the command button at that location and open the **Command Button Wizard**. See Figure 9.12.

A command button provides you with a way to perform an action by clicking the button. Attaching your macro to the command button allows you to execute your macro without closing the form.

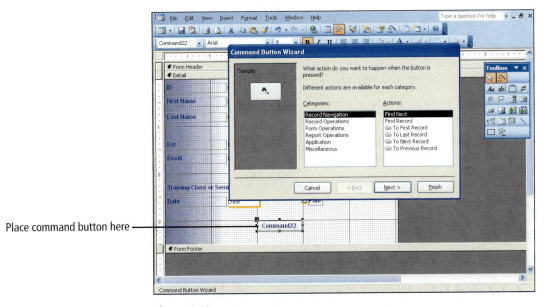

Place command button here

Figure 9.12

5 In the **Command Button Wizard**, under **Categories**, click **Miscellaneous** and under **Actions**, click **Run Macro**. See Figure 9.13.

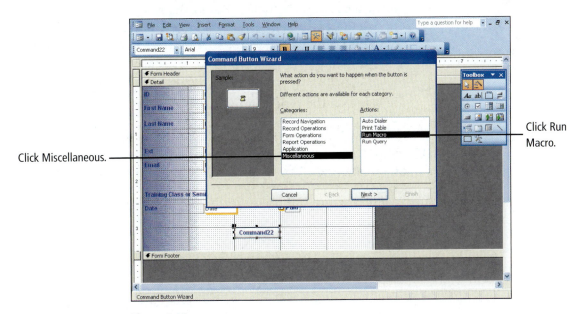

Click Miscellaneous.

Click Run Macro.

Figure 9.13

Project 9A: Medical Center | **Access**

6 Click **Next**.

Here you select the macro that you want to run when the button is clicked.

7 Click your **Public Seminars Report** macro, and then click **Next**. If necessary, click the **Picture** option button, and then click **Run Macro**.

The left side of the Command Button Wizard dialog box displays a picture of the button. A command button can be formatted to display either text or a picture. The text or picture helps to identify the purpose of the command button. You may select a Microsoft picture or you may select any bitmap picture you have saved on your computer.

8 Click **Next** to assign a meaningful name to your button. Type **Run Public Seminars Report Macro** and then click **Finish**.

A command button with a scroll and an exclamation point is displayed on your form. The scroll icon represents a macro. The picture displays as a reminder that the command button runs a macro when clicked.

9 On the **View** menu, click **Page Header/Footer**. On the Toolbox toolbar, click **Label**. In the Page Footer, drag the label from the upper left of the footer to the lower right of the footer. In the label, type **9A Employee Training and Seminar Enrollments Firstname Lastname**

10 Switch to **Form view** and examine the updated form. At the bottom of the form, click **New Record**. Using your own information and in the appropriate fields, type **Firstname** and **Lastname** and type **315** as your extension (Ext). For the email, use your name and type **Lastname_Firstname@universitymed.com**

11 Click the **Command Button** at the bottom of the form to run your macro. Click **OK** in the first Message box, click **Yes** to run the make-table query, and then click **Yes** in the warning message confirming the deletion of the previous table. Type **12/12/2005** for the starting date and click **OK**. Click **Yes** to paste two rows into a new table, and then click **OK** to open the report.

12 Click anywhere on the report to zoom in, and notice that two seminars are listed on the report. Notice that the date of the Women's Health Update seminar is 12/30/2005, and then **Close** the report.

13 In the **Training Class or Seminar** box, type **Women's Health Update** and in the **Date** box, type **12/30/2005** Compare your form with Figure 9.14.

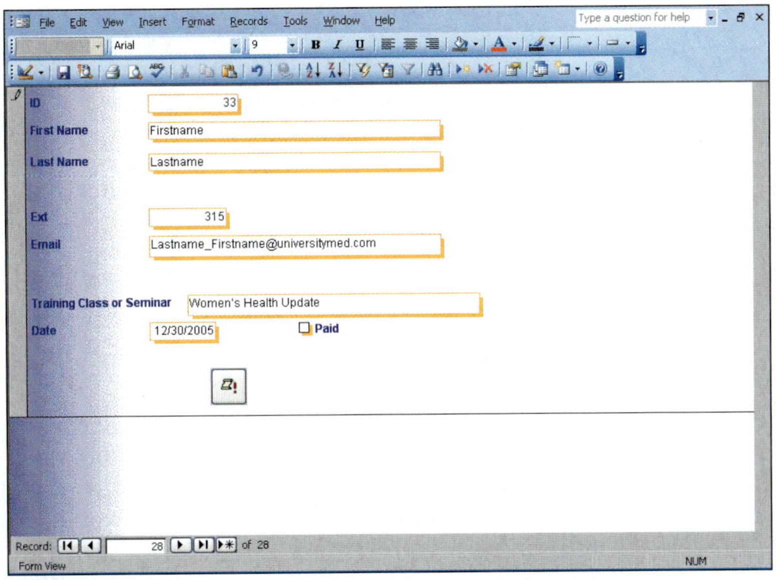

Figure 9.14

14 From the **File** menu, click **Print**. Under **Print Range**, click the **Selected Record(s)** option button, and then click **OK**. **Close** ⊠ the form and save your changes. Leave the database open for the next activity.

Objective 3
Run a Macro in Response to an Event

Actions you perform on or within objects are called *events*. An event is any significant action that can be detected by a system. Some examples of events include clicking a button, moving a mouse, or opening a form. A macro can run automatically when an event occurs.

Activity 9.5 Running a Macro in Response to an Event

When enrolling in one of the seminars, payment must be received seven days before the scheduled date of the seminar. In this activity, you will create a macro to update a Due Date text field to seven days before the seminar date in the Employee Training and Seminar Enrollments form. The due date needs to be updated for each form. Updating the due date automatically when the form opens is efficient and ensures that all of the forms are updated when viewed.

1 If necessary, open your file **9A_Medical_Center_Firstname_Lastname** and select the **Forms** object. Right-click the **Employee Training and Seminar Enrollments** form, and then click **Design View**. If necessary **Maximize** ▢ the window. Be sure the Toolbox toolbar is displayed. If the Toolbox is not displayed, click the Toolbox button on the Form Design toolbar.

2 On the Toolbox toolbar, click the **Text Box** button. Position the plus sign attached to the pointer at **1.5 inches on the horizontal ruler** and directly under the Date control and click. Use Ctrl plus any of the directional arrow keys to adjust the position if necessary.

3 Right-click the text box label and click **Properties**. Click the **Format tab**, and then change the **Caption** to **Payment Due: Close** the properties sheet. With the label still selected, use the left and right resizing handles to resize the label to match the Date label above it as shown in Figure 9.15.

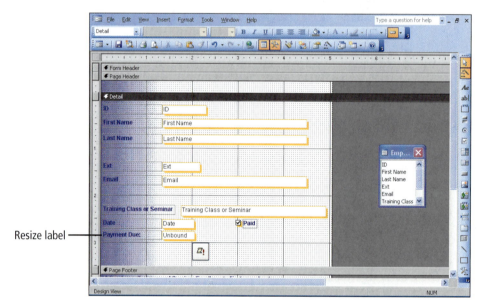

Figure 9.15

4 Right-click the **Unbound text box control** and click **Properties**. Click the **All tab** and change the **Name** to **Payment Due Date** Click the **Data tab** and change **Locked** to **Yes**. **Close** the sheet. With the text box control still selected, click the **Align Right** button to right align the text within the control. **Close** the Form window and click **Yes** to save your changes.

By changing Locked to Yes, the user is prevented from manually entering a date into this control.

5 On the Objects bar, click **Macros**. In the Database window, click **New**.

6 In the **Action** column, in the first box, type **SetValue** Alternatively, select *SetValue* from the list. As the comment, type **Sets the Payment Due Date to the Date minus 7 days** Press F6 to move to the **Action Arguments**. At the right end of the **Item** box, click the **Build** button.

The Expression Builder helps you build your expression if you do not know the field or control names. The item box holds the control to be set.

7 In the lower half of the **Expression Builder** dialog box, double-click **Forms** to expand the folder, and then double-click **All Forms**. After the *All Forms* folder is expanded, click the third folder, **Employee Training and Seminar Enrollments** folder, to open it. See Figure 9.16.

When an object is opened in the first column of the Expression Builder, the controls from the object are displayed in the second column. When you click on a control in the second column, the control's properties are displayed in the third column.

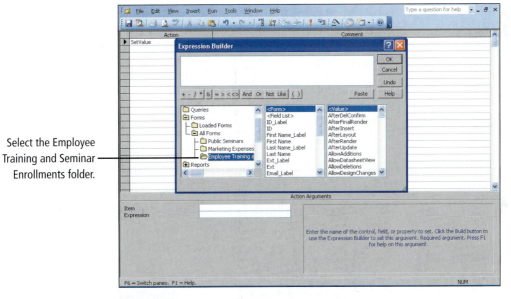

Select the Employee Training and Seminar Enrollments folder.

Figure 9.16

8 In the second column, scroll down and double-click **Payment Due Date** to place it in the **Expression Builder** box. See Figure 9.17.

The Payment Due Date needs to be set to seven days before the Seminar Date.

Payment Due Date placed in Expression Builder

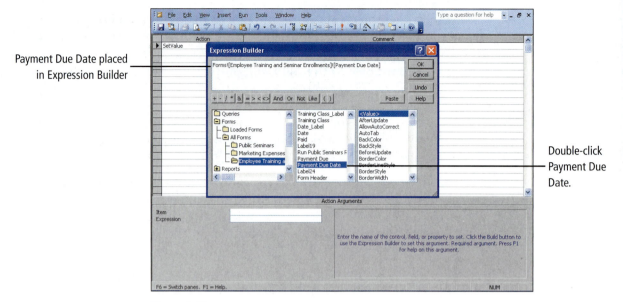

Double-click Payment Due Date.

Figure 9.17

9 Click **OK**. Press Tab to move to the **Expression argument**. Click the **Build** button. In the first column, double-click **Forms**. After the Forms folder is expanded, double-click **All Forms**. Click the third folder, **Employee Training and Seminar Enrollments** folder, to open it.

All of the controls on the Employee Training and Seminar Enrollments form are displayed in the second column.

10 In the second column, scroll down and double-click **Date**, to place it in the Expression Builder box. Be sure that the insertion point is blinking at the end of the Expression Builder box and type **-7** to subtract 7 from the seminar date. See Figure 9.18.

The expression subtracts seven from the value in the date field and places the new date in the Payment Due Date text field.

Expression added to the Expression Builder

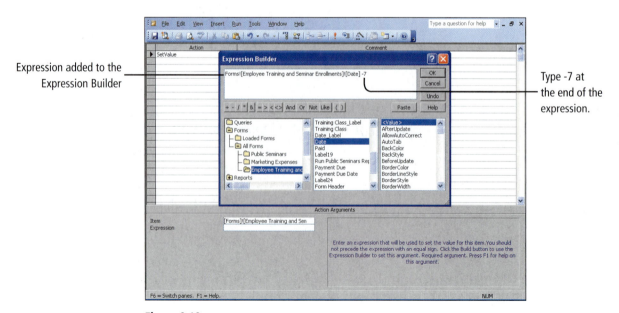

Type -7 at the end of the expression.

Figure 9.18

11. Click **OK** to close the Expression Builder. Click **Save** and name the macro **Set Due Date** Click **OK**, and then **Close** the macro.

12. On the Objects bar, click **Forms**. Open the **Employee Training and Seminar Enrollments** form in **Design view**. If necessary, **Maximize** the window.

13. To the left of the horizontal ruler, **right-click** on the **Form Selector** button and click **Properties**. See Figure 9.19.

    The Form Selector button is used to select the form or change its properties.

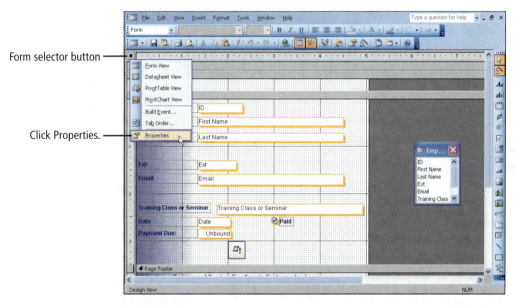

Figure 9.19

14. Click the **Event tab**. Click the **On Current arrow** and from the displayed list, click **Set Due Date**. **Close** the Properties sheet.

    By setting the On Current event, the Set Due Date macro will run every time a form is viewed. The due date will be calculated when the form is opened to ensure the date is accurate. The macro will not run when a new seminar date is entered in the form.

15. Switch to **Form view** and scroll through the 28 records, and then notice that the Payment Due date is set for each record. Click the **Last Record** button, change the **Date** to **12/22/2005** and then press Tab. Notice that the Payment Due is not updated.

16. Switch to **Design view**. Right-click the **Date control,** and then click **Properties**. Click the **Event tab**. Click in the **After Update** box, click the **arrow**, and then click the **Set Due Date** macro. **Close** the Property sheet.

    By changing the properties of the Date control to After Update, the Set Due Date macro will run as soon as the date changes.

Project 9A: Medical Center | **Access** 563

17 Switch to **Form view**. Click the **Last Record** button and change the **Date** textbox to **6/20/2005** and press Tab. Notice the Payment Due is now updated.

18 **Close** the form and save your changes. Leave the database open for the next activity.

Activity 9.6 Using Condition Expressions in Macros

When you create a macro, you may not want the macro to run automatically. In the previous activity, you created a macro to calculate a payment due date. The macro ran automatically when the form opened. However, if a seminar participant has already paid, it is not necessary to display the payment due date. In this activity, you will use a ***conditional expression*** to determine if the participant has paid for the seminar. A conditional expression is a test that evaluates a condition of true or false and performs a function based on the answer. You will set the macro to perform one function—hide the due date—if the fee has been paid, which is the *true* condition. You will set the macro to perform a different function—display the due date—if the fee has not yet been paid, which is the *false* condition.

1 On the Objects bar, click the **Macros** object, right-click the **Set Due Date** macro, and then click **Design View**.

2 On the Macro Design toolbar, click the **Conditions** button.

Notice that a new column is inserted in front of the Action column. See Figure 9.20.

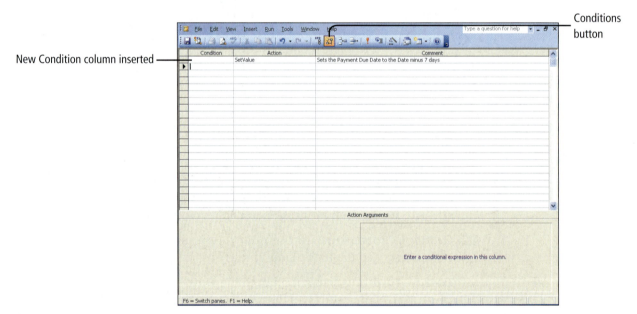

Figure 9.20

3 Under **Condition** in the *second* row, type **[Paid]=Yes**

Recall that in an expression, square brackets are used to denote a field name. This conditional expression will test to see if the Paid field was checked. When a relational operator such as an equal sign, less than sign, or a greater than sign is used, the expression is evaluated to be true or false.

4 Press Tab and type **SetValue** Press Tab and in the comment section, type **Hides the Payment Due Date control if fee is already paid** Press F6 to move to the Action Arguments and next to **Item**, type **[Payment Due Date].[Visible]**

Instead of using the expression builder, you can type the field name and properties directly into the Item box if you know the exact names. Every control on your form has many properties. One of these properties allows you to hide the controls. The Visible property can be set to Yes or No, which will determine if the control will be visible on the form. When typing an expression, first list the field to modify. Then, type a period to separate the field and the property, and then list the property to modify. This method may be used to change any of the field properties. Recall that you can see a list of field properties by right-clicking on the field and then clicking on Properties.

5 Press Tab. Type **No** next to **Expression** to set the visible property to No. See Figure 9.21.

The control has now been set to hide the Payment Due Date if the seminar fee has been paid.

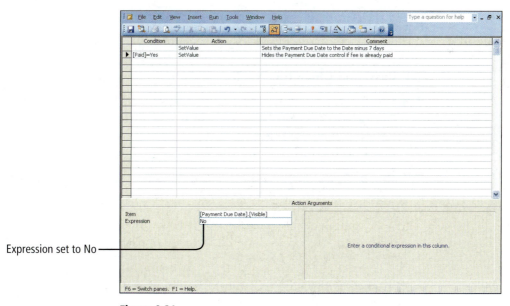

Expression set to No

Figure 9.21

6 Press F6 to return to the Action column. Press Tab to move to the next Condition. Type **[Paid]=No** Press Tab and type **SetValue** Press Tab and in the comment section, type **Displays the Payment Due Date control if fee has not been paid** Press F6 and next to **Item**, type **[Payment Due Date].[Visible]**

7 Press Tab. Type **Yes** next to **Expression** to set the visible property to Yes. See Figure 9.22.

The control has now been set to display the Payment Due Date if the seminar fee has not yet been paid.

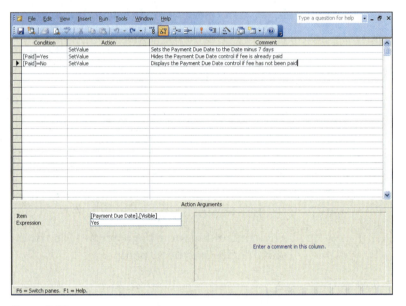

Figure 9.22

8 **Save** and **Close** the **Set Due Date** macro.

9 On the Objects bar, click the **Forms** object. Double-click the **Employee Training and Seminar Enrollments** form. Scroll through all the records and notice that the **Payment Due** control only displays on the forms when the **Paid** field is not selected.

10 **Close** the form and leave the database open for the next activity.

Objective 4
Create a Macro Group

In the previous activities, you practiced how to create a macro. As you continue to create more macros, you may want to group related macros together. You can do this by creating a **Macro Group**. A Macro Group is a set of macros grouped together by a common name.

Activity 9.7 Creating a Macro Group

In this activity, you will create three macros and group them together in a Macro Group called Open Forms. One macro will open a new record in the Employee Training and Seminar Enrollment form, one macro will open the Marketing Form, and one macro will open the Public Seminars form.

1 On the Objects bar, click **Macros**, and in the Database window, click **New**.

2 On the Macro Design toolbar click **Macro Names**.

Notice that a new column is inserted in front of the Action column. See Figure 9.23.

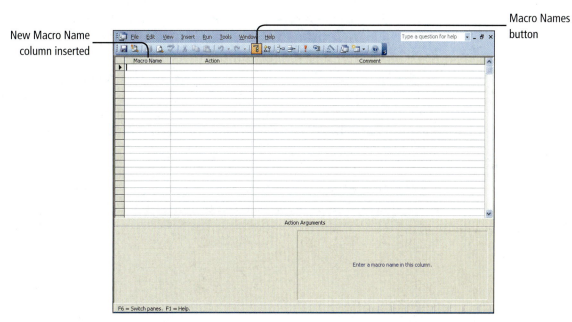

Figure 9.23

3 In the first row under **Macro Name**, type **Enrollments** and then press [Tab] and type **OpenForm** Then press [Tab] and type **Open the Employee Training and Seminar Enrollments form** Press [F6]. Click the **Form Name arrow**, and then click the **Employee Training and Seminar Enrollments** form. Click the **Data Mode arrow** and click **Edit** to allow the user to insert or change the records. Press [F6]. Press [Tab] to move to the second row of the macro.

4 Press [Tab] to move the insertion point to the second row under **Action**. Type **GoToRecord** and press [F6]. Click the **Object Type arrow** and click **Form**. Click the **Object Name arrow**, then click **Employee Training and Seminar Enrollments**. Click the **Record arrow**, and then click **New**.

5 Press [F6], and then press [Tab] to position the insertion point in the **GoToRecord Comment** column. Under **Comment**, type **Go to a new form in the Enrollments form** Press [Tab].

Since the GoToRecord action does not have a macro name in front of it, the action will be run when the Enrollments macro is executed. Each additional action will be run until a new macro is defined.

6 In the third row under **Macro Name**, type **Expenses** Press [Tab] and type **OpenForm** and then press [Tab] and type **Open the Marketing Expenses form** Press [F6], and then click the **Form Name arrow**. Click the **Marketing Expenses** form. Click the **Data Mode arrow**, and then click **Edit**. Press [F6], and then press [Tab] to move to the fourth row in the Macro Name column.

7 In the fourth row under **Macro Name**, type **Seminars** Press [Tab] and type **OpenForm** and then press [Tab] and type **Open the Public Seminars form** Press [F6], and then click the **Form Name** arrow. Click the **Public Seminars** form. Click the **Data Mode** arrow, and then click **Edit**. See Figure 9.24.

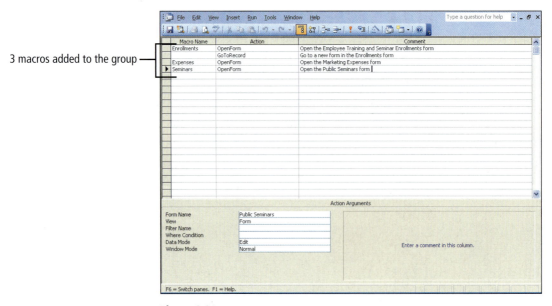

3 macros added to the group

Figure 9.24

8 On the Macro Design toolbar, click **Save**. In the **Macro Name** box, type **Open Forms** and then click **OK**. **Close** the macro.

9 In the Database window, if necessary, click to select the **Open Forms** macro. On the **Tools** menu, point to **Macro**, and then click **Run Macro**. Click the **Macro Name arrow**.

If necessary, move the small scroll box to the top of the scroll bar. Notice that four different macros are associated with the **Open Forms** macro. See Figure 9.25.

To run a macro from the group, type the macro group name, a period, and then the macro name. If you run the Open Forms macro, only the first macro to open the Employee Training and Seminar Enrollments form will be executed.

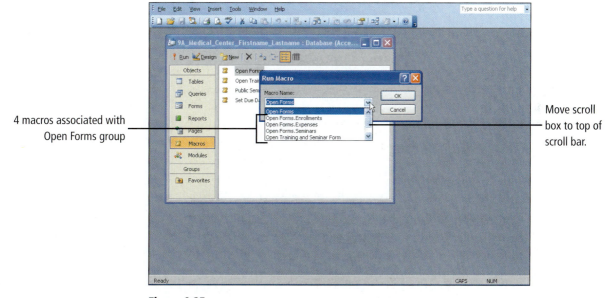

Figure 9.25

10 Click on the **Open Forms.Seminars** macro and click **OK** to run the macro. **Close** the **Public Seminars** form.

11 **Close** the database and close Access.

End You have completed Project 9A

Project 9B

Databases are often utilized by multiple individuals who must have easy access to the forms and reports, but who should not be able to change any of the tables, queries, or macros. In this project you will create a ***switchboard*** to provide controlled access to the objects in the Medical Center database. A switchboard is a form that displays when the database is opened and allows individuals to open only the objects that have been set up on the form.

In Activities 9.8 through 9.11, you will create, enhance, and run a switchboard to automate the Medical Center Database. You will save your database as *9B_Switchboard_Firstname_Lastname*.

Figure 9.26
Project 9B—Switchboard

Objective 5
Create a Switchboard Page

When you create a switchboard in Access, you are creating a new interface for individuals who use the database. People using the database will no longer have to navigate through all of the Access objects; they will be able to select the object to open directly from the switchboard.

Activity 9.8 Creating a Switchboard Page

In this activity, you will create a new switchboard page to be displayed when the Medical Center database is opened.

1 Using **My Computer**, navigate to the student files that accompany this textbook and locate the Access database **a09B_Switchboard**. Copy and paste the file to the Chapter 9 folder you created, and rename the file **9B_Switchboard_Firstname_Lastname** Remove the Read-only property from the file. Start Access and open the database you just renamed.

2 On the **Tools** menu, point to **Database Utilities**, and then click **Switchboard Manager**. See Figure 9.27.

Your database does not currently contain a switchboard. Thus, the Switchboard Manager displays a message indicating that a valid switchboard could not be found. After you create a switchboard, this message will not display.

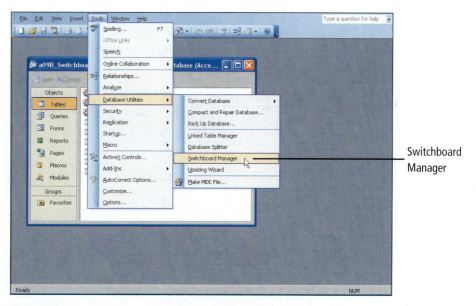

Figure 9.27

3 In the message box, click **Yes** to create a new switchboard.

When you create a new switchboard, a main switchboard is created and it is set as the default page. The default page is the switchboard page that initially displays when the database opens.

4 In the **Switchboard Manager** dialog box, click **Edit** to change the Main Switchboard. See Figure 9.28.

Project 9B: Switchboard | **Access**   571

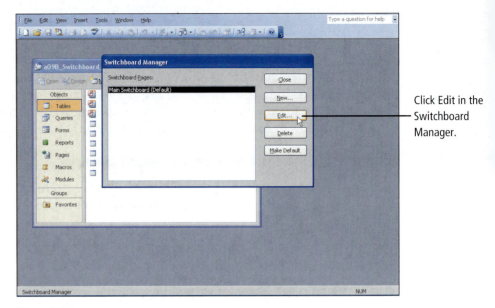

Figure 9.28

5. In the **Switchboard Name** box, type **Medical Center Switchboard**

   The name of the switchboard will display on the title bar of the switchboard. Changing the name will differentiate between the database and the switchboard.

6. Click **New** to add an item to the switchboard. See Figure 9.29.

   You will add shortcuts that will allow individuals to open the forms directly from the switchboard. Each shortcut must be added one at a time.

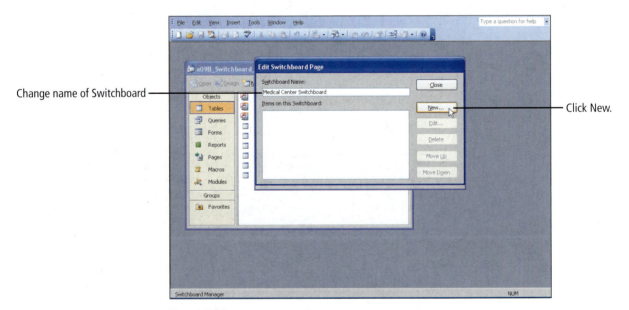

Figure 9.29

572   Access | Chapter 9: Macros and Switchboards

7 In the **Text** box, type **&Employee Training and Seminar Enrollments**

This text displays on the switchboard to indicate what the shortcut does. The & creates a keyboard accelerator, or keyboard shortcut, with the letter it precedes. The letter will be underlined on the switchboard. You can click the name of the shortcut on the switchboard to open the form; or, use the keyboard accelerator Alt + E to open the form.

8 Click the **Command arrow**, and then click **Open Form in Edit Mode**. Click the **Form arrow**, and then click **Employee Training and Seminar Enrollments**. Compare your dialog box with Figure 9.30. Click **OK**.

By opening a form in edit mode you can edit current records and add additional records to your database. When a form is opened in Add Mode, you can only add to records to the database.

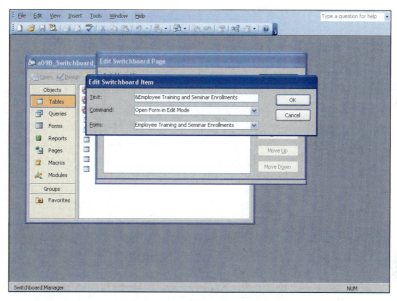

Figure 9.30

9 In the **Edit Switchboard Page** dialog box, add the remaining forms to the switchboard as follows, repeating Steps 6–8 to add switchboard items to each of the remaining forms: **Marketing Expenses**, **Media Contacts**, **Public Seminars**, and **Speakers**. For each **Text** box, type respectively:
&Marketing Expenses
Media &Contacts
&Public Seminars
&Speakers
Compare your switchboard with Figure 9.31.

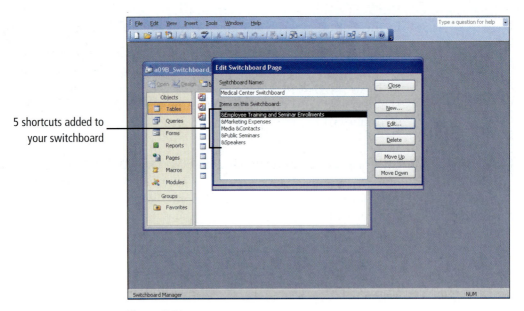

5 shortcuts added to your switchboard

Figure 9.31

10 In the **Edit Switchboard Page** dialog box, click **New** to add an additional item to your switchboard from which you can exit the application. In the **Text** box, type **E&xit Access** to create a keyboard accelerator Alt + X , because Alt + E was already used. In the **Command** box, type **Exit Application** Click **OK**, and then click **Close** to close the **Edit Switchboard Page** dialog box. Click **Close** to close the **Switchboard Manager** dialog box.

11 On the Objects bar, click **Forms**, and notice that an additional form has been added to your database named *Switchboard*. Double-click on the **Switchboard** form to open it.

Each of the shortcuts that you created displays in the switchboard. Notice the underlined letter in each shortcut. Recall that the ampersand (&) preceded the underlined letter when you typed the text in the Edit Switchboard Page dialog box.

12 Open each of the forms (except the *Exit Access* form) by clicking on the name of the form or by using the keyboard accelerator to be sure each of the items on your switchboard works properly. To use a keyboard accelerator, press and hold down Alt , and then press the underlined letter in the title. After you view a form, close it.

13 Close ❎ the **Switchboard** and leave the database open for the next activity.

Activity 9.9 Enhancing the Switchboard

In this activity, you will modify the layout and look of the switchboard in Design view.

1 On the Objects bar, be sure **Forms** is selected. Right-click the **Switchboard** form and click **Design View**. **Maximize** 🗖 the window.

Alert!

Editing the Switchboard Design

Editing the switchboard design is accomplished by editing the design just as you would any other form. When editing the switchboard design, it is important not to change any of the command buttons in the form. Changing the command buttons may cause the switchboard to function incorrectly.

2 In the title section of the form, click the label **9B_Switchboard_Firstname_Lastname**, and then press Delete. A second label was placed on the switchboard to create a shadow effect. Click the second label and press Delete.

3 If necessary, display the Toolbox toolbar. On the Toolbox toolbar click **Label**. Starting at the upper left corner of the title section, drag to the lower right corner of the title section to create a label just above the command buttons. See Figure 9.32.

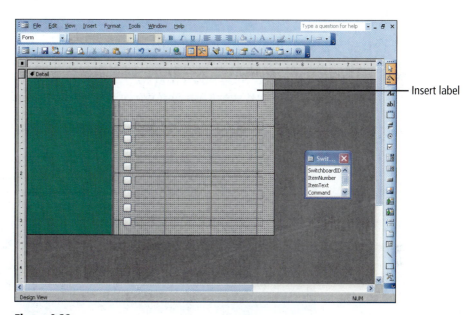

Figure 9.32

4 In the label, type **Medical Center** and press Enter. On the Formatting toolbar, click the **Font Size arrow**, and then click **24 point**. Click **Center** to center the title in the label. On the Formatting toolbar, click the **Font/Fore Color arrow**, and then in the fourth row, click the third color—**Yellow**. On the Formatting toolbar, click the **Special Effect arrow** and click **Special Effect: Shadowed**. Compare your form with Figure 9.33.

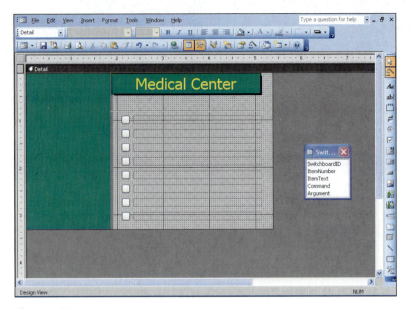

Figure 9.33

5 On the Toolbox toolbar, click the **Image** button . On the left border of the detail section, and at the **1-inch mark on the vertical ruler**, drag down and to the right to draw a box that extends to the **2-inch mark on the vertical ruler** and to the **1.75-inch mark on the horizontal ruler**. See Figure 9.34.

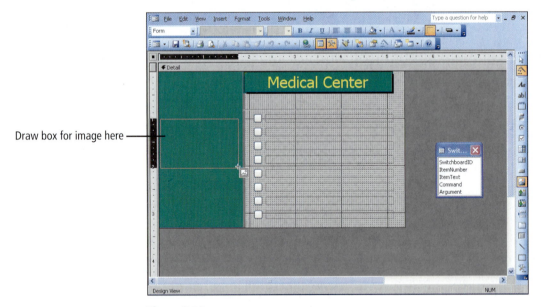

Draw box for image here

Figure 9.34

6 In the **Insert Picture** dialog box, navigate to your student files, and double-click the **a09_Medical.jpg** file to insert the picture into your form. Right-click the image and click **Properties**. On the **Format tab**, change the **Size Mode** to **Stretch**.

Remember that Stretch will enlarge or shrink an image to fit the box. It may distort a picture, whereas Zoom will keep the sizes in perspective.

7 **Close** the properties sheet. Switch to **Form View** to view your updated form. **Close** the form and save the changes, and leave the database open for the next activity.

Activity 9.10 Adding a Second Page to the Switchboard

In this activity, you will add a second page to your switchboard for your queries, macros, and reports.

1 On the **Tools** menu, point to **Database Utilities**, and then click **Switchboard Manager**.

2 Click **New**. In the **Switchboard Page Name** box, type **Queries, Macros and Reports** Click **OK**. Under **Switchboard Pages**, click **Queries, Macros and Reports**, and then click **Edit**. See Figure 9.35.

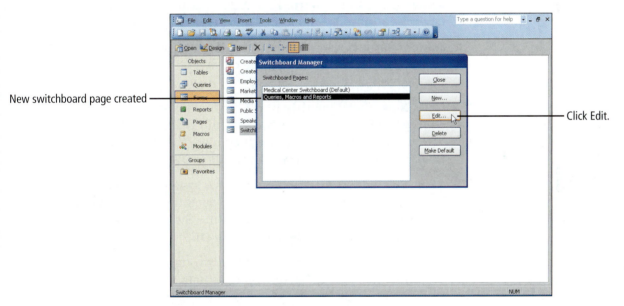

New switchboard page created

Click Edit.

Figure 9.35

3 Click **New** to add an item to your switchboard page. In the **Text** box, type **&Employment Training and Seminar Enrollments Report** Click the **Command arrow**, and then click **Open Report**. Click the **Report arrow**, and then click **Employee Training and Seminar Enrollments**. See Figure 9.36. Click **OK**.

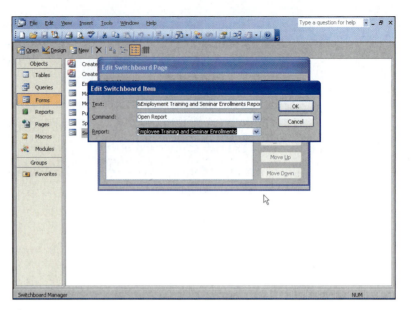

Figure 9.36

■4 In the **Edit Switchboard Page** dialog box, click **New**. In the **Text** box, type **&Seminars by Speaker Query** and then click the **Command arrow**. Click **Run Macro**, and then click the **Macro arrow**. Click **Open Seminars by Speaker Query**, and then click **OK**.

Switchboards do not have a run query command, so you must first create a macro that will run the query and then run the macro from the switchboard.

■5 Click **New** to add another new item to your switchboard. In the **Text** box, type **&Public Seminars by Date** and then click the **Command arrow**. Click **Run Macro**, and then click the **Macro** arrow. Click the **Public Seminars by Date** macro. Click **OK**.

■6 Click **New** to add the last item to your switchboard page. In the **Text** box, type **&Return to Main** and then click the **Command arrow**. Click **Go to Switchboard**, and then click the **Switchboard arrow**. Click **Medical Center Switchboard**. Click **OK**.

Because the user will be navigating through the database using the switchboards, you must set commands to navigate between the switchboards.

■7 In the **Edit Switchboard Page** dialog box, click **Close**. In the **Switchboard Manager** dialog box under **Switchboard Pages**, click **Medical Center Switchboard**, and then click **Edit**. Click **New** to add an item to your switchboard page. In the **Text** box type **&Open Queries, Macros and Reports Switchboard** Click the **Command arrow**, and then click **Go to Switchboard**. Click the **Switchboard arrow**, and then click **Queries, Macros and Reports**. Click **OK**.

The new switchboard item is added to the bottom of the Items on this Switchboard list. The switchboard is easier to use if the Exit Access option is the last option. Thus, the Open Queries, Macros and Reports Switchboard must be moved up in the list.

8 Click to select the **&Open Queries, Macros and Reports Switchboard** item, and then click **Move Up** to move the item above the E&xit Access item. See Figure 9.37.

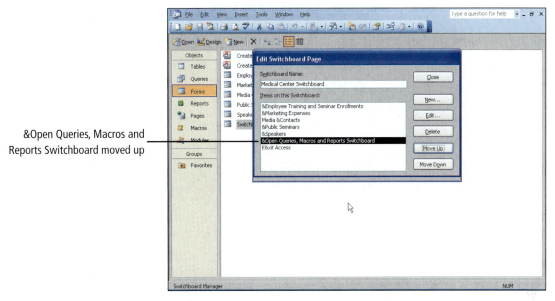

&Open Queries, Macros and Reports Switchboard moved up

Figure 9.37

9 Click **Close** to close the **Edit Switchboard Page** dialog box, and then click **Close** to close the Switchboard Manager. If necessary, on the Objects bar click the **Forms** object, and then double-click the **Switchboard** form. Click to test several of the switchboard items, but do not click the Exit Access item.

When you are finished, **Close** ⊠ the Switchboard. Leave the database open for the next activity.

Activity 9.11 Changing Switchboard Properties

Recall that one reason for creating a switchboard is to allow access to the reports and forms in a database. To limit individuals to Switchboard use, the Switchboard properties must be modified. In this activity, you will change the properties of your switchboard to prevent anyone from resizing the switchboard or closing the switchboard. You will also change the startup settings so that the switchboard will automatically display when the database opens.

1 On the Objects bar, be sure **Forms** is selected. Right-click the **Switchboard** form and click **Design View**.

2 In the upper left corner of the form to the left of the horizontal ruler, right-click the **Form selector**, and then click **Properties**. See Figure 9.38.

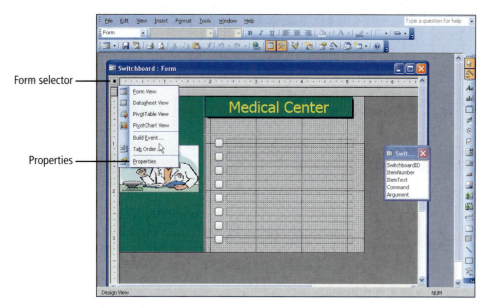

Figure 9.38

3 Click the **Format tab**, and then change the **Auto Resize** setting to **No**. Scroll the Format properties list, and then change the **Border Style** to **Dialog**. Scroll the Format properties list, and then change the **Close Button** to **No**.

The form will not be resized when the form opens and anyone using the form will not be able to resize or close the form.

4 **Close** the property sheet, and then **Close** ☒ the switchboard and save changes.

5 Double-click the **Switchboard** form to open it. Notice that the **Close** button ☒ and **Maximize** button ☐ are disabled. See Figure 9.39.

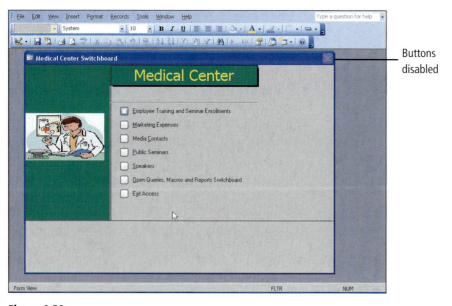

Figure 9.39

6 Press Ctrl + F4 to close the switchboard without closing the database.

The Close button is not active on the form, so you must use an alternative method to close the form without closing the database.

7 On the **Tools** menu, click **Startup**. Click the **Display Form/Page arrow**, and then click **Switchboard**. See Figure 9.40. Click **OK**.

By changing the startup properties, the Switchboard will start each time the database is opened.

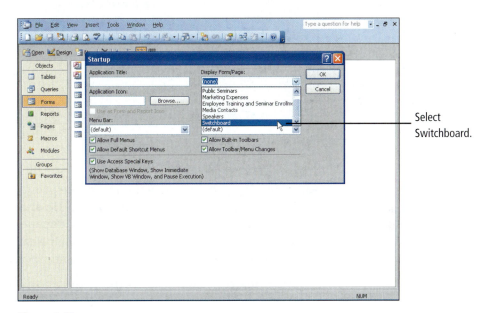

Figure 9.40

8 **Close** the database and leave Access open. On the Database toolbar click **Open** and from your Chapter 9 folder, double-click your **9B_Switchboard** database.

Notice that the switchboard displays when the database opens.

9 Press Ctrl + F4 to close the switchboard.

10 Click the **Reports** object. Double-click **Create report by using wizard**. Under **Tables/Queries** click **Table: Switchboard Items**. Move all the fields to the **Selected Fields** box by clicking the **All Fields** button. See Figure 9.41.

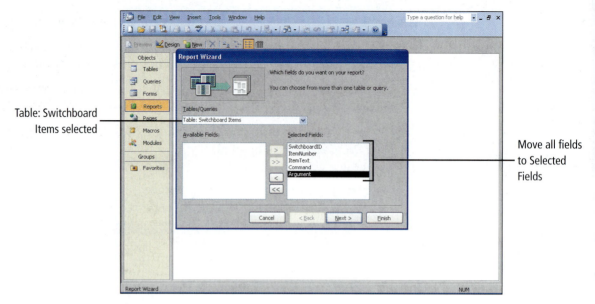

Figure 9.41

11 Click **Next**. None of the items will be grouped; click **Next**. None of the items will be sorted; click **Next**. Be sure the **Layout** is **Tabular** and change the **Orientation** to **Landscape**, and then click **Next**. Click the **Formal** style, and then click **Next**. Name the report **Switchboard Items Firstname Lastname** Click **Finish**.

The report will show all of the items on the switchboard on a single page.

12 On the **File** menu, click **Print**. Click **OK**. **Close** ⊠ the report and if necessary save your changes. **Close** ⊠ the database and close Access.

End You have completed Project 9B

Summary

Access provides a variety of ways to automate your work. In this chapter, you practiced creating, modifying, and running macros that opened reports and forms and that ran queries. You also created a Command Button in a form and attached a macro to the Command Button. You practiced creating a macro and running the macro in response to an event.

In this chapter, you also practiced creating and using a switchboard. A switchboard is a form that displays when the database is opened and allows you to open only the objects that have been set up on the form. You practiced enhancing a switchboard by adding a graphic and modifying some of the form controls on the switchboard. You also practiced changing the switchboard properties.

In This Chapter You Practiced How To

- View the Macro Window
- Create a New Macro
- Run a Macro in Response to an Event
- Create a Macro Group
- Create a Switchboard Page

Concepts Assessments

Matching Match each term in the second column with its correct definition in the first column. Write the letter of the term on the blank line to the left of the correct definition.

____ 1. A control tied to a field in an underlying table or query.

____ 2. A form that appears when the database is opened and allows you to open only the objects that have been set up on the form.

____ 3. Indicates the type of icon that will be displayed when a message box is displayed.

____ 4. Any significant action that can be detected by a system.

____ 5. Provides you with a way of performing an action by simply clicking on it.

____ 6. Additional information required by some macro actions that give Access additional information on how to carry out the action.

____ 7. A set of one or more actions.

____ 8. Allows you to see the conditions, actions, and argument values as each action is performed

____ 9. A window where you add commands in a step-by-step manner until you have completed your macro.

____ 10. Contains the text that will be displayed in the title bar of the message box.

A Action argument
B Bound control
C Command Button
D Event
E Macro
F Macro window
G Single step
H Switchboard
I Title argument
J Type argument

Concepts Assessments (continued)

Fill in the Blank Write the correct answer in the space provided.

1. Clicking a button, moving a mouse, or opening a form are examples of _____.

2. By changing the _____ settings you can set the switchboard to automatically display when the database opens.

3. The Message argument, Beep argument, Type argument, and Title argument are examples of _____.

4. A(n) _____ is the basic building block of a macro.

5. _____ are important when creating macros, because they describe what each action of your macro is doing.

6. _____ will enlarge or shrink an image to fit the box, but it may distort a picture.

7. A set of macros grouped together by a common name is called a _____.

8. Editing the switchboard design is done the same way as editing any other _____.

9. By opening a form in _____ mode you can modify current records and also add additional records to your database.

10. The _____ button is located on the upper left corner of the form in Design view and is used to select the form or change its properties.

Skill Assessments

Project 9C—Marketing Expenses

Objective: *Create a New Macro.*

In the following Skill Assessment, you will create a macro to run a Make Table query that creates a table of marketing expenses. The macro will then open a report to display the table. You will rename the database as *9C_Marketing_Expenses_Firstname_Lastname* in the folder you have created for this chapter. Your completed macro will look similar to Figure 9.42.

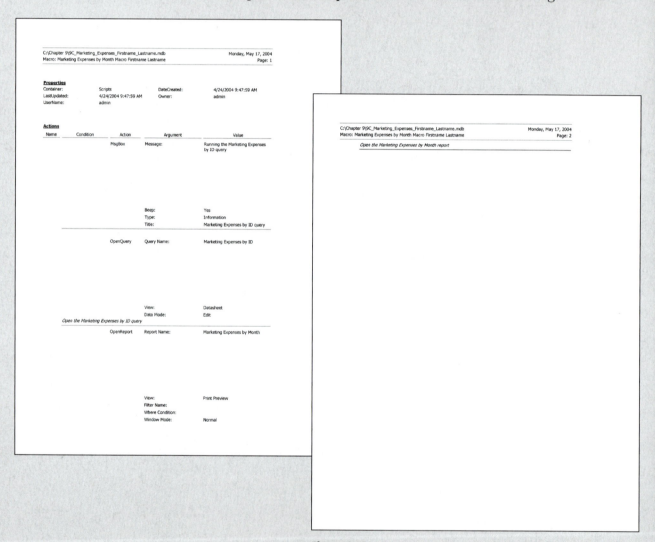

Figure 9.42

1. Locate the file **a09C_Marketing_Expenses** in your student files, and copy and paste the file to the Chapter 9 folder you created. Remove the Read-only property from the file and rename the file as **9C_Marketing Expenses_Firstname_Lastname** Start Access and open the database you just renamed. On the Objects bar, click **Macros**. On the Database toolbar, click **New**.

(**Project 9C**–Marketing Expenses continues on the next page)

Skill Assessments (continued)

(Project 9C–Marketing Expenses continued)

2. In the first box of the **Action** column, type **msgBox** Press F6 to move the insertion point to the **Action Arguments** section. In the **Message** box, type **Running the Marketing Expenses by ID query** Press Tab to move to the **Beep** box and leave **Yes** in the box. Press Tab again to move to the **Type** box. Click the **Type arrow**, and from the displayed list, click **Information**. Press Tab, and in the **Title** box type **Marketing Expenses by ID query** as the message box title.

3. Press F6 to move back to the **Action** column in the Macro window. Press Tab twice to move to the next **Action** box. In the second **Action** box, type **OpenQuery** and then press Tab. In the **Comment** column type **Open the Marketing Expenses by ID query**

4. Press F6. Click the **Query Name arrow** to display a list of existing queries, and then click **Marketing Expenses by ID**. Press Tab, click the **View arrow**, and then click **Datasheet**. Press Tab again, and then click the **Data Mode arrow** and click **Edit**.

5. Press F6 to move back to the **Comment** column in the Macro window. Press Tab to move to the next **Action** box. In the third **Action** box, type **OpenReport** and press Tab. In the **Comment** column type **Open the Marketing Expenses by Month report**

6. Press F6. Click the **Report Name arrow** to display a list of existing reports, and then click **Marketing Expenses by Month** report. Press Tab, click the **View arrow** and click **Print Preview**, and leave the default settings for the remaining three arguments.

7. On the Macro Design toolbar, click **Save**. Save the macro as **Marketing Expenses by Month Macro Firstname Lastname** and then click **OK**. On the Macro Design toolbar, click the **Run** button.

8. When the message box displays indicating the action that Access is taking, click **OK**. When the warning message box displays before creating the table, click **Yes**. In the second warning message box, click **Yes**.

9. In the **Enter the ID** box, type **5** to run a report for expense, type **5** and then click **OK**. In the displayed warning box, click **Yes** to paste a row into a new table. Preview the report. **Close** the report.

10. On the **File** menu, click **Print**. Be sure that **Properties** and **Actions and Arguments** are selected and that **Permissions by User and Group** is *not* selected. Click **OK**. **Close** the macro and **Close** Access.

End You have completed Project 9C

Skill Assessments (continued)

Project 9D—Medical Center Reports

Objective: *Create a Switchboard Page.*

In the following Skill Assessment, you will create a switchboard to allow the user to open and view the reports when the database opens. You will rename and save your database as 9D_*Medical_Center_Reports_Firstname_Lastname*. Your completed switchboard will look similar to Figure 9.43.

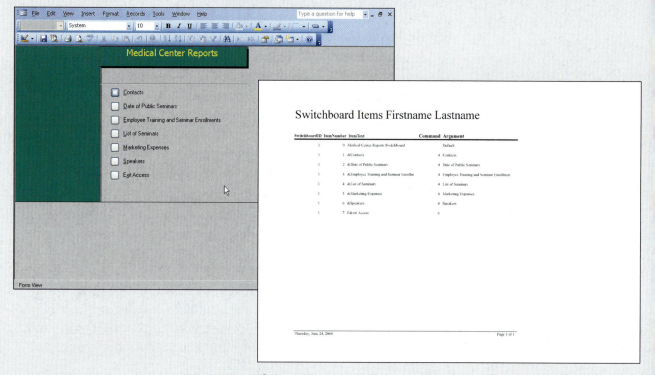

Figure 9.43

1. Locate the file **a09D_Medical_Center_Reports** in your student files, and copy and paste the file to the Chapter 9 folder you created. Remove the Read-only property from the file and rename the file **9D_Medical_Center_Reports_Firstname_Lastname** Start Access and open the database you just renamed.

2. On the **Tools** menu, point to **Database Utilities**, and then click **Switchboard Manager**. In the message box, click **Yes** to create a new switchboard.

3. In the **Switchboard Manager** dialog box, click **Edit** to change the Main Switchboard.

4. In the **Switchboard Name** box, type **Medical Center Reports Switchboard**

(**Project 9D**–Medical Center Reports continues on the next page)

Skill Assessments (continued)

(Project 9D–Medical Center Reports continued)

5. Click **New** to add an item to the switchboard.

6. In the **Text** box, type **&Contacts**

7. Click the **Command arrow**, and then click **Open Report**. Click the **Report arrow**, and then click the **Contacts** report. Click **OK**.

8. In the **Edit Switchboard Page** dialog box, repeat Steps 5–7 to add switchboard items to open the remaining reports: **Date of Public Seminars**, **Employee Training and Seminar Enrollments**, **List of Seminars**, **Marketing Expenses**, and **Speakers**. You will name your shortcuts **&Date of Public Seminars &Employee Training and Seminar Enrollments &List of Seminars &Marketing Expenses** and **&Speakers** respectively.

9. In the **Edit Switchboard Page** dialog box, click **New** to add an additional item to your switchboard. For the **Text** to display, type **E&xit Access** and then for the **Command**, click **Exit Application** Click **OK**, and then click **Close** to close the **Edit Switchboard Page** dialog box. Click **Close** to close the **Switchboard Manager** dialog box.

10. On the Objects bar click the **Forms** object button, if necessary. Double-click on the **Switchboard** form to open it.

11. Open each of the reports by clicking on the name of the report or by using the keyboard accelerator to be sure each of the items on your switchboard works properly. Recall that to use a keyboard accelerator, you can press [Alt] and the underlined letter in the title at the same time.

12. On the Form View toolbar, switch to **Design view**. From the upper part of the form, click the label **9D_Medical_Center_Reports_Firstname_Lastname** and press [Delete]. A second label was placed on the switchboard to create a shadow effect. Click the second label and press [Delete].

13. If necessary, display the Toolbox toolbar. On the Toolbox toolbar click **Label**. Starting at the upper left corner of the title section, drag to the lower right corner of the title section to create a label just above the command buttons.

14. In the label, type **Medical Center Reports** and press [Enter]. On the Formatting toolbar click the **Font Size arrow**, and then click **14**. Click **Center** to center the title in the label. Change the **Font/Fore Color** to **Yellow**. Click the **Special Effect arrow** and click **Shadowed**. Switch to **Form view** to examine your changes. **Close** the form and save your changes.

(Project 9D–Medical Center Reports continues on the next page)

Skill Assessments (continued)

(Project 9D–Medical Center Reports continued)

15. On the Objects bar click the **Reports** object. Double-click **Create report by using wizard**. Under **Tables/Queries** click **Table: Switchboard Items**. Move all the fields to the **Selected Fields** by clicking the **All Fields** button.

16. Click **Next**. None of the items will be grouped; click **Next**. None of the items will be sorted; click **Next**. Be sure the **Layout** is **Tabular** and change the **Orientation** to **Landscape**, and then click **Next**. Select the **Formal** style, then click **Next**. Name the report **Switchboard Items Firstname Lastname** Click **Finish**.

17. From the **File** menu, click **Print**. Click **OK**. **Close** the report and save your changes if necessary. **Close** the database.

End You have completed Project 9D

Skill Assessments (continued)

Project 9E—Macro Group

Objective: *Create a Macro Group.*

In the following Skill Assessment, you will create a macro group. You will create a macro to open each of the queries in the database and group them together in a group called Open Queries macro. Your completed macro will look similar to Figure 9.44. You will rename and save your database as *9E_Macro_Group_Firstname_Lastname*.

Figure 9.44

(**Project 9E**–Macro Group continues on the next page)

Skill Assessments (continued)

(Project 9E–Macro Group continued)

1. Locate the file **9E_Macro_Group** in your student files, and copy and paste the file to the Chapter 9 folder you created. Remove the Read-only property from the file and rename the file as **9E_Macro_Group_Firstname_Lastname** Start Access and open the database you just renamed.

2. On the Objects bar, click **Macros**, and from the Database window, click **New**.

3. On the Macro Design toolbar, click **Macro Names**.

4. In the first row under **Macro Name**, type **Florida Media** Press [Tab] and type **OpenQuery** and then press [Tab] and type **Open the Florida Media Contacts Query** Press [F6]. Click the **Query Name arrow**, click the **Florida Media Contacts Query**, and then press [Tab]. Click the **View arrow** and click **Print Preview**. Press [Tab], and then click the **Data Mode arrow** and click **Read Only**. Press [F6]. Press [Tab] two times to move to the second row of the macro.

5. Repeat Step 4 to add macros to open the remaining queries: **Speakers with Seminars Query**, **Total Marketing Expenses Query**, and the **Unpaid Enrollments** with the same Action Arguments.

6. On the Macro Design toolbar click **Save**. Name the macro **Open Queries** Click **OK**. **Close** the macro. From the **Tools** menu, point to **Macro**, and then click **Run Macro**. Click the **Macro Name arrow**.

7. Click the **Open Queries.Florida Media** macro and click **OK** to run the macro. **Close** the **Florida Media** query.

8. In the Database window, be sure the macro is selected. On the Database window toolbar, click Design to open the macro in Design view. From the **File** menu, click **Print**. Be sure **Properties** and **Actions and Arguments** are selected. Click **OK**. **Close** the macro and **Close** Access.

 You have completed Project 9E

Performance Assessments

Project 9F — Media Contacts

Objective: Create a Switchboard Page.

In the following Performance Assessment, you will enhance a switchboard page and change the properties of the switchboard. Your completed switchboard will look similar to Figure 9.45. You will rename and save your database as 9F_Media_Contacts_Firstname_Lastname.

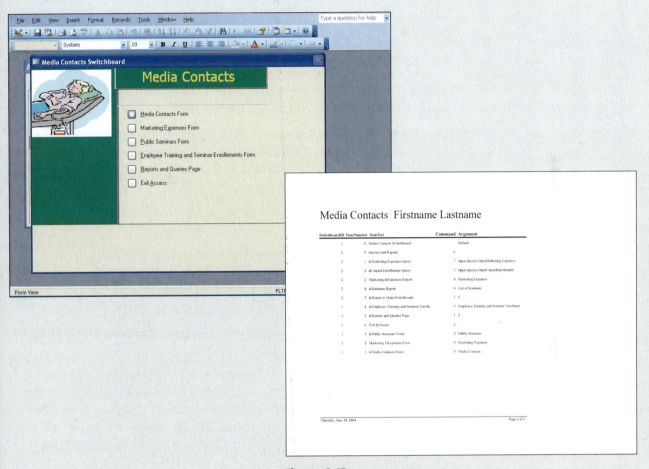

Figures 9.45

1. Locate the file **a09F_Media_Contacts** in your student files, and copy and paste the file to the Chapter 9 folder you created. Remove the Read-only property from the file and rename the file as **9F_Media_Contacts_Firstname_Lastname** Start Access and open the database you just renamed.

2. On the Objects bar, be sure **Forms** is selected. Double-click the **Switchboard** form, and then click **Reports and Queries Page** to view the second page of the switchboard. Switch to **Design view** and **Maximize** the window.

(**Project 9F**–Media Contacts continues on the next page)

Performance Assessments (continued)

(Project 9F–Media Contacts continued)

3. In the upper part of the form, click the label **a09F_Media_Contacts** and press Delete. Click the second label and press Delete. Be sure the Toolbox toolbar is displayed and on the Toolbox toolbar, click **Label**. Starting at the upper left corner of the title section, drag to the lower right corner of the title section to create a label just above the command buttons.

4. In the label, type **Media Contacts** and press Enter. Change the **Font Size**, to **22 point**, and then **Center** the label. Change the **Font/Fore Color** to **Yellow** and add a **Raised Special Effect**.

5. From the Toolbox toolbar, click the **Image** button. From the upper left corner of the form drag down to the **1.5-inch mark on the vertical ruler** and to the right to the **1.75-inch mark on the horizontal ruler** to make a box for the image.

6. In your student files, locate the **a09_Medical_Bed.jpg** file. Double-click the file to insert it into your form. Right-click the image and click **Properties**. On the **Format tab**, change the **Size Mode** to **Stretch**. **Close** the **Properties** box.

7. In the upper left corner of the form, right-click the **Form selector** and click **Properties**.

8. Click the **Format tab**, if necessary, and change the **Auto Resize** setting to **No**. Use the scroll bar to scroll down the properties and click the **Border Style arrow** and click **Dialog**. Scroll down and change the **Close Button** to **No**. Close the property sheet.

9. From the **Tools** menu click **Startup**. Click the **Display Form/Page arrow** and click **Switchboard**. Click **OK**.

10. **Close** the form and save the changes. **Close** the database and leave Access open. From the Database toolbar click **Open**. Navigate to find and open your **9F_Media_Contacts_Firstname_Lastname** database. Notice that the switchboard is automatically displayed when the database opens. Press Ctrl + F4 to close the switchboard without closing the database.

11. Click the **Reports** object. Double-click **Create report by using wizard**. Under **Tables/Queries** click **Table: Switchboard Items**. Move all the fields to the selected fields by clicking the **All Fields** button.

12. Click **Next**. None of the items will be grouped; click **Next**. None of the items will be sorted; click **Next**. Be sure the **Layout** is **Tabular** and change the **Orientation** to **Landscape**, and then click **Next**. Select the **Formal** style, then click **Next**. Name the report **Media Contacts Firstname Lastname** Click **Finish**.

13. From the **File** menu, click **Print**. Click **OK**. **Close** the report and save your changes if necessary. Close the database and close Access.

You have completed Project 9F

Performance Assessments (continued)

Project 9G—Conditional Expressions

Objective: *Run a Macro in Response to an Event.*

The Medical Center has $15,000 budgeted for each of the marketing expenses. In the following Performance Assessment, you will create a conditional expression to display an over budget control if more than $15,000 was spent on any marketing expense or hide the control if the amount is less than $15,000. Your completed macro will look similar to Figure 9.46. You will rename and save your database as *9G_Conditional_Expressions_Firstname_Lastname*.

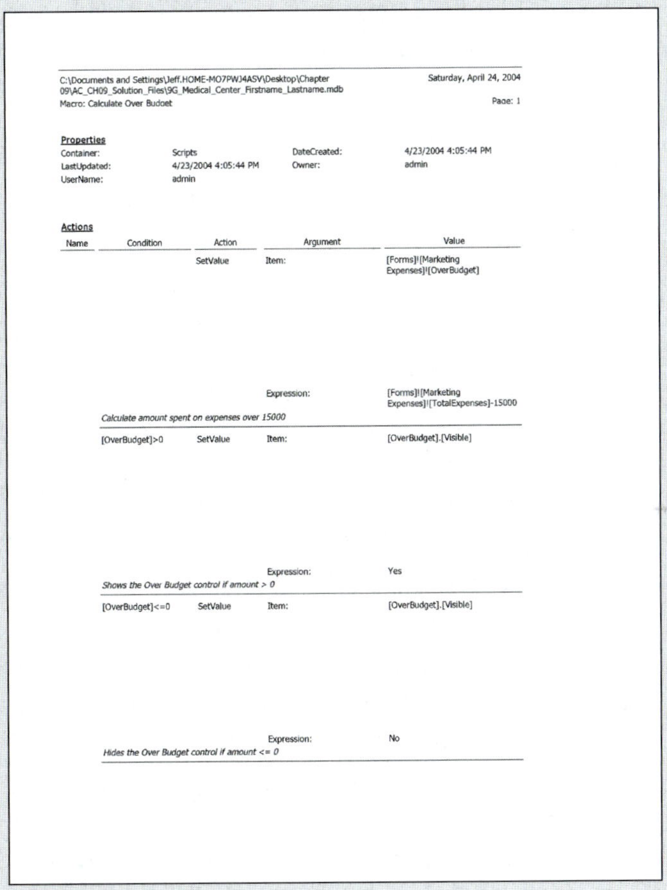
C:\Documents and Settings\Jeff.HOME-MO7PWJ4ASV\Desktop\Chapter 09\AC_CH09_Solution_Files\9G_Medical_Center_Firstname_Lastname.mdb — Saturday, April 24, 2004

Macro: Calculate Over Budget — Page: 1

Properties

Container:	Scripts	DateCreated:	4/23/2004 4:05:44 PM
LastUpdated:	4/23/2004 4:05:44 PM	Owner:	admin
UserName:	admin		

Actions

Name	Condition	Action	Argument	Value
		SetValue	Item:	[Forms]![Marketing Expenses]![OverBudget]
			Expression:	[Forms]![Marketing Expenses]![TotalExpenses]-15000
	Calculate amount spent on expenses over 15000			
	[OverBudget]>0	SetValue	Item:	[OverBudget].[Visible]
			Expression:	Yes
	Shows the Over Budget control if amount > 0			
	[OverBudget]<=0	SetValue	Item:	[OverBudget].[Visible]
			Expression:	No
	Hides the Over Budget control if amount <= 0			

Figure 9.46

1. Locate the file **a09G_Conditional_Expressions** in your student files, and copy and paste the file to the Chapter 9 folder you created. Remove the Read-only property from the file and rename the file as **9G_Conditional_Expressions_Firstname_Lastname** Start Access and open the database you just renamed.

(Project 9G–Conditional Expressions continues on the next page)

Performance Assessments (continued)

(Project 9G–Conditional Expressions continued)

2. On the Objects bar, if necessary, click the **Forms** object, and then double-click the **Marketing Expenses** form. Preview the 10 records and notice the Total Expense for the Year and the Over Budget controls. The Over Budget Control subtracts 15000 from the Total Expense for Year. Many of the Over Budget controls display negative numbers.

3. Now you will create a conditional expression for the **Calculate Over Budget** macro. On the Objects bar, click the **Macros** object. Right-click the **Calculate Over Budget** macro and click **Design View**. On the Macro Design toolbar click the **Conditions** button.

4. Under **Condition**, in the *second* row, type **[OverBudget]>0** Press Tab and type **SetValue** Press Tab and in the comment section type **Shows the Over Budget control if amount > 0**

5. Next you need to tell Access what to do if the OverBudget values are greater than 0. Press F6 to move to the **Action Arguments** and next to **Item** type **[OverBudget].[Visible]** Press Tab. Next to **Expression** type **Yes**

6. Next you will enter a test condition to look for OverBudget items that are less than or equal to 0. Press F6 to return to the Comment column. Press Tab to move to the next action row. In the first cell in the third row, type **[OverBudget]<=0** Press Tab and type **SetValue** Press Tab and in the comment section type **Hides the Over Budget control if amount <= 0** Press F6 to move to the **Action Arguments** and next to **Item** type **[OverBudget].[Visible]** Press Tab. Next to **Expression** type **No**

7. **Close** the macro and **Save** the changes.

8. On the Objects bar, click the **Forms** object. Double-click the **Marketing Expenses** form. Scroll through all the records and notice the **Over Budget** control only displays on the forms when the over budget amount in greater than zero. **Close** the form.

9. On the Objects bar, click **Macros**. Right-click the **Calculate Over Budget** macro and click **Design View**. From the **File** menu, click **Print**. Be sure **Properties** and **Actions and Arguments** are selected. Click **OK**. **Close** the macro and **Close** Access.

End You have completed Project 9G

Performance Assessments (continued)

Project 9H — Public Seminars

Objective: *Create a Switchboard Page.*

In the following Performance Assessment, you will create a new switchboard page. The switchboard will contain two pages. The first page will contain shortcuts to all of the forms, and the second page will display shortcuts to the queries in the database. Your completed switchboard page and printed report will look similar to Figure 9.47. You will rename and save your database as *9H_Public_Seminars_Firstname_Lastname*.

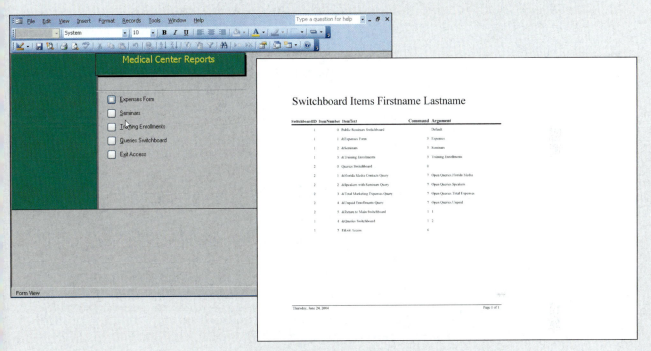

Figure 9.47

1. Locate the file **a09H_Public_Seminars** in your student files, and copy and paste the file to the Chapter 9 folder you created. Remove the Read-only property from the file and rename the file as **9H_Public_Seminars_Firstname_Lastname** Start Access and open the database you just renamed.

2. From the **Tools** menu, point to **Database Utilities**, and then click **Switchboard Manager**. In the message box, click **Yes** to create a new switchboard. In the **Switchboard Manager** dialog box, click **Edit** to change the Main Switchboard.

3. In the **Switchboard Name** box, change the name of the switchboard to **Public Seminars Switchboard**

4. Click **New** to add an item to the switchboard. In the **Text** box, type **&Expenses Form** Click the **Command arrow** and click **Open Form in Edit Mode**, then click the **Form arrow**, and then click the **Expenses** form. Click **OK**.

(**Project 9H**–Public Seminars continues on the next page)

Performance Assessments (continued)

(Project 9H–Public Seminars continued)

5. Repeat Step 4 to add shortcuts to the **Seminars** and the **Training Enrollments** forms. Name the shortcuts **&Seminars** and **&Training Enrollments** Open the forms in Edit Mode.

6. **Close** the **Edit Switchboard Page** dialog box. In the **Switchboard Manager**, click **New**. In the **Switchboard Page Name** box, type **Queries Switchboard** Click **OK**. In the **Switchboard Pages** list, double-click the **Queries Switchboard**.

7. In the **Edit Switchboard Page** dialog box, click **New**. In the **Text** box type **&Florida Media Contacts Query** Click the **Command arrow** and select **Run Macro**, and then click the **Macro arrow** and select **Open Queries.Florida Media**. Click **OK**.

8. In the **Edit Switchboard Page** dialog box, repeat Step 7 to add switchboard items to run the remaining queries: **Speakers with Seminars Query**, **Total Marketing Expenses Query**, **Florida Media Contacts Query**, **Speakers with Seminars Query**, and **Unpaid Enrollments Query**. You will name your shortcuts, respectively:

    &Speakers with Seminars Query

    &Total Marketing Expenses Query

    &Unpaid Enrollments Query

9. Click **New** to add the last item to your switchboard page. For the **Text** to display type **&Return to Main Switchboard** For the **Command** click **Go to Switchboard**, and for the **Switchboard** click the **Public Seminars Switchboard**. Click **OK**. Click **Close**.

10. In the **Switchboard Manager**, double-click the **Public Seminars Switchboard**. In the **Edit Switchboard Page** dialog box, click **New** to add an additional item to your switchboard. For the **Text** to display type **&Queries Switchboard** For the **Command** click **Go to Switchboard**, and for the **Switchboard** click the **Queries Switchboard**. Click **OK**.

11. Click **New**. In the **Text** box type **E&xit Access** and then for the **Command**, type **Exit Application** Click **OK**, and then click **Close** to close the **Edit Switchboard Page** dialog box. Click **Close** to close the **Switchboard Manager** dialog box.

12. On the Objects bar click the **Forms** object button, if necessary. Double-click the **Switchboard** form to open it.

13. Open each of the forms to be sure that each of the items on your switchboard pages works properly.

14. Switch to **Design view**. In the upper part of the form, click the label **9H_Public_Seminars_Firstname_Lastname** and press Delete. A second label was placed on the switchboard to create a shadow effect. Click the second label and press Delete.

(Project 9H–Public Seminars continues on the next page)

Performance Assessments (continued)

(Project 9H–Public Seminars continued)

15. Be sure the Toolbox toolbar is displayed and on the Toolbox toolbar click **Label**. Starting at the upper left corner of the title section, drag to the lower right corner of the title section to create a label just above the command buttons.

16. In the label, type **Medical Center Reports** and press . **Center** the label and change the **Font Size** to **14**. Change the **Font/Fore Color** to **Yellow** and add a **Shadowed Special Effect**. **Close** and save the form.

17. On the Objects bar click the **Reports** object. Double-click **Create report by using wizard**. Under **Tables/Queries** click **Table: Switchboard Items**. Move all the fields to the **Selected Fields** by clicking the **All Fields** button.

18. Click **Next**. None of the items will be grouped; click **Next**. None of the items will be sorted; click **Next**. Be sure the **Layout** is **Tabular** and change the **Orientation** to **Landscape**, and then click **Next**. Select the **Formal** style, and then click **Next**. Name the report **Switchboard Items Firstname Lastname** Click **Finish**.

19. From the **File** menu, click **Print**. Click **OK**. **Close** the report and save your changes if necessary. **Close** the database.

End You have completed Project 9H

Mastery Assessments

Project 9I—Speakers

Objectives: *Create a Macro Group and Create a Switchboard Page.*

In the following Mastery Assessment, you will create a macro group to run each of the queries in the Speakers database. You will use the macro group to add the shortcuts to your queries on a switchboard page along with the forms and reports. Your completed switchboard and printed table will look similar to Figure 9.48. You will rename and save your database as *9I_Speakers_Firstname_Lastname*.

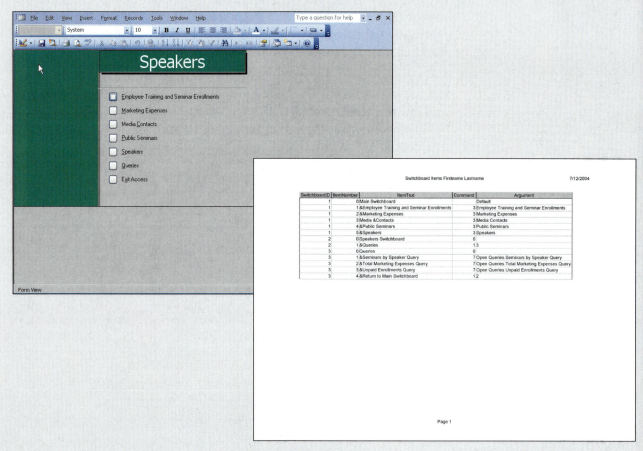

Figure 9.48

1. Locate the file **a09I_Speakers** in your student files, and copy and paste the file to the Chapter 9 folder you created. Remove the Read-only property from the file and rename the file as **9I_Speakers_Firstname_Lastname** Start Access and open the database you just renamed.

2. On the Objects bar, click **Macros**, and then in the Database window click **New**. From the Macro Design toolbar, click **Macro Names**. **Maximize** the window.

(**Project 9I**–Speakers continues on the next page)

Mastery Assessments (continued)

(Project 9I–Speakers continued)

3. In the first **Macro Name** box, type **Seminars by Speaker Query** In the first **Action** box, type **OpenQuery** and then in the first **Comment** box type **Run Seminars by Speaker Query** Move down to the Action Arguments for this macro. For the **Query Name** click **Seminars by Speaker** and be sure the **View** is **Datasheet** and the **Data Mode** is **Edit**.

4. Using the technique above, create new macros in the group that will run the **Total Marketing Expenses Query** and the **Unpaid Enrollments Query**.

5. Save the Macro Group as **Open Queries** and **Close** the Macro window.

6. Display the **Switchboard Manager**.

7. Create a new switchboard and name the switchboard page **Speakers Switchboard**, click **OK**, select the new switchboard, and then click **Edit**.

8. Click **New**. In the **Text** box, type **&Employee Training and Seminar Enrollments** and click the **Command arrow**. Click **Open Form in Edit Mode**, click the **Form arrow**, and then click the **Employee Training and Seminar Enrollments** form. Click **OK**.

9. Repeat Step 8 and add the remaining four forms to your switchboard page (do not include the Switchboard form). Name the shortcuts:

    &Marketing Expenses

    Media &Contacts

    &Public Seminars

    &Speakers

10. **Close** the **Edit Switchboard Page** dialog box. Click **New** to add a second switchboard page and name the page **Queries** Click **OK**. In the **Switchboard Pages** list, click **Queries**. Click **Edit**.

11. Click **New** to add a shortcut to your page. In the **Text** box type **&Seminars by Speaker Query** Click the **Command arrow** and click **Run Macro**, and then click the **Macro arrow** and click **Open Queries.Seminars by Speaker Query**. Click **OK**.

12. Repeat Step 11 to add the remaining two macros from your macro group. Name the shortcuts **&Total Marketing Expenses Query** and **&Unpaid Enrollments Query**

13. Click **New**. In the **Text** box, type **&Return to Main Switchboard** Be sure that the **Command** box displays **Go to Switchboard**, and then click the **Switchboard arrow** and click **Speakers Switchboard**. Click **OK**. **Close** the **Edit Switchboard Page**.

(Project 9I–Speakers continues on the next page)

Mastery Assessments (continued)

(Project 9I–Speakers continued)

14. If necessary, click the **Speakers Switchboard**, and then click **Edit**. Add a new shortcut to the switchboard page to open the **Queries** switchboard page. In the textbox type **&Queries**

15. On the **Speaker Switchboard**, add a shortcut to exit Access. Click **New**, and then in the **Text** box type **E&xit Access** and in the **Command** box click **Exit Application**. Click **OK**. **Close** the Switchboard Manager.

16. On the Objects bar, click **Forms**. Open the Switchboard in **Design view** and change the title to **Speakers**. Change the to **Font Size** to **26 point**, change the **title** to **White**, and then **Center** and add a **Shadowed** effect. Switch to **Form view** and test each of the shortcuts on the Switchboard pages. **Close** the Switchboard and save the changes.

17. On the Objects bar, click **Tables**. Right-click the **Switchboard Items** table, click copy and then paste the new table with the structure and data. As the table name, type **Switchboard Items Firstname Lastname** Open the table. Select all of the columns. From the **Format** menu, click **Column Width**, and then click **Best Fit**.

18. From the **File** menu, click **Page Setup**. Click the **Page tab** and change the **Orientation** to **Landscape**. **Print** the table. Close the table and save your changes. **Close** the database and close Access. If necessary, clear the Office Clipboard.

 You have completed Project 9I

Mastery Assessments (continued)

Project 9J—Macros

Objectives: *Create a New Macro and Run a Macro in Response to an Event.*

In the following Mastery Assessment, you will create a macro to open the Public Seminars table, and then you will attach the macro to a command button in the Speakers form. Your completed form will look similar to Figure 9.49. You will rename and save your database as *9J_Macros_Firstname_Lastname*.

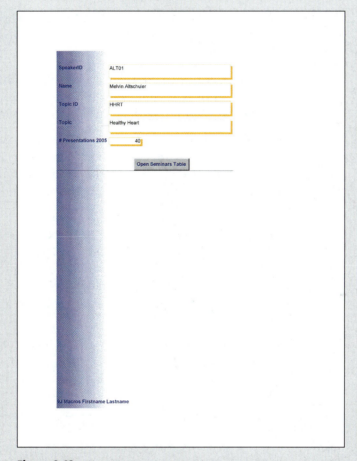

Figure 9.49

1. Locate the file **a09J_Macros** in your student files, and copy and paste the file to the Chapter 9 folder you created. Remove the Read-only property from the file and rename the file as **9J_Macros_Firstname_Lastname** Start Access and open the database you just renamed.

(*Project 9J*–Macros continues on the next page)

Mastery Assessments (continued)

(Project 9J–Macros continued)

2. On the Objects bar, click **Macros**, and then in the Database window click **New**. In the first action box, type **OpenTable** and in the first **Comment** box, type **Open the Public Seminars Table** Press to move to the **Action Arguments**.

3. In the **Table Name** box, click **Public Seminars** and leave the **View** set to **Datasheet** and the **Data Mode** set to **Edit**.

4. Save the macro as **Open Public Seminars Table** and close the macro. On the Objects bar, click **Forms**.

5. Open the **Speakers** form in **Design view**. **Maximize** the window. Extend the **Detail section** down to the **2.5-inch mark on the vertical ruler**.

6. From the Toolbox toolbar, click **Command Button**. Move the mouse pointer to approximately **2.25 inches on the vertical ruler** and **2 inches on the horizontal ruler**, and then click.

7. In the **Categories** list, click **Miscellaneous** and from the **Actions** list, click **Run Macro**. Click **Next**. The **Open Public Seminars Table** is highlighted. Click **Next**. In the **Text** box type **Open Seminars Table** Click **Next**. Name the Command Button **Run Public Seminar Macro** Click **Finish**.

8. From the **View** menu, click **Page Header/Footer**. From the Toolbox toolbar, click **Label**. In the **Page Footer**, drag the label from the upper left area of the footer to the lower right area of the footer. In the label, type **9J Macros Firstname Lastname** Switch to **Form view** and click the **Open Seminars Table** command button. **Close** the table.

9. On the **File** menu, click **Print**. Under **Print Range**, select **Selected Record(s)**. Click **OK**. Close your form and save the changes. Close the database, and then close Access.

End You have completed Project 9J

Problem Solving

Project 9K—Multiple Switchboards

Objective: *Create a Switchboard Page.*

In the following Problem Solving exercise, you will create a Switchboard with multiple pages.

1. Locate the file **a09K_Multiple_Switchboards** in your student files, and copy and paste the file to the Chapter 9 folder you created. Remove the Read-only property from the file and rename the file as **9K_Multiple_Switchboards_Firstname_Lastname** Start Access and open the database you just renamed.

2. Open the different objects in the database and examine all of the tables, forms, and queries.

3. Create multiple Switchboard pages to organize all of the objects in your database. (Hint: You will have to create macros to open each of the tables and queries first.)

4. Enhance the Switchboard by adding a graphic and changing the title.

5. Change the Startup options so the Switchboard will display when the database opens.

6. Make a copy of the Switchboard Items table and name the table **Switchboard Items Firstname Lastname** Print the table.

7. Close the table, saving any changes. Close the database, and then close Access.

End You have completed Project 9K

Problem Solving (continued)

Project 9L—Conditional Macro

Objective: *Run a Macro in Response to an Event.*

The Medical Group is currently only using URLs for the Magazines media. In the following Problem Solving exercise, you will create a macro with a conditional expression to display the media URL in the Media Contacts form only if the media type is a magazine.

1. Locate the file **a09L_Conditional Macro** in your student files, and copy and paste the file to the Chapter 9 folder you created. Remove the Read-only property from the file and rename the file as **9L_Conditional_Macro_Firstname_Lastname** Start Access and open the database you just renamed.

2. Open the **Media Contacts** form and view the controls. You will create a conditional expression that will check the media type for each record to see if it is a magazine. Add a URL control and a URL label. Hide or display the **URL** and **URL_Label** controls if the **Type** is equal to **Magazine**.

3. Create a macro with conditional statements. Go back to the form and change the events so the macro will run when the form opens and when the Type is updated.

4. Add your name in the page footer of the form. Print page 2 of the forms, and then close the form, saving any changes. **Close** the database, and then close Access.

End You have completed Project 9L

On the Internet

Getting More Information About Macros

The Microsoft Web page contains a variety of information about macros in Access. Go to the Microsoft site at **www.microsoft.com** and click Search. Search for Access macros and examine the information on macros. Print any information that is of interest to you.

GO! with Help

Debugging Macros

In this chapter you created and ran macros. If the macro does not run the way you planned, you will need to debug the macro. In this Help activity, you will use Help to learn ways to help you debug a macro.

1. Start Access. In the *Type a question for help* box, type **debug macro** and press Enter.
2. In the **Search Results** task pane, click **Troubleshoot macros**.
3. Click each of the links to expand the information on the screen. Read each of the steps in debugging a macro.
4. Print the Help information if you want to keep a copy of it. Close the Help window, and then close Access.

Access 2003

chapter ten
Access Tools

In this chapter, you will: complete these projects and practice these skills.

Project 10A **Creating a Database with a Wizard**	**Objective** • Use the Database Wizard
Project 10B **Using Access Tools**	**Objectives** • Analyze Data with the Table Analyzer • Use the Performance Analyzer • Manage and Secure a Database
Project 10C **Replicating a Database**	**Objective** • Create a Replica of a Database

Oceana Palm Grill

Oceana Palm Grill is a chain of 25 upscale, casual, full-service restaurants based in Austin, Texas. The company opened its first restaurant in 1975 and now operates 25 outlets in the Austin and Dallas areas. Plans call for 15 additional restaurants to be opened in North Carolina and Florida by 2008. These ambitious plans will require the company to bring in new investors, develop new menus, and recruit new employees, all while adhering to the company's strict quality guidelines and maintaining its reputation for excellent service.

© Getty Images, Inc.

Access Tools

Microsoft Access 2003 provides several tools that you can use to improve the performance and security of your database. You can save space by eliminating duplicate data and you can improve performance by preventing inconsistent data. Additionally, you can restrict access to database information or functions in order to protect the integrity of your database, thus ensuring that your data is accurate.

10A Project 10A New Contacts

The Oceana Palm Grill is planning to open 15 new restaurants by 2008. In order to manage the new restaurant contacts, you will create a new database for Felicia Mabry, President of Oceana Palm Grill.

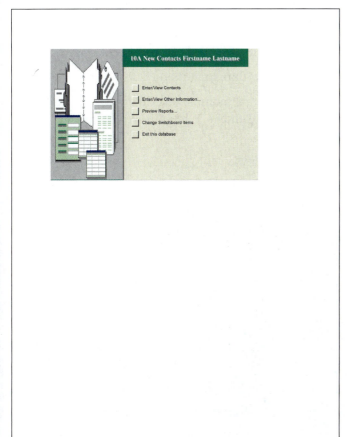

In Activity 10.1, you will create a new database using the Database Wizard. You will save your database as *10A_New_Contacts_Firstname_Lastname*. See Figure 10.1.

Figure 10.1
Project 10A—New Contacts

Objective 1
Use the Database Wizard

When creating a new database, you can save time by using the **Database Wizard**. The Database Wizard allows you to choose and customize a built-in template. The wizard walks you through the steps necessary to create a set of tables, queries, forms, and reports, and a switchboard for the database. You can use this method to create a database if one of the built-in templates closely matches your requirements.

Activity 10.1 Using the Database Wizard

In this activity, you will create a new database using the Database Wizard.

1. Start Access and on the Database toolbar, click **New**. In the **New File** task pane, under **Templates**, click **On my computer**. See Figure 10.2.

    The Templates dialog box displays.

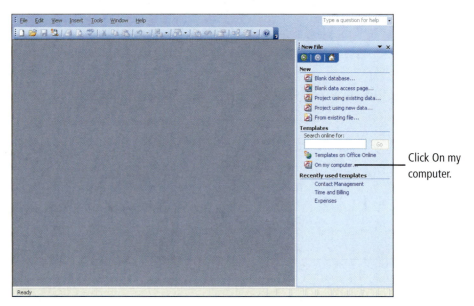

Figure 10.2

2. Click the **Databases tab**.

    In this dialog box, you can choose the template that is most similar to the type of database that you want to create.

3. Click the **Contact Management** template, and then click **OK** to display the **File New Database** dialog box. Navigate to your storage location, create a new folder for Chapter 10, and then name the database **10A_New_Contacts_ Firstname_Lastname** Click **Create**.

    The Database Wizard dialog box displays the data to be stored in the database. In the Contact Management template, the data includes Contact and Call information.

4 Click **Next** to display the second dialog box.

Notice that under *Tables in the database*, three tables display. Under *Fields in the table*, the required and optional fields associated with the selected table display.

5 If necessary, under **Tables in the database**, click **Contact information**. Scroll the **Fields in the table** list to view all of the fields.

The selected fields are required in the database. The optional fields are not selected and display in italic. See Figure 10.3.

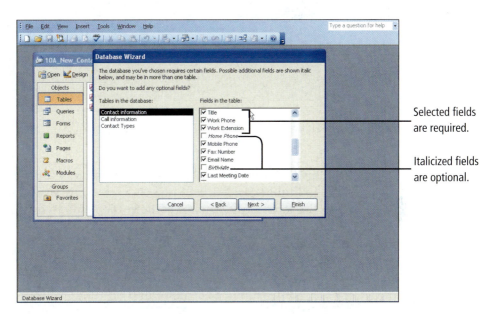

Figure 10.3

More Knowledge — Adding Optional Fields to Tables Using the Database Wizard

The optional fields that display in the *Fields in the table* list can be added to the table by selecting the field check box. To add the field, be sure to click the check box, not the field name.

---

6 Click **Next** to display a list of screen styles that determine the way that forms will display in your database. Click each style to view the available screen displays, and then click **Blends**. Click **Next** to display a list of printed report styles. Click **Corporate**, and then click **Next**. In the **What would you like the title of the database to be?** box, type **10A New Contacts Firstname Lastname** using your own first and last name. If necessary, clear the **Yes, I'd like to include a picture** check box. Click **Next**. Verify that the **Yes, start the database** check box is selected, and then click **Finish**.

The Database Wizard creates the tables, reports, and forms, and the Objects window is minimized, displaying the Main Switchboard. Recall that a switchboard is a user-friendly form that provides a way to access all of the tables, forms, queries, and reports in your database. See Figure 10.4.

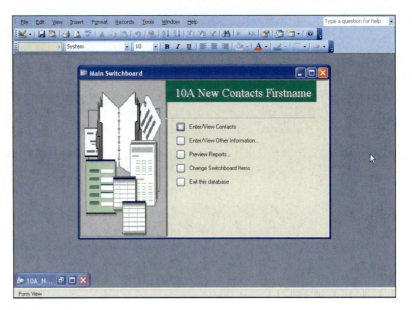

Figure 10.4

7 Click each of the switchboard options to navigate through the different tables, forms, and reports created by the wizard. Notice the tables, forms, and reports contain the fields that you selected from the wizard. Do not exit the database.

8 On the Form view toolbar, click **Design View**, and then **Maximize** the form. Click the title label **10A New Contacts Firstname Lastname** and on the Formatting toolbar, click the **Font Size arrow**, and then click **12**. Click **Bold**.

Notice that a second label forms a shadow effect behind the title.

9 Press Shift + Tab to select the second label. On the Formatting toolbar, click the **Font Size** arrow, and then click **12**. Click **Bold**. See Figure 10.5.

Change Font Size to 12.

Apply Bold.

Select label.

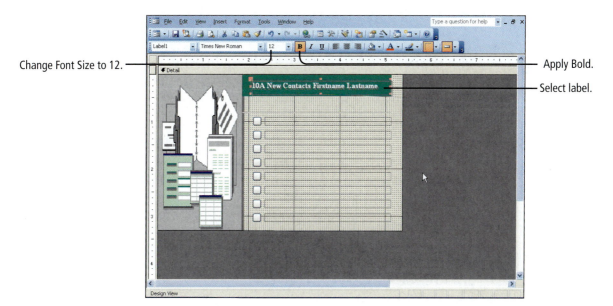

Figure 10.5

10 On the Form view toolbar, click **Form view**. From the **File** menu, click **Print**. Click **OK** to print the form. **Close** the form, click **Yes** to save the changes, and **Close** the database.

End **You have completed Project 10A**

Project 10B Security

Microsoft Access 2003 includes a number of tools that you can use to improve the performance of your database. You can also apply security and protection features that will ensure the integrity of your data.

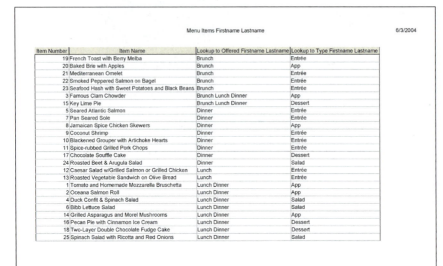

In Activities 10.2 through 10.5, you will analyze your database to improve its performance and you will set security levels to protect your data. You will save your database as *10B_Security_Firstname_Lastname*. See Figure 10.6.

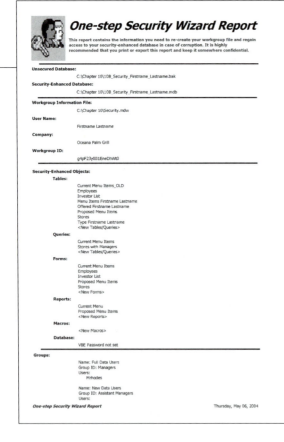

Figure 10.6
Project 10B—Security

Objective 2
Analyze Data with the Table Analyzer

You can improve the performance of your database and prevent data errors by using the *Table Analyzer*. The Table Analyzer divides a table that has repeated information into separate tables so that each type of information is stored only once. This process improves database efficiency, makes it easier to update, and reduces database size.

Activity 10.2 Using the Table Analyzer

In this activity, you will use the Table Analyzer to eliminate repeated information and split the Current Menu Items table into three more efficient tables.

1 Using **My Computer**, navigate to the student files that accompany this textbook and locate the Access database **a10B_Security**. Copy and paste the file to the Chapter 10 folder you created, and rename the file **10B_Security_Firstname_Lastname** Remove the Read-only property from the file. Start Access and open the database you just renamed.

2 If necessary, click the **Tables** object, and double-click the **Current Menu Items** table to open it. **Maximize** the table and examine the **Offered On Menu** and **Category** fields. Notice the duplicate names under these two fields. See Figure 10.7. **Close** the table. Notice there are currently five tables in your database.

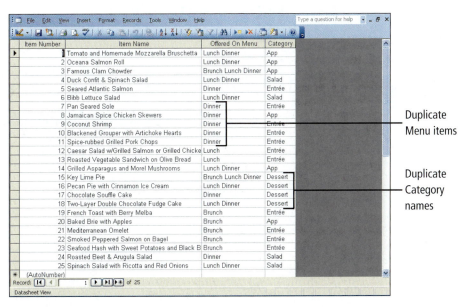

Figure 10.7

3 On the **Tools** menu, point to **Analyze**, and then click **Table** to start the Table Analyzer Wizard. Read the first page of the Table Analyzer Wizard, which describes potential problems associated with duplicate table information. Click each of the **Show me an example** buttons. Read the information boxes that display, and then close each box.

Project 10B: Security | **Access** **617**

Another Way

To Start the Table Analyzer

You can also start the Table Analyzer from a toolbar. On the Database toolbar, click the Analyze arrow, and then click Analyze Table.

4 Click **Next** to display the second page of the Table Analyzer Wizard, which describes how the Table Analyzer solves the problem of duplicate data. Read the second page of the wizard, and then click each of the **Show me an example** buttons. Read the information boxes that display, and then close each box.

5 Click **Next**.

In this step, you must identify the table that contains fields with values that are repeated in many records.

6 If necessary, click **Current Menu Items**, and then click **Next**. Verify that the **Yes, let the wizard decide** option button is selected. Click **Next**.

The Table Analyzer examines the table, looks for repeated information, and then splits the table into multiple tables where the information will be stored only once. If the information needs to be updated, you need only update it in one location. In this instance, the wizard determined that the *Offered On Menu* and *Category* fields have repeated information. The wizard will set up the tables and the one-to-many relationships between the tables. Additionally, the wizard creates a primary key for both new tables, called **Generated Unique ID.** See Figure 10.8.

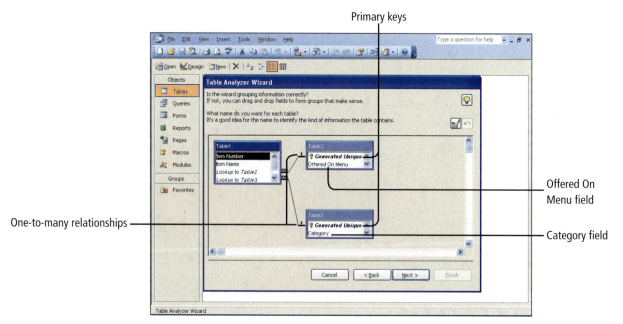

Figure 10.8

7 Double-click on the **Table1** title bar to display the **Table Analyzer Wizard** dialog box, in which you can change the table name. In the **Table Name** box, type **Menu Items Firstname Lastname** and then click **OK**. Repeat the process to change the name of **Table2** to **Offered Firstname Lastname** and **Table3** to **Type Firstname Lastname**

Each of the tables is renamed and the Lookup fields from the Menu table are updated. See Figure 10.9.

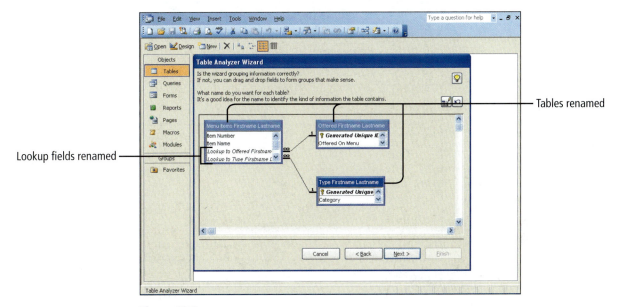

Figure 10.9

8 Click **Next**.

On this page of the wizard, you can change the primary key in the proposed tables. In this case, you will accept the Generated Unique ID fields created by the wizard.

9 Click **Next**. On the last page of the wizard, verify that the **Yes, create the query** option is selected. Click **Finish**, noticing that the Microsoft Office Access Help window displays, describing the query created

by the Table Analyzer. Read the Help page, and then **Close** ⊠ the Help window.

The query displays fields from all three tables and allows you to work with the data in one location, just as you did before in the table. To change the data, open the query and enter, update, or delete data the same way you did in the original table. When you change a repeated field in the query, the rest of the fields will automatically be updated in the tables. Any forms or reports that were dependent on the original table will automatically be converted to be dependent on the query.

10 **Close** the query.

11 On the **Objects** bar, if necessary, click **Tables**.

Notice that three new tables have been added to the list: **Menu Items Firstname Lastname**, **Offered Firstname Lastname**, and **Type Firstname Lastname**. Also, the name of the original table has been changed to **Current Menu Items_OLD**. See Figure 10.10.

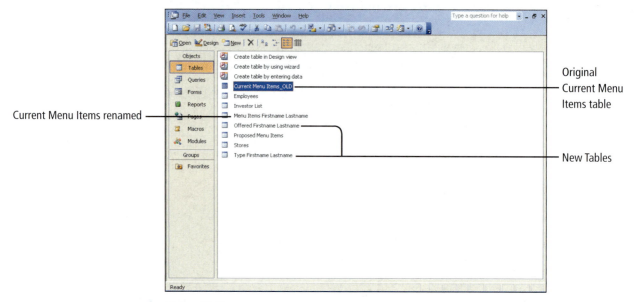

Figure 10.10

12 Double-click your **Type** table to open it. In the first row next to **App**, click the **Expand** button to view all the appetizers from your **Menu Items** table. **Close** the table.

13 Double-click your **Offered** table to open it. In the first row next to **Brunch**, click the **Expand** button to view all the brunch items from your **Menu Items** table. **Close** the table.

14 Double-click your **Menu Items** table to open it. Move the mouse pointer to the **Item Number** field title so that the down-pointing black arrow displays. Press and hold down the left mouse button and drag to the right to select all of the columns. On the **Format** menu, click **Column Width**. In the **Column Width** dialog box, click **Best Fit**.

Each column is resized to accommodate the largest entry or field name.

15 On the **File** menu, click **Page Setup**. Click the **Margins tab**, if necessary, and under **Margins**, next to **Left** type **0.5** and then next to **Right** type **0.5** Click the **Page tab**, and then under **Orientation**, click **Landscape**. Click **OK**. From the **File** menu, click **Print**. Click **OK**. **Close** the table, click **Yes** to save the changes to the layout, and leave the database open for the next activity.

Objective 3
Use the Performance Analyzer

In the previous activity, you ran the Table Analyzer to examine a specific table. Microsoft Access 2003 includes another tool called the ***Performance Analyzer***. The Performance Analyzer evaluates objects in your database and makes suggestions on how you might improve the performance of your database. You can select the objects you want to analyze and the Performance Analyzer will provide three different types of advice: ***Recommendations***, ***Suggestions***, and ***Ideas***. Recommendations are marked with a red exclamation point and point out ways that your database can be optimized. Suggestions are indicated by a question mark and provide possible ways to improve the performance of the database. Ideas are marked with a light bulb and offer additional tips for enhancing performance. Access can perform Recommendation and Suggestion optimizations for you. You must perform Idea optimizations yourself. By following these steps in the Performance Analyzer, you may find ways to improve the performance of your database and get ideas to help you design future databases.

Activity 10.3 Using the Performance Analyzer

In this activity, you will use the Performance Analyzer to improve the performance of your database.

1 On the **Tools** menu, point to **Analyze**, and then click **Performance**.

Another Way

To Start the Performance Analyzer

You can also start the Performance Analyzer from a toolbar. On the Database toolbar click the Analyze arrow, and then click Analyze Performance.

2 Click the **All Object Types tab**, and then click **Select All** to select all the objects in the database. See Figure 10.11. Click **OK**.

In the Analysis Results section of the Performance Analyzer dialog box, three items display. To the left of each item, an icon displays indicating the type of advice suggested by Performance Analyzer, and a key to the icons displays below the Analysis Results. In this case, the three light bulbs indicate that the three items are Ideas. In the lower section of the dialog box, the Analysis Notes display information about the proposed optimization.

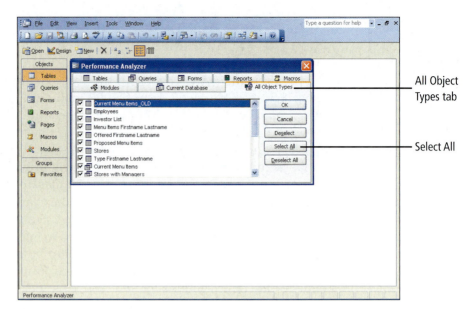

Figure 10.11

[3] In the **Analysis Results** section, click on each idea and read the Analysis Notes at the bottom of the dialog box. See Figure 10.12.

Recall that you must perform Idea optimizations yourself. Thus, the Optimize button is not available. Remember, the ideas are generated by the wizard and it may not be possible to use all of the ideas. In this example, the Investor List table does not contain any related fields so a relationship cannot be made to another table.

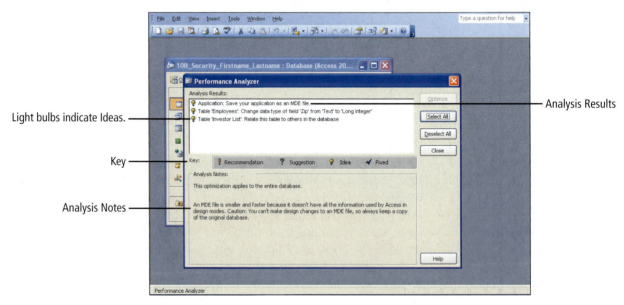

Figure 10.12

> **More Knowledge** — MDE Files
>
> The first Idea displayed in the Analysis Results section is *Save your application as an MDE file*. An MDE file compiles all modules, removes all editable source code, and compacts the destination database. Once a file is saved as an MDE file you will not be able to view, modify, or create forms, reports, or modules in Design view; add, delete, or change references to object libraries or databases; change code; or import or export forms, reports, or modules. You can, however, continue to update data and run reports.

4 **Close** the Performance Analyzer.

5 Right-click the **Employees** table and on the shortcut menu, click **Design View**. Locate the **Zip** field, and then click in the Data Type column. Click the **Data Type arrow**, and then click **Number**.

Close ✕ the table and click **Yes** to save the changes.

6 On the **Tools** menu, point to **Analyze**, and then click **Performance**. Click the **All Object Types tab**, and then click **Select All** to select all of the objects in the database. Click **OK**. Notice the analysis results show only two ideas instead of three. **Close** the **Performance Analyzer** dialog box, **Close** ✕ your database, and leave Access open for the next activity.

Objective 4
Manage and Secure a Database

A database often contains sensitive information, such as wages and social security numbers. Databases that are shared with multiple users or that are accessible to many people may require security precautions that limit the amount of information available to users. You can set different security levels depending on the sensitivity of your data and the access restrictions that you wish to employ. It is not necessary to secure every database that you create. For example, a database that you create for your own personal use may not require the application of security precautions. Thus, when you create a database, consider the data, the users, and the accessibility of the system when deciding whether or not to implement security precautions.

Activity 10.4 Setting a Database Password

Passwords provide a simple method of securing your database. Passwords restrict access to a database by requiring a user to type a specified combination of letters, numerals, spaces, or symbols in order to open the database. A password is case sensitive and can be up to 15 characters long. If your database is shared among a small group of users or is on a single computer, setting a password is often all that is required to secure the database. Once a password is set, a dialog box that requests the password displays whenever the database is opened. Only users who type the correct password will be allowed to open the database. Once a database is password protected, you cannot open the file if you lose or forget the password. In this activity, you will set a password for your 10B_Security_Firstname_Lastname database.

1 On the Database toolbar, click **Open**. Navigate to your saved files and click your **10B_Security_Firstname_Lastname** database so that it is selected. In the lower right corner of the **Open** dialog box, click the **Open arrow**, and then click **Open Exclusive**. See Figure 10.13.

When a database is shared, you must open it in exclusive mode before *encrypting* it. Encrypting a file alters the file using a secret code so it is unintelligible to unauthorized parties. The exclusive mode prevents others from opening the database.

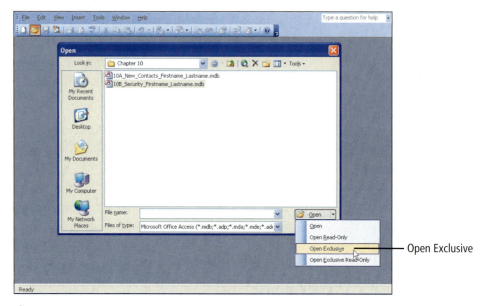

Figure 10.13

2 On the **Tools** menu, point to **Security**, and from the submenu click **Set Database Password**.

3 In the **Password** box, type **Oceana** and then press Tab. In the **Verify** box, type **Oceana** noticing that instead of the word *Oceana*, asterisks display in the **Set Database Password** dialog box. Click **OK**.

Alert!
Your Passwords Don't Match!
If a message box displays after you set the database password, then the two passwords that you typed did not match. Retype the passwords making sure that you use the same capitalization in both passwords, and then click OK.

4 **Close** the database and leave Access open.

To unset—change or remove—a password you must open the database in exclusive mode.

5 On the Database toolbar, click **Open**. From your saved files, click your **10B_Security_Firstname_Lastname** database so it is highlighted. Click the **Open arrow**, and then click **Open Exclusive**.

A dialog box displays asking you to enter the database password.

6 Type **Oceana Grill** and click **OK**.

A message box displays indicating that an invalid password was entered.

7 Click **OK**. In the **Password Required** dialog box, type **Oceana** and then click **OK** to open the database.

8 On the **Tools** menu, point to **Security**, and then click **Unset Database Password**. Type **Oceana** and then click **OK**. **Close** [X] the database and leave Access open.

Activity 10.5 Establishing User-Level Security

The most flexible and extensive method of implementing security measures for a database is ***user-level security***. By implementing user-level security, you can establish different levels of access to sensitive data and objects in your database. Each user is identified by a unique identification code. The level of access and the objects to which a user has access are established based on the individual's identification code and password. In this activity, you will create three levels of user-level security using the Security Wizard. You will create a group for Managers, Assistant Managers, and Employees. You will then create a user to add to each of the groups. Your report will look similar to Figure 10.14.

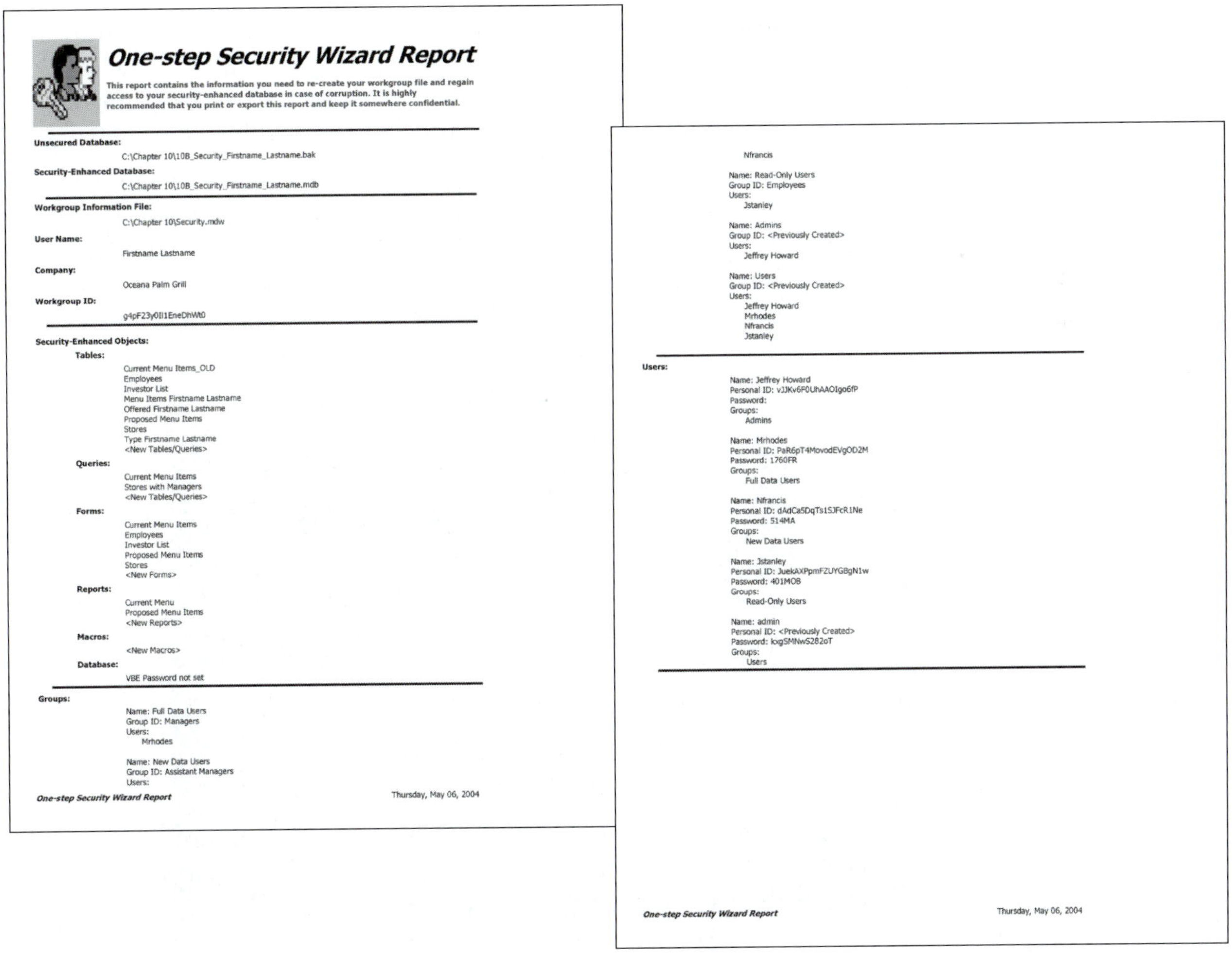
One-step Security Wizard Report

This report contains the information you need to re-create your workgroup file and regain access to your security-enhanced database in case of corruption. It is highly recommended that you print or export this report and keep it somewhere confidential.

Unsecured Database:
C:\Chapter 10\10B_Security_Firstname_Lastname.bak
Security-Enhanced Database:
C:\Chapter 10\10B_Security_Firstname_Lastname.mdb

Workgroup Information File:
C:\Chapter 10\Security.mdw
User Name:
Firstname Lastname
Company:
Oceana Palm Grill
Workgroup ID:
g4pF23y0Il1EneDhWt0

Security-Enhanced Objects:
Tables:
Current Menu Items_OLD
Employees
Investor List
Menu Items Firstname Lastname
Offered Firstname Lastname
Proposed Menu Items
Stores
Type Firstname Lastname
<New Tables/Queries>
Queries:
Current Menu Items
Stores with Managers
<New Tables/Queries>
Forms:
Current Menu Items
Employees
Investor List
Proposed Menu Items
Stores
<New Forms>
Reports:
Current Menu
Proposed Menu Items
<New Reports>
Macros:
<New Macros>
Database:
VBE Password not set

Groups:
Name: Full Data Users
Group ID: Managers
Users:
Mrhodes

Name: New Data Users
Group ID: Assistant Managers
Users:

One-step Security Wizard Report Thursday, May 06, 2004

Nfrancis

Name: Read-Only Users
Group ID: Employees
Users:
Jstanley

Name: Admins
Group ID: <Previously Created>
Users:
Jeffrey Howard

Name: Users
Group ID: <Previously Created>
Users:
Jeffrey Howard
Mrhodes
Nfrancis
Jstanley

Users:
Name: Jeffrey Howard
Personal ID: vJJKv6F0UhAAOIgo6fP
Password:
Groups:
Admins

Name: Mrhodes
Personal ID: PaR6pT4MovodEVgOD2M
Password: 1760FR
Groups:
Full Data Users

Name: Nfrancis
Personal ID: dAdCa5DqTs1SJFcR1Ne
Password: 514MA
Groups:
New Data Users

Name: Jstanley
Personal ID: JuekAXPpmFZUYGBgN1w
Password: 401MOB
Groups:
Read-Only Users

Name: admin
Personal ID: <Previously Created>
Password: kxgSMNwS282oT
Groups:
Users

One-step Security Wizard Report Thursday, May 06, 2004

Figure 10.14

1 On the Database toolbar, click **Open**. If necessary, navigate to your saved files. Double-click your **10B_Security_Firstname_Lastname** database to open it.

2 On the **Tools** menu, point to **Security**, and then click **User-Level Security Wizard**.

The User-Level Security Wizard will help you create your own groups of users and assign or remove *permissions* for each group of database users. Permissions determine the type of access a user has to the different objects in the database. Because you currently do not have a *workgroup* created, *Create a new workgroup information file* is selected in the first Security Wizard step. A workgroup is a group of users in a multiuser environment who share data and the same *workgroup information file*. A workgroup information file contains information about users in the workgroup, including their passwords, account names, and groups to which they belong.

3 Click **Next**.

The Security Wizard creates a workgroup information file with the default filename Security.mdw. A default *workgroup ID* is also created. The workgroup ID, or WID, is a unique, case-sensitive string of characters that uniquely identifies the workgroup. The WID is needed to copy the workgroup information file.

4 In the **Your name** box, type your **Firstname Lastname** and in the **Company** box, type **Oceana Palm Grill** At the bottom of the dialog box, be sure that the **I want to create a shortcut to open my security-enhanced database** option is selected. See Figure 10.15.

By selecting the *I want to create a shortcut to open my security-enhanced database* option, you are indicating that you want to use this workgroup information file exclusively for this database. Thus, you do not want to set this file as the default workgroup information file. This will also place a shortcut to your database on your desktop.

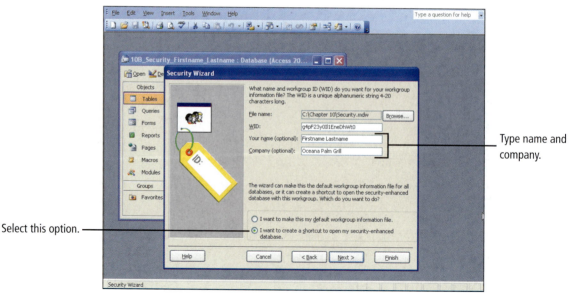

Figure 10.15

5 Click **Next**.

In this page of the wizard, you can select the objects that you want to secure. By default, all objects are selected.

6 Verify that all objects are selected, and then click **Next**.

In this page of the wizard, you can specify the groups to which you wish to assign permissions.

7 Click on each of the seven group names and read the description of each group in the Group permissions section of the dialog box. Do *not* select the check boxes.

8 Click the **Full Data Users** check box and in the **Group ID** box, type **Managers** See Figure 10.16.

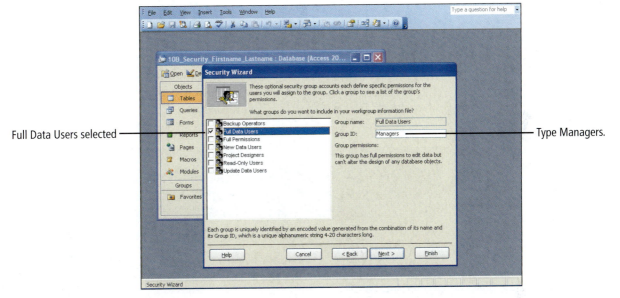

Full Data Users selected

Type Managers.

Figure 10.16

9 Click the **New Data Users** check box and in the **Group ID** box, type **Assistant Managers**

10 Click the **Read-Only Users** check box and in the **Group ID** box, type **Employees** Click **Next**.

In this page of the wizard, you can assign permission to specific users. By default, no permissions are assigned to Users.

11 Verify that the **No, the Users group should not have any permissions** option is selected. Click **Next**.

In this page of the wizard, you can add users to your workgroup information file. Each user can be assigned a password and personal ID. Notice that your name, or the current log in name, displays in the list. Your name is set as the default administrator. As an administrator, you will have full access to the database.

Project 10B: Security | **Access** 627

12 Click **Add New User**. In the **User name** box, type **Mrhodes** and then press Tab to move the insertion point to the **Password** box. Type **1760FR** Click **Add This User to the List**.

Mrhodes is added to the user list.

> ### More Knowledge — Selecting Passwords
>
> Use strong passwords that combine upper and lowercase letters, numbers, and symbols. Weak passwords don't mix these elements. An example of a strong password isY6dh!et5, and a weak password would be House27. Use a strong password that you can remember so that you don't have to write it down. User names can range from 1 to 20 characters, and can include alphabetic characters, accented characters, numbers, spaces, and symbols.

13 In the **User Name** box, type **Nfrancis** and then press Tab. In the **Password** box, type **514MA** and then click **Add This User to the List**. Repeat this technique to add **Jstanley** with the password **401MOB** and notice that the list includes the three users that you added. See Figure 10.17. Click **Next**.

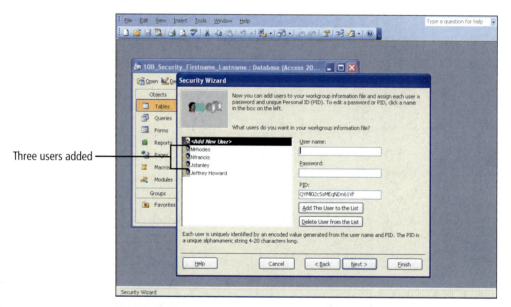

Three users added

Figure 10.17

14 Verify that the **Select a user and assign the user to groups** option is selected. Click the **Group or user name arrow** and click **Mrhodes**. Click the **Full Data Users** check box.

Recall that the Managers group has full data access. By assigning Mrhodes to the Full Data Users group, you have specified full data access permission.

15 Repeat the process to assign **Nfrancis** to the **New Data Users** group and **Jstanley** to the **Read-Only Users**. Click **Next** to display the last **Security Wizard** dialog box. Do *not* change the default backup name of the unsecured database. Click **Finish**.

The wizard creates the workgroup information file, the secured database, an unsecured backup copy of the database, and a report named One-step Security Wizard Report. The report contains the information contained in your workgroup information file, including group IDs, User names, IDs, passwords, and security-enhanced objects. The report will help you recreate the workgroup file in case of corruption.

16 From the **File** menu, click **Print** to print the **One-step Security Wizard Report**. Click **OK**. **Close** ⊠ the report. In the **Security Wizard** message box, click **Yes** to save a snapshot of the report. **Close** the snapshot viewer. In the message box, click **OK** to close the database.

17 **Close** ⊠ Access. From the windows desktop, double-click the shortcut to your **10B_Security_Firstname_Lastname** file. In the **Name** box, type **Jstanley** and in the **Password** box, type **401MOB** See Figure 10.18. Click **OK**.

By default, the previous user's name will display in the Name box.

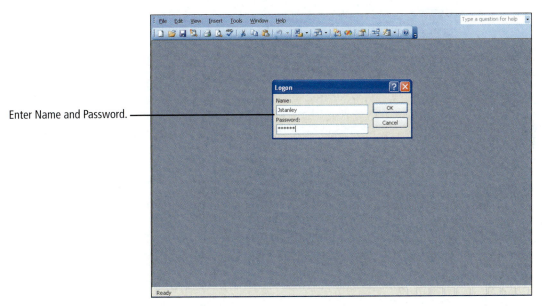

Enter Name and Password.

Figure 10.18

> **Alert!**
>
> **Passwords Are Case Sensitive!**
> The user passwords that you created are case sensitive. If a message box displays indicating that you have entered an invalid account name or password, type the password again and be sure to use the correct capitalization.

18 On the **Objects** bar, click **Forms**. Double-click the **Employees** form.

If necessary, **Maximize** the form. At the bottom of the form in the **Record** box, type **5** and press Enter. In the **Rate** box, try to replace the 7.00 by typing **10.00** and notice that the data cannot be changed.

Recall that Jstanley has read-only properties. Thus, none of the data can be changed.

19 **Close** the form, **Close** the database, and then **Close** Access.

20 On the Windows desktop, double-click the shortcut to your **10B_Security_Firstname_Lastname** file. In the **Name** box, type **Mrhodes** and in the **Password** box, type **1760FR** and then click **OK**.

21 On the **Objects** bar, click **Forms**. Double-click the **Employees** form.

If necessary, **Maximize** the form. At the bottom of the form in the **Record** box, type **5** and press Enter. In the **Rate** box, select the 7.00 and type **10.00**

Mrhodes is a full data user, and as such can make changes to data in the database.

22 **Close** the form, **Close** the database, and then **Close** Access.

23 On the desktop, right-click the shortcut that you created, click **Delete**, and then click **Delete Shortcut**.

End You have completed Project 10B

Project 10C Replica

The managers at each Oceana Palm Grill restaurant should be able to view, input, and update information to the Oceana Palm Grill database, but they should not be able to change the design. Thus, you must protect the design of the database.

In Activities 10.6 and 10.7, you will protect the design of your database by replicating it and by applying additional security measures. You will save your replicated database as *10C_Replica_Firstname_Lastname*. See Figure 10.19.

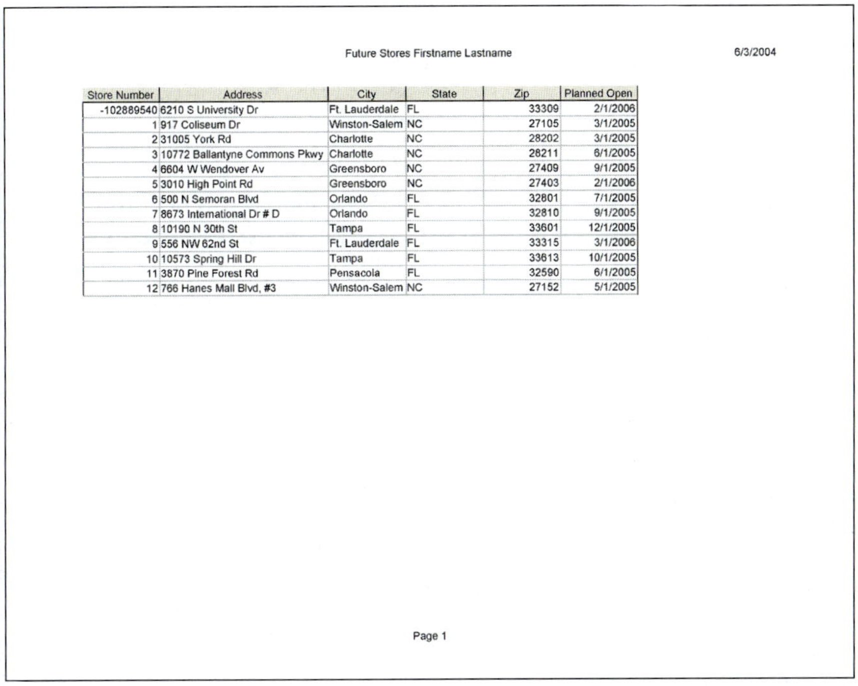

Future Stores Firstname Lastname

6/3/2004

Store Number	Address	City	State	Zip	Planned Open
-102889540	6210 S University Dr	Ft. Lauderdale	FL	33309	2/1/2006
1	917 Coliseum Dr	Winston-Salem	NC	27105	3/1/2005
2	31005 York Rd	Charlotte	NC	28202	3/1/2005
3	10772 Ballantyne Commons Pkwy	Charlotte	NC	28211	6/1/2005
4	6604 W Wendover Av	Greensboro	NC	27409	9/1/2005
5	3010 High Point Rd	Greensboro	NC	27403	2/1/2006
6	500 N Semoran Blvd	Orlando	FL	32801	7/1/2005
7	8673 International Dr # D	Orlando	FL	32810	9/1/2005
8	10190 N 30th St	Tampa	FL	33601	12/1/2005
9	556 NW 62nd St	Ft. Lauderdale	FL	33315	3/1/2006
10	10573 Spring Hill Dr	Tampa	FL	33613	10/1/2005
11	3870 Pine Forest Rd	Pensacola	FL	32590	6/1/2005
12	766 Hanes Mall Blvd, #3	Winston-Salem	NC	27152	5/1/2005

Page 1

Figure 10.19
Project 10C—Replica

Objective 5
Create a Replica of a Database

You can protect the design of your database by creating a *replica*. A replica is a copy of a database that allows users in multiple locations to update data, while restricting changes in the database design to one location. The location in which design changes may be performed is called the *Design Master*. By having one Design Master, you could create a different replica to send to each manager.

Activity 10.6 Creating a Replica of a Database

In this activity, you will protect the design of your database by creating a single replica.

1. Using **My Computer**, navigate to the student files that accompany this textbook and locate the Access database **a10C_Oceana_Palm_Grill**. Copy and paste the file to the Chapter 10 folder you created, and rename the file **10C_Oceana_Palm_Grill_Firstname_Lastname** Remove the Read-only property from the file. Start Access and open the database you just renamed.

2. From the **Tools** menu, point to **Replication**, and then click **Create Replica** to display an information dialog box stating that the database must be closed to create a replica. Click **Yes**.

   The database closes and after a few moments an information box indicates *Converting a database into a Design Master results in changes to your database.* It is strongly recommended that you make a backup of it for reference. When you replicate a database, a Design Master is created. The Design Master is the only database in which changes to the design can be made. Because you will be modifying the database, it is a good idea to create a backup of the original database.

3. Click **Yes** to create a backup of your database, which Access will name *10C_Oceana_Palm_Grill_Firstname_Lastname.bak*.

   An information box may display indicating that the database is being converted to a Design Master. The Location of New Replica dialog box displays. In the File name box, the name Replica of *10C_Oceana_Palm_Grill_Firstname_Lastname* displays.

4. If necessary, use the Save in arrow to navigate to your chapter folder. Then, delete the text in the **File name** box and type **10C_Replica_Firstname_Lastname** Select the **Prevent deletes** check box to prevent users from deleting any records in the replica. See Figure 10.20, and then click **OK**.

   When the replication is complete, an information box displays indicating that the file has been converted to a Design Master.

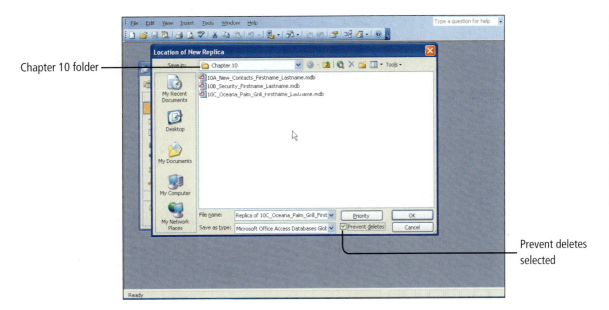

Figure 10.20

5. In the information box, click **OK**.

   Notice that the icons next to each table in the Design Master have changed, indicating that the tables are replicated.

6. **Close** your database. **Open** your **10C_Replica_Firstname_Lastname** database. From the **Objects** bar, be sure **Tables** is selected. Right-click the **Future Stores** table and click **Design View**.

   A warning box displays indicating that you cannot change the design of the table.

7. Click **No** so that you do not open the table in Design view in read-only mode.

8. Double-click the **Future Stores** table to open it. On the navigation bar, click the **New Record** button. Press Tab to move the insertion point to the **Address** field and type **6210 S University Dr** Press Tab and type **Ft. Lauderdale** Press Tab and type **FL** Press Tab and type **33309** Press Tab, and then type **2/1/2006** See Figure 10.21.

   Because there may be many replicas, the New Store ID should be a unique ID so that when all of the databases are replicated, there will not be a conflict. Thus, your store ID will likely differ.

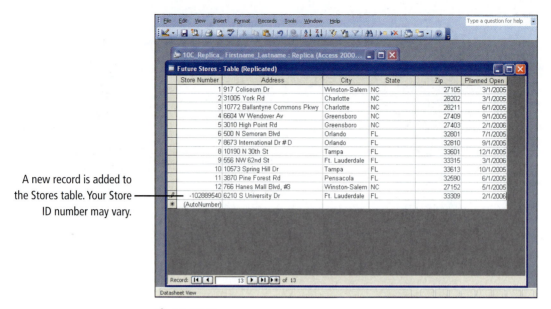

A new record is added to the Stores table. Your Store ID number may vary.

Figure 10.21

9. **Close** ![X] the table, and **Close** ![X] the database. On the Database toolbar, click **Open**. From your Chapter 10 folder, double-click on your **10C_Oceana_Palm_Grill_Firstname_Lastname** to open it.

10. If necessary, from the **Objects** bar, click **Tables**. Double-click the **Future Stores** table to open it and notice that the table contains 12 records. The new store ID has been added to a replica but not added to the permanent Design Master copy of the database.

11. **Close** ![X] the table. From the **Tools** menu, point to **Replication**, and then click **Synchronize Now**. In the **Directly with Replica** box, be sure that your file **10C_Replica_Firstname_Lastname** displays. Click **OK**. Click **Yes** to close the database and begin the synchronization. When the synchronization is complete, click **OK**.

Alert! — **Verify the File Name**
If your 10C_Replica_Firstname_Lastname database is not entered in the box, click Browse, and then navigate to your replicated database.

12. Right-click the **Future Stores** table, click **Rename**, and name the table **Future Stores Firstname Lastname** Double-click your **Future Stores Firstname Lastname** table to open it.

Notice that the new store added to the file 10C_Replica_Firstname_Lastname has been added to the table. See Figure 10.22.

A new record is added to the Design Master. The position in the table may be different on your screen due to the AutoNumber assigned.

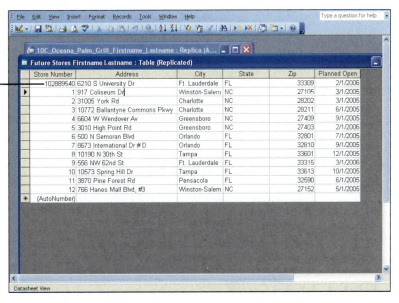

Figure 10.22

> **Note** — **Synchronizing Databases**
>
> The synchronization feature updates each replica. The update includes changes to the data and Design Master. It is important to synchronize often so your data will be current in each database.

13 From the **File** menu, click **Page Setup**, click the **Page tab**, and then under **Orientation**, click **Landscape**. Click **OK**. From the **File** menu, click **Print**, and then click **OK**. **Close** ⊠ the table and **Close** ⊠ the database, and leave Access open for the next activity.

Activity 10.7 Encrypting a Database

In the last activity, you created a replica of your Oceana Palm Grill database. You can email replicas to other users so that they can make changes to the database. To provide additional protection of your database, you will **encrypt** the database before sending it. Encryption, or encoding, is the simplest form of protection of your database. Encrypting a database compacts the database file and helps protect it from being read by a word processor or utility program. It is particularly useful when you transmit a database electronically, or when you store it on floppy disk or compact disc. In this activity, you will encrypt your 10C_Replica_Firstname_Lastname database.

1 On the Database toolbar, click **Open**. Click your file **10C_Replica_Firstname_Lastname**. Click the **Open arrow**, and then click **Open Exclusive**.

2 From the **Tools** menu, point to **Security**, and then click **Encode/Decode Database**.

3 In the **Encode Database As** dialog box, navigate to your files and select your **10C_Replica_Firstname_Lastname** file. Click **Save**. A warning message displays asking if you want to replace the existing file. Click **Yes**.

The database is now encoded. You may now send the file electronically or store it. The file is compacted and encrypted.

> **More Knowledge** — Decoding a Database
>
> To decode a database, repeat the process that you used to encode the database. The Decode Database As dialog box will display in place of the Encode Database As dialog box.

4 **Close** the database and close Access.

End You have completed Project 10C

Summary

Access contains a variety of tools to help you improve the performance of a database and also to protect your database. In this chapter, you practiced creating a database using the Database Wizard. By using the wizard, you can design a database with tables, forms, reports, and a switchboard very quickly. You also practiced using the Table Analyzer and the Performance Analyzer. By analyzing your database, you may find ways to improve the performance of your database and decrease the likelihood of data errors.

In this chapter, you also practiced protecting your database. You saved a database with a password and you also created different levels of users that can access your database. By creating different levels of users, you can control how much access each user has to the database. You practiced replicating your database. By replicating your database you can allow users in many locations to update, view, and add data without the design of the database changing.

In This Chapter You Practiced How To

- Use the Database Wizard
- Analyze Data with the Table Analyzer
- Use the Performance Analyzer
- Manage and Secure a Database
- Create a Replica of a Database

Concepts Assessments

Matching Match each term in the second column with its correct definition in the first column. Write the letter of the term on the blank line to the left of the correct definition.

___ 1. A specified combination of letters, numerals, spaces or symbols that an individual types for the purpose of restricting access to a database.

___ 2. A tool that divides a table that has repeated information into separate tables so that each type of information is stored only once.

___ 3. A process by which the type of access a user has to the different objects in the database is determined.

___ 4. A unique, case-sensitive string of characters that identifies the workgroup.

___ 5. A copy of a database that allows users in multiple locations to update data, while restricting changes in the database design to one location.

___ 6. A Microsoft Acess database file that compiles all modules, removes all editable source code, and compacts the destination database.

___ 7. The process of compacting a database file to help protect it from being read by a word processor or utility program.

___ 8. A method of implementing database security measures that establishes different levels of access to sensitive data and objects in your database based on an individual's identification code and password.

___ 9. A tool that evaluates objects in your database and makes suggestions on how you might improve the performance of your database.

___ 10. A tool that walks you through the steps necessary to create a set of tables, queries, forms, and reports, and a switchboard for the database.

A Database Wizard
B Encryption
C MDE file
D Password
E Performance Analyzer
F Permissions
G Replica
H Table Analyzer
I User-level security
J Workgroup ID

Concepts Assessments (continued)

Fill in the Blank Write the correct answer in the space provided.

1. A _____ is a user-friendly form that provides a way to access all of the tables, forms, queries, and reports in your database.

2. In a replicated database, the _____ is the only database in which changes to the design can be made.

3. If your database is on a single computer, setting a _____ is often all that is required to secure the database.

4. Once a file is saved as an MDE file, you will not be able to view, modify, or create forms, reports, or modules in _____.

5. By using the Table Analyzer, you can improve database efficiency, make the database easier to update, and reduce _____.

6. _____ are marked with a red exclamation point and point out ways that your database can be optimized.

7. The _____ feature updates each replica in a replicated database.

8. You should create _____ passwords that combine upper and lowercase letters, numbers, and symbols.

9. When creating user-level security, the level of access and the objects to which a user has access are established based on the individual's _____ and password.

10. Encrypting a database is particularly useful when you transmit a database _____.

Skill Assessments

Project 10D — Ledger

Objective: *Use the Database Wizard.*

In the following Skill Assessment, you will create a new database using the Database Wizard. The database will be used to organize the accounts and transactions for the restaurant. You will name the database *10D_Ledger_Firstname_Lastname* in the folder you have created for this chapter. The switchboard in your completed database will look similar to Figure 10.23.

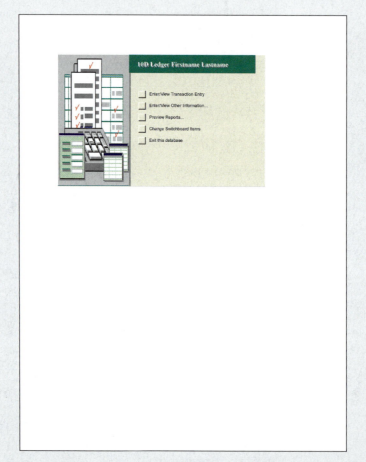

Figure 10.23

1. Start Access and on the Database toolbar, click **New**. In the **New File** task pane, under **Templates**, click **On my computer** to display the **Templates** dialog box.

2. Click the **Databases tab**.

(**Project 10D**–Ledger continues on the next page)

Skill Assessments (continued)

(Project 10D–Ledger continued)

3. Click the **Ledger** template, and then click **OK** to display the **File New Database** dialog box. Save the database as **10D_Ledger_Firstname_Lastname** in your Chapter 10 folder. Click **Create**.

4. Click **Next** to display the second page of the wizard. Notice the three tables the wizard will create.

5. If necessary, under **Tables in the database**, click **Transaction information**. Select the **Taxable** check box to add it to the table as a field. Click the **Accounts** and **Classifications of account numbers** tables and notice the field list in each table.

6. Click **Next** to display a list of screen styles. Click **Blends**. Click **Next** to display a list of printed report styles. Click **Formal**, and then click **Next**. In the **What would you like the title of the database to be?** box, type **10D Ledger Firstname Lastname** using your own first and last name. If necessary, *clear* the **Yes, I'd like to include a picture** check box. Click **Next**. Verify that the **Yes, start the database** check box is selected, and then click **Finish**.

7. Click each of the switchboard options to navigate through the different tables, forms, and reports created by the wizard. Notice the tables, forms, and reports contain the fields you selected from the wizard. Do not exit the database.

8. On the Form view toolbar, click **View**, and then **Maximize** the form. Click the title label **10D New Contacts Firstname Lastname** and on the Formatting toolbar, change the **Font Size** to **12** and apply **Bold**.

9. Press [Shift] + [Tab] to select the second label. Change the **Font Size** to **12** and apply **Bold**.

10. On the Form Design toolbar, click **View**. From the **File** menu, click **Print**. Click **OK** to print the form. **Close** the form, click **Yes** to save the changes, and **Close** the database.

End You have completed Project 10D

Skill Assessments (continued)

Project 10E—Stores

Objective: *Analyze Data with the Table Analyzer.*

In the following Skill Assessment, you will use the Table Analyzer to examine and divide the Stores table so duplicate information is stored only once. You will use the query created by the analyzer to view the information. You will rename and save your database as *10E_Stores_Firstname_Lastname*. Your completed table will look similar to Figure 10.24.

Stores Main Firstname Lastname — 5/6/2004

Store #	Address	Address2	Zip	Manager	Lookup to Stores City Firstname Lastname
13	3220 N. Capital Dr.	#500	73301	Lisa Holt-King	Austin, TX
14	1620 W. 35th St.		73344	Hayward Kahn	Austin, TX
15	1024 Spicewood Sprin		78708	Erin Posner	Austin, TX
16	9407 W. Hwy. 290	#460	78708	Louisa Choy-Day	Austin, TX
17	736 Jefferson St.		78712	Michael Amendola	Austin, TX
18	6415 Parkcrest Dr.		78715	Garrett Zerunyan	Austin, TX
19	323 N Lamar Blvd	#G	78718	Mark Williams	Austin, TX
20	7002 E Riverside Dr	#200	78719	Michelle Biderman	Austin, TX
21	8211 Directors Blvd		78720	Charlotte Denham	Austin, TX
22	1060 Airport Blvd		78741	Shar Emanuel	Austin, TX
23	450 W William Cannon		78735	Rob Handler	Austin, TX
24	3341 Burnet Rd		78755	Grace Imre	Austin, TX
25	902 E Pecan St	#1	78785	Rachel Hoffman	Austin, TX
1	17941 Preston Road	#100	75214	Jonathan Arbisser	Dallas, TX
2	3050 Routh St		75245	Fabio Camara	Dallas, TX
3	3125 E Mockingbird Lane		75378	Nancy Cohen Sher	Dallas, TX
4	5140 Lemmon Avenue	#A	75342	Sherry Fesler	Dallas, TX
5	2674 W Ledbetter Dr		75376	Gordon Wang	Dallas, TX
6	1619 Greenville Ave		75396	Tomas Groban	Dallas, TX
7	7158 Camp Bowie Boul		76107	Amy Songstad	Ft. Worth, TX
8	5491 N Main St		76123	Oscar Tosetti	Ft. Worth, TX
9	3355 E Loop 820 St	#200	76124	Yvette Swanson	Ft. Worth, TX
10	7121 W Magnolia Ave		76140	Gerald Pekich	Ft. Worth, TX
11	3181 W Berry Sreett		76161	Marvin Levine	Ft. Worth, TX
12	401 Houston St		76192	Nina Marangi	Ft. Worth, TX

Page 1

Figure 10.24

1. Using **My Computer**, navigate to the student files that accompany this textbook and locate the Access database **a10E_Stores**. Copy and paste the file to the Chapter 10 folder you created, and rename the file **10E_Stores_Firstname_Lastname** Remove the Read-only property from the file. Start Access and open the database you just renamed.
2. If necessary, click the **Tables** object, and double-click the **Stores** table to open it. **Maximize** the table and examine the **City** and **State** fields. Notice the duplicate data under these two fields. **Close** the table.

(Project 10E–Stores continues on the next page)

Skill Assessments (continued)

(Project 10E–Stores continued)

3. On the **Tools** menu, point to **Analyze**, and then click **Table** to start the Table Analyzer Wizard.

4. Click **Next** to display the second page of the Table Analyzer Wizard, which describes how the Table Analyzer solves the problem of duplicate data. Click **Next**.

5. If necessary, click **Stores**, and then click **Next**. Verify that the **Yes, let the wizard decide** option button is selected. Click **Next**. The Table Analyzer creates a second table with the City and State fields.

6. Double-click in the **Table1** title bar to display a **Table Analyzer Wizard** dialog box in which you can change the table name. In the **Table Name** box, type Stores Main Firstname Lastname and then click **OK**. Repeat the process to change the name of **Table2** to Stores City Firstname Lastname Click **Next**.

7. Click **Next**. On the last page of the wizard, verify that the **Yes, create the query** option is selected, and then click **Finish**. **Close** the Microsoft Office Access Help window.

8. **Close** the query.

9. On the **Objects** bar, click **Tables**.

10. Double-click your **Stores City Firstname Lastname** table to open it. In the first row next to **Austin** click the **Expand** button to view all the restaurants in Austin from the **Stores Main Firstname Lastname** table. **Close** the table.

11. Double-click your **Stores Main** table to open it. Move the mouse pointer to the **Store #** field title so that the down-pointing black arrow displays. Press and hold down the left mouse button and drag to the right to select all of the columns. On the **Format** menu, click **Column Width**. In the **Column Width** dialog box, click **Best Fit**.

12. On the **File** menu, click **Page Setup**. Click the **Page tab**, and then under **Orientation**, click **Landscape**. Click **OK**. From the **File** menu, click **Print**. Click **OK**. **Close** the table, click **Yes** to save the changes to the layout, and **Close** the database.

 You have completed Project 10E

Skill Assessments (continued)

Project 10F — Security Report

Objective: *Manage and Secure a Database.*

In the following Skill Assessment, you will create three levels of security for the Oceana Palm Grill database. Your completed security report will look similar to Figure 10.25. You will rename and save your database as *10F_Security_Report_Firstname_Lastname*.

Figure 10.25

1. Using **My Computer**, navigate to the student files that accompany this textbook and locate the Access database **a10F_Security_Report**. Copy and paste the file to the Chapter 10 folder you created, and rename the file **10F_Security_Report_Firstname_Lastname** Remove the Read-only property from the file. Start Access and open the database you just renamed.

(Project 10F–Security Report continues on the next page)

Skill Assessments (continued)

(Project 10F–Security Report continued)

2. On the **Tools** menu, point to **Security**, and then click **User-Level Security Wizard**. Click **Next**.

3. In the **Your name** box, type your **Firstname Lastname** and in the **Company** box, type **Oceana Palm Grill** At the bottom of the wizard page, be sure that the **I want to create a shortcut to open my security-enhanced database** option is selected. Click **Next**.

4. Verify that all objects are selected, and then click **Next**.

5. Click the **Full Permissions** check box and in the **Group ID** box, type **Manager** Click the **New Data Users** check box and in the **Group ID** box, type **Floor Manager** Click the **Read-Only Users** check box and in the **Group ID** box, type **Host** Click **Next**.

6. Verify that the **No, the Users group should not have any permissions** option is selected. Click **Next**.

7. Click **Add New User**. In the **User name** box, type **Jpena** and then press [Tab] to move the insertion point to the **Password** box. Type **Jp1645L** Click **Add This User to the List**.

8. In the **User name** box, type **Ctorosian** and then press [Tab]. In the **Password** box, type **Ct718W** and then click **Add This User to the List**. Repeat this technique to add **Mramirez** with the password **Mr1049S** and notice that the list includes the three users that you added. Click **Next**.

9. Verify that the **Select a user and assign the user to groups** option is selected. Click the **Group or user name arrow** and click **Jpena**. Click the **Full Permissions** check box.

10. Repeat the process to assign **Ctorosian** to the **New Data Users** group and **Mramirez** to the **Read-Only Users**. Click **Next** to display the last **Security Wizard** page. Do *not* change the default backup name of the unsecured database. Click **Finish** and wait for the Security Report to display.

11. On the **File** menu, click **Print**, and then click **OK** to print the **One-step Security Wizard Report**. **Close** the report. In the **Security Wizard** message box, click **Yes** to save a snapshot of the report. **Close** the snapshot viewer. In the message box, click **OK** to close the database.

12. **Close** Access. From the Windows desktop, double-click the shortcut to your **10F_Security_Report** file. In the **Name** box, type **Mramirez** and in the **Password** box, type **Mr1049S** and then click **OK**.

13. On the **Objects** bar, click **Tables**. Double-click the **Employees** table. If necessary, **Maximize** the table. In the first record of the table under **Rate**, try to replace the 4250 by typing **5000** and notice that the data cannot be changed.

14. **Close** the table and close Access. On the desktop, right-click the shortcut and click **Delete**.

End You have completed Project 10F

Access chapter ten

Performance Assessments

Project 10G—Oceana

Objective: *Create a Replica of a Database.*

In the following Performance Assessment, you will create a replica of your database, change the data in the replica, and then synchronize your databases. Your report will look similar to Figure 10.26. You will rename and save your database as *10G_Oceana_ Firstname_Lastname*.

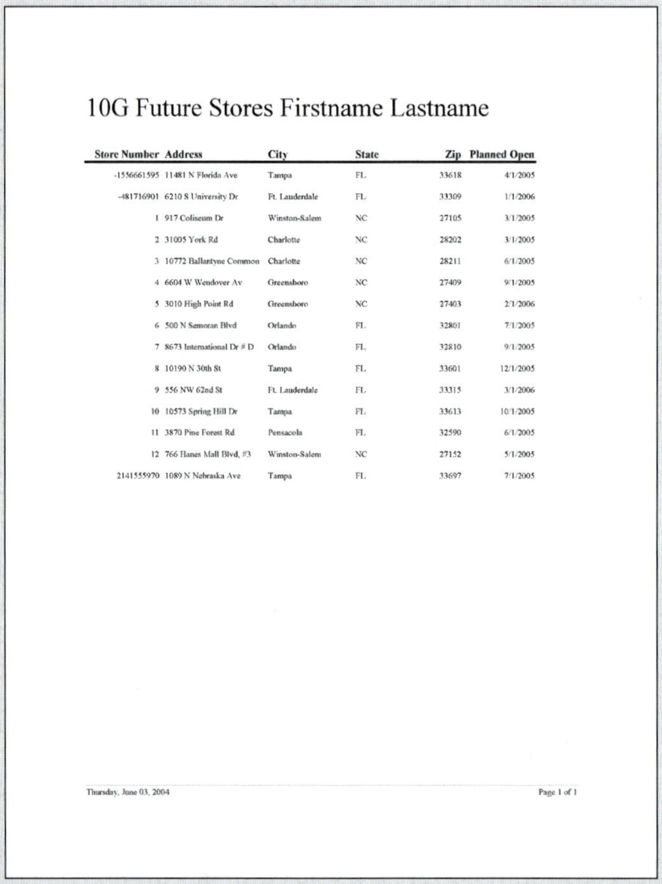

Figure 10.26

1. Using **My Computer**, navigate to the student files that accompany this textbook and locate the Access database **a10G_Oceana**. Copy and paste the file to the Chapter 10 folder you created, and rename the file **10G_Oceana_ Firstname_Lastname** Remove the Read-only property from the file. Start Access and open the database you just renamed.

2. From the **Tools** menu, point to **Replication**, and then click **Create Replica** to display an information dialog box stating that the database must be closed to create a replica. Click **Yes**.

(**Project 10G**–Oceana continues on the next page)

Performance Assessments (continued)

(Project 10G–Oceana continued)

3. Wait a few moments, and then click **Yes** to create a backup of your database, which Access will name *10G_Oceana_Firstname_Lastname.bak*.

4. If necessary, use the Save in arrow to navigate to your Chapter 10 folder. In the File name box, delete the existing text and type **10G_Oceana_Replica_Firstname_Lastname** Select the **Prevent deletes** check box to prevent users from deleting any records in the replica, and then click **OK**.

5. Click **OK**. **Close** your database.

6. Open your **10G_Oceana_Replica_Firstname_Lastname** database. From the **Objects** bar, be sure **Tables** is selected. Double-click the **Oceana Palm Grill Future Stores** table.

7. Add the following three stores to the table: **11481 N Florida Ave Tampa FL 33618 4/1/2005**; **1089 N Nebraska Ave Tampa FL 33697 7/1/2005**; **6210 S University Dr Ft. Lauderdale FL 33309 1/1/2006**

8. **Close** the table, and **Close** the database. From the Database toolbar, click **Open**. From your Chapter 10 folder, double-click your **10G_Oceana_Firstname_Lastname** database to open it.

9. On the **Tools** menu, point to **Replication**, and then click **Synchronize Now**. In the **Directly with Replica** box, be sure that your file **10G_Oceana_Replica_Firstname_Lastname** displays. Click **OK**. Click **Yes** to close the database and begin the synchronization. When the synchronization is complete, click **OK**.

10. From the **Objects** bar, click **Reports**. Double-click **Create report by using wizard**. Select your **Table: Oceana Palm Grill Future Stores** and move all the fields to the selected fields. Click **Next**. Leave the default settings for grouping, sorting, and layout. For the report style, click **Formal**. Name the report **10G Future Stores Firstname Lastname** Click **Finish**. The position of the records in your table may differ from the figure due to the AutoNumber assigned.

11. From the **File** menu, click **Print**, and then click **OK**. **Close** the report, **Close** the database, and then **Close** Access.

 You have completed Project 10G

Performance Assessments (continued)

Project 10H — Performance

Objective: *Use the Performance Analyzer.*

In the following Performance Assessment, you will use the Performance Analyzer to improve the performance of your database. You will save the database as an MDE file, change a data type, and create relationships suggested by the analyzer. You will print the relationships window. Your relationships will look similar to Figure 10.27. You will rename and save your database as *10H_Performance_Firstname_Lastname*.

Figure 10.27

1. Using **My Computer**, navigate to the student files that accompany this textbook and locate the Access database **a10H_Performance**. Copy and paste the file to the Chapter 10 folder you created, and rename the file **10H_Performance_Firstname_Lastname** Remove the Read-only property from the file. Start Access and open the database you just renamed.

2. On the **Tools** menu, point to **Analyze**, and then click **Performance**. Click the **All Object Types tab**, and then **Select All** the objects in the database. Click **OK**. The analyzer lists six ideas and one suggestion. Read through all of the ideas and the suggestion.

3. Click the suggestion to relate the table **Stores** to the table **Employees**. Click **Optimize**. This will create a relationship between the two tables.

(**Project 10H**–Performance continues on the next page)

Performance Assessments (continued)

(Project 10H–Performance continued)

4. **Close** the Performance Analyzer.

5. Display the **Employees** table in **Design view**. In the **Field Name** list locate **Rate** field, and then change the **Data Type** to **Number**. Change the **Field Size** property to **Double**. **Close** the table and click **Yes** to save the changes.

6. On the Database toolbar, click **Relationships**. On the Relationship toolbar, click **Show All Relationships**. Click the **Show Table** button, and add the **Current Menu Items** and the **Proposed Menu Items** tables to the window. In the two tables you just added, create a relationship between the **Category** fields in each of the tables. Do not enforce Referential Integrity. From the **File** menu, click **Print Relationships**. From the **File** menu, click **Print**, and then click **OK**. **Close** the window, click **Yes** to save the changes, and then click **OK**. **Close** the **Relationships** window.

7. On the **File** menu, click **Database Properties**. If necessary, click the **General tab**. Notice the file type and that the size of the database is over 2.3 MB. The Performance Analyzer suggested saving the database as an MDE file. Click **OK** to close the dialog box.

8. Recall that you can create an MDE file so that the destination database will be compacted. Once you save the file as an MDE file, you will not be able to view, modify, or create forms, reports, or modules in Design view; add, delete, or change references to object libraries or databases; change code; or import or export forms, reports, or modules. To create an MDE file, the database must first be converted to the 2002-2003 file format. On the **Tools** menu, point to **Database Utilities**, then point to **Convert Database**, and then click **To 2002-2003 File Format**. Navigate to your chaper folder, and then name the database **10H_Performance_2003_Firstname_Lastname** and then click **Save**. A message box displays indicating that the database cannot be shared with Access 97 and Access 2000 users. Click **OK**. **Close** the current database and open your **10H_Performance_2003** database.

9. On the **Tools** menu, point to **Database Utilities**, and then click **Make MDE File**. Do not change the file name. Click **Save**. **Close** the current database and open your **10H_Performance_2003.mde** database—the file icon displays a small lock. From the **File** menu, click **Database Properties**. If necessary, click the **General tab**. Notice the file type is now an MDE file, and the size of the database is approximately 1.0 MB. Click **OK** to close the dialog box.

10. On the **Tools** menu, point to **Analyze**, and then click **Performance**. Click the **All Object Types tab**, and then **Select All** of the objects in the database. Click **OK**. Notice the Analysis results area contains no suggestions. **Close** the **Performance Analyzer** dialog box, **Close** the database, and **Close** Access.

End You have completed Project 10H

Performance Assessments (continued)

Project 10I — Employees

Objective: *Analyze Data with the Table Analyzer.*

In the following Performance Assessment, you will use the Table Analyzer to examine and divide the Employees by Restaurant table so that duplicate information is stored only once. You will use the query created by the analyzer to view the information. You will rename and save your database as *10I_Employees_Firstname_Lastname*. Your completed table will look similar to Figure 10.28.

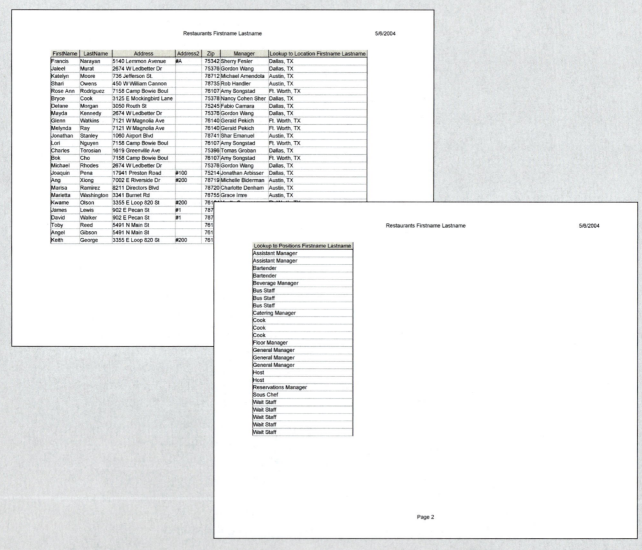

Figure 10.28

(**Project 10I**–Employees continues on the next page)

Performance Assessments (continued)

(Project 10I–Employees continued)

1. Using **My Computer**, navigate to the student files that accompany this textbook and locate the Access database **a10I_Employees**. Copy and paste the file to the Chapter 10 folder you created, and rename the file **10I_Employees_Firstname_Lastname** Remove the Read-only property from the file. Start Access and open the database you just renamed.

2. If necessary, click the **Tables** object, and double-click the **Employees by Restaurant** table to open it. **Maximize** the table and examine the fields. Notice any duplicate data. **Close** the table.

3. On the **Tools** menu, point to **Analyze**, and then click **Table** to start the Table Analyzer Wizard.

4. Click **Next** to display the second page of the Table Analyzer Wizard, which describes how the Table Analyzer solves the problem of duplicate data. Click **Next**.

5. Click **Employees by Restaurant**, and then click **Next**. Verify that the **Yes, let the wizard decide** option button is selected. Click **Next**.

6. Rename **Table1 Restaurants Firstname Lastname** and rename **Table2 Positions Firstname Lastname** and then rename **Table3 Location Firstname Lastname** Click **Next**.

7. The wizard found similar names in the tables. These are unique names. Next to each position in the correction column, click the selection arrow and choose **(Leave as is)** for each of the fields. Click **Next**. Be sure **Yes, create the query** is selected, and then click **Finish**.

8. **Close** the Help window. **Close** the query. On the **Objects** bar, click **Tables**.

9. Double-click your **Restaurants Firstname Lastname** table to open it. Select all of the columns in the table. On the **Format** menu, click **Column Width**. In the **Column Width** dialog box, click **Best Fit**.

10. On the **File** menu, click **Page Setup**. Click the **Page tab**, and then under **Orientation**, click **Landscape**. Click **OK**. From the **File** menu, click **Print**. Click **OK**. **Close** the table, click **Yes** to save the changes to the layout, and **Close** the database.

End You have completed Project 10I

Mastery Assessments

Project 10J—Expenses

Objectives: *Use the Database Wizard and Manage and Secure a Database.*

In the following Mastery Assessment, you will create a new database using the Database Wizard, and then establish user-level security for the database. Your completed report will look similar to Figure 10.29. You will save your database as *10J_Expenses_Firstname_Lastname*.

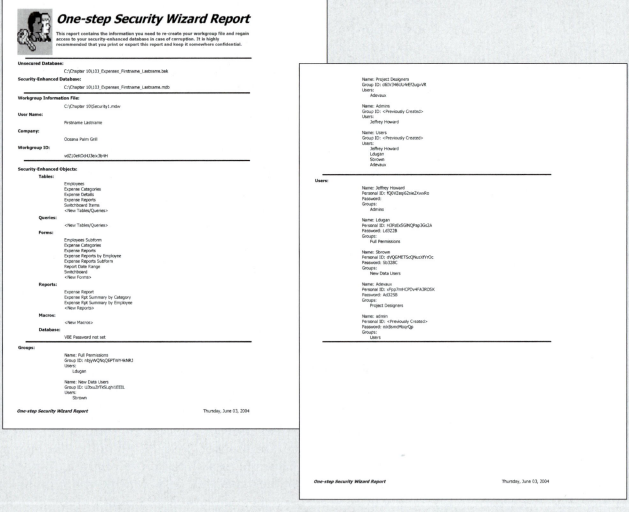

Figure 10.29

1. Start Access. From the **File** menu, click **New**. Under **Templates**, click **On my computer**. Click the **Databases tab**, and then double-click **Expenses**.

(**Project 10J**–Expenses continues on the next page)

Mastery Assessments (continued)

(Project 10J–Expenses continued)

2. Navigate to your chapter folder and then name the new database, which will be based on the Expenses template, **10J_Expenses_Firstname_Lastname** In the **Database Wizard**, do not change the default fields in the tables and use the **Blends** style for the forms and **Formal** style for the report. Title the database **10J Expenses Firstname Lastname** and then start the database.

3. Switch to Design view, and then **Maximize** the form. Change the formatting of the title and the second label to a **12-point** font and apply **Bold**. Close the switchboard and save the changes.

4. Start the **User-Level Security Wizard**, and click **Yes** to open the database in shared mode.

5. In the **Your name** box, type your **Firstname Lastname** and in the **Company** box, type **Oceana Palm Grill** At the bottom of the dialog box, be sure that the **I want to create a shortcut to open my security-enhanced database** option is selected.

6. Verify that all objects are selected for security, and then include the **Full Data Users**, **New Data Users**, and the **Project Designers** in the workgroup information file. Do not change the default Group IDs. Verify that the **No, the Users group should not have any permissions** option is selected.

7. Add the following new users and passwords: **Ldugan** with password **Ld322B Sbrown** with password **Sb328C** and **Adevaux** with password **Ad325B**

8. Verify that the **Select a user and assign the user to groups** option is selected. Assign **Ldugan** as a **Full Data User**, **Sbrown** as a **New Data User**, and **Adevaux** as a **Project Designer**. Do not change the default backup name of the database. Click **Finish**.

9. **Print** the **One-step Security Wizard Report**. **Close** the report. Save a snapshot of the report, and then **Close** the snapshot viewer. In the message box, click **OK** to close the database. **Close** Access.

10. On the desktop, right-click your 10J_Expenses shortcut, click **Delete**, and then click **Delete Shortcut**.

End You have completed Project 10J

Mastery Assessments (continued)

Project 10K—Import

Objective: *Create a Replica of a Database.*

In the following Mastery Assessment, you will create a replica of your database, import information into a table in the replica, and then synchronize your databases. Your report will look similar to Figure 10.30. You will rename and save your database as *10K_Import_Firstname_Lastname*.

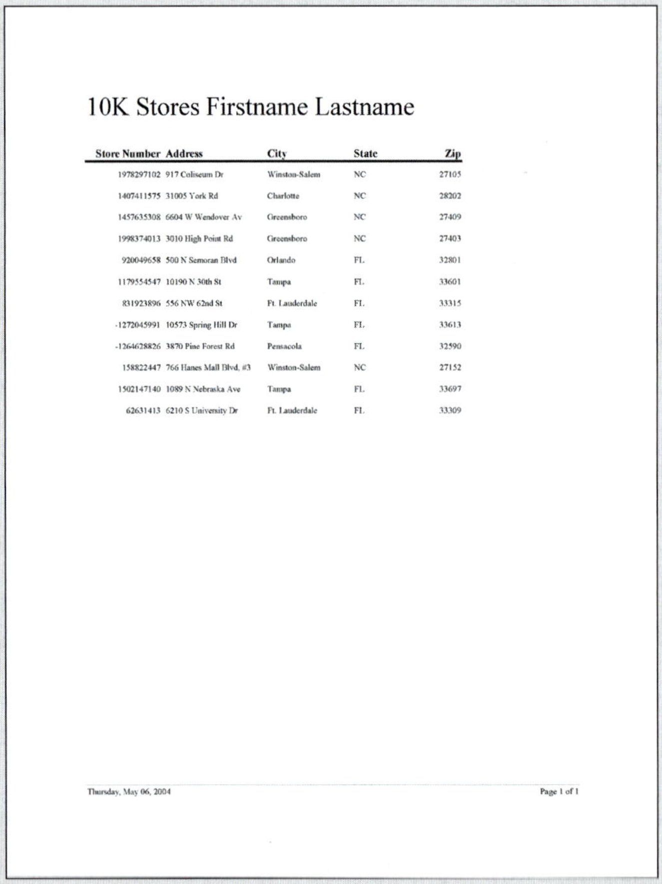

10K Stores Firstname Lastname

Store Number	Address	City	State	Zip
1978297102	917 Coliseum Dr	Winston-Salem	NC	27105
1407411575	31005 York Rd	Charlotte	NC	28202
1457635308	6604 W Wendover Av	Greensboro	NC	27409
1998374013	3010 High Point Rd	Greensboro	NC	27403
920049658	500 N Semoran Blvd	Orlando	FL	32801
1179554547	10190 N 30th St	Tampa	FL	33601
831923896	556 NW 62nd St	Ft. Lauderdale	FL	33315
-1272045991	10573 Spring Hill Dr	Tampa	FL	33613
-1264628826	3870 Pine Forest Rd	Pensacola	FL	32590
158822447	766 Hanes Mall Blvd, #3	Winston-Salem	NC	27152
1502147140	1089 N Nebraska Ave	Tampa	FL	33697
62631413	6210 S University Dr	Ft. Lauderdale	FL	33309

Thursday, May 06, 2004 Page 1 of 1

Figure 10.30

1. Using **My Computer**, navigate to the student files that accompany this textbook and locate the Access database **a10K_Import**. Copy and paste the file to the Chapter 10 folder you created, and rename the file **10K_Import_Firstname_Lastname** Remove the Read-only property from the file. Start Access and open the database you just renamed.

(Project 10K–Import continues on the next page)

Mastery Assessments (continued)

(Project 10K–Import continued)

2. Create a replica and a backup of the database. Save the replica as **10K_Import_Replica_Firstname_Lastname** in your Chapter 10 folder. Select the **Prevent deletes** check box to prevent users from deleting any records in the replica. Close the Design Master, and then open the replica. **Close** your database.

3. Open your **10K_Import_Replica_Firstname_Lastname** database. From the **File** menu, point to **Get External Data**, and then click **Import**. Change the **Files of type** to **Text Files**. From the student files that accompany this textbook, double-click the **a10K_Future_stores.txt** file.

4. In the first page of the **Import Text Wizard**, verify that **Delimited** is selected, and then click **Next**. Be sure **Tab** is selected, and then select the **First Row Contains Field Names** check box. Click **Next**. Import the data into the existing table, **Oceana Palm Grill Future Stores**. Click **Next**. Click **Finish**.

5. **Close** the table, and **Close** the database. When one of the replicas has been changed, you should synchronize the database from the Design Master. From your Chapter 10 folder, open your **10K_Import_Firstname_Lastname** database.

6. **Synchronize** the database with the **10K_Import_Replica_Firstname_Lastname** file.

7. From the **Objects** bar, click **Reports**. Start the **Report Wizard** using all the fields in the **Table: Oceana Palm Grill Future Stores** table. Do not change the default settings for grouping, sorting, and layout. Select the **Formal** report style, and then name the report **10K Stores Firstname Lastname** Click **Finish**. The position of the records in your table may differ from the figure due to the AutoNumber assigned.

8. From the **File** menu, click **Print**, and then click **OK**. **Close** the report, **Close** the database, and **Close** Access.

End You have completed Project 10K

Problem Solving

Project 10L — Time and Billing

Objectives: *Use the Database Wizard and Manage and Secure a Database.*

In the following Mastery Assessment, you will create a new database using the Database Wizard, and then establish user-level security for the database. You will save your database as *10L_Time_and_Billing_Firstname_Lastname*.

1. Use the **Database Wizard** to create a new database based on the Time and Billing template on your computer. Name the database **10L_Time_and_Billing_Firstname_Lastname**

2. In the **Information about Employees** table, add the **Employee Number** and **Email name** fields. Choose the styles of your choice and entitle your database **10L Time and Billing Firstname Lastname** Fill in the Company name and address when prompted to do so.

3. **Close** the Switchboard.

4. Add User-Level Security to the database by creating accounts for Owners, Managers, Assistant Managers, and Workers. Pick appropriate levels of security for each level. Add one user name and password for each level.

5. **Print** the **One-step Security Wizard Report** and **Print** the Switchboard form.

6. **Close** the form, **Close** the database, and then **Close** Access.

End You have completed Project 10L

Problem Solving (continued)

Project 10M — Expansion

Objective: *Create a Replica of a Database.*

The Oceana Palm Grill is continuing to expand, and multiple replicas will be made to send to each restaurant. In the following Problem Solving exercise, you will create a Switchboard for the database, and then you will create a replica to send out to a new restaurant. You will save the database as *10M_Expansion_Firstname_Lastname*.

1. Locate the file **a10M_Expansion** from your student files, and copy and paste the file to the Chapter 10 folder you created. Remove the Read-only property from the file and rename the file as **10M_Expansion_Firstname_Lastname** Start Access and open the database you just renamed.

2. Create a switchboard with multiple pages to make a user-friendly interface for the manager of the restaurant. Name the switchboard page **10M_Switchboard_Firstname_Lastname**

3. Create a **Replica** of the database and save the new database as **10M_Expansion_Replica_Firstname_Lastname Close** the database and open your replica.

4. Open the Switchboard form in the replica. **Print** the form, and then **Close** the form. **Close** the database, and then **Close** Access.

 You have completed Project 10M

On the Internet

Improving Database Performance

The Microsoft Web page contains a variety of information about improving the performance of your databases. Go to the Microsoft site at **www.microsoft.com**. In the Search box, type **Improve Performance in Access** and click Go. Examine the information on improving the performance in your database. Print any information that is of interest to you.

GO! with Help

Splitting a Database

In this chapter, you learned how to improve the performance and security of your database. Another way to improve your database is to split the database into a front-end and a back-end database. In this Help activity, you will use Help to learn how to split a database.

1. Start Access. In the *Type a question for help* box, type **splitting a database** and press Enter.

2. In the Search Results taskbar, click **Split an Access database (MDB)**.

3. Read the information on how to split a database.

4. Print the Help information if you want to keep a copy of it. Close the Help window, and then close Access.

Access 2003

chapter eleven

Visual Basic for Applications

In this chapter, you will: complete these projects and practice these skills.

Project 11A
Working With Procedures

Objectives
- Convert a Macro to VBA Code
- Modify an Existing Procedure
- Use Immediate Window to Test Statements
- Write a Procedure

Project 11B
Using Structures in a Procedure

Objectives
- Define Variables in a Procedure
- Use the Selection Structure
- Use the Select Case Structure

University Medical Center

The University Medical Center is a premier patient-care and research institution serving the metropolitan area of Orange Beach, Florida. It provides preventive and routine care through innovations and state-of-the-art programs. The Office of Public Affairs (OPA) promotes the services and achievements of the medical staff. The OPA conducts community health seminars, maintains a speakers bureau of health experts, and provides up-to-date information to local and national media.

© Photosphere Images Ltd.

Visual Basic for Applications

When working with Access, you can create simple Access applications without writing any programming code, but when you need to create more sophisticated applications, you will need to use Visual Basic for Applications (VBA) code. In this chapter, you will customize your database by using VBA code.

Project 11A Medical Center

The Medical Center database has been very helpful in organizing the training, seminars, expenses, and speakers. Mike Martinez, the Director of Public Affairs, wants you to customize, using VBA code, the Medical Center database so the forms and reports interact with one another.

In Activities 11.1 through 11.5, you will view an existing procedure, modify a procedure, and write your own procedure. You will save your database as *11A_Medical_Center_Firstname_Lastname*.

```
Converted Macro- Open Training and Seminar Form Firstname Lastna - 1

Option Compare Database
'--------------------------------------------------------------
' Open_Training_and_Seminar_Form_Firstname_Lastname
'--------------------------------------------------------------
Function Open_Training_and_Seminar_Form_Firstname_Lastname()
    Beep
    MsgBox "This Macro will open the Form Employee Training and Seminar Enrollments to the first record.", vbInformation, "Employee Training and Seminar Enrollments form"
    ' Open the Employee Training and Seminar Enrollments form
    DoCmd.OpenForm "Employee Training and Seminar Enrollments", acNormal, "", "", , acNormal
    ' Move to the first record
    DoCmd.GoToRecord acForm, "Employee Training and Seminar Enrollments", acFirst
    Beep
    MsgBox "The macro will now create a new record", vbInformation, " Employee Training and Seminar Enrollments form"
    ' Go to New record
    DoCmd.GoToRecord acForm, "Employee Training and Seminar Enrollments", acNewRec
    Beep
    MsgBox "The macro will now maximize the form if it isn't already maximized", vbInformation, " Employee Training and Seminar Enrollements form"
    ' Maximize form
    DoCmd.Maximize
    Beep
    MsgBox "The macro will now close the Employee Training and Seminar Enrollment form", vbInformation, " Employee Training and Seminar Enrollments form"
    ' Close the Employee Training and Seminar Enrollments form
    DoCmd.Close acForm, "Employee Training and Seminar Enrollments"
    ' Display the Office Assistant
    MsgBox "The macro will now display the Office Assistant.", vbInformation, "Office Assistant"
    Assistant.On = True
    MsgBox "The Office Assistant will move to upper left corner of the window."
    Assistant.Move 20, 50
    MsgBox "The Office Assistant will now close."
    Assistant.On = False
End Function
```

```
Form_Employee Training and Seminar Enrollments_Firstname_Lastname - 1

Private Sub Form_BeforeUpdate(Cancel As Integer)
    'Update DateModified field after the form is updated
    DateModified = Date
    'Update TimeModified field after the form is updated
    TimeModified = Time
End Sub

Private Sub Form_Close()
    'Display Message
    MsgBox "Remember to print the updated Seminar report."
    'Open report in Print Preview
    DoCmd.OpenReport "Employee Training and Seminar Enrollments", acViewPreview
End Sub
```

Figure 11.1
Project 11A—Medical Center

Objective 1
Convert a Macro to VBA Code

Recall that a ***macro*** is a series of commands and instructions grouped together as a single command to accomplish one or more tasks automatically. When you create macros, you can perform tasks when an ***event*** occurs. An event is any significant action that can be detected by a system, for example, a mouse click, a change in data, or a form opening or closing. Macros, however, are limited by the actions already programmed within Access.

Visual Basic for Applications, also known as ***VBA***, is a programming language used to write computer applications within the Microsoft Windows environment. Macros you create are stored in a ***module*** using Visual Basic for Applications. A module is a group of related ***procedures***, which are units of computer code that perform some action. Procedures consist of a group of VBA ***statements***. A statement is a single VBA instruction. By putting multiple statements together in a VBA procedure, you are no longer limited to simple macros. Rather, you can create specific, customized instructions.

Activity 11.1 Converting a Macro to VBA Code

In this activity, you will convert a macro to VBA code and view the procedure in VBA. The advantage to the VBA function is that you can customize the code.

1 Using **My Computer**, navigate to the student files that accompany this textbook and locate the Access database **a11A_Medical_Center**. Copy and paste the file to your storage location, creating a new folder for Chapter 11 if you want to do so. Rename the file **11A_Medical_Center_Firstname_Lastname** Remove the Read-only property from the file. Start Access and open the database you just renamed.

2 On the Objects bar, click **Macros**, right-click the **Open Training and Seminar Form** macro, and then click **Rename**. Rename the macro **Open Training and Seminar Form Firstname Lastname** and then open the macro in **Design View**. **Maximize** the window and examine the macro. Click on each action and examine each of the action arguments, as shown in Figure 11.2.

Recall that when you create a macro, the action arguments specify the properties of each of the actions.

Click each action.

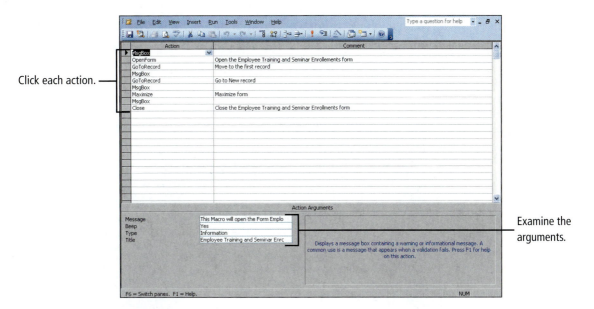

Figure 11.2

3 On the Macro Design toolbar, click **Run**. Read the first message box, and then click **OK**. Repeat this process for the remaining three message boxes. **Close** the macro window.

4 From the **Tools** menu, point to **Macro**, and then click **Convert Macros to Visual Basic** as shown in Figure 11.3.

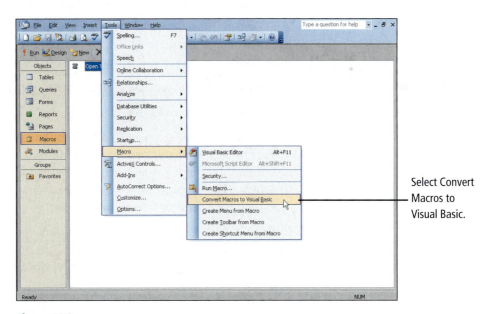

Select Convert Macros to Visual Basic.

Figure 11.3

Project 11A: Medical Center | **Access** 663

5 In the **Convert macro** dialog box, clear the **Add error handling to generated functions** check box as shown in Figure 11.4.

This action will limit the lines of viewable code to those that are included in the actual macro.

Clear the check box for *Add error handling to generated functions.*

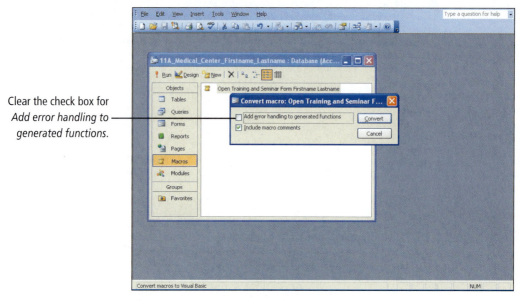

Figure 11.4

6 Click **Convert**. When the conversion is finished, click **OK**.

The *Visual Basic Editor* window opens after the conversion is finished. In the Visual Basic Editor, you can view, create, and modify VBA code.

7 **Maximize** the window if necessary. On the Standard toolbar, click **Project Explorer**.

The Project Explorer pane displays on the left and displays a hierarchical list of the projects and all of the items contained and referenced by each project. A module and a function procedure, or function, was created for you. The function is called *Converted Macro-Open Training and Seminar Form*.

8 In the **Project Explorer** pane, right-click the **Converted Macro-Open Training and Seminar Form** function, and from the shortcut menu, click **View Code**. Alternatively, double-click on the function name. See Figure 11.5.

Right-click the *Converted Macro-Open Training and Seminar Form* to display the shortcut menu.

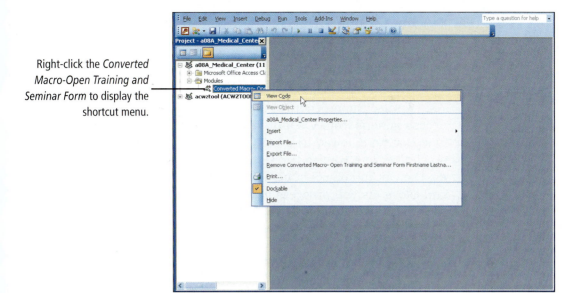

Figure 11.5

9 In the upper right corner of the **Project Explorer** pane, click **Close** ⊠.

By closing the Project Explorer pane you will be able to view more of the Code window.

10 In the displayed *Open_Training_and_Seminar_Form_Firstname_Lastname* function, examine the first *MsgBox* statement.

Each action in the macro is now converted to its VBA code, and each action argument is included with the action. The action consists of the *MsgBox*, followed by the action arguments in this order: message, the type of icon, and the title. See Figure 11.6.

First message box statement

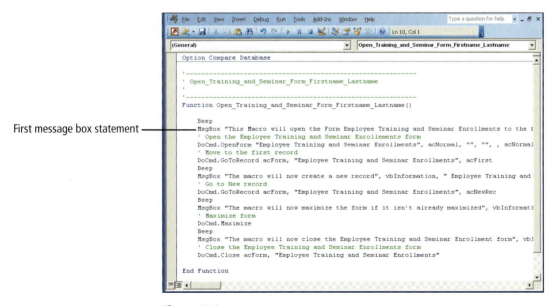

Figure 11.6

Project 11A: Medical Center | **Access** 665

11 Examine the first line of green text under the first MsgBox. The green statements are comments. These comments are from the Comment section of the macro.

12 Examine the remaining lines of VBA code.

You can use the procedures of the *DoCmd* object to run Microsoft Access actions from Visual Basic. To use the procedures, you can type *DoCmd* followed by a period, and then select the name of the procedure you want to run. Examine each of the procedures following the DoCmd object such as *OpenForm*, *GoToRecord*, *Maximize*, and *Close*. As you progress in your study of Access in this chapter, you will practice using these statements. See Figure 11.7.

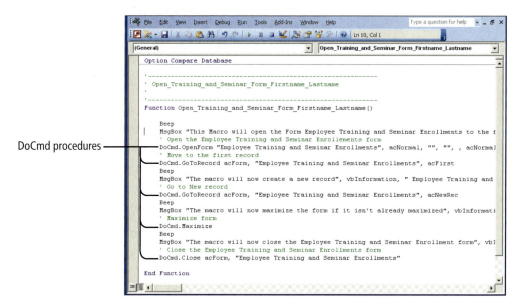

Figure 11.7

13 Click in the Code window inside the function. On the Standard toolbar, click **Run Sub/UserForm**. This will run the function to test whether the function works in the same manner as the macro. In each of the message boxes, click **OK**.

The VBA function runs in the same manner that the macro does.

14 Close the Visual Basic Editor and leave the database open for the next activity.

Objective 2
Modify an Existing Procedure

After a procedure is created, either from converting a macro or creating the procedure, you can open the Visual Basic Editor to modify the procedure. If a procedure does not work the way you intended it to, you must edit the procedure and test it to be sure it works as you intended.

Activity 11.2 Modifying an Existing Procedure

In this activity, you will edit your *Converted Macro-Open Training and Seminar Form* procedure to display the Office Assistant, ask the Office Assistant a question, and then close the Office Assistant.

1 From the **Tools** menu, point to **Macro**, and then click **Visual Basic Editor**. If necessary, redisplay your function code from the project pane, and then close the project pane.

2 Locate the last line—*End Function*—and then click to position the insertion point on the blank line directly above it as shown in Figure 11.8.

The Visual Basic Editor functions like a word processor. You can type your statements one at a time. If you type an incorrect statement, the font will display in red to indicate that the Visual Basic Editor cannot interpret your statement.

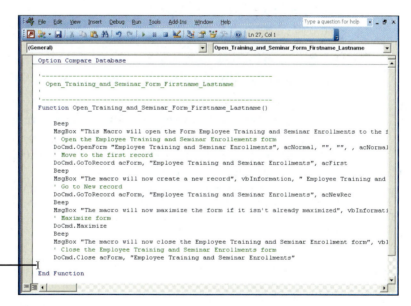

Position the insertion point here.

Figure 11.8

3 Press Tab. Insert a new comment by typing **' Display the Office Assistant.** Press Enter.

Text that you type following an apostrophe is considered by Visual Basic as a comment, not actual code. When you press Enter, the comment text displays in green to indicate that this statement is a comment, as shown in Figure 11.9.

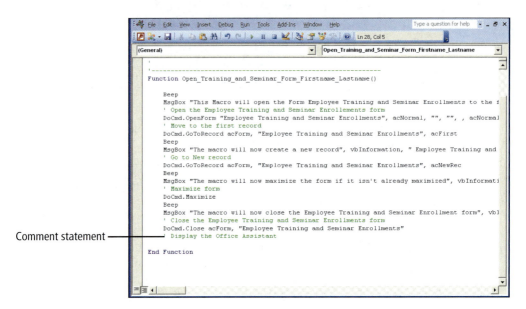

Comment statement

Figure 11.9

4 Insert a new message box by typing **MsgBox "The macro will now display the Office Assistant.", vbInformation,"Office Assistant"** Press Enter.

The editor is not case sensitive. You can type in uppercase or lowercase letters; however, any text enclosed in quotes outputs exactly as it is written. When you are typing in the Visual Basic Editor, the editor will attempt to assist you by showing the arguments for the MsgBox procedure. See Figure 11.10. When entering a MsgBox statement, only the message or prompt is required. The other arguments are optional.

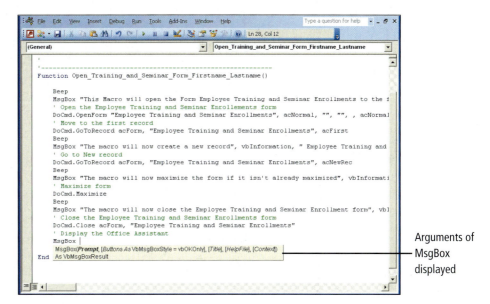

Figure 11.10

5 To display the Office Assistant, type **Assistant.On = True** Press [Enter].

Recall that when typing a statement, you must first identify the object, then type a period, and then type the procedure you want to run; or, select the procedure from the list. In this case, the *On* procedure must be set to *True* or *False*.

6 You will type two statements to show a message box, and then move the Office Assistant to the upper left corner of the window. Type **MsgBox "The Office Assistant will move to upper left corner of the window."** Press [Enter], and then type **Assistant.Move 20, 50** Press [Enter].

The Office Assistant will display in the same location each time unless it is moved by the mouse or a VBA statement. The numbers *20* and *50* indicate coordinates—points on the screen—measured in pixels. The editor starts counting pixels from the upper left corner of the window. The first coordinate—20—represents how many pixels to move to the right and the second coordinate represents how many pixels to move down.

7 Type **MsgBox "The Office Assistant will now close."** Press [Enter], and then type **Assistant.On = False** which will turn the Office Assistant off. Compare your completed function with Figure 11.11.

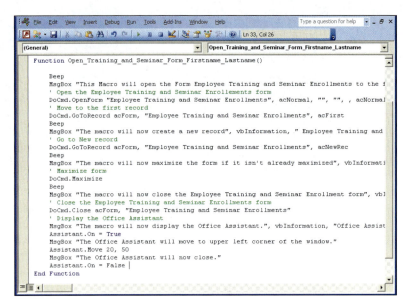

Figure 11.11

8 On the Standard toolbar, click **Save**, and then on the Standard toolbar, click **Run Sub/UserForm**.

Alert! — If an Error Message Displays

If you made a mistake in entering the code, you will see a dialog box informing you of the error. The message will vary, depending on the error that you have made. If this happens, return to the Visual Basic Editor window, and the line of code with the error will be highlighted in yellow. Examine the code and compare it with the instructions. Look for a typing error, a missing character, or a missing line of code. Correct the error and then click the Run Sub/UserForm button again. If you are unable to resolve the error, seek assistance from your instructor or lab coordinator.

9 Read the message boxes as they appear, and then click **OK** for each message box.

The beginning of your code has not changed, but after the Employee Training and Seminar Enrollments form closes, the Office Assistant will display, move, and then close.

10 With the code redisplayed on your screen, from the **File** menu, click **Print**. Under **Range**, be sure that **Current Module** is selected and under **Print What**, **Code** is selected. Click **OK**.

Your code prints. Note that longer lines of code wrap to the edge of the paper. Because code is not frequently printed, it is not necessary to adjust the alignment at this time.

11 **Close** the module, and then **Close** the Visual Basic Editor. Leave the database open for the next activity.

Objective 3
Use Immediate Window to Test Statements

Because writing procedures in VBA code is a complex process, it is helpful to test your statements before you type the statement into your module. To do this, the Visual Basic Editor contains an **Immediate window** to help you test your statements. The Immediate window is a window in the Visual Basic Editor in which you can run individual lines of Visual Basic code for the purpose of testing and **debugging**. Debugging is the process of locating and correcting errors in a program. The Immediate window displays information resulting from commands typed directly into the window. You can type the statement into the window and then run the statement to see the results of the statement.

Activity 11.3 Using Immediate Window to Test Statements

In this activity, you will use the Immediate window to display the results of statements typed into the window.

1 From the **Tools** menu, point to **Macro**, click **Visual Basic Editor**, and, if necessary, **Maximize** the window. Alternatively, open the Visual Basic Editor by pressing [Alt] + [F11].

2 From the **View** menu, click **Immediate Window**.

A blank window opens at the bottom of the Visual Basic Editor, as shown in Figure 11.12.

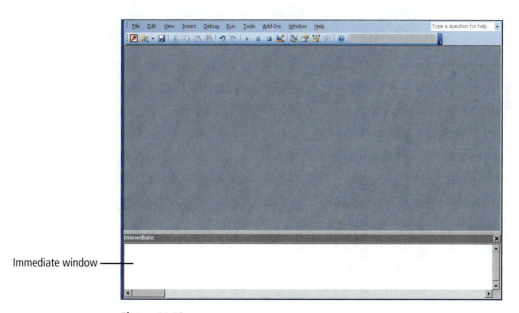

Immediate window

Figure 11.12

3 Click in the Immediate window, and then type **MsgBox "You can test VB statements in the Immediate window",vbInformation,"Immediate window"** Press Enter. The message box displays on the screen with your message, title, and Information icon—an instant test of your typed statement. Click **OK** to return to the Immediate window.

By using the Immediate window, there is no need to put the statement into a procedure and run the procedure to test the statement. The results of a single statement can be tested before putting multiple statements together.

> **More Knowledge** — Using a Procedure's Member List
>
> In the Visual Basic Editor, when you type an object name followed by a period, a member list will display. If the member list does not display, the editor does not recognize the object name or this option is turned off. To turn the option on, from the Tools menu, click Options, click the Editor tab, and then select Auto List Members.

4 If necessary, click on the blank line below the MsgBox statement in the Immediate window. Type **? 8 + 15** Press Enter. The result of the statement is 23. See Figure 11.13.

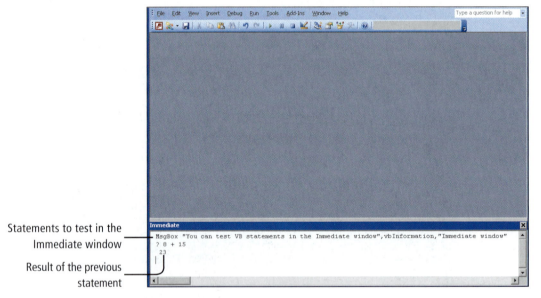

Statements to test in the Immediate window
Result of the previous statement

Figure 11.13

5 Type **? Date** and then press Enter. Type **? Time** and then press Enter.

The editor displays the current date and time from the computer's clock in the Immediate window.

6 In the Immediate window, at the far right end of its title bar, click **Close** ☒. **Close** ☒ the Visual Basic Editor and leave the database open for the next activity.

Objective 4
Write a Procedure

In the previous activities, you ran and edited an existing procedure and tested statements in the Immediate window. You can also create your own procedures to customize your database. In the following Activities, you will create two **event procedures**. Event procedures run when a specific event occurs. Recall that an event can be a mouse click, a change in data, a form opening or closing, among others. An event is usually the result of a user action. When creating an event procedure, Access automatically creates a procedure template for you.

Activity 11.4 Writing a Procedure

When looking at information in a form, it may be useful to see how current the information is on the form. Thus, it would be helpful to place a date and a time field on the form to display when the form was last updated. In this activity, you will create a procedure to update the DateModified field and TimeModified field after the form is updated.

1 On the Objects bar, click **Forms**. Right-click the **Employee Training and Seminar Enrollments** form and click **Rename**. Rename the form **Employee Training and Seminar Enrollments Firstname Lastname** Right-click on the form name again and click **Design View**. If necessary, **Maximize** the form window.

2 Locate, at the bottom of the form, where the **DateModified** and **TimeModified** fields are located.

These two fields belong to the Employee Training and Seminar Enrollments table. The fields must belong to the table so that the date and time for each record can be saved when the record is updated. The fields are also locked so the user cannot change them. See Figure 11.14.

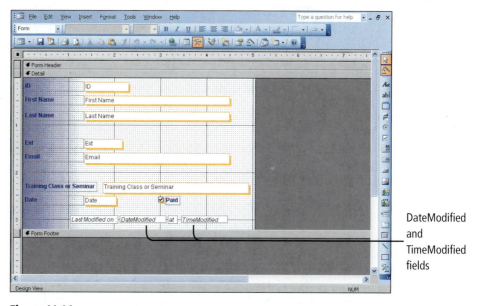

Figure 11.14

3️⃣ To the left of the horizontal ruler, right-click the **Form selector** and click **Properties** as shown in Figure 11.15.

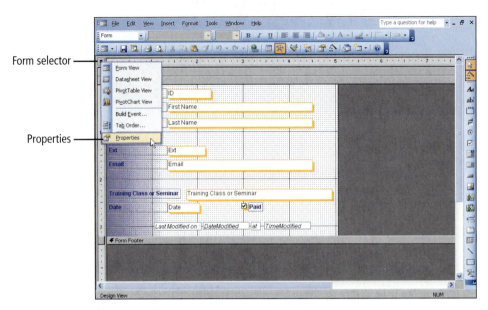

Figure 11.15

4️⃣ On the displayed Properties sheet, click the **Event tab**, and then click in the **Before Update** text box.

To the right of the text box, click **Build**. In the displayed **Choose Builder** dialog box, click **Code Builder** and then click **OK**.

The Visual Basic Editor opens and a procedure named *Form_BeforeUpdate* displays. This procedure has been created for you. You can enter your VBA code in the procedure and the code will be executed when the event occurs—in this case, the *Before Update* event.

5️⃣ If necessary, click to position the insertion point on the blank line above *End Sub*. Press Tab, and then type **'Update DateModified field after the form is updated** Recall that the apostrophe creates a comment line, not a line of code. Press Enter.

6️⃣ Type **DateModified = Date** Press Enter.

DateModified is the field from the table. Recall from the Immediate window that the Date statement copies the current date from your computer's internal clock and calendar. This statement copies the current date from your computer to the DateModified field in your form.

7️⃣ Type the comment line **'Update TimeModified field after the form is updated** Press Enter, and then to update the TimeModified field, type **TimeModified = Time** Compare your completed procedure with Figure 11.16.

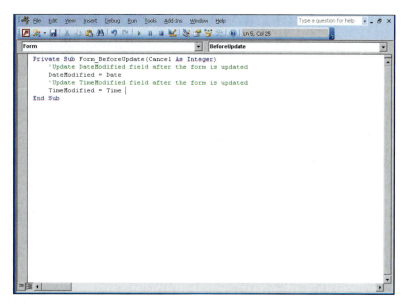

Figure 11.16

8 **Close** ☒ the Visual Basic Editor, **Close** ☒ the properties sheet, and then switch to **Form View** 🔲. In the Record navigation box at the bottom of the screen, type **6** then press Enter to go to record 6. In the form, select the **Paid** check box to indicate that Thomas Brookfield has now paid for the seminar.

The date and time correspond to the DateModified and TimeModified fields, respectively. The next time this form is displayed, the values will be displayed.

9 Click **Next Record** ▶, and then click **Previous Record** ◀. Notice that the date and time are updated at the bottom of the form. See Figure 11.17.

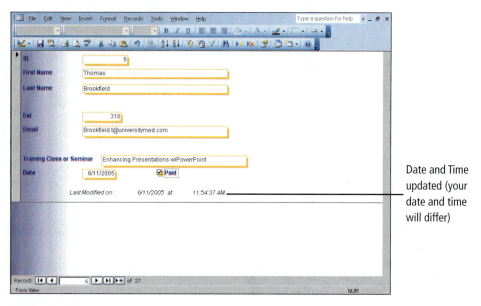

Date and Time updated (your date and time will differ)

Figure 11.17

10 Switch to **Design View** 📐 and leave the form open for the next activity.

Activity 11.5 Writing a Second Procedure

In this activity, you will create a procedure to remind the user to print the Employee Training and Seminar Enrollments report when they are finished updating the Employee Training and Seminar Enrollments form.

1 To the left of the horizontal ruler, right-click the **Form selector** and click **Properties** to display the properties sheet. If necessary, click the Event tab.

2 Expand the properties sheet if necessary, click in the **On Close** box, and then click **Build** . Double-click **Code Builder**.

A second procedure template is created below your *Form_BeforeUpdate* procedure.

3 In the blank line below *Private Sub Form_Close()*, press Tab, and then type the comment **'Display Message** Press Enter.

4 To enter the statement that causes the message box to display, type **MsgBox "Remember to print the updated Seminar report."** Press Enter.

5 Type the comment **'Open report in Print Preview** and then press Enter.

6 To enter the statement to cause the report to open in print preview, type **DoCmd.OpenReport "Employee Training and Seminar Enrollments",** After you type the comma, in the displayed shortcut menu, point to and then double-click **acViewPreview** to insert the text without typing it. See Figure 11.18.

Recall that to open a form or a report, you must put the DoCmd statement before the object you want to open.

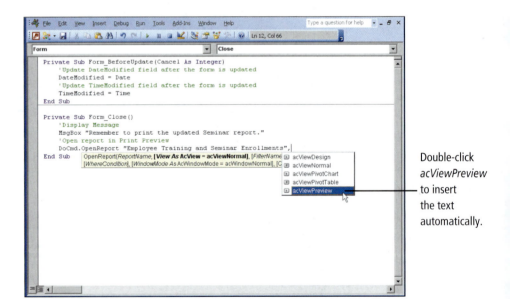

Figure 11.18

7 On the Standard toolbar, click **Save**, and then **Close** the Visual Basic Editor. **Close** the properties sheet, and then switch to **Form View**.

8 To test the procedure, you must close the form to run the *On Close* event. **Close** the form. If prompted, click **Yes** to save changes. Read the first message box, and then click **OK**.

The Employee Training and Seminar Enrollments report displays in Print Preview mode.

9 **Close** the report.

10 Press [Alt] + [F11] to redisplay the VBA code for the two procedures you created. From the **File** menu, click **Print**. Be sure **Current Module** is selected and **Code** is selected. Click **OK**. **Close** the Visual Basic Editor, close your database, and then close Access.

End You have completed Project 11A

Project 11B Medical Center Update

As you develop your skill in writing VBA code, you will find more ways to customize your database. You will find more objects and more properties that can be modified and also more ways to run your code. You will also want to run statements in your code based on whether certain conditions are true. Recall when you created a macro, in an earlier chapter, it was necessary to test certain conditions before the macro was executed.

In Activities 11.6 through 11.9, you will continue writing more VBA procedures to customize your database. Your results will look similar to those shown in Figure 11.19. You will name your database *11B_Medical_Center_Update_Firstname_Lastname*.

Figure 11.19
Project 11B—Medical Center Update

Objective 5
Define Variables in a Procedure

To perform calculations in your VBA code, you must create *variables*. A variable is a temporary holding location for a value in your procedure. A variable must have a unique name and must also have a data type associated with it. By declaring variables in your procedure, you can manipulate data, calculate formulas, and input information.

Activity 11.6 Defining a String Variable in a Procedure

In this activity, you will create an Input Box to allow the user to type in his or her name. Then you will store the person's name in a *string* variable, and then place the person's name on the form. A string is a variable that stores zero or more characters enclosed in quotation marks (" ").

1. From the student files that accompany this textbook, locate the Access database **a11B_Medical_Center_Update**, and then copy and paste the file to the folder where you are storing your projects for this chapter. Remove the Read-only property from the file, and rename the file as **11B_Medical_Center_Update_Firstname_Lastname** Start Access and open the database you just renamed.

2. On the Objects bar, click **Forms**. Right-click the **Public Seminars** form and click **Rename**. Change the name of the form to **Public Seminars Firstname Lastname** Right-click your **Public Seminars** form and click **Design View**. **Maximize** the form window. Notice in the bottom right corner of the form, there is an **UpdatedBy** field. This field will contain the name of the person who updates the form.

3. To the left of the horizontal ruler, right-click the **Form selector** and click **Properties** to display the properties sheet. If necessary, click the **Event tab**. Click in the **Before Update** box, and then click **Build**. Double-click **Code Builder**.

4. In the first blank line of the event procedure, press Tab. Type **Dim strName As String** and then press Enter.

    When declaring a variable, you start by typing *Dim*. Dim is a VBA statement used to reserve a procedure-level variable. The computer reserves enough space in memory for a variable of that data type. Notice this data type is a string. Each type of variable takes up different amounts of memory, so the data type must be specified. The standard method of naming variables is to begin the name with three letters representing the data type, followed by a unique identifier. In this variable, *str* is short for *string* and *Name* is a unique identifier.

5. To get the user's name from an Input Box, type **strName = InputBox ("Please type in your full name", "Get User's Name")** Press Enter.

    An Input Box displays a prompt in a dialog box similar to a message box, waits for the user to input text or click a button, and then returns a String containing the contents of the text box. The contents will be stored in the strName variable.

6 To set the field **UpdatedBy** in the form, type **UpdatedBy = strName** Compare your completed procedure to Figure 11.20.

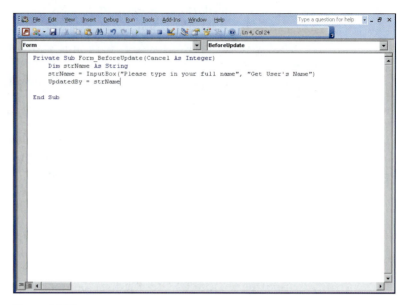

Figure 11.20

7 **Close** ☒ the Visual Basic Editor. **Close** ☒ the properties sheet, and then switch to **Form view** ▦ ▾.

8 Navigate to record **3** and update the **Expense Amt** from $75 to **$80** Press [Tab]. The Input Box displays and asks for your name. Type your **Firstname Lastname** See Figure 11.21. Click **OK**.

Access advances to the next record. To view the results of your VBA code, you must go back to the previous record.

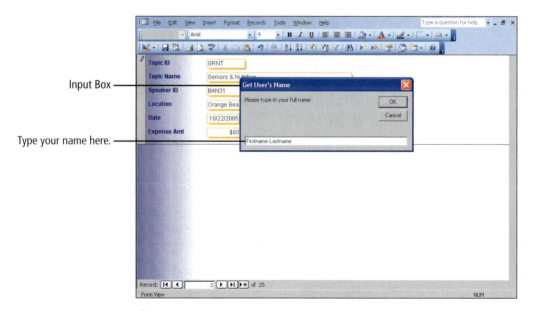

Figure 11.21

9 Click **Previous Record** . Notice that your name is displayed on the form under the *Updated By* label as shown in Figure 11.22.

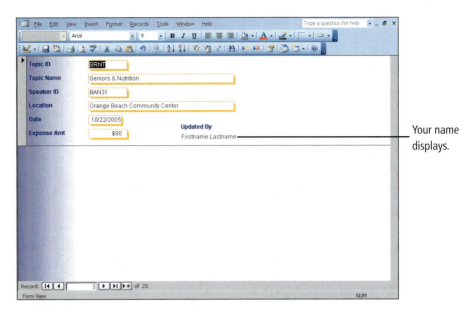

Your name displays.

Figure 11.22

10 From the **File** menu, click **Print**. Under **Print Range**, click the **Selected Record(s)** option button, and then click **OK**. **Close** the form, and save your changes. Leave your database open for the next activity.

Activity 11.7 Defining a Numeric Variable in a Procedure

In the previous activity, you defined a string variable to store a person's name. There are many different types of variables in VBA. Another type of variable is a ***numeric variable***. A numeric variable is a storage location that can store a single number. There are many different types of numbers, so when declaring a numeric variable you should choose the most appropriate type of numeric variable. The two numeric variables you will use are **Long** and **Single**. A Long variable can store a whole number from negative 2 billion to positive 2 billion. A Single variable is used to store a number containing a decimal value.

Some of the Medical Center's expenses are paid for by donations. To predict how much money must be raised from donations, you must write a procedure to total an expense for the year, ask the user what percentage of the expense will be paid for by donations, and then calculate and display this amount.

1 On the Objects bar, click **Forms**, if necessary. Right-click the **Marketing Expenses** form and click **Rename**. Name the form **Marketing Expenses Firstname Lastname** and then right-click your **Marketing Expenses** form and click **Design View**.

2 To the left of the horizontal ruler, right-click the **Form selector** and click **Properties** to display the properties sheet. If necessary, click the **Event tab**. Click in the **On Current** box, and then click **Build** . Double-click **Code Builder**.

3 On the blank line under the title of the procedure, press Tab, and then type the comment **'Declare variables** Press Enter and then on the next three lines type the following three variable declarations: **Dim sngTotal As Single** Press Enter then type **Dim strPercent As String** Press Enter and then type **Dim sngPercent As Single** Press Enter two times to place an extra line before the next section of the code. Compare your screen with Figure 11.23.

The first variable, *sngTotal*, contains the total cost of the expense for the 12-month period. The second variable, *strPercent*, contains the percent the user types in the Input Box. Recall that when a user types something in an Input Box, a string value is returned. You will convert the percent from a string to a value and store it in the final variable—*sngPercent*.

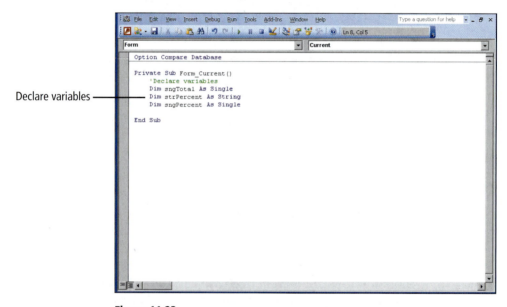

Declare variables

Figure 11.23

4 Type the comment **'Calculate total amount of expense for the year and display in form** Press Enter.

When typing a procedure, it is helpful to add a blank line before each section of the procedure. This makes the code easier to read and to correct if there is an error.

5 To calculate the total amount spent on the expense for the year, type the following formula: **sngTotal = Jan + Feb + Mar + Apr + May + Jun + Jul + Aug + Sep + Oct + Nov + Dec** Press Enter two times.

6 Type the comment **'Input percentage of expense to come from donations** Press [Enter], and then add the following code to create an Input Box: **strPercent = InputBox("What percent of this expense comes from donations?", "Donations", 0.25)** Press [Enter].

The value the user types for the percent will be saved as a string value in the *strPercent* variable. The third value listed in the Input Box is 0.25. This represents the default value, or the value that automatically displays in the text box.

7 To convert the percentage from a string to a percent, you will use the ***Val*** function. On the next line, type **sngPercent = Val(strPercent)** Press [Enter].

A string cannot be used in any calculations. The Val function converts a string to its numeric value. The string must be a numeric value like *123*.

8 To calculate the final result, you will multiply the total by the percent entered by the user. To accomplish this, type **sngTotal = sngTotal * sngPercent** Press [Enter] two times.

The editor multiplies the original total by the percent and saves the result as the updated total.

9 Type the comment **'Output Result** Press [Enter] and then to output the result in a message box, type **MsgBox "You must raise $" & sngTotal & " from donations."** Click anywhere to close the ScreenTip, and then compare your procedure to Figure 11.24.

The & symbol allows you to add multiple statements to the message box. The values in quotes will be output exactly as they are, and because *sngTotal* is not in quotes, the editor outputs the value of the variable.

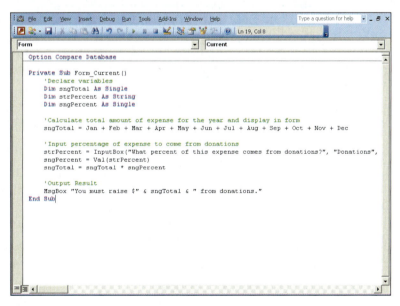

Figure 11.24

10 Close ☒ the Visual Basic Editor. Close ☒ the properties sheet, and then switch to **Form view** 🔲.

11 In the first Input Box, replace the default value of 0.25 with **0.15** and then click **OK**. A message box displays, indicating that $5535 must be raised from donations. Click **OK**. Click **Next Record** ▶ and in the Input Box, type **0.10** and then click **OK**. A message box displays, indicating that $2400 must be raised from donations. Click **OK**.

12 Press [Alt] + [F11] to display the VBA code for your procedure. From the **File** menu, click **Print**. Be sure **Current Module** is selected and **Code** is selected. Click **OK**. Close ☒ the Visual Basic Editor, Close ☒ the form, saving any changes, and leave your database open for the next activity.

Objective 6
Use the Selection Structure

In the previous activities, you wrote procedures using a **sequence** structure where each of the procedure's statements was processed in order. In some procedures, a statement to be processed may depend on certain conditions. You can use **selection** structure when you want a procedure to make a decision or comparison, and then based on the result of the decision or comparison, select one of two paths.

Activity 11.8 Using the Selection Structure

In this activity, you will write a procedure to output a reminder message if an individual enrolled in one of the seminars has not paid.

1 On the Objects bar, click **Forms**. Right-click the **Employee Training and Seminar Enrollments** form and rename the form **Employee Training and Seminar Enrollments Firstname Lastname** Right-click the form, and then open the form in **Design View**. If necessary, **Maximize** 🔲 the form window.

2 To the left of the horizontal ruler, right-click the **Form selector** and click **Properties**. If necessary, click the Event tab. Click in the **On Current** box, and then click **Build** […]. Double-click **Code Builder**.

3 In the blank line following the procedure title, press [Tab], and then type the comment **'Determine if the fee has been paid** Press [Enter].

4 Type your conditional statement **If (Paid = No) Then** and then press Enter, then press Tab, and then type the statements to run if the condition is true as follows: **MsgBox "Send a reminder to " & [First Name] & " " & [Last Name], vbExclamation, "Not Paid"** Press Enter.

Visual Basic Editor compares the value of the Paid field to see if it equals No, and then if an individual has not paid, a message box will display with the name of the individual.

5 Press Bksp to decrease the indent to line up with the If statement. Then, because this is the only statement to run if the condition is true, type **End If**

Visual Basic Editor allows you to place multiple statements in the If statement. If the condition is false, everything in the If statement will be skipped. Compare your procedure to Figure 11.25.

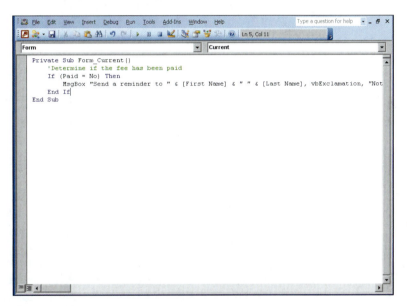

Figure 11.25

6 **Close** the Visual Basic Editor. **Close** the properties sheet, and then switch to **Form view**.

7 Navigate through each record by clicking **Next Record** and notice that when one of the participants has not paid, a message box displays. After you read each message box that displays, click **OK** to close each message box. See Figure 11.26.

Message box displays —

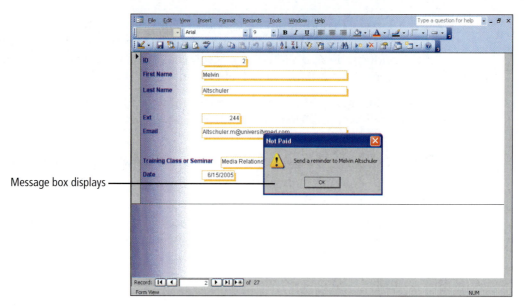

Figure 11.26

8 Press [Alt] + [F11]. Your VBA code redisplays. From the **File** menu, click **Print**. Be sure **Current Module** is selected and **Code** is selected. Click **OK**. **Close** ⊠ the Visual Basic Editor, **Close** ⊠ the form saving changes, and leave your database open for the next activity.

Objective 7
Use the Select Case Structure

In the previous activity, you used an If statement to test a condition, and then, based on the condition, selected one of two paths. While it is possible to write an If statement when there are more than two paths, it is usually simpler to use a **Select Case** statement. A Select Case statement has a single test but allows for many different paths that can be followed.

Activity 11.9 Using the Select Case Structure

The Medical Center frequently sends large packages of promotional materials to the media. In this activity, you will use the Select Case structure to calculate the shipping cost to each Media Contact based on the state where the contact is located.

1 On the Objects bar, click **Forms**. Right-click the **Media Contacts** form and rename the form **Media Contacts Firstname Lastname** Right-click the form and open the form in **Design View**. If necessary, Maximize the form window.

2 Right-click the **Form selector** and click **Properties**. If necessary, click the Event tab. Click in the **On Current** box, and then click **Build** ⋯ . Double-click **Code Builder**.

3 In the blank line following the name of the procedure, press Tab, and then type **'Declare variables** Press Enter, and then type **Dim sngPostage As Single** to declare a variable to store the cost of postage. Press Enter two times.

4 Type **'Calculate postage** and press Enter, and then start the Select Case structure by typing **Select Case State** and then press Enter.

Select Case will compare the value in the State field with all of the Case statements to determine what path to use in the code.

5 Press Tab. For the first Case statement, type **Case "AZ"** press Enter, press Tab, and then type **sngPostage = 12** Press Enter. Press Bksp to decrease the indent for the next Case statement.

6 Repeat Step 5 to create a Case for **"CA"** to set sngPostage to **10** a Case for **"FL"** to set sngPostage to **5** a Case for **"IL"** to set sngPostage to **8** a Case for **"MA"** to set sngPostage to **9** and a Case for **"NY"** to set sngPostage to **7** Press Enter after the last line, press Bksp three times to move the insertion point to the left edge of the screen, and then compare your procedure to Figure 11.27. Press Tab. Type **End Select** to end the Select Case structure. Press Enter two times.

The Select Case statement will assign the appropriate postage to the variable *sngPostage*. Only one path in a Select Case statement can be run. When a path is executed, the remaining statements are skipped by the Visual Basic Editor.

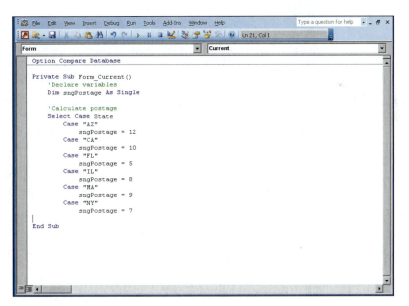

Figure 11.27

7 Type in the comment **'Output Postage** Press Enter, and then type the code to output the postage in a message box as follows: **MsgBox "The postage will cost $" & sngPostage, vbInformation, "Postage"**

8 Press Enter. **Close** ☒ the Visual Basic Editor. **Close** ☒ the properties sheet, and then switch to **Form view** ▦ ▾.

9 Click **OK**, and then navigate through each record by clicking **Next Record** ▶ and notice the postage is displayed for each media contact based on the state where the contact is located. See Figure 11.28. Click **OK** to close each message box as it is displayed.

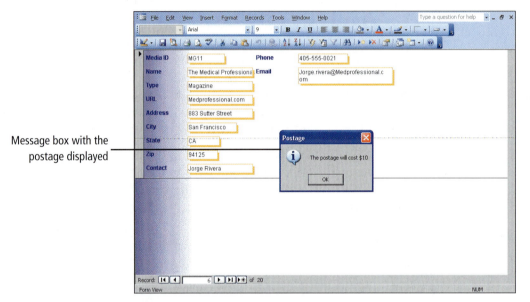

Message box with the postage displayed

Figure 11.28

10 Press Alt + F11 to redisplay your VBA code. From the **File** menu, click **Print**. Be sure **Current Module** is selected and **Code** is selected. Click **OK**. **Close** ☒ the Visual Basic Editor, **Close** ☒ your form saving changes, close your database, and close Access.

End You have completed Project 11B

Summary

In this chapter, you learned how to customize your database using Visual Basic for Applications (VBA). By using VBA code, you can modify data, input data, and output data using new techniques.

When you need to create a more sophisticated database, many times the only way to accomplish this task is by using VBA code. You practiced viewing and modifying a VBA procedure. You created event procedures to run when certain events on the forms were executed. You practiced creating message boxes to display information and created input boxes to get information from the user. You also practiced defining different types of variables to store information in your procedures. In this chapter, you also wrote If statements and Select Case statements to test conditions to determine different paths of code to run in your procedures.

In This Chapter You Practiced How To

- Convert a Macro to VBA Code
- Modify an Existing Procedure
- Use Immediate Window to Test Statements
- Write a Procedure
- Define Variables in a Procedure
- Use the Selection Structure
- Use the Select Case Structure

Concepts Assessments

Matching Match each term in the second column with its correct definition in the first column by writing the letter of the term on the blank line in front of the correct definition.

____ 1. A single VBA instruction used in a procedure.

____ 2. Related procedures that are grouped together.

____ 3. VBA statements that are grouped together.

____ 4. A statement that has a single test, but allows many different paths that can be followed.

____ 5. A window in the Visual Basic Editor in which you can run individual lines of Visual Basic code for the purpose of testing and debugging.

____ 6. A program used to view, create, and modify VBA code.

____ 7. A structure where each of the procedure's statements is processed in order.

____ 8. A variable that can store a whole number from negative 2 billion to positive 2 billion.

____ 9. A VBA statement used to reserve a procedure-level variable.

____ 10. A dialog box that waits for the user to input text or click a button, and returns a string containing the contents of the text box.

____ 11. A variable that stores zero or more characters enclosed in quotation marks (" ").

____ 12. A pane in the Visual Basic Editor window that displays a hierarchical list of the projects and all of the items contained and referenced by each project.

____ 13. A structure used when you want to make a decision or comparison, and then based on the result of the decision or comparison, select one of two paths.

____ 14. A temporary holding location for a value in a procedure.

____ 15. A variable used to store a number containing a decimal value.

A Dim
B Immediate window
C Input Box
D Long
E Module
F Procedure
G Project Explorer
H Select Case
I Selection
J Sequence
K Single
L Statement
M String
N Variable
O Visual Basic Editor

Concepts Assessments (continued)

Fill in the Blank Write the correct answer in the space provided.

1. After a procedure is created, either from converting a macro or coding the procedure, you can open the _____ to modify the procedure.

2. A _____ must have a unique name and must also have a data type associated with it.

3. _____ are limited by the actions already programmed in Access.

4. A storage location that can store a single number is called a _____ variable.

5. The _____ function converts a string to its numeric value.

6. The _____ allows you to add multiple statements to the message box.

7. When typing a statement, you must first identify the _____, type a period, and then type the procedure you want to run.

8. The Visual Basic editor does not consider anything on a line following the _____ to be code; rather, it is a comment.

9. You can use the procedures of the _____ object to run Microsoft Access actions from Visual Basic.

10. When creating an event procedure, Access automatically creates a _____.

Access chapter eleven

Skill Assessments

Project 11C — Marketing Expenses

Objective: *Write a Procedure.*

In the following Skill Assessment, you will create a VBA procedure to add the total amount spent for each marketing expense and display the result in a message box when the form for the expense displays. You will rename and save your database as *11C_Marketing_Expenses_Firstname_Lastname*. Your completed procedure will look similar to Figure 11.29.

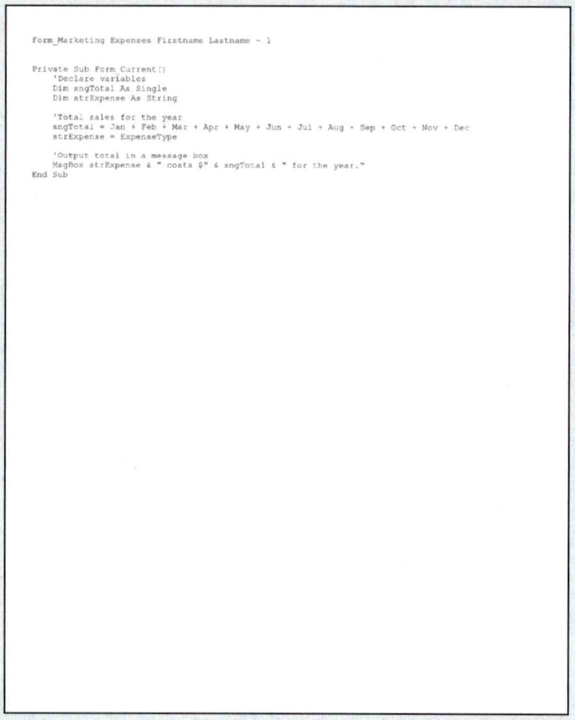

```
Form_Marketing Expenses Firstname Lastname - 1

Private Sub Form_Current()
    'Declare variables
    Dim sngTotal As Single
    Dim strExpense As String

    'Total sales for the year
    sngTotal = Jan + Feb + Mar + Apr + May + Jun + Jul + Aug + Sep + Oct + Nov + Dec
    strExpense = ExpenseType

    'Output total in a message box
    MsgBox strExpense & " costs $" & sngTotal & " for the year."
End Sub
```

Figure 11.29

1. Using **My Computer**, navigate to the student files that accompany this textbook and locate the Access database **a11C_Marketing_Expenses**. Copy and paste the file to your chapter folder. Rename the file **11C_Marketing_Expenses_Firstname_Lastname** Remove the Read-only property from the file. Start Access and open the database you just renamed.

2. On the Objects bar, click **Forms**. Right-click the **Marketing Expenses** form and rename the form **Marketing Expenses Firstname Lastname** and then right-click the form and click **Design View**. **Maximize** the form window. Notice the form currently lists all 12 months for each expense.

3. To the left of the horizontal ruler, right-click the **Form selector** and click **Properties**. If necessary, click the **Event tab**.

4. Click in the **On Current** box and click the **Build** button. Click **Code Builder**, and then click **OK**.

(Project 11C–Marketing Expenses continues on the next page**)**

Skill Assessments (continued)

(Project 11C–Marketing Expenses continued)

5. Be sure the insertion point is positioned in the blank line following the heading for the *Form_Current* procedure. You will use two variables for this procedure. One variable stores the total expenses for the year and the second variable stores the expense name. Press Tab. Type **'Declare variables** press Enter, type **Dim sngTotal As Single** press Enter, then type **Dim strExpense As String** and then press Enter two times.

6. You must store the values for your two variables by using the current values in the form. Type **'Total sales for the year** and press Enter; then to total all 12 months, type **sngTotal = Jan + Feb + Mar + Apr + May + Jun + Jul + Aug + Sep + Oct + Nov + Dec** and press Enter. To assign the expense name from the form to your variable, type **strExpense = ExpenseType** and then press Enter two times.

7. Type **'Output total in a message box** and press Enter. Then, type **MsgBox strExpense & " costs $" & sngTotal & " for the year."**

8. **Close** the Visual Basic Editor. **Close** the properties sheet, and then click the **View** button to switch to **Form view**. A message box displays showing the total expense for Printing–Brochures for the year. Click **OK**, and then navigate through all 10 records and read each message box.

9. Press [Alt] + [F11] to redisplay your code. From the **File** menu, click **Print**. Be sure **Current Module** is selected and **Code** is selected. Click **OK**. **Close** the Visual Basic Editor, close the form, save your changes, close your database, and then close Access.

End You have completed Project 11C

Project 11D — Convert Macro

Objective: *Convert a Macro to VBA Code.*

In the following Skill Assessment, you will convert an existing macro to VBA code so it will be easier to modify in the future. You will rename and save your database as *11D_Convert_Macro_Firstname_Lastname*. The code for your converted macro will look similar to Figure 11.30.

1. From your student files, locate the database file **a11D_Convert_Macro**, and then copy and paste the file to your chapter folder. Remove the Read-only property from the file and rename the file **11D_Convert_Macro_Firstname_Lastname** Start Access and open the database you just renamed.

2. On the Objects bar, click **Macros**, and then right-click the **Open List of Seminars report** macro and click **Design View**.

3. Click in each **Action** box and notice the Action Arguments for each action. **Close** the macro.

(Project 11D–Convert Macro continues on the next page)

Skill Assessments (continued)

(Project 11D–Convert Macro continued)

Figure 11.30

4. From the **Tools** menu, point to **Macro**, and then click **Convert Macros to Visual Basic**. Clear the **Add error handling to generated functions** check box. Click **Convert**. When the conversion is finished, click **OK**.

5. If your Project Explorer pane is not displayed, from the **View** menu, click **Project Explorer**. In the **Project Explorer**, under **Modules**, double-click the **Converted Macro-Open List of Seminars report**.

6. Read through each of the lines in the new function and notice how the Action Arguments were converted to VBA code.

7. Click anywhere in the VBA code window. On the Standard toolbar, click the **Run Sub/UserForm** button. Read the first message box and click **OK**. Read the next two message boxes and click **OK** for each of the messages.

8. Click on the first line under the title of the procedure—under the word *Function*—and insert the comment **'Procedure created by Firstname Lastname** From the **File** menu, click **Print**. Be sure **Current Module** is selected and **Code** is selected. Click **OK**. **Close** the Visual Basic Editor, close your database, save any changes, and then close Access.

End You have completed Project 11D

Skill Assessments (continued)

Project 11E — Select Case

Objective: *Use the Select Case Structure.*

In the following Skill Assessment, you will use the select case structure to display a reminder of what material to send to each Media Contact. The VBA code for your select case structure will look similar to Figure 11.31. You will rename and save your database as *11E_Select_Case_Firstname_Lastname*.

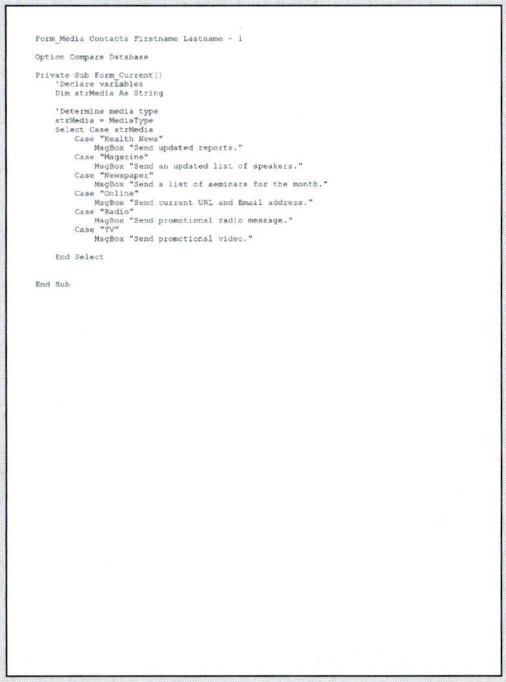

```
Form_Media Contacts Firstname Lastname - 1
Option Compare Database

Private Sub Form_Current()
    'Declare variables
    Dim strMedia As String
    
    'Determine media type
    strMedia = MediaType
    Select Case strMedia
        Case "Health News"
            MsgBox "Send updated reports."
        Case "Magazine"
            MsgBox "Send an updated list of speakers."
        Case "Newspaper"
            MsgBox "Send a list of seminars for the month."
        Case "Online"
            MsgBox "Send current URL and Email address."
        Case "Radio"
            MsgBox "Send promotional radio message."
        Case "TV"
            MsgBox "Send promotional video."
    End Select

End Sub
```

Figure 11.31

1. From your student files, locate the database file **a11E_Select_Case**, and then copy and paste the file to your chapter folder. Remove the Read-only property from the file and rename the file **11E_Select_Case_Firstname_Lastname** Start Access and open the database you just renamed.

2. On the Objects bar, click **Forms**. Right-click the **Media Contacts** form, rename the form **Media Contacts Firstname Lastname** and then right-click the form and click **Design View**. **Maximize** the form. Right-click the **Form selector** and click **Properties**. If necessary, click the **Event tab**. Click in the **On Current** box, and then click **Build**. Double-click **Code Builder**.

3. In the first line of the procedure press [Tab], type **'Declare variables** and press [Enter], and then type **Dim strMedia As String** to declare a variable to store the media type. Press [Enter] two times.

(**Project 11E**–Select Case continues on the next page)

Skill Assessments (continued)

(Project 11E–Select Case continued)

4. Type **'Determine media type** press Enter, then type **strMedia = MediaType** and press Enter. Start the Select Case structure by typing **Select Case strMedia** and then press Enter.

5. Press Tab. For the first Case statement, type **Case "Health News"** press Enter, press Tab, and then type **MsgBox "Send updated reports."** Press Enter.

6. Press Bksp to decrease the indent. Repeat Step 5 to create a Case for **"Magazine"** to display a message **"Send an updated list of speakers."**, a Case for **"Newspaper"** to display a message **"Send a list of seminars for the month."**, a Case for **"Online"** to display a message **"Send current URL and Email address."**, a Case for **"Radio"** to display a message **"Send promotional radio message."**, and a Case for **"TV"** to display a message **"Send promotional video."** and press Enter at the end of the last case.

7. Press Bksp two times. Type **End Select** and then press Enter two times.

8. **Close** the Visual Basic Editor. **Close** the properties sheet, and then switch to **Form view**.

9. Click **OK** in the first message box. Navigate through each record by clicking **Next Record** and notice the message displayed for each media contact based on the media type.

10. Press Alt + F11. From the **File** menu, click **Print**. Be sure **Current Module** is selected and **Code** is selected. Click **OK**. **Close** the Visual Basic Editor, close your database, save changes, and then close Access.

End You have completed Project 11E

Performance Assessments

Project 11F—Updated Expenses

Objective: *Write a Procedure.*

In the following Performance Assessment, you will write a procedure to insert a date stamp on the Marketing Expenses form. Your completed form will look similar to Figure 11.32. You will rename and save your database as *11F_Updated_Expenses_Firstname_Lastname*.

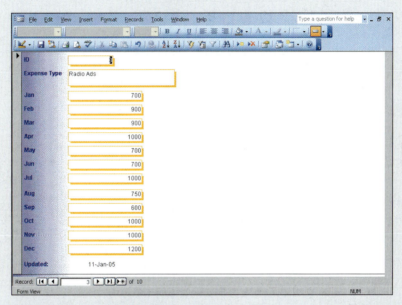

Figure 11.32

1. From your student files, locate the database file **a11F_Updated_Expenses**, and then copy and paste the file to your chapter folder. Remove the Read-only property from the file and rename the file as **11F_Updated_Expenses_Firstname_Lastname** Start Access and open the database you just renamed.

2. On the Objects bar, click **Forms**. Rename the **Marketing Expenses** form **Marketing Expenses Firstname Lastname** Open the form in **Design View** and **Maximize** the form window.

3. Display the **Properties** sheet. Click the **Event tab**, click in the **Before Update** box, and then click the **Build** button. Double-click **Code Builder**.

4. If necessary, click on the first line after the title of the procedure, press Tab and type **'Assign current date to Updated field after the form is modified** Press Enter.

5. Type **Updated = Date** Press Enter.

(**Project 11F**–Updated Expenses continues on the next page)

Performance Assessments (continued)

(Project 11F–Updated Expenses continued)

6. **Close** the Visual Basic Editor, close the properties sheet, and then switch to **Form view**. In the record navigation box, type **3** then press Enter to go to record 3. Change the amount in the **Dec** field to **1200**

7. Click **Next Record** and then click **Previous Record**. The updated field displays the current date.

8. From the **File** menu, click **Print**. Under **Print Range**, click the **Selected Record(s)** option button, and then click **OK**. **Close** the form, save your changes, close the database, and then close Access.

End You have completed Project 11F

Project 11G—Over Budget

Objective: *Use the Selection Structure.*

In the following Performance Assessment, you will write a procedure to determine if the marketing expenses have gone over budget and then display an appropriate message. Your updated form will look similar to Figure 11.33. You will rename and save your database as *11G_Over_Budget_Firstname_Lastname*.

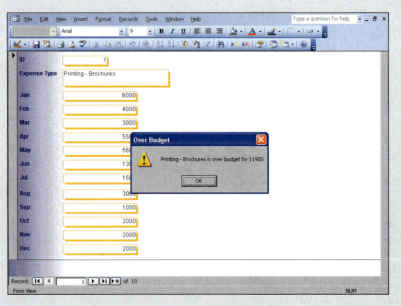

Figure 11.33

(Project 11G–Over Budget continues on the next page)

Performance Assessments (continued)

(Project 11G–Over Budget continued)

1. From the student files that accompany this textbook, locate the database file **a11G_Over_Budget**, copy and paste the file to your chapter folder, and then rename the file **11G_Over_Budget_Firstname_Lastname** Start Access and open the database you just renamed.

2. On the Objects bar, click **Forms**. Rename the Marketing Expenses form **Marketing Expenses Firstname Lastname** and open it in **Design View**. **Maximize** the form window.

3. Display the **Properties** sheet and click the **Event tab**. Click in the **On Current** box, and then click **Build**. Double-click **Code Builder**.

4. Click under the heading for the *Form_Current* procedure. Press Tab, and then type **'Define variable** press Enter, type **Dim sngTotal As Single** and then press Enter two times.

5. Type **'Total expenses for the year** press Enter, type **sngTotal = Jan + Feb + Mar + Apr + May + Jun + Jul + Aug + Sep + Oct + Nov + Dec** and then press Enter two times.

6. To compare the total expenses with the value in the budget field, type the conditional statement **If (sngTotal > Budget) Then** and press Enter, then press Tab and type the statement to run if the condition is true as follows: **MsgBox [Expense Type] & " is over budget by " & sngTotal - Budget, vbExclamation, "Over Budget"** Press Enter, press Bksp to decrease the indent, and then type **End If**

7. Press Enter and type the second conditional statement **If (sngTotal < Budget) Then** and press Enter, press Tab, and then type the statement to run if the condition is true as follows: **MsgBox [Expense Type] & " is under budget by " & Budget - sngTotal, vbExclamation, "Under Budget"** Press Enter, press Bksp to decrease the indent, and then type **End If**

8. **Close** the Visual Basic Editor. **Close** the properties sheet, and then switch to **Form view**.

9. Click **OK** in each message box, and navigate through each record by clicking **Next Record** and read each message box that displays.

10. Press Alt + F11 to redisplay your VBA code. From the **File** menu, click **Print**. Be sure **Current Module** is selected and **Code** is selected. Click **OK**. **Close** the Visual Basic Editor, **Close** the form, save your changes, close the database, and then close Access.

End You have completed Project 11G

Performance Assessments (continued)

Project 11H — Email

Objective: *Write a Procedure.*

When sending reminders to the employees through email, many of the reminders were returned because the email address was incorrect. In the following Performance Assessment, you will write a procedure to prompt the user to read and confirm that the email address is correct. If it is not correct, the user should correct the address. Your updated form will look similar to Figure 11.34. You will rename and save your database as *11H_Email_Firstname_Lastname*.

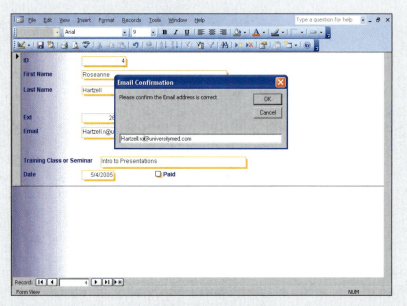

Figure 11.34

1. From the student files that accompany this textbook, locate the database file **a11H_Email**, copy and paste the file to your chapter folder, and then rename the file **11H_Email_Firstname_Lastname** Start Access and open the database you just renamed.

2. On the Objects bar, click **Forms**. Rename the **Training Enrollments** form **Training Enrollments Firstname Lastname** and then open the form in **Design View**. **Maximize** the form window.

3. Display the properties sheet and click the **Event tab**. Click in the **On Current** box, and then click the **Build** button. Double-click **Code Builder**.

4. Click under the heading for the *Form_Current* procedure. Type **'Define variable** and press Enter, type **Dim strEmail As String** and then press Enter two times.

(**Project 11H**–Email continues on the next page)

Performance Assessments (continued)

Project 11H–Email continued)

5. You will create an Input Box to show the current email address and allow the user to view and, if necessary, change the address. Type **'Create input box** and press Enter. Type **strEmail = InputBox("Please confirm the Email address is correct", "Email Confirmation", Email)** The default for the Input Box is the current value from the Email field. Press Enter two times.

6. Now you can assign the email address from the Input Box to the Email field. Type **'Assign current Email address to Email field** and then press Enter. Type **Email = strEmail**

7. **Close** the Visual Basic Editor. **Close** the properties sheet, and then switch to **Form view**.

8. Navigate through the first three records by clicking **Next Record** and read each message box that displays. When record 4 displays, change the email address in the input box to **Hartzell.ro@universitymed.com** Click **OK** and notice that the email in the form is updated.

9. Press Alt + F11. From the **File** menu, click **Print**. Be sure **Current Module** is selected and **Code** is selected. Click **OK**. **Close** the Visual Basic Editor, **Close** the form, save your changes, and then close the database and close Access.

End You have completed Project 11H

Mastery Assessments

Project 11I — Seminars

Objective: *Use the Selection Structure.*

In the following Mastery Assessment, you will write a procedure that asks the user if they want to print the updated List of Seminars report when they close the Public Seminars form. Your form will look similar to Figure 11.35. You will rename and save your database as *11I_Seminars_Firstname_Lastname*.

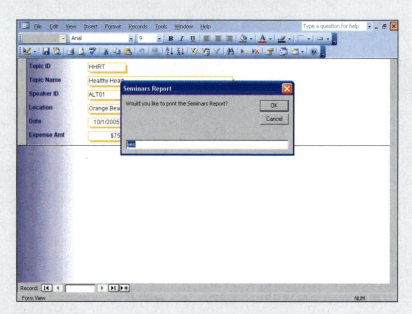

Figure 11.35

1. From the student files, locate the database file **a11I_Seminars**, and then copy and paste the file to your chapter folder. Remove the Read-only property from the file and rename the file as **11I_Seminars_Firstname_Lastname** Start Access and open the database you just renamed.

2. On the Objects bar, click **Forms**. Rename the **Public Seminars** form **Public Seminars Firstname Lastname** and then open the form in **Design View**.

3. On the **Properties** sheet, change the **On Close** event to run a VBA procedure.

4. Write a comment, and then declare a String variable called **strReport** Set the strReport variable equal to an Input Box with the prompt **"Would you like to print the Seminars Report?"** and the title **"Seminars Report"** and a default value of **"yes"**

(**Project 11I**–Seminars continues on the next page)

Mastery Assessments (continued)

(Project 11I–Seminars continued)

5. Write a comment to explain the comparison statements, and then write an If statement to evaluate if strReport = "Yes". If strReport is Yes, then use the **DoCmd** to open the report in **acViewPreview**. End the If statement.

6. **Close** the Visual Basic Editor. **Close** the properties box, and then switch to **Form view**.

7. Leave the text "yes" in the text box and click **OK**. View and then **Close** the report.

8. Open the VBA editor and print your procedure. **Close** the editor, close the form, save any changes, and then close Access.

 You have completed Project 11I

Project 11J—Bonus

Objective: *Use the Select Case Structure.*

In the following Mastery Assessment, you will create a procedure to calculate the bonus amount for each of the speakers based on how many presentations the speaker has given. Your form will look similar to Figure 11.36. You will rename and save your database as *11J_Bonus_Firstname_Lastname*.

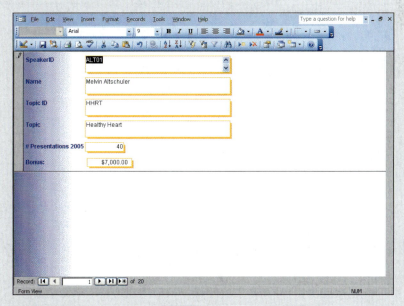

Figure 11.36

(**Project 11J**–Bonus continues on the next page)

Mastery Assessments (continued)

(Project 11J–Bonus continued)

1. From the student files, locate the Access database **a11J_Bonus**, and then copy and paste the file to your chapter folder. Remove the Read-only property from the file and rename the file as **11J_Bonus_Firstname_Lastname** Start Access and open the database you just renamed.

2. On the Objects bar, click **Forms**. Rename the **Speakers** form **Speakers Firstname Lastname** and then open the form in **Design View**.

3. Create an event procedure for the **On Current** event for the form.

4. Write a **Select Case** structure to compare the field **# Presentations 2005** and set the **Bonus** field to 0 if the # of presentations is from **0 To 9**. You can set up a range in a Case statement by using the word *To*.

5. Set up five more Case statements for the following ranges: 10 To 19 set Bonus = 1000, 20 To 29 set Bonus = 2500, 30 To 39 set Bonus = 4000, 40 To 49 set Bonus = 7000, and use the Else statement set Bonus = 10000. The Else statement covers any values not satisfied by the other cases.

6. Switch to **Form view** and navigate through each record to confirm that each Bonus is correct.

7. Open the VBA editor and print your procedure. **Close** the editor, close the form, save any changes, and then close Access.

End You have completed Project 11J

Problem Solving

Project 11K — Switchboard

Objective: *Write a Procedure.*

In the following Problem Solving exercise, you will write procedures to open each of the tables and queries in the database. Then you will create a Switchboard to open each of the tables and queries by running the procedures you created. You will rename and save your database as 11K_Switchboard_Firstname_Lastname.

1. From the student files, locate the Access database **a11K_Switchboard**, and then copy and paste the file to your chapter folder. Remove the Read-only property from the file and rename the file as **11K_Switchboard_Firstname_Lastname** Start Access and open the database you just renamed.

2. Create a Switchboard to open the Tables, Queries, Forms, and Reports from the database. Write procedures to open each table and query. Use the **Run Code** command to open each of the objects from the Switchboard. This method is similar to running a Macro to open a table or query.

3. Open the VBA editor, add a comment at the top of the window to add your name to the top of the procedures, and then print your procedures. **Close** the editor, close the form, and then close Access.

End You have completed Project 11K

Project 11L — Updated Seminars

Objective: *Use the Selection Structure.*

In the following Problem Solving exercise, you will write a procedure to run when the Public Seminars form displays and ask the user if they are interested in the seminar. If they are interested, ask how many people would attend the seminar, and display a message box with the final cost of attending the seminar.

1. From the student files, locate the Access database **a11L_Updated_Seminars**, and then copy and paste the file to your chapter folder. Remove the Read-only property from the file and rename the file as **11L_Updated_Seminars_Firstname_Lastname** Start Access and open the database you just renamed.

2. Open the **Public Seminars** form, and rename the form **Public Seminars Firstname Lastname** Create an **On Current** event procedure. The procedure should display an Input Box asking the user if he or she is interested in the seminar. If the response is Yes, display a second Input Box and ask the user how many people would be attending the seminar, and then display the total cost for the seminar. You should multiply the number of people by the cost of the seminar.

3. Open the VBA editor, add a comment at the top of the window to add your name to the top of the procedures, and then print your procedures. **Close** the editor, close the form, save any changes, and then close Access.

End You have completed Project 11L

On the Internet

Getting Information About VBA

The Microsoft Web site contains a variety of information about using VBA in Access. Go to the Microsoft site at http://msdn.microsoft.com/vba/. Search the site and learn more about VBA in Access. Print any information that is of interest to you.

GO! with Help

Other VBA Objects

In this chapter, you worked with functions and procedures. VBA has many procedures and functions already written that you can use when you need them.

1. Start Access. Press Alt + F11 to open the Visual Basic editor.
2. On the Standard toolbar, click **Microsoft Visual Basic Help**.
3. In the Search text box, type **Functions** and then press Enter.
4. View the list of functions and open and view any of the functions that may be helpful to you. Print the Help information if you want to keep a copy of it. Close the **Help** window, close the VBA window, and then close Access.

Access 2003

chapter twelve

Exporting and Advanced Integration

In this chapter, you will: **complete these projects** and **practice these skills.**

Project 12A
Exporting Data

Objectives
- Export an Access Table to Excel
- Export an Access Table to Word
- Create a Report Snapshot

Project 12B
Working with Data Access Pages

Objectives
- Create a Custom Data Access Page
- Place a PivotTable in a Data Access Page

Project 12C
Working with XML

Objectives
- Export Access Data as an XML Document
- Import an XML Document into Access

Lake Michigan City College

Lake Michigan City College is located along the lakefront of Chicago—one of the country's most exciting cities. The college serves its large and diverse student body and makes positive contributions to the community through relevant curricula, partnerships with businesses and not-for-profit organizations, and learning experiences that allow students to be full participants in the global community. The college offers three associate degrees in 20 academic areas, adult education programs, and continuing education offerings on campus, at satellite locations, and online.

© Getty Images, Inc.

Exporting and Advanced Integration

When working with Access, you are not limited to the functionality of Access to analyze your data. By using the various export functions in Access, you can use the features of other programs, such as Excel and Word, to view, format, and analyze your data.

Access also allows you to export and share information by publishing data to the Web. By creating a data access page, you can create a Web page to view, analyze, and enter data. Microsoft Office 2003 has incorporated new methods to export, share, and analyze data. The latest technique for sharing information across different computer platforms or applications is to export your Access tables, queries, or forms using XML, which is a markup language similar to HTML, the markup language used to create Web pages.

In this chapter, you will work with data from Lake Michigan City College. You will export data from Access to Microsoft Word and Excel. You will publish a data access page as a Web page, and then manipulate the data using your browser. Finally, you will import an XML database and export data from Access and save the data in XML format.

Project 12A LMCC Health Sciences

The Health Sciences Division at Lake Michigan City College includes the Dental Assisting and Radiology programs. The Dean of the Division wants to export some of the Division's data into Word and Excel where it is more easily analyzed and formatted. The Dean also wants to distribute Access reports to individuals who do not have Access on their computers.

In Activities 12.1 through 12.4, you will export Access tables to Excel and to a Word table for analysis and formatting. You will also create a file to distribute an Access report to individuals who do not have Access on their computers. You will save your database as *12A_LMCC_Health_Sciences_Firstname_Lastname*.

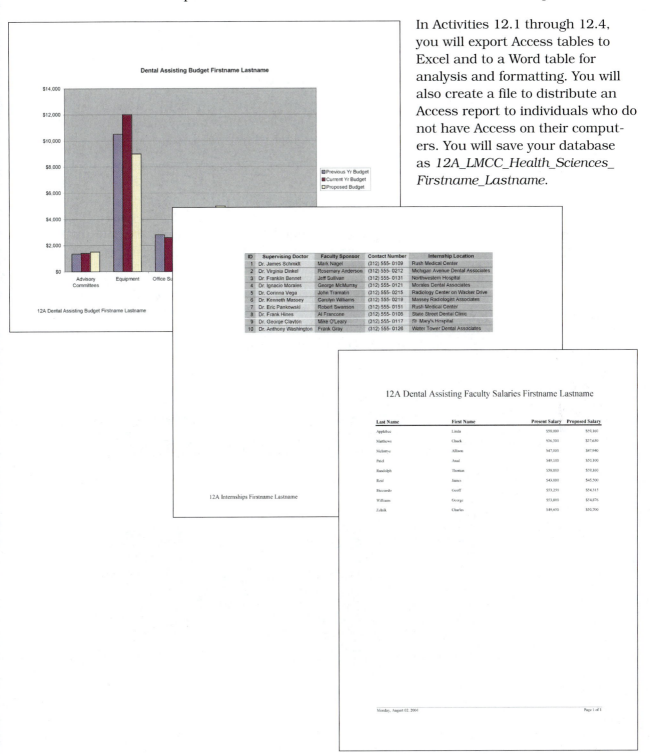

Figure 12.1
Project 12A—LMCC Health Sciences

Objective 1
Export an Access Table to Excel

To analyze Access data using Microsoft Excel, use the Microsoft Access tool *Analyze It with Microsoft Excel* to export the data to an Excel worksheet. This tool copies the data from your table or query into an Excel worksheet. After the data is in Excel, you can use Excel's analysis tools to view, analyze, or edit the data. No link between the Excel worksheet and the database is established; thus, any changes made to the data in the Excel worksheet will not affect your original table or query.

Activity 12.1 Exporting Data to Excel

In this activity, you will export the Dental Assisting Budget to Excel. With the data in an Excel spreadsheet, the Dean can use Excel's financial analysis tools to make decisions about the budget.

1 Using **My Computer**, navigate to the student files that accompany this textbook and locate the Access database **a12A_LMCC_Health_Sciences**. Copy and paste the file to your storage location, creating a new folder for Chapter 12 if you want to do so. Rename the file **12A_LMCC_Health_Sciences_Firstname_Lastname** Remove the Read-only property from the file. Start Access and open the database you just renamed.

2 On the Objects bar, click **Tables**, and then double-click the **Dental Assisting Budget** table to open it. Notice the columns that refer to the three different budgets: Previous Year, Current Year, and Proposed, as shown in Figure 12.2.

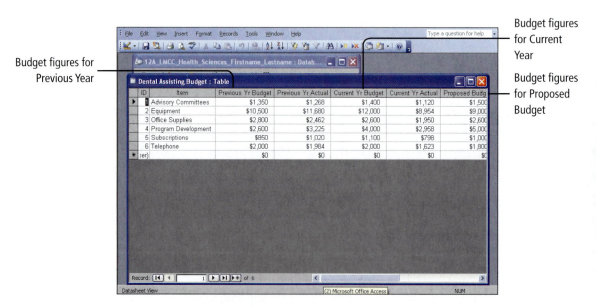

Figure 12.2

3 Close the table. Right-click the **Dental Assisting Budget** table and click **Rename**. Rename the table **12A Dental Assisting Budget Firstname Lastname** and press Enter. Be sure the table is still selected.

4 On the Database toolbar, click the **OfficeLinks** arrow . From the displayed list, point to **Analyze It with Microsoft Office Excel** as shown in Figure 12.3, and then click. If a message indicates that the file already exists, click **Yes**.

Microsoft Excel opens and the data from the Dental Assisting Budget table displays in a new worksheet. The worksheet and the workbook are named *12A Dental Assisting Budget Firstname Lastname* and are saved in your current directory.

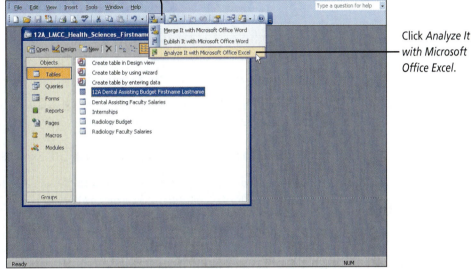

Figure 12.3

5 From the **File** menu, click **Save As**, navigate to your chapter folder, and then click the **Save** button. From the Excel **View** menu, click **Header and Footer**. Click the **Custom Footer** button.

6 With the insertion point in the **Left section**, in the row of buttons above the sections, click the **File name** button, and then compare your screen with Figure 12.4.

&[File] indicates that the name of the file will be placed in the left section of the footer.

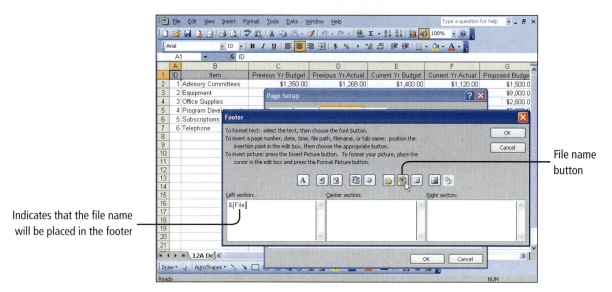

Figure 12.4

7 Click **OK** to close the **Footer** dialog box, and then click **OK** to close the **Page Setup** dialog box. Click **Save** and leave your Excel worksheet open for the next activity.

Activity 12.2 Creating a Chart to Analyze Data in Excel

In this activity, you will create a *chart* in Excel to examine the figures from the Dental Assisting Budget table. A chart is a graphic representation of data in a worksheet. Data presented in a chart is usually easier to understand than a table of numbers. Excel has excellent charting tools; thus, when you want a visual representation of data in an Access table, it is useful to export the table to Excel.

1 Click in any cell in **column D**. From the **Format** menu, point to **Column**, and then click **Hide**. Use the same technique to hide **column F**.

The remaining columns display the three budgets to be analyzed.

2 Click in cell **C2** and drag over and down to cell **G7** to select the range **C2:G7**. The selected cells represent the budget numbers. On the Formatting toolbar, click the **Decrease Decimal** button two times to remove the decimal point and the following two zeros from the budget numbers.

3 Click in cell **B1** and drag over and down to cell **G7** to select the range **B1:G7**. This represents the data to chart, as shown in Figure 12.5.

Range B1:G7 selected

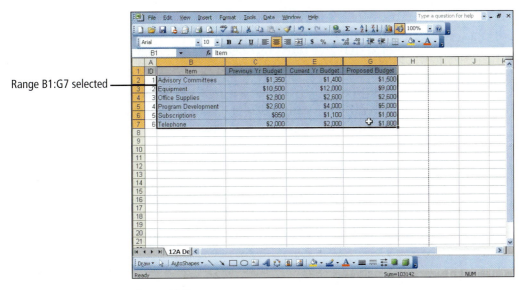

Figure 12.5

4 On the Standard toolbar, click the **Chart Wizard** button as shown in Figure 12.6.

The Chart Wizard displays the first of four steps to assist you in creating a chart from the selected cells in the worksheet.

Click Chart Wizard.

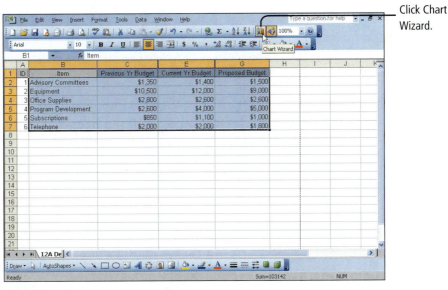

Figure 12.6

5 In the **Chart type** list, be sure **Column** is selected, and under **Chart sub-type**, leave the default **Clustered Column** chart selected. Click **Next**.

The most commonly used chart types are ***column charts***, which are used to make comparisons among related numbers. Step 2 of the wizard displays and your selected data is surrounded by a moving border.

6 Check to be sure the **Data range** box indicates the worksheet name followed by the range *$B$1:$G$7* and if it does not, click in the box and edit as necessary. Click **Next**.

7 In the **Chart title** box, type **Dental Assisting Budget Firstname Lastname** as shown in Figure 12.7.

After a moment, the title of the chart displays in the preview window.

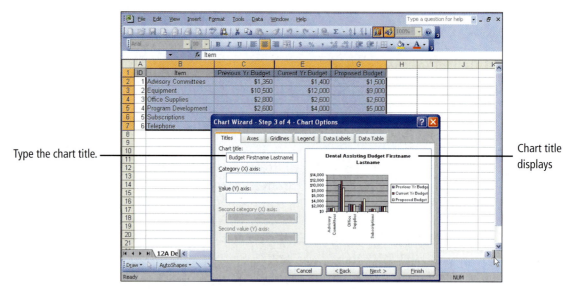

Type the chart title.

Chart title displays

Figure 12.7

8 Click **Next**. In the displayed **Step 4 of 4** dialog box, click the **As new sheet** option button, which will place the chart in a new worksheet. Replace the worksheet name *Chart 1* by typing **Dental Assisting Budget Chart** and then click **Finish**.

Your chart displays on a new worksheet. Recall that a chart is a visual representation of numbers. As shown in Figure 12.8, you can see that *Equipment* is the largest budget item, and you can also see that the budget for *Equipment* in the *Current Yr Budget* is larger than that of the *Previous Yr Budget*. The ***legend*** defines the colors used in the chart and identifies the data series, which are the various budget names.

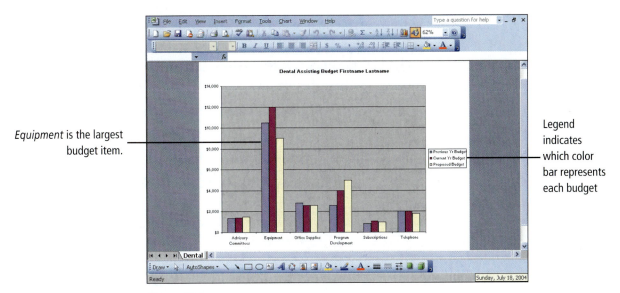

Equipment is the largest budget item.

Legend indicates which color bar represents each budget

Figure 12.8

9. From the **View** menu, click **Header and Footer**. Click the **Custom Footer** button.

10. With the insertion point in the **Left section**, in the row of buttons above the sections, click the **File name** button. Click **OK** twice to close the dialog boxes.

11. On the **Standard** toolbar, click the **Save** button. From the **File** menu, click **Print**. In the displayed **Print** dialog box, under **Print range**, be sure **All** is selected and under **Print what**, Active sheet(s) is selected. Click **OK**.

12. **Close** Excel and leave Access and your database open for the next activity.

Objective 2
Export an Access Table to Word

If you want to share the information contained in an Access table, export it into Word to form a Word document. In this manner, you can e-mail a single Word document rather than e-mailing the entire database. Exporting an Access table to Word is also helpful if you have a table of information that you want to format in a more formal way than you can by just printing an Access table.

Activity 12.3 Exporting an Access Table to Word

Word provides many ways to format information attractively. In this activity, you will export the Internships table to Microsoft Word so that the Dean can format it in an attractive manner.

1. On the Objects bar, be sure **Tables** is selected. Right-click the **Internships** table and click **Rename**. Rename the table **12A Internships Firstname Lastname** and press Enter.

2 With the table still selected, on the Standard toolbar, click the **OfficeLinks** arrow, which may now display the Excel icon, and then click **Publish It with Microsoft Office Word**. If a message box displays stating the file already exists, click **Yes** to replace it.

As shown in Figure 12.9, your table is copied to a Word document.

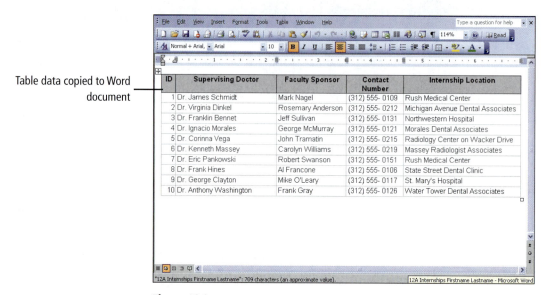

Table data copied to Word document

Figure 12.9

> **Another Way**
>
> **To Export an Access Table to Word**
>
> With your database displayed, open Microsoft Word. From the taskbar, switch back to your database. Be sure your table name is selected. Drag the table name down and over the Word Document1 button on the taskbar, keep holding the left mouse button down while Word displays, and then move the mouse pointer into the blank document area and release the mouse button. The table data is copied into the Word document.

3 From the **File** menu, click **Save As**, navigate to your chapter folder, and then click the **Save** button.

4 From the Word **Table** menu, point to **Select**, and then click **Table**. With the table selected, from the **Table** menu, click **Table AutoFormat**. In the **Table styles** list, scroll as necessary, and then click **Table 3D effects 3**. At the bottom of the dialog box, under **Apply special formats to**, be sure that all of the check boxes are cleared, as shown in Figure 12.10.

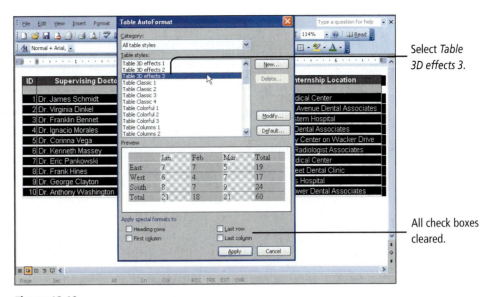

Figure 12.10

5 Click **Apply**, and then with the table still selected, on the Formatting toolbar, click the **Center** button. From the **Table** menu, point to **AutoFit**, and then click **AutoFit to Contents**. Click anywhere in the document to cancel the selection.

Because Word flags words that are not in its dictionary, you may notice wavy red lines under some proper names. These lines do not print.

6 From the **View** menu, click **Header and Footer**. On the displayed toolbar, click the **Switch Between Header and Footer** button. On the same toolbar, click the **Insert AutoText** button, and from the displayed list click **Filename**. **Close** the Header and Footer toolbar.

7 From the **File** menu, click **Page Setup**, click the **Margins tab**, and then under **Orientation**, click **Landscape**. Click **OK**. From the **File** menu, click **Print**, and then click **OK**.

After the table is in Word, it is easy to print and include it with a letter, to attach it to an e-mail message, or to share the document in other ways. Because a link was not established between the Access table and the Word table, changes made to the table in Word will *not* affect the original table in Access.

8 Click the **Save** button, and then **Close** Microsoft Word. Leave the database open for the next activity.

Objective 3
Create a Report Snapshot

Thus far, you have exported a table into Excel and a table into Word. Another export option is to create a ***report snapshot***. A report snapshot is a file that contains a high-fidelity copy of each page of an Access *report*. It preserves the two-dimensional layout, graphics, and other embedded objects of the report.

The benefit of a report snapshot is that you can view, print, store, publish, distribute, and archive a report snapshot without having the Access program on your computer. Thus, you can send the report to individuals who do not have Access. They can view it using a combination of Snapshot Viewer and Microsoft Windows Explorer, an e-mail program, or a Web browser. This is an easy way to distribute Access reports to others electronically. Snapshot Viewer can be downloaded for free from http://office.microsoft.com/downloads.

Activity 12.4 Using the Export Command to Create a Snapshot

In this activity, you will create a report snapshot from the Dental Assisting Faculty Salaries report so that it can be e-mailed to and viewed by college administrators who do not have Access on their computers.

1 On the Objects bar, click **Reports**. Right-click the **Dental Assisting Faculty Salaries** report and click **Rename**. Rename the report **Dental Assisting Faculty Salaries Firstname Lastname** and press [Enter].

2 Right-click your **Dental Assisting Faculty Salaries Firstname Lastname** report and click **Design View**. In the Report Header, click to select the **Dental Assisting Faculty Salaries** label box, click to the left of *Dental* and type **12A** and press [Spacebar]. Click to the right of the word *Salaries*, press [Spacebar], and then type **Firstname Lastname** Press [Enter] to accept the changes and leave the label selected, change the **Font Size** to **18**, and then click the **Center** button. Compare your screen with Figure 12.11.

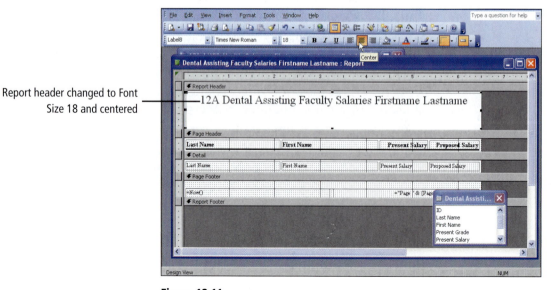

Report header changed to Font Size 18 and centered

Figure 12.11

3 Close the report window. Click **Yes** to save the changes. After the report closes, leave the report name selected. From the **File** menu, click **Export**. In the displayed **Export Report** dialog box, navigate to your chapter folder. At the bottom of the dialog box, click the **Save as type arrow**, and then click **Snapshot Format**. Select the **Autostart** check box to view the file in the Snapshot Viewer when you export the file. Leave the default file name as *Dental Assisting Faculty Salaries Firstname Lastname*. Compare your screen with Figure 12.12.

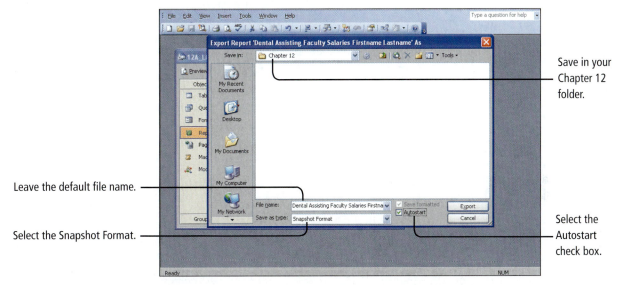

Figure 12.12

4 Click **Export**. After a moment, the Snapshot Viewer opens.

Maximize the Snapshot Viewer window.

5 From the **File** menu, click **Print**. Under **Page Range**, click the **Pages** option button, and then in the **Pages** box, type **1** At the bottom of the dialog box, click **Print** to print the report from the **Snapshot Viewer**.

6 Close the Snapshot Viewer. Close your database and close Access. Click **Yes** if a message displays regarding emptying the Clipboard.

 **You have completed Project 12A**

Project 12B Summer Schedule

Organizations increasingly place information on the Internet. Access data can be stored and distributed on the Web using data access pages. Data access pages allow you to place Access data on Web pages. Additionally, the pages can be displayed or edited from the Web. Data access pages combine features of a form and a report so the data may be viewed, analyzed, and input while working in your browser.

In Activities 12.5 through 12.7, you will create a data access page so that the summer course schedule for the Business and Computer Information Systems Division can be viewed from the Internet by the public, and to allow college officials to enter data from a Web page. You will also rearrange information in a PivotTable. Your completed output will look similar to Figure 12.13. You will name your database *12B_Summer_Schedule_Firstname_Lastname*.

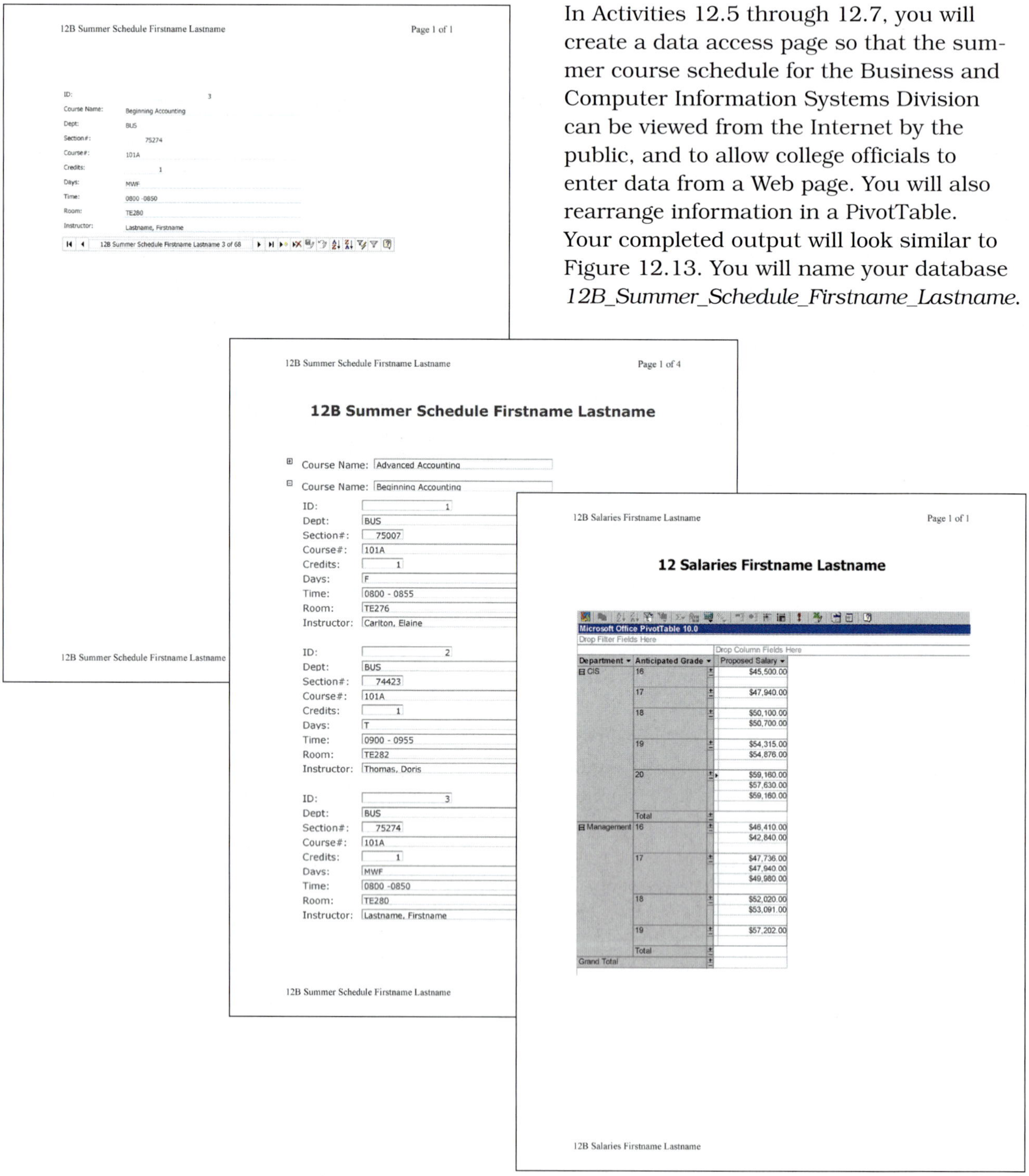

Figure 12.13
Project 12B—Summer Schedule

Objective 4
Create a Custom Data Access Page

A ***data access page*** is a special type of Web page designed for viewing and working with Access data on the Internet or on an organization's intranet. A data access page is a separate file that is stored outside Access; however, when you create the file, Access automatically adds a shortcut to the file in the Database window. Data access pages are stored as HTML files. Because they are stored as HTML files, the pages may be opened using a browser; or they can be opened from the shortcut in Access.

Activity 12.5 Creating a Custom Data Access Page

In this activity, you will create a data access page for the Summer Schedule table using the wizard. College officials will be able to change the data from the college's intranet. Members of the public will be able to view the Summer Schedule on the Web and even arrange the data in a manner that is useful to them. However, appropriate protection will be applied so that public viewers on the Web cannot change the actual data in the database.

1. From the student files that accompany this textbook, locate the Access database **a12B_Summer_Schedule**, and then copy and paste the file to the folder where you are storing your projects for this chapter. Remove the Read-only property from the file, and rename the file as **12B_Summer_Schedule_Firstname_Lastname** Start Access and open the database you just renamed.

2. On the Objects bar, click **Tables**, if necessary. Right-click the **Salaries** table, click **Rename**, and name the table **12B Salaries Firstname Lastname** Right-click the **Summer Schedule** table, click **Rename**, and name the table **12B Summer Schedule Firstname Lastname** On the Objects bar, click **Pages**. Double-click **Create data access page by using wizard**.

3. In the displayed **Page Wizard** dialog box, click the **Tables/Queries arrow**, and then click **Table: 12B Summer Schedule Firstname Lastname**. Click the **All Fields** button to move all the fields to the **Selected Fields** list. Click **Next**.

4. No grouping levels are necessary, so click **Next** to display the sort order page of the wizard. No sort order is necessary, so click **Next** to display the final page of the wizard.

5. In the center of the dialog box, click the **Open the page** option button. Leave the default title for your page. Click **Finish**. The data access page opens with the first record displayed. **Maximize** the window and compare your screen with Figure 12.14.

First record displayed

Navigation bar

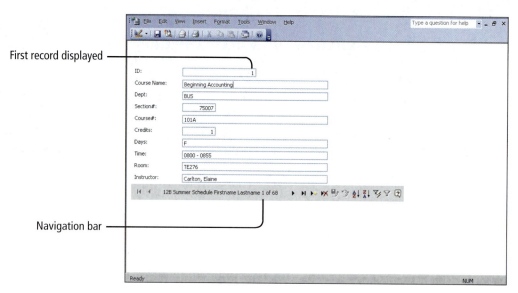

Figure 12.14

6 Notice the Navigation bar at the bottom of the screen. Use the navigation buttons to scroll through some of the records.

The navigation buttons in a data access page function in the same manner as the navigation buttons in a table or form.

7 Navigate to **record 3**, change the **Days** field to **MWF** and change the **Time** field to **0800 – 0850** and change the **Instructor** field to your **Lastname, Firstname** In the Navigation bar at the bottom of the page, click the **Save** button to save the changes. Compare your screen with Figure 12.15.

Changed fields

Type your name here.

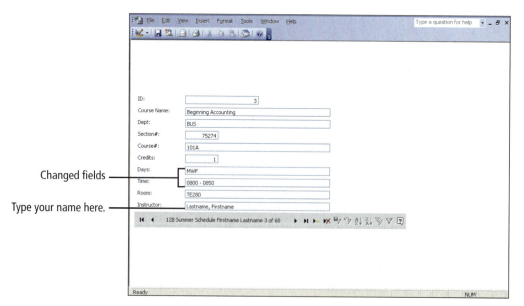

Figure 12.15

722   Access | Chapter 12: Exporting and Advanced Integration

8 **Close** ⊠ the data access page and click **Yes** to save the changes. Accept the default file name, be sure the **Save in** box displays your chapter folder, and be sure the **Save as type** box indicates *Microsoft Data Access Pages*. Click **Save**.

A warning message indicates that the **connection string** is an absolute path. A connection string is text that specifies the name and location of the database on the computer used to connect the data page to its Access database. Because the data access page is not part of the database, the connection string is used to link the two files together. Both the data access page and the Access database must be in a location that is accessible by the Web or intranet server so that the page can be viewed on the Internet.

9 Click **OK**. A shortcut to the data access page is added to the Pages area of the database window.

10 Right-click your **12B Summer Schedule Firstname Lastname** data access page shortcut and click **Web Page Preview** to open the data access page in your Web browser. Navigate to **record 3**.

11 From the **File** menu, click **Page Setup**. In the **Footer** box, clear any existing text and type **12B Summer Schedule Firstname Lastname** and then click **OK**. From the **File** menu, click **Print**. At the bottom of the dialog box, click **Print** to print the record from your Web browser.

Close ⊠ your Web browser and leave your database open for the next activity.

Activity 12.6 Modifying a Data Access Page

In the previous activity, you created a data access page using a wizard. You can customize your page in a manner similar to customizing a form or report. In this activity, you will customize your existing data access page.

1 On the Objects bar, be sure the **Pages** object is selected. Right-click your **12B Summer Schedule Firstname Lastname** data access page shortcut and click **Design View**.

2 If necessary, **Maximize** ▢ the window. With the cursor in front of *Click here and type title text*, type **12B Summer Schedule Firstname Lastname** Your text may wrap to two lines.

3 From the **Format** menu, click **Theme**. In the **Choose a Theme** list, click **Compass**, leave the other default settings, and then click **OK**. Select the title text that you typed and change the **Font Size** to **18**.

You can change any of the settings individually, but selecting a theme is a quick way to format your page.

4 Under the **ID** field, right-click the white text box next to **Course Name** (*Name* may not be visible), and from the displayed shortcut menu, click **Promote**.

The **Course Name** field moves up under the Header as shown in Figure 12.16. Promoting this field creates an alphabetic grouping based on the Course Name. The different sections of each class will be grouped by the course name.

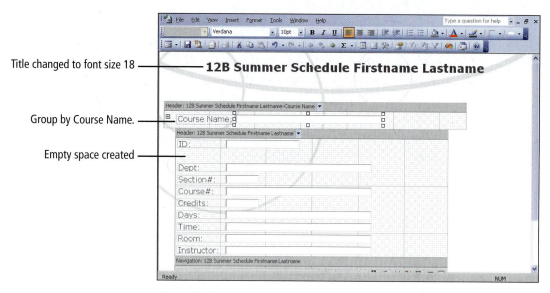

Figure 12.16

5. Notice the empty space created under the **ID** field. Select the text box to the right of **Dept**, hold down Shift, and beginning with the **Section** text box, select the remaining text boxes as shown in Figure 12.17.

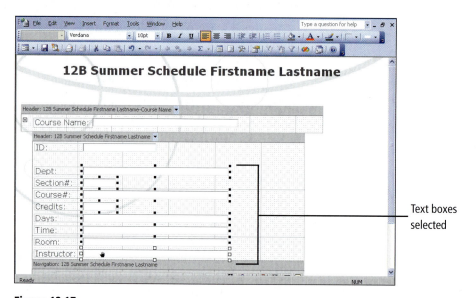

Figure 12.17

6. With the group selected and the **Hand pointer** displayed, drag the selection up slightly to fill in the empty space that was created under the **ID** field. Alternatively, you can use the up arrow to move the fields. Compare your screen with Figure 12.18.

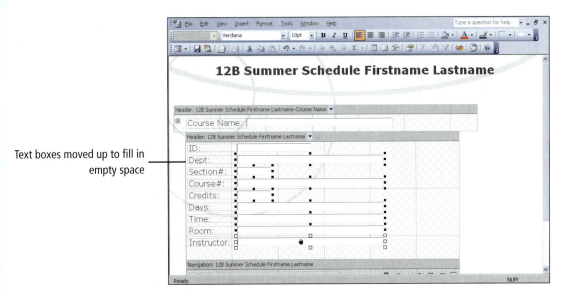

Text boxes moved up to fill in empty space

Figure 12.18

7 Click in the white space under the page title to cancel the selection.

On the Page Design toolbar, click **View**, and if necessary, scroll to the bottom to view the Navigation bar.

The page displays the courses in alphabetical order by *Course Name* and in groups of 10. Notice that there are 12 different course names as shown in Figure 12.19.

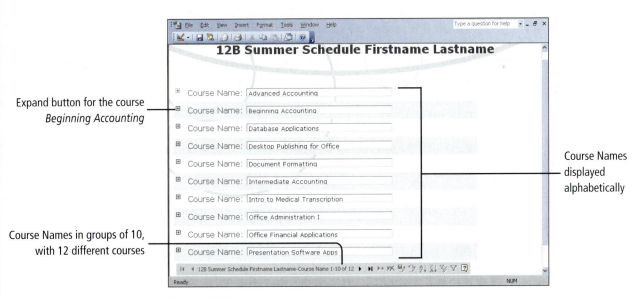

Expand button for the course *Beginning Accounting*

Course Names displayed alphabetically

Course Names in groups of 10, with 12 different courses

Figure 12.19

8 To the left of *Beginning Accounting*, click the **Expand** button and scroll as necessary to view the various sections of this class that will be offered. Click the **Collapse** button—the same button but now displaying a minus sign—to collapse (hide) the detailed information.

You can see that formatting the data access page in this manner is likely more useful to those viewing the information on the Internet.

9 **Close** the data access page, save your changes, and after a few moments, the database window redisplays. Right-click your **12B Summer Schedule Firstname Lastname** data access page shortcut again, and from the menu, click **Web Page Preview**.

10 **Expand** the Beginning Accounting course, which includes Section# 75274 that you modified.

11 From the **File** menu, click **Page Setup** and verify that the footer still displays *12B Summer Schedule Firstname Lastname* and if not, edit as necessary. Click **OK**. From the **File** menu, click **Print**. Under **Page Range**, click the **Pages** option button, and in the box to the right, type **1** to print only page 1. Click **Print**.

12 **Close** your Web browser and leave the database open for the next activity.

Objective 5
Place a PivotTable in a Data Access Page

Individuals who view your data access page on the Internet or on an internal intranet can rearrange the data in different ways if you incorporate a **PivotTable**. A PivotTable is a table that can show the same data in more than one arrangement. Viewers of your data access page can rearrange the data, without using the Design view, by simply dragging different information into the columns and rows, or by dragging information on and off the table.

Activity 12.7 Placing a PivotTable in a Data Access Page

In this activity, you will create a new data access page that contains a PivotTable. Using the PivotTable, college officials can analyze the different salaries of the summer school faculty by viewing the data in various ways.

1 On the Objects bar, click **Pages**. Double-click **Create data access page in Design view**. A warning message displays indicating that the data access page cannot open in Design view in Access 2000; click **OK**. If necessary, **Maximize** the window.

2 Be sure the Toolbox toolbar is displayed; if necessary, on the Page Design toolbar, click the **Toolbox** button. On the Toolbox toolbar, click **Office PivotTable**. Move the mouse pointer into the upper left corner of the grid under the word *Drag*, and click to place the PivotTable. The Field List will display. If necessary, click to select the PivotTable and use the vertical resize pointer to expand the lower edge, as shown in Figure 12.20.

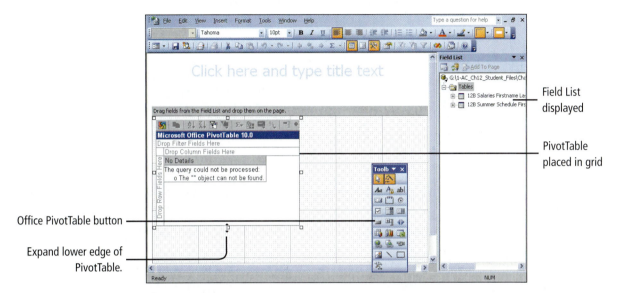

Figure 12.20

3 In the **Field List**, click the plus sign (+) next to **12B Salaries Firstname Lastname** to expand the list, and then click **Department**. Drag the *Department* into the PivotTable and over the text *Drop Row Fields Here,* as shown in Figure 12.21, and then when the border of the box is highlighted, release the mouse button.

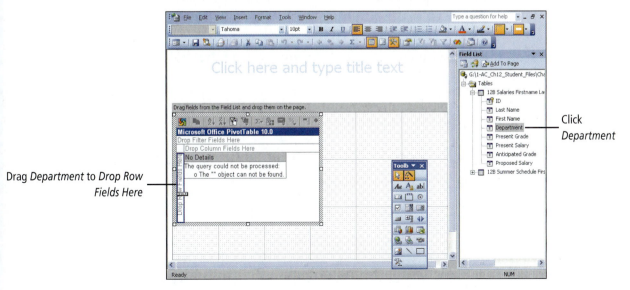

Figure 12.21

4 In the **Field List**, click **Present Grade** and drag the field to the PivotTable over *Drop Column Fields Here* and release the mouse button.

The PivotTable will compare the salaries of faculty members in the CIS and Management Departments based on the faculty member's present salary grade.

5 From the **Field List**, drag **Present Salary** and release it over *Drop Totals or Detail Fields Here*. **Close** ⊠ the **Field List** and drag the lower right corner of the PivotTable down and to the right until the complete PivotTable is visible. Compare your screen with Figure 12.22.

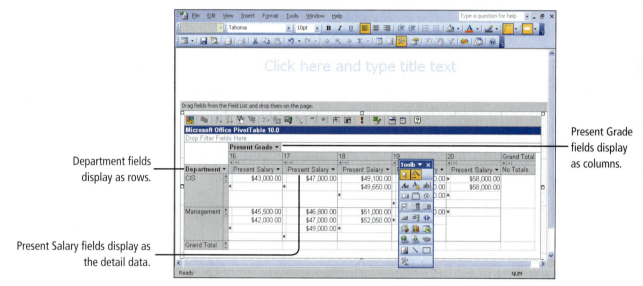

Figure 12.22

6 In the PivotTable, click the **Present Grade** field, drag it upward into the white space below *Click here and type title text*, and then release the mouse button. As you drag, a red X displays on the mouse pointer. Use the same technique to drag the **Present Salary** off the table.

You can drag and exchange any of the fields in the rows, columns, or details.

7 From the **View** menu, click **Field List** to redisplay the list. From the **Field List**, click **Anticipated Grade** and drag it to the *Drop Column Fields Here* section of the PivotTable. Drag **Proposed Salary** to the *Drop Totals or Detail Fields Here* section of the PivotTable.

8 To compare the salaries in columns instead of rows, in the PivotTable, click **Anticipated Grade** and drag the field to the right of the **Department** field as shown in Figure 12.23, and then release the mouse button.

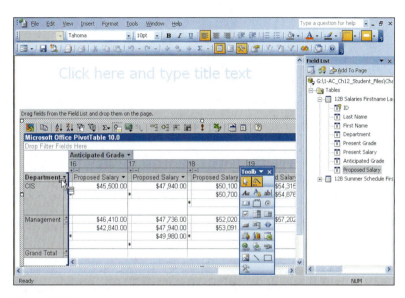

Figure 12.23

9 Close ⊠ the **Field List** and the Toolbox toolbar. Resize the PivotTable by dragging the bottom border of the table down until the entire table is visible—you will likely have to use the scroll bar to scroll down several times as you expand the table. Be sure that you can see *Grand Total* at the bottom. Scroll up and click in the title placeholder text, type **12B Salaries Firstname Lastname** and then select the text and change the **Font Size** of the title to **18**. Compare your screen with Figure 12.24.

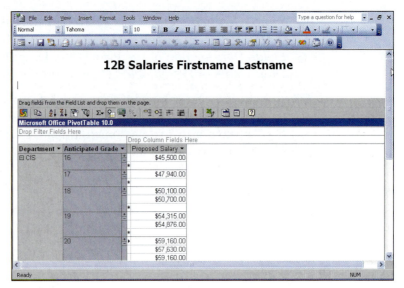

Figure 12.24

10 **Close** ☒ the data access page, and save it in your Chapter 12 folder as **12B Salaries Firstname Lastname** Click **Save**, and then click **OK**. Open the new data access page in Web Page Preview. The Pivot Table can also be modified in the browser by dragging fields on and off the table.

11 Display the **Page Setup** dialog box, and in the **Footer** box, type **12B Salaries Firstname Lastname** and then click **OK**. From the **File** menu, click **Print**. Leave the default settings in the **Print** dialog box and click **Print**. **Close** ☒ your Web browser, close your database, and close Access.

End You have completed Project 12B

Project 12C Internships

With so many different people at the college trying to share data from many different applications, a common format is needed so the data can be exchanged, combined, and analyzed. The data also needs to be in a format that can be uploaded to the college's Web site. Moving information across the Internet and between applications has been difficult in the past because of all the different data formats. With Microsoft Office 2003, moving information across the Internet and between software applications is easier because of the introduction of a markup language called XML.

In Activities 12.8 through 12.9, you will export data as an XML document, and then in Activity 12.10 you will import an XML document into your database. You will produce output that will look similar to Figure 12.25. You will name your database *12C_Internships_Firstname_Lastname*.

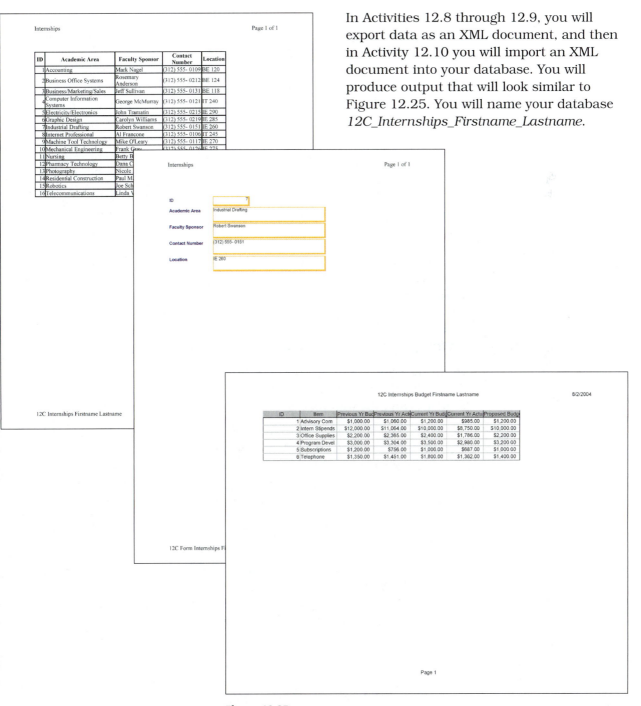

Figure 12.25
Project 12C—Internships

Objective 6
Export Access Data as an XML Document

XML, which stands for *eXtensible Markup Language*, is the standard language for describing and delivering data on the Web. In a manner similar to HTML, which uses tags to indicate how a Web browser should display text and graphics, XML uses tags to organize and present data. Unlike HTML, which has *one* set of standard tags to identify types of screen formatting, XML lets you create your own set of tags for the types of data that you work with. XML code can be generated from any Access table, query, or form. By creating an XML document, the data can be reported on a Web page, included in a Word document, analyzed in Excel, imported into a different database, or imported into many other programs that recognize XML files.

When you export data to XML, multiple files are created. An XML *schema* is a document that defines the elements, entities, and content allowed in the document. It uniquely identifies the tag names and defines the order, relationships, and data type you use with each tag. If you plan to import the XML data into another Access database, the schema is essential to ensure that all of the table relationships and data types are preserved when the data is imported. An XML document is not formatted to be viewed directly in a Web browser. Recall that the standard language for viewing Web pages is HTML. Additional files are created so the data is viewable in a Web browser. **Presentation** files allow you to view the data in a tabular format in a Web browser. Two presentation files are created. A stylesheet (.xsl) transforms the generated XML data to HTML for presentation. Another file applies the stylesheet used by the Web server.

Activity 12.8 Exporting Access Data as an XML Document

In this activity, you will export the Internships table as an XML document. The internship information can then be imported into Word to e-mail to students and the information can also be posted on the college's Web site.

1. From the student files that accompany this textbook, locate the Access database **a12C_Internships**, and then copy and paste the file to your chapter folder. Remove the Read-only property from the file, and then rename the file as **12C_Internships_Firstname_Lastname** Start Access and open the database you just renamed.

2. On the Objects bar, click **Tables**. Double-click the **Internships** table to open it.

3. From the **File** menu, click **Export**. In the **Export Table** dialog box, use the **Save in arrow** to navigate to your chapter folder. At the bottom of the dialog box, click the **Save as type arrow** and click **XML**. In the **File name** box type **12C_Internships_Firstname_Lastname** Compare your screen with Figure 12.26.

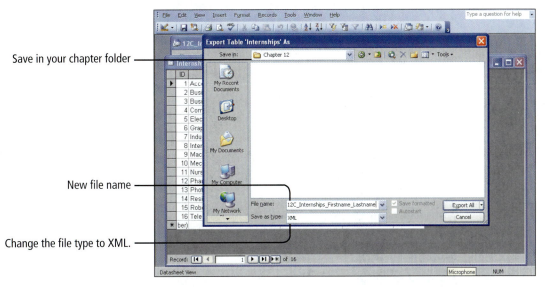

Save in your chapter folder

New file name

Change the file type to XML.

Figure 12.26

4 Click **Export All**. In the displayed **Export XML** dialog box, be sure the **Data (XML)** and **Schema of the data (XSD)** check boxes are selected, and then click to select the **Presentation of your data (XSL)** check box.

5 Click **OK**. **Close** the **Internships** table. On the Microsoft Access title bar, click **Minimize** Access, and then using **My Computer**, navigate to and open your chapter folder. Notice that four new files have been created from your *Internships* table.

6 In **My Computer**, display the **Tools** menu, and then click **Folder Options**. In the displayed **Folder Options** dialog box, click the **View tab**. Under **Advanced settings**, clear the **Hide extensions for known file types** check box, if necessary. Compare your screen with Figure 12.27.

Revealing the extensions for known file types enables you to see the file extensions for all files.

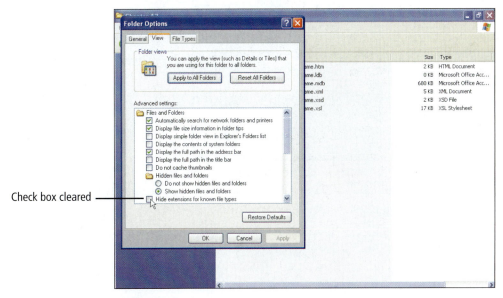

Check box cleared

Figure 12.27

Project 12C: Internships | **Access**   733

7 Click **OK** and compare your screen with Figure 12.28.

Four new files, with the extensions *.htm*, *.xml*, *.xsd*, and *.xsl* are listed.

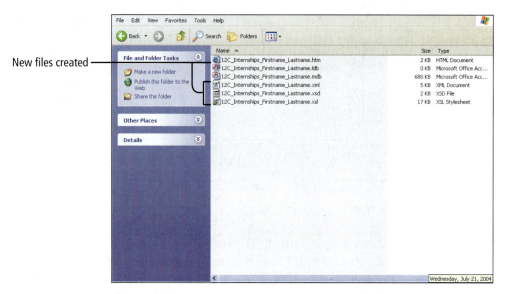

New files created

Figure 12.28

8 Point to and then double-click to open your **12C_Internships_Firstname_Lastname.htm** file to view the table in your Web browser. The *.htm* file was created as one of the presentation files.

9 From the **File** menu, click **Page Setup**, and in the **Footer** box, type **12C Internships Firstname Lastname** as shown in Figure 12.29.

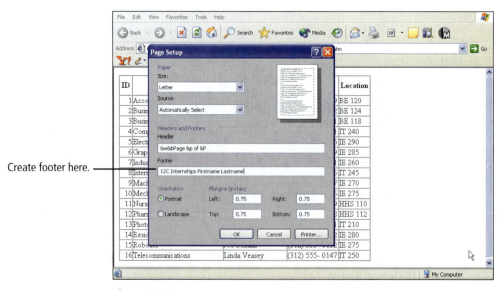

Create footer here.

Figure 12.29

10 Click **OK** to close the **Page Setup** dialog box. From the **File** menu, click **Print**. At the bottom of the dialog box, click **Print** to print the table from your Web browser. **Close** ☒ your Web browser and **Close** ☒ the **My Computer** window. On the taskbar, click your database to maximize it, and leave your database open for the next activity.

Activity 12.9 Exporting Forms

In the previous activity, you exported the Internship table. In this activity, you will export a single record form as an XML document. The form will be forwarded in an e-mail message to a student interested in a particular internship.

1 On the Objects bar, click **Forms**. Double-click **Create form by using wizard**.

2 Click the **Tables/Queries arrow**, and then click **Table: Internships**.

3 Click **All Fields** [>>] to move all the fields to the **Selected Fields** list. Click **Finish**.

4 At the bottom of the form, in the navigation text box, type **7** and then press [Enter] to navigate to **record 7**.

5 From the **File** menu, click **Export**. In the **Export Form** dialog box, be sure you are saving in your chapter folder, change the **Save as type** to **XML**, and for the **File name** type 12C_Form_Internships_Firstname_Lastname

6 Click **Export All**. Click as necessary to select all three check boxes, and then click the **More Options** button.

7 In the displayed **Export XML** dialog box, click the **Data tab**. On the right side of the dialog box, under **Records to Export**, click the **Current Record** option button. Click **OK**.

> **More Knowledge** — Exporting Other Objects from Access
>
> You can also export queries and reports from Access. Exporting a query is useful when you want to limit the number of columns you want to export from a table, or if you want to display or filter information from the table before exporting it. Exporting a report is useful when you want to display the data from the table in a different format.

8 **Close** ☒ the form. **Minimize** ▬ Access and open your Web browser. From the **File** menu, click **Open**. Click **Browse**. Navigate to your chapter folder and double-click your **12C_Form_Internships_Firstname_Lastname.htm**. In the displayed **Open** dialog box, click **OK**.

[9] From the **File** menu, click **Page Setup**. In the **Footer** box, type **12C Form Internships Firstname Lastname** and click **OK**. Display the **File** menu again and click **Print**. Leave the default settings in the **Print** dialog box and click **Print**.

[10] **Close** your Web browser. On the taskbar, click your Access database to maximize it. Leave the database open for the next activity.

Objective 7
Import an XML Document into Access

In the previous activities, you exported data from your database as an XML file. You can also *import* data saved in XML format into your database. For example, many of the faculty members at the college use other applications to manage and analyze data. If the application the faculty member uses can export the data as an XML document, the data can be shared across many applications. In the following activity, you will import an XML document into a new table in your database.

Activity 12.10 Importing an XML Document into Access

In the following activity, you will import an XML file to create a new table to include the Internships Budget data.

[1] From the **File** menu, point to **Get External Data**, and then click **Import**.

[2] In the displayed **Import** dialog box, navigate to the student files that accompany this textbook, click the **Files of type arrow**, and then click **XML**. Click **a12C_Internships_Budget.xml**, and then compare your screen with Figure 12.30.

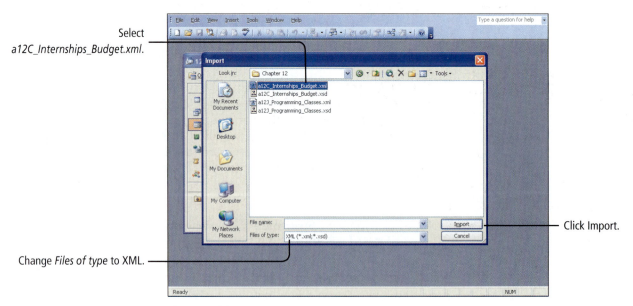

Figure 12.30

3 Click the **Import** button. In the displayed **Import XML** dialog box, click the **Expand button** next to *Internships Budget*, examine the fields that will be imported into the table, and then click **OK**.

4 When the table is finished importing, in the message box, click **OK**.

5 On the Objects bar, click **Tables**, if necessary. Right-click the **Internships Budget** table and rename the table **12C Internships Budget Firstname Lastname**

6 Double-click your **12C Internships Budget Firstname Lastname** table to open it.

7 From the **File** menu, click **Page Setup**. Click the **Page tab** and change the **Orientation** to **Landscape**. Click **OK**.

8 From the **File** menu, click **Print**. Leave the default settings in the **Print** dialog box and click **OK**. **Close** the table. Close your database and close Access.

9 Open **My Computer**. From the **Tools** menu, click **Folder Options**, and then click the **View tab**. Click to select the **Hide extensions for known file types** to return the system to the original settings. Click **OK** and close **My Computer**.

End **You have completed Project 12C**

Summary

Access has export functions with which you can use other programs, such as Microsoft Word or Microsoft Excel, to view, format, and analyze data. In this chapter, you practiced exporting an Access table to Excel and then analyzing the data by creating an Excel chart. You practiced exporting an Access table to Word and then used Word's AutoFormat and other formatting features to create an attractive report. You created a report snapshot, which produces a high-fidelity copy of each page of an Access report. The benefit is that individuals who do not have the Access software installed on their computers can view an Access report using the report snapshot.

A data access page is a special type of Web page designed for viewing and working with Access data on the Internet or on an organization's intranet. In this chapter, you practiced using a wizard to create a custom data access page. After a data access page is placed on the Web, individuals who view your data access page can rearrange the data in a format that is useful to them. In this chapter, you practiced using a PivotTable to place data on a data access page. Viewers of your data can then rearrange the data by simply dragging different information into the columns and rows.

In this chapter, you practiced exporting Access data as an XML document. XML, or eXtensible Markup Language, is the standard language for describing and delivering data on the Web. To do this, tags are used in a manner similar to HTML. By creating an XML document, the data can be reported on a Web page, included in a Word document, analyzed in Excel, imported into a different database, or imported into many other programs that recognize XML files. You also imported an XML document into Access.

In This Chapter You Practiced How To

- Export an Access Table to Excel
- Export an Access Table to Word
- Create a Report Snapshot
- Create a Custom Data Access Page
- Place a PivotTable in a Data Access Page
- Export Access Data as an XML Document
- Import an XML Document into Access

Concepts Assessments

Matching   Match each term in the second column with its correct definition in the first column by writing the letter of the term on the blank line in front of the correct definition.

____ 1. The standard language for describing and delivering data on the Web.

____ 2. A file that contains a high-fidelity copy of each page of an Access report.

____ 3. A tool to copy data from a table or query into an Excel worksheet.

____ 4. A graphic representation of data in a worksheet.

____ 5. Defines the colors used in the chart and identifies the data series.

____ 6. A table that can show the same data in more than one arrangement.

____ 7. Text that specifies the name and location of the database on the computer used to connect the data page to its Access database.

____ 8. A file that allows you to view data in a tabular format in a Web browser.

____ 9. A special type of Web page designed for viewing and working with Access data on the Internet or on an organization's intranet.

____ 10. A document that defines the XML elements, entities, and content allowed in the document.

A   Analyze It with Microsoft Office Excel

B   Chart

C   Connection string

D   Data access page

E   eXtensible Markup Language

F   Legend

G   PivotTable

H   Presentation

I   Report snapshot

J   Schema

Concepts Assessments (continued)

Fill in the Blank Write the correct answer in the space provided.

1. Data presented in a _____ is usually easier to understand than a table of numbers.

2. When you export an Access table to Excel, no _____ is established between the spreadsheet and the table.

3. Exporting a _____ is useful when you want to limit the columns you want to export from a table.

4. The most commonly used chart type is the _____ _____, which is used to make comparisons among related numbers.

5. _____ uses tags to indicate how a Web browser should display text and graphics.

6. A _____ transforms the generated XML data to HTML for presentation.

7. If you want to share the information contained in an Access table, _____ it into Word to form a Word document.

8. You can view, print, store, publish, distribute, and archive a _____ without having the Access program on your computer.

9. A markup language that lets you create your own set of tags for the types of data that you work with is called _____.

10. Viewers of a data access page can rearrange the data without using the _____.

Access chapter twelve

Skill Assessments

Project 12D — LMCC

Objectives: *Export an Access Table to Excel, Export an Access Table to Word, and Create a Report Snapshot.*

In the following Skill Assessment, you will export an Access table to Excel and create a chart, export an Access table to Word and format it, and create a report snapshot. The Faculty Senate at Lake Michigan City College wants to publish a comparison of average salaries across the departments on campus. To accomplish this, they must export the available data from an Access table into Excel to create a chart that is easy to understand. The same database also contains a table of student information that must be formatted differently and e-mailed to different departments without e-mailing the entire database. The easiest way to accomplish this is to export the Student table to Word, format it, and then e-mail it as an attachment. There is also a report in the database that contains some information from the ClassSchedule table. This must be available to individuals on campus that do not have Access on their computers. To accomplish this, you will create a Snapshot report that can be viewed by those individuals on campus that do not have Access on their computers. Your completed files will look like the ones shown in Figure 12.31. You will rename and save the database as *12D_LMCC_Firstname_Lastname*.

1. Using **My Computer**, navigate to the student files that accompany this textbook and locate the Access database **a12D_LMCC**. Copy and paste the file to your Chapter 12 folder. Rename the file **12D_LMCC_Firstname_Lastname** Remove the Read-only property from the file. Start Access and open the database you just renamed.

2. Be sure the **Tables** object is selected. Right-click the **Faculty** table and click **Rename**. Rename the table **12D Faculty Firstname Lastname** and press [Enter]. Be sure the table is still selected. On the Database toolbar, click the **OfficeLinks** arrow. Click **Analyze It with Microsoft Office Excel**.

3. From the **File** menu, click **Save As**. In the **Save As** dialog box, navigate to your chapter folder and click **Save**.

4. Click in cell **A1** and drag to select the range **A1:B13**. On the Standard toolbar, click the **Chart Wizard** button. In the **Chart type** list, be sure **Column** is selected and under **Chart sub-type** use the default **Clustered Column** chart. Click **Next** two times.

5. In the **Chart title** box, type Average Faculty Salaries by Department Click the **Legend tab** and clear the **Show legend** check box so that it will not display. Click **Next**. Click the **As new sheet** option and name the sheet Faculty Salaries Chart and then click **Finish**.

(**Project 12D**–LMCC continues on the next page)

Skill Assessments (continued)

(**Project 12D**–LMCC continued)

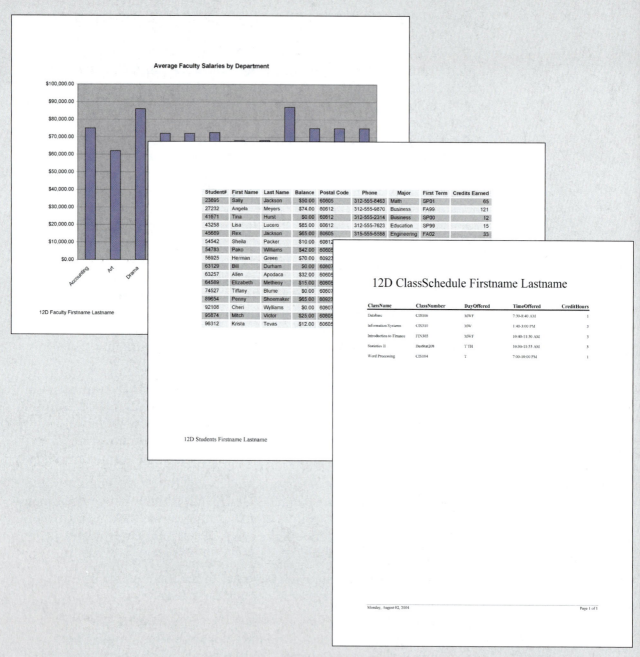

Figure 12.31

6. From the **View** menu, click **Header and Footer**. Click the **Custom Footer** button. In the **Left section**, click the **File name** button. Click **OK** twice to close the dialog boxes.

7. On the **Standard** toolbar, click **Save**. From the **File** menu click **Print**. In the displayed **Print** dialog box, under **Print range**, be sure **All** is selected and under **Print what**, **Active sheet(s)** is selected. Click **OK**. **Close** Excel, save changes if prompted, and leave Access open.

(**Project 12D**–LMCC continues on the next page)

Skill Assessments (continued)

(Project 12D–LMCC continued)

8. On the Objects bar, be sure **Tables** is selected. Right-click the **Students** table and rename it as **12D Students Firstname Lastname**

9. On the Standard toolbar, click the **OfficeLinks arrow**, and then click **Publish It with Microsoft Office Word**.

10. From the **File** menu, click **Page Setup**, click the **Margins tab**, and change the **Orientation** to **Landscape**.

11. From the **File** menu click **Save As**. In the **Save As** dialog box, navigate to the folder where you are saving your Chapter 12 files and click **Save**.

12. From the **Table** menu, point to **Select**, and then click **Table**. With the table selected, from the **Table** menu, click **Table AutoFormat**. In the **Table styles** list, click **Table Contemporary**. At the bottom of the dialog box, under **Apply special formats to**, be sure that all of the check boxes are cleared. Click **Apply**, and then with the table still selected, click the **Center** button on the Formatting toolbar. From the **Table** menu, point to **AutoFit**, and then click **AutoFit to Contents**.

13. From the **View** menu, click **Header and Footer**. Click the **Switch Between Header and Footer** button. Click the **Insert AutoText** button and click **Filename**. **Close** the Header and Footer toolbar.

14. From the **File** menu, click **Print**, and then click **OK**. Click the **Save** button, and then **Close** Microsoft Word. Leave the database open.

15. On the Objects bar, click **Reports**. Right-click the **ClassSchedule** report and rename as **12D ClassSchedule Firstname Lastname**

16. Right-click the **12D ClassSchedule Firstname Lastname** report and click **Design View**. Maximize the window if necessary. In the Report Header, click the **ClassSchedule** label to select it, and then change the name in the label to **12D ClassSchedule Firstname Lastname** Press Enter to accept the changes and leave the label selected. Click the **Center** button. Resize the label box to the right if necessary to make the label fit on one line.

17. **Close** the report window and save the changes. With the report name selected, from the **File** menu, click **Export**. Navigate to your chapter folder. At the bottom of the dialog box, click the **Save as type arrow**, and then click **Snapshot Format**. Select the **Autostart** check box to view the file in the Snapshot Viewer when you export the file. Click **Export**. When the Snapshot Viewer opens, **Maximize** the Snapshot Viewer window.

18. From the **File** menu, click **Print**. At the bottom of the dialog box, click **Print** to print the report from the **Snapshot Viewer**.

19. Close the Snapshot Viewer, close your database, and close Access.

End You have completed Project 12D

Skill Assessments (continued)

Project 12E — Distance Learning

Objectives: *Create a Custom Data Access Page and Place a PivotTable in a Data Access Page.*

In the following Skill Assessment, you will create a custom data access page, modify a data access page, and place a PivotTable in a data access page. The Extended Studies department at Lake Michigan City College is responsible for all distance learning courses. The department has a list of all Business courses that will be offered as distance learning courses in the Fall term. You will make this available to students on the Internet so that they know what courses are available and in what departments. There is also a partial list of textbooks required for these distance learning courses and the textbook price. You will create a PivotTable in a data access page that can be placed on the college's intranet so departments can compare their prices to other departments. Your completed files will look similar to the ones shown in Figures 12.32. You will rename and save the database as *12E_Distance_Learning_Firstname_Lastname*.

1. Using **My Computer**, navigate to the student files that accompany this textbook and locate the Access database **a12E_Distance_Learning**. Copy the file to your Chapter 12 folder. Rename the file as **12E_Distance_Learning_Firstname_Lastname** Remove the Read-only property from the file. Start Access and open the database you just renamed.

2. Be sure the **Tables** object is selected. Right-click the **Courses** table and click **Rename**. Rename the table as **12E Courses Firstname Lastname** and press [Enter]. Right-click the **Business Textbooks** table and click **Rename**. Rename the table as **12E Business Textbooks Firstname Lastname** and press [Enter]. On the Objects bar, click **Pages**. Double-click **Create data access page by using wizard**.

3. In the displayed **Page Wizard** dialog box, click the **Tables/Queries arrow**, and then click **Table: 12E Courses Firstname Lastname**. Click the **All Fields** button to move all fields to the **Selected Fields** list. Click **Next**. Click **Next** two more times to display the final page of the wizard.

4. In the center of the dialog box, click the **Open the page** option button. Leave the default title for your page. Click **Finish**. The data access page opens with the first record displayed. **Maximize** the window.

5. On **record 1**, change the **CreditHours** field to **2** Navigate to **records 2** and **3** and change both of the **CreditHours** fields to **2** In the Navigation bar at the bottom of the page, click the **Save** button to save the changes.

(**Project 12E**–Distance Learning continues on the next page)

Skill Assessments (continued)

(Project 12E–Distance Learning continued)

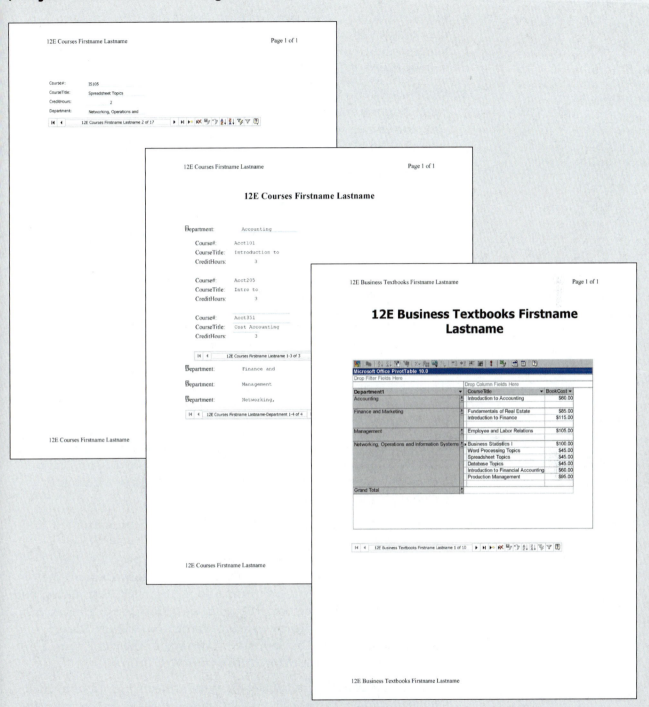

Figure 12.32

(Project 12E–Distance Learning continues on the next page)

Access Chapter twelve — Skill Assessments (continued)

(Project 12E–Distance Learning continued)

6. **Close** the data access page and click **Yes** to save the changes. Accept the default File name, be sure the **Save in** box displays your chapter folder, and be sure the **Save as type** box indicates *Microsoft Data Access Pages*. Click **Save**. Click **OK** to the warning message.

7. Right-click your **12E Courses Firstname Lastname** data access page shortcut and click **Web Page Preview** to open the data access page in your Web browser. Navigate to **record 2**.

8. From the **File** menu, click **Page Setup**. In the **Footer** box, type **12E Courses Firstname Lastname** Click **OK**. From the **File** menu, click **Print**. At the bottom of the dialog box, click **Print** to print the record from your Web browser. **Close** your Web browser.

9. Right-click your **12E Courses Firstname Lastname** data access page shortcut and click **Design View**. **Maximize** the window.

10. With the insertion point blinking in front of *Click here and type title text*, type **12E Courses Firstname Lastname** From the **Format** menu, click **Theme**. In the **Choose a Theme** list, click **Blends**, and then click **OK**. Select the title text that you typed and change the **Font Size** to **18**.

11. Right-click the white text box next to **Department**, and from the displayed shortcut menu, click **Promote**. Click the label box that contains *Group Of Department*. Click twice to position the insertion point within the box, and then delete *Group Of*.

12. On the Page Design toolbar, click **View**. To the left of *Accounting*, click the **Expand** button and scroll as necessary to view the various course offerings of the department. Click the **Collapse** button to collapse the detailed information.

13. **Close** the data access page, save your changes, and after a few moments, the database window redisplays. Right-click your **12E Courses Firstname Lastname** data access page shortcut again, and from the menu, click **Web Page Preview**. **Expand** the **Accounting** Department. From the **File** menu, click **Page Setup** and confirm that the **Footer** box still indicates *12E Courses Firstname Lastname*. From the **File** menu, click **Print**. Under **Page Range**, click the **Pages** option button, and in the box to the right, type **1** to print only page 1. Click **Print**. **Close** your Web browser.

14. Be sure that **Pages** is still selected on the Objects bar. Double-click **Create data access page in Design view**. Click **OK** to the warning message. **Maximize** the window.

15. Be sure the Toolbox toolbar is displayed. On the Toolbox toolbar, click **Office PivotTable**. Move the mouse pointer into the upper left corner of the grid and click to place the PivotTable.

(Project 12E–Distance Learning continues on the next page)

Skill Assessments (continued)

(Project 12E–Distance Learning continued)

16. In the **Field List**, if necessary, click the plus sign (+) next to **12E Business Textbooks Firstname Lastname** to expand the list, and then click **Department**. Expand the lower edge of the PivotTable to occupy at least three grid rows. Drag *Department* into the PivotTable and over the text *Drop Row Fields Here*, and then release the mouse button. Drag the lower right sizing handle on the PivotTable down and to the right until you can see the *Drop Column Fields Here* area and the *Drop Totals or Detail Fields Here* area In the **Field List**, click **CourseTitle** and drag the field to the PivotTable over *Drop Column Fields Here* and release the mouse button. From the **Field List**, drag **BookCost** and release it over *Drop Totals or Detail Fields Here*.

17. To compare course titles in columns instead of rows, in the PivotTable, click **CourseTitle** and drag the field to the right of the **Department** field, and then release the mouse button. Resize the PivotTable by dragging the lower right sizing handle of the table down and to the right until the entire table is visible. Close the **Field List** and the Toolbox toolbar.

18. Scroll up and click in the title placeholder text, type **12E Business Textbooks Firstname Lastname** and then change the **Font Size** of the title to **18**. Close the data access page, and save it in your chapter folder as **12E Business Textbooks Firstname Lastname** Click **Save**. Click **OK** to the warning message. Open the new data access page in Web Page Preview.

19. From the **File** menu, click **Page Setup** and change the footer to **12E Business Textbooks Firstname Lastname** From the **File** menu, click **Print**. Leave the default setting in the **Print** dialog box and click **Print**. Close your Web browser, close your database, and close Access.

 You have completed Project 12E

Skill Assessments (continued)

Project 12F — Employees

Objective: *Export Access Data as an XML Document.*

In the following Skill Assessment, you will export Access data as an XML document and export a single form as an XML document. The Human Resources department at Lake Michigan City College wants to convert information from the employee database to XML so that it can be delivered to the college intranet. You will export the employee table as an XML document and then export a single form as an example as to how the form will look when it is complete. Your completed files will look similar to the ones shown in Figure 12.33. You will rename and save the database as *12F_Employees_Firstname_Lastname*.

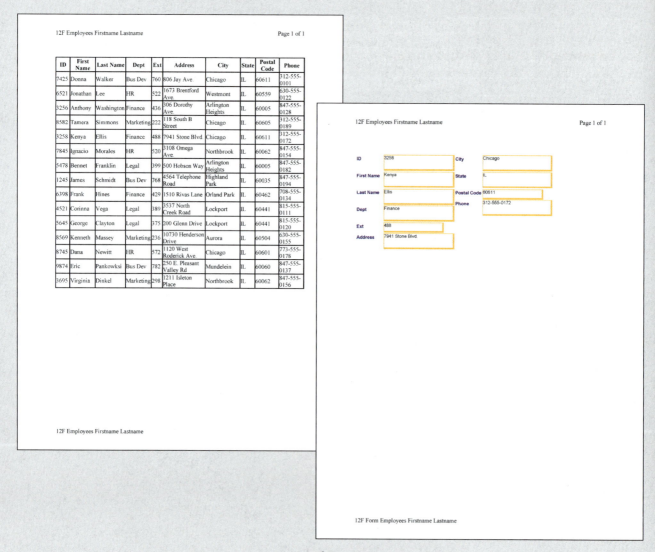

Figure 12.33

(**Project 12F**—Employees continues on the next page)

Skill Assessments (continued)

(Project 12F–Employees continued)

1. Using **My Computer**, navigate to the student files that accompany this textbook and locate the Access database **a12F_Employees**. Copy the file to your Chapter 12 folder. Rename the file as **12F_Employees_Firstname_Lastname** Remove the Read-only property from the file. Start Access and open the database you just renamed.

2. On the Objects bar, click **Tables**. Right-click the **Employees** table and click **Rename**. Rename the table as **12F Employees Firstname Lastname** and press [Enter]. Double-click the table to open it.

3. From the **File** menu, click **Export**. In the **Export Table** dialog box, use the **Save in arrow** to navigate to your chapter folder. At the bottom of the dialog box, click the **Save as type arrow** and click **XML**. If necessary, in the **File name** box type **12F_Employees_Firstname_Lastname**

4. Click **Export All**. In the displayed **Export XML** dialog box, be sure the **Data (XML)** and **Schema of the data (XSD)** check boxes are selected, and then click to select the **Presentation of your data (XSL)** check box to select it.

5. Click **OK**. **Close** your **Employees** table. **Minimize** Access, and then using **My Computer**, navigate to and open your chapter folder. Notice that four new files have been created from your **Employees** table.

6. In **My Computer**, display the **Tools** menu, and then click **Folder Options**. Click the **View tab**. Under **Advanced settings**, if necessary, clear the **Hide extensions for known file types** check box. Click **OK**.

7. Point to and then double-click to open your **12F_Employees_Firstname_Lastname.htm** file to view the table in your Web browser.

8. From the **File** menu, click **Page Setup**, and in the **Footer** box type **12F Employees Firstname Lastname** Click **OK** to close the **Page Setup** dialog box.

9. From the **File** menu, click **Print**. At the bottom of the dialog box, click **Print** to print the table from your Web browser. **Close** your Web browser and close the **My Computer** window.

10. **Maximize** your database. On the Objects bar, click **Forms**. Double-click **Create form by using wizard**.

11. Click the **Tables/Queries arrow**, and then click **Table: 12F Employees Firstname Lastname**. Click the **All Fields** button to move all the fields to the **Selected Fields** list. Click **Finish**.

12. At the bottom of the form, in the navigation text box, type **3** and then press [Enter] to navigate to **record 3**.

(Project 12F–Employees continues on the next page)

Skill Assessments (continued)

(Project 12F–Employees continued)

13. From the **File** menu, click **Export**. In the **Export Form** dialog box, be sure you are saving in your chapter folder, change the **Save as type** to **XML**, and as the **File name** type 12F_Form_Employees_Firstname_Lastname

14. Click **Export All**. Click as necessary to select all three check boxes, and then click the **More Options** button. Click the **Data tab**. On the right side of the dialog box, under **Records To Export**, click **Current record**, and then click **OK**.

15. **Close** the form. **Minimize** Access and open your Web browser. From the **File** menu, click **Open**. Click **Browse**. Navigate to your chapter folder and double-click your **12F_Form_Employees_Firstname_ Lastname.htm** file. In the displayed **Open** dialog box, click **OK**.

16. From the **File** menu, click **Page Setup**. In the **Footer** box type **12F Form Employees Firstname Lastname** and click **OK**. Display the **File** menu again and click **Print**. Leave the default setting in the **Print** dialog box and click **Print**. Close your Web browser, close your database, and close Access.

17. Open **My Computer**. From the **Tools** menu, click **Folder Options**, click the **View tab**, and then click to select the **Hide extensions for known file types** check box. Click **OK** and close **My Computer**.

 You have completed Project 12F

Access chapter twelve

Performance Assessments

Project 12G — Inventory

Objectives: *Export an Access Table to Excel, Export an Access Table to Word, and Create a Report Snapshot.*

In the following Performance Assessment, you will export an Access table to Excel and create a chart, export an Access table to Word and format it, and create a Report Snapshot. Lake Michigan City College officials want to chart how last year's computer budget was spent by category. This information is available in an Access database. They also want information about the quantity and location of all computers by department. You will export this information from Access to Word so that it can be formatted and later e-mailed to college officials. Finally, the college would like information about the office supply inventory at the bookstore. This information is available in an Access report, but some college officials do not have Access on their computers. You will create a Report Snapshot that can be e-mailed. Your completed files will look similar to the ones shown in Figure 12.34. You will rename and save the database as *12G_Inventory_Firstname_Lastname*.

1. Using **My Computer**, navigate to the student files that accompany this textbook and locate the Access database **a12G_Inventory**. Copy the file to your Chapter 12 folder. Rename the file as **12G_Inventory_Firstname_Lastname** Remove the Read-only property from the file. Start Access and open the database you just renamed.

2. Be sure the **Tables** object is selected. Rename the **Computer Inventory** table as **12G Computer Inventory Firstname Lastname** On the Database toolbar, click the **OfficeLinks arrow**. Click **Analyze It with Microsoft Office Excel**.

3. In Microsoft Excel, display the **Save As** dialog box. Navigate to your chapter folder and save the file using the default file name.

4. Select the range **A1:B5**. On the Standard toolbar, click the **Chart Wizard** button. In the **Chart type** list, click **Pie** and under the **Chart sub-type** use the **Pie with a 3-D visual effect**—in the first row, the second chart. Click **Next** twice.

5. In the **Chart title** box, type **Computer Spending by Category** Click the **Legend tab** and clear the **Show legend** check box. Click the **Data Labels tab** and select the **Category name** and **Percentage** check boxes. Click **Next**. Place the chart on a new sheet and name the sheet **Computer Spending Chart**

6. Display the **Header and Footer** dialog box and add the file name to the **Left section** of the custom footer. On the Standard toolbar, click the **Save** button. From the **File** menu click **Print**. In the displayed **Print** dialog box, under **Print range**, be sure **All** is selected and under **Print what**, **Active sheet(s)** is selected. Click **OK**. **Close** Excel, save your changes if prompted, and leave Access open.

(**Project 12G**–Inventory continues on the next page)

Performance Assessments (continued)

(Project 12G–Inventory continued)

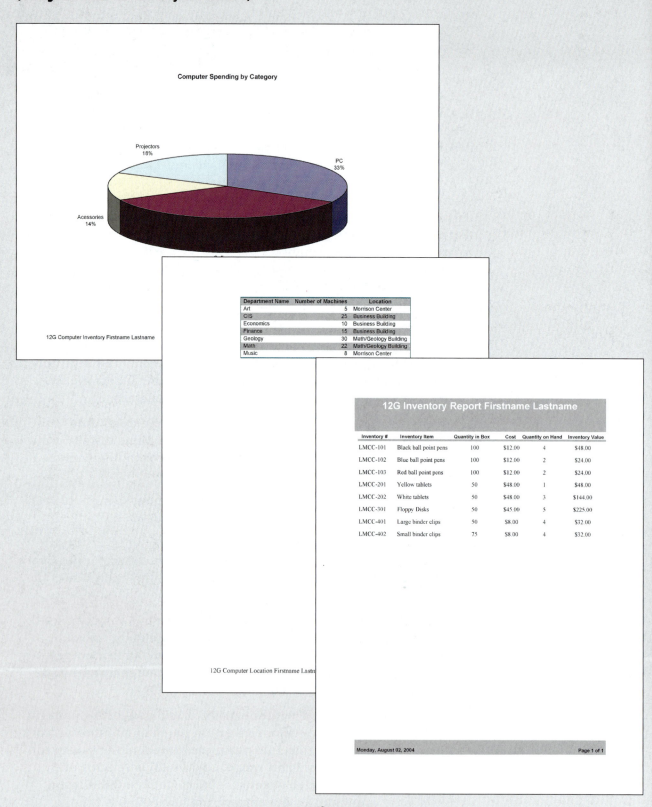

Figure 12.34

(Project 12G–Inventory continues on the next page)

Performance Assessments (continued)

Project 12G–Inventory continued)

7. Be sure the **Tables** object is selected. Rename the **Computer Location** table as **12G Computer Location Firstname Lastname** On the Standard toolbar, click the **OfficeLinks arrow**, and then click **Publish It with Microsoft Office Word**.

8. In Microsoft Word, from the **View** menu, click **Header and Footer**. Click the **Switch Between Header and Footer** button. Click the **Insert AutoText** button and click **Filename**. **Close** the Header and Footer toolbar. Open the **Save As** dialog box. Navigate to your chapter folder, and save the file using the default file name.

9. Change the first two column labels to read **Department Name** and **Number of Machines** Select the table and **AutoFit to Contents**. With the table selected, from the **Table** menu, click **Table AutoFormat**. In the **Table styles** list, click **Table List 1**. At the bottom of the dialog box, under **Apply special formats to**, be sure that all of the check boxes are cleared. Click **Apply**, and then with the table still selected, click the **Center** button on the Formatting toolbar.

10. From the **File** menu, click **Print**, and then click **OK**. Click the **Save** button, and then close Microsoft Word. Leave the database open.

11. On the Objects bar, click **Reports**. Rename the **Inventory Report** as **12G Inventory Report Firstname Lastname**

12. Right-click the **12G Inventory Report Firstname Lastname** report and click **Design View**. In the Report Header, click to select the **Inventory Report** label box, and change the name of the report to **12G Inventory Report Firstname Lastname** Change the **Font Size** to **18**. Click the **Center** button. Press [Enter] to accept the changes.

13. **Close** the report window and save the changes. With the report name selected, from the **File** menu, click **Export**. Navigate to your chapter folder. At the bottom of the dialog box, click the **Save as type arrow**, and then click **Snapshot Format**. Select the **Autostart** check box to view the file in the Snapshot Viewer when you export the file. Click **Export**. When the Snapshot Viewer opens, **Maximize** the Snapshot Viewer window.

14. From the **File** menu, click **Print**. At the bottom of the dialog box, click **Print** to print the report from the Snapshot Viewer.

15. Close the Snapshot Viewer, close your database, and close Access.

End You have completed Project 12G

Performance Assessments (continued)

Project 12H—Music Orientation

Objectives: *Create a Custom Data Access Page and Place a PivotTable in a Data Access Page.*

In the following Performance Assessment, you will create a custom data access page, modify a data access page, and place a PivotTable in a data access page. The Music Department at Lake Michigan City College has a music orientation session the week before classes begin for new students who are interested in playing in the orchestra. The department has a list of instruments that are available for rent. You will make this available to students on the Internet so that they know what instruments are available for rent, if they need special permission for this instrument, and the location of the instruments so they can plan for the music orientation. There is also a list of audition times during the week. You will create a PivotTable in a data access page that can be placed on the college's intranet so advisors can access different views of the data to use for advising students attending the music orientation. Your completed files will look similar to the ones shown in Figures 12.35. You will rename and save the database as *12H_Music_Orientation_Firstname_Lastname*.

1. Using **My Computer**, navigate to the student files that accompany this textbook and locate the Access database **a12H_Music_Orientation**. Copy the file to your Chapter 12 folder. Rename the file as **12H_Music_Orientation_Firstname_Lastname** Remove the Read-only property from the file. Start Access and open the database you just renamed.

2. Be sure the **Tables** object is selected. Rename the **Auditions** table as **12H Auditions Firstname Lastname** Rename the **Rental Instruments** table as **12H Rental Instruments Firstname Lastname** On the Objects bar, click **Pages**. Double-click **Create data access page by using wizard**.

3. In the displayed **Page Wizard** dialog box, click the **Tables/Queries arrow**, and then click **Table: 12H Rental Instruments Firstname Lastname**. Click the **All Fields** button to move all fields to the **Selected Fields** list. Click **Next**. Click **Next** two more times to display the final page of the wizard. Click the **Open the page** option button. Leave the default title for your page. Click **Finish**. The data access page opens with the first record displayed. **Maximize** the window.

4. Navigate to **record 6** and change the **Total Quantity** field to **12** Navigate to **record 8** and turn **off** the **Special Permission** check box. In the navigation bar at the bottom of the page, click the **Save** button to save the changes. **Close** the data access page and save changes when prompted. Accept the default file name, be sure the **Save in** box displays your chapter folder, and be sure the **Save as type** box indicates *Microsoft Data Access Pages*. Click **Save**. Click **OK** to the warning message.

(**Project 12H**–Music Orientation continues on the next page)

Performance Assessments (continued)

Project 12H–Music Orientation continued)

Figure 12.35

(**Project 12H**–Music Orientation continues on the next page)

Project 12H: Music Orientation | **Access** 755

Access Chapter Twelve

Performance Assessments (continued)

(Project 12H–Music Orientation continued)

5. Right-click your **12H Rental Instruments Firstname Lastname** data access page shortcut and click **Web Page Preview** to open the data access page in your Web browser. Navigate to **record 6**. From the **File** menu, click **Page Setup**, change the **Footer** to 12H Rental Instruments Firstname Lastname and click **OK**. From the **File** menu, click **Print**. At the bottom of the dialog box, click **Print** to print the record from your Web browser. **Close** your Web browser.

6. Right-click your **12H Rental Instruments Firstname Lastname** data access page shortcut and click **Design View**. **Maximize** the window. Click *Click here and type title text* and type 12H Rental Instruments Firstname Lastname From the **Format** menu, click **Theme**. Click **Eclipse**, and then click **OK**. Select the title text that you typed and change the **Font Size** to **14**.

7. Right-click the white text box next to **Type**, and click **Promote**. Edit the textbox *Group Of Type* to be *Type*. Select the text box to the right of **Total Quantity**, hold down [Shift], and beginning with the **Special Permission** text box, select the remaining text boxes. Drag the selection up to fill in the empty space.

8. On the Page Design toolbar, click **View**. To the left of *Brass*, click the **Expand** button to view the various instruments of that type. Click the **Collapse** button to collapse the detailed information.

9. **Close** the data access page and save your changes. Right-click your **12H Rental Instruments Firstname Lastname** data access page shortcut and click **Web Page Preview**. **Expand** the **Woodwind Type**. From the **File** menu, click **Print**. Click the **Pages** option button, and in the box to the right, type **1** to print only page 1. Click **Print**. **Close** your Web browser.

10. Be sure that **Pages** is still selected on the Objects bar. Double-click **Create data access page in Design view**. If necessary, click **OK** to the warning message. **Maximize** the window.

11. Display the Toolbox toolbar. On the Toolbox toolbar, click **Office PivotTable**. Move the mouse pointer into the upper left corner of the grid and click to place the PivotTable.

12. Expand the lower edge of the PivotTable about halfway into the third grid. In the **Field List**, if necessary, click the plus sign (+) next to **12H Auditions Firstname Lastname** to expand the list, and then click **Type**. Drag *Type* over the text *Drop Row Fields Here*, and then release the mouse button. In the **Field List**, click **Date** and drag the field over *Drop Column Fields Here*. From the **Field List**, click **Time**, press [Shift] and click **Location**. Drag both of these fields and release them over *Drop Totals or Detail Fields Here*.

(Project 12H–Music Orientation continues on the next page)

Performance Assessments (continued)

Project 12H–Music Orientation continued)

13. Close the **Field List** and the Toolbox toolbar. Resize the PivotTable by dragging the lower right sizing handle of the table down and to the right until the entire table is visible. Do *not*, however, display the Grand Total column at the right. If it displays, resize to the left so that it does not display.

14. Scroll up and click in the title placeholder text, type **12H Auditions Firstname Lastname** and then change the **Font Size** of the title to **14**. Close the data access page, and save it in your chapter folder as **12H Auditions Firstname Lastname** Click **Save**. Click **OK** to the warning message. Open the new data access page in **Web Page Preview**.

15. From the **File** menu, click **Page Setup**. Change the **Orientation** to **Landscape** and change the **Left** and **Right** margins to **0.25** Change the footer to **12H Auditions Firstname Lastname** Click **OK**. From the **File** menu, click **Print**. Leave the default setting in the **Print** dialog box and click **Print**. Close your Web browser, close your database, and close Access.

End You have completed Project 12H

Access chapter twelve

Performance Assessments (continued)

Project 12I — Spanish Club

Objective: *Export Access Data as an XML Document.*

In the following Performance Assessment, you will export Access data as an XML document and export a single form as an XML document. The Spanish Club at Lake Michigan City College wants to convert information from their database to XML so that it can be delivered to the college intranet. You will export the Club Events table as an XML document and then export a single form from the Members form as an example of how the form will look when it is complete. Your completed files will look similar to the ones shown in Figure 12.36. You will rename and save the database as *12I_Spanish_Club_Firstname_Lastname*.

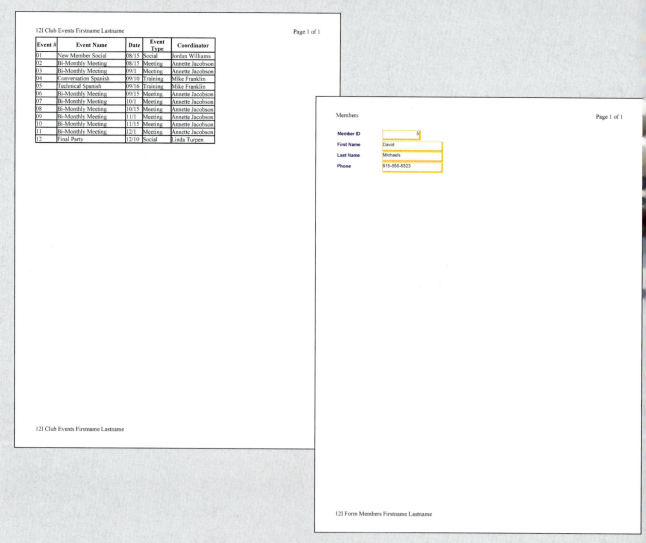

Figure 12.36

(**Project 12I**–Spanish Club continues on the next page)

758 Access | Chapter 12: Exporting and Advanced Integration

Performance Assessments (continued)

(Project 12I–Spanish Club continued)

1. Using **My Computer**, navigate to the student files that accompany this textbook and locate the Access database **a12I_Spanish_Club**. Copy the file to your Chapter 12 folder. Rename the file as **12I_Spanish_Club_Firstname_Lastname** Remove the Read-only property from the file. Start Access and open the database you just renamed.

2. Be sure the **Tables** object is selected. Rename the **Club Events** table as **12I Club Events Firstname Lastname** Double-click the table to open it.

3. From the **File** menu, click **Export**. Use the **Save in arrow** to navigate to your chapter folder. Click the **Save as type arrow** and click **XML**. Name the file **12I_Club_Events_Firstname_Lastname** Click **Export All**. Click as necessary to select all three check boxes. Click **OK**.

4. **Close** your **12I Club Events** table. **Minimize** Access, and then using **My Computer**, navigate to and open your chapter folder. Notice that four new files have been created from your **12I Club Events** table.

5. In **My Computer**, display the **Tools** menu, and then click **Folder Options**. Click the **View tab**. If necessary, clear the **Hide extensions for known file types** check box. Click **OK**. Open your **12I Club Events Firstname Lastname.htm** file to view the table in your Web browser.

6. From the **File** menu, click **Page Setup**, and in the **Footer** box type **12I Club Events Firstname Lastname** Click **OK** to close the **Page Setup** dialog box. From the **File** menu, click **Print**. At the bottom of the dialog box, click **Print** to print the table from your Web browser. **Close** your Web browser and **Close** the **My Computer** window.

7. **Maximize** your database. On the Objects bar, click **Forms**. Double-click **Create form by using wizard**. Click the **Tables/Queries arrow**, and then click **Table: Members**. Click the **All Fields** button to move all the fields to the **Selected Fields** list. Click **Finish**. Navigate to **record 5**.

8. From the **File** menu, click **Export**. Be sure you are saving in your chapter folder, change the **Save as type** to **XML**, and name the file **12I_Form_Members_Firstname_Lastname**

9. Click **Export All**. Click as necessary to select all three check boxes, and then click the **More Options** button. Click the **Data tab**. Click the **Current record** option button. Click **OK**.

(**Project 12I**–Spanish Club continues on the next page)

Performance Assessments (continued)

(Project 12I–Spanish Club continued)

10. **Close** the form. **Minimize** Access and open your Web browser. From the **File** menu, click **Open**. Click **Browse**. Navigate to your chapter folder and double-click your **12I_Form_Members_Firstname_Lastname.htm**. In the displayed **Open** dialog box, click **OK**.

11. From the **File** menu, click **Page Setup**. In the **Footer** box type **12I Form Members Firstname Lastname** and click **OK**. Display the **File** menu again and click **Print**. Leave the default setting in the **Print** dialog box and click **Print**. **Close** your Web browser, close your database, and close Access. Open **My Computer**, from the **File** menu click **Tools**, click the **View tab**, and then select the **Hide extensions for known file types** check box. Click **OK** and close **My Computer**.

 You have completed Project 12I

Mastery Assessments

Project 12J — Programming Classes

Objective: *Import an XML Document into Access.*

In the following Mastery Assessment, you will import the schedule of programming classes. The file is currently saved as an XML document. After the data has been imported, you will create a data access page to share the information on the college's intranet. Your data access page will look similar to Figure 12.37. You will save your database as *12J_Programming_Classes_Firstname_Lastname*.

Figure 12.37

(**Project 12J**–**Programming Classes continues on the next page)**

Mastery Assessments (continued)

(Project 12J–Programming Classes continued)

1. Start Access and create a new blank database and save the file as **12J_Programming_Classes_Firstname_Lastname** In **My Computer**, display the file extensions for all files.

2. From the **File** menu, point to **Get External Data**, and then click **Import**. Navigate to your student files and select the **a12J_Programming_Classes.xml** file to import. Finish importing the **Programming Classes** table.

3. Rename the table as **12J Programming Classes Firstname Lastname**

4. Create a new data access page using the wizard. Use your **Programming Classes** table and include all the fields from the table on your page.

5. After the data access page has been created, modify the page to use the **Network** theme, change the title of the page to **12J Programming Classes Firstname Lastname** Change the **Font Size** of the title to **18** point, and then **Promote** the **Programming Classes** field. Eliminate the space created by promoting the **Programming Classes** field by dragging the lower four fields up to fill the empty space.

6. Switch to **Page view**. Click the **Expand** button to the left of **Advanced Java Programming** to view the two sections of this class.

7. Change the **Top** and **Bottom** margins to **0.5** inches. Print your data access page.

8. **Close** the data access page and save the page as the default name **12J Programming Classes Firstname Lastname.htm** Close the database, and then close Access.

End You have completed Project 12J

Mastery Assessments (continued)

Project 12K — Faculty

Objective: *Export an Access Table to Word.*

In the following Mastery Assessment, you will export an Access table to Word and format the table. By exporting the table to Word, it can easily be e-mailed to faculty members so they will have an updated contact list. Your document will look similar to Figure 12.38. You will save your database as *12K_Faculty_Firstname_Lastname*.

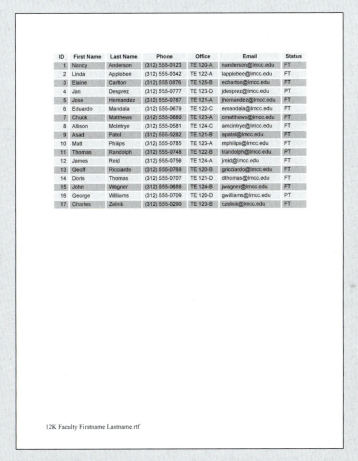

Figure 12.38

1. From the student files, locate the Access database **a12K_Faculty**, and then copy and paste the file to your chapter folder. Remove the Read-only property from the file and rename the file as **12K_Faculty_Firstname_Lastname** Start Access and open the database you just renamed.

(**Project 12K** – Faculty continues on the next page)

Mastery Assessments (continued)

(Project 12K–Faculty continued)

2. On the Objects bar, click **Tables**. Rename the **Faculty** table **12K Faculty Firstname Lastname** Leave the table selected.

3. On the Standard toolbar, click the **OfficeLinks arrow**, and then click **Publish It with Microsoft Office Word**.

4. Use **Table AutoFormat** to format your table with the **Table Contemporary** style.

5. Change the **Left** and **Right** margins to **0.75** inches. Resize the columns to fit each of the fields.

6. Center the table horizontally on the page and display the file name in the footer section of the page.

7. Print your Word table. Close Word, saving the changes, and then close Access.

End You have completed Project 12K

Problem Solving

Project 12L — Schedule

Objective: *Export Access Data as an XML Document.*

In the following Problem Solving exercise, you will export the schedule of computers classes as an XML document so the schedule can be posted on the college's Web site. You will rename and save your database as *12L_Schedule_Firstname_Lastname*.

1. From the student files, locate the Access database **a12L_Schedule**, and then copy and paste the file to your chapter folder. Remove the Read-only property from the file and rename the file as **12L_Schedule_Firstname_Lastname** Start Access and open the database you just renamed.

2. Export the **Schedule** table as an XML document. Name the document **12L_Schedule_Firstname_Lastname** Export the XML document, the Schema, and the **Presentation** files.

3. Navigate to your chapter folder and double-click on the **12L_Schedule_Firstname_Lastname.htm** file to preview the table in your browser. From the Page Setup, in the footer section, type **12L_Schedule_Firstname_Lastname**

4. Print the table from your browser. Close the browser, and then close Access.

End You have completed Project 12L

Problem Solving (continued)

Project 12M — Budgets

Objective: *Export an Access Table to Excel.*

In the following Problem Solving exercise, you will export the budgets of three departments to Excel so the information can be viewed in an Excel chart. You will rename and save your database as *12M_Budgets_Firstname_Lastname*.

1. From the student files, locate the Access database **a11M_Budgets**, and then copy and paste the file to your chapter folder. Remove the Read-only property from the file and rename the file as **12M_Budgets_Firstname_Lastname** Start Access and open the database you just renamed.

2. Export the three budgets, Nursing, Radiology, and Dental Assisting, to Excel. Create a Line chart for each of the budgets. Name the charts **Nursing Firstname Lastname Radiology Firstname Lastname** and **Dental Assisting Firstname Lastname** respectively.

3. Print the three charts. Close Excel, save your changes, and then close Access.

End You have completed Project 12M

On the Internet

Getting Information on XML in Access

The Microsoft Web site contains a variety of information about using XML in Access. Go to the Microsoft site at http://www.microsoft.com. In the **Search Microsoft.com for** text box type **XML in Access 2003** and click on any of the links that may help you. Print any information that is of interest to you.

GO! with Help

Exporting Objects

In this chapter, you worked with exporting Access objects to Excel, Word, and XML documents. Access can export to many different programs with a variety of formats.

1. Start Access. Press F1 to open Access Help.
2. In the **Search** text box, type **exporting formats** and then press Enter.
3. Click the link **Data formats you can export to**. View the list of formats and click any of the links to expand the information that interests you. Print the Help information if you want to keep a copy of it. Close the **Help** window, and then close Access.

Access 2003 Task Guide

Each book in the *GO! Series* is designed to be kept beside your computer as a handy reference, even after you have completed all the activities. Any time you need to recall the sequence of steps or a shortcut needed to achieve a result, look up the general category in the alphabetized listing that follows and then find your task. To review how to perform a task, turn to the page number listed in the second column to locate the step-by-step exercise or other detailed description. Additional entries without page numbers describe tasks that are closely related to those presented in the chapters.

Access Task	Page	Mouse	Menu Bar	Shortcut Menu	Shortcut Keys
Action, add to macro	553	Click arrow in Action column; select action			
Action query, create	454	on Query Design toolbar; click one of the action query types	Query | Action Query type	Right-click Query window; Query Type | Action Query type	
Analyze, performance	320		Tools | Analyze | Performance		
Analyze, table	317		Tools | Analyze | Table		
Append query, create	456	Create query; on Query Design toolbar; click Append Query	Create query; Query | Append Query	Right-click Query window; Query Type | Append Query	
AutoForm, close	89	in form window	File | Close		Ctrl + F4 or Ctrl + W
AutoForm, create	87	On Objects bar, click Forms, and then click New and select an AutoForm Select a table, and then click on Database toolbar	Insert | Form, and then select an AutoForm		
AutoFormat, data exported to Word	715		In Word: Table | Table AutoFormat		
Best fit, apply to table columns	490	Select columns; double-click border between column headings	Format | Column Width, Best Fit		
Calculated field, create for group in report	429	in Toolbox; click in group footer; click Control Source box;			

769

Access Task	Page	Mouse	Menu Bar	Shortcut Menu	Shortcut Keys
Calculated field, create in report	434	[abl] in Toolbox; click in report footer; click Control Source box; [...] Click group footer's calculated field; [icon] on Report Design toolbar; click Report Footer section bar; [icon] on Report Design toolbar			
Chart, create in Excel	712	In Excel: [icon]	In Excel: Insert | Chart		
Close, database	54	[X] in the Database window	File | Close		Ctrl + F4 or Ctrl + W
Close, Database window	23	[X] in Database window	File | Close		Ctrl + F4 or Ctrl + W
Close, query	20, 161	[X] in query window	File | Close		Ctrl + F4 or Ctrl + W
Close, table	18	[X] in table window	File | Close		Ctrl + F4 or Ctrl + W
ControlTip, add to form	373	Display property sheet, click Other tab, then enter value in ControlTip Text box			
Create, new blank database	28	[icon] then click Blank database in New File task pane	File | New		Ctrl + N
Create, table in Design view	29	On Objects bar, click Tables; double-click Create table in Design view or click [New], and then click Design view	Insert | Table, Design View	Right-click Create table in Design View command, and then click Open	
Crosstab query, add conditions	450		In Query Design view, enter condition(s) in Criteria row		
Crosstab query, create	447	On Objects bar, click Query; click New; click Crosstab Query Wizard	Insert | Query; select Crosstab Query Wizard		
Data access page, add new record	265	[icon] on Navigation bar			
Data access page, browse records	263	First [icon], Previous [icon], Next [icon], Last [icon] on Navigation bar			
Data access page, change theme	723		In Design view: Format | Theme		

Access Task	Page	Mouse	Menu Bar	Shortcut Menu	Shortcut Keys
Data access page, create using Design view	726	On Objects bar, click Pages; double-click *Create data access page in Design view* OR Click arrow on [icon]; Page; Design View OR [New]; Design View	Insert | Page; Design View		
Data access page, create using wizard	721	On Objects bar, click Pages; double-click *Create data access page by using wizard* OR [icon] drop-down arrow on Database toolbar; Page; Page Wizard OR [New]; Page Wizard	Insert | Page; Page Wizard		
Data access page, create with Page Wizard	260	On Objects bar, click Pages; click [New], Page Wizard OR double-click *Create data access page by using wizard*	Insert | Page, Page Wizard		
Data access page, delete record	263	[icon] on Navigation bar			
Data access page, filter records in Page view or Web page preview	263	Click in filter field, [icon] on Navigation bar			
Data access page, insert PivotTable	726	[icon] on Toolbox in Design view; drag fields from Field List to PivotTable	In Design view: Insert | Office PivotTable; drag fields from Field List to PivotTable		
Data access page, open in Design view	263, 723	Click data access page name then [Design]		Right-click data access page name; click Design View	
Data access page, open in Page view	263	Click data access page name then [Open] Double-click data access page name		Right-click data access page name; click Open	
Data access page, promote object	723	[icon] on Page Design toolbar		Promote	

Access Task	Page	Mouse	Menu Bar	Shortcut Menu	Shortcut Keys
Data access page, remove filter	263	on Navigation bar			
Data access page, save record	265	on Navigation bar			
Data access page, sort records in Page view or Web page preview	263	Click in sort field, click or on Navigation bar			
Data access page, switch to Design view	263		View	Design View		
Data access page, switch to Page view	263		View	Page View	Right-click data access page title bar; click Page View	
Data access page, view in browser (Web page preview)	263, 723	Click arrow on or , click Web Page Preview	File	Web Page Preview	Right-click data access page name; click Web Page Preview	
Data type, change	228	In Table Design view, click a field's Data Type box, then select from drop-down list			
Data type, select	29	In Table Design view, click a field's Data Type box, and then select from drop-down list			
Database, clear Read-only property	4		In My Computer, File	Properties; clear Read-only	In My Computer, right-click database file name, and then click Properties; clear Read-only	
Database, close	54	in the Database window	File	Close		
Database, compact	326		Tools	Database Utilities	Compact and Repair Database		
Database, convert from previous version of Access	267		Tools	Database Utilities	Convert Database	(choose a format)		
Database, copy	4		In My Computer, select file, Edit	Paste in same or other folder	In My Computer, right-click database file name, and then click Copy; right-click in file name area of destination folder, and then click Paste	Ctrl + C and Ctrl + V In My Computer, select file
Database, create new (blank)	28	and then click Blank database in New File task pane	File	New		Ctrl + N

Access Task	Page	Mouse	Menu Bar	Shortcut Menu	Shortcut Keys
Database, create using wizard	612	on Database toolbar; click *On my computer* in New File task pane; Databases tab	File	New; click *On my computer* in New File task pane; Databases tab		Ctrl + N; click *On my computer* in New File task pane; Databases tab
Database, encode/decode	324, 635		Tools	Security	Encode/Decode Database		
Database, encrypt	635		Tools	Security	Encode/Decode Database		
Database, open existing	6		File	Open		Ctrl + O
Database, protect with password	322		Tools	Security	Set Database Password		
Database, remove password	322		Tools	Security	Unset Database Password		
Database, rename	4		In My Computer, File	Rename	In My Computer, right-click database file name, and then click Rename	
Database, repair	326		Tools	Database Utilities	Compact and Repair Database		
Database, replicate	327, 632		Tools	Replication	Create Replica		
Database, set password	623		Tools	Security	Set Database Password		
Database, synchronize	634		Tools	Replication	Synchronize Now		
Database window, close	23	in Database window			
Database window, restore	23				
Database Wizard, use	612	on Database toolbar; click On my computer in New File task pane; Databases tab	File	New; click On my computer in New File task pane; Databases tab		Ctrl + N; click *On my computer* in New File task pane; Databases tab
Delete, record	45	in Table Datasheet view	Edit	Delete Record, and then click Yes to confirm	Right-click selected record, and then click Delete Record	Delete
Delete, record in data access page	263	on Navigation bar			
Delete, table field	39	In Table Design view, click record selector and then	Edit	Delete Rows Edit	Delete	Right-click a field name, and then click Delete Rows	Delete

Task Guide | Access 773

Access Task	Page	Mouse	Menu Bar	Shortcut Menu	Shortcut Keys
Delete query, create	444	Create query; [icon] on Query Design toolbar; click Delete Query	Create query; Query | Delete Query	Right-click Query window; Query Type | Delete Query	
Display, first record in form	84	[icon]	Edit | Go To | First		Ctrl + Home
Display, last record in form	84	[icon]	Edit | Go To | Last		Ctrl + End
Display, next record in form	21	[icon]	Edit | Go To | Next		PageDown
Display, previous record in form	84	[icon]	Edit | Go To | Previous		Page Up
Display, print preview of form	110	[icon]	File | Print Preview	Right-click form name, and then click Print Preview	
Display, Total row in query design grid	201	Σ	View | Totals	Totals	
Display/close, field list	115	[icon] [icon] to close	View | Field List		
Display/hide report's page header/footer	124		View | Page Header/Footer	Page Header/Footer	
Display/hide report's report header/footer	124		View | Report Header/Footer	Report Header/Footer	
Display/hide, form header/footer	98, 110		View | Form Header/Footer	Form Header/Footer	
Edit, record	44	In Table Datasheet view, click in a field, and then type			Delete or Bksp to delete text
Encode/decode, database	324, 635		Tools | Security | Encode/Decode Database		
Enforce referential integrity	301		In Relationship window, Relationship | Edit Relationship, select Enforce Referential Integrity check box	In Relationship window, right-click relationship line, click Edit Relationship, select Enforce Referential Integrity check box	
Excel chart, insert in Access form	514		In form Design view, Insert | Object; select Create from File; browse and select Excel file		

Access Task	Page	Mouse	Menu Bar	Shortcut Menu	Shortcut Keys
Excel chart, link to Access report	519		In report Design view, Insert | Object; select Create from File; browse and select Excel file; click Link check box		
Excel, import worksheet data in Access	496		Files | Get External Data | Import; select Excel file; click Import and follow wizard steps		
Excel, export table to	710	drop-down arrow on Database toolbar, Analyze It with Microsoft Office Excel	Tools | Office Links | Analyze It with Microsoft Office Excel OR File | Export; Save as type: Microsoft Excel 97-2003 (*.xls)		
Exit, Access	54	in the Access window	File | Exit		Alt + F4
Export, data as XML document	732		File | Export; Save as type: XML	Export; Save as type: XML	
Export, form as XML	735		File | Export; Save as type: XML	Export; Save as type: XML	
Export, object as XML document	735		File | Export; Save as type: XML	Export; Save as type: XML	
Export, selected table to Excel	710	drop-down arrow on Database toolbar, Analyze It with Microsoft Office Excel	Tools | Office Links | Analyze It with Microsoft Office Excel OR File | Export; Save as type: Microsoft Excel 97-2003 (*.xls)		
Export, selected table to Word	715	drop-down arrow on Database toolbar, Publish It with Microsoft Office Word OR Drag Access table to minimized Word document in Windows taskbar	Tools | Office Links | Publish It with Microsoft Office Word		
Export, snapshot of object	718		File | Export; Save as type: Snapshot Format (*.snp)		
Expression Builder, use	246	Type an expression or use the buttons to insert characters into the expression			
Field list, display/close	115	to close	View | Field List		
Field, add to form	356	In Design view, drag field from field list to form			

Access Task	Page	Mouse	Menu Bar	Shortcut Menu	Shortcut Keys
Field, add to table	41	In Table Design view, [icon], and then type field name Click in first field of next available row, and then type field name	Insert | Rows (Design View)	Right-click a field name or blank row, and then click Insert Rows	
Field, change size	232	In Table Design view, click field name; click Field Size box, enter number			
Field, create input mask	242	In Table Design view, click field name; type input mask characters in Input Mask box			
Field, create input mask using wizard	240	In Table Design view, click field name; click Input Mask box, click [icon] button		In Table Design View, click field name; right-click Input Mask box, and then click Build	
Field, create lookup using wizard	250	In Table Design view, click a field's Data Type box, then select Lookup Wizard			
Field, create validation text	248	In Table Design view, click field name; type text message in Validation Text box			
Field, format	237	In Table Design view, click field name; click Format box, then click down arrow and select a format			
Field, format in lowercase	235	In Table Design view, click field name; click Format box, type < followed by letter mask character (L or ?)			
Field, format in uppercase	235	In Table Design view, click field name; click Format box, type > followed by letter mask character (L or ?)			
Field, require entry	244	In Table Design view, click field name; click Required box, then click down arrow and select Yes			
Field, set default value	234	In Table Design view, click field name; click Default Value box, type value			
Field, validate using Expression Builder	246	In Table Design view, click field name; click Validation Rule box, click [icon], button		In Table Design View, click field name; right-click Validation Rule box, and then click Build	
Filter, by form	257	In Table Datasheet view, [icon], type text (use wildcard) or select from field's drop-down list, then [icon]	In Table Datasheet View, Records | Filter | Filter By Form; type or select text; Filter | Apply Filter/Sort	In Table Datasheet View, right-click field, right-click any field, click Filter By Form; right-click in table, Apply Filter/Sort	

Access Task	Page	Mouse	Menu Bar	Shortcut Menu	Shortcut Keys
Filter, by selection	255	In Table Datasheet view, click in field that has the value, [icon]	In Table Datasheet View, click in field that has the value, Records | Filter | Filter By Selection	In Table Datasheet View, right-click field, click Filter By Selection	
Filter, by selection in data access page	263	Click in filter field, [icon] on Navigation bar			
Filter, remove	255	[icon] on Table Datasheet toolbar	In Table Datasheet View, Records | Remove Filter/Sort	In Table Datasheet View, right-click field, right-click any field, click Remove Filter/Sort	
Filter, remove in data access page	263	[icon] on Navigation bar			
Find, value in column	252	Click in column to be searched; [icon] on Table Datasheet toolbar	Select column; Edit | Find	Right-click column heading, then click Find	Ctrl + F
Find, value in table	254	[icon] on Table Datasheet toolbar; click Look in box, select table name	Select column; Edit | Find; click Look in box, select table name	Right-click any column heading, then click Find; click Look in box, select table name	Ctrl + F
Form, add combo box	374	[icon] on Toolbox in Design view			
Form, add custom ControlTip	373	Display property sheet, click Other tab, then enter value in ControlTip Text box			
Form, add field	356	In Design view, drag field from field list to form			
Form, add form footer	110	In Design view, add a label to Form Footer section			
Form, add form header	98	In Design view, add a label to Form Header section			
Form, add label	98	[icon] on Toolbox in Design view			
Form, add new record	90	[icon]	Insert | New Record (in Datasheet View)		Ctrl + +
Form, add record using subform	390	Display record in form, add record to related subform			
Form, add status bar instructions	371	Display property sheet, click Other tab, then enter value in Status Bar Text box			
Form, add subform	388	in Design view, [icon] on Toolbox			

Access Task	Page	Mouse	Menu Bar	Shortcut Menu	Shortcut Keys
Form, add title	386	In Design view, add a label [Aa] on Toolbox to Form Header section	View | Form Header/Footer, add a label	Form Header/Footer, add a label	
Form, apply border to control	363	In Design view, click control, arrow on Formatting toolbar, then click a border width			
Form, change background color	361	In Design view, click a Section selector, on Formatting toolbar, then click a color		Right-click a Section selector, Fill/Back Color arrow, then click a color	
Form, change background color of control	361	In Design view, click control, arrow on Formatting toolbar, then click a color		Right-click control, Fill/Back Color arrow, then click a color	
Form, change background to picture	385	Double-click form selector, click Format tab, Picture box, [...]		Right-click form title bar, Properties | Format tab, Picture box, Build button	
Form, change font color	359	In Design view, click control, [A] arrow on Formatting toolbar, then click a color		Right-click control, Font/Fore Color arrow, then click a color	
Form, change tab order	379		View | Tab Order	Tab Order	
Form, close	21, 84	[X] in form window	File | Close		Ctrl + F4 or Ctrl + W
Form, close AutoForm	89	[X] in form window	File | Close		Ctrl + F4 or Ctrl + W
Form, close when maximized	110	[x]	File | Close	Right-click title bar, and then click Close	Ctrl + F4 or Ctrl + W
Form, create AutoForm	87	On Objects bar, click Forms, and then click [New] and select an AutoForm. Select a table, and then click on Database toolbar	Insert | Form, and then select an AutoForm		
Form, create in Design view	382	On Objects bar, click Forms, then click [New], Design view. Double-click *Create form in Design view*	Insert | Form, Design View		

Access Task	Page	Mouse	Menu Bar	Shortcut Menu	Shortcut Keys
Form, create with Form Wizard	96	On Objects bar, click Forms, and then click [New], Form Wizard Double-click *Create form by using wizard*	Insert | Form, Form Wizard		
Form, delete record	91	on toolbar	Edit | Delete Record	Right-click record selector, and then click Cut	Delete
Form, display first	84		Edit | Go To | First		Ctrl + Home
Form, display last record	84		Edit | Go To | Last		Ctrl + End
Form, display next record	21		Edit | Go To | Next		PageDown
Form, display previous record	84		Edit | Go To | Previous		Page Up
Form, display print preview	110		File | Print Preview	Right-click form name, and then click Print Preview	
Form, display/hide form header/footer	98, 110		View | Form Header/Footer	Form Header/Footer	
Form, display/hide rulers	98		View | Ruler (Design View)	Ruler	
Form, display/hide Toolbox	98	on Form Design toolbar	View | Toolbox	Toolbox	
Form, export	735		File | Export; Save as type: XML	Export; Save as type: XML	
Form, insert Excel chart	514		In form Design view, Insert | Object; select Create from File; browse and select Excel file		
Form, insert hyperlink to a Word document	497	In Word, select text to be destination of hyperlink, click [icon]. In Access form Design view, click Edit | Paste as Hyperlink	In Word, select text to be destination of hyperlink, click Edit | Copy	In Word, right-click selected text; click Copy. In Access form Design view, click Edit | Paste as Hyperlink	In Word, select text; Ctrl + C
Form, insert hyperlink to an Excel worksheet	500	on Form Design toolbar; select the Excel file	In form Design view, Insert | Hyperlink; select the Excel file		Ctrl + K

Access Task	Page	Mouse	Menu Bar	Shortcut Menu	Shortcut Keys
Form, link to an Excel worksheet	505	Click Tables in Objects bar; click [New]; click Link Table; select Excel file and click Link; follow wizard steps	Insert | Table; click Link Table; select Excel file and click Link; follow wizard steps	Right-click Tables in Objects bar; Link Tables; select Excel file and click Link; follow wizard steps	
Form, maximize window	98	Or double-click title bar			
Form, move a field	103	In Design view, display, drag border			
Form, move text box control separately from label	103	In Design view, display, drag large black handle			
Form, open in Design view	21	Click form name and then Design		Right-click form name, and then click Design View	
Form, open in Form view	21, 84	Click form name and then Open Double-click form name		Right-click form name, and then click Open	
Form, print	110		File | Print	Right-click form name, and then click Print	Ctrl + P
Form, resize a field	103	In Design view, drag a selection handle	Format | Size	Right-click field, and then click Size	
Form, save design	89	on Form design toolbar Switch views, and then click Yes	File | Save		Ctrl + S
Form, select multiple controls	359	Shift + click each control In Design view, drag to draw a box around fields or drag in a ruler			
Form, switch to Design view	21, 98		View | Design View	Right-click form title bar, and then click Form Design	
Form, switch to Form view	21, 98		View | Form View	Right-click form title bar, and then click Form View	
Form, use Format Painter to format control	363	on Standard toolbar (double-click to apply repeatedly)			Ctrl + Shift + C and Ctrl + Shift + V

Access Task	Page	Mouse	Menu Bar	Shortcut Menu	Shortcut Keys
Go to, first field of first record in datasheet	53	Click in first field			Ctrl + Home
Go to, first record in datasheet	53	[icon]	Edit | Go To | First		Ctrl + Page Up and then Ctrl + Home
Go to, last field of last record in datasheet	53	Click in last field			Ctrl + End
Go to, last record in datasheet	53	[icon]	Edit | Go To | Last		Ctrl + PageDown and then Ctrl + End
Go to, next record in datasheet	52, 53	[icon]	Edit | Go To | Next		↓
Go to, previous record in datasheet	52, 53	[icon]	Edit | Go To | Previous		↑
Hyperlink to Excel, insert in Access form	500	[icon] on Form Design toolbar; select the Excel file	In form Design view, Insert | Hyperlink; select the Excel file		Ctrl + K
Hyperlink to Word, insert in Access form	497	In Word, select text to be destination of hyperlink, click [icon]. In Access form Design view, click Edit | Paste as Hyperlink	In Word, select text to be destination of hyperlink, click Edit | Copy	In Word, right-click selected text; click Copy. In Access form Design view, click Edit | Paste as Hyperlink	In Word, select text; Ctrl + C
Immediate window, use	671		In VBA window: View | Immediate Window		Ctrl + G in Visual Basic window
Import, data from a Word table	484		In Word: Table | Convert | Table to Text; save as a plain text file. In Access: Files | Get External Data | Import; select the text file; click Import and follow wizard steps		
Import, data from an Excel worksheet	496		Files | Get External Data | Import; select Excel file; click Import and follow wizard steps		
Import, XML file to table	736		File | Get External Data | Import		
Index field, create with duplicates	295	In Table Design view, click Indexed box, select Yes (Duplicates OK)			
Index field, create without duplicates	294	In Table Design view, click Indexed box, select Yes (No Duplicates)			

Access Task	Page	Mouse	Menu Bar	Shortcut Menu	Shortcut Keys
Indexes, display	295	in Table Design view	In Table Design view, View | Indexes	Right-click table title bar in Design View, Indexes	
Input mask, create in Design view	242	In Table Design view, click field name; type input mask characters in Input Mask box			
Input mask, create	240	In Table Design view, click field name; click Input Mask box, click [...] button		In Table Design view, click field name; right-click Input Mask box, then click Build	
Link databases	510	Click Tables in Objects bar; click New; click Link Table; select database file and click Link; follow wizard steps	Insert | Table; click Link Table; select database file and click Link; follow wizard steps	Right-click Tables in Objects bar; Link Tables; select database file and click Link; follow wizard steps	
Link form and Excel worksheet	505	Click Tables in Objects bar; click New; click Link Table; select Excel file and click Link; follow wizard steps	Insert | Table; click Link Table; select Excel file and click Link; follow wizard steps	Right-click Tables in Objects bar; Link Tables; select Excel file and click Link; follow wizard steps	
Lookup Wizard, use for field lookup	250	In Table Design view, click a field's Data Type box, then select Lookup Wizard			
Macro, assign to command button	556	in Toolbox; click form; specify macro in wizard steps			
Macro, convert to VBA code	662		Tools | Macro | Convert Macros to Visual Basic		
Macro, create	551	On Objects bar, click Macros; New	Insert | Macro		
Macro, debug	556	on Macro Design toolbar	Run | Single Step		
Macro, insert row in Design view	553	Select row;	Insert | Rows	Right-click row; Insert Rows	
Macro, open in Design view	548, 662	On Objects bar, click Macros; click macro; Design		Right-click macro name; Design View	
Macro, run	554, 663	on Macro Design toolbar, or in Database window Double-click macro name	Tools | Macro | Run Macro OR Run | Run		
Macro, run in response to event	559	on Form Design toolbar; select Form; click Event tab; select macro for an event		In Design view, right-click form selector; Properties | Event tab; select macro for an event	

Access Task	Page	Mouse	Menu Bar	Shortcut Menu	Shortcut Keys
Macro, save	554	on Macro Design toolbar			Ctrl + S
Macro, step through	556	on Macro Design toolbar	Run | Single Step		
Macro, use conditional expression	564	on Macro Design toolbar; enter condition	In macro Design view, View | Conditions; enter condition		
Macro group, create	567	on Macro Design toolbar; enter macro name	In macro Design view, View | Macro Names; enter macro name		
Mail merge, insert merge field	491	In Mail Merge task pane or on Mail Merge toolbar, click ; click a field and then click Insert			
Make-table query, create	454	Create query; on Query Design toolbar; click Make-Table Query	Create query; Query | Make-Table Query	Right-click Query window; Query Type | Make-Table Query	
Merge, Access table with a Word document	491	on Database toolbar; click Merge It with Microsoft Office Word; follow wizard and task pane steps	Tools | Office Links | Merge It with Microsoft Office Word; follow wizard and task pane steps		
Minimize, Access window	497	in title bar		Right-click title bar; Minimize	
Move, field in form	103	In Design view, display , drag border			
Move, query field	190	Drag column selector left or right			
Move, report field and label in different sections in Design view	117	Select using Shift, and then drag			→, ←, ↑, ↓
Move between panes in macro Design view	551	Click pane			F6
Open, existing database	6		File | Open		Ctrl + O
Open, form in Design view	21	Click form name and then Design		Right-click form name, and then click Design View	

Task Guide | **Access**

Access Task	Page	Mouse	Menu Bar	Shortcut Menu	Shortcut Keys
Open, form in Form view	21, 84	Click form name and then Open Double-click form name		Right-click form name, and then click Open	
Open, query in Datasheet view	20, 162, 189	Click query name and then Open Double-click query name		Right-click query name, and then click Open	
Open, query in Design view	20, 162	Click query name and then Design		Right-click query name, and then click Design View	
Open, report in Design view	23	Click report name and then Design		Right-click report name, and then click Design View	
Open, table in Datasheet view	14, 38	Click table name and then Open Double-click table name		Right-click table name, and then click Open	
Open, table in Design view	14	Click table name and then Design		Right-click table name, and then click Design View	
Page setup, check margins	42	In Print dialog box, click Setup	File	Page Setup		
Parameter query, create	452		In Query Design view, enter condition(s) in Criteria row within [ ]		
Password, set for database	623		Tools	Security	Set Database Password		
Performance, analyze	320		Tools	Analyze	Performance		
Performance Analyzer, use	621	drop-down arrow on Database toolbar; Analyze Performance	Tools	Analyze	Performance		
Picture from file, insert in field	228	Data type must be OLE object; in Table Datasheet view, Insert	Object, Create from File, Browse; locate and double-click picture file		Data type must be OLE object; right-click field in Table Datasheet View, then click Insert Object; click Create from File, then click Browse; locate and double-click picture file	
Picture, view OLE object in table	228	In Table Datasheet view, double-click Package in field		In Table Datasheet View, right-click Package in field; Package Object	Activate Contents	
PivotTable, insert in Data access page	726	on Toolbox in Design view; drag fields from Field List to PivotTable	In Design view: Insert	Office PivotTable; drag fields from Field List to PivotTable		

Access Task	Page	Mouse	Menu Bar	Shortcut Menu	Shortcut Keys
Primary key, create	34	In Table Design view, click a field name, and then	Edit | Primary Key	Right-click a field name, and then click Primary Key	
Print, snapshot file	719		In Snapshot Viewer: File | Print		In Snapshot Viewer: Ctrl + P
Print, table	42	in Table Datasheet view	File | Print	Right-click table name, and then click Print	Ctrl + P
Print, form	110		File | Print	Right-click form name, and then click Print	Ctrl + P
Print, landscape/portrait orientation	42		File | Landscape or Portrait		
Print, query results	172		File | Print		Ctrl + P
Print, report	23	on Print Preview toolbar	File | Print	Right-click on report, and then click select Print	Ctrl + P
Print relationships	304	Display Relationships report,	In Relationships window, File | Print Relationships	Right-click Relationships report, Print	
Project Explorer, close	665	in Project Explorer window			
Project Explorer, open	664	on Visual Basic Standard toolbar	View | Project Explorer		Ctrl + R in Visual Basic window
Property sheet, display in Design view	366	on Form Design toolbar Double-click control or section of form	View | Properties	Properties	Alt + Enter
Property sheet, set format properties	366, 369	on Form Design toolbar, click Format tab, select property, enter value	View | Properties | Format tab, select property, enter value	Properties | Format tab, select property, enter value	Alt + Enter, Format tab, select property, enter value
Query, add calculated field	196	Type expression in Field row, enclosing field names in brackets		Right-click in Field row, choose Zoom, type expression	
Query, add fields to design grid	156	Double-click field name in field list Drag field to grid Click in Field row, and then select from list			

Access Task	Page	Mouse	Menu Bar	Shortcut Menu	Shortcut Keys
Query, add table in Design view	156	, click Add	Query | Show Table, Add	Show Table	
Query, clear the design grid	180		Edit | Clear Grid		
Query, close	20, 161	in query window	File | Close		Ctrl + F4 or Ctrl + W
Query, create action query	454	on Query Design toolbar; click one of the action query types	Query | *Action Query type*	Right-click Query window; Query Type | *Action Query type*	
Query, create append query	456	Create query; on Query Design toolbar; click Append Query	Create query; Query | Append Query	Right-click Query window; Query Type | Append Query	
Query, create crosstab query	447	in Database window; click Crosstab Query Wizard	Insert | Query; select Crosstab Query Wizard		
Query, create delete query	444	Create query; on Query Design toolbar; click Delete Query	Create query; Query | Delete Query	Right-click Query window; Query Type | Delete Query	
Query, create Find Duplicates	313	, Query, Find Duplicates Query Wizard On Object bar, click Queries; click New ; click Find Duplicates Query Wizard	Insert | Query, Find Duplicates Query Wizard		
Query, create Find Unmatched	315	, Query, Find Unmatched Query Wizard On Objects bar, click Queries; click New ; click Find Unmatched Query Wizard	Insert | Query, Find Unmatched Query Wizard		
Query, create in Design view	156	On Objects bar, click Queries; click New ; click Design view double-click *Create query in Design view*	Insert | Query, Design View		
Query, create make-table query	454	Create query; on Query Design toolbar; click Make-Table Query	Create query; Query | Make-Table Query	Right-click Query window; Query Type | Make-Table Query	
Query, create parameter query	452		In Query Design view, enter condition(s) in Criteria row within [ ]		

Access Task	Page	Mouse	Menu Bar	Shortcut Menu	Shortcut Keys
Query, create update query	440	Create query; [icon] on Query Design toolbar; click Update Query	Create query; Query | Update Query	Right-click Query window; Query Type | Update Query	
Query, delete selected field(s)	163	[icon]	Edit | Delete Columns	Cut	Delete
Query, display Total row	201	Σ	View | Totals	Totals	
Query, format calculated field	196	[icon]	View | Properties	Properties	Alt + Enter
Query, group data	201	In Total row, click Group By			
Query, hide field from result	180	In the Show row under the field, clear the check box			
Query, move field	190	Drag column selector left or right			
Query, open in Datasheet view	20, 162, 189	Click query name and then [Open] Double-click query name		Right-click query name, and then click Open	
Query, open in Design view	20, 162	Click query name and then [Design]		Right-click query name, and then click Design View	
Query, print results	172	[icon]	File | Print		Ctrl + P
Query, run	161, 443, 445, 453, 456	[icon] in Design view	Query | Run		
Query, save design	161	[icon] Switch views, and then click Yes	File | Save		Ctrl + S
Query, save to new name	166		File | Save As	Right-click name, and then click Save As	
Query, sort by multiple fields in Design view	190	Move fields in order of sort; in Sort row, select Ascending or Descending for each sort field			
Query, sort in Datasheet view	189	[A↓] or [Z↓]			
Query, sort in Design view	190	In Sort row, select Ascending or Descending			

Task Guide | **Access** 787

Access Task	Page	Mouse	Menu Bar	Shortcut Menu	Shortcut Keys
Query, specify * wildcard criteria	174	Type under field in Criteria row, substituting * for multiple characters			
Query, specify ? wildcard criteria	178	Type under field in Criteria row, substituting ? for single characters			
Query, specify criteria using AND	187	Type under each field in Criteria row			
Query, specify criteria using comparison operators	184	Type under field in Criteria row with operators			
Query, specify criteria using OR	188	Type under field in Criteria and *or* rows			
Query, specify text or numeric criteria	166, 183	Type under field in Criteria row			
Query, switch to Datasheet view	20	on Query Design toolbar	View | Datasheet View	Right-click query title bar, and then click Datasheet View	
Query, switch to Design view	20, 162		View | Design View	Right-click query title bar, and then click Query Design	
Query, use functions	203	In Total row, click Sum, Avg, Min, Max, etc.			
Query, view in SQL	458		Open Query; View | SQL View	Right-click Query window; SQL View	
Record, add to table	36	In Table Datasheet view, , and then type Click in first field of next available record, and then type Click in last field of last record, and then press Tab and type	Insert | New Record	Right-click selected record, and then click New Record	Ctrl + +
Record, delete	45	in Table Datasheet view	Edit | Delete Record, and then click Yes to confirm	Right-click selected record, and then click Delete Record	Delete
Record, edit	44	In Table Datasheet view, click in a field, and then type			Delete or Bksp to delete text
Record, insert in data access page	265	on Navigation bar			
Record, search in column	252	Click in column to be searched; on Table Datasheet toolbar	Select column; Edit | Find	Right-click column heading, then click Find	Ctrl + F

788 Access | Task Guide

Access Task	Page	Mouse	Menu Bar	Shortcut Menu	Shortcut Keys
Record, search table to find record	254	on Table Datasheet toolbar; click Look in box, select table name	Select column; Edit | Find; click Look in box, select table name	Right-click any column heading, then click Find; click Look in box, select table name	Ctrl + F
Records, browse in data access page	263	First, Previous, Next, Last on Navigation bar			
Records, find duplicates	313	, Query, Find Duplicates Query Wizard	Insert | Query, Find Duplicates Query Wizard		
Records, find unmatched	315	, Query, Find Unmatched Query Wizard	Insert | Query, Find Unmatched Query Wizard		
Referential integrity, enforce	301		Relationships | Edit Relationships	Right-click relationship line, Edit Relationships	
Relationship, edit	301, 304, 307	Double-click relationship line	Relationships | Edit Relationships	Right-click relationship line, Edit Relationships	
Relationship, establish	301, 304, 307	Drag a field from one table to a related field in another table	Relationships | Edit Relationships	Right-click relationship line, Edit Relationships	
Relationships, display content of table	296	Drag border of table window			
Relationships, display window	296	on Database toolbar	Tools | Relationships	Right-click Database window, Relationships	
Relationships, hide table	296		Relationships | Hide Table	Right-click table, Hide Table	
Relationships, print	304	Display Relationships report,	File | Print Relationships	Right-click Relationships report, Print	
Relationships, show all	296	in Relationships window	Relationships | Show All	Right-click Relationships window, Show All	
Relationships, show table	304	in Relationships window	Relationships | Show Table	Right-click Relationships window, Show Table	
Replica, create	632		Tools | Replication | Create Replica		
Report, add page footer or report	124	, drag in Page Footer or Report Footer section			
Report, change setup	115	on Print Preview toolbar	File | Page Setup		

Access Task	Page	Mouse	Menu Bar	Shortcut Menu	Shortcut Keys
Report, change width	117	Drag right edge of report [icon], click Format tab, Width			
Report, close	23	[X] in report window	File | Close		Ctrl + F4 or Ctrl + W
Report, create from crosstab query	437	Click Reports in Objects bar; double-click *Create report by using wizard*; click a query in the Tables/Queries list; complete the wizard steps [New] in Database window; click Report Wizard; click a query in the Tables/Queries list; complete the wizard steps	Insert | Report; select Report Wizard; select a query in the Tables/Queries list; complete the wizard steps		
Report, create subreport	423	[icon] in Toolbox; click in Detail section in Design view; follow the wizard steps			
Report, create with Report Wizard	112	On Objects bar, click Report; click [New], Report Wizard Double-click *Create report by using wizard*	Insert | Report, Report Wizard		
Report, display/hide page header/footer	124		View | Page Header/Footer	Page Header/Footer	
Report, display/hide report header/footer	124		View | Report Header/Footer	Report Header/Footer	
Report, group data	427	[icon] on Report Design toolbar	View | Sorting and Grouping	Right-click report in Design view; Sorting and Grouping	
Report, link to an Excel chart	519		In report Design view, Insert | Object; select Create from File; browse and select Excel file; click Link check box		
Report, maximize window	23	[icon] Or double-click title bar			
Report, move field and label in different sections in Design view	117	Select using Shift, and then drag			→, ←, ↑, ↓
Report, nudge object in Design view	117				Ctrl + (→, ←, ↑, ↓)

790 Access | Task Guide

Access Task	Page	Mouse	Menu Bar	Shortcut Menu	Shortcut Keys
Report, open in Design view	23	Click report name and then Design		Right-click report name, and then click Design View	
Report, preview	23	Click report name, and then Preview or [icon] Double-click report name		Right-click report name, and then click Print Preview	
Report, print	23	[icon]	File	Print	Right-click on report, and then click	Ctrl + P
Report, save design	115	[icon] Switch views, and then click Yes	File	Save		Ctrl + S
Report, set margins	433	Setup on Print Preview toolbar	File	Page Setup	Margins tab		
Report, set properties (Design view)	435	[icon] on Report Design toolbar	View	Properties	Right-click section heading bar; Properties	Alt + Enter
Report, switch to Design view	23, 115	[icon]	View	Design View	Right-click report title bar, and then click Report Design	
Report, switch to Print preview	23, 115	[icon] or [icon]	View	Print Preview	Right-click report title bar, and then click Print Preview	
Report, zoom to size	23	Fit on Print Preview toolbar	View	Zoom	Right-click on report, and then choose zoom setting	
Resize, column	46	Drag vertical line between column headings left or right	Format	Column Width	Right-click column heading, and then click Column Width	
Resize, column to fit widest entry	46	Double-click vertical line between column headings at right of field	Format	Column Width, Best Fit	Right-click column heading, and then click Column Width; choose Best Fit	
Resize, form field	103	A selection handle	Format	Size	Right-click field, and then click Size	
Resize, multiple columns	46	Select multiple columns; drag vertical line between column headings left or right	Format	Column Width	Right-click column heading, and then click Column Width	
Resize, row height	46	Drag horizontal line between row up or down	Format	Row Height	Right-click, and then click Row Height	
Resize, row height to default	46		Format	Row Height, Standard Height	Right-click, and then click Row Height; choose Standard Height	
Save, form design	89	[icon] on Form Design toolbar Switch views, and then click Yes	File	Save		Ctrl + S

Task Guide | Access

Access Task	Page	Mouse	Menu Bar	Shortcut Menu	Shortcut Keys
Save, query design	161	🖫 on Query Design toolbar Switch views, and then click Yes	File | Save		Ctrl + S
Save, query design to new name	166		File | Save As	Right-click report name, and then click Save As	
Save, record in data access page	265	🖫 on Navigation bar			
Save, report design	115	🖫 on toolbar Switch views, and then click Yes	File | Save		Ctrl + S
Save, table design	33	🖫 on Table Design toolbar Switch views, and then click Yes	File | Save		Ctrl + S
Security, remove password	322		Tools | Security | Unset Database Password		
Security, set database password	322		Tools | Security | Set Database Password		
Security, set user-level	625		Tools | Security | User-Level Security Wizard		
Snapshot, export object	719		File | Export; Save as type: Snapshot Format (*.snp)		
Snapshot, print	719		In Snapshot Viewer: File | Print		
Sort, query by multiple fields in Design view	190	Move fields in order of sort; in Sort row, select Ascending or Descending for each sort field			
Sort, query in Datasheet view	189	⬇ or ⬆			
Sort, query in Design view	190	In Sort row, select Ascending or Descending			
Sort, records in ascending order	51	Select one or more adjacent columns, and then click ⬇	Records | Sort | Sort Ascending	Right-click anywhere in selected column(s), and then click Sort Ascending	
Sort, records in data access page	263	Click in sort field, ⬇ or ⬆ on Navigation bar			
Sort, records in descending order	51	Select one or more adjacent columns, and then click ⬆	Records | Sort | Sort Descending	Right-click anywhere in selected column(s), and then click Sort Descending	

Access Task	Page	Mouse	Menu Bar	Shortcut Menu	Shortcut Keys
SQL, view query	458		Open Query; View	SQL View	Right-click Query window; SQL View	
Start, Access	6	**start** on Windows taskbar, and then locate and click Microsoft Office Access 2003	Start	All Programs	Microsoft Office	Microsoft Office Access 2003		
Status bar, add instructions to form	371	Display property sheet, click Other tab, then enter value in Status Bar Text box			
Subform, add record	390	Display record in form, add record to related subform			
Subform, add to form	388	In Design view, [icon] on Toolbox			
Subreport, embed in report	423	[icon] on Toolbox; click in Detail section in Design view; follow the wizard steps			
Switchboard, add image	576	[icon] in Toolbox; drag on form; double-click image file	In form Design view, Insert	Picture		
Switchboard, add label	575	[icon] in Toolbox; drag on form			
Switchboard, add page	577		Open Switchboard in Design view; Tools	Database Utilities	Switchboard Manager; New		
Switchboard, change properties	579	[icon] on Form Design toolbar; select Form; click Format tab		In Design view, right-click form selector; Properties	Format tab	
Switchboard, close	580		File	Close		Ctrl + F4
Switchboard, create	571		Tools	Database Utilities	Switchboard Manager		
Switchboard, display when database opens	581		Tools	Startup; click Display Form/Page; select Switchboard		
Synchronize, database	634		Tools	Replication	Synchronize Now		
Table, add field	41	In Table Design view, click [icon], and then type field name Click in first field of next available row, and then type field name	Insert	Rows	Right-click a field name or blank row, and then click Insert Rows	

Task Guide | **Access**

Access Task	Page	Mouse	Menu Bar	Shortcut Menu	Shortcut Keys
Table, add record	36	In Table Datasheet view, click , and then type Click in first field of next available record, and then type Click in last field of last record, and then press Tab and type	Insert | New Record	Right-click selected record, and then click New Record	Ctrl + +
Table, analyze	317		Tools | Analyze | Table		
Table, close	18	in table window	File | Close		Ctrl + F4 or Ctrl + W
Table, create in Design view	29	On Objects bar, click Tables; double-click Create table in Design view or click New, and then click Design view	Insert | Table, Design View	Right-click Create table in Design View command, and then click Open	
Table, delete field	39	In Table Design view, click record selector and then	Edit | Delete Rows Edit | Delete	Right-click a field name, and then click Delete Rows	Delete
Table, deselect	46	Click anywhere in the table			
Table, enter description for field	29	In Table Design view, click a field's Description column, and then type text			
Table, export as XML	732		File | Export; Save as type: XML	Export; Save as type: XML	
Table, export to Word	715	drop-down arrow on Database toolbar, Publish It with Microsoft Office Word OR Drag Access table to minimized Word document in Windows taskbar	Tools | Office Links | Publish It with Microsoft Office Word		
Table, hide columns	49		Format | Hide Columns	Right-click column heading, and then click Hide Columns	
Table, import from XML file	736		File | Get External Data | Import		
Table, move down one screen	53	Click below scroll box in vertical scroll bar			PageDown
Table, move to first field in datasheet	53	Click in first field			Ctrl + Home
Table, move to first record in datasheet	53		Edit | Go To | First		Ctrl + Page Up and then Ctrl + Home

794 Access | Task Guide

Access Task	Page	Mouse	Menu Bar	Shortcut Menu	Shortcut Keys
Table, move to last field in datasheet	53	Click in last field			Ctrl + End
Table, move to last record in datasheet	53	[>|]	Edit | Go To | Last		Ctrl + PageDown and then Ctrl + End
Table, move to next record in datasheet	52, 53	[>]	Edit | Go To | Next		↓
Table, move to previous record in datasheet	52, 53	[<]	Edit | Go To | Previous		↑
Table, move up one screen	53	Click above scroll box in vertical scroll bar			Page Up
Table, open in Datasheet view	14, 38	Click table name and then Open Double-click table name		Right-click table name, and then click Open	
Table, open in Design view	14	Click table name and then Design		Right-click table name, and then click Design View	
Table, print	42	[icon] in Table Datasheet view	File | Print	Right-click table name, and then click Print	Ctrl + P
Table, remove sort	51		Records | Remove Filter/Sort	Right-click anywhere in table, and then click Remove Filter/Sort	
Table, save design	33	[icon] on Table Design toolbar Switch views, and then click Yes	File | Save		Ctrl + S
Table, select column	14	Click column heading			
Table, select data type	29	In Table Design view, click a field's Data Type column, and then select from drop-down list			
Table, select row	14	Click row selector			
Table, sort records in ascending order	51	Select one or more adjacent columns, and then click [A↓]	Records | Sort | Sort Ascending	Right-click anywhere in selected column(s), and then click Sort Ascending	
Table, sort records in descending order	51	Select one or more adjacent columns, and then click [Z↓]	Records | Sort | Sort Descending	Right-click anywhere in selected column(s), and then click Sort Descending	

Access Task	Page	Mouse	Menu Bar	Shortcut Menu	Shortcut Keys
Table, switch to Datasheet view	18, 33	(icon)	View | Datasheet View	Right-click table title bar, and then click Datasheet View	
Table, switch to Design view	18	(icon)	View | Design View	Right-click table title bar, and then click Design View	
Table, unhide columns	49		Format | Unhide Columns, and then select boxes for columns to unhide	Right-click table title bar, and then click Unhide Columns	
Table Analyzer, use	617	(icon) drop-down arrow on Database toolbar; Analyze Table	Tools | Analyze | Table		
Test VBA statement	672		In VBA window: View | Immediate Window		Ctrl + G in Visual Basic window
Toolbox, display/hide	374, 556	(icon) on Form Design toolbar	View | Toolbox	Toolbox	
Update query, create	440	Create query; (icon) on Query Design toolbar; click Update Query	Create query; Query | Update Query	Right-click Query window; Query Type | Update Query	
User-level security, establish	625		Tools | Security | User-Level Security Wizard		
VBA function, run	666	(icon) on Visual Basic Standard toolbar	In VBA window: Run | Run Sub/UserForm		In VBA window: F5
VBA module, close	670	(icon) in VBA window			
VBA procedure, create (for form)	673, 676	In Form Design view, click Form selector; (icon); Event tab; click an event property; (icon); double-click Code Builder	In Form Design view, View | Properties | Event tab; click an event property; (icon); double-click Code Builder	In Form Design view, right-click Form selector; Event tab; click an event property; (icon); double-click Code Builder	In Form Design view, Alt + Enter; Event tab; click an event property; (icon); double-click Code Builder
VBA procedure, define numeric variable	681	In VBA window, type a statement beginning with *Dim* followed by the variable name, and ending with a numeric type (such as Single or Long); example: *Dim sngTotal As Single*			
VBA procedure, define string variable	679	In VBA window, type a statement beginning with *Dim* followed by the variable name, and ending with As *String*; example: *Dim strName As String*			

Access Task	Page	Mouse	Menu Bar	Shortcut Menu	Shortcut Keys
VBA procedure, modify	667	Open procedure in Visual Basic editor; type to edit code			
VBA procedure, print	670		In VBA window: File	Print		Ctrl + P in Visual Basic window
VBA procedure, save	670	on Visual Basic Standard toolbar	In VBA window: File	Save		Ctrl + S in Visual Basic window
VBA procedure, use case structure	686	In VBA window, type a *Select Case* statement, including multiple *Case* conditions and paths			
VBA procedure, use selection structure	684	In VBA window, type an *If…Then* statement, including a condition and a true/false path; example: If (Paid = No) Then MsgBox "Send a reminderto " & [Name], vbExclamation, "Not Paid"			
VBA statement, test	672		In VBA window: View	Immediate Window		Ctrl + G in Visual Basic window
Visual Basic editor, close	670		File	Close and Return to Microsoft Office Access		Alt + Q
Visual Basic editor, open	667	on Database toolbar On Objects bar, click Modules; click module name; click Design button on Database toolbar	Tools	Macro	Visual Basic Editor	Right-click module name; Design View	Alt + F11
Word, export table to	715	drop-down arrow on Database toolbar, Publish It with Microsoft Office Word OR Drag Access table to minimized Word document in Windows taskbar	Tools	Office Links	Publish It with Microsoft Office Word		
Word, import data into Access	484		In Word: Table	Convert	Table to Text; save as a plain text file. In Access: Files	Get External Data	Import; select the text file; click Import and follow wizard steps		

Access Task	Page	Mouse	Menu Bar	Shortcut Menu	Shortcut Keys
Word, mail merge with Access table	491	on Database toolbar; click Merge It with Microsoft Office Word; follow wizard and task pane steps	Tools	Office Links	Merge It with Microsoft Office Word; follow wizard and task pane steps		
XML, export selected form	735		File	Export; Save as type: XML	Export; Save as type: XML	
XML, export selected table	732		File	Export; Save as type: XML	Export; Save as type: XML	
XML, import to table	736		File	Get External Data	Import		

Glossary

Action A self-contained instruction that can be combined with other actions to automate tasks.

Action arguments Additional information required by some macro actions; they give Access additional information on how to carry out the action.

Action query A query that changes data in a table.

Aggregate functions A function that groups and performs calculations on multiple fields.

Analyze It with Microsoft Excel A tool to copy data from a table or query into an Excel worksheet.

Append query A query that adds new records to an existing table by importing data from another Access database, from another program such as Microsoft Excel, or from a table in the same database.

Ascending order Sorts text alphabetically (A to Z) and sorts numbers from the lowest number to the highest number.

AutoForm A feature that creates a form, with minimal formatting, using all available fields from an existing table.

AutoNumber A data type that assigns a number to each record as it is entered into the table.

Beep argument Will sound a beep when the message box is displayed—if it is selected.

Binary Pertains to a numbering system that uses two digits; Access databases are binary, meaning they are constructed of mostly unreadable characters.

Bound Linked.

Bound controls Controls in a report that are tied to a field in an underlying table or query.

Browser A program such as Microsoft Internet Explorer that enables you to view Web pages.

Chart A graphic representation of data in a worksheet.

Column chart A chart used to make comparisons among related numbers.

Combo box A control that allows the user to either type the information in the field or choose a selection from a predefined list; a combo box combines the features of a textbox and a list box.

Command button Provides you with a way of performing an action by simply clicking on it.

Compacting Reduces the size of a file and removes deleted objects from the database.

Compound criteria Two or more criteria in a query. Compound criteria are used to create more specific criteria and refine the query's results.

Conditional expression A test that evaluates as to true or false.

Connection string Text that specifies the name and location of the database on the computer used to connect the data page to its Access database.

Control An object such as a label or text box in a form or report that allows you to view or manipulate information stored in tables or queries.

ControlTip Displays when a user pauses the mouse pointer over a control in a form.

Criteria (1) The specifications that determine what records will be displayed. (2) The conditions specified to Access so it can find matching fields and records.

Crosstab query A special type of query that performs calculations on data that is grouped by two types of information.

Crosstab report A report generated from a Crosstab query that displays calculated data grouped by two types of information.

Data Facts about people, events, things, or ideas.

Data access page A special type of Web page designed for viewing and working with Access data on the Internet or on an organization's intranet.

Data entry Typing data into the database.

Data source In a mail merge operation, the Access table that contains the names and addresses of the individuals to whom the document is being sent.

Data type The type of data that can be entered in a field: text, memo, number, date/time, currency, AutoNumber, Yes/No, OLE object, and hyperlink. Specifies how Access organizes and stores data in a field.

Database A collection of data related to a particular topic or purpose.

Database window The window from which all database objects can be manipulated or accessed. The Database window displays when a database is open.

Database Wizard A tool that walks you through the steps necessary to create a set of tables, queries, forms, and reports, and a switchboard for the database.

Datasheet view The view in which the information in a table or query can be viewed and manipulated. Datasheet view displays all the records in a table in a format of columns (fields) and rows (records).

Delete query A type of action query that removes records from a table.

Delimited text file A file containing data where individual field values are separated by a character, such as a comma or a tab.

Delimiter character The character, such as a comma or a tab, that separates individual field values in a converted text file.

Descending order Sorts text in reverse alphabetic order (Z to A) and sorts numbers from the highest number to the lowest.

Design The number and content of the fields in the table. Good design ensures that a database is easy to maintain.

Design grid The lower pane of the Select Query window.

Design Master A copy of the original database that is created when a database is replicated and is the only copy to which structural changes can be made.

Design view The view in which the structure of a table or query can be viewed and manipulated.

Destination file An Office program to which the source file can be linked or embedded.

Detail In Design view of a form or report, the section that contains the fields and records that display in the form or report.

Detail section The area of a report or form that contains the main body of the data, and which is repeated for each record in the underlying record source.

Dim A VBA statement used to reserve a procedure-level variable.

Embedded Objects that are placed in the database object; used with the OLE data type.

Encode Scrambling a file so the file is unreadable.

Encryption The process of compacting a database file to help protect it from being read by a word processor or utility program.

Event Any significant action that can be detected by a system.

Event procedures Procedures that run when a specific event occurs.

Exclusive use Exclusive use means that nobody else can have the database open at that time.

Expression Combination of functions, field values, constants, and operators that bring about a result.

Expression builder A feature used to create formulas (expressions) in query criteria, form and report properties, and table validation rules.

eXtensible Markup Language The standard language for describing and delivering data on the Web, abbreviated XML.

External data source A file in a program other than Access.

Extracting Pulling out specific information from a database based on the specified criteria.

Field An individual item of information that describes a record and is the same type for all records in the table. In Access, fields are located in vertical columns.

Field Properties Pane that is in the lower portion of the table window in Design view where individual characteristics for a field can be set.

Filter By Form Allows you to locate records by typing the desired values into one or more fields on a blank form.

Filter By Selection Allows you to locate records based on data in a field.

Fit An entire page of a report displays on screen at one time, giving an overview of what the printed pages will look like.

Flat file database A database that stores different types of information in one table and usually contains data about one particular item in multiple places.

Foreign key In a relationship, the field in the second table that is linked to the primary key in the first table; the field on the many side of a one-to-many relationship.

Form A database object used to enter, edit, and manipulate information in a table.

Form Footer Displays only at the end of a form when it is viewed in Form view or when the form is printed.

Form Header Displays only at the beginning of a form when the form is viewed in Form view or when the form is printed.

Form selector Used to select the entire form to perform form-level operations.

Form Wizard Creates a form in a manner that gives you much more flexibility in the design, layout, and number of fields included in the form. The Form Wizard asks the user questions and then creates a form based on the answers provided.

Generated Unique ID A primary key created by the table analyzer to relate the tables created by the wizard.

Hyperlink A pointer from one object to another.

Ideas Advice from the performance analyzer marked with a light bulb offering additional tips for enhancing performance.

Immediate window A window that displays information resulting from commands typed directly into the window.

Import To copy data from a text file like Microsoft Word, a spreadsheet file like Microsoft Excel, or a database table from another Access database, and then insert it into an Access table.

Index A special list that is created in Access to speed up searches and sorting.

Information Data that has been organized in a useful manner.

Input box A dialog box that waits for the user to input text or click a button, and returns a string containing the contents of the text box.

Input mask Field property that determines the data that can be entered, how the data displays, and how the data is stored.

Intranet A privately owned Web-based network used by companies and organizations to share information.

Junction table The third table in a many-to-many relationship.

Label control The field name attached to a text box control in a form or report; can also be a text description in a form or report.

Landscape orientation Refers to the printed page layout when the page is wider than it is high.

Legend Defines the colors used in the chart and identifies the data series.

Line chart A chart that shows trends over time.

Link To insert information from a an external source into an Access table in a way that, when the Access table is updated, the original file is also updated, and vice versa.

Linked Objects that have only a link in the database object to an external file, such as a graphic; used with the OLE data type.

List box A control that displays a scrollable list of selections.

Logical operators Boolean operators. AND, OR, and NOT.

Long A variable that can store a whole number from negative 2 billion to positive 2 billion.

Lookup field Allows you to display a list of values from a field in another table.

Macro Automates common tasks and is a set of one or more actions.

Macro Group A set of macros grouped together by a common name

Macro window A window in which you create and modify macros, where you add commands in a step-by-step manner until you have completed your macro.

Mail merge To create a group of form letters by combining a main document created in Microsoft Word with a data source created in Access.

Main document In a mail merge operation, the Word document that contains the text of the letter or memo.

Main form The form that contains a subform.

Make-table query An action query that creates a new table based on existing tables.

Many-to-many A relationship that involves two tables that each have a one-to-many relationship to a third table, called a junction table.

MDE file A Microsoft Access database file that compiles all modules, removes all editable source code, and compacts the destination database.

Message argument Indicates the message that will be displayed when the macro is started.

Module Related VBA procedures that are grouped together.

Nudge To move in small increments; especially useful in Design view to move elements with precision.

Numeric variable A storage location that can store a single number.

Object The primary component of an Access database, such as a table, form, query, or report.

Object Linking and Embedding A program-integration technology for sharing information between Office programs, abbreviated OLE.

Objects bar Located on the left side of the Database window and contains the buttons to access the objects in the database.

OLE Object Linking and Embedding; data type that is used for a field that contains external objects, such as Word documents, spreadsheets, and graphics.

One-to-many A relationship between two tables where one record in the first table corresponds to many records in the second table.

One-to-one A relationship that requires that for every record in one table, there can be only one matching record in the other table.

Optimize Improve performance by increasing efficiency.

Page Footer Contains information that displays at the bottom of every page of a form or report in Print Preview or when printed.

Page Header Contains information that displays at the top of every page of a form or report in Print Preview or when printed.

Pages The database object that enables users to view information contained in a database from the Internet or a company intranet.

Parameter query A query that will prompt you for criteria before running the actual query.

Passwords A specified combination of letters, numerals, spaces, or symbols that an individual types for the purpose of restricting access to a database.

Performance Analyzer A tool to evaluate objects in your database and makes suggestions on how you might improve the performance of your database.

Permissions A process by which the type of access a user has to the different objects in the database is determined.

Pie chart A chart that shows the contributions of parts to a whole.

PivotTable A table that can show the same data in more than one arrangement.

Populate Fill a table with data.

Portrait orientation Refers to the printed page layout when the printed page is taller than it is high.

Presentation A file that allows you to view data in a tabular format in a Web browser.

Primary key In a database table, the field that uniquely identifies a record in a table.

Primary sort field The field that Access sorts by initially during a sort operation.

Procedures VBA statements that are grouped together.

Project Explorer A window that displays a hierarchical list of the projects and all of the items contained and referenced by each project.

Properties Characteristics that determine the appearance, structure, and behavior of a control as well as the characteristics of the text or data it contains.

Property sheet Where users can view a control's properties.

Query (1) A database object that locates information based on specified criteria so that the information can be viewed, changed, or analyzed in various ways. (2) A question formed in a manner that Access can interpret.

Recommendations Advice from the performance analyzer marked with a red exclamation point; they point out ways that your database can be optimized.

Record All the items of information (fields) that pertain to one particular thing such as a customer, employee, or course. In Access, records are located in horizontal rows.

Record selector The gray bar along the left edge of a table or form, that when clicked, selects the entire record.

Record source Between two bound objects, the record source is the object from which the actual data comes.

Referential integrity A set of rules that Access uses to ensure that the data between related fields is valid.

Relational database A database that contains several tables that are related, or connected, to each other by common fields.

Relationship The connection between two fields in separate tables within a relational database.

Relationship line The line that connects two related objects in the Relationships window.

Relationships window The location where relationships can be viewed, created, and modified.

Replica A copy of a database that allows users in multiple locations to update data, while restricting changes in the database design to one location.

Replica set Consists of the Design master and any replicas of a database when a database is replicated.

Replicating The process of creating copies, or replicas, of a database.

Report A database object that displays the fields and records from the table (or query) in an easy-to-read format suitable for printing or viewing on the screen. It is useful for summarizing information in a database in a professional-looking manner.

Report footer An optional area in a report useful for displaying report totals, and that appears only once—at the end of the report.

Report header An optional area in a report frequently used for a logo, report title, or print date, and that appears only once—at the beginning of the report.

Report snapshot A file that contains a high-fidelity copy of each page of an Access report.

Report Wizard Creates a report by asking a series of questions and then constructs the report based on the answers provided.

Row selector The small gray box at the left end of a row that, when clicked, selects all the cells in the row.

Schema A document that defines the elements, entities, and content allowed in the document.

ScreenTip The button name that displays when the mouse pointer is positioned over the button.

Secondary sort field The field that Access uses to sort records that have matching primary sort fields during a sort operation.

Section selectors Used to select entire sections of a form to perform section-level operations, such as adding background colors.

Select Case A statement that has a single test, but allows many different paths that can be followed.

Selection structure A structure used when you want to make a decision or comparison, and then based on the result of the decision or comparison, select one of two paths.

Select query A query that retrieves and displays data from one or more tables based on criteria that you specify and then displays the results.

Sequence structure A structure where each of the procedure's statements is processed in order.

Single A variable used to store a number containing a decimal value.

Single step Allows you to see the conditions, actions, and argument values as each action is performed.

Sizing handles The small squares surrounding a control that indicate that the control is selected.

Sorting The process of rearranging records in a specific order. Records can be sorted either ascending or descending.

Source file A file created in one Office program that can be linked to or embedded in another Office program, the destination file.

SQL The acronym and commonly used term for structured query language.

SQL-specific queries Cannot be created in the design grid but must be created directly in SQL view.

SQL statement What your query, created in design view, is translated into, in order for Access to run your query.

Statement A single VBA instruction used in a procedure.

Status bar The horizontal bar at the bottom of the screen directly above the task bar.

String A variable that stores zero or more characters enclosed in quotation marks (" ").

Structured query language A database sublanguage used in querying, updating, and managing relational databases in database programs such as Microsoft Access.

Subform A form that is embedded within another form (the main form).

Subreport A report inserted into a control, and the control is then embedded in another report.

Suggestions Advice from the performance analyzer indicated by a question mark, providing possible ways to improve the performance of the database.

Switchboard A form that will appear when the user opens the database and will allow the user to open only the objects that have been set up on the form.

Synchronization The process of merging the replicas with the Design Master database.

Tab order The order in which the fields on a form are selected when the Tab key is pressed.

Table The database object that stores the data in a database. Data is organized in a format of horizontal rows (records) and vertical columns (fields).

Table Analyzer A tool that divides a table that has repeated information into separate tables so that each type of information is stored only once.

Table area The upper pane of the Select Query window.

Table Design toolbar The toolbar that displays when a table is displayed in Design view.

Task pane A window within a Microsoft Office application that provides commonly used commands.

Text box control A control on a form or report where data from the corresponding table is displayed when the form or report is viewed.

Title argument Indicates the text that will be displayed in the title bar of the message box.

Toolbox The toolbar that contains the controls that can be added to forms or reports.

Type argument Indicates the type of icon that will be displayed when a message box is displayed.

Unbound controls Controls in a form or report that have no data source, but that display information such as labels that identify a field's contents.

Update query A type of action query that replaces existing data.

User-level security A method of implementing database security measures that establishes different levels of access to sensitive data and objects in your database based on an individual's identification code and password.

Validation rule An expression that precisely defines the information that will be accepted in a field.

Validation text Displays the correct format for a field that has a validation rule.

Val function A function that converts a string to its numeric value.

Variable A temporary holding location for a value in a procedure.

View A view is a way of looking at something for a specific purpose, such as Design view or Datasheet view.

Visual Basic Editor A program used to view, create, and modify VBA code.

Wildcard characters A placeholder for an unknown character or characters in search criteria.

Workgroup A group of users in a multi-user environment who share data and the same workgroup information file.

Workgroup ID A unique, case-sensitive string of characters that uniquely identifies the workgroup.

Workgroup information file A file containing information about users in the workgroup, including their passwords, account names, and groups to which they belong.

XML An abbreviation that stands for eXtensible Markup Language.

Zoom An option to make the page view larger or smaller.

Index

Symbols

& (ampersand)
    add multiple statements, 683
    input mask character, 244
    keyboard accelerator, 573–574
' (apostrophe), VBA comments, 668
* (asterisk)
    adding fields to queries, 159
    password character, 323
    query wildcard, 174, 257, 450
\ (backslash), input mask character, 244
: (colon), using calculated fields in queries, 197
= (equal)
    comparison operator, 184–186
    in formulas, 431
=Now( ) control, 422, 438
="Page" control, 422, 438
! (exclamation point)
    input mask character, 244
    recommended optimization, 621
> (greater than)
    comparison operator, 184–186
    input mask character, 240, 244
∞ (infinity sign), on relationship lines, 299
< (less than)
    comparison operator, 184–186
    input mask character, 244
- (minus sign), collapse indicator, 297
+ (plus sign)
    expand indicator, 296
    line in report, 433
 # (pound sign), input mask character, 244
? (question mark)
    input mask character, 240, 244
    query wildcard, 178–179
    suggested optimization, 621
" (quotation marks)
    strings, 235
        string variables, 679
    text in VBA, 668
[ ] (square brackets)
    in formulas, 431
    using calculated fields in queries, 196–197
0, input mask character, 244
1, on relationship lines, 299
    1:∞ relationship, 299, 301–303
        in subreports, 420, 424
9, input mask character, 244

A

A, input mask character, 244
Abbreviation field, 251
Access
    closing, 54
    converting previous versions, 267
    parts of Access window, 7–8, 11–12
    relational database, 292, 296
    starting, 6–7
access restrictions, 623
Action column in Macro window, 549, 552, 561
action queries, 440, 454
actions, 548
    action argument, 665
        section in Macro window, 549–554, 561
acViewPreview, 676
Add Generated Key button (Table Analyzer Wizard), 319
Add New User (Security Wizard), 628
administrator, default, 627
aggregate functions, 201, 203–205
Align Right button, in text box control, 560
Alignment, picture property, 384
All Fields button
    Form Wizard, 96
    Page Wizard, 260–261
    Report Wizard, 113. 437–438, 581
    Subform Wizard, 387
ampersand (&)
    add multiple statements, 683
    input mask character, 244
    keyboard accelerator, 573–574
Analysis Results section (Performance Analyzer), 621–623
Analyze arrow (Database toolbar)
    Analyze Performance, 621
    Analyze Table, 618
Analyze command (Tools menu)
    Performance, 320, 623
    Table, 317, 617
analyzing
    data, 617–620
    performance, 621–623
AND logical operator, 187–188
Any Part of Field, 254
apostrophe ('), VBA comments, 668
Append Query, 456–457
appending data in a table, 488

Apply Filter button (Table Datasheet toolbar), 258
arrows
    curved, in Database window, 263
    double-headed
        in Relationships window, 298
        resizing Form Header section, 100
        resizing table columns/rows, 46
    downward-pointing
        in Design view, 228–229
        in Field Properties, 235–236
        in Required box, 244–245
        in State field, 250–251
    right-pointing, in database tables, 15
    zoom, 420
ascending (sort) order, 51, 251
ask a question. *See* queries
asterisk (*)
    adding fields to queries, 159
    password character, 323
    query wildcard, 174, 257, 450
AutoFit command (Table menu, Word), 717
AutoForms, 87
    closing, 89
    creating, 87–89
    saving, 89
AutoNumber data type, 35, 232
AVG aggregate function, 201–204

B

Back Color box (Section: Detail dialog box), 436
Back Style property box, 367
backgrounds, forms
    color, 88, 359–361
        transparent, 367
    pictures, 383
backslash (\), input mask character, 244
backup, database, 326, 632
    and delete query, 446
Beep argument, 549–550, 552
Before Section (Section: Detail dialog box), 436
Best Fit, 490, 497, 507
binary file, 324
blank line in code, 682
Blends form style, 500, 508
Bold button (Formatting toolbar), 614–615
bold text, primary key, 300, 309
borders on controls, 361–363
    Border Color box, 367
    Border Width box, 367
bound controls, 421–422
    resizing, 501, 520
bound form to table, 354

brackets ([ ])
    in formulas, 431
    using calculated fields in queries, 196–197
Browse dialog box, 515
browser, viewing data access page, 259, 263–265
Build button
    Back Color box, 436
    Control Source box, 431
    Field Properties box, 234, 237–238, 246–247
    Item box, 561–562
    Picture box, 384
built-in template, 612
buttons
    in database window, 11–12
    navigating to records, 53, 85–86
    for records, 22

C

C, input mask character, 244
calculated fields
    crosstab query, 449
    groups, 429–433
    queries, 196–201
    reports, 434–435
capital letters in input mask, 240
cascade, 304
Cascade Delete Related Records check box (Edit Relationships dialog box), 304, 307–308
Cascade Update Related Fields check box (Edit Relationships dialog box), 303, 307–308
case-sensitivity
    passwords, 323, 629
    VBA, 668
Center button (Formatting toolbar), 385
Chart Wizard, 87, 713–714
charts
    Excel
        creating, 712–715
        embedding, 514–518
        linking into Access report, 519–520
    types of, 514
Choose Builder dialog box, 674
Choose from a list option button (Subreport Wizard), 424
clearing design grid, 182
Close button, 495
    Access window, 93
    data access page window, 262
    Database window, 54, 93
    Field Properties dialog box, 200
    forms, 86
    picture window, 231

query result, 162
query window, 171, 177–179, 189, 200, 205
subreport window, 426, 435
table, 20

closing
Access, 54
AutoForms, 89
databases, 54
Header and Footer toolbar, 492
Immediate window, 672
queries, 161–162
tables, 37–38
Visual Basic Editor, 670

Code Builder, Visual Basic Editor, 674, 676
Collapse button, 726
collapse indicators, 297
colon (:), using calculated fields in queries, 197
color
font, 357–359
form backgrounds, 88, 359–361, 367
palette, 358, 360–361
VBA statements
  green, 666, 668
  red, 667

Color dialog box, 367, 436
column charts, 514, 714
Column, Hide command (Format menu, Excel), 712
Column Width dialog box, 490–491, 507
Columnar layout, 500, 508, 512
columns, database tables, 15–16
headings, 41
hiding, 49–50, 712
resizing, 46–48, 490–491

combo box, adding to form, 369, 372–376
Command arrow, 573
Command button (Toolbox toolbar), 557
attaching a macro, 556–558
editing switchboard design, 575
running a macro, 558

command icons
Create form by using wizard, 95
Create query in Design view, 156
Create report by using wizard, 112
Create table in Design view, 30

commands
Edit menu. *See* Edit menu commands
File menu. *See* File menu commands
Format menu. *See* Format menu commands
Insert menu, Hyperlink, 502
Records menu, Remove Filter/Sort, 52
shortcut menu. *See* shortcut menu commands

Table menu (Word)
  AutoFit, 717
  Select, 716
Tools menu. *See* Tools menu commands
View menu. *See* View menu commands

comments in macros, 549, 552, 666, 668
Compact Database Into dialog box, 326
comparison operators, 184–186
compound criteria, 187–189
conditional statement, 685
conditional expressions in macros, 564–566

Conditions button (Macro Design toolbar), 564
connection string, 723
Control Source property box, 375, 431–432
controls
bound vs. unbound, 422
embedded in reports, 420, 422, 438
forms, 100, 354. See also forms
  applying borders, 361–363
  changing text properties with property sheets, 364–366
  font color, 357–359

ControlTips, creating, 371–372
Convert Database Into dialog box, 268
Convert macro dialog box, 664
convert table to text, 484–485
coordinates, 669
Copy button
Report Design toolbar, 434
Standard toolbar, 497–498

copying databases, 4
Create form by using wizard command icon, 95
Create from File option button (Microsoft Office Access dialog box), 514
Create query in Design view, 310, 444
command icon, 156

Create report by using wizard, 581
command icon, 112

Create table in Design view command icon, 30
criteria, 154–155
adding to crosstab query, 450–452
compound, 187–189
create a delete query, 444
from field not in query result, 180–182
numeric, 183
prompting with parameter query, 452–454
record query, 21
text, 166–171
update queries, 440
using calculated fields, 196–201
using comparison operators, 184–186
using wildcard characters, 174–179

Index | **Access** 807

Criteria row, in query design grid, 166
crosstab query, 437–438, 447–450
    adding conditions, 450–452
Currency
    data type, 36, 232
    formatting, 200, 432
current date, in report footers, 124
curved arrow in Database window, 263
Customize command (Tools menu), 10

D

data, 3
    analyzing, 617–620
    entering, 84
        error reduction, 227, 229
        validation, 246–248
    mail merge source, 491
    redundancy, 293, 296, 312
    restrictions, 227
    sorting, 189–194
    types of data, 32, 232
        AutoNumber, 35
        changing, 228–231
        Currency, 36
        Date/Time, 229, 232, 235–237
        Hyperlink, 229
        Number, 31, 183
        numeric variables, 681–682
        OLE Object, 230
        required, 679
        State, 250
        string variables, 679
        text, 31, 166
data access pages, 259, 721
    adding records, 265–266
    creating, 260–263, 721–723
    modifying, 723–726
    placing a PivotTable, 726–729
    viewing with browser, 263–265
Data Mode, Edit, 554, 568
Data Type column, 31, 228
Database to Compact From dialog box, 326
Database toolbar
    in Access window, 7–8
    Analyze arrow
        Analyze Performance, 621
        Analyze Table, 618
    New button, 28, 440, 612
    New Object AutoForm button, 89
    New Object button arrow, 313–316
    OfficeLinks arrow
        Analyze It with Microsoft Office Excel, 711
        Merge It with Microsoft Office Word, 491

    Open button, 8, 268, 624
    Print button, 93, 172, 178–179, 189, 194
    Relationships button, 297–298, 305
Database Utilities command (Tools menu)
    Compact and Repair Database, 326
    Convert Database, 268
    Switchboard Manager, 571, 577
database window toolbar, New button, 380, 551
Database Wizard, 28, 612–614
databases, 3
    backing up, 326, 446, 632
    closing, 54
    compacting, 326
    converting old to new, 267
    copying, 4
    creating, 27–29
        using Database Wizard, 612–614
    encoding and decoding, 324–325, 635–636
    extracting information, 20
    file extension, 4
    flat file, 296
    linking, 510–513
    opening, 6–11
    optimizing, 320–321, 621–622
    protecting, 321–323, 631–632
    relational, 292, 296
    renaming, 4–6
    replicating, 327–329, 631–635
    resizing columns, 490–491
    saving, 54
    synchronizing, 329, 634–635
    viewing the window, 12–14
Datasheet view
    adding records, 33
    opening a table, 38
    viewing a table, 18–19
Date statement
    display in Immediate window, 672
    use in procedure, 674
Date/Time data type, 229, 232, 235–237
dates
    formats, 235–237
    in report footers, 124
debugging
    macros, 556
    VBA program, 671
Decimal Places, 432
decoding databases, 324–325, 636
Decrease Decimal button (Formatting toolbar, Excel), 712
defaults
    administrator, 627
    field values, 234
    query type, 441

Security.mdw filename, 626
user permissions, 627
workgroup ID, 626
Delete Query, 444–446
Delete Record button, 46, 92, 264
deleting
   fields, 39–41
   records from tables, 46, 92
Delimited option button, 487
delimited text file, 484
descending (sort) order, 51
Description column, 32
descriptive text on controls, 371
design. *See also* **tables, table design**
   design errors, 317–319
   design grid
      adding fields to query, 170
      clearing, 182
      creating query from joined tables, 310–311
      query window, 441
      Select Query window, 156–158
Design button, 39, 163
Design Master, 327–329, 632–635
Design view
   adding hyperlinks, 498
   creating
      Delete Query, 444
      queries, 156, 158
   data access page, 261, 263
   embedding subreports, 420
   forms, 98–99, 103, 673, 675
      adding fields, 354
      creating, 380–383
   macros, 662
   reports, 115–117
      moving and resizing fields, 117–124
   Section Selector, 359–360
   switchboard
      enhancing, 574–577
      properties, 579
   tables
      creating new, 28–30
      opening, 38
      viewing, 18–19
Design view button (Form view toolbar), 614
desktop, viewing from Access, 12–13
destination file, linking and embedding, 513
Detail section
   forms, 99
   reports, 420–425
Develop application (MOD), 329
Diagonal Resize pointer, 515, 521
dialog boxes. *See also* **messages**
   Append, 457
   Browse, 515
   Choose Builder, 674

Color, 367, 436
Column Width, 490–491, 507
Command Button Wizard, 558
Compact Database Into, 326
Convert Database Into, 268
Convert macro, 664
Convert Table to Text, 485
Database to Compact From, 326
Database Wizard, 612
Decode Database As, 325, 636
Edit Relationships, 301–303, 306–308
Edit Switchboard Page, 573–574, 578–579
Encode Database As, 324, 636
Encode/Decode Database, 325
Export Form, 735
Export Report, 719
Export Table, 732
Export XML, 733, 735
Expression Builder, 246–247, 431, 561–563
Field Properties, 198–199
File Conversion, 486
File New Database, 29
Find and Replace, 253–254
Folder Options (My Computer), 773, 737
Footer, 712
Form Wizard, 95
Import, 487, 496, 736
Import XML, 737
Indexes, 295
insert an object, 231
Insert Merge Field, 493–494
Insert Picture, 384, 577
Link, 506, 511
Link Tables, 511
Location of New Replica, 327, 632
Make Table, 455
Microsoft Office Access, 514
New Form, 87, 380
New Query, 313–315, 447–448
New Table, 506, 511
Open, 10, 624
Page Setup
   Columns tab, 92
   Footer box, 723
   Margins tab, 44, 438
   Page tab, 116, 304
Page Wizard, 721–723
Password Required, 323, 625
Paste Table As, 440
Performance Analyzer, 320–321, 621–623
Print, 42, 57
Properties, 5, 43
Row Height, 48
Save As, 89, 162, 167, 177, 179, 188–189, 205
Save As Data Access Page, 262

Section: Detail, 436
Set Database Password, 322–323, 624
Show Table, 156–157, 168, 174, 178–180, 187, 201, 305, 307, 310, 440
Sorting and Grouping, 428
Switchboard Manager, 571–572, 574, 578
Tab Order, 377–378
Table Analyzer Wizard, 619
Table AutoFormat (Word), 716
Templates, 612
Theme, 261
Unhide Columns, 49, 440
Zoom, 196–198

dictionary, Word, 485
Dim statement, 679
Directly with Replica box, 634
DoCmd statement, 666, 676
double-headed arrows
in Find Unmatched Query Wizard, 315–316
Form Footer bar, 500–501, 509
in Relationships window, 298
resizing Form Header section, 100
resizing table columns/rows, 46

downward-pointing arrow
in Design view, 228–229
in Field Properties, 235–236
in Required box, 244–245
in State field, 250–251

drag and drop
exporting an Access table to Word, 716
fields in PivotTable, 727–729
fields in query design grid, 170

duplicate records, 313–315, 617
duplicates in indexes, 294–295

E

Edit menu commands
Clear Grid, 182
Paste as Hyperlink, 498
Select All, 363
Select Form, 383

Edit Relationships dialog box, 301–303, 306–308
Edit Switchboard Page dialog box, 573–574, 578–579
editing
information in a record, 44–45
queries, 163–165

efficiency of database, 320–321
Email addresses, 228–229
embedding, 230, 513
Excel chart in Access form, 514–518
subreports in reports, 420–427

encoding databases, 324–325, 635–636

encrypting databases, 624, 635–636
End Function, 667
End Select statement, 687
Enforce Referential Integrity check box, 303, 307–308
entering data, 84
equal (=)
comparison operator, 184–186
in formulas, 431

equations, in calculated fields, 196
error messages
blank records in table, 490
Visual Basic Editor, 670

errors
data, 293, 312
design, 317–319
reducing in fields, 227–229

Esc key, remove entry or record, 243
events, 662
event procedures, 673
in macros, 559
  running macros, 559–563

Excel, 506–507
charts, 712–715
  creating, 712–715
  embedding in Access form, 514–518
  linking into Access report, 519–520
data
  exporting from Access table, 710–711
  importing into Access table, 496–497
worksheets
  hyperlinks from Access form, 500–503
  linking to Access, 505–507, 509–510

exclamation point (!)
input mask character, 244
recommended optimization, 621

exclusive mode, 322, 624
Existing File or Web Page (Insert Hyperlink dialog box), 502
Expand button, 620, 726
expand indicators, 296–297
Expedition form style, 512
Export command (File menu), 719, 732
Export Form dialog box, 735
Export Report dialog box, 719
Export Table dialog box, 732
Export XML dialog box, 733, 735
exporting
data to Excel, 710–711
reports, report snapshots, 718–719
tables to Word, 715–717
as XML documents
  forms, 735–736
  queries, 735
  reports, 735
  tables, 732–734

Expression Builder dialog box, 246–247, 431, 561–563
expressions, 176, 246
eXtensible Markup Language (XML). See XML (eXtensible Markup Language)
external data source, linking to Access, 505
extracting information from database, 20

F

Field List command (View menu), 355, 727–729
Field Name column, 232
Field Properties, 565
    default value, 234
    Expression Builder box, 246–247
    field size, 232–234
    format, 235–236
    Indexed, 294–295
    Input Mask box, 237–238, 240–242
    Required box, 244–245
    Validation Rule box, 246–247
    Validation Text box, 248
Field Properties dialog box, 198–199
fields, 16
    adding, 41
        to forms, 354–357
        to query design grid, 170
    deleting, 39–41
    describing in database table, 32
    formats, 235
        vs. input masks, 242
    moving and resizing
        in forms, 103–109
        in reports, 117–124
    removing from query table, 163–165
    required, 244–245
    restricting data size, 232–233
    rows in query design grid, 159, 170, 196
    searching for record, 252–254
    sorting multiple, 190–194
    table lists, 613
File Conversion dialog box, 486
file extensions
    .htm, 734
    .mdb, 4
    .xsl, 732, 734
File menu commands
    Export, 719, 732
    Get External Data, 487, 496
        Import, 736
    New, Folder, 4
    Open, 10
    Page Setup, 116, 438
    Print, 42, 172
        Print Range, 378, 436, 559, 681
        VBA code, 670, 677
    Print Relationships, 304
File name button (Footer dialog box), 711
file names, using spaces, 5
File New Database dialog box, 29
Files of type arrow (Import dialog box), 487
Fill/Back Color button arrow (Formatting toolbar), 360–361, 383
Filter By Form button (Table Datasheet toolbar), 257
Filter By Selection button
    Navigation bar, 265
    Table Datasheet toolbar, 255–256
Filter Toggle button (Navigation bar), 265
filters. *See also* queries
    displaying specific records, 255–258
Find and Replace dialog box, 252–254
Find Duplicates Query Wizard, 313–315
Find Unmatched Query Wizard, 315–316
Finish button
    Form Wizard, 97
    Lookup Wizard, 251
FIRST aggregate function, 201
First Record button, 85, 264
First Row Contains Field Names check box (Import Text Wizard), 487–488
Fit display setting, 24
flat file databases, 296
Folder Options dialog box (My Computer), 733, 737
Font/Fore Color button arrow (Formatting toolbar), 358
Font Name property box, 365
Font Size arrow (Formatting toolbar), 614–615
fonts
    changing text properties with property sheets, 364–366
    color, 357–358
Footer dialog box, 712
footers, forms, 99, 110. *See also* form headers
Force New Page property, 436
foreign key
    in table, 301
    referential integrity, 303–304
Form arrow, 573
Form Design toolbar
    Field List button, 355
    Properties button, 364
    Toolbox button, 101, 556, 559
    View button, 109
Form Footer section, 99
Form Header section, 99

Form Header/Footer command (View menu), 384
form headers, 98–102, 110
Form Name arrow/box, 89, 568
Form selector, 383, 563
form types, by wizard creation, 87
Form view, 675
    adding
        fields, 354
        hyperlinks, 499
    of forms, 98
Form View toolbar
    Delete Record button, 92
    Design view, 614
    Print Preview button, 111
    View button, 98, 102
Form Wizard, 87, 94, 735
    creating forms, 95–97
Format box in Field Properties, 235–236
Format menu commands
    Access
        Hide Columns, 49–50, 443
        Row Height, 48
        Theme, 723
        Unhide Columns, 49–50, 440, 443
    Excel, Column, Hide, 712
Format Painter button (Formatting toolbar), 363
Format tab on property sheet, 364–365, 435–436
Formatting toolbar
    Access
        Bold button, 614–615
        Center button, 385
        Fill/Back Color button arrow, 360–361, 383
        Font/Fore Color button arrow, 358
        Font Size arrow, 614–615
        Format Painter button, 363
        Line/Border Width button arrow, 361–362
    Excel, Decrease Decimal button, 712
forms, 82–83
    adding
        combo boxes, 372–376
        fields, 354–357
        form headers, 99–102
        instructions to status bars, 369–371
        page footers, 110–111
        records to tables, 90–91
        titles, 384–386
    backgrounds, 88
        color, 88, 359–361, 367
        pictures, 383
    changing tab order, 378
    ControlTips, creating, 371–372

    creating
        in Design view, 380–383
        with Form Wizard, 95–97
    customizing, 353
    deleting records from tables, 91–93
    embedding Excel chart, 514–518
    entering information, ease of use, 82, 84
    exporting as XML documents, 735–736
    headers, 98–102, 110
    hyperlinks
        to Excel worksheet, 500–503
        to Word document, 497–499
    linking to Excel worksheet, 505–510
    modifying, 98
    moving and resizing fields, 103–109
    navigating to records, 84–86
    selecting, 383, 563
    style, 96
        Blends, 508
        Expedition, 512
    text properties, 364–366
    switching between views, 98, 102–103
    viewing, 21–22, 82, 84
Forms button, 21, 84
Forms (Objects bar), Rename command, 673
formulas, 176
    in calculated field, 431–432, 434
Full Data Users check box (Security Wizard), 627–628
full menu, 9–10
functions
    aggregate or statistical, 201–205
    VBA, 664

G

Generated Unique ID, 618–619
Get External Data command (File menu), 487, 496
    Import, 736
graphic lines on reports, 123
greater than (>)
    comparison operator, 185
    input mask character, 240, 244
green text, in VBA, 666, 668
grid pattern
    Detail section of forms, 99
    reports, 115
Group Footer box, 428
Group ID box, 627
grouping data
    crosstab queries, 447
    queries, 201–202
    reports, 427–428

groups bar in database window, 11–12
groups, creating calculated fields, 429–433

H

hand pointer
    charts, 517
    control borders, 104–107, 501–502
    Page Footer section, 520
    pasted hyperlinks, 498
Header and Footer command (View menu, Excel), 711
Header and Footer toolbar
    Close button, 492
    Switch Between Header and Footer button, 492
headers, forms, 98–102, 110
help box in Access window, 7
help system, Access, 55–57
Hide Columns command (Format menu), 49–50, 443
Hide extensions… setting (Folder Options dialog box, My Computer), 733, 737
hiding
    columns, 49–50, 443
    tables, 300
Horizontal Resize pointer, 501
horizontal rulers
    in Design view of forms, 101
    select controls, 359
HTML, compared to XML, 732
Hyperlink data type, 229, 232
hyperlinks
    expanding information, 55
    from form to Excel worksheet, 500–503
    from form to Word document, 497–499

I

I-beam pointer, 85
Ideas
    Performance Analyzer, 321
    optimizations, 621–622
If statement, 685
Image button (Toolbox toolbar), 576
Immediate window, 671
    Close, 672
    testing statements, 671–672
Import dialog box, 487, 496, 736
Import Spreadsheet Wizard, 496
Import Text Wizard, 487–488

Import to Table box, 489, 497
Import XML dialog box, 737
importing
    data
        Excel worksheet, 496–497
        vs. linking, 505
        Word table, 484–487, 489–490
    XML documents into Access tables, 736–737
Indexed arrow, 489
indexing fields
    with duplicates, 295
    without duplicates, 294–295
infinity sign (∞) on relationship lines, 299
information, 3
    extracting from database, 20
Input Box, 679–680, 682–683
Input Mask box in Field Properties, 237–242
input mask characters, 237, 244
Input Mask Wizard, 237–240
input masks, 237
    capital letters vs. lowercase text in, 240, 244
    numeric, 242
    phone number, 238
    Social Security Number, 238
    vs. field formats, 242
    zip codes, 238–240
Insert button (Insert Merge Field dialog box), 493
Insert Hyperlink button, 502
Insert menu commands, Hyperlink, 502
Insert Merge Field dialog box, 493–494
Insert New Record, 499
Insert Object dialog box, 231
Insert Picture dialog box, 384, 577
Insert Rows button (Macro Design toolbar), 553–554
inserting text automatically, 676
instructions, adding to status bars of forms, 369–370
intranet, 259
Item box, Build button, 561–562

J-K

joined tables, creating queries, 310–311
junction tables, 307–309

Keep Together box, 428, 436
Key area of Performance Analyzer, 321
keyboard shortcuts
    ampersand (&), 573–574
    navigating records, 53

L

L, input mask character, 240, 244
Label button (Toolbox toolbar)
    Form Header section, 100, 384
    Page Footer section, 110, 355, 422, 438, 558
    title section, 575
label controls, in Design view of forms, 102, 104, 354–355
Landscape orientation, 43
    reports, 116
LAST aggregate function, 201
Last Record button, 53, 85, 91, 264, 563–564
legend, 714–715
less than (<)
    comparison operator, 185
    input mask character, 244
light bulb for idea optimization, 621–622
Like term in SQL, 176
Line/Border Width button arrow (Formatting toolbar), 361–362
Line button (Toolbox toolbar), 433
line charts, 514
Link dialog box, 506, 511
Link Select pointer, 229
Link Spreadsheet Wizard, 506
Link Tables dialog box, 511
linking
    data vs. importing, 505
    databases, 510–513
    Excel to Access
        chart in report, 519–520
        worksheet to form, 505–510
    objects, 230
    tables, 301
list boxes, 372
lists, locating items, 252
Location of New Replica dialog box, 327, 632
logical operators, 187
Long Date format, 235–236
Long variable, 681
Look In box, 254
Lookup Wizard, 250–252
    data type, 232
lowercase text in input mask, 240

M

Macro command (Tools menu)
    Convert Macros to Visual Basic, 663
    Visual Basic Editor, 667, 671
Macro Design toolbar
    Conditions button, 564
    Insert Rows button, 553–554
    Macro Names button, 567
    Run button, 550, 553–554, 663
    Save button, 553–554, 569
    Single Step button, 556
Macro Groups, 567–569
Macro window, 548
    Action Arguments section, 549–554, 561
    Action column, 549, 552, 561
    Comment column, 549, 552
    viewing, 548–551
macros, 546, 662
    adding actions, 553–555
    attaching to command button, 556–558
    comments, 549, 552, 666, 668
    conditional expressions, 564–566
    converting to VBA code, 662–666
    creating new, 551–553
    debugging, 556
    event response, 559–563
    running, 554
        with Command Button, 558
Macros (Objects bar), Rename command, 662
magnifying glass pointer, 425
Mail Merge task pane, 492–494
Mail Merge Wizard, 491–492
main document, mail merge, 491
main form, 386–390
Make-Table Query, 454–456
many-to-many relationship, 307–309
margins
    report margins, 433
    setting, 518
Match box, 254
MAX aggregate function, 201–204
maximizing window, 13–14, 23–24, 498
MDE file, 623
Media field, 265
Medium Date format, 236–237
member list of procedure, 672
Memo data type, 232
menu bar in Access window, 7–8
merging table with Word document, 491–495
Message argument, 549–552
messages
    blank records in table, 490
    Confirm File Rename, 5
    data integrity rules, 245–246
    database conversion, 268
    earlier version of Access, 267
    exclusive use, 322
    field size changed, 233–234
    hyperlinks harmful to computer, 499, 503
    invalid value, 229–230
    record search complete, 254
    Security Warning, 11
    There is no primary key defined, 34
    validation rule violation, 247

Microsoft Access. *See* Access
Microsoft Excel. *See* Excel
Microsoft Office Access dialog box, 514
Microsoft Word. *See* Word
MIN aggregate function, 201–204
minimizing window, 12–13, 497–498
minus sign (-), as collapse indicator, 297
modifying data access pages, 723–726
modules, 662
More items button (Mail Merge task pane), 493–494
mouse pointers. *See also* pointers
    ControlTips, 371–372
    text box control, 106
MsgBox, 549, 552–554
    MsgBox statement, 665–668

N

naming files, 5
navigating to records
    in tables, 52–54
    using forms, 84–86
navigation areas
    main forms and subforms, 388–389
    results from queries, 161
Navigation bar on data access page, 264
    Filter By Selection button, 265
    New button, 265
    Save button, 266
    Sort Ascending button, 265
    Sort Descending button, 265
navigation buttons, 264, 420, 426, 436
New button
    Database toolbar, 28, 440, 612
    Database window toolbar, 380, 551
    Navigation bar, 265
New Data Users check box (Security Wizard), 627
New File task pane, 28, 612
New Form dialog box, 87, 380
New Object AutoForm button, 89
New Object button arrow (Database toolbar), 313–315
New Query dialog box, 313–315, 447–448
New Record button, 86, 90, 264
New Table dialog box, 506, 511
New, Folder command (File menu), 4
Next Record button, 22, 53, 91, 264–265
nudging objects, in Design view of reports, 121, 125, 422
number (numeric) data types, 31, 232
    as criteria in queries, 183
numeric input mask, 242
numeric variables, defining in procedures, 681–682

O

Object Linking and Embedding (OLE), 230–232, 513
Object Name arrow, 568
Object Type arrow, 568
objects, 12, 14, 513
    selecting all, 621
Objects bar
    database window, 11–14
    Forms, 21, 354, 380, 556, 563, 574, 579
        Rename command, 673
    Macros, 548, 551, 554, 560, 564, 567
        Rename command, 662
    Pages, 259–260, 721
    Queries, 20, 156, 310, 440
    Reports, 23, 420, 437, 581, 718
    Tables, 14, 228, 420, 440, 710
Office Assistant, 55
    used in VBA procedure, 667–669
Office PivotTable button (Toolbox toolbar), 727
OfficeLinks arrow
    Database toolbar
        Analyze It with Microsoft Office Excel, 711
        Merge It with Microsoft Office Word, 491
    Standard toolbar, Publish It with Microsoft Office Excel, 716
OLE (Object Linking and Embedding), 230–232, 513
One Field Back button, 113
One Field button, 96, 113, 251, 314–316, 423, 448
One-step Security Wizard Report, 629
one-to-many relationship, 299, 301–303, 386
    subreports, 420, 424
one-to-one relationship, 304–307
Open button
    Database toolbar, 8, 268
    Objects bar, 14, 84
Open dialog box, 10, 322
Open Exclusive, 624
Open Form in Edit Mode, 573
OpenForm box, 550
OpenQuery Comment row, 554
OpenReport action, 552
opening
    databases, 6–11
    queries, 162–163
    tables, 14–18, 38–39
operators
    comparison, 184–186
    logical, 154, 187–189
optimizing databases, 320–321, 621–622
optional digits in input mask, 238–240
Options command (Tools menu), Auto List Members, 672

OR logical operator, 187–189
ORDER BY in SQL statement, 459

P

Page Design toolbar
    Toolbox button, 727
    View button, 263, 725
Page Footer, 421
    forms, 110–111
    reports, 124–125
        created by Report Wizard, 115–116
Page Header, 421
    in reports created by Report Wizard, 115–116
Page Header/Footer command (View menu), 110, 355, 558
page navigation buttons, 420, 426, 436
page numbers in report footers, 124
Page Setup dialog box
    Columns tab, 92
    Footer box, 723
    Margins tab, 44, 438
    Page tab, 116, 304
Page view of data access page, 263
Page View toolbar, View button, 263
Page Wizard, 260, 721–723
pages
    data access, 259. *See also* data access pages
    Web data access
        creating, 721–723
        modifying, 723–726
        placing a PivotTable, 726–729
panes, of query window, 441
paperclip character (Office Assistant), 55
parameter query, 452–454
Password Required dialog box, 323, 624–625
passwords
    case sensitivity, 629
    for database security, 623–624
    don't match, 624
    input mask character, 244
    protecting databases, 321–323
    selecting, 628
Paste as Hyperlink command (Edit menu), 498
Paste button (Report Design toolbar), 434
Paste Table As dialog box, 440
pencil image in database tables, 17–18
percentage, conversion from string, 683
Performance Analyzer, 320–321, 621–623
permissions, 626
Phone Number input mask, 238
Picture Size Mode box, 384
pictures
    adding to background, 383
    properties, 384
    in records, 230–231

pie charts, 514
PivotTable, placing in data access page, 726–729
pixels, 669
placeholder. *See* wildcard characters
Plain Text type (Save As dialog box), 486
plus sign (+)
    expand indicator, 296
    and letter A pointer, 101
pointers
    Diagonal Resize, 515, 521
    double-headed, 500–501, 509
    hand
        charts, 517
        control borders, 104–107, 501–502
        Page Footer section, 520
        pasted hyperlinks, 498
    I-beam, 85
    magnifying glass, 425
    plus sign and letter A, 101
    pointing hand, 106, 356
    two-headed, 491
populate a table, 29
Portrait orientation, 43
Position label, 425
postage cost in variable, 687–688
pound sign (#), input mask character, 244
presentation files, 732
Previous Record button, 85, 264
primary key, 34–35, 243–244, 489–490
    bold text, 300, 309
    changing in wizard, 619
    index field, 294
    in many-to-many relationship, 307, 309
    referential integrity, 303–304
primary sort field, 52
Print button
    Access Help window, 57
    Database toolbar, 93, 172, 178–179, 189, 194
    Print Preview toolbar, 111, 126
    queries, 172
    reports, 25
    Standard toolbar, 42, 258
Print command (File menu), 42, 172
    Print Range, 436
        Selected Records, 378, 559, 681
    VBA code, 670, 677
Print dialog box, 42, 57
Print Macro Definition box, 555
Print Preview, 425
    forms, 111
    macros, 552–553
    reports, 677
Print Preview toolbar
    Print button, 111, 126
    View button, 115

Print Relationships command (File menu), 304
printing
    query results, 172
    Relationships window, 304
    report styles, 613
    reports, 23–26, 126
        Relationships, 309
        Snapshot Viewer, 719
    tables, 42–44
procedures in VBA, 662
    adding blank lines, 682
    defining variables
        numeric, 681–684
        string, 679–680
    modifying in VBA, 667–670
    Select Case structure, 686–688
    selection structure, 684–685
    template, 673
    writing, 673–677
Project Explorer pane, 664–665
Promote command (shortcut menu), 723
properties
    controls, 364–368
    date control, 563
    fields, 227
    form controls, 565
    formatting, 577, 580
    Forms, 674, 676
    groups, 428
    switchboard, 579–581
    text box label, 560
    Unbound text box control, 560
Properties button, 43
    Form Design toolbar, 364
    text box control, 369
Properties dialog box, 5, 43
property sheets
    closing, 433
    form controls, 364–368, 431
    formatting, 430, 432, 435–436
Property Update Options smart tag, 235–236
protecting databases, 321–323, 631–632

Q

queries, 154–156. *See also* **filters**
    action, 440, 454
    adding all fields, 159–160, 166
    calculated fields, 196–201
    creating, 156–160
        append query, 456–457
        crosstab, 437–438, 447–452
        delete query, 444–446
        forms in Design view, 380
        from joined tables, 310–311
        make-table query, 454–456
        update query, 440–443

criteria
    compound, 187–189
    from field not in query result, 180–182
    numeric, 183
    text, 166–171
    with comparison operators, 184–186
    with wildcard characters, 174–179
design modification, 190–194
exporting as XML documents, 735
grouping data, 201–202
opening, 162–163
printing results, 172
prompting with parameter query, 452–454
removing fields from table, 163–165
running, saving, and closing, 161–163
selecting, 156
sorting data
    with multiple fields, 190–194
    with single field, 189–190
switching between views, 162–163
viewing, 20–21
Queries object, 20
Query Datasheet toolbar
    Sort Ascending button, 189
    Sort Descending button, 190
    View button, 163, 165, 176–177, 181–182, 185
Query Design toolbar
    Query Type button, 441–442
    Run button, 161, 165–167, 170, 177, 182–183, 186, 189, 193, 198–203, 443
    Totals button, 202
Query Name arrow, 554
Query Type, 441–442
Query Type command (shortcut menu)
    Append Query, 457
    Delete Query, 445
question mark (?)
    input mask character, 240, 244
    query wildcard, 178–179
    suggested optimization, 621
quotation marks (")
    strings, 235
        string variables, 679
    text in VBA, 668

R

Read-only attribute on databases, 5–6
Read-Only Users check box (Security Wizard), 627
readable characters, 324
Recommendations
    optimization, 621
    Performance Analyzer, 321
Record arrow, 568

records, 16
  adding to tables, 36–37
    using data access page, 265–266
    using forms, 90–91
    using subforms, 388–390
  changing information, 44–45
  deleting from tables, 45–46, 243
    using forms, 91–93
  displaying using filters, 255–258
  duplicate, 313–315
  editing, 44–45
  finding in table, 252–254
  forms, 22
    selecting, 92
  navigating
    using keyboard, 53–54
    using navigation area, 52
    and viewing using forms, 84–86
  source, 354
  unmatched, 315–316
Records menu commands, Remove Filter/Sort, 52
red statement, in VBA, 667
redundancy, data, 293, 296, 312
referential integrity, 301, 303, 307–308
relational database, 292, 296
relationship line in tables, 299, 302–303
  deleting relationships, 309
Relationship toolbar
  Show All Relationships button, 299
  Show Table, 305
relationships
  and delete query, 446
  deleting, 309
  many-to-many, 307–309
  one-to-many, 301–303
    subreports, 420, 424
  one-to-one, 304–307
  viewing in database, 296
Relationships button (Database toolbar), 297–298, 305
Relationships window, 297–300, 308
  printing, 304
Remove Filter button (Table Datasheet toolbar), 256–258
Remove Filter/Sort command (Records menu), 52
renaming
  databases, 4–6
  forms, 673
  macros, 662
  tables, 318–319, 619
repeated information, 617
replica set, 327
replicating databases, 327–329, 631–635

Replication command (Tools menu)
  Create Replica, 327, 632
  Synchronize Now, 634
Report Design toolbar
  Copy button, 434
  Paste button, 434
  Sorting and Grouping button, 427
  View button, 116
Report Footer, 124–125, 421, 434
Report Header, 421
Report Name arrow, 552
report snapshots, 718–719
Report view, 115
Report Wizard, 112–114, 581
reports, 23, 82
  creating
    calculated fields, 434–435
    from crosstab query, 437–438
    Report Wizard, 112–114
  Design view, 115–117
  ease of use, 82
  embedding subreports, 420–427
  exporting as XML documents, 735
  grouping data, 427–428
  linking Excel chart, 519–520
  moving and resizing fields in Design view, 117–124
  One-step Security Wizard, 629
  Page and Report Footers, 124–125
  printing, 23–26, 126
    Print Preview mode, 677
    print styles, 613
  Relationships, 304, 309
  Report view, 115
  saving, 115
  setting properties, 435–436
  viewing, 23–26
Reports button, 23
required digits in input mask, 238–240
required field, 244–245
resizing
  bound controls, 501, 520
  fields
    in forms, 103–109
    in reports, 117–124
  Form Header section, 100
  Report Footer section, 520
  Report Header section, 520
  table columns/rows, 46–48, 490–491
  text box controls, 509
Restore Window button, 14, 26, 112, 263, 426, 436
right-pointing arrows in database tables, 15
Row Height dialog box, 48
row selector, 17

rows, database tables, 15–16
   resizing, 46–49
Ruler command (View menu), 101
rulers in Design view of forms, 101, 359
Run button
   Macro Design toolbar, 550, 553–554, 663
   Query Design toolbar, 161, 165–167, 170, 177, 182–183, 186, 189, 193, 198–203, 443
running
   macros
      alternative methods, 554
      by events, 559–563
      with Command Button, 558
   queries, 161–163

S

Save As Data Access Page dialog box, 262
Save As dialog box, 89, 162, 167, 177, 179, 188–189, 205
Save as type arrow (Save As dialog box), 486
Save button
   Macro Design toolbar, 553–554, 569
   Navigation bar, 266
Save in box, 29
saving
   AutoForms, 89
   databases, 54
   queries, 161–162
   Relationships report, 309
   reports, 115
   tables, 33, 37–38
schemas, XML, 732
screen styles, 613
ScreenTips
   ControlTips, 371–372
   Open, 8
   Zoom, 24
Search Results task pane, 55
Search, in Help system, 55
secondary sort field, 52
Section: Detail dialog box, 436
Section Selector for Detail section, 359–360, 383
security
   database, 623, 631
   default file name (Security.mdw), 626
   precautions, 623
   user-level, 625–630
   warning messages, 11
Security command (Tools menu)
   Encode/Decode Database, 324–325, 635
   Set Database Password, 624, 322
   Unset Database Password, 625
   User-Level Security Wizard, 626

Security Wizard, 625–629
Select All command (Edit menu), 363
Select Case structure in VBA procedures, 686–688
Select command (Table menu, Word), 716
Select Form command (Edit menu), 383
SELECT in SQL statment, 459
select queries, 156, 440
Select Query window, 156–159
Selected Fields list, 423
Selected Records option button, 378
selection structure in VBA procedures, 684–685
sequence structure, 684
Set Database Password dialog box, 322–323, 624
Set Unique Identifier button, 319
Setup button, 44
Short Date format, 237
short menu, 9
shortcut menu commands
   to data access page, 263
   Delete Shortcut, 630
   Promote, 723
   Properties, 5, 430
   Query Type, 442
      Append Query, 457
      Delete Query, 445
   Show Table, 305
   tables, 300, 303
   View Code, 664
shortcuts
   database, 626, 630
   forms from switchboard, 572–573
Show All Relationships button (Relationship toolbar), 299
Show check box, 181
Show me an example buttons, 617–618
Show Table dialog box, 156–157, 168, 174, 178–180, 187, 201, 305, 307, 310, 440
Single Step button (Macro Design toolbar), 556
Single variable, 681, 687
Size Mode, 577
sizing buttons
   in Access window, 7–8, 11
   in database window, 11–12
sizing handles
   label box in Design view of forms, 102
   subreports, 425
smart tags, Property Update Options, 236
Snapshot Viewer, 718–719
   printing reports, 719
Social Security Number input mask, 238
Sort Ascending button
   Navigation bar, 265
   Query Design toolbar, 51–52, 189

Sort Descending button
    Navigation bar, 265
    Query Design toolbar, 190
sorting data
    by groups in reports, 427–428
    with multiple fields in queries, 190–194
    with single field, 189–190
    sort order
        in abbreviation field, 251
        on data access page, 261
    table records, 51–52
source file, linking and embedding, 513
spaces in file names, 5
specifications, criteria for record query, 21
spelling errors, 197, 485
SQL (Structured Query Language), 176, 458–459
square brackets ([ ])
    in formulas, 431
    using calculated fields in queries, 196–197
Standard Height check box, 48–49
Standard toolbar
    Chart Wizard button, 713
    OfficeLinks arrow (Publish It with Microsoft Office Excel), 716
    Print button, 258
    Project Explorer button, 664
    Run Sub/UserForm button, 666, 670
    View button, 42
Start menu, 6
starting Access, 6–7
startup properties of switchboard, 581
State field, 250–252
statements
    as VBA instructions, 662
    Date statement, 672, 674
    DIM statement, 679
    DoCmd statement, 666, 676
    End Select statement, 687
    If statement, 685
    MsgBox statement, 665–666, 668
    testing, 671–672
    Time statement, 672, 674
    typing in VBA, 669
statistical functions in queries, 201–205
Status Bar Text property box, 370
status bars, 7–8
    adding instructions to status bars of forms, 369–371
STDEV aggregate function, 201
stretching a picture, 384, 577
strings, 176
    quotation marks, 235
    string variables, defining in procedures, 679
Structured Query Language (SQL), 176, 458–459

stylesheets, 732
SubForm Wizard, 386–387
subforms, 352, 386
    adding records, 388–390
    creating, 386–387
subreport labels, 424–425
SubReport Wizard, 423–427
subreports
    creating, 420
    embedding in report, 420–427
Suggestions
    optimization, 621
    Performance Analyzer, 321
SUM aggregate function, 201–204
Sum calculation function, 449
summary of data, with crosstab query, 447
Switch Between Header and Footer button (Header and Footer toolbar), 492
switching between views
    forms, 98, 102–103
    queries, 162–163
    reports, 115–117
    tables, 33
switchboard, 546, 570
    adding second page, 577–579
    changing properties, 579–581
    creating, 571–574
    enhancing, 574–577
    startup properties, 581
Switchboard Manager, 571–572, 577–579
synchronizing databases, 329, 634–635

T

tab characters, 485
Tab key, 247
tab order of fields on form, 369, 377–378
Table Analyzer, 317–319, 617–620
table area
    of query window, 441
    of Select Query window, 157
Table AutoFormat dialog box (Word), 716
Table Datasheet toolbar
    Apply Filter button, 258
    Filter By Form button, 257
    Filter By Selection button, 255–256
    Find button, 252–254
    Remove Filter button, 256–258
    Undo button, 230
    View button, 18–19, 35
Table Design toolbar, 34
    View button, 19, 33
Table menu commands (Word)
    AutoFit, 717
    Select, 716

tables, 6, 12
  adding records, 36–37
    with Append Query, 456–457
    using data access page, 265–266
    using forms, 90–91
  closing, 37–38
  creating, 29–33
  deleting records using forms, 91–93
  exporting
    to Excel, 710–711
    to Word, 715–717
    as XML documents, 732–734
  hiding, 300
  importing
    Excel data, 496–497
    Word data, 484–487, 489–490
    XML documents, 736–737
  linking
    databases, 510–513
    Excel worksheet to form, 505–510
  make-table query, 454–456
  merging with Word document, 491–495
  modifying design of, 39–41
  opening, 14–18, 38–39
  naming, 619
  populating, 29
  printing, 42–44
  resizing columns/rows, 46–48
  saving, 33, 37–38
  searching for record, 254
  sorting records, 51–52
  switching between views, 33
  table design
    adding fields, 41
    deleting fields, 39–41
    error checking, 317–319
  viewing, 18–20
Tables/Queries arrow, 423
Tabular layout, 519
task panes, 7
  in Access window, 7–8
  Mail Merge, 492–494
  New File, 28, 612
  Search Results, 55
templates
  built-in, 612
  event procedure template, 673
testing
  VBA functions, 666, 670
  VBA program, 671
Text Box button (Toolbox toolbar), 429, 560
text box controls
  background colors, 361
  forms, 103–104, 354–356, 370
  resizing, 509
text criteria in queries, 166–171

Text data type, 31, 232
Text Files type, 487
Text Label, 430
text properties, 364–366
Theme command (Format menu), 723
Theme dialog box, 261
Tiling, picture property, 384
Time statement
  display in Immediate window, 672
  use in procedure, 674
Tips button (Table Analyzer Wizard), 318
tips (ControlTips), creating, 371–372
Title argument, 549–550, 565
title bar
  Access window, 7–8
  database window, 268
Title box, 552
titles
  forms, 384–386
  pages, 262
toolbars
  Database. *See* Database toolbar
  Database window, New button, 380, 551
  Form Design. *See* Form Design toolbar
  Form View. *See* Form View toolbar
  Formatting. *See* Formatting toolbar
  naming, 34
  Page Design. *See* Page Design toolbar
  Page View, View button, 263
  Print Preview. *See* Print Preview toolbar
  Query Datasheet. *See* Query Datasheet toolbar
  Query Design. *See* Query Design toolbar
  Relationship, Show All Relationships button, 299
  Report Design. *See* Report Design toolbar
  Standard. *See* Standard toolbar
  Table Datasheet. *See* Table Datasheet toolbar
  Table Design. *See* Table Design toolbar
  Toolbox. *See* Toolbox toolbar
Toolbox button
  Form Design toolbar, 101, 556, 559
  Page Design toolbar, 727
Toolbox command (View menu), 101
Toolbox toolbar
  Combo Box button, 372–373
  Command button, 557
  displaying, 556, 559
  in forms Design view, 98–100
  Image button, 576
  Label button, 100, 110, 355, 384, 422, 438, 558, 575
  Office PivotTable button, 727
  Subform/Subreport button, 386, 423
  Text Box button, 429, 560

Tools menu commands
  Analyze
    Performance, 320, 623
    Table, 317, 617
  Customize, 10
  Database Utilities, 268, 326, 571, 577
  Macro
    Convert Macros to Visual Basic, 663
    Visual Basic Editor, 667, 671
  Options, Auto List Members, 672
  Replication
    Create Replica, 327, 632
    Synchronize Now, 634
  Run Macro, 554, 569
  Security
    Encode/Decode Database, 324–325, 635
    Set Database Password, 624, 322
    Unset Database Password, 625
    User-Level Security Wizard, 626
  Startup, 581
Total row, in query design, 201–202
Totals button (Query Design toolbar), 202
transparent background color, 367
two-headed pointer, 491
Type a question for help box, 7–8, 56
Type argument, 549–550
Type, picture property, 384

U

unauthorized users, 321, 324
unbound controls, 421–422, 431, 434
unbound object, 375
Unbound text box control, 560
underscores in file names, 5
Undo button (Table Datasheet toolbar), 230, 248
Unhide Columns dialog box, 49–50, 440, 443
unmatched records, 315–316
Unset Database Password, 324
Update Query, 440–443
uppercase text in input mask, 240
Use existing Tables and Queries option button (Subreport Wizard), 423
User Name box (Security Wizard), 628
user-level security, 625–630
Users group permissions, 627

V

Val function, 683
validate data entry, 246–248
validation rule, 246–247

validation text, 248
VAR aggregate function, 201
variables, 679
VBA. *See* **Visual Basic for Applications (VBA)**
Vertical Resize pointer, 424
vertical rulers
  Design view of forms, 101
  select controls, 359
View button
  Form Design toolbar, 109
  Form View toolbar, 98, 102
  Page Design toolbar, 263
  Page View toolbar, 263–264, 725
  Print Preview toolbar, 115
  Query Datasheet toolbar, 163, 165, 176–177, 181–182, 185
  Report Design toolbar, 116
  Table Datasheet toolbar, 18–19, 35
  Table Design toolbar, 19, 33
View Code command (shortcut menu), 664
View menu commands
  Access
    Field List, 355, 727, 729
    Form Header/Footer, 384
    Immediate window, 671
    Page Header/Footer, 110, 355, 558
    Ruler, 101
    SQL View, 459
    Tab Order, 377
    Toolbox, 101
  Excel, Header and Footer, 711
viewing
  database window, 12–14
  forms, 21–22
  Macro window, 548–551
  queries, 20–21
  records, 84–86
  reports, 23–26
  tables, 18–20
views, switching between, 18
  forms, 98, 102–103
  queries, 162–163
  reports, 115–117
  tables, 33
Visible property, 565
Visual Basic Editor
  Close, 670
  Code Builder, 674, 676
  error messages, 667, 670
  open in alternate way, 671
  procedures
    member list, 672
    modification, 667
  typing text, 668
  VBA code, 664